A MANUAL OF
MODERN SCHOLASTIC PHILOSOPHY
VOL. II.

Toussaint 1915.

Mon Révérend Père,

Vous avez eu l'amabilité de traduire, à l'intention du public de langue anglaise, le cours élémentaire de philosophie édité par les professeurs de l'Institut saint Thomas à Louvain.

Bien que les travaux absorbants de mon ministère ne me permettent plus de suivre d'aussi près que je le voudrais les publications philosophiques,

Facsimile of letter from Cardinal Mercier to one of the translators.

tout ce qui intéresse l'Institut saint
Thomas me tient toujours fort à
coeur. Aussi suis-je particulièrement
heureux de savoir combien votre
traduction est fidèle, élégante,
et à la portée de la jeunesse
studieuse que vous visiez en
l'écrivant.

Je me fais un plaisir de vous en
exprimer toute ma reconnaissance
et je vous prie d'agréer, Mon Révérend
Père, l'assurance de mes sentiments
cordialement dévoués.

† D. J. card. Mercier, arch. de Mal.

A MANUAL OF MODERN SCHOLASTIC PHILOSOPHY

By

CARDINAL MERCIER

And

PROFESSORS OF THE HIGHER INSTITUTE OF
PHILOSOPHY, LOUVAIN

Authorized Translation, and Eighth Edition, by
T. L. PARKER, M.A., and S. A. PARKER, O.S.B., M.A.

With a Preface by
P. COFFEY, Ph.D. (Louvain)
Professor of Philosophy at Maynooth College, Ireland

Vol. II

NATURAL THEOLOGY (THEODICY), LOGIC,
ETHICS, HISTORY OF PHILOSOPHY

WITH FACSIMILE LETTER

LONDON
KEGAN PAUL, TRENCH, TRUBNER & CO., LTD.
St. Louis: B. HERDER
1917

Nihil obstat :
    J. Cuthbertus Almond, O.S.B.

Imprimi potest :
    E. Cuthbertus Butler,
        Abbas Præses Congr. Angl. O.S.B.
            die 16 Junii, 1917.

Nihil obstat :
    C. Schut, S.T.D.
        Censor deputatus.

Imprimatur :
    Edm : Can : Surmont
        Vic. Gen.
    Westmonasterii, die 24 Septembris, 1917.

Of this work four French editions have already been published, as well as Italian (two editions) and Spanish translations.

This translation has been made from the fourth French edition, with the aid of the second Italian. Prof. de Wulf has amplified the History, and has read the proofs.

iv

CONTENTS OF THE MANUAL

VOL. I.

VOL. II.

ILLUSTRATIONS.

Analytical Contents of Volume II

NATURAL THEOLOGY

PART I

The Existence of God

CHAP. I. IDEA OF THE DIVINE BEING

CHAP. II. THE EXISTENCE OF GOD

ART. I. CRITICAL EXAMINATION OF THE DOCTRINES OPPOSED TO THE PROOF OF GOD'S EXISTENCE

ART. II. THE PROOFS OF THE EXISTENCE OF GOD

PART II

The Nature of God

PART III

The Activity of God

LOGIC

ETHICS

PART I

General Ethics :
A Theory of Good and Evil

CHAP. I. THE NATURAL END OF MAN

CHAP. II. FREE-WILL

CHAP. III. THE MORAL ORDER

CHAP. IV. CONSCIENCE

PART II

Special Ethics :
A Theory of Right and Duty

CHAP. I. RIGHTS OF THE INDIVIDUAL

OUTLINES OF THE HISTORY OF PHILOSOPHY

PART I

The Philosophy of India and China

APPENDIX

Contemporary Philosophy

NATURAL THEOLOGY
OR
THEODICY

INTRODUCTION *

1. Meaning of Natural Theology.—Natural theology or, as it is sometimes called, *theodicy*[1] is the philosophical study of God. It establishes the existence of a first efficient Cause of all things, and then investigates the nature of this Cause. It derives its principles and its methods from the light of natural reason alone, and on this account is distinguished from *Christian theology*. This latter starts from data which the human reason if left to its own resources is quite incapable of discovering but which are given to it by divine revelation ; the mind endowed with Christian belief has elaborated these revealed data by means of reflection, deduction and co-ordination, and has gradually worked them all up into a systematized whole which we know by the name of theology.

2. Place of Natural Theology among the Branches of Philosophic Study.—We have already seen how philosophic studies have been classified by Aristotle and the Scholastics (*Introduction*, **9**, and *Gen. Metaphysics*, **1**). Philosophy, they tell us, deals with (1) *what is*—this is speculative philosophy ;

---

* Books for study or consultation :—
Garrigou-Lagrange, *Dieu, son existence et sa nature* (Beauchesne, Paris, 1915).
BOEDDER, *Natural Theology* (Longmans, London, 2nd ed., 1896).
AVELING, *The God of Philosophy* (C. T. S., London, 2nd ed., 1914).
DRISCOLL, *Christian Philosophy : God* (Benziger, New York, 2nd ed., 1902).
MOYES, *The Existence of God* (brochure : Sands, London, 1906).
MICHELET, *D eu et L'Agnosticisme contemporain* (Lecoffre, Paris, 1909).
CALDECOTT and MACKINTOSH, *Selections from the Literature of Theism* (Clark, Edinburgh, 1904).
A large edition of *Théodicée* as a volume of the *Cours* was announced by the Institut Supérieur de Philosophie as in preparation before the destruction of Louvain.

[1] Etymologically the word is derived from an ' advocate's plea ' on the subject of God, Θεοῦ δίκη. We find it first used by Leibniz in his *Essai de théodicée sur la bonté de Dieu, la liberté de l'homme et l'origine du mal* (Amsterdam, 1710) ; and here it is of God as known by revelation that he speaks. Kant took the word in the same sense ; but since then *theodicy* has been used to signify the *purely philosophical* study of God, as distinguished from theology which is confined to the study of God as known to us by revelation. Theodicy in this present-day sense is also often called rational, or natural, theology ; by Aristotle it was catalogued as ἡ θεολογική φιλοσοφια. [The word is also used in the narrower meaning of 'God's Justice,' His Providence : ROSMINI, *Theodicy*, 3 vols. (Longmans, London, 1912).—TRS.].

(2) *what ought to be*—this is practical philosophy. Speculative philosophy investigates the nature of *movement*, of *quantity*, of *substance*. Hence we have the treatises that correspond, namely, *physics, mathematics* and *metaphysics*.

If we ask what is the place of natural theology in speculative philosophy, we find that it belongs both to physics and to metaphysics. (1) To physics, because the fundamental proof of the existence of the First Being is to be found, as we shall see, in the consideration of *movement* or the transition from potentiality to actuality, as we observe it in the things that come within our experience ; and *movement* was the particular subject-matter of the physics of the ancients. (2) To metaphysics, because the First Cause, the real existence of which is made known to us by the fact of movement, in no way needs the intervention of a being anterior to itself for the explanation of its existence and its activity ; for it has in itself all the perfections that constitute it. It can admit of no transition from potentiality to actuality ; or, to use the concise and expressive terms of the Scholastics, it is in no sense *moved*, but it is the *Unmoved*.

Since the First Being does not admit of being other than it is, of the possibility of passing from potency to actuality, it is wholly and entirely actual, *actus purus ;* and consequently admits neither of potentiality nor of materiality; in other words, it is *immaterial* (*Gen. Metaphysics*, **123**). Now the formal object of metaphysics, we saw (**3**), is *substance* considered without any reference to change or to those characteristics which are proper to matter ; it investigates being as immaterial—negatively or positively—and immobile. It follows, then, that if we take the division of philosophy according to the ancients, natural theology is not really a distinct branch of study : the existence of God is the ultimate conclusion, the highest flight of the study of physics, and the study of His nature is an application of general metaphysics to a particular being, the Being that is absolutely perfect. We conclude, then, that there is no special philosophic science of God.

Moreover, a distinct science would require a formal object of its own and special principles. Yet all the concepts that we can form regarding God are not applicable exclusively to Him, at least *in regard to their positive content*. All our positive, proper concepts are drawn from the material world that comes within the scope of our experience (*Psychology*, **90**). Therefore whatever *positive* notions we form concerning immaterial beings, and concerning God in particular, can only be applications of the concepts we have previously drawn from the material world around us, and all the knowledge we may have about an immaterial being can be at best *analogical.* The ideas we apply solely to spiritual beings and to God are *negative* ones : we limit down the extension of concepts originally apprehended in the material world and make them applicable to God, by eliminating from them all the imperfections that are characteristic of the finite and contingent beings which human knowledge proportionately and adequately represents. Hence, as the content of the notions we possess about God in so far as it is *positive* is shared also by finite and material beings, natural theology has no formal object to call its own.

Again, the principles from which this study sets out are not applicable *exclusively* to God. For, the principles of a science are the fundamental relations that the mind establishes between the different concepts which it has previously drawn from the analysis of the formal object of the science in question ; and where there is no formal object special to the science, there can be no principles peculiar to it to constitute it a special science.

Natural theology, then, belongs both to physics and to metaphysics : in so far as it is metaphysical, it is an application of the concepts and principles of general metaphysics to the First Cause, the existence of which is made known to us by the study of movement.

3. Division of Natural Theology.—Theodicy proves the *existence* of God ; it inquires into the *nature* of God and into the *activity* of the First Cause. To these three problems there correspond the three chief parts of natural theology.

PART I

The Existence of God

Before attempting to prove the existence of God we must first define what we are to understand by the Sovereign Being which is to be the object of our proof. Accordingly this first part of Natural Theology we divide into two chapters, —the one dealing with the *idea of the divine Being*; the other, with the *existence of God*.

CHAPTER I

IDEA OF THE DIVINE BEING

4. The Idea of an Infinite God.—The notion of an infinite God, possessing in Himself every perfection, is found amongst those who live in a Christian environment ; but if our study of natural theology is to be *methodical* it should begin with a notion of God that is common to all men without distinction, whether they are acquainted with a revealed religion or not.

This notion of God we may know as it exists, in the first place, in the *spontaneous consciousness of the individual* ; next, in the *original signification of the names* which serve to portray it ; and lastly, in the *religious notions* entertained by the different races of mankind.

1. We find that men, whether professing belief or not, instinctively and without any reflection use such expressions as : 'Would to God that . . . !' 'Thank God!' 'God only knows!' This implies that God is regarded as the Supreme Master whose will disposes all things, whose wisdom penetrates all things.

2. There are two well-defined groups of languages, the *Semitic* and the *Indo-Germanic*. Philologists have shown that in both these groups the roots of the words that stand for God indicate either the power of a Supreme Master of the universe (*El, Elohim, Allah,* in the Semitic group) ; or else the permanence, the immutability of a Being who remains the self-same in the midst of all change (Ζεὺς from the Sanskrit root *dyut,* meaning to beam, radiant heaven, the shining one, in the Indo-Germanic group) ; or again, a Being who when called upon hearkens to petition (Θεός from θέσσομαι, I invoke).

3. Anthropologists (e.g. De Quatrefages, Lang, Chantepie) who have studied the religious conceptions of the various civilized and savage peoples, agree that everywhere, both in the past and in the present, there is to be found the idea of

8

one or more powerful divinities, above the order of mankind, who reward good and punish evil.

It is the philosopher's task to ascertain whether this universally accepted notion comes from a purely *anthropomorphic* tendency of the human mind or whether there really exists one or several beings which correspond to it. Whatever may be said about the existence of God, which will be examined in Chapter II, we must first establish the following proposition.

5. The Idea of a Supreme Being, Superior to the World, the Guardian of the Moral Order, is an Idea of an Absolutely Simple Perfection ; and is therefore Sufficient to provide Natural Theology with a Proper Object.—We have to explain these terms and prove the proposition.

Put briefly our argument is this : An idea of God is sufficiently characteristic of its object when it comprises an absolutely simple perfection. Now although the spontaneous idea of God we have described above does not contain the *explicit* notion of the Infinite, nevertheless it comprises several perfections that are absolutely simple, especially those of absolute sovereignty, of immutability in the midst of change, and of a being who is guardian of the moral order. An idea such as this is sufficient to provide natural theology with a proper formal object.

Perfections are of different kinds, as has been shown in General Metaphysics **(174, 175)**. We distinguish between *mixed*, *simple* and *absolutely simple* perfections. (1) The first kind formally contain an imperfection, e.g. the power of reasoning which is the characteristic perfection of man. (2) A simple perfection (*simplex*) is one which does not, by its very definition, imply any imperfection, yet at the same time does not exclude it ; e.g. the perfection of intelligence or of life. (3) By an absolutely simple perfection (*simpliciter simplex*) is meant one whose concept formally excludes all imperfection whatsoever. The perfections of God belong to this third category. They are characteristic of the divine Being, since in them we can find neither trace of admixture nor of limitation.

Nevertheless, the absolutely simple perfections which we recognize in God either from spontaneous knowledge or as the result of philosophic argumentation do not contain in an *explicit* way the character of infinity of perfection. It is only by a further deduction that we draw from these first concepts the idea of this eminent perfection. The infinite nature of pure Actuality is found contained in them in an *implicit* way.

According to Descartes and the ontologists who follow him the human mind has positive and proper concepts of what is immaterial, especially of the Infinite. For, with them, the notion of the Infinite is primordial ; arguing as they do that the idea ' finite ' bespeaks limitation, and that limitation is a negative idea that entails a previous acquaintance with the positive of which it is the denial : hence the idea of God is a primary idea as well as a positive and proper one. In his *Méditations métaphysiques,* Descartes argues that it is by a way of limitation applied to this primordial concept we have of the Infinite that we know all finite beings ; the human mind is primarily conscious of the subsistent Infinite Being.

Descartes' theory of innate ideas is erroneous. The truth is, as we have seen in Psychology (**90-97**), that the formal object of our intelligence is abstract natures which underlie what we perceive by the senses. But none of the notes that formally belong to the world perceived by our senses can be predicated in the same sense of the divine Being, which even Descartes himself allows is supersensible and infinite. Not one, then, of the positive and proper notions of the mind can be applied *as such* to God, nor, in consequence, can they give natural theology the formal object which it demands. We can have but a negative and analogical knowledge of what is by nature spiritual.

Again, the finite intelligence of man is capable only of receiving finite intelligible forms. It is clearly impossible for any finite intelligible form to represent the Infinite in a positive and proper way. Our finite intelligence, then, cannot conceive a proper idea of the Infinite. The Beatific Vision, the promise faith gives us of life eternal, cannot be by means of *concepts*. It is not given to imperfect beings such as we are to reach God by the way suggested by Descartes. We must, therefore, fall back on the longer yet more secure way taught by the Scholastic system.

Kant was aware of a line of argument for establishing the existence of an Infinite God which proceeds first to assert the existence of a necessary Being and then to conclude from it His Infinity ; but he would not allow its validity on the ground that the leap from the *necessity* to the *infinity* of God involved an appeal to the very ontological argument which he combated—an argument which we also refuse to accept. Consequently he argued that all rigorous philosophical demonstration of the existence of God by the Theoretic Reason must necessarily imply the direct affirmation of the Infinite. Recognizing, and quite rightly, that this is impossible, he arrived at the conclusion that the Practical Reason alone, from the postulates that it makes, can lead us to posit the fact of God's existence.

Later we shall show that the criticisms of Kant, based as they are on the necessity of recourse to the ontological argument for passing from the first to the second stage in the proof of an Infinite God, are without any foundation (25).

We assert, then, against Kant that we *can*, against Descartes that we *must*, take as our starting point for our proof of the existence of God a notion of the infinite Being that is not a positive and proper one.

6. Triple Process of Attribution, Elimination and Transcendence.—We are justified in predicting of God the *simple* perfections that are presented to us in the consideration of the world and of man ; for the divine Being is the supreme efficient cause of them, and surely in the cause must be found the perfections of the effect.

But further we must submit all perfections as we know them in the world to a process of elaboration if we wish to predicate them of God in a way that they will belong to Him alone.

This process involves three stages. (i) First we affirm of the primary Cause all *simple* perfections. This is the process of attribution. (ii) We then immediately exclude from these perfections all idea of imperfection. This is the process of elimination. (iii) These perfections, purified from all alloy, we attribute to God, affirming that they belong to Him in a *different* way from that in which they belong to the contingent beings from which we have apprehended them. They are in Him in a supereminent way. This is the process of transcendence.

Thus purified and exalted by the processes of elimination and transcendence, these simple perfections become *absolutely simple* (5), or, more strictly, they manifest to us under different aspects one and the same absolute perfection.

7. This Process is neither Fallacious nor Useless.—A difficulty is raised by the employment of this threefold process of attribution, elimination and transcendence. The objection may be made that the different notions of the divine essence as they are given to us by this method are either without meaning or they are erroneous ; for either these different concepts represent one and the same formality or else formalities that are quite different from one another. In the first hypothesis there is no ground for any multiplicity ; in the second hypothesis, they lead us into error inasmuch as their multiplicity cannot represent the divine essence which is above composition of any kind.

This difficulty, long ago put by Duns Scotus against the teaching of St. Thomas, can be solved only by attending to the *virtual incomplete* distinction that exists between the different perfections that we attribute to the divine Being. Let us recall what has been said on the subject of distinctions (*General Metaphysics*, **48**).

Distinctions correspond to compositions, and these are either real or existing only in the mind. (1) A composition is *real* when quite independently of any consideration by the mind it implies a plurality of things ; it exists between this thing and that thing, *inter rem et rem*. In order that there may be a real distinction, it is not at all necessary that the things, though distinct, be really separable. By their very nature they may be incapable of existing apart from one another and yet they may be in reality distinct, e.g. essence and existence, thought and the faculty of thinking. (2) We have a *logical* distinction when there are, in the mind, several different concepts of the same thing. A logical distinction may be either one of pure reason, or a virtual one. (*a*) It is one of *pure reason* or *rationis ratiocinantis* when the two concepts have *the same formal* as well as material object, although one of them may be more explicit than the other. Thus there is a distinction of pure reason between the concepts of man and rational animal. (*b*) A logical distinction is *virtual* or a *distinctio rationis ratiocinatae* when the concepts have the same material object but *not the same formal object ;* they regard one and the same entity, but they view it under different aspects or distinct formalities—as, for example, the distinction between the spirituality and the simplicity of the soul. Further, this logical virtual distinction may be complete or incomplete—(a) *complete*, when the formal object of each of these distinct concepts is *realizable separately*, e.g. the mind can distinguish in the case of the human soul its intellectual, its animal and its vegetative life ; (β) *incomplete* when each formally distinct object implicitly comprises the others.

With these terms defined, we recognize among the divine perfections an *incomplete virtual distinction*. The divine essence, which is simple in itself, may be represented to us by concepts which have a formally distinct content ; nevertheless, the formal object which each of these concepts represents contains in an implicit manner the objects represented by the other concepts. Moreover, the divine perfections are attributed to an infinite being ; each of them because it is infinite must comprise the others. The virtual distinction that we recognize between the divine perfections must, then, be imperfect or incomplete [2].

For the very reason that this distinction is incomplete, our knowledge of the divine Being is not, in the first place, fallacious ; for the concept of each perfection, since it implies infinity, implicitly contains all the other perfections. Our knowledge would be untrue only if it represented as *distinct* those perfections which constitute a *real* unity.

In the second place, this notion of the perfect Being is anything but useless ; for each concept which goes to form it brings before us, in an explicit manner, *some different aspect* of the divine essence.

If we inquire what is the real foundation for this incomplete virtual distinction that we make between the perfections of God, we find that it certainly cannot be in the divine essence viewed in an absolute manner, for God in Himself is above all composition ; but it is to be found in the divine essence viewed in a *relative* manner—relatively, that is, to the world, of which God is the primary efficient cause as well as the supereminent archetypal cause, and relatively to our intelligence whose proper object is the essence of material beings, and whose manner of knowing, being abstract and fragmentary,

---

[2] The same incomplete virtual distinction is seen amongst the transcendental attributes of being. *Gen. Metaphysics*, **76**.

prevents it from taking in at a single glance the simple perfection of God. On account of this infirmity of the human
mind we can only know the nature of God in His relations to
creation which we see. From the order of finality established
and maintained in the cosmos we rise to the idea of God's
intelligence and *wisdom*, and from the contingency of the beings
that surround us we rise to the idea of the *power* of God who
created them. God, then, inasmuch as He is regarded by the
mind as the primary and archetypal cause of created things,
is the foundation of that composite knowledge, which is at
once true and useful, that we piece together concerning His
nature.

CHAPTER II

THE EXISTENCE OF GOD

ART I. CRITICAL EXAMINATION OF THE DOCTRINES OPPOSED TO THE PROOF OF GOD'S EXISTENCE

8. General Sketch.—(1) Positivism asserts that the immaterial world, and God in particular, cannot be the object of human knowledge. (2) Traditionalism holds the view that since the mind is incapable of proving the existence of God, this truth can be received only by an act of faith based upon revelation. (3) On the other hand, ontologism asserts that to reach God it is not neccesary to use a method of discursive reasoning, but that we have an immediate intuition of the divine essence. (4) We may reduce to ontologism whatever positive content there is in the New Philosophy as expounded chiefly by Bergson and Le Roy. According to the latter, who deals specially with the question of God, there is no method available for demonstrating God's existence ; we do not prove His existence by any process of reasoning, but we *affirm God* intuitively by means of *Thought-Action* (la Pensée-Action), that fundamental reality which Bergson calls the vital *Elan* or impulse which is also the abundant source of Being. God does not afford a proof of Himself, but each and every man has within himself a vital experience of Him[3]. (5) Lastly, we must at least speak briefly of those who make the affirmation of God's existence rest on a subjective sentiment.

Before dealing directly with the proofs for the existence of God, we must examine these various teachings and show both

---

[3] In other respects the New Philosophy has some affinity with positivism and with Kantianism ; it is ultimately reducible to an evolutionistic monism most akin to Hegelian idealism and the phenomenalism of Heraclitus. See BALTHASAR, *Le problème de Dieu d'après la Philosophie nouvelle.* (Reprint from the *Rev. Néo-Scolastique*, Louvain, 1908.)

the possibility and the necessity of proving the existence of the divine Being.

9. Positivism and Agnosticism.—On this question of the existence of God we find that the positivist school is divided into two groups. The one deals with the possibility of our knowledge of what is immaterial and, by way of consequence only, of our knowledge of God in particular ; the other deals directly with the question of the existence of the Supreme Being.

Those positivists who deny that we have any notion about the immaterial which is of scientific value base their argument on different considerations. Some set out with a simple affirmation which they maintain is perfectly self-evident and must be taken as a postulate, namely, that the human mind is capable of thinking only in positive ideas. With regard to the soul, God; and in general all things that are not clothed with material conditions, they profess a necessary ignorance, sometimes waiving the question whether they exist or not, sometimes disposing of them by a categorical denial. Other philosophers, dominated by Kantianism, put forward as their reason for eliminating all idea of the immaterial from human thought the fact that there is a *law* of our understanding enforcing this. It is part, indeed, of the Kantian system that only those of our cognitions are scientific which are synthetic a priori judgments, and these are conditioned by pure intuitions of time and space. As what is immaterial is, by its nature, withdrawn from such conditions, it follows that the human mind cannot have a scientific knowledge of such beings.

Those philosophers whose purpose is a direct criticism of the knowledge that we affirm we can have of God, rest their contention chiefly on considerations of fact. According to Comte the history of ideas as shown to us both in the development of ages and in the life of each individual reveals that the conceptions of the human mind are governed in their progress by a law—his famous ' law of the three stages '. Our knowledge, he says, passes through three successive stages. The first is the theological stage, in which the mind is inclined to absolute cognitions : phenomena are regarded by it as the resultants of the direct action of supernatural free agencies, and, in consequence, as subject to no fixed law. This is the period when everything is ascribed to deities. Subsequent to this is the metaphysical stage, when recourse is no longer had to supernatural realities for the explanation of phenomena, but instead to invisible powers or forces, which are nothing more than abstractions accredited with reality. Lastly comes a stage, the positive stage, at which the mind recognizes the impossibility of attaining absolute notions, of knowing the inmost causes of phenomena, and confines itself exclusively to gaining a knowledge of the invariable relations of succession and similarity which unite them.

It is not the place here to appraise the worth of Kant's criticism and of his unproved claim that our knowledge has no scientific value except as formulated in synthetic a priori judgments.[4] We must confine our attention to a refutation of agnosticism and the positivism of Comte.

10. Criticism of the Agnostic Position.—The agnostic asserts as an a priori truth, anterior to all examination concerning the object of our knowledge, and as self-evident, that our cognitive faculties cannot rise above what is of the sensible order. But, we may ask, is it thus evident without any inquiry into the extent of human knowledge that the mind cannot attain to immaterial beings, should such happen to exist ? The object of intellectual knowledge is simply thing, something ; the intellectual apprehends what-a-thing-is, quiddity, being (*Psychology*, 88). A very elementary introspection proves this, that being, and not necessarily material being, is the object of intelligence : it is not being, thing, as *material* which it grasps, but simply as being ; its object is not necessarily characterized by material conditions. But we are far from asserting that what we learn from an elementary inquiry about our cognitive faculty warrants our declaring that we are able to know immaterial being positively ; it only shows that it is incorrect to infer, as do the positivists, that material things are the only object of intellectual knowledge[5]. Their postulate therefore is both a priori and gratuitous. If indeed after mature reflection we find that the material world requires for its *adequate* interpretation that immaterial things also exist, we shall not be wrong in listening to what our reason informs us about those immaterial things.

[4] See *Criteriology*, 39, 40 ; and cp. *Crit. gén.* (Cours Supérieur), 98 f.
[5] Cp. *Critériologie générale* (Cours Supérieur), 116.

The positivist of the Spencerian type may rejoin by asserting that, granted it is a priori and arbitrary to rule out all immaterial beings from the domain of knowledge, still any such knowledge we may acquire of such beings, and therefore of the divine Being, cannot be of any scientific value ; only what is known in terms of extension, number and weight can be the subject-matter of certain and positive science : the little we know of God is only enough to let us know that He is the ' Unknowable '.

We do not wish to deny an important aspect of the truth which is concealed under the above objection. We readily admit that our mind finds in the material world the object which is proportionate to its capabilities ; sensible things are what we know in a proper and positive way. And if the philosopher in defining his terms—where undoubtedly there is scope for what is arbitrary—calls scientific only those representations which possess these characteristics, then assuredly the immaterial cannot be the object of science.

But, having said this, we must never forget that, over and above the notions we have concerning the material world, our minds are capable of possessing analogical and negative conceptions of God. We are not, indeed, able to predicate positively of Him what is common also to material beings ; nevertheless these concepts which we have taken originally from the material world of things we refine by means of a process of negation which eliminates from them every element of imperfection. Without strictly signifying what in a positive manner is peculiar to God, these concepts are in reality applicable to Him alone, and thus they afford us a true knowledge of the divine Being.

11. Criticism of Comte's ' Law of the Three Stages ' and the Agnostic Mentality it produces.—Comte endeavoured to establish his ' law of the three stages ' on various considerations : (1) The general history of the sciences shows that this law really exists. All knowledge has gone through or is still going through these three stages of human thought. (2) The historical argument is corroborated by an argument from analogy. The life of every man reveals in its course three successive stages. Childhood marks that of credulity and theological belief. Youth is a prey to metaphysical illusions. Mature age turns a man to the physical order.   (3) Finally there is an intrinsic argument to show the necessity of this law.   The human mind feels a need of connecting, by some theory or other, the facts which come under its experience.   Along with this mental need there also discloses itself, in the early stages of rational development, the inability to discover a theory suggested by facts observed.   If, therefore, a man wanted to find scope for the employment of his intellectual activity, he had to invent from the information at hand some interpretation that would serve to unify the phenomena he observed : theology served him this purpose.   This prepared the way to the metaphysical theory of nature, whence humanity has been enabled to arrive at this stage of positive science, which is the final stage.

To-day there are not many of the followers of Comte who hold by this celebrated law.   Indeed, it is not very difficult to show by various historical facts that it is false.   In the days of old the Greeks were by no means unfamiliar with the study of natural phenomena.   Though Aristotle was a giant in metaphysical speculations, he was also the compiler of all the observations both in physics and politics of his times. And in mediaeval times the West, engrossed in theological speculations, has given us, besides such metaphysicians as St. Thomas and Duns Scotus, a physicist of the calibre of Roger Bacon.

Again, it is no less false to maintain that each individual passes through the three stages of theology, metaphysics and the positive sciences.   The child by no means dreams of explaining the phenomena that attract his attention by the agency of divine beings.   In this sense—and it is Comte's— he is not at all naturally inclined to religion.   Youth, in general, shows very little bent for metaphysical abstractions.   On the contrary we meet with powerful minds for whom philosophical studies are the final stage of a career which has been devoted chiefly, if not entirely, to the study of the physical sciences. Such, for example, was Helmholz, who was first a physiologist and then devoted himself to philosophy after passing an intermediary stage of mathematical study.   So too Kant wrote a universal history of the nature of the heavens, a sketch on some considerations concerning fire, various studies on earthquakes, on the theory of winds, and an essay on headaches, before he reached the final stage of his thought in which he elaborated his two *Critiques*.

Again, Comte's *logical* proof of the *necessity* of the ' law of the three stages ' derives all its value from his empirical proof. Isolated from history, it would be a *petitio principii*. For he makes the assertion that the first hypotheses which the human mind constructed were necessarily theological. But on what grounds does he base his assertion ? It is true that the observer of nature does read some theory into his facts, that he constructs some hypothesis concerning the nature of the connexions binding facts together and directs his observations and experiments to the verification of this hypothesis ; it is true that this premature theory, this provisionary hypothesis, may be theological, and indeed, as Spencer remarks, certain ' unaccustomed ' ' anomalous ' phenomena may well have led primitive man to adopt some theory of this kind : but there is nothing to warrant our saying that recourse was had to such an explanation as a general rule.

Moreover, Comte takes it for granted, without offering adequate proof, that the positive stage of knowledge is the final and perfect one, and yet this is an essential part of his ' law of the three stages '. What—apart from historical considerations—is the proof he adduces ? That, on the one hand, positive explanations cannot co-exist with theological or metaphysical ones, since they are mutually exclusive ; and that, on the other hand, positive science cannot precede or be inferior, since the human mind is subject to a law of indefinite progress and retrogression is impossible. But is this an adequate proof ? Why may not the perfection of knowledge, the final stage, be a synthesis of all, theological, metaphysical and positive ? And what grounds are there for the assertion that progress is indefinite and that it is impossible for the human race to fall back ? Either this is a mere assertion without proof, and in this case his pretended law of the three stages is merely a corollary of a non-proven postulate ; or it is an attempt at proof based on the historical grounds that everywhere and always theological and metaphysical explanations have given way to positive ones : in which case what was claimed as a *logical* proof is found to be really an empirical one, and apart from historical observation has no value at all.

It is interesting, moreover, to note that for the foundation of his positivism Comte had to have recourse to a necessary and universal law, namely the necessity of the mind to bind facts together by a theory, in order to prove precisely from this that there are no such things as necessary laws but only associations that are more or less constant. A positivist can pronounce about *what is*, he cannot speak of *what ought to be*.

Though as a matter of fact the ' law of the three stages ' has been abandoned by the majority of philosophers, even by the positivists themselves, it has yet left a heritage of considerable influence. Many thinkers who are engrossed in the study of the natural sciences and confine themselves to the use of experimental methods, consider every metaphysical or religious inquiry as vain and illusory. The method of the positive sciences they make to consist in a complete disregard for any such speculation. And their method, they assure us, has proved its value. To it we are indebted for those marvellous conquests in the realms of the unknown which have enlarged man's horizon both in knowledge and in action. And to Comte, it is said, belongs the glory of all these modern achievements ; to him as the founder of positivism we must be grateful for revealing the method of observation which has exercised such a powerful influence on the various branches of the sciences.

But is it really true that the credit is due to the positive method extolled by Comte for the progress in the sciences which is the object of our admiration and the source of abundant blessings ? This eulogy of positivism is due in great part to the confusion which Comte created between the positive method and the experimental method, which is the real source of the discoveries of modern times. This confusion is pure sophistry, as Pasteur showed in his celebrated Inaugural Address to the French Academy. Comte put the observer face to face with nature and left him to consider the manifold antecedents of a phenomenon in the complex conditions in which they find their play. This method, by not allowing an inquiry into what antecedent amongst them is the cause of the phenomenon to be explained, enables us merely to pass, more or less legitimately, from *what has been* to *what can be*. The experimental method, which alone is of value in the physical sciences, starts out, on the contrary, from *a directive idea* which the experimenter endeavours to *verify* by his study of the phenomena.

He varies *artificially* the conditions under which the phenomenon appears ; he sets aside certain antecedents, and modifies the intensity of action in certain others. The positivistic method leaves the observer passive, with the result that his conclusions are subject to the conditions under which the phenomenon he is studying presents itself ; the experimental method leads him actively to search for the laws that natural agents obey.

Finally we must remember that the dream of a positive science supplanting philosophy in every respect has already passed out of fashion. H. Poincaré, Duhem, Le Roy and other writers on the ' *critique of the sciences* ' have done much to humble the proud claims made by scientists. Metaphysical, ethical and theological speculations have again taken their proper place beside and above the experimental sciences, which fail to satisfy the ultimate questionings of the human mind.

12. Criticism of Traditionalism.—There are two schools of traditionalism : (1) The radical school who regard the human reason as incapable of demonstrating the existence of God, which they make the object of an act of faith based on a primitive revelation handed on to us by society. Since the coming of Christ this revealed deposit has been entrusted to the Church. (2) The semi-traditionalists who likewise maintain that in the first instance unaided reason is incapable of attaining to a knowledge of the existence of God, but differ from the former school by professing that after a revelation of the fact it is now possible to demonstrate by rational proof.

To establish their fideism the traditionalists point chiefly to the errors shown in the history of philosophy. De Bonald, the most able thinker amongst them, had recourse to a psychological argument. We cannot think, he says, without words ; and to create language man had to think and, consequently, must already have had the use of words. (An evident vicious circle.) Since reason was in itself incapable of creating language and of making an act of thought which is really its own, it is necessary for the explanation of these activities in man to have recourse to a primitive revelation, the teachings of which we receive by faith.

We see that by way of a reaction from a revolutionary rationalism the traditionalists took a most exaggerated view of the weakness of the human mind. The truth is that the many errors displayed by the history of philosophy are no cogent proof of the total incapacity of our reason. Such a radical conclusion would only be justified if it could be shown that the laborious speculations of all thinkers in all ages were nothing more than one long delirium. Only if this were established could we assert that there has been no progress towards the truth. But to take such a pessimistic view of the great systems of philosophy is absolutely to falsify history. Revelation is indeed *morally* necessary for humanity to preserve the body of speculative ethical truths it has inherited ; but it is not *physically* necessary. In any case, as we shall show, the existence of God cannot be simply the object of an act of divine faith.

As to de Bonald's argument from an appeal to the origin of language, which he maintained must be due to revelation, we may remark, in the first place, that the very thorny problem (which it is not given us here to discuss) of how language came into existence, he solved not by induction but purely a priori. And even if we grant, in spite of all that is to be said to the contrary, this first premiss of his argument, namely, that language together with all the notions that it embodies could result only from a divine teaching made known to the first members of the human race ; we have still to remark (*a*) that a teaching is not necessarily a revelation : the former may be the appeal made by a master to the intelligence of his disciple, whilst the latter is an appeal to the faith of a believer. (*b*) That, if we suppose the human mind to be absolutely incapable, a revelation is not sufficient to explain how we are able to arrive at a certain knowledge of the existence and nature of God. If we receive a revealed truth, this is not by an act of blind credence but only after we have satisfied ourselves about the claims that this proposition has to be received by faith ; and it is only by the exercise of our reason that we can satisfy ourselves about its credibility. Yet traditionalism is based on the assertion that the reason is totally incapable. The believer, in reality, admits the object of his faith by relying on the authority of God[6]. This very act, then, *presupposes* that he has a rational knowledge of God's existence and of the

---

[6] We say advisedly *on the authority of God* and not *on the evidence* which we have of that authority. The latter, the motives of credibility, are necessarily finite ; the former, which is the motive of faith, is unlimited, and faith is a supernatural gift.

historical fact of revelation (*Criteriology*, **69**). Therefore traditionalism can never succeed in establishing the proposition that the existence of God is accepted *by faith* ; it drives man back to an agnostic position.

Semi-traditionalists, on the other hand, by recognizing that the reason has a limited capacity, are carried on, in spite of themselves, to the same opinion as we uphold ; for by logically following out their conclusions they are forced to acknowledge that a proof of the existence of God is possible.

Their contention is that the human reason can arrive at this proof under the guidance of the light of revelation. But the intellectual operation of the mind which discovers the existence of God is *intrinsically* just the same as the operation which enables it to accept as a rational truth the knowledge that it has acquired by revelation. Undoubtedly, after the revelation of a truth that our intellectual faculties are capable of attaining by their own power, the *extrinsic* difficulties of its proof become less. But since the discursive act of the reason which is necessary for the attainment of a truth hitherto unknown is *in itself* the same as the act by which we prove a truth already known, it follows that to grant that reason has the power to make this last operation is also to admit its intrinsic capability of producing the first operation. The intermediate position which the semi-traditionalists have taken up is untenable ; they must, if they are logical, either return to that of radical traditionalism and therefore ultimately fall back to agnostic scepticism, or else they must carry to its ultimate consequences the concession they have made to the rationalistic position of the Scholastics and acknowledge that a proof of God's existence is possible.

After this conclusion regarding the possibility of proving God's existence, we must, against the ontologistic school, show the *necessity* of demonstrating it.

13. Criticism of Ontologism.—According to the teaching of Rosmini and Gioberti, God is not the term of a syllogism but the object of an intuition. This immediate knowledge of the divine Being is primordial in man ; only subsequently are contingent beings known, by means of a comprehensive view through which the mind directly sees the divine essence and in it the eternal archetypes of all created beings.

This theory is based by its proponents chiefly on two

arguments : (1) It is quite impossible that God should be represented under any finite form ; consequently the human intelligence, which as a matter of fact does know His existence, can gain this knowledge only from an immediate vision. (2) For knowledge to be true, it must be in conformity with the object known. But in the order of real beings, God is the primary Being and all created things are posterior. So also in the order of knowledge, we must first know God and afterwards contingent beings.

1. Ontologism sets out from an erroneous theory of ideas. The proper object of the intelligence, as we have shown elsewhere (*Psychology*, **89**), consists in the intelligible forms as apprehended in the world presented to our senses. To see God as He is in Himself constitutes the Beatific Vision, which is the goal promised *by faith* to the *supernatural* life of grace. Under the limitations of our knowledge in this present life we can know immaterial beings only by applying, by means of the processes we have already spoken of (**6**), the notions which we have first drawn from the material world. Experience attests that we have no intuition of the infinite Being. Moreover if we could gaze upon the very essence of God, we should by the enjoyment of this supreme happiness be absorbed in the contemplation of the inexhaustible perfections of God and lost in the love of the infinite Goodness. At the same time our minds would not be subject to the least error about God, and we should be more certain of His existence than of that of anything else. Since such consequences are belied by facts, the theory from which they necessarily follow stands condemned.

2. In the second place, the ontologists are at fault in their logic : (*a*) They maintain that God can in no way be represented in our knowledge by a finite form. Undoubtedly this is true if it is a question of a knowledge that is positive, proper and adequate ; but this is no argument against our attainment of knowledge of God that is analogical and negative, by means of finite forms. (*b*) Again, truth by its very definition is the conformity of the mental cognition with the thing known, and from this they argue that the order in which our knowledge arises in the mind must necessarily follow the precise order in which things really exist. But this inference they draw from the definition of truth is unwarrantable. The truth of an *individual* cognition does require the conformity of *this* cognition with the

particular thing cognized ; but for the *system* of our cognitions to be true, there is no need for us to represent everything in the order of its logical succession. Such a condition is needed for the perfection of our scientific system, not for its truth : a thing is true when what we say of it is in conformity with what it is ontologically. What we affirm of God, although it is by ideas which are mediate and drawn originally from the world of sensible experience, is that He is the First Cause and Last End of this world (5).

14. Meaning of the ' New Philosophy '[7].—According to Le Roy[8], God is infinite becoming. The essence of reality is ' movement ', becoming. In so far as He has already become within us, He is the immanent divine ; in so far as He will ceaselessly continue to develop Himself, He is the transcendent divine. Now I have within myself an immediate intuition of a becoming, of a tendency to become more and more perfect, more and more moral. This supremacy of the moral law which I feel within myself constitutes the affirmation of the existence of God. There are, accordingly, no atheists properly so-called, since every man feels within himself an aspiration towards what is better ; or rather, we should say, every one experiences a season of atheism whensoever he is doing what is evil and not advancing towards the ideal. The only true reality is an incessant becoming, conscious of itself in varying degrees—and this is known as *Thought-Action* (la Pensée-Action). Our reasoning as it were congeals this continuous flow of reality and so changes its nature. To use the metaphorical language of this philosophy, reality is a continuous curve, reasoning is a tangent which at any moment stops its movement ; the mind owing to its utilitarian or practical tendency ' scatters ' reality, and breaks it up—this is *matter ;* it then unifies by *reasoning* these scattered elements that were created by Thought-Action. Here we have as it were an echo of the underlying fundamental continuity of the one and eternal becoming which is the only reality, namely, Thought-Action. Besides matter and reason it is necessary to posit a directive element which draws us on to perfection—this is the principle

---

[7] Here we confine ourselves to some fundamental criticisms. For further details, see BALTHASAR, *op. cit.*

[8] E. LE ROY, *A New Philosophy : Henri Bergson*, tr. V. Benson (Williams & Norgate, London, 1913).

of growth, or moral reality. This reality, spirit of our spirit, cannot be reduced to any other form of reality ; it is at the very source of existence. It is necessary to posit its supremacy, and it is this which constitutes the affirmation of God. The New Philosophy is, then, opposed to ' *philosophia perennis* ' as the philosophy of becoming is opposed to that of being. It is *idealist*, for it is all consciousness ; it is *evolutionist*, for the fundamental reality is a more and more perfect becoming, which is necessitated by its own nature ; being is a dynamic welling-up, an effort to develop.

1. This system of philosophy which claims to correct common sense and to go beyond it by asserting as a postulate that thought cannot reach out beyond itself or know an object other than thought itself, must logically terminate in pantheism, notwithstanding what may be affirmed to the contrary. For God is made to live within us, to realize Himself in us ; by the higher part of our being we are in fact God, since we know Him and since thought can know nothing but itself.

2. We are conscious, it is said, of a tendency towards self-realization, of being drawn to perform the good. This, however, cannot be a *vital experience of God*, unless indeed we are ourselves God. For if there exists a tendency in my nature towards working what is just and noble and good, it is legitimate to argue that this finite impulse towards the ideal is contingent like my nature, and therefore requires for its explanation a Necessary Being already self-perfected and not needing to acquire further reality ; but this is a proof of God from causality and not by any vital experience of Him.

3. It is not true that the abstract principles of thought change the nature of reality. Granted they do not apprehend all reality, that they abstract from many elements in reality, nevertheless they do apply to reality and they truly express the laws of reality. It is thus that the becoming, or the acquisition of reality, cannot be adequately explained without recourse to an unmoved being which in some way possesses this perfection of reality. We shall return to this point when we deal with the argument *a motu* for the existence of God. We cannot say that becoming is the fundamental reality without at the same time denying the objective application of the principle of sufficient reason. The New Philosophy does

not shrink from this extreme consequence and so utters its own condemnation.

We must here confine ourselves to these fundamental criticisms. The New Philosophy cannot establish the affirmation of God by a vital experience without reducing God to the level of finite things, and thereby despoiling Him of what is divine.

15. Examination of the Religion of Sentiment.—The word *immanence* is extraordinarily prominent in present-day philosophy. The New Philosophy tells us that man cannot get beyond his states of consciousness ; he has an intuition of the real by virtue of an operation which is at once thought and action. Other philosophers distinguish between thought and sentiment and they posit the existence of God by virtue of a purely subjective sentiment which cannot be reduced to thought. The development of these ideas is to be ascribed partly to the influence of Protestantism, partly to the disintegrating action of the ' Critique of Pure Reason ', and partly also to the vague impression that everything is subject to a law of rhythmic evolution, that nothing is absolute, and that truth is but the fruit of the will [9].

It is sufficient for us to remark that in the solution of the problems to which the study of consciousness gives rise the reflecting reason must always have the last word. Feeling or sentiment of its very nature is blind ; it is the province of reason to show that it is right. Man can be obliged to admit God only if he *proves* His existence. The worship man pays to Him is meritorious only if it is founded on reason and conviction. The classical piece of advice that Pascal gave to the free-thinker, that without any use of his reason he should throw in his lot on the side of religion, as preferable to taking the opposite side, is obviously of no avail. Reason alone affords a criterion by which to judge the truth or the falsity of a doctrine ; sentiment, unless it makes an appeal to reason, is powerless to decide.

[9] We may rank as falling under this conception the ideas of Renan and Sabatier, and even, in a certain degree, the ideas of some Catholic advocates of a new apologetic which they associate with the name of Pascal ; they disparage the part played by the reason in religious questions and particularly in the question of God's existence, and place undue emphasis upon the part played by the will and the feelings.

ART. II.   THE PROOFS OF THE EXISTENCE OF GOD

16. Division of this Article.—Proofs are of three kinds—
a priori, a posteriori, and a simultaneo.   (*a*) An *a priori* proof
is one that proceeds from cause to effect, from reason to consequent.   Such, for instance, is a syllogism establishing the
goodness of the end of the universe by starting out from the
idea of a first Cause infinitely wise and good.   (*b*) An *a posteriori*
proof goes to work in just the opposite way, from an effect
to a cause or principle.   Such, for example, is the proof, in
psychology, of the spirituality of the soul from the immaterial
nature of the acts of the mind and the will.   (*c*) An *a simultaneo*
demonstration is the proof of one thing by another which is not
distinct from it in reality but which is conceived by the
mind as preceding it : e.g. the immortality of the soul
as demonstrated by its spirituality.   This threefold division
of proofs, it is clear, is founded on the relation that exists
between things as they are in reality and the way in which
they unfold themselves in our concepts.

It is not difficult to see that there is only one form of
proof that is possible and valid for the existence of God, namely,
an a posteriori proof. (For, in the first place, we cannot conceive of any a priori proof ; it would be absurd to suppose a
being anterior to the First Being.) In the second place, although
an a simultaneo demonstration has been put forward, that
known in history as the ontological argument of St. Anselm,
this argument leads to no justifiable conclusion.   We shall
state and examine it, and then pass on to review the proofs
that are capable of demonstrating the existence of God.

I. THE ONTOLOGICAL ARGUMENT OF ST. ANSELM

17. Statement of the Argument.—The celebrated argument
to which St. Anselm has given his name may be briefly formulated thus : Every man possesses the concept of that being
which is the greatest possible.   But existence in the ontological
order is a perfection.   Therefore we must, unless we violate the
law of contradiction, grant that the being which is the greatest
possible, which is absolutely perfect, has this perfection.   We
conclude then that God does exist.

This argument has been taken up by various well-known

philosophers—Descartes [10], Bossuet, Leibniz. This last, who could not help feeling some weakness in the argument, tried to strengthen it. He gave it a new foundation, in the possibility of the divine essence. God, he alleged, if He is, can only exist of Himself. His essence, if it is possible, is so not inasmuch as it is realizable but inasmuch as it comprises in itself existence. Consequently, if the divine essence in which existence is necessarily involved is possible, God must exist. But It is possible. Therefore God does exist.

18. Criticism of the Ontological Argument.—1. *In general.*—The idea we have of an absolutely perfect being we form synthetically, that is to say, we form it by apprehending the various perfections in creatures, subtracting all limitations and imperfections from such ideas, and then combining them together into a single concept, which is that of the divine being. Now to argue deductively from this idea, to analyse this synthetic notion of God, is to do nothing else than to unwrap again the elements that originally went to form it. Hence from the analysis of our idea of ' infinite ' we can never draw the note of ' existence ' of God. For the idea of the ' existence ' of God could only have been introduced into our synthetic notion of ' infinite ' if in forming it we had either seen it or proved it or postulated it. Outside these three hypotheses

---

[10] Descartes used two further arguments for God's existence.

(1) I have in me the idea of God, i.e. of the Being that is infinitely perfect. But this idea could not have had its origin in me, since I am limited in my being. Therefore I am forced, in order to give a causal explanation of this idea, to admit the existence of God. (*Third Meditation.*)—This argument would be valid if the idea that we have of God represented the Infinite to us in a positive and proper way. But this is not so, as we have already seen. My finite idea of the Infinite is explained by finite causes.

(2) I exist and I have the idea of the perfect Being. From these two truths of fact it is easy to draw a proof of God's existence. For if I had given my being to myself, I should have given myself all the perfections of which I can conceive. Therefore the reason of my existence cannot lie with me but must lie with God. And further it is not difficult to see that there is no power in us by which we are able to subsist or preserve ourselves in being even for a single moment. The contingent nature, then, of our being requires the existence of a necessary Being. (*Principles of Metaphysics*, 20 and 21.)—The second part of this argument comprises, in a confused way, the proof drawn from becoming which we shall explain later (**21**). Still we may here object against Descartes that the fact of our existence and our idea of God is not at all the basis on which we may expect to found the argument from contingency. Whilst it is true that we have not in ourselves the reason of our own being, we come to know this not by observing with Descartes that if a being which possesses the notion of the infinite had given itself its own being it would have given it to itself without any limits : such a line of thought would presuppose that it is at least possible for a being to cause itself, and this involves the absurd supposition that a being can be *anterior* to itself.

it could not have been there. Now an advocate of St. Anselm's argument would certainly shrink from admitting that he has had an intuition of this existence, inasmuch as this would be to profess ontologism ; moreover the question is of *proving* God's existence. In the second place, it is equally impossible, in the very act of forming the synthetic conception of God, to prove His existence ; for this, as we say, is just what is in question. And the third hypothesis, which is the only one left, namely, that in forming our idea we postulated the existence of God, would make the argument a glaring *petitio principii*.

2. *In particular.*—(*a*) The argument of St. Anselm.—It is not sufficient for refuting the argument of so able a thinker as St. Anselm merely to observe that he jumps quite unjustifiably from the ideal order to the real order. Indeed St. Anselm himself considered that existence in *the ontological order* is necessarily contained in the very concept of the infinite Being. Consequently he did not consider that he was leaping the abyss that separates the ideal order from the real, and this objection left him unmoved. For him the premiss from which he was starting was already related to the real order.

The reasoning of St. Anselm is based on this major : ' It is necessary to conceive the perfect Being as existing '. This we do not venture to contradict. He then goes on to infer : ' Consequently the perfect Being exists '. This inference is illogical. From the antecedent on which his reasoning is based, all that can be inferred with regard to the real order is the following consequent : Given that the concept of the infinite Being includes real existence under pain of self-contradiction, if this Being exists, this existence belongs to It necessarily, and the predicate ' existence ' in the proposition must be united to the subject ' perfect Being ' by a necessary nexus. St. Anselm did not perceive that the necessity of real existence which our concept of infinity includes is only a hypothetical necessity. If I conceive the most perfect possible being, I can only conceive it as necessarily existent. But this is no proof that it really exists.

(*b*) The argument as emended by Leibniz.—As the divine essence is possible, and this essence includes existence, it follows that the divine essence exists : so runs the new form in which St. Anselm's argument is clothed. It has the same essential flaw as before. Leibniz confuses the various kinds of possibilities that we have already distinguished (*Gen. Metaphysics*, **19**). We have seen that *intrinsic* possibility is different from *extrinsic* possibility. The former we may call a *non-impossibility*, in other words, the absence of contradiction between the notes that constitute an essence. The latter implies the existence of a being which is the sufficient reason for the production of an essence that is intrinsically possible ; or, in the case of the Being that does not admit of being produced, the presence of a reason for us to posit the existence of this being which we cannot know properly. Hence, when Leibniz asserts that the divine essence, conceived by the intelligence, is possible, he cannot be referring to its extrinsic possibility, as this would be either to presuppose the very question at issue, or to lapse into the fallacy of St. Anselm that we have just refuted. He must be speaking only of intrinsic possibility. Now it is true to say that if we saw positively that there was no repugnance in the *idea* of God's existence, we should *ipso facto* be seeing His existence. For this we should have to possess a positive and proper view of His essence which implies existence : and this would be to fall into the ontologism that Leibniz himself does not admit. In point of fact we have a priori no more reason for affirming that God is possible than for affirming that He is impossible. Our state of mind is absolutely negative ; all that we can say when we argue from the negative and analogical concept that we possess of God is this, that we do not see that He is impossible. So long, however, as we have no reason for asserting that He exists, we cannot affirm that He is intrinsically possible. Indeed it is from existence that we draw our notion of intrinsic possibility ; and we see in a positive way the intrinsic possibility of those beings alone of whose properties and nature we have a direct knowledge (*Gen. Metaphysics*, **20**). Thus the analysis that Leibniz made of the possibility of God, despite the apparent correctness of his logic, conceals the same fundamental flaw as the argument of St. Anselm.

II. St. Augustine's Argument from our Knowledge of Possible Essences

19. Statement and Criticism of the Argument.—*Neither the notes of metaphysical truth nor the objective laws of criteriology nor the necessary possibility of possibles nor their unlimited* *number supply an immediate sufficient reason for the existence of a necessary and infinite Being.*

The truth, St. Augustine somewhere says, is one in itself, independent of all contingent beings. No one speaks of *my* truth, but of *the* truth. It is a norm anterior to all created existences. It is immutable, eternal, necessary. It cannot, then, be explained by a contingent existence ; there must be, for the explanation of its notes, a Being that is necessary, eternal, infinite.

This same line of argument was followed by St. Bonaventure and adopted by Bossuet, Balmès, and d'Hulst. And most modern Scholastics allow its validity. Fr. Lepidi especially sees in the objectivity and in the extramental reality of ideal truth the stumbling-block of Kantian philosophy.

The opinion that Bossuet put forward in one of his ' Eléva-tions ', that metaphysical truth, or the world of possibles, is something divine, even God Himself, seems not far removed from the error of ontologism. For would it not follow that if the truth ' 2 + 2 = 4 ' is the truth of God, when we apprehend it we should be seeing God in Himself ? Such a consequence has not escaped modern exponents of the argument, who are explicit in asserting that this world of possibles is not God Himself but only an *effect* of God. Alongside the world of existences there is, they say, the world of metaphysical truth, of the abstract essences of possible being, equally *real* with it although not *existential ;* and the notes of necessity, eternity, universality of this world would directly lead us, by virtue of the principle of causality, to affirm the existence of God, since in no other way can we account for these notes. Such is the modern version of the argument. It behoves us to examine what are the characteristics and nature of possible essences, and then to ask ourselves if we may not explain them without recourse to God[11].

1. The immutability of truth, the necessity of the laws of logic, the necessary possibility of possibles and their unlimited number are *conditional* and not *absolute*.

2. Possible essences belong to the realm of logical assertions and not to that of actual beings ; or as the old Scholastics

[11] For a fuller statement and criticism of the argument, see P. COFFEY, *Ontology* (Longmans, London), pp. 89-95, and S. REINSTADLER, *Elementa Philosophiae Scholasticae* (Herder, London), II, pp. 232-235.

would have expressed it, ' Necessitatem habent hypotheticam
in praedicando et non absolutam in essendo '.

Now this necessity of relations can be adequately explained
by the faculty of abstraction and universalization which our
finite and contingent mind possesses (*Psychology*, **89-92**).
It does not; then; constitute the immediate sufficient reason
for the existence of a Being absolutely necessary and, in consequence, infinite. What happens is this : the mind leaves
on one side all the individuating notes of a thing and so
*constitutes norms which once posited are regarded as in-
dependent of contingent conditions and even of our very existence.* Whether I exist or not, 2+2 still make 4, it is still
possible that I should exist. If, however, there were no mind,
there would be no truth and 2+2 would not make 4 ; there
would be no possibles ; it would not be possible that I exist.

The objection may be raised that precisely because 2+2
necessarily make 4, because I am necessarily possible, and
finite intelligences are contingent, there is demanded a necessary and infinite intelligence so that 2+2 should always make
4 and that it should always be possible that I exist. We
reply that if we know that God exists, we know also that the
truth is always present before Him ; but that as long as we do
not know the fact of His existence (this is the very point in
question) we have quite an adequate explanation of the truth
that 2+2 always make 4 because in our very statement of it
we suppose the two terms of the proposition always to be presented to some intelligence or other. Since my mind makes
abstraction from the conditions of time and space in its considerations, it sees, granted that it is in possession of these
terms, that always and everywhere 2+2=4.

In our opinion, to give to the ideal world a reality outside
the mind that conceives it is to multiply beings without necessity ; and the objectivity of the ideal order is sufficiently
safeguarded against those who hold a purely subjective view
by the presence in the mind of essences that are drawn from the
sensible world. Kant's view is that we actively constitute
the truth, since the principles that guide us in its search are
a priori ; it is sufficient to reply to him that we abstract our
concepts from reality, that we are passive in the elaboration
of them and of the relations that unite them to one another
(*Criteriology*, **39** f.).

These reasons, it seems to us, force us to assert that there is not, alongside the world of existences, a world of possibles which in some special way leads us to affirm the existence of a necessary Being.

III. Proofs of the Existence of God

20. General Statement of St. Thomas's Proofs.—When we consider a being, we perceive in it its essence, its existence, and its action. The individual *essence* of a being is the sum of the perfections that constitute it, whether they are essential or accidental. *Existence* is that actuality or final determination whereby this constitutive perfection is made to be actual, which determines individual essence into being. By its *action*, the being becomes an efficient cause, and thus manifests its essential perfections and tends towards its end by putting into operation the means that lead to it.

St. Thomas Aquinas in his *Summa Theologica* deals with each of these aspects, static and dynamic, of being to arrive at arguments for the existence of God. (i) The fact that the essential perfection of a finite being is received provides the basis of the *argument from movement*. (ii) The conditional activity of beings leads to the conclusion that there exists a first cause of their action, which is the *argument from efficient causality*. (iii) The becoming of beings shows their contingency and demands the existence of a necessary being : this is the *argument from contingency*.

To these three basic arguments which are known as the ' metaphysical ' proofs of the existence of God St. Thomas adds two others : (iv) The one is connected with the proof drawn from metaphysical movement and is the *argument from the degrees of perfection* that we find in the world. (v) The other shows that the orderliness and purpose manifest in the cosmos demand a supreme designer as cause : an argument known as the *physico-theological argument*.

21. Argument drawn from Metaphysical Movement.—I. The reality from which St. Thomas sets out is metaphysical movement[12], that is to say, the passing from potentiality to actuality. There are beings, he says, in the world around us which, at first without some formal perfection yet capable of

[12] For further explanation of the metaphysical ideas utilized in this argument, see *Gen. Metaphysics*. **112-121.**

possessing it, do acquire this perfection : what happens is that
potentiality is made determinate by its actuality. This
actuality is not the activity of efficient causality ; it is the
perfection which the formal cause gives to a being by an intrinsic self-communication. And this perfection which completes a being may be essential or accidental ; thus food is
digested and transformed into the very substance of the man that
takes it a thought received by a pupil perfects his intelligence.

II. Now a being in a state of potency is not able itself to
be the principle or source of the perfection it acquires. For
before receiving this formal determination the being is without
it. To suppose that it is itself the principle of its perfection
is to assert that it already possesses it. This amounts to the
self-contradiction of saying that the being which is in potentiality
to receive some perfection and does not yet possess it, already
possesses it. Consequently the passing from potentiality to
actuality can be explained only by the action of some other
being already in actuality.

III. Now a series of beings each subject to an external action
cannot mount up *ad infinitum*, without ever coming to a stop
at a first term which itself has in no way acquired the essential
perfections that characterize it. For not one of these moved
beings, taken individually, would have in itself the reason of
the perfections which it receives, and the same would be true
with regard to the whole series which they go to form, for even
in this whole series we could not find the principle of the movement which in it communicates itself from one being to another.
Consequently these formal determinations could not have
produced themselves, and we are forced, for the explanation
of the passing from potentiality to actuality which we observe
in the beings around us, to have recourse to a First Being who
is the principle of it and who does not receive from any other
being His own essential perfections. And as in this Being
there is no metaphysical movement possible, there is no potentiality ; and since His formal determinations are not received
in passive potentiality, He is purely actual or Pure Actuality.
Such is the first proof developed by St. Thomas in his *Summa
Theologica*. We give the text.

> ' The first and most manifest way is the argument from
> motion. It is certain and evident to our senses that some
> things are in motion. Whatever is in motion is moved by

another, for nothing can be in motion except it have a potentiality for that towards which it is being moved ; whereas a thing moves inasmuch as it is actual. By " motion " we mean nothing else than the reduction of something from a state of potentiality into a state of actuality. Nothing, however, can be reduced from a state of potentiality into a state of actuality, unless by something already in a state of actuality. Thus that which is actually hot, as fire, makes wood, which is potentially hot, to be actually hot, and thereby moves and changes it. It is not possible that the same thing should be at once in a state of actuality and potentiality from the same point of view, but only from different points of view. What is actually hot cannot simultaneously be only potentially hot ; still, it is simultaneously potentially cold. It is therefore impossible that from the same point of view and in the same way anything should be both moved and mover, or that it should move itself. Therefore, whatever is in motion must be put in motion by another. If that by which it is put in motion be itself put in motion, then this also must needs be put in motion by another, and that by another again. This cannot go on to infinity, because then there would be no first mover, and, consequently, no other mover—seeing that subsequent movers only move inasmuch as they are put in motion by the first mover ; as the staff only moves because it is put in motion by the hand. Therefore it is necessary to arrive at a First Mover, put in motion by no other ; and this everyone understands to be God ' [13].

To recapitulate : (I) There are beings that are ' moved ' (II) The reason of the formal determinations which they

[13] ' *Prima* autem, et manifestior via est, quae sumitur ex parte motus. Certum est enim, et sensu constat, aliqua moveri in hoc mundo : omne autem, quod movetur, ab alio movetur. Nihil enim movetur, nisi secundum quod est in potentia ad illud, ad quod movetur : movet autem aliquid, secundum quod est actu. Movere enim nihil aliud est, quam educere aliquid de potentia in actum. De potentia autem non potest aliquid reduci in actum, nisi per aliquod ens in actu : sicut calidum in actu, ut ignis, facit lignum, quod est calidum in potentia, esse actu calidum, et per hoc movet, et alterat ipsum. Non autem est possibile, ut idem sit simul in actu et potentia secundum idem, sed solum secundum diversa ; quod enim est calidum in actu, non potest simul esse calidum in potentia, sed est simul frigidum in potentia. Impossibile est ergo, quod secundum idem, et eodem modo aliquid sit movens et motum, vel quod moveat seipsum : omne ergo, quod moveatur, oportet ab alio moveri. Si ergo id, a quo movetur, moveatur, oportet et ipsum ab alio moveri, et illud

acquire is not found in themselves ; it is therefore extrinsic.
(III) To explain how these perfections are acquired it is
necessary to admit, outside the series of agents that are moved,
an agent that is not itself subject to any external action.
Because, if there existed only beings that are moved, the total
series that they go to form would not give the *raison d'être* of
the movement which comes before our experience. We must
then admit the existence of a motor Cause, withdrawn from
all movement, which is itself the principle of its own determinations.

It is important to grasp the exact scope and validity of this
argument. It leads us to place at the head of each series of
perfections that we find before us in the world a formal cause
that possesses in a plenary degree these perfections. But it
does not prove that these pure actualities placed at the top
of each series of perfections converge in such a way as to constitute only one being. We are not at all yet justified in asserting that there is one first Being or that there are many first
Beings. A further analysis of the notion to which this argument leads us is necessary for our enlightenment on this point.

In the same way we cannot immediately state the manner
in which the perfective reality communicates itself to the subject it perfects. Does the first Being communicate itself *intrinsically* to the potentiality that it perfects ? Or is not this
mode of communication impossible, and does not the nature
of pure Actuality require that it should determine the moved
being that it completes in an eminent manner and not as
being itself one of the series ? These questions can only
be answered by analysis.

We must note also that this argument drawn from metaphysical movement is a fundamental one. From it we may
deduce the two arguments that follow, the one drawn from
the conditional causality of beings, the other from their
contingency. For the power to act is also a formal perfection,

ab alio : hic autem non est procedere in infinitum, quia sic non esset aliquod
primum movens, et per consequens nec aliquod aliud movens, quia moventia
secunda non movent nisi per hoc, quod sunt mota a primo movente, sicut
baculus non movet, nisi per hoc, quod est motus a manu ; ergo necesse est
devenire ad aliquod primum movens, quod a nullo moveatur ; et hoc omnes
intelligunt Deum '. *Summa Theologica*, I, q. 2, a. 3.

The above and most of the following translations are taken from the
Dominican translation of St. Thomas (Washbourne, London, 1914).

and again existence is a perfective actuality. In consequence the argument which is based on the intrinsic determinations that the formal cause communicates to the being in potentiality has the same value when applied to action and existence also.

22. Objections to the Preceding Argument.—(a) *The principle of movement.* A difficulty may be put in this form : A being that passes from potentiality to actuality does not find in itself but in some other being the reason of the perfection that it acquires, or ⟨*Quidquid movetur ab alio movetur* ⟩ but this principle, which is the staple of the argument given above, admits of exceptions. For there are some beings which pass from potency to actuality without however being subject to any external agency, e.g. living beings, the characteristic of which lies in the spontaneity of their immanent action. The cell nourishes itself, and is certainly the principle of its own nutrition.

The objection rests on the false assumption that life is spontaneous in its activity ; and certain French spiritualist philosophers are quite wrong in maintaining that the characteristic of a living being consists in this. The truth is that it possesses immanence of action, not spontaneity. In it the efficient cause is identical with the subjective cause, in other words, the subject that receives the activity is the same as the principle that produces it ; but in the whole scale of living beings we do not find any spontaneous action which is not subordinated to an external influence. The vegetable acts only in consequence of certain actions coming from outside itself. Animal life presupposes excitation caused by the external world and received by the sensitive cognitional faculty. The mind of man has knowledge only when determined concurrently by the active intellect and the senses ; and his will is solicited by the good which his mind puts before it. After an excitation of this kind the living being reacts, it acquires a perfection not possessed before, and this reaction—which is distinct from the action undergone—this increase of actuality can find its adequate explanation only in the pre-motion of the Being that is pure Actuality. ⟩ This point will be explained more in detail in the last part of this treatise. The objection we are considering does not, then, in any way overthrow the principle ' Quidquid movetur ab alio movetur '. The passage from ' power ' to ' act ' in a living being presupposes an excitation exterior to the faculty that acts and beyond this excitation itself the pre-motion from the first Cause.

(*b*) The New Philosophy raises the objection that the foundation of being is nothing static but movement, becoming ; change is the fundamental, necessary reality. Reality is ' continuous becoming ' and being is ' perpetual spring '. The advocates of this theory are willing to grant that if all movement must necessarily be derived from something static, then the ultimate principle of explanation would certainly be found only in a supreme Unmoved. But as the case is otherwise, *as things are themselves self-movement and nothing but movement, there is no further need to ask how they received it.*

The reply to this objection is that a solution of this kind leads logically to the denial of the objective validity of the principle of sufficient reason or, in ultimate analysis, of the principle of contradiction. For, to become is to acquire something. A thing cannot become what it already is. And since nothing can give itself what it does not already possess, it must necessarily receive it from some being that does possess it, and ultimately from some being which has not itself received it from another—otherwise this want of having would be traced from one to another indefinitely and there would never be an end. Unless, then, we are to introduce a contradiction into the very heart of metaphysics and to maintain that reality is self-contradictory, we must posit at the source of movement an Unmoved Being.

23. Argument drawn from Efficient Causality.—I. The metaphysical reality which forms the basis of this proof is the subordinated causality which we can observe in the things that surround us, ' in istis sensibilibus ', to use St. Thomas's phrase. We see beings acting ; they depend essentially on other agents, both for activity and for the very being which is the source of their activity. For example, a piece of coal gives out only the heat with which it has previously been heated ; a plant grows and flowers and bears fruit by means of the earth from which it draws nourishment and the rain and the sun.

II. Now none of these causes can contain within itself the principle of its own causal activity. For, to suppose this would involve the contradiction of asserting on the one hand that it depends for its activity on an extrinsic principle, and on the other that it is not subject to any external action since it has the reason of its own efficiency in itself. Moreover, to say that an efficient cause is the principle of its own being is to assert that it acts before it exists ; it is therefore dependent also for its very being upon some cause extrinsic to itself. A conditional efficient cause, then, presupposes the action of a distinct being.

III. It is useless to trace causality *ad infinitum* down a series of dependent causes, since each new cause imagined far from solving the difficulty merely renews it. An infinite series can do no more than complicate the problem indefinitely. On the other hand, mentally to unite the chain of causes so as to make of them a single congeries, gives rise to a dilemma : either the whole is dependent on some cause distinct from it and independent of any other cause—which is to give the same solution as ourselves ;—or it is dependent on some subordinate cause in the series and is thus dependent upon itself. We are therefore forced to the conclusion that there is a Cause independent of all action of an extrinsic cause.

The second way is from the formality of efficient causation. In the world of sense we find there is an order of efficient causation. There is no case known (neither is it, indeed, possible) in which a thing is found to be the efficient cause of itself ; for so it would be prior to itself, which is impossible. In efficient causes it is not possible to go on to infinity, because in all efficient causes following in order, the first is the cause of the intermediate cause, and the intermediate is the cause of the ultimate cause, whether the intermediate cause be several, or one only. To take away the cause is to take away the effect. Therefore, if there be no first cause among efficient causes, there will be no ultimate cause, nor any intermediate. If in efficient causes it is possible to go on to infinity, there will be no first efficient cause, neither will there be an ultimate effect, nor any intermediate efficient causes ; all of which is plainly false. Therefore it is necessary to put forward a First Efficient Cause, to which everyone gives the name of God "[14].

---

[14] ' *Secunda* via est ex ratione causae efficientis. Invenimus enim in istis sensibilibus esse ordinem causarum efficientium, nec tamen invenitur, nec est possibile, quod aliquid sit causa efficiens sui ipsius, quia sic esset prius seipso, quod est impossibile : non autem est possibile, quod in causis efficientibus procedatur in infinitum, quia in omnibus causis efficientibus ordinatis

Here we must speak of the possibility of the world having existed *ab aeterno*. Some great philosophers, with St. Thomas at their head, maintain that we cannot establish by reason alone that the world must have had a beginning. If the world had a beginning in time, there must evidently exist an eternal self-subsisting Being to have caused it : for out of complete nothingness nothing could have come. But even if science could demonstrate that the actual state of this world as we find it had a commencement ; if geological data, etc., could trace the history of the past and show that at a certain stage of the cosmic evolutions life was impossible, if the law of entropy could establish as a fact that the forces of the world have had an origin in far-off ages, reason alone could never be sure that this state was not endlessly preceded by some other state of which science is entirely ignorant through absence of data. In any case it is imprudent, seeing the difficulty of the question and the state of uncertainty of the best philosophers with regard to these matters, to identify the question of the existence of God with that of the commencement of the world. Whether the world has always existed or not, it is necessary to posit, beyond the series of caused causes, even if such be infinite, the existence of an uncaused Cause. A problem is not solved by the fact of proposing it an endless number of times.

In the passage just quoted St. Thomas says that reason forbids us to regress to infinity in the series of causes *in which there is to be found the adequate reason of the dependent causality* ; in another passage he calls such causes *causae subordinatae per se*, that is to say, causes dependent in the very act of causing [15]. But it did not seem to him impossible that in a series of causes dependent *per accidens*, that is to say, in a series of exactly similar causes, there need ever be any limit. In this case there is in the whole sum in reality only a single cause which is replaced again and again *per accidens*, as for example a number of hammers that keep breaking in the hands of the workman

primum est causa medii, et medium est causa ultimi, sive media sint plura, sive unum tantum : remota autem causa, removetur effectus ; ergo, si non fuerit primum in causis efficientibus, non erit ultimum, nec medium. Sed, si procedatur in infinitum in causis efficientibus, non erit prima causa efficiens, et sic non erit nec effectus ultimus, nec causae efficientes mediae, quod patet esse falsum. Ergo est necesse ponere aliquam causam efficientem primam ; quam omnes Deum nominant '. *Sum. Theol.*, I, q. 2, a. 3.

[15] Cp. *Sum. Theol*, I, q. 46, a. 2, ad 7.

using them. In the first case the action depends on the series as such and consequently cannot be infinite, ' nam infinitum non est transire '; in the second the action depends only on a single cause.

It is no argument, then, against St. Thomas's proof to say, as is so often said, that there is nothing unreasonable in the world having existed *ab aeterno ;* such a retort would be nothing but an *ignoratio elenchi.* The necessity of a first Cause laid down by St. Thomas in no way supposes that God is put on the same level with secondary causes, even if they are multiplied *ad infinitum.* Outside and above the series which they form there must be a primary Cause which is not univocal with them but analogical.

To recapitulate : (I) There are dependent efficient causes. (II) Their *raison d'être* cannot be found in themselves. (III) Consequently it is necessary to posit, outside the series of causes, even if it be infinite, an uncaused Cause which gives the adequate explanation of their action.

24. Argument drawn from the Contingency of Beings.— I. There are beings which begin to be, which pass from non-being to being ; the man yonder and myself are both instances of beings who at one time did not exist.

II. A being which begins to be does not possess in itself the reason of its own existence, for in this hypothesis it has not begun to be but always has been. Consequently the transition from non-being to being is only explained by the action of a distinct, anterior being.

III. It is useless to continue the series of contingent beings *ad infinitum* without ever admitting a first Being which is itself the reason of its own existence. If none of the beings that constitute the series gives the reason of the existence that is found in it, there cannot, without a first Being, be any existence. Consequently the causal explanation of contingent existences requires a Being that is independent and is itself the reason of its own existence.

St. Thomas gives the argument from contingency under a slightly different form. He breaks up the reasoning into two syllogisms, one of which follows from the other. He proves in the first place the existence of necessary beings. Amongst these some are ' necessary ' in the sense that their nature is above the law of transformation that affects all corporeal substances ; yet these are indebted to some other being for their necessary nature (e.g. the human soul, which of itself is naturally incorruptible) ; it may also be that there is a necessary being whose necessity finds its explanation in itself. A being of this sort, which has its source of being within itself, is then inevitably arrived at by a second syllogism. The argument, however, can well be shortened by the omission of one middle term, namely, the beings whose necessity is dependent, and we pass directly from contingent beings to the being that is necessary by itself. This is what we have done in the statement of our proof.

' The third way is taken from possibility and necessity, and runs thus. We find in nature things that could either exist or not exist, since they are found to be generated, and then to corrupt ; and, consequently, they can exist, and then not exist. It is impossible for these always to exist, for that which can one day cease to exist must at some time have not existed. Therefore, if everything could cease to exist, then at one time there could have been nothing in existence. If this were true, even now there would be nothing in existence, because that which does not exist only begins to exist by something already existing. Therefore, if at one time nothing was in existence, it would have been impossible for anything to have begun to exist ; and thus even now nothing would be in existence—which is absurd. Therefore, not all beings are merely possible, but there must exist something the existence of which is necessary. Every necessary thing either has its necessity caused by another, or not. It is impossible to go on to infinity in necessary things which have their necessity caused by another, as has been already proved in regard to efficient causes. Therefore we cannot but postulate the existence of some being having of itself its own necessity, and not receiving it from another, but rather causing in others their necessity. This all men speak of as God ' [16].

[16] ' *Tertia* via est sumpta ex possibili, et necessario (quae talis est). Invenimus enim in rebus quaedam, quae sunt possibilia esse, et non esse, cum quaedam inveniantur generari et corrumpi, et per consequens possibilia esse, et non esse. Impossibile est autem omnia, quae sunt talia, semper esse, quia quod possibile est non esse, quandoque non est. Si igitur omnia sunt possibilia non esse, aliquando nihil fuit in rebus. Sed si hoc est verum, etiam nunc nihil esset, quia quod non est, non incipit esse, nisi per aliquid, quod est. Si igitur nihil fuit ens, impossibile fuit, quod aliquid inciperet esse, et sic modo nihil esset : quod patet esse falsum. Non ergo omnia entia sunt possibilia,

To recapitulate : (I) There are beings which begin to be. (II) These contingent beings are only accounted for by some being external to themselves. (III) No explanation of their dependent existence is found by endlessly tracing a series of beings that do not contain their *raison d'être* in themselves. Therefore we must posit a Being which shall contain within itself the reason of their existence, in a word, a necessary Being [17].

25. Conclusion Common to these Three Proofs.—Is it possible to merge into a single conclusion these three arguments from movement, action and contingency, presenting as they do the same reasoning and differing only in the points from which they start ?

The last two conclusions involve each other, inasmuch as an uncaused cause must exist of itself. Is the first also involved ? Is it evident that pure Actuality draws from itself the reason of its own being ? The answer will appear if we try to conceive a being that is devoid of all potentiality—such is Pure Actuality —and yet is not its own explanatory, sufficient reason : such a being is inconceivable, since the purely Actual Being, were it contingent, would be at one time only capable of being, potential to existence, and thus not simply and solely actuality. There is, then, a common conclusion to the three arguments we have developed, namely, that there exists a Being which contains within itself the reason of its own existence and action, and whose perfections are all actual, so that it is potential to receiving no further reality.

These proofs, however, do not yet warrant us in deciding whether the Being which is purely Actual is infinite or finite, whether it has the perfection of uniqueness or involves many pure actualities. These further points will be determined

---

sed oportet aliquid esse necessarium in rebus. Omne autem necessarium vel habet causam suae necessitatis aliunde, vel non habet. Non est autem possibile, quod procedatur in infinitum in necessariis, quae habent causam suae necessitatis, sicut nec in causis efficientibus, ut probatum est (*in jam dictis in ipso art.*) : ergo necesse est ponere aliquid, quod sit per se necessarium, non habens causam necessitatis aliunde, sed quod est causa necessitatis aliis : quod omnes dicunt Deum '. *Sum. Theol.*, I, q. 2, a. 3.

[17] To say that a being exists, but is not self-existent and, in consequence, is subject to change and destruction, is tantamount to saying that it has its *raison d'être* in some other being. The principle of sufficient reason is ultimately reducible to the principle of contradiction. The Kantian school cannot call it synthetic a priori, since between *esse a se* and *esse non a se* or, in other words, *esse ab alio*, it is evident that there is no middle term.

by a careful analysis of what is contained in these first notions that we have acquired about God. We may also here remark against Kant that the transition from the Being necessarily existent in the ontological order to the Infinite Being does not involve an appeal to the ontological argument. This latter jumps from the *concept* of the greatest possible being to the *fact* of its real existence. But in the argument which we are putting forward, we first demonstrate that the necessary Being exists, and then whatever further analysis reveals must, by the very fact of this previous demonstration, refer to the real order ; for our concepts are not in their building up or in their further analysis the resultants of subjective forms, are not a priori syntheses.

26. Corollary.—We are now able to draw from the three proofs of the existence of God which we have established, an important moral consequence ; namely, the foundation of religion. If we are indebted to a first Being for our essential perfections, our activity and our existence, there is a moral obligation on us of worshipping that Being. The act of worship whereby we confess that God alone is *He who is* and that our being and perfections are essentially dependent upon Him is that of adoration. And adoration, which embraces the internal avowal of the human soul that it is subordinate to Him and the external manifestation of this avowal, is the fundamental act of natural religion.

27. Argument drawn from the Grades of Perfection manifested in Beings.—St. Thomas's exposition of this proof is as follows :—

' The fourth way is taken from the gradation to be found in things. Among beings there are some more and some less good, true, noble, and the like. But ' more ' and ' less ' are predicated of different things, according as they resemble in their different ways something which is in the degree of ' most ', as a thing is said to be hotter according as it more nearly resembles that which is hottest ; so that there is something which is truest, something best, something noblest, and, consequently, something which is uttermost being ; for the truer things are, the more truly they exist. What is most complete in any genus is the cause of all in that genus ; as fire, which is the most complete form of heat, is the cause whereby all things are made hot.

Therefore there must also be something which is to all beings the cause of their being, goodness, and every other perfection ; and this we call God ' [18].

At first sight St. Thomas's proof seems to be this : We notice in beings which are the object of our knowledge a graduated scale of perfections : virtue, nobleness, goodness, etc., appear before us in varying degrees. But we judge the degree of perfection that we find, according as it approximates to or falls away from a supreme type. Therefore, since every comparative presupposes a superlative, this ideal of perfection must exist.

To such a proof the objection might very well be raised that this absolute perfection which we use as the standard for judging the degree of perfection realized in the things we know, is merely a concept of our mind. Is there not latent in St. Thomas's proof the old fallacy of the ontological argument, a jump from the existence of this ideal in the mind to its existence in the real order ?

As a matter of fact the proof, we think, has in the mind of Aquinas quite another meaning [19] :—

I. We discover that in beings there are graduated perfections.

II. The limitation of virtue, goodness, nobleness, etc., shows that these perfections do not belong to the beings of themselves, in virtue of their essences. For an essence—i.e. that which makes a being what it is—cannot be partly verified in a being ; the perfection possessed in virtue of its essence is wholly present or else not at all : a being is a man or not a man, and cannot be partly a man. Conversely, anything that is present in a being in a way that admits of more or less cannot belong to it in virtue of its essence, but must have for its reason something else other than the essence. For it would

[18] ' *Quarta* via sumitur ex gradibus, qui in rebus inveniuntur. Invenitur enim in rebus aliquid magis, et minus bonum, et verum, et nobile, et sic de aliis hujusmodi. Sed magis, et minus dicuntur de diversis, secundum quod appropinquant diversimode ad aliquid, quod maxime est : sicut magis calidum est, quod magis appropinquat maxime calido. Est igitur aliquid, quod est verissimum, et optimum, et nobilissimum, et per consequens maxime ens. Nam quae sunt maxime vera, sunt maxime entia, ut dicitur 2. Metaph. Quod autem dicitur maxime tale in aliquo genere, est causa omnium, quae sunt illius generis ; sicut ignis, qui est maxime calidus, est causa omnium calidorum, ut in eodem libro dicitur. Ergo est aliquid, quod omnibus entibus est causa esse, et bonitatis, et cujuslibet perfectionis, et hoc dicimus Deum '. *Sum. Theol.*, I, q. 2, a. 3.

[19] Our interpretation is founded on other passages from St. Thomas, especially *Sum. cont. Gent.*, II, c. 15, and *De Potentia*, q. 3, a. 5.

indeed be a contradiction to hold that that by which wisdom is wisdom is likewise the formal reason of the absence of wisdom. Wherever, therefore, we find a perfection in a limited degree it is true to say that this perfection does not belong to the being by virtue of its essence, but that it has been *communicated* to it and consequently presupposes the intervention of some causal agent other than itself.

III. But there is no justification for supposing an indefinitely long series of perfections caused by an extrinsic action. As we have established in the three arguments above, it is necessary for their explanation to posit a being which is the reason of its own perfections, the Being we call God.

We have seen the extrinsic reason why the perfections in a being are limited, viz. their dependence on an extrinsic cause. We have yet to inquire what is the intrinsic reason. It is found in the fact that the essence is that which is actualized by existence, and the actuality of existence is limited by the material cause in which it is received. This is a case where we must apply the general principle of Scholastic metaphysics : *Receptum est in recipiente ad modum recipientis.* A being's existence is limited to the essential perfections it is its rôle to make actual. The receptivity of a being is the intrinsic reason why it is not being itself but has just that much being which corresponds to its potentiality, or to its receptivity. It is for this reason it is finite in its existence. God, on the contrary, who is self-existent and receives not His existence from another, is subject to no limitation in His essential perfections.

We must be careful to notice the limits of this argument drawn by St. Thomas from the degrees observable in the perfections of things. In the first place, he does not say that at the head of each series of graduated beings there is a being which possesses in an eminent degree their essential type. This is the realistic conception of Plato, not the thought of the Angelic Doctor. The latter asserts that the perfections we find in varying degrees in the world carry our mind up to absolute perfections, as the principles of these limited perfections in the world. Secondly, he makes no further statement as to whether these total perfections are united in a single Being or whether there exist several beings each possessing

certain perfections in a supreme degree, or even whether there
are several absolutely perfect beings.

28. Argument drawn from the Order of the Universe.—
That there is order in the universe is abundantly manifest ;
the many elements and activities composing the world are
adapted to make one harmonious and enduring whole. This
order demands an intelligent and free cause, first to have
conceived its design, then to have chosen to carry it into execution. Now this cause is either a necessary cause or it is not.
If it is necessary, the existence of God is proved. If it is contingent, it leads us in its last analysis to a necessary cause and
thus again we come to the divine Being.—Such is the fifth
argument that St. Thomas develops in his *Summa Theologica*.

'The fifth way is taken from the governance of the
world ; for we see that things which lack intelligence, such
as natural bodies, act for some purpose, which fact is evident from their acting always, or nearly always in the same
way, so as to obtain the best result. Hence it is plain that
not fortuitously, but designedly, do they achieve their purpose. Whatever lacks intelligence cannot fulfil some purpose, unless it is directed by some being endowed with intelligence and knowledge ; as the arrow is shot to its mark
by the archer. Therefore some intelligent being exists by
whom all natural things are ordained towards a definite
purpose ; and this being we call God ' [20].

We must first establish the major and the minor of this
argument.

I. We have already examined the notion of order and the
order of the universe (*Gen. Metaphysics*, **169** ff.).

Order supposes manifold elements all leading in some way
to unity. By the principle of unification we distinguish two
kinds of order, that of co-ordination or æsthetical order, that
of subordination or teleological order. In the first the different
elements constitute the parts of one and the same whole.
In the second the elements are means arranged in view of one

[20] '*Quinta* via sumitur ex gubernatione rerum : Videmus enim, quod aliqua,
quae cognitione carent, scilicet corpora naturalia, operantur propter finem,
quod apparet ex hoc, quod semper, aut frequentius eodem modo operantur,
ut consequantur id, quod est optimum. Unde patet, quod non a casu, sed
ex intentione perveniunt ad finem. Ea autem, quae non habent cognitionem,
non tendunt in finem, nisi directa ab aliquo cognoscente et intelligente, sicut
sagitta a sagittante ; ergo est aliquis intelligens, a quo omnes res naturales
ordinantur ad finem, et hoc dicimus Deum'. *Sum. Theol.*, I, q. 2, a. 3.

and the same end. In reality these are but two aspects of the same order ; for every being is made for action. The elements are so arranged as to form one harmonious whole, and they tend to realize the same end. The order of co-ordination, which is static, exists in view of the order of subordination, which is dynamic. Now turning to order in the universe we notice the following various ways in which it is exhibited :—
(a) Every living organism displays wonderful order in the nice adjustment of its various parts. All its organs are perfectly arranged and work together for the welfare of the whole living being. Each organ too is made up of an immense number of elements displaying forces that are different yet so interconnected and subordinated as to subserve the good of the entire organism. This class of phenomena presents an orderliness that we may term an *absolute particular order*—one that has reference only to the individual being of which it is a characteristic. (b) Furthermore, things do not fulfil the end of their being in a state of isolation. They are bound up with certain other things and in such a way that their mutual adaptations present an orderliness which, as distinguished from the above, may be called *relative particular order*. An example is to be found in the wonderful proportion existing between the anatomical structure of the eye and the physiological working of the visual organ on the one hand and its physical agent, light, on the other. (c) There are discernible even still wider classes of combinations, the different kingdoms of beings which exhibit further mutual relations, static and dynamic. The interdependence of all the parts of the universe constitutes a *relative universal order*. The world is a poem instinct with action and life, and displaying a marvellous harmony, known to the Greeks as the Cosmos. The existence of order in the universe is the basis of the physical sciences, and the invariable result of scientific progress is a fresh revelation of this order. (d) Lastly, this order, absolute and relative, particular and universal, is not a passing phase but something continuous and *constant*. The universe is animated with incessant movement, the individual characters and the scenes shift rapidly ; yet in the perpetual flux types remain constant, ends do not alter, the good alike of individuals and of the whole steadily continues to be attained.

To guard against any misconception of the meaning of these

assertions, it must be noted that we do not say that every-thing in the universe is orderly, that there are no elements which do not perhaps appear as sources of disorder and evil. In the major as we lay it down it is merely asserted that order is as a general rule the characteristic phenomenon and the most universal phenomenon exhibited by the universe and by the parts of which it is made up.

II. The order in the universe is contingent. Reason forbids us to assign such an effect to chance. It therefore demands an intelligent cause as its designer. Indeed to account for it by an adequate cause, we must admit the existence of a mind to have designed and a will to have chosen this subordination of the multifarious component elements to one end. (a) Let us suppose those elements exhibiting what we have called *particular order* to be the sport of chance and directed in their mutual convergence by no sort of controlling principle. In such a supposition inorganic and organic substances would act at random, combining and disintegrating anyhow; there would no longer be any motive making them combine according to strictly fixed proportions in a way that would render vital activity possible. We must conclude, then, that chance can offer no explanation of this kind of order we observe. Nay more, it would be positively detrimental to any such effect. Left to themselves these elements would be causes not merely indifferent to all order but productive of positive disorder. For instance, if each cell in an organism received no influence from the rest of the body, it would work for its own immediate end : the muscular tissues would contract indefinitely, the glandular tissues would go on secreting without control, the epithelial cells would keep on growing, and all these activities being devoid of any sort of direction would never achieve the well-being of the organism as a whole. Chance, then, far from sup-plying the sufficient reason for what we observe in this parti-cular order, would furnish only a reason for its impossibility. In order to find a sufficient reason for this wonderful order, since our observation meets with a multitude of elements which of themselves are indifferent to entering into any com-bination and yet are drawn to such a felicitous and purposeful union, we must look for it not in the elements themselves but in some overruling, controlling cause. Furthermore, the ar-rangement of so many elements with a view to an end, and their nice proportions, imply a mind that conceived the plan and an act of will that has carried it into execution; that is, this designing cause must be an agent endowed with intelligence and will. (b) And chance offers no better explanation of the *relative order* manifest in the universe. To take but one example : the breathing of animals and the action of chlorophyl in plants keeps our atmosphere constantly adapted to the life of both kingdoms. The chemical bodies composing the air are in themselves indifferent to forming either a useful or a noxious admixture, and therefore they cannot be accountable for this effect. Neither are plants and animals if left to themselves the sole causes, for there is nothing to stop plants from indefinitely absorbing the carbonic acid with their green parts and animals from breathing it out in unlimited quantities, and thus militating against the very relative order of which their joint action is an example. The only sufficient reason of the phenomena of this kind is to be found once again in a controlling cause outside of the beings themselves which exhibit this order. (c) The *universe taken as a whole* is like an immense drama where the general success of the innumerable scenes that succeed one another is secured by the harmonious setting and development of all its parts. This likewise requires for its adequate cause an intelligence as designer. (d) Finally, the evolution of the world counts well-nigh numberless phases, and yet in these similar though not identical situations there ever reappears that interplay of parts which is conducive to the welfare of the whole. Here the inadequacy of chance is the most apparent ; for the cosmic order is persistent despite the multiplicity of parts that are concerned in it, despite the variety of phases in which it manifests itself. Suppose, for the sake of argument, that some elements indifferent to any particular action did at some moment combine harmoniously ; what prevented this order from being hopelessly broken up at the next moment ? The reason of the *persistence* of this order must be sought in a supreme controlling force, and since we have to account for a phenomenon which undoubtedly evidences intelligence and will, this being must have a life that is endowed with intelligence and will. Hence we come to the general conclusion that the only cause which explains the order we observe in nature is to be found in a principle which determines throughout the universe the combination of elements and beings towards the good of species, of kingdoms and of the whole universe.

III. Now such an intelligent, voluntary cause, even if you allow it to be only contingent in its nature, must necessarily presuppose the existence of an anterior Being that has in Itself the reason of Its own being and of Its own perfection.

29. Corollaries.—1. We have established the existence of an efficient cause of the wonderful order which we observe is in the world around us. We question now whether this cause is really distinct from the design which is being worked out and the end to which it is progressing. If this exemplary cause and this final cause which we have been bound to postulate are necessary in their nature, then they are identical with the necessary efficient cause from which the order of the universe proceeds. If they are contingent, they must depend on the necessary cause and, consequently, it is in this latter that we shall have *ultimately* to place the design and the purpose of the universe, for creatures can neither exist nor act without the intervention of the necessary cause. We thus come to acknowledge a necessary Being that is at once the efficient, exemplary and final cause of the world He has brought into being.

2. The next question in this physico-theological argument is whether the controlling, ordinating cause of the universe is one or many. In reference to this question we may remark, in the first place, that there is no need to postulate several designers in order to explain the tendency towards the good that we observe : one alone is sufficient. In the second place, from the unity of the order which the cosmos reveals the legitimate inference is that it is a single God who presides over the governance of the world. Certainly it is possible to conceive two beings with identically the same end in view in their ruling of the world and using exactly the same means of bringing it about. But it would be gratuitous to assert the actual existence of two such beings : if the end and action of the two governing causes are identical, one of them is useless. Hence we have here at least a presumption in favour of there being only one God.

30. Note.—The proof we have just developed is not merely an argument from analogy. If some are inclined to think so, the reason is to be found in the faulty exposition given of this proof by certain authors. They argue that we judge the intellectual capacity of our fellow-men by the adaptation of the means they choose to their ends, that order or adaptation is an indication of intelligence ; that the universe manifests supreme order ; therefore, etc. Argument of this kind need cause no misgiving. The example given embodies simply a single application of the principle of order on which the physico-theological argument is based ; the real argument is that the order which obtains between elements that are in themselves indifferent can only be explained by a cause which arranges them by its intelligence (*Gen. Metaphysics*, **171** ff.). Our argument is based not on analogy but on the principle of sufficient reason.

After having thus examined the proofs for the existence of God which St. Thomas draws from the *different aspects of being* and from *beings as a whole*, we must notice briefly some other arguments which are not infrequently brought forward.

31. Scientific Proofs of the Existence of God.—The proofs we refer to are such as these : that life has had a commencement on the earth ; that a simple intrinsic evolution of matter is not capable of accounting for vegetable life in the first place, and then for sensitive life and still less for intellectual life ; that the law of entropy shows that the cosmic forces tend towards an equilibrium of condensation and proves that they must have had a commencement in time, or else that state of equilibrium would have been reached. These and kindred considerations of a *scientific* nature are valuable indications that over and above the actual universe there is something which explains this acquisition of forces and directs this evolution. They are different aspects of a process of reality which is not self-explanatory ; but by themselves they have no cogency unless supported by the *philosophical*, metaphysical argument which demonstrates that this principle of explanation taken to its last analysis must be pure Actuality, necessary Being, first Cause, subsistent Perfection, and highest Intelligence.

32. Proof drawn from the Common Consent of Mankind.— In the fact that all races of men acknowledge the existence of God some see a spontaneous declaration on the part of humanity, and this, they argue, cannot be fallacious. This argument, we think, calls for two remarks.

In the first place, during the course of ages many erroneous conceptions have been entertained, and therefore a unanimous verdict is not always infallible. Nevertheless, for *psychological* reasons special weight does attach to this universal testimony regarding the existence of God. It is a question, as Pascal very well observes, that is of the utmost importance. It has a great bearing on the direction of a man's life if he knows that there is a Master who claims his service and who punishes what he does amiss. Human passion has ever sought to liberate itself from this Guardian of the moral law. If then, in spite of this natural bias, we find among all races and throughout all times men of every temperament, learned and unlearned, cultured and illiterate, all acknowledging the existence of God, it would seem that we have here no mere anthropomorphism but a *morally certain indication* that there are proofs warranting the assertion that God exists. This is an argument which is *indirect* and *extrinsic*, but perfectly sound for a man who has not the time or mental energy for examining the intrinsic proofs of God's existence.

In the second place, since human ideas of God vary very much among different peoples, this argument does not in reality demonstrate more than that there is above men one or more higher beings ruling the destinies of mankind. In brief, we have to guard against two excesses : the argument is sometimes made to prove too much, and sometimes it is despised as having no value. Its real value is that it supplies a presumption that valid proofs do exist.

33. Proof from the Higher Aspirations of Mankind.— ' Irrequietum est cor nostrum donec requiescat in te ' writes St. Augustine, and we find the echo in the *Mélanges philosophiques* of the unfortunate Jouffroy, ' All earthly satisfaction gradually exhausts itself and ends in disappointment and disgust '. Man, it is argued, has been made for the true and the good ; he yearns for that yet-to-be when virtue will be clasped in the embrace of happiness and its present divorce for ever ended. Such happiness can only consist in the contemplation of the true, and since the true is found in God alone He must therefore exist. Is this a valid proof ?

Granted that human nature is not vitiated by some radical flaw, undoubtedly God must exist as the end of its higher activities. But can we postulate that our nature is so made ?

Is it not precisely because it is God who made it that we know it is a perfect production? How, in consequence, can we affirm the existence of God by basing it on the needs of our nature? It is true we can say that, if God did not exist, man alone of all creatures would be irremediably unhappy. But this is only an argument from analogy that scarcely carries with it more than a probability.

Again, why have we need of God as the satisfaction of our nature except because He is necessary as an explanation of the world? We are thus led back to examine the traditional proofs of God's existence, and to weigh in the light of the objective evidence of the principle of sufficient reason the motives leading us to posit His existence.

34. Proof drawn from Moral Obligation.—Man feels that he is morally bound to practise good and to avoid evil. God must then exist, for without a legislator there can be no law. A law so universal, so imperious as the moral law presupposes a supreme, eternal and all-powerful Legislator.

We must remark, first of all, that this proof does not *demonstrate* the existence of God. It merely declares that the man who admits the moral obligation has already admitted God as the Legislator who imposes His will. The certitude of God's existence is the same as that of the moral law. With the spectacle of nature and humanity before his eyes man spontaneously acknowledges that there is a higher Being who obliges him to do his duty. If the existence of God is not admitted, his feeling of moral obligation is a pure illusion, and there is no further question of duty. This proof, if it were valid, would not be *a posteriori*, but *a simultaneo* (**16**), like the argument of St. Anselm.

In the second place, the fact of moral obligation could, in our opinion, be sufficiently explained without having recourse to a divine Legislator. Human nature because it is human, strives *by its own natural tendency* after the true and the good. To fail in its human dignity, to disregard the requirements of justice towards our fellow-men, is self-degradation, and a falling short *of its own law*. For the word ' law ' may be used in two senses. Either it is the ordinance of a superior who prescribes this or that means for gaining a special end ; or it is the natural tendency of a being towards its own end—so, e.g., we speak of chemical or physical laws. Now to say that the law of our nature would not be a law if there were no supreme Legislator, is to suppose that in our case the word ' law ' cannot be used in the second sense, and this surely is to beg the whole question. *Whether we wish it or not*, we feel that when we do what is wrong we are offending against the intimate requirements of our human nature merely considered in itself. And in this it would seem that there is a sufficient reason for a *real* obligation which is yet consistent with the play of liberty, since the good that is presented to us in the conditions of our present life always carries with it at the same time the possibility of doing wrong. Certainly, if considered ontologically, this law of our nature is the work of God, but until we are aware that God exists we must perforce be ignorant of this. For God does not manifest His will openly as do human legislators, but He ingrains it in the very tendencies of our nature (*Ethics*, **40**). Hence it appears that no special argument can be drawn from moral obligation requiring a divine Legislator for its immediate explanation. The proof which is adduced is not an independent one, but is reducible to the fourth developed by St. Thomas (**27**) : namely, that our conscience informs us that we are more or less good, more or less virtuous, and therefore we must have a share of the perfections of a Being who is subsistent Goodness. Moreover as the necessary Being cannot feel himself to be under obligation, we can see here also a particular aspect of contingency or of movement.

Furthermore, the argument may take the form of a consideration of man as a whole, not simply of the moral obligation he recognizes as incumbent upon him but also of a tendency towards happiness precisely as a reward, or sanction, of virtue. The performance of duty we feel must lead to complete happiness which must consist in the contemplation of God in another life (*Ethics*, **10-13**), or if not, if there were no moral sanction, our nature would be an imperfect production, and we might just as well set at naught the call of duty and abandon ourselves to the pleasures of the senses and of the present life as surrender these enjoyments to follow the strait path of duty. Presented in this form the ethical argument for the existence of God is reducible to the proof from the natural aspirations of man, and subject therefore to the same criticisms [21].

---

[21] These different points cannot be fully discussed here in this manual ; they are to be treated *ex professo* in the larger work on *Natural Theology*.

PART II

The Nature of God

Natural theology falls into three divisions : the first treats of the preliminary question of *our knowledge* of God and then proves His *existence ;* the second studies His *nature ;* the third, the *attributes* of God or the divine activity.

We have already spoken of our knowledge of the supreme Being and demonstrated His existence ; we now pass to the second part, treating of the divine essence or the *nature* of the divine Being. We shall see, first of all, *in what His essence consists* (Chapter I) ; then what, as far as we are concerned, are the *notions immediately connected* with that of the essence of God (Chapter II).

CHAPTER I

THE METAPHYSICAL ESSENCE OF GOD

35. Meaning of Metaphysical Essence.—The essences of things which form the object of our knowledge, no matter whether they really exist in the world of contingent beings or are merely possible, may be regarded from a *relative* or an *absolute* point of view. From the former, essence is seen on the side of its extension, that is to say, in its relation to the number of subjects to which it can be applied. From the latter it is regarded in itself, absolutely, as comprising so many notes in its comprehension.

From this second point of view, which is the only one that concerns us here, every essence appears as a combination of a certain number of notes or perfections that are indissolubly united, and, in this sense, it constitutes a necessary, fixed type.

When this essential type is a material substance, we may define it by expressing the really distinct physical parts that enter into its constitution, namely, primary matter and substantial form ; and this is its *physical essence*.

But we may also, for the sake of clearness and logical consistency, consider an essence as a single whole made up of metaphysical or logical parts, and may set about defining the whole by analysing it into these parts. Thus we can say that sensitive life and reason (animal rationale, animalitas et rationalitas) are the proximate genus and the specific difference of man regarded as a *metaphysical essence*. For a good definition of metaphysical essence all the properties of a being need not, and indeed cannot, be given explicitly, but to avoid being defective or misleading it must contain them all *implicitly*, so that analysis and further reasoning may without difficulty discover them.

The problem before us is to ascertain what is the metaphysical essence of God, what is that which makes God what He is, and different from every other being, just as sensitive life and reason make man to be man and to hold a distinct place in the scale of beings.

At first sight the question may appear to be futile, seeing that in the absolutely simple perfection of God there is no complexity, and therefore no matter for analysis. However, since the supereminent perfection of the Infinite Being is *in our thought* equivalent to a metaphysical whole of a very vast comprehension, it is quite possible for us to make a logical analysis of ' God ' *like* that we make of the essences of finite things when we define them by their metaphysical parts and so reduce to fundamental constituents the reality which they each severally contain. Consequently our endeavour here is to ascertain what *from our point of view* is that divine perfection the explicit concept of which takes precedence over all others as the characteristic of the supreme Being, so that from the mere analysis of this first perfection we may deduce all the perfections belonging tc the divine Being.

36. Solution of the Question: ' Deus est Ipsum Esse Subsistens '.—Four answers that deserve our attention have been given to this question [22].

1. The modern philosophers who follow the thought of Descartes and Leibniz make the essence of God to consist in the *sum* of all His attributes raised to their highest power, that is to say, to *infinity* understood in an *extensive* sense. Some, however, hark back to the Platonic philosophy and seem to have a preference for absolute *goodness*.

2. The School of Duns Scotus [23] places the characteristic of the divine essence in the *intensive infinity* of God, i.e. in that *fundamental* attribute of God which is the root of all possible perfections.

3. Billuart [24] and some Thomists of recent date make it consist in intellectual *thought*.

4. But more commonly, with St. Thomas, the metaphysical essence of God is considered to lie in the very being of God,

---

[22] We should not exaggerate the importance of this discussion, which is in reality only a simple question of scientific method. Its chief merit, it seems to us, is that it emphasizes the simplicity of God, inasmuch as if philosophers are constrained by the very limits of the human mind to study the divine perfection from this or that particular aspect, they at once evince their conviction that at bottom these divine perfections are but one and the same.

[23] *In I Sent.*, dist. 3.

[24] *Cursus Theol.*, I, Diss. 2, a. 2, § 2.—Cp. GONET, *Clypeus*, Tr. I, Disp. 2, a. 1.

' *esse irreceptum* ', or, to adopt a Latinism commonly made use of, in His *aseity*, ' *esse a se* '[25]. St. Thomas says :—

' Absolute being, that is to say, being considered as including the whole perfection of being, surpasses both the perfection of life and every other definite perfection. And therefore absolute being contains eminently in itself all other perfections '. It is clear that St. Thomas is here speaking of the absolute Being, *esse irreceptum, esse a se*, for he immediately adds : ' But being which is received in particular things that do not possess the whole perfection of being but have a limited being, as the being enjoyed by a creature, is less perfect than that which has a determined perfection added to it. This is why the pseudo-Dionysius says that living beings are more perfect than beings which exist without life and beings endowed with intelligence more perfect than those which are merely living '[26].

37. Proof of St. Thomas's Opinion.—To enjoy its full force this proof should find its place in a sequence of reasonings proper to a larger treatise and not appear by itself as here, presuming as it does on truths we have yet to establish. Nevertheless it will be convenient here to notice the drift of it. It falls into two parts, in the first of which it is shown that actual absolute existence is part of the metaphysical essence of God, and in the second that actual absolute existence is the whole of the metaphysical essence.

I. *Actual absolute existence belongs to the metaphysical essence of God.*—We have seen that the First Being is Pure Actuality, Necessary Being. Since it is evident that such a being is itself the reason of its existence, it is unwarrantable to postulate outside of this being a prior and further reason for its actual perfections and existence. Must it not be that one who is essentially Being must be Actual Being ? Does not the principle of identity come in here ?

[25] Zigliara has tried to reconcile the two last opinions and to show that they were intended to complete each other ; but his attempt seems to have met with but doubtful success ; he appears to have evaded the discussion rather than to have ended it. (*Summa Phil.*, Vol. II, p. 325.)

[26] ' Esse simpliciter acceptum, secundum quod includit in se omnem perfectionem essendi, praeeminet vitae et omnibus perfectionibus subsequentibus. Sic igitur ipsum esse praehabet in se omnia bona subsequentia. Sed si consideretur ipsum esse, prout participatur in hac re vel in illa, quae non habent totam perfectionem essendi, sed habent esse imperfectum, sicut est esse cujuslibet creaturae ; sic manifestum est quod ipsum esse cum perfectione superaddita est eminentius. Unde Dionysius dicit, quod viventia sunt meliora existentibus, et intelligentia viventibus '. I-II, q. 2, a. 5, ad. 2.

2. *Actual absolute existence is the whole metaphysical essence of God.*—Firstly, to be essentially existent, to be subsistent absolutely, is ground for a sufficient and explicit distinction between God and contingent things ; secondly, from such absolute essential existence, as we shall presently see, can be deduced by analysis and reasoning all the divine perfections, even including infinity and intelligence [27].

38. Criticism of the Opinions Opposed to St. Thomas's Thesis.—The other opinions we have mentioned fail to give what is required for a true metaphysical essence of the divine Being.

1. Each of the perfections the *union* of which according to this first opinion constitutes the essence of God, is evidently anterior to this union itself.

Those who make the metaphysical essence of God consist in His absolute *goodness* can only be referring to the sum-total of His perfections ; consequently they lay themselves open to the same criticism as the Cartesian view above. Moreover, the notion of goodness is one superadded to the notion of being and is not prior to it.

2. The *infinity* of God is not a principle which reveals to us the necessity of the existence of the self-subsistent Being, but it is a conclusion to be inferred from this necessity itself, as will be seen presently.

3. When Billuart maintains that the metaphysical essence of God must be found in the most noble reality known to us and consequently that it cannot be found in subsistence, he is labouring under a confusion of ideas, already exposed by St. Thomas, between the essential and concrete subsistence of God and the abstract and contingent existence of creatures (see **36**, the passage quoted from the *Summa*). Further,

[27] St. Thomas gives the reason for this when he says : ' Existence is that which makes every form or nature actual ; for goodness or humanity is only spoken of as actual, when it is spoken of as existing. It is necessary, therefore, that existence should stand to essence, which is distinct from it, in the same relation as actuality to potentiality. Therefore, since in God there is no potentiality, it follows that in Him essence does not differ from existence. Therefore His Essence is His Existence '.

' Esse est actualitas omnis formae vel naturae ; non enim bonitas vel humanitas significatur in actu, nisi prout significamus eam esse. Oportet igitur quod ipsum esse comparetur ad essentiam quae est aliud ab ipso sicut actus ad potentiam. Cum igitur in Deo nihil sit potentiale, sequitur quod non est aliud in eo essentia quam suum esse. Sua igitur essentia est suum esse '. *Sum. Theol.*, I. q. 3, a. 4.

how can the notion of intelligence as such lead to the concept
of the immensity, eternity and all-powerfulness of God ?
It could do so only in virtue of the fact that this intelligence
is infinite or essentially subsistent ; in other words, the advocates of this opinion are ultimately driven back to the former
one (2) or to that which we are ourselves maintaining (4).

Conclusion : The name which properly connotes God and
brings before us His metaphysical essence is that which He
Himself made known : when asked by Moses, He replied :
' I am Who am (Jahweh) ; thou shalt say to the people of
Israel : He Who is (ὅ ὤν) hath sent me to you. Ego sum qui
sum Ait : sic dices filiis Israel, qui est misit me ad vos ' [28].

[28] *Exod.*, III, 14.—' Hoc nomen, *qui est*, triplici ratione est maxime proprium nomen Dei.—Primo quidem propter sui significationem. Non enim
significat formam aliquam, sed ipsum esse. Unde cum esse Dei sit ipsa ejus
essentia, et hoc nulli alii conveniat, ut supra ostensum est (q. 3, art. 4),
manifestum est quod inter alia nomina hoc maxime proprie nominat Deum.
Unumquodque enim denominatur a sua forma.—Secundo propter ejus univer-
salitatem. Omnia enim alia nomina vel sunt minus communia ; vel si con-
vertantur cum ipso, tamen addunt aliquid supra ipsum secundum rationem.
Unde quodammodo informant et determinant ipsum. Intellectus autem
noster non potest ipsam Dei essentiam cognoscere in statu viae, secundum
quod in se est ; sed quemcumque modum determinet circa id quod de Deo
intelligit, deficit a modo quo Deus in se est. Et ideo quanto aliqua nomina
sunt minus determinata, et magis communia et absoluta, tanto magis proprie
dicuntur de Deo a nobis. Unde et Damascenus dicit (*Orth. fid.*, lib. I, cap. 9) :
Quod " principalius omnibus quae de Deo dicuntur nominibus, est, *qui est*.
Totum enim in seipso comprehendens habet ipsum esse velut quoddam pelagus
substantiae infinitum et indeterminatum." Quolibet enim alio nomine determinatur aliquis modus substantiae rei ; sed hoc nomen, *qui est*, nullum modum
essendi determinat, sed se habet indeterminate ad omnes. Et ideo nominat
ipsum pelagus substantiae infinitum.—Tertio vero ex ejus consignificatione.
Significat enim esse in praesenti : et hoc maxime proprie de Deo dicitur,
cuius esse non novit praeteritum vel futurum '. *Sum. Theol.*, I, q. 13, a. 11

CHAPTER II

IDEAS INTIMATELY CONNECTED WITH THAT OF THE ESSENCE OF GOD

39. These notions, which are sometimes called *absolute* attributes of God, complete the thought of St. Thomas on the question of the essence of God. They are as follows : His simplicity, His infinity, His immensity, His immutability, His eternity, and His unicity or character of being unique.

I. THE SIMPLICITY OF GOD

40. Meaning of Simplicity.—The idea *simplicity* we conceive by the negation of *composition* ; ' We can speak of simple things only as though they were like the composite things from which we derive our knowledge ' [29]. By the idea of composition we mean the *union* of things that are distinct ; and these are known as *formal* or *virtual* parts of the compound, according as they are really distinct in the object independently of any consideration by the mind, or are merely *distinguishable* by reason of the different aspects under which the object may in fact be viewed by the mind.

41. God is Absolutely Simple.—1. *Argument from induction.* God is absolutely simple, since in Him there are none of the types of composition that we find in natural beings ; we do not find (i) extended parts, (ii) matter and form, (iii) nature and personality, (iv) essence and existence, (v) nor, strictly speaking, genus and difference, (vi) substance and accident.

(i) In God there are no extended parts. ' God is not a body ; and this can be shown in three ways : (*a*) Because no body is in motion unless previously moved by something else, as is evident from induction. It has been already proved that God is the Prime Mover ; and is Himself unmoved. Therefore it is

---

[29] *Sum. Theol.*, I, q. 3, a. 3, ad 1.

clear God is not a body. (b) Because the First Being must of necessity actually exist, and in no way remain in a state of potentiality. Although in any single thing that passes from a state of potentiality to a state of actuality, the potentiality is prior in time to the actuality ; nevertheless, absolutely speaking, actuality is prior to potentiality ; for whatever is in potentiality can only be reduced into actuality by some actual being. It has already been proved that God is the First Being. It is therefore impossible that in God there should be any potentiality. But every body is in potentiality, because whatever is continuous, formally considered, is divisible to infinity ; it is therefore impossible that God should be a body. (c) Because God is the most noble of beings. It is impossible to admit that any body is the most noble of beings ' [30].

(ii) There is in God no composition of matter and form. To quote St. Thomas again : (a) ' Whatever is composed of matter and form is a body ; for extended dimensions are the first quality of matter. But God is not a body ; therefore He is not composed of matter and form. (b) Matter is necessarily in a state of potentiality. But God is pure Actuality (Actus Purus), without any potentiality. Hence it is impossible that God should be composed of matter and form ' [31].

(iii) There is in God no composition of nature and personality or hypostasis, that is to say, there is no need to add anything to the essence of God to make Him an individual Being (cp. Gen. Metaphysics, 87-91). We never conceive of an

[30] ' Deum non esse corpus, tripliciter ostendi potest. 1° Quia nullum corpus movet non motum, ut patet inducendo per singula. Ostensum est autem supra (q. 2, art. 3) quod Deus est primum movens immobile. Unde manifestum est quod Deus non est corpus.—2° Quia necesse est, id quod est primum ens, esse in actu, et nullo modo in potentia. Licet enim in uno et eodem quod exit de potentia in actum, prior sit tempore potentia quam actus, simpliciter tamen prior est actus quam potentia ; quia quod est in potentia non reducitur in actum, nisi per ens actu. Ostensum est autem supra (quaest. praec., art. 3) quod Deus est primum ens. Impossibile est igitur quod in Deo sit aliquid in potentia. Omne autem corpus est in potentia ; quia continuum, in quantum hujusmodi, divisibile est in infinitum. Impossibile est igitur Deum esse corpus.—3° Quia Deus est id quod est nobilissimum in entibus, ut ex dictis patet. Impossibile est autem aliquod corpus esse nobilissimum in entibus '. St. Thomas, Sum. Theol., I, q. 3, a. 1.

[31] ' (a) Omne compositum ex materia et forma est corpus ; quantitas enim dimensiva est quae primo inhaeret materiae. Sed Deus non est corpus, ut ostensum est (art. praec.). Ergo Deus non est compositus ex materia et forma.— (b) Materia est id quod est in potentia. Deus autem est purus actus, non habens aliquid de potentialitate. Unde impossibile est quod Deus sit compositus ex materia et forma '. Loc. cit., a. 2.

existing being except as an individual. But the essence of God is His actual, existential being. He cannot then be a composition of nature and hypostasis.

(iv) There is in Him no composition of essence and existence. See above, **36, 37,** *Sum. Theol.,* I, q. 3, a. 4.

(v) God excludes all composition of genus and difference. (*a*) ' The formality from which we draw the notion of specific difference, and thence that from which the difference constituting the species is derived, is always related to that from which the genus is derived, as actuality is related to potentiality. Since in God actuality cannot be said to be added to potentiality, it is impossible that He should be in any genus as a species. (*b*) Since the existence of God is His essence, if God were in any genus, He would be in the genus " being ", because, since it is predicated of its nature, genus refers to the essence of a thing. The Philosopher has shown (*Metaph.*, Bk. III, 10) that being cannot be a genus, for every genus has differences distinct from its generic essence. No difference can exist distinct from being ; for non-being cannot be a difference. It follows that God is not in a genus ' [32].

(vi) Lastly, there is in God no composition of substance and accidents. ' A subject is compared to its accidental qualities as potentiality to actuality ; for a subject is in some sense made actual by its accidental qualities. But there can be no potentiality in God ' [33].

2. ' In every compound there must be potentiality and actuality ; for the different parts that constitute a being can only go to form a substantial unit on the condition that some are in potentiality and others in actuality. Beings in actuality are only united to one another if they are, as it were, mutually

---

[32] ' (*a*) Semper enim id a quo sumitur differentia constituens speciem, se habet ad illud unde sumitur genus, sicut actus ad potentiam. Unde cum in Deo non adjungatur potentia actui, impossibile est quod sit in genere tanquam species.—(*b*) Quia cum esse Dei sit ejus essentia, ut ostensum est (art. praec.) ; si Deus esset in aliquo genere, oporteret quod genus ejus esset ens. Nam significat essentiam rei, cum praedicetur in eo quod quid est. Ostendit autem Philosophus (*Metaph.* lib. III, text. 10) quod ens non potest esse genus alicujus. Omne enim genus habet differentias, quae sunt extra essentiam generis. Nulla autem differentia potest inveniri quae esset extra ens ; quia non ens non potest esse differentia. Unde relinquitur quod Deus non sit in genere '. *Loc. cit.*, a. 5.

[33] ' Subjectum enim comparatur ad accidens sicut potentia ad actum ; subjectum enim secundum accidens est aliquo modo in actu ; esse autem in potentia, omnino removetur a Deo '. *Loc. cit.*, a. 6.

bound together and form a group ; in which case they form
not a substantial but an accidental union.   Yet they may
be in potentiality relatively to the whole which they form ;
for they are actually united after having been in potentiality to possible union.   But since in God there is no
potentiality there is in Him no composition of substance
and accident ' [34].

3. ' So, again, every composite thing is posterior to its
component parts and is dependent on them.   But God is the
first Being ' [35].

4. ' Every compound presupposes a being that has made it ;
for a compound is the union proceeding from several parts.
But these parts which are in themselves multiple come together
to form a unity only under the unifying action of another being.
If God were a compound there would be need of another being
to have made him.   He could not have compounded himself ;
no being ˙ a cause unto itself, since in this case there would
be the contradiction of a being prior to itself.   But a being
which compounds another being is its efficient cause.   God
would then have an efficient cause and would not be the first
Cause ' [36].

42. Corollaries.—1. It is impossible to give a strict definition
of the divine Being (*Logic*, **78-81**). ' God cannot be defined,
for every definition is by genus and specific difference ' [37].
' God and creature are not distinguished by any specific differences which we can predicate of them as though they belonged
to the same genus ; they differ by their whole reality ; whence,
strictly speaking, we cannot say there is a difference between

[34] ' In omni composito oportet esse actum et potentiam.   Non enim plura
possunt simpliciter fieri unum, nisi aliquid ibi sit actus et aliquid potentia.
Quae enim actu sunt non uniuntur, nisi quasi colligata vel sicut congregata :
quae non sunt unum simpliciter, in quibus etiam ipsae partes congregatae
sunt sicut potentia respectu unionis.   Sunt enim unitae in actu, postquam
fuerint in potentia unibiles.   In Deo autem nulla est potentia ; non est igitur
in eo aliqua compositio '.

[35] ' Item omne compositum posterius est suis componentibus et dependens
ex eis.   Deus autem est primum ens '.   I, q. 3, a. 7.

[36] ' Omnis compositio indiget aliquo componente ; si enim compositio est,
ex pluribus est.   Quae autem secundum se sunt plura, in unum non conveniunt, nisi ab aliquo componente uniantur.   Si igitur compositus esset Deus,
haberet componentem ; non enim ipse seipsum componere posset, quia nihil
est causa sui ipsius ; esset enim prius seipso, quod est impossibile.   Compo-
nens autem est causa efficiens compositi.   Ergo Deus haberet causam efficientem ; et sic non esset causa prima '.   *Cont. Gent.*, I, 18.

[37] *Cont. Gent.*, I, 25.

them but a complete diversity ; diversity marks an absolute opposition, difference a relative opposition ' [38]

2. Care must be taken that the true meaning be given to the pregnant saying of Catholic theology : ' Esse omnium est, quae esse super esse est, Deitas ' ; which St. Thomas interprets thus : ' Deitas dicitur esse omnium effective et exemplariter, non autem per essentiam ' [39].

3. God is a pure spirit [40].

II. The Infinite Perfection of God

43. Meaning of Perfection.—Our imagination naturally represents a simple being as an unknowable monad very akin to an abstraction, but reflection tells us that God is called simple because He *is* all that He has. ' Deus ideo simplex dicitur quia quidquid habet hoc est ' [41].

We have then to ascertain what God has, that is to say, what plenitude of perfection He possesses in His simplicity. St. Thomas answers that God is (I) *perfect*, and therefore *good* ; (II) God possesses *all perfection* to be found in creatures ; (III) God is *infinite* in perfection.

44. I. God is Perfect.—We say that a thing is *perfect* when it is completely made, when it has everything possible for its action and natural requirements (*Gen. Metaphysics*, **173**). When we say that a thing is perfection we do not signify directly the nobility of its rank, but its intrinsic mode of being, the manner in which it possesses the properties that it has, whatever be the degree that it occupies in the scale of beings. The question therefore whether God is perfect is in other words this : Does God actually possess all the perfection which His nature implies ? or on the contrary is the perfection that He enjoys capable of being increased, is it yet further perfectible ? ' Perfectum dicitur cui nihil deest secundum modum suae perfectionis ' ; ' quaerere utrum Deus sit perfectus, est quaerere utrum Deus id quod est sit optimo modo ' [42].

---

[38] ' Deus et esse creatum non differunt aliquibus differentiis utrique (tanquam eidem generi) additis, sed se ipsis : unde nec proprie dicuntur differre, sed diversa esse ; diversum enim est absolutum, sed differens relativum '. *I Sent.*, dist. 3, q. 1, a. 2, ad 3.

[39] *Sum. Theol.*, I, q. 3, a. 8, ad 1.

[40] Cp. *Cont. Gent.*, I, 18, 3, and 20, 5.

[41] St. Augustine, *De Civitate Dei*, II, 10 ; Monsabré, *Conf. de N.-D.*, 7me Conf.

[42] St. Thomas, *Sum. Theol.*, I, q. 4, a. 3 ; and Cajetan, *Comment. in h.l.*

45. Proof.—God is pure actuality ; the perfection which He has is removed from all potentiality. But perfectibility pre-supposes a certain potentiality : ' Existenti in potentia deest id quod in actu esse potest : existenti autem in actu ut sic nihil deest' [43]. Therefore the perfection of God is no longer perfectible but He enjoys the plenitude of His natural per-fection.

46. II. God possesses united in Himself all the Perfections belonging to His Works.—' It must be said that all created perfections are in God. Hence He is spoken of as universally perfect, because He lacks not any excellence which may be found in any genus. This may be seen from the consideration that whatever perfection exists in any effect must be found in the effective cause : either in the same formality, or in a more eminent degree. It is plain that the effect pre-exists virtually in the causative agent. Although to pre-exist in the potentiality of a material cause is to pre-exist in a more imperfect way, since matter as such is imperfect, and an agent as such is perfect ; still to pre-exist virtually in the causative agent is not to pre-exist in a more imperfect, but in a more perfect way. Since God is the first effective Cause of things, the perfections of all things must pre-exist in God in a more eminent way. Dionysius implies the same line of argument by saying of God : It is not that He is this but not that, but that He is all, as the cause of all ' [44].

' Nothing acts except inasmuch as it is in actuality : action therefore follows the measure of the actuality in the agent. It is impossible therefore for any effect that is brought into being by action to be of a nobler actuality than is the actuality of the agent. It is possible however for the actuality of the

---

[43] CAJETAN, *loc. cit.*

[44] ' Dicendum quod in Deo sunt perfectiones omnium rerum. Unde et dicitur universaliter perfectus, quia non deest ei aliqua nobilitas, quae inveniatur in aliquo genere. Et hoc quidem ex eo considerari potest quia quidquid perfectionis est in effectu, oportet inveniri in causa effectiva vel secundum eamdem rationem, vel eminentiori modo. Manifestum est enim quod effectus praeexistit virtute in causa agente. Praeexistere autem in virtute causae agentis non est praeexistere imperfectiori modo, sed perfectiori ; licet praeexistere in potentia causae materialis sit praeexistere imperfectiori modo ; eo quod materia, inquantum hujusmodi, est imperfecta ; agens vero, inquantum hujusmodi, est perfectum. Cum ergo Deus sit prima causa effectiva rerum, oportet omnium rerum perfectiones praeexistere in Deo secundum eminentiorem modum. Et hanc rationem tangit Dionysius (*De div. nom.*, cap. 5, lect. 1), dicens de Deo, quod "non quidem hoc est, hoc autem non est ; sed omnia est ut omnium causa "'. ST. THOMAS, *Sum. Theol.*, I, q. 4, a. 2.

effect to be less perfect than the actuality of the acting cause, inasmuch as action may be weakened on the part of the object to which it is terminated, or upon which it is spent. Now in the category of efficient causation everything is reducible ultimately to one cause which is God, of Whom are all things. Everything therefore that actually is in any other thing must be found in God much more eminently than in the thing itself (though the converse is not true) ; God then is most perfect ' [45].

This proof used in connexion with what we said at the beginning (4 f.) on the way the perfections of creatures can be predicated of God leads us to the conclusion that the Divine Being possesses in a supereminent way all the perfections to be found in creation.

47. Corollary.—The teaching that St. Thomas develops in Question 5 and Question 6 of the *Summa Theologica* (de bono in communi, de bonitate Dei) is only a more express statement of the preceding theories about the perfection of the divine Being. Hence there is no need to do more than give as a corollary the leading ideas of these Questions.

1. ' Goodness and being are really the same, and differ only logically ; which is clear from the following argument. The formality of goodness consists in this, that it is in some way *desirable*. Hence the Philosopher says : Goodness is what all desire. It is clear that a thing is desirable in so far as it is perfect ; for all desire their own perfection '.

2. ' Since goodness is that which all men desire, and since this has the formal aspect of an end, it is clear that goodness implies the formal aspect of an *end* '.

3. ' Good is attributed to God, inasmuch as all desirable perfections flow from Him as from their first Cause. Therefore as good is in God as in the first, but not the univocal, cause of all things, it must be in Him more excellently ; and therefore He is called the Supreme Good or *Summum Bonum* '.

---

[45] ' Nihil agit nisi secundum quod est in actu ; actio igitur consequitur modum actus in agente. Impossibile est igitur effectum, qui per actionem educitur, esse in nobiliori actu quam sit actus agentis. Possibile est tamen effectum imperfectiorem esse, quam sit actus causae agentis, eo quod actio potest debilitari ex parte ejus in quod terminatur. In genere autem causae efficientis fit reductio ad unam causam, quae Deus dicitur, ut ex dictis patet, a quo sunt omnes res, ut in sequentibus ostendetur. Oportet igitur quidquid actu est in quacumque re alia, inveniri in Deo multo eminentius, quam sit in re illa ; non autem e converso. Est igitur Deus perfectissimus '. *Id., Cont. Gent.,* I, 28. (Trs. RICKABY, *Of God and His Creatures,* p. 22.)

4. '*God alone is good by His own Essence*. Everything is called good according to its perfection. . . . But perfection belongs to no creature by its own essence ; it belongs to God only, in whom alone Essence is His Existence . . . for He is not ordered to anything else as His end ; but He Himself is the last end of all things. Hence it is manifest that God alone has every kind of perfection by His own Essence ; therefore He Himself alone is good by His own Essence '.

5. '*Everything is called good from the Divine Goodness*, inasmuch as God is the first exemplary, efficient and final principle of all goodness ' [46].

48. III. God is Infinite in Perfection.—The ideas *finite* and *infinite* are originally derived from material extension, and then applied by analogy to the goodness and perfection of spiritual beings. When we say, then, that God is infinite, we mean that the goodness or perfection of the divine Being is not finite, has no limits. Now limit itself we do not conceive distinctly, as when we compare two or more beings of different size or perfection. There is then no better way of getting a clear and distinct idea of the infinite than by saying : God is a being so good and so perfect that there cannot be a better or more perfect than He. Whilst it is not against reason in the case of a finite being, even if it is perfect, for it to be inferior to another, it would be self-contradictory to suppose an infinite being that is inferior to anything else [47].

[46] 1° ' Bonum et ens sunt idem secundum rem ; sed differunt secundum rationem tantum. Quod sic patet. Ratio enim boni in hoc consistit, quod sit aliquid *appetibile*. Unde Philosophus dicit quod " bonum est quod omnia appetunt ". Manifestum est autem quod unumquodque est appetibile secundum quod est *perfectum ;* nam omnia appetunt suam perfectionem '. q. 5, a. 1.

2° ' Cum bonum sit quod omnia appetunt, hoc autem habeat rationem finis, manifestum est quod bonum rationem *finis* importat '. *Ibid.*, a. 4.

3° ' Bonum Deo attribuitur, inquantum omnes perfectiones desideratae effluunt ab eo sicut a prima causa. Sic ergo oportet, cum bonum sit in Deo, sicut in prima causa omnium non univoca, quod sit in eo excellentissimo modo. Et propter hoc dicitur *summum bonum* '. q. 6, a. 2.

4° ' *Solus Deus est bonus per suam essentiam.* Unumquodque enim dicitur bonum secundum quod est perfectum. Perfectio autem nulli creato competit secundum suam essentiam, sed soli Deo, cujus solius essentia est suum esse. Ipse etiam ad nihil aliud ordinatur sicut ad finem, sed ipse est ultimus finis omnium rerum. Unde manifestum est quod solus Deus habet omnimodam perfectionem secundum suam essentiam. Et ideo ipse solus est bonus per suam essentiam '. *Ibid.*, a. 3.

5° ' *Unumquodque* dicitur *bonum bonitate divina*, sicut primo principio exemplari, effectivo et finali totius bonitatis '. *Ibid.*, a. 4.

[47] ' Infinitum quantitatem sequitur . . . sed non potest infinitas Deo attribui nisi secundum spiritualem magnitudinem : quae quidem spiritualis magnitudo

This infinity, of which we have been speaking, we attribute in the first place to the divine *Being*, then to the divine *perfection* : the divine Being is infinite, God is the absolute plenitude of being ; God is infinite in perfection, He is eminently all pure perfection, ' omnis perfectio simplex '.

49. Proof.—First we must call to mind the leading thesis on which all our first discussion was based : that our idea of God does not furnish us with any positive characteristic, but by way of *negation* we come to distinguish God and creatures [48]. It would then be against all reason to try to establish a proof the conclusion of which would contain a positive concept of infinity and show directly the manner of God's existence ; any argument that makes such a claim must necessarily be ruled out of court. Nevertheless it will not be sufficient merely to prove that God could not have limited Himself, and, since He is the first Being, could not have been limited by another being prior to Himself ; the point is to establish that *intrinsically* God knows no limit.

1. *First Argument.*—The leading idea of the fundamental argument of St. Thomas is summed up in these two lines : ' Since the divine Being is not a being received in anything but is His own subsistent Being, it is clear that God Himself is infinite and perfect ' [49].

He develops this proof under more than one form in the *Summa contra Gentiles* : ' God is not other than His self-existence ; He is therefore the infinitely perfect being, and by this I mean the being to whom no kind of perfection is wanting.

' Indeed a being is endowed with perfection in the measure in which it has existence, e.g. a man would have no perfection

---

quantum ad duo attenditur, scil. quantum ad *potentiam* et quantum ad propriae *naturae bonitatem* sive completionem. Dicitur enim aliquid magis vel minus album secundum modum quo in eo sua albedo compleatur ; pensatur etiam magnitudo virtutis ex magnitudine virtutis vel factorum. Harum autem magnitudinum una aliam consequitur ; nam ex hoc ipso quod aliquid *in actu* est, *activum* est ; secundum igitur modum quo in actu suo completur, est modus magnitudinis suae virtutis ; et sic relinquitur res spirituales magnas dici secundum modum suae completionis : nam in his quae non mole magna sunt, illud omne est majus quod est melius. Ostendendum est igitur secundum hujus magnitudinis modum Deum infinitum esse, . . . quia nullus est perfectionis suae terminus, sive finis, sed est summe perfectus '. *Cont. Gent.*, I, 43 ; cp. SUAREZ, *De Deo*, lib. II, c. 1, n. 5.

[48] Cp. **2** ; ST. THOMAS, *Cont. Gent.*, I, 14.

[49] ' Cum esse divinum non sit esse receptum in aliquo, sed ipse sit *suum esse subsistens*, manifestum est quod ipse Deus sit infinitus et perfectus.' *Sum. Theol.*, I, q. 7, a. 1.

in virtue of his wisdom if he were not *himself* made wise by his wisdom ; and so of his other perfections. Whence the degree of being that a thing has determines the degree of its perfections, and the limits of the being of a thing determine the limits of its perfection. Therefore if there is a being which has the total perfection of being, no perfection of any kind whatsoever can be wanting to it. Now the Being which is its own being must have the total perfection of being ; just as if whiteness be supposed to be self-existent, none of the properties and degrees of whiteness would be wanting to it ; whereas to any particular white thing some degrees of whiteness may be wanting, and this because the subject which receives the whiteness is imperfect, since it receives this whiteness conformably with the limitations of its own nature and not wholly and entirely according to the full perfection of whiteness. Therefore God, who because He is His own being possesses being in all its fullness, cannot be wanting in any possible perfection.

' Moreover, just as every dignity and perfection belong to a thing in proportion as it has being, so any defect is found in it in the measure that it lacks being. So in regard to God, just as He has being wholly, so is He wholly removed from non-being ; for in proportion as a thing is being, it is removed from non-being. Therefore defect of any kind has no place in God ; consequently He is wholly perfect. On the other hand, things whose being is limited are imperfect not because of the imperfection of being considered in itself, absolutely, but by this that they do not possess being in all its fullness ; they are imperfect because they have received being in a particular and inferior grade '[50].

[50] ' Deus qui non est aliud quam suum esse, est universaliter ens perfectum. Et dico universaliter perfectum, cui non deest alicujus generis nobilitas.—Omnis enim nobilitas cujuscumque rei est sibi secundum suum esse ; nulla enim nobilitas esset homini ex sua sapientia, nisi per eam sapiens esset, et sic de alio. Sic ergo secundum modum quo res habet esse, est suus modus in nobilitate. Nam res, secundum quod suum esse contrahitur ad aliquem specialem modum nobilitatis, majorem vel minorem, dicitur esse secundum hoc nobilior vel minus nobilis. Igitur si aliquid est cui competit tota virtus essendi, ei nulla virtus nobilitatis deesse potest, quae alicui rei conveniat. Sed rei, quae est suum esse, competit esse secundum totam essendi potestatem ; sicut si esset aliqua albedo separata, nihil ei de virtute albedinis deesse posset. Nam alicui albo aliquid de virtute albedinis deesse potest, ex defectu recipientis albedinem, qui eam secundum modum suum recipit, et fortasse non secundum totum posse albedinis. Deus igitur qui est totum suum esse, ut supra probatum est, habet esse secundum totam virtutem ipsius esse ; non potest ergo carere aliqua nobilitate, quæ alicui rei conveniat. Sicut autem omnis nobilitas et perfectio inest rei, secundum quod est, ita omnis

This reasoning may be put in the following syllogistic form. I. We say first that God is the absolute plenitude of being, an infinite Being.

God, whose existence we have proved, is of Himself, in virtue of His essence, what He is, ' esse divinum est *suum esse subsistens, irreceptum* '. But a being which is, by virtue of its essence, what it is, suum esse subsistens, cannot but be the absolute plenitude of being. Therefore God is the absolute plenitude of being ; God is infinite.

Proofs of the minor : A self-subsistent being cannot but be the absolute plenitude of being. (*a*) If you go through the whole series of beings, actual or possible, you find that all are inevitably limited. Now the one and only cause which accounts for this universal and inevitable limitation is that each being, realized or realizable, is a subject which is not formally existent in virtue of its intrinsic constitution, but is susceptible of existence, an essential type being presupposed to mark out beforehand what shall be the definite sphere of the being to be produced ; so that the essence which existence presupposes is the sole reason of the precise degree in which

defectus inest rei, secundum quod aliqualiter non est. Deus autem sicut habet esse totaliter, ita ab eo totaliter absistit non esse ; quia per modum per quem habet aliquid esse deficit a non esse. A Deo ergo omnis defectus absistit ; est igitur universaliter perfectus. Ista vero quae tantum sunt, non sunt imperfecta propter imperfectionem ipsius esse absoluti, non enim ipsa habent esse secundum totum suum posse, sed quia participant esse per quemdam particularem modum, et imperfectissimum '. *Cont. Gent.*, I, 28, and cp. with *ibid.*, 43 : ' Omnis actus alteri inhaerens terminationem recipit ex eo in quo est ; quia quod est in altero est in eo per modum recipientis. Actus igitur in nullo existens, nullo terminatur : ut puta si albedo esset per se existens, perfectio albedinis in ea non terminaretur, quominus haberet quidquid de perfectione albedinis haberi potest. Deus autem est actus nullo modo in aliquo existens ; quia non est forma in materia, ut probatum est (c. 26 et 27), nec esse suum inhaeret alicui formae vel naturae, quum ipse sit suum esse, ut supra (c. 21) ostensum est. Relinquitur ergo ipsum esse infinitum '. Also : ' Deus est actus infinitus ; quod patet ex hoc quod actus non finitur nisi dupliciter. Uno modo ex parte agentis ; sicut ex voluntate artificis recipit quantitatem et terminum pulchritudo domus. Alio modo ex parte recipientis ; sicut color in lignis terminatur et quantitatem recipit secundum dispositionem lignorum. Ipse autem divinus actus non finitur ex aliquo agente, quia non est ab alio sed est a seipso ; neque finitur ex alio recipiente, quia cum nihil potentiae passivae ei admisceatur, ipse est actus purus non receptus in aliquo ; est enim Deus *ipsum esse suum* in nullo receptum. Unde patet quod Deus est infinitus ; quod sic videri potest. Esse enim hominis terminatum est ad hominis speciem, quia est acceptum in natura speciei humanae ; et simile est de esse cujuslibet creaturae. Esse autem Dei, cum non sit in aliquo acceptum sed sit esse purum, non limitatur ad aliquem modum perfectionis essendi, sed totum esse in se habet ; et sic sicut esse in universali acceptum ad infinita se potest extendere, ita divinum esse infinitum est'. *Id.*, *De potentia*, q. 1, art. 2.

a thing participates in the fullness of being. Therefore, the self-subsistent being which is not a subject realized or realizable and in which there is no essence presupposed before existence, is not subject to the cause we have mentioned which universally and inevitably limits creatures ; it is outside every conceivable limit [51], it does not participate by way of degree at all in being but it is itself the absolute fullness of being. (b) The same proof may assume a different form : If God, the self-subsistent being, were not *all being*, not only would it be reasonable to represent Him as susceptible of being and of perfection, but it would be unreasonable to represent Him otherwise. 'Existence is the actuality of every form and every nature ; goodness or humanity are actual only if we can say that they are existent. It is necessary, then, that existence should stand to essence, which is really distinct from it, in the same relation as actuality to potentiality ' [52]. Now in God there is no distinction between essence and existence ; in the case of God, His essence, which is the first thing conceivable in a being, is identical with His existence, which is the last thing that it is possible to conceive. 'Since in God there is no potentiality, it follows that in Him essence does not differ from existence. Therefore His essence is His existence ' [53]. The self-subsistent Being is then *all being*, the fullness of being.

II. Next we say that the infinite Being is *infinite in perfection*.

Proofs : (a) 'A being has perfection and dignity according to the measure in which it is ; and imperfection according to the measure in which it is not ' [54]. But God is the fullness of being. Therefore He is being comprising all the modes of being, being in every respect, and consequently His being

[51] As we conceive the Infinite by way of negation of the finite, we may not exclude from the subsistent being limitations of which we have no concept ; to attempt to consider limits of some other kind than those of which we can derive an idea from things that exist or are intelligible would be to play with words and to be attempting the impossible. ' Dicimur in fine nostrae cognitionis Deum tamquam ignotum cognoscere '. St. Thomas, *In Boëth. de Trin.*, q. 1, a. 2, ad 1.

[52] ' Esse est actualitas omnis formae vel naturae, non enim bonitas vel humanitas significatur in actu, nisi prout significatur eam esse. Oportet igitur quod ipsum esse comparetur ad essentiam quae est aliud ab ipso sicut actus ad potentiam '. St. Thomas, *Sum. Theol.*, I, q. 3, a. 4.

[53] ' Cum igitur in Deo nihil sit potentiale, sequitur quod non est aliud in eo essentia quam suum esse. Sua igitur essentia est suum esse '. *Ibid.*

[54] ' Sicut omnis nobilitas et perfectio inest rei, secundum quod est, ita omnis defectus inest ei, secundum quod aliqualiter non est '. *Id., Cont. Gent.*, I, 28.

embraces, without any limits, every pure perfection. (*b*) The existence of a contingent perfection presupposes the existence of a pure actuality corresponding to it which possesses this perfection essentially. Now to affirm the existence of a perfection such that it is in a state of pure actuality is to affirm that this perfection is identical with the subsistent Being. Therefore all-perfection, when in a state of pure actuality, is identical with the subsistent being. Hence God who is the subsistent being is *eo ipso* all-perfection. Now He is the plenitude of being. Therefore He is the plenitude of all perfection ; He is infinite in perfection.

2. *Second Argument.*—Our first argument was an *a priori* (διότι) proof of the infinity of God ; the following one is drawn from a psychological fact, namely the *necessary and supreme tendencies of the soul towards the Infinite*[55].

The soul by its higher faculties spontaneously aspires towards what is more and more perfect ; ' no finite thing can satiate the desires of the mind ' ; the soul of man, then, tends towards the infinite. Now there are two alternatives : either this tendency has a real end corresponding to it or it is a matter of illusion. If it is illusory, then we are face to face with an inexplicable fact : we see the spectacle of man, ' a small and feeble creature whom all the powers of body, mind and heart, combined with the refinement of art, not only fail to satisfy but ever awaken to a deeper sense of emptiness and disappointment '[56] ; and we should therefore have to conclude that, whilst

---

[55] ' Intellectus noster ad infinitum in intelligendo extenditur, cujus signum est quod qualibet quantitate finita data intellectus noster majorem excogitare possit ; frustra autem esset haec ordinatio intellectus ad infinitum nisi esset aliqua res intelligibilis infinita ; oportet igitur esse aliquam rem intelligibilem infinitam, quam oportet esse maximam rerum, et hanc dicimus Deum. Deus igitur est infinitus '.
' Omni finito potest aliquid majus cogitari ; ex quo declaratur quod intellectus noster habet quandam infinitatem respectu sui intelligibilis. Intelligibile autem est res. Omni autem potentiae respondet suus actus, cum potentia ad actum dicatur. Cum igitur intelligibile sit actus et perfectio intellectus, oportet ponere aliquam rem intelligibilem infinitam. Infiniti autem principium non potest esse aliquid finitum cum nihil agat ultra seipsum '. *Id., Cont. Gent.*, I, 43.
' Nihil finitum, desiderium intellectus quietare potest, quod exinde ostenditur, quod intellectus quolibet finito dato, aliquid ultra molitur apprehendere ; unde qualibet linea finita data, aliquam majorem molitur apprehendere, et similiter in numeris, et haec est ratio infinitae additionis in numeris et lineis mathematicis '. *Ibid.*, III, 50.
[56] VAN WEDDINGEN, *Eléments Raisonnés de Religion*, p. 374. Cp. also *Essai sur la philosophie de S. Anselme*, pp. 307 and 320. This author remarks that one cannot but be struck by the oft recurrence of the noblest minds to

harmony and finality govern the lower beings of this world, man alone, the master-piece of creation, is an anomaly, nay more, a monstrosity in nature.

The fact, then, of these natural tendencies of the human soul proves the existence of what will satisfy them. Consequently there must really exist an infinite Being who is the object of our intellect under the form of the true, and of our will under the form of the good ; and since dependence of any kind is incompatible with infinity, the only being that can be identified with the infinite is God ; therefore God whom we conceive as living and caring for us is infinite.

50. Objections.—Tiberghien, a disciple of Krause, lays the charge of asserting a contradiction against those who maintain that God is infinite and distinct from the world. The infinite, he argues, must be all that is ; for, if we could conceive anything outside of or beside God, He would not be infinite, since in that case the whole of reality would be divided into two parts. But the advocates of the dualistic position maintain that God is not all that is, for they postulate a created world as a reality distinct from Him ; therefore they are guilty of saying that the Infinite is not infinite [57].

We reply by distinguishing two meanings in the major premiss of his argument : (a) in the sense that the Infinite must be, in the ineffable super-eminence of His nature, the formal reason of His own being and the supreme efficient exemplary and final *cause* of all that there is outside of Him, we grant ; (b) in the sense that the Infinite must be *formally*, that is to say must intrinsically constitute, all that exists, we deny. In the same way we contradistinguish his minor ; and accordingly refuse assent to the conclusion.

St. Thomas foresaw and propounded the same objection : ' The being which is of a nature such that it is distinct from all other beings and does not possess their entity, is a finite substance. But God is of such a nature and is really distinct from other beings ; He is clearly not stone or wood. Consequently God is not an infinite substance '. And to this he

St. Anselm's argument. The reason is that the objective element in the idea of the infinite appears to them with such vivid clearness that its light seems to envelop the subjective notion as well, p. 307.

[57] See the works of the author *passim*, especially *Introduction à la Philosophie*, pp. 50 and 54 (Brussels, 1888), and *Esquisse de Phil. Mor.*, pp. 48, 54, and 65.

replied : ' Because God exists of Himself, because we must predicate infinity of Him, He must necessarily be distinct from all other beings and they must not be confounded with Him ' [58]. In other words, we assent to the proposition that that being is finite which is determined and distinct from other beings, because its nature realizes a perfection which is exclusive of the perfections of some other ; but we do not allow that that being is finite which is determinate and distinct from all others not by reason of some exclusive perfection but because its nature is such that it embraces all modes of being, and thus surpasses every other being because it comprises everything *eminently* in its absolute substance.

A *rejoinder* might be made : Finite beings are not pure non-entity, they have their own endowment of reality. Since this is so, there is no reason why they should not be added to the infinite being. But if this addition were made, we should have a total which is greater than infinity—which is absurd. Therefore the infinite implies a contradiction.

To this we reply by denying the supposition which underlies the major. Addition is possible only of terms which are units of the same genus ; and between God, the transcendent Being, and creatures that enjoy only an existence analogous to that of God there is nothing common in the same genus : therefore the supposed addition is intrinsically impossible. Furthermore, even were such an addition intrinsically possible, which we do not allow, the resultant would be *more beings*, that is to say more natures as opposed to nothing, not *more being*, i.e. more excellence ; in fact it would necessarily imply less excellence, inasmuch as a being susceptible of any kind of composition would be inferior to that whose absolute simplicity permits of none.

III. The Immensity of God

51. Meaning of Immensity.—For a being to be *somewhere*, that is to say, for it to exercise its activity upon other beings, is certainly a perfection ; and therefore, since both spiritual

---

[58] ' Quod ita est hoc quod non est aliud, est finitum secundum substantiam. Sed Deus est hoc et non est aliud. Non enim est lapis nec lignum. Ergo Deus non est infinitus secundum substantiam.
R. Dicendum quod ex hoc ipso quod esse Dei est per se subsistens non receptum in aliquo, prout dicitur infinitum, distinguitur ab omnibus aliis et alia removentur ab eo '. *Sum. Theol.*, I, q. 7, a. 1, ad 3.

and material created substances have this perfection, God too must possess it. However to be *only somewhere*, to have a limited presence and a *definite* sphere of action in space like spirits and still more to be *circumscribed* by ambient space like material bodies, implies an imperfection which cannot apply to the Being without division or limit. In order to gain as complete an idea as possible of the divine perfection which corresponds to the presence of a created being in space, we must examine in turn (1) on what grounds, (2) to what extent, (3) in what manner, (4) for what fundamental reason, we must say that God is present in the midst of His works. This examination will consist in analysing the manner in which a creature is present and then in freeing this conception from every element of imperfection that we find included in it.

1. In a wider sense of the expression, a being is said to be present by reason of its *active influence*, and in this sense it is present to the objects under the control of its power, and even to the things falling within the scope of its perception ; more strictly and in the proper sense of the expression a being is present only where it is *substantially*. The presence that we attribute to a creature on these different grounds, we can and we must attribute to God. God is naturally present to the works He has created, which He preserves in being, which He knows and which He governs. ' Therefore, God is in all things by His *Power*, inasmuch as all things are subject to His Power ; He is in all things by His *Presence*, as all things are bare and open to His eyes ; He is in all things by His *Essence*, inasmuch as He is the cause of existence to all things ' [59]. ' God is in all things ; not, indeed, as part of their essence, nor as an accident ; but as an agent is present to anything upon which it works. . . . God causes existence in things not only when they first begin to exist, but as long as they are preserved in existence. Therefore as long as a thing exists, God must be present to it, according to its mode of existence. Now existence (esse) is what is most intimate to a thing and what is at

---

[59] ' Sic ergo Deus est in omnibus per *potentiam*, inquantum omnia ejus potestati subduntur ; est per *praesentiam* in omnibus, inquantum omnia nuda sunt et aperta oculis ejus ; est in omnibus per *essentiam*, inquantum adest omnibus ut causa essendi, sicut dictum est (art. 1) '. St. Thomas, *Sum. Theol.*, I, q. 8, a. 3.

the very bottom of all things, inasmuch as it is the final determination of whatever is in a thing. Hence it must be that God
is in all things intimately ' [60].

2. Further, *omnipresence* or *ubiquity* is an attribute of God.
' God is in every place ; which means to exist everywhere.
First, He is so in all things as giving them being, and power,
and operation ; for He is in every place as giving it existence
and locative power. Also, things placed are in place, inasmuch
as they fill place ; and God fills every place ; not, indeed, like
a body ; for a body is said to fill place, inasmuch as it does not
suffer the co-presence of another body ; whereas by God
being in a place, others are not thereby excluded from it ;
indeed, by the very fact that He gives existence to everything
in every place, He fills every place ' [61].

3. The quotation just cited also indicates the *manner* of
God's presence everywhere. St. Thomas continues : ' Although corporeal things are said to be in anything as in that
which contains them, nevertheless spiritual things contain
those things in which they are ; as the soul contains the body.
Hence also God is in things as containing them ; nevertheless
by a certain similitude to corporeal things, it is said that all
things are in God, inasmuch as they are contained by Him ' [62].
' Incorporeal things are not in place by contact of dimensive
quantity, as bodies are ; but by contact of power ' [63]. ' Hence

---

[60] ' Deus est in omnibus rebus, non quidem sicut pars essentiae, vel sicut
accidens, sed sicut agens adest ei in quod agit. Deus causat esse in rebus,
non solum quando primo esse incipiunt, sed quamdiu in esse conservantur.
Quamdiu igitur res habet esse, tamdiu oportet quod Deus adsit ei secundum
modum quo esse habet. Esse autem est illud quod est magis intimum cui-
libet, et quod profundius omnibus inest ; cum sit formale respectu omnium
quae in re sunt. Unde oportet quod Deus sit in omnibus rebus et intime '.
I, q. 8, a. 1.

[61] ' Deus est in omni loco, quod est esse ubique. Primo quidem sicut est
in omnibus rebus, ut dans eis esse, et virtutem, et operationem, sic etiam
est in omni loco, ut dans ei esse, et virtutem locativam. Item, locata sunt in
loco inquantum replent locum ; et Deus omnem locum replet ; non sicut
corpus, corpus enim dicitur replere locum, inquantum non compatitur secum
aliud corpus, sed per hoc quod Deus est in aliquo loco, non excluditur quin
alia sint ibi ; imo per hoc replet omnia loca, quod dat esse omnibus locatis
quae replent omnia loca '. I, q. 8, a. 2.

[62] ' Licet corporalia dicantur esse in aliquo sicut in continente, tamen
spiritualia continent ea in quibus sunt ; sicut anima continet corpus. Unde
et Deus est in rebus, sicut continens res. Tamen per quamdam similitudinem
corporalium dicuntur omnia esse in Deo, inquantum continentur ab ipso '
I, q. 3, a. 1, ad 2.

[63] ' Incorporalia non sunt in loco per contactum quantitatis dimensivae,
sicut corpora, sed per contactum virtutis '. I, q. 3, a. 2, ad 1.

according as their power can extend itself to one or to many, to a small thing, or to a great one ; in this way it is in one or in many places, and in a small or large place ' [64]. ' As the soul is whole in every part of the body, so is God whole in all things and in each one ' [65].

4. The omnipresence of God is a simple corollary of His immensity which is a higher absolute perfection prior to His creative activity : ' It belongs to anything to be everywhere absolutely (per se) when, on any supposition, it must be everywhere. This properly belongs to God alone. For whatever number of places are supposed, even if an infinite number were supposed besides what already exist, it would be necessary that God should be in all of them ; for nothing can exist except by Him ' [66].

Although we cannot form a proper and positive representation of God's immensity, yet we can conceive that there must be in the infinite Being, in an eminent manner, some perfection that corresponds to what local presence gives to finite beings, some intrinsic and absolute exigence that involves His substantial presence in all the worlds that He has created or ever will create, where His omnipotence, His omniscience and His supreme providential action have to be exercised.

52. Proof of the Immensity of God.—The proof of the immensity of God is evident from what we have just said. The infinite Being comprises every absolutely pure perfection ; immensity is an absolutely pure perfection ; therefore the infinite Being is immense.

Proof of the minor premiss : To be endowed with an absolutely pure perfection means to possess a perfection which excludes all imperfections that can detract from it. Now the presence of a thing somewhere, inasmuch as it is something positive, is a perfection ; immensity is just this same perfection without the other impairing elements that are mixed with it when

---

[64] ' Secundum quod virtus ejus se potest extendere ad unum vel ad multa, ad parvum vel ad magnum, secundum hoc substantia incorporea est in uno vel pluribus locis, et in loco parvo vel magno '. *Ibid.*, ad. 2.

[65] ' Sicut anima est tota in qualibet parte corporis, ita Deus totus est in omnibus et singulis entibus '. *Ibid.*, ad. 3.

[66] ' Per se convenit esse ubique alicui, quando tale est quod, qualibet positione facta, sequitur illud esse ubique. Et hoc proprie convenit Deo ; quia quotcumque loca ponantur, etiamsi ponerentur infinita praeter ista quae sunt, oporteret in omnibus esse Deum ; quia nihil potest esse nisi per ipsum '. I, q. 8, a. 4.

realized in creatures. In the case of a creature, presence involves imperfection for the double reason that it is a mode of being which depends on the creature itself, and that, as it is circumscribed or in some other way restricted, it is essentially subject to limitation. The immensity, however, of God is identical with His substantial being ; that being has no extended parts but is indivisible reality unlimited in every line, and excluding by its very essence every limit, no matter what may be the number and size of the worlds to which His action extends.

Therefore immensity is an absolutely simple perfection.

What connexion is there, we may ask, between the action of God on things outside Himself and His presence in place ? Undoubtedly there is a relation of constant concomitance between the two ; for since God is immense it cannot be that His action should terminate in something to which He is not present. But is there between the action of God and His presence in place a necessary connexion, in such a way that we can logically infer the latter from the former ?

Many writers answer in the affirmative, arguing from the impossibility of ' action at a distance ' : Cajetan, St. Bonaventure, the Dominican School in general, Suarez, Kleutgen, are supporters of this view, and they claim in general the support of St. Thomas's authority. On the other hand, Scotus, Vasquez and some others hold to a negative answer, and assert that the principle on which their opponents rely does not apply to the question.

Vasquez (*Disp.*, 28, c. 3) argues that the action by which God preserves the world in being is no other than the continuation of the act of creation ; but the creative act requires that there be no pre-existing subtrate since it produces the created thing from nothingness ; therefore it is absurd to suppose the action of God necessarily demands His presence in the object of His action. And he goes on to say that the impossibility of action at a distance proves at most only a presence of continuous juxtaposition, whereas what needs proof in the case of God is an inmost presence which penetrates the creature in a most fundamental sense. From these premises he concludes that it is not logical to infer from the action of God that He is substantially present in place.

These criticisms seem to us well founded and the inference

they oppose seems illogical ; the presence of God to an object that His creative action deals with appears posterior to the action itself and consequently is not a prerequisite condition ; and therefore, in order to show that there is a necessary connexion between the substantial presence of God and His action on things without, it would be necessary either to go back to some principle which is anterior to both the one and the other, or else to establish each by proofs that are mutually independent.

Moreover we think we are in agreement with the whole teaching of St. Thomas on the act of creation. True, the passage we have already quoted may be brought against us : ' God is in all things, as an agent is present to what it acts upon. For it is necessary that every agent should be united to what is immediately subjected to its action and that it should touch it by his operation. Whence it follows that immediate contact is necessary between an agent moving and an object moved ' [67]. But to this we reply that St. Thomas reasons by way of analogy. The action of corporeal agents presupposes their presence in the spot where they act ; consequently, on any hypothesis, it is legitimate to reason in this wise : Just as the action of exterior objects reveals to us their presence in a place, so the action of God which manifests itself in the created universe justifies us in asserting analogically that the divine Being comprises in Himself something which corresponds in an eminent way to the perfection denoted by the local presence of finite agents [68]

IV. The Absolute Immutability of God

53. Meaning and Proof.—We cannot do better than give without comment the concise and clear statement of St. Thomas.

1. *God is immutable :* ' From what precedes, it is shown that God is altogether immutable. (*a*) First, because it was shown above that there is some first Being, whom we call God ; and

---

[67] ' Deus est in omnibus rebus, sicut agens adest ei in quod agit. Oportet enim omne agens conjungi ei in quod immediate agit, et sua virtute illud contingere. Unde probatur quod motum et movens oportet esse simul '. I, q. 8, a. 1.
[68] Cp. *Cont. Gent.*, II, 16, 7, and 17. ' Quod creatio non est motus neque mutatio '.

that this first Being must be purely Actual (Actus Purus), without any potentiality ; for the reason that potentiality is absolutely posterior to actuality. Everything which is in any way changed, is in some way a potentiality. Hence it is evident that it is impossible for God to be in any way change-able. (*b*) Secondly, because everything which is moved, remains as it was as regards some term, and passes away as regards some other term ; as what is moved from whiteness to blackness, remains the same in substance ; thus in everything which is moved, there is some kind of composition to be found It has been shown above that in God there is no composition ; for that He is absolutely simple. Hence it is manifest that God cannot be moved. (*c*) Thirdly, because everything which is moved acquires something by its motion, and attains to what it had not attained previously. As God is Infinite, compre-hending in Himself the plenitude of perfection of all Being, He cannot acquire anything new, nor extend Himself to any-thing whereto He was not extended previously. Hence motion in no way belongs to Him ' [69].

2. *God alone is absolutely immutable :* ' Thus in every creature there is a potentiality to change either as regards substantial existence, as in the case of things corruptible ; or as regards locality only, as in the case of the celestial bodies [which in the physics of the ancients were considered incorruptible] ; or as regards the order of their end, and the application of their powers to divers objects, as is the case with the angels ; and further the whole order of creatures taken together is capable of being changed, since the Creator has power to maintain them in existence or to annihilate them. But as God alone is in none of

---

[69] ' Ex praemissis (q. 2, a. 3) ostenditur Deum esse omnino immutabilem : 1° Quidem, quia supra ostensum est (*loc. cit.*) esse aliquod primum ens, quod Deum dicimus ; et quod hujusmodi primum ens oportet esse purum actum absque permixtione alicujus potentiae ; eo quod potentia simpliciter est posterior actu. Omne autem quod quocumque modo mutatur, est aliquo modo in potentia. Ex quo patet quod impossibile est Deum aliquo modo mutari.—2° Quia omne quod movetur, quantum ad aliquid manet, et quan-tum ad aliquid transit ; sicut quod movetur de albedine in nigredinem, manet secundum substantiam. Et sic in omni eo quod movetur, attenditur aliqua compositio. Ostensum est autem supra (q. 3, a. 7) quod in Deo nulla est compositio, sed est omnino simplex. Unde manifestum est quod Deus moveri non potest.—3° Quia omne quod movetur, motu suo aliquid acqui-rit, et pertingit ad illud ad quod prius non pertingebat. Deus autem, cum sit infinitus, comprehendens in se omnem plenitudinem perfectionis totius esse, non potest aliquid acquirere ; nec extendere se in aliquid ad quod prius non pertingebat. Unde nullo modo sibi competit motus '. I, q. 9, a. 1.

these ways mutable, it belongs to Him alone to be altogether immutable '[70].

V. The Eternity of God

54. Meaning of Divine Eternity.—The idea of eternity at once appears to everyone as a duration without imperfection. In proportion as our concept of it becomes clearer there stands out as its distinctive characteristics the absence of (a) commencement, (b) limit, (c) vicissitude. These features have become fixed in the definition which since Boëthius has been universally received by the Scholastics : ' Eternity is the full and perfect possession of an interminable life ; Interminabilis vitae tota simul et perfecta possessio '.

Let us go through the ascending scale of contingent beings in such a way as to eliminate one by one from our concept of the duration of God all imperfections that are found in them.

1. At the bottom stand *corporeal substances,* which (a) come into being at a particular moment as the result of a natural disintegration or combination, (b) constantly manifest accidental changes (phenomena), until (c) sooner or later their very substance combines or decomposes under the action of some extrinsic action, to form one or more new substances (*temporary duration, tempus*).

2. Higher in the scale come *spiritual beings* which, though unchangeable in their substantial nature and therefore naturally imperishable, (a) are no less subject to variations in the development of their faculties, and (b) are dependent at each moment on the omnipotence of God for their preservation in the being they have received (c) at the commencement of their life (*permanent duration, aevum*). It does not here concern us whether this dependence involves a positive succession of real parts (St. Bonaventure) or simply a succession of possible parts (St. Thomas, Suarez) in the duration of a spiritual being.

3. Although such is *as a matter of fact* the condition of every spiritual substance, yet it is not repugnant to the mind to

[70] ' Sic igitur in omni creatura est potentia ad mutationem ; vel secundum esse substantiale sicut corpora corruptibilia : vel secundum esse locale tantum (sicut corpora coelestia) ; vel secundum ordinem ad finem, et applicationem virtutis ad diversa, sicut in angelis ; et universaliter omnes creaturae communiter sunt mutabiles secundum potentiam creantis, in cujus potestate est esse et non esse earum. Unde, cum Deus nullo istorum modorum sit mutabilis, proprium ejus est omnino immutabilem esse '. *Ibid.*, a. 2.

conceive a spirit created from all eternity and raised at the first instant to the possession of its end ; such a being would know neither date of origin nor change in action from the point of view of the enjoyment of its supreme end ; but does it follow that it would be eternal ?

Strictly speaking it would not be ; for even allowing that there were no variation in its acts and no real development in the duration of its existence, such a favoured spirit would still always be liable to annihilation and, consequently, radically subject to the law of successive duration.

In order to perfect this negative idea that we have of eternity we must raise *the fact* of this perpetual and unvarying existence of a spirit, however great such a dignity, to the height of an *essential right,* and exclude, as being intrinsically incompatible with the nature of an eternal being, not only the fact but even the possibility of a commencement, of an end, or of any kind of a series of successive events in the course of its existence. ' O my God,' writes St. Augustine, ' Thy years neither come nor go ; they stand together, nor are departing thrust out by coming years, for they pass not away. Thy years are one day ; and Thy day is not daily, but To-day, seeing Thy To-day gives not place unto to-morrow, for neither doth it replace yesterday. Thy To-day, is Eternity ' [71].

It follows from what we have said that the *eternity* of God is absolute, that is to say, independent of all relation to time, just as His immensity is independent of all relation to space ; and therefore the *co-existence* of God with the past, the present and the future of His creatures is only a corollary following from His eternity [72].

---

[71] *Confessions,* XI, 13.

[72] ' Conveniens definitio aeternitatis est ea quam ponit Boetius dicens quod aeternitas est interminabilis vitae tota simul et perfecta possessio '. ' Sicut in cognitionem simplicium oportet nos venire per composita, ita in cognitionem aeternitatis oportet nos venire per tempus ; quod nihil aliud est quam numerus motus secundum prius et posterius. Cum enim in quolibet motu sit successio, et una pars post alteram ; ex hoc quod numeramus prius et posterius in motu, apprehendimus tempus, quod nihil aliud est quam numerus prioris et posterioris in motu. In eo autem quod caret motu, et semper eodem modo se habet, non est accipere prius et posterius. Sicut igitur ratio temporis consistit in numeratione prioris et posterioris in motu, ita in apprehensione uniformitatis ejus quod est omnino extra motum, consistit ratio aeternitatis. Item ea dicuntur tempore mensurari, quae principium et finem habent in tempore, ut dicitur (*Phys., lib.* IV, text. 70). Et hoc ideo, quia in omni eo quod movetur, est accipere aliquod principium et aliquem finem. Quod vero est omnino immutabile, sicut nec successionem,

55. God is Eternal.—' The idea of eternity follows immutability, as the idea of time follows movement, as appears from the preceding. Hence as God is supremely immutable, it supremely belongs to Him to be eternal. Nor is He eternal only : but He is His own eternity, whereas no other being is its own duration, as no other is its own existence. God is His own uniform Being, and hence as He is His own essence, so is He His own eternity ' [73].

God alone is Eternal. ' Eternity really and properly speaking is in God alone, for eternity follows immutability. And God alone is absolutely immutable ' [74].

VI. THE UNICITY OF GOD

56. Proof.—We may show that polytheism is an error and that there are not and cannot be several gods answering to the concept of the supreme Being.

ita nec principium aut finem habere potest. Sic ergo ex duobus notificatur aeternitas : 1° Ex hoc quod id quod est in aeternitate, est interminabile, id est principio et fine carens ; ut terminus ad utrumque referatur. 2° Per hoc quod ipsa aeternitas successione caret, tota simul existens '. *Sum. Theol.*, I, q. 10, a. 1.

' In tempore est duo considerare, scilicet ipsum tempus, quod est successivum, et nunc temporis quod est imperfectum. Dicitur ergo aeternitatis *tota simul*, ad removendum tempus ; et *perfecta* ad excludendum nunc temporis '. *Ibid.*, ad 5.

' Cum aeternitas sit mensura esse permanentis, secundum quod aliquid recedit a permanentia essendi, secundum hoc recedit ab aeternitate. Quaedam autem sic recedunt a permanentia essendi, quod esse eorum est subjectum transmutationis, vel in transmutatione consistit, esse hujusmodi mensurantur tempore, sicut omnis motus, et etiam esse omnium corruptibilium. Quaedam vero recedunt minus a permanentia essendi ; quia esse eorum nec in transmutatione consistit, nec est subjectum transmutationis ; tamen habent transmutationem adjunctam vel in actu vel in potentia : sicut patet de angelis qui habent esse intransmutabile quantum ad eorum naturam pertinet, cum transmutabilitate secundum electionem, et cum transmutabilitate intelligentiarum et affectionum et locorum suo modo. Et ideo hujusmodi mensurantur aevo, quod est medium inter aeternitatem et tempus. Esse autem quod mensurat aeternitas, nec est mutabile, nec mutabilitati adjunctum. Sic ergo *tempus* habet prius et posterius ; *aevum* autem non habet in se prius et posterius, sed ei conjungi possunt ; *aeternitas* autem non habet prius neque posterius, neque ea compatitur '. I, q. 10, a. 5.

[73] ' Ratio aeternitatis consequitur immutabilitatem, sicut ratio temporis consequitur motum, ut ex dictis patet (art. praec.). Unde cum Deus sit maxime immutabilis, sibi maxime competit esse aeternum. Nec solum est aeternus, sed est sua aeternitas ; cum tamen nulla alia res sit sua duratio, quia non est suum esse. Deus autem est suum esse uniforme. Unde sicut est sua essentia, ita sua aeternitas '. I, q. 10, a. 2.

[74] ' Aeternitas vere et proprie in solo Deo est : quia aeternitas immutabilitatem consequitur. . . . Solus autem Deus est omnino immutabilis, ut est superius ostensum '. *Ibid.*, a. 3.

We have already seen that the unity of plan and purpose that is manifested by the universe as we know it affords an indication of the unicity of Him who presides over its governance[75]. This affords a presumption in favour of His unicity, which we may confirm by two arguments.

1. From the fact that God is His self-subsistence.—It is impossible that the *actual being* of an individual, e.g. my own personal being, should be shared by others, communicated to several. But the divine nature is absolutely and entirely identical with His personal actual being. Therefore it is impossible that the divine nature should be shared by several gods.

In other words, a plurality of gods would only be possible if the divine essence were a type, distinct from His existence, that could be realized, and could be identified with several species or with several individuals falling within it. But the divine Being is not a specific type capable of being shared by several individuals. Therefore there can only be one God[76].

Infinite simplicity is identical with infinite unity ; in virtue of His infinite simplicity God not only is one God, but that oneness, uniqueness is His essentially. And as the whole of the essence of God is His actual being, there is nothing in it that can be communicated to several, nothing that is not numerically one and unique.

2. It is impossible that there should be *two infinite beings*, whether we suppose them different from one another or absolutely alike. For if we suppose them to be different, one then has a perfection that the other lacks, and therefore the latter is, to say the least, not infinite. If we suppose them to be perfectly alike, we are faced with two alternatives : either

[75] Cp. *Sum. Theol.*, I, q. 11, a. 3 ; *Cont. Gent.*, I, 42, 3 and 6.
[76] ' Deum esse unum demonstratur *ex ejus simplicitate*. Manifestum est enim quod illud unde aliquid singulare est *hoc aliquid*, nullo modo est multis communicabile. Illud enim unde Socrates est homo, multis communicari potest, sed id, unde est hic homo, non potest communicari, nisi *uni tantum*. Si ergo Socrates per id esset homo, per quod est hic homo, sicut non possunt esse plures Socrates, ita non possent esse plures homines. Hoc autem convenit Deo. Nam ipse Deus est sua natura, ut supra ostensum est '. *Sum. Theol.*, I, q. 3, a. 3 ; q. 11, a. 3.
' Natura significata hoc nomine Deus, aut est per seipsam individuata in hoc Deo, aut per aliquid aliud. Si per aliud, oportet quod ibi sit compositio ; si per seipsam, ergo impossibile est quod alteri conveniat. Illud enim quod est individuationis principium, non potest esse pluribus commune. Impossibile est igitur esse plures deos '. *Cont. Gent.*, I, 42.

the second infinite is dependent on God or it is not. In the former case, it is not infinite. In the latter, God is no longer infinite, for in order to be so He must definitely be the *raison d'être* of all that exists and must comprise, in an eminent degree, everything that has being. We conclude then that in any hypothesis there cannot be two infinite beings [77].

[77] 'Deum esse unum probatur ex infinitate ejus perfectionis. Ostensum est enim supra (q. 4, a. 2) quod Deus comprehendit in se totam perfectionem essendi. Si ergo essent plures dii, oporteret eos differre. Aliquid ergo conveniret uni quod non alteri. Si autem hoc esset, perfectio alteri eorum deesset. Et sic ille in quo esset privatio, non esset simpliciter perfectus. Impossibile est ergo esse plures deos '. *Sum. Theol.*, I, q. 11, a. 3.

PART III

The Activity of God

57. Nature and Action of God.—The essence of a being is the intrinsic reason of what it is ; the nature is this same essence considered as a principle of activities.

In the case of a finite being this nature acts through the medium of operative powers. The latter, together with their actions, are *accidental* determinations of its nature. In God, however, there is no trace of what is accidental ; throughout the whole of His being He is substance. For an accident implies imperfection, since in order to exist it needs to inhere in a substance and depends on it ; and in proportion to its dependence it is imperfect.

Nevertheless, from another point of view an accident is the perfecting of a substance that can be perfected ; for this reason it is a perfection.

God, who is all-perfect, has both the independence proper to a substance and also the perfections which belong to the accidental determinations of creatures. The transcendent nature of God is a self-active substance, a substantial activity.

58. Life in God.—The actions of creatures are of two kinds, transitive and immanent ; the highest manifestations of the latter are knowledge and volition.

Beings which act on other natural beings are in their turn subject to the law of reaction ; now there is no reason why God should not act transitively ' ad extra ', that is, on things outside Himself, but since He is actuality without any potentiality He is not subject to reaction from them. Moreover He is the First Being and is what He is before anything exists and has power to act.

There is no need to point out that the lower degrees of life, both vegetable and sensitive, are incompatible with the pure essential actuality of God. Intellectual life, however—

knowledge and will—does not formally contain an imperfection; it is a *simple* perfection (5) and, on this account, may be attributed to God. And, moreover, for three positive reasons it must be attributed to Him : (*a*) The world manifests design and order, and we know that the first Cause of this order is endowed with intelligence and will (28). (*b*) Among contingent beings in this world there are some that are endowed with power of thought and will ; wherefore their Author must enjoy the same perfections. (*c*) Beatitude by its definition is the full and conscious possession of the most perfect good that a being is capable of enjoying. So understood, it is something purely positive, and must therefore belong to the infinitely perfect Being. And this intellectual life belongs to Him without any imperfection ; it is therefore the infinite possession of an infinite good. This infinite good cannot be other than the divine essence.

But the infinite possession of this good can find its activity only in thought and love, in such a way that the intelligibility of the divine essence is its own intellection, its lovableness, its own actual love.

Therefore there are in God thought and love : this love inspires the works that are exterior to God, and this thought directs them.

According to this very brief argument we divide Part III into three chapters : Thought in God (I) ; Will in God (II) ; The work of God (III).

CHAPTER I

THOUGHT IN GOD

59. Intellectual Life of God.—The intellectual life of God, in other words His knowledge or science, may be considered in itself or in its object.

Considered subjectively, in itself, it does not consist in the exercise of a faculty, since in God there is no composition of a substance and faculties; nor is it the fruit of a process of reasoning, for the faculty of ratiocination goes from truths known to a truth unknown, and in God in whom there is no potentiality there is no intellectual growth; nor again is it an abstractive operation which employs a series of compositions and divisions of abstract ideas, for in a Being who is actually and perfectly His own entire perfection there is neither fragmentary knowledge nor multiplicity of acts nor succession of action. The divine knowledge is a single act of adequate comprehension, that is to say an act which exhausts at a glance the whole intelligibility of its object.

Considered objectively, looked at in its term, the divine knowledge is, primarily, of the very nature of God, and, secondarily, of all other things that exist or may exist.

60. God's Knowledge is the Actual Comprehension of His Nature.—1. This proposition rests on the *simplicity* of the divine Being. In God there is no intellective potentiality capable of being determined to intellection : His intellection is His essence. Now actual intellection or understanding and the actual being understood are one and the same thing. Therefore the divine substance, being actual intellection, is also the actual object of this intellection.

2. It rests on the *infinity* of the divine perfection. This infinity of perfection implies (*a*) an infinitely intelligible essence, (*b*) an infinite power of knowing, and (*c*) a union of the power of knowing with its infinitely perfect object in such a way that there is an adequate correspondence between the one and the other. Consequently the exercise of the power of knowing

93

that is proper to an infinite Being consists in the adequate perception of this Being, in a word, in a ' comprehensive ' view of the divine Being.

61. God knows all Things Actual and Possible.—In *Meta-physics*, Bk. XII, Aristotle lays down that God can know nothing but Himself.   In this opinion he was followed by his Arabian commentators, Avicenna and Averroës, the plea being urged that the knowledge of a secondary object is incompatible with the absolute perfection of the divine Being : an act of knowledge, they argued, is one which perfects the knower, and therefore, did God know other objects besides His essence, His perfection would be due to something else than His essential perfection.   A second argument is that, in order to know such objects, the divine intelligence would require to be determined by them, to receive some sort of intelligible impression from them ; and this would imply potentiality in Him, whereas He is pure Actuality.   Finally, Aristotle concludes that there are some things that it is better not to know than to know.

This objection is founded on a misunderstanding, which will be more apparent after we have established our own thesis.

1. *A posteriori proof :* The physico-theological argument for the existence of God has revealed to us an Author of nature acting with intelligence and purpose.   Therefore at least the beings He has called into existence were present to the thought of the Creator and were considered as suitable for existence.

Further, it would be arbitrary to suppose that only the beings actually created were present to His mind, since the beings which have been created, having been so by an act of free-will, must have been chosen from all possible beings.   God therefore knows ' alia a se ', i.e. everything that has been created or could have been created by Him.

2. *A priori proof :* God's knowledge of His nature would not be ' comprehensive ' if it did not know this nature under all the aspects under which it is knowable.   Now it is essential to the divine nature that it should be imitable, albeit imperfectly[78], in an indefinite number of ways by an indefinite number

[78] A Franciscan writer, Pieralisi, maintains that it is not possible to speak of imitations of the divine essence because a copy of such a divine exemplar would necessarily be infinite ; and yet a production of an infinite is a contradiction in terms.   This objection is a mere playing with words.   Certainly neither St. Augustine nor St. Thomas overlooked the fact that the Infinite cannot be adequately imitated, yet they did not hesitate to regard the possibility of creatures being the ' imagines et similitudines Dei ' or the ' vestigia Dei '.

of creatures ; this imitability is an intrinsic characteristic of
the divine nature. It follows, then, in the first place that the
knowledge of the divine essence would not be ' comprehensive '
if it perceived this essence exclusively as an absolute object
without at the same time seeing it under the indefinitely
great number of intelligible aspects that it presents as the
exemplary cause of all the possible imitations of the divine
Being. In the second place, that what He must know is
the formal and proper being that creatures would possess if
they existed ; for this formal and proper being is that by
which the creature images the divine Being, it is the expression
of the mode according to which the creature imitates the essence
of its Creator. And in the third place, that He possesses a
distinct knowledge of creatures ; all the perfections, alike
essential and accidental, which their being represents, in their
generic, specific and individual essence ; all without any
exception are before the thought of God in their proper formalities because all without exception are so many definite
imitations of the Being whose imitability God ' comprehends '.

Before passing on we must remark that it is not strictly
correct to say that God knows the essences of things *because
He is the almighty cause of all His creatures.* For He sees Himself as the supereminent exemplary causes of all the ideal types
of creation before He sees Himself as the power that actually
creates them. Hence we have given our first proof as an
a posteriori argument, but the second alone gives the causal
reason of the intelligibility of beings distinct from God.

The objection of Aristotle and his Arabian commentators
falls to the ground before this explanation. Whilst things outside
God are the object of the divine knowledge, they are nevertheless *not a determining principle superadded* to the essence of
God, after the manner of the accidental intelligible determination which completes the potential faculty of the human intellect when as yet it is intrinsically incomplete (*Psychology*, **101** f.).
The divine essence by itself corresponds to the intelligible
impression or *species* that the later Scholastics have called
' species impressa ' ; in other words, it is in itself its own
determining principle of intellection, ' medium quo intellec-
tionis ' ; whilst it is also itself the intelligible counterpart,
the ' species expressa ', or that in which the cognoscibility

of a real thing is manifested, ' medium in quo objective relucet quidquid est intelligibile '.

Moreover, when St. Thomas distinguishes a primary object and a derived object of the divine knowledge, he does not suppose that in God there is any process of discursive reasoning ; for this—*dis-currere*—implies a succession of cognitive acts which proceed *ex alio* ad aliud ; the divine knowledge is a single act which sees the divine essence and, in this essence—in alio—sees whatever has a necessary connexion with it.

62. The Divine Ideas.—An ' idea ' in Scholastic language connotes (*a*) the *essential reasons* of things, ' rationes rerum,' which are present to the thought of God, and (*b*) their formal character as *models* of things to be created. So that, whilst the ' species intelligibilis ' is considered as a *subjective* form, the idea is the *objective* terminus of the divine intuition. The former in God is single ; the latter are manifold, inasmuch as things being manifold to infinity and having an indefinitely great number of mutual relations of causality, finality, etc., are so many distinct modes according to which the infinite perfection of the divine Being is imitable.

It must not be thought, however, that these ideas are so many realities *in God* ; their reality is identical with that of the divine essence considered as the supreme archetype of things ; God sees them in His own essence. But in virtue of its rôle as archetype, the divine essence presents to the mind of God what is distinct from Him under the guise of a multitude of intelligible objects resembling those which can be produced ' ad extra '. In this sense the ideas of the divine intellect are many in number.

63. The Objects of the Divine Knowledge.—The expression ' Everything actual and possible '; which we have purposely left vague, comprises objects that can be distinguished into various groups.

One distinction, which we have already noticed, is that between the *primary* object of the divine knowledge, namely, the very nature of God considered absolutely, and the *derived object* or the *derived objects*, namely, what God knows in His essence considered as imitable ' ad extra'.

These objects of this secondary knowledge are *possible* things as well as things *existent* which have come into being at some definite moment of time. ' Possibles ', whether considered without reference to actual existence or as definitely excluding it (sive praecisive sive exclusive) form the object of what the Schoolmen call *simple intelligence*, objectum scientiae *simplicis intelligentiae*. Things which have existed, exist or will exist, form the object of *intuitive* knowledge, objectum scientiae *visionis*.

In the controversies that have taken place about the knowledge of God there is the further question of an ' *intermediate knowledge* ', *scientia media*, which deals with objects termed ' conditional futurables ', that is to say, things which would have existed or would exist if, under certain conditions, the action of some definite cause had taken place, were taking or should take place. Those who advocate this third kind of knowledge maintain that ' conditional futurables ' do not fall either under the ' knowledge of pure intelligence ', seeing that they are ' futurables ' and not mere ' possibles '; or under God's intuitive ' knowledge of vision ', seeing that they do not belong to the class of definite and true future things; they must then be ranked, they say, as the object of a knowledge distinct from these other two, in a sense midway between them : they are the objects of a ' scientia media.'

The ' knowledge of simple intelligence ' is sometimes called also *necessary* knowledge, since its object is not conditioned by any free act either on the part of God or on the part of the creature ; the ' knowledge of vision ' is also known as *free* knowledge, since its object is dependent on the free *fiat* of the creative act ; the ' intermediate knowledge ' again appears distinct from these other two, since its object consists in those things of the future that are dependent on human liberty but considered as belonging to the purely hypothetical order of things, called by the Scholastics ' free conditional future things '.

In God we may also distinguish a *speculative* knowledge, the object of which is the divine nature and the possibles which are not and never will be realized, from a *practical* knowledge, which directs either the will or the activity ' ad extra ' of God.

64. God possesses a Knowledge of Possible Things.—Of possibility there may be distingushed two kinds (see *Gen. Metaphysics*, **18** f.). *Intrinsic* possibility is verified when an object presents elements which from the compatibility of their nature allow of existence ; *extrinsic* possibility means the existence of a cause capable of producing what is intrinsically possible. In the case of God who is almighty whatever is intrinsically possible is also extrinsically possible.

The divine ideas are types that are formally imitable ' ad extra ', outside the divine essence. Now God knows these ideas perfectly. Therefore He knows them as formally imitable ' ad extra '. But to know that these ideas are imitable ' ad extra ' is to know that there is no contradiction in the existence of things that imitate the model ideas conceived by the divine intelligence ; in brief, it is to know things as intrinsically possible.

Further, God knows His Nature adequately and sees it all-powerful, capable of realizing things after the archetypal ideas which His intelligence conceives. Now to know Himself as capable of realizing what is intrinsically possible is to know the extrinsic possibility of things. Therefore God sees possible things both in their negative and in their positive possibility.

65. God possesses ' the Knowledge of Vision '.—God is omniscient with regard to all that will happen in the future and knows with infallible knowledge every free act which is going to be performed. The knowledge of vision that He has embraces everything which for us would be of the present, past or future. With God, however, His knowledge of our present or past does not date from the actual time that these events take place, but because His knowledge is unchangeable He sees them all in advance, so that from this point of view the knowledge of vision would be more appropriately named after our manner of thinking and speaking as that of *prevision*. It embraces all things that take place, whether necessary or dependent on the free-will of man. Yet the chief point of interest is mainly in reconciling the infallible certitude of this foreknowledge with man's freedom of action, and therefore the thesis we have now to establish will deal mainly with free future acts.

God is the perfect Ruler of this universe, and in this universe a high place is occupied by beings that are endowed with intelligence and free-will. To establish this order and to maintain it, two things are obviously indispensable, namely the knowledge of the end of the universe and of the means suitable for the attainment of this end ; and in order to guarantee this order, the author of it must know, not partially and by way of conjecture, but adequately and with certainty, both the end and the means to it ; and the greater the perfection of the order is, the more perfect both in penetration and in certitude must be the knowledge of the elements that constitute it. Further, the universe comprises a physical order and a moral order, with the former in subordination to the latter, and therefore the supreme Designer of both must possess complete and infallible knowledge of all moral acts. This knowledge must be complete from the very first, since in God there can be no change or progress. If God knew what happens only after it has come about, it would be necessary sooner or later, for the maintenance of the order in the whole of His work, for Him to modify His end and to vary the means necessary for its realization ; in a word, take away God's foreknowledge and the stability of the order of nature would be compromised. God, therefore, eternally possesses a full, infallible, clear vision of the order of the universe and of the acts of free creatures in particular.

66. How does God know the Object of His ' Knowledge of Simple Intelligence ' ?—The reply to this first question has been given above : by His intellect God knows in His essence the internal possibility of everything possible, and in the unlimited power of His will their external possibility.

An infinite number of possible worlds and the infinite number of ways in which circumstances may be arranged in them are, then, eternally present before God. Now among these combinations there are some which are conditioned by the free *fiat* of God's creative act ; there are others which are dependent on a possible *fiat* that as a matter of fact will never be carried into execution. In order to explain God's knowledge of this latter class of combinations, some have introduced—uselessly, we think—the ' scientia media ', different both from that of simple understanding or intelligence and from that of intuition or vision.

67. How does God know the Object of His ' Knowledge of Vision ' ?—1. God knows in the decrees of His will the future effects of causes that are *necessary :* by knowing the causes that He has created He knows infallibly their nature and their forces, as well as the play of their combination, and in consequence their effects.

2. How does He know the future effects of causes that are

free ? Some of these effects are really future, 'free contingent futures ' (futura contingentia) ; others are called by those responsible for the invention of His 'scientia media ' ' free conditional futures ' (futura essent sub conditione possibili), or 'futurables' (futurabilia). The freedom of these acts seems to exclude the possibility of an infallible knowledge of them in their causes. To understand the difficulty let us consider the example of the French Revolution of 1789. We know the causes which, in the light of after events, explain the revolution : the philosophy of the eighteenth century, the abuses of the ancient regime, the weakness of Louis XVI, etc. These causes supply us to-day with the sufficient reason why the men of that time so acted as to bring about that epoch-making event. But no one with even the most thorough knowledge of these causes, both in themselves and in their whole setting, would have been able to predict with infallible foresight the effect which they have produced. To say that any-one could have done so would be tantamount to the assertion that the antecedents clearly manifested in themselves the reason that necessitated their consequent ; and it would follow that the men who brought about the Revolution of '89 were not able to avoid bringing it about, and the event would appear not to have been free but necessary. Similarly with all the free actions of my individual life : does the adequate knowledge of my nature, my faculties, my temperament, my character, the circumstances affecting my will, necessarily imply an infallible knowledge of my free act—as, for example, the act I am at this moment performing in writing these lines, which I persuade myself I have the power not to write ? If the answer is in the affirmative, it would follow that, given my complex state previous to my decision, I am powerless to decide otherwise than to write them. How would my decision to write still remain free on such conditions as these ? My free-dom would be nothing more than an illusion, a word without any meaning. But granted that, on the contrary, my nature and the circumstances which have led me to my present action have no necessary connexion with this action, it follows then that though anyone should know with the most perfect possible knowledge both my nature and the conditions of its operation, he could never be certain of reading in them the decision I shall eventually make.

To solve this real and perhaps insoluble difficulty, Molina, Lessius and other theologians have introduced the ' scientia media ' of God. They reason as follows : The Apostle Peter yielded to the voice of a woman and denied his Master. He need not have done so ; he denied Him freely. Since he has denied Him, it was true from all eternity that he would deny Him. The divine essence, which necessarily reflects all truth, is a mirror in which the divine intelligence apprehends the truth, ' Peter denies his Master at a certain precise moment of history '. The divine knowledge has thus for its necessary object all the eternal truths that are connected with free actions in the future ; in other words, the divine essence is for God the means (medium in quo) by which He knows free future events. Moreover the divine essence represents the truth of conditional future events with the same clearness, and for the same reason, as it represents that of absolute events in the future. This explanation, they say, enables us to reconcile God's infallible knowledge of vision with the perfect free-will on the part of the object of His knowledge [79].

Unfortunately their explanation is quite indefensible. (a) In the first place, the existence of an eternal truth in the case of free futures if they are considered without reference to the divine intelligence is a mere fancy. Truth depends upon reality ; it is a transcendental property of being. Where being does not exist there is no truth. Leave out of consideration the divine intelligence, and where was Peter previous to the

---

[79] ' According to our view we regard the free act before and also after the decree of creation ; before the decree the act is conditionally future, and the object of the " scientia media " ; after the decree it is counted as being present to the eternal vision of God.

' If the will decides to posit, in time, a free act, the proposition in which this decision is expressed has a truth which is eternal. But unless the divine knowledge knew all truth such as the divine essence represented it, it would follow that the divine essence would not be the complete representation of all truth and the divine knowledge would not be infinite. The future act, though it has a temporal existence, has an eternal truth for the divine knowledge.

' The same thing happens with regard to future conditional events—they are intelligible from all eternity, since it is true from eternity that, should such and such conditions come about, this determinate choice would be made. So from eternity it was true that Peter the Apostle when questioned by the Jews should deny his divine Master. Similarly, one of the two following propositions was true from eternity : If the first man is tempted by the serpent, he will yield ; or again, when tempted by the serpent, the first man will not yield. If propositions are true from all eternity God must know them as they are in themselves (in seipsis) '. DUPONT, *Théodicée*, Thèse LVII, pp. 101-102.

first century A.D. ? Nowhere ; he did not exist. And since
he was not in existence, he could not put forth an act which
should be the ontological foundation of a truth. The moment
that it is admitted that God exists and thinks, there is room for
an eternal truth in God ; but outside God, eternally there is
nothing : and consequently there is no truth. ' Etiam si
intellectus humanus non esset, adhuc res dicerentur verae,
in ordine ad intellectum divinum. Sed si uterque intellectus,
quod est impossibile, intelligeretur auferri, nullo modo veritatis ratio remaneret ' [80]. (b) In the second place, even supposing that an objective truth were eternally existing, it would
not be a term for God's thought unless we suppose that it
exercises an active influence on His intelligence. But such
a supposition is untenable, since God cannot be subject to the
action of any cause. It is then *in God Himself, ab intra*, that
we must look for the reason of the divine knowledge.

This reason Thomists find in the decrees of the divine will.
Although the free acts of man are not antecedently determined
ad unum, they say, and although the divine motion which
applies the free-will of man to its definite act is not a necessitating motion, nevertheless a divine motion is necessary to the
will to make it pass, although in a manner consistent with its
freedom, from the power of willing to the act of volition.
There is an infallible connexion between the divine motion and
the human free act of will, although the former does not destroy
the freedom of the latter. Far from compromising the liberty
of the free act, the divine motion is the first cause of this liberty,
says St. Thomas, because God works in all things according
to the mode of being that is proper to each. ' By moving
voluntary causes God does not deprive their actions of being
voluntary ; but rather is He the cause of this very thing in them :
for He operates in each thing according to its own nature ' [81].

---

[80] St. Thomas, *De veritate*, q. 7, a. 2.

[81] ' Liberum arbitrium est causa sui motus : quia homo per liberum arbitrium seipsum movet ad agendum. Non tamen hoc est de necessitate liber-
tatis, quod sit prima causa sui id quod liberum est : sicut nec ad hoc quod
aliquid sit causa alterius requiritur quod sit prima causa ejus. Deus igitur
est prima causa movens et naturales causas et voluntarias. Et sicut naturalibus causis movendo eas, non aufert quin actus earum sint naturales : ita
movendo causas voluntarias, non aufert quin actiones earum sint volunta-
riae ; sed *potius hoc in eis facit : operatur enim in unoquoque secundum ejus
proprietatem'. Sum. Theol.*, I, q. 83, a. 1, ad 3.

Bossuet, in his *Traité du libre arbitre* (chap. 8), has a remarkably clear
exposition of this theory and the fundamental reason which underlies it :

This latter theory respects both the divine omnipotence and the liberty of the created will ; and herein lies its merit. But does it offer any rational explanation which reconciles the two terms ? We fail to see how it does. We are led rather to think that in this delicate question it is necessary frankly to avow the incapacity of human reason. No explanation yet put forward seems to give satisfaction ; and we have not even the hope of ever finding a more satisfactory solution. Bossuet seems to us to have said the very last word on this subject :

' My conclusion is,' he says, ' that by the natural light of reason two things are evident ; one is, that we are free, the other is, that the actions which we do freely are included in the decrees of divine providence, which has means to conduct them to its purposes. Nothing can throw doubt on these two important truths, because both are established by reasons which it is impossible to overthrow ; for whoever knows anything of God cannot doubt that His providence as well as His foreknowledge extends to everything ; and whoever reflects on his own nature will recognize his own freedom with such plain evidence that nothing can succeed in obscuring the conviction he has of it. It is easy to see that two truths established by such convincing reasons cannot be destructive of each other, for truth cannot destroy truth ; and however difficult it may be to succeed in reconciling them, the failure to understand such high matters is no reason for a diminished certainty in regard to the truths which we recognize so plainly. Really, if we had to abandon either free-will on account of God's providence or God's

' Freedom has its place in the soul,' he says, ' not only inasmuch as the soul has the power to choose, but further during the actual exercise of its power of choice, and God, who is the immediate cause of our freedom, must needs produce it in its ultimate act. This ultimate act being the actual choice, that choice must come from God, and as such must be included in the divine will : for there is nothing in the creature, however small the degree of being it has, which does not hold from God all that it has. Now, the more actual anything is, the more " being " it will have ; it follows then that the more actual it is, the more it must get from God. So, our soul when we regard it as actually exercising its power of choice, is for that very reason more under the divine action than it was before. This would be unintelligible unless it be granted that this very exercise comes immediately from God. God is the maker of all being and all perfection ; if then in each free act there is any being and any perfection, it is God who renders the act worthy of the description " free " ; and the infinite efficacy of His action, that is of His will, reaches—if one may use the phrase—even to that quality by which it is placed in the category of free acts '.

providence on account of free-will, we should not know
where to begin, so necessary are they both, so sure and
evident are the ideas we have about them ; for if reason
should appear to set above question that which we attribute
to God, on the other hand experience is so much more
complete of that which we attribute to man : so that both
these truths must be considered as equally incontestable.

'Let our conclusion be, then, that it is possible, even in
matters of which we are most certain, to find difficulties
which we cannot overcome. We should not be able to start
anywhere, if we were to call in question those known truths
which we cannot reconcile together, since all the difficulties
which we discover when we use our reason can only have
their source in the nature of reason itself, and truth cannot
be attacked except on some principle that has its source in
reason itself.

'I do not know whether we have grounds for believing
that there is any truth which we comprehend exhaustively
and in such a way that there is no difficulty left to be
solved ; but even though there be some truths that we can
thus thoroughly comprehend, it would be rash to presume
that all truths are in the same case. We should be no less
mistaken if we rejected all knowledge as soon as we found
our minds baffled ; for such is the nature of our mind that it
is necessary for it to pass by degrees from what is clear to
what is obscure, and from what is certain to what is doubtful, and that without rejecting the former as soon as it en-
counters the latter. Whenever we begin to reason, we must
grasp this principle, that we can have knowledge of matters
whose issues and consequences nevertheless escape the
range of our intelligence. The first rule of our logic should
be this : that we must not loose hold of any truths which we
know for certain, whatever difficulty there may be in reconciling some of them with others ; we must, so to say, hold
on tightly to both ends of the chain, though we cannot see
the middle of it, nor follow it with our eyes from end to end.

'Still, we may look about for means of reconciling these
truths, provided we are determined not to abandon any of
them ; whatever happens in the search—the good which we
actually hold must not be let loose, merely because success
does not attend our pursuit of some other. "Disputare vis,

nec obest, si certissima praecedat fides ", said S. Augustine.
Following this thought we proceed to search for means of
reconciling our free-will with the decrees of Providence. We
may enumerate the different views held by theologians in
the hope of finding something which will satisfy us ' [82].

Before passing to the study of the divine will we must reply
to an objection.

**68. A Difficulty : the Foreknowledge of God and the Free-
dom of Free Future Acts.**—We have made the statement that
God foresees with an infallible knowledge free future acts.
But the infallibility of knowledge implies that between this
knowledge and its object there exists a necessary connexion
which cannot be other than it is. Therefore future acts
forming as they do the object of a divine infallible knowledge
must be as they are foreknown and, in consequence, it would
seem, are necessitated. Briefly, either the future acts are
entirely necessary, and then the divine knowledge is explained
only at the expense of human liberty ; or there are truly free
acts, and then they cannot be infallibly seen by God.

Certain writers, led by a passage [83] of the *Summa Theologica*
—which, if we read aright, they misinterpret—argue thus :
With God there is neither past nor future, but an eternal
present. God is like to a man who looks down from the
summit of a hill upon a plain below where he sees travellers
passing around its foot. The travellers pass at different times
by various points of the circumference, but the onlooker who
sees them, sees them all simultaneously. So it is with God. Men
pass along, centuries succeed one another, but the movement
exists only in the created things ; the divine thought is eternal
and co-exists with all the moments of time.

And when a man plunges into a river before my eyes, does
his act, for the reason that I see him plunge in, cease to be a

---

[82] Bossuet, *op. cit.*, ch. 4.

[83] ' Omnia quae sunt in tempore sunt Deo ab aeterno praesentia, non solum
ea ratione qua habet rationes rerum apud se praesentes, ut quidam dicunt, sed
quia ejus intuitus fertur ab aeterno supra omnia, prout sunt in sua praesen-
tialitate. Unde manifestum est quod contingentia infallibiliter a Deo cog-
noscuntur, in quantum subduntur divino conspectui secundum suam prae-
sentialitatem, et tamen sunt futura contingentia, suis causis proximis com-
parata '. *Sum. Theol.*, I, q. 14, art. 13, c.—' Ille qui vadit per viam, non
videt illos qui post eum veniunt ; sed ille qui ab aliqua altitudine totam viam
intuetur, simul videt omnes transeuntes per viam '. *Ibid.*, ad 3.

free act ? Similarly do the acts which God sees taking place cease to be free because God sees them ? Evidently not.

In this reply is the key to the solution of the difficulty, but it requires to be properly handled. The principle involved is right : Knowledge neither creates nor influences its object ; it merely knows it such as it is : if it is a necessary event, it knows it as such, as necessary ; if it is free, it knows it as a free event.

When we may suppose the knowledge to be faithful, it is quite right, in putting it in the logical order, to argue : A mind possesses a certain and definite knowledge of an event, be it necessary or free ; therefore the event is a matter of fact. But, in the ontological order, the certain knowledge of the event has a place only because the event was real.

Consequently, when it is a question of reconciling the certain foreknowledge of free events with the freedom of these events, the only special difficulty to be solved is to know *by what means* something which does not yet exist in itself can be present to the mind of God.

This difficulty is not solved by merely stating : Free acts which succeed one another in the course of time are all present before God ; or, which is the same, God has immutably and eternally the actual knowledge of them. We willingly grant this : there is not, there cannot be succession in the thought of God. But the real difficulty still remains : how are things which do not yet exist present to the divine thought ? In what does God see them ?

It seems to us to be a contradiction in terms to say that a future act, considered in its own being, has an existence in the present. We cannot, then, say that the omniscience of God has for its term this non-existent entity. Moreover, even if future things had an entity in the present, it would be necessary to explain how they could be the term of a mind which, inasmuch as it is not determined by them, cannot, it would seem, be in communication with them.

Our conclusion is that the determining principle of the divine knowledge can only be *within God Himself.* What we think this is we have already suggested. We have adopted the opinion which holds that God sees the occurrence of future free acts *in His Will to cause them to exist according to their free mode of being.* Certainly it is difficult to reconcile this freedom with the sovereign efficacy of the divine motion, but this problem is distinct from that which we are at present considering. Putting aside the question how God knows future events, it is a certain fact that He does know them, that is to say, He sees them according to the nature that they actually have : if they come to pass freely He sees them, with an infallible foreknowledge, take place freely. Granted that He sees them, I am able, in the logical order, to argue from His act of vision to the real existence of its object, but, in the onto‑ logical order, the reality of the object is anterior to the divine knowledge of it [84].

[84] A letter of St. Thomas to the abbot of Monte Cassino gives the answer to this difficulty we are considering. He is considering the case of a sinner who dies impenitent. His sin, he says, is a free act ; but the knowledge that God has of the free acts of a sinner is necessary *ex necessitate consequenti*, that is to say, through the free acts being posited. His exact words are :

' Quia homo subjacet mutationi et tempori, in quo prius et posterius locum habent ; successive cognoscit res, quaedam prius et quaedam posterius ; et inde est, quod praeterita memoramur, videmus praesentia, et pronostica‑ mur futura. Sed Deus, sicut liber est ab omni motu, secundum illud Malachiae : " Ego Dominus, et non mutor " ; ita omnem temporis successionem excedit, nec in eo inveniuntur praeteritum et futurum ; sed praesentialiter omnia futura et praeterita ei adsunt ; sicut ipse Moysi famulo suo dicit : " Ego sum qui sum ". Eo ergo modo ab aeterno praescivit hunc tali tempore moriturum, ut modo nostro loquimur ; cum tamen ejus modo dicendum esset, videt eum mori, quomodo ego video Petrum sedere, dum sedet. Manifestum est autem, quod ex hoc, quod video aliquem sedere, nulla ingeritur et neces‑ sitas sessionis. Impossibile est haec duo simul esse vera, quod videam aliquem sedentem, et ipse non sedeat ; et similiter non est possibile quod Deus praesciat aliquid esse futurum, et illud non sit : nec tamen propter hoc futura ex necessitate eveniunt '.

CHAPTER II

WILL IN GOD

69. Meaning.—In the creature we have to distinguish between the *faculty* by which we will, the *good* as an object towards which the faculty tends, the *union* of the faculty of will with its object. This union constitutes the *act of will* or volition.

To will the good is *to love*. The tendency of a created being towards a good which it does not possess is *desire ;* the satisfaction of desire by the union of the will with its object gives rise to *enjoyment*, delight.

In God these manifold elements of human appetition find no place ; the faculty of will, the good, the act of will constitute the same transcendental reality. In this act of the will there is no desire, because in the divine will there is no want ; the divine act of will is perfect love always present, plenary enjoyment.

Although we recognize this simplicity in the divine will, yet we apply to it by way of analogy, in order better to understand its fullness, the distinction founded on the composite character of the human will.

It is perhaps superfluous to add that there is nothing in God analogous to the human emotions, or passions, which we experience on account of evil—hate, aversion, sadness ; for all evil is excluded from the infinite Goodness.

The will is concerned with two classes of objects, its *formal* or primary object, and *material* or secondary objects. The primary object is the good which by uniting itself to the will gives it the perfection which it is capable of receiving ; the secondary objects are the goods which the will is capable of loving because it loves its formal object.

In God, the primary object of His will is the goodness of the divine essence ; the secondary objects are created goods. Not that God loves these goods in order to acquire them, for nothing is wanting to Him ; if He is pleased to love them, this

is because He wishes to give them : the good is self-diffusive—
bonum est sui diffusivum.

70. In God there is a Will.—We have already, at the beginning of Chapter I, brought forward two reasons based on fact
which prove that there is a will in God : (i) the order which
reigns in the universe requires a Cause which has designed and
brought it into effect ; (ii) the existence of beings endowed with
intelligence and free-will proves that there is a Cause which
possesses in a supereminent manner both intelligence and free-
will. (iii) A third reason may be deduced from the necessity
of attributing supreme happiness to God. Happiness is a
perfection, indeed the sum-total of perfections. Now the
intellect knows the good, but its function is to present it as
an object before the will rather than itself to seek union with
it ; it is for the will to make for that identification with it
of which the fruit is enjoyment. Therefore God, who is supreme
happiness, possesses that perfection which in the case of a creature we call *will*. St. Thomas presents the argument thus :—
Every form carries with it a tendency—the substantial form
of the human body involves a ' tendency of nature ' (*intentio
naturae*) ; knowledge acquired by the senses induces a sensitive
appetite, that of the intelligence gives rise to an intellective
appetite : therefore the divine knowledge would seem to be
followed by a *love* towards the object of it on the part of God,
and this constitutes an act of will.

**71. The Formal Object of the Will of God is the Goodness
of the Divine Essence.**—As in God, the self-subsisting Being,
there is nothing accidental, His will is identical with the substance of His divine Being. But His will is not distinct from
the object He loves, otherwise this object would be an accidental
determination produced in His will by the good. Therefore
the object He loves is the substance of His divine Being.

Again, the perfection of the divine will is necessarily infinite,
and this could not be so unless the good that He loves is infinite.
If God were not drawn by the power of His love towards
His own infinite self but were necessarily drawn to something
else, He would be subordinate to that and dependent upon it
—which is a supposition that conflicts with the true idea of
His nature. Thus it is that all races have shown a preference
to speak of God as the Summum Bonum, as Goodness itself :
compare the expressions ' le bon Dieu ' ; ' Goodness knows ', etc.

72. Whatever participates in the Divine Goodness can be a Secondary Object of the Will of God.—God is the Author of the world, and far from having made it without a purpose He has disposed all things with wisdom. Therefore He has willed whatever good exists in His created works.

God loves His essence infinitely, that is to say, to the full extent to which it is an object of love. In itself it is an object of love to an infinite degree, but further, it is an object of love inasmuch as His goodness is to a certain degree, though ever imperfectly, communicable to creatures. Whence the divine goodness, in so far as it is *communicable* to creatures, is for the will of God a necessary object of love, but the *communication* of this goodness to contingent beings is not a necessary but a *free* act of His will.

73. God loves the Goodness of His Essence necessarily, and the Goodness of Created Beings freely.—1. The *first proposition* is easy to prove : All is good in God, and therefore all in Him is an object of love. Consequently, God who comprehends Himself as He is sees that there is nothing in His nature which is not an object of love ; the whole of His nature forces Him to love Himself, in a word, He loves Himself necessarily.

In the case of a created will, the act of volition may be withheld on account of the finite nature of the good which is presented to it : under one aspect—in so far as it presents its goodness—it is an object of love ; under another aspect— in so far as it falls short—it is not an object of love. The created will, then, is able to love or not to love an object, that is, its love of finite goods is not a necessary love. In the case of God, this duality of aspects in the infinite goodness of the divine essence is not possible ; whence the love of God for Himself must, we see, be a necessary love.

Again, the happiness essential to God requires that He has not merely the faculty of enjoying what is His good, but also that He has the actual enjoyment of it. Therefore God has not the freedom of loving or not loving Himself, but He loves Himself with a necessary love.

2. The *second proposition* may be proved thus : God loves with a necessary love only His essence, for this is an infinite good which adequately corresponds to what we may call the infinite capacity for enjoyment in the divine will ; and no created good is capable of adding anything to the infinite Good,

for the will of God, which is an act of volition always substantially accomplished, cannot receive any accidental perfection from any created good.   Yet on the other hand the will which produced and designed the world did not exercise its activity without a purpose and consciousness ; the supreme intelligence which directed the will of the Author of nature must accordingly have presented creation as a good, or God could not have willed it ; but it could not have presented it as a good *necessary* to His divine happiness, since creation is able to add nothing to the essential and perfect happiness of God who is all-good. Therefore the supreme intelligence which directed the will of the Author of all things presented them to Him as a good though not as a good lovable by necessity but with a *free* love.

In this connexion Cajetan's observation [85] is worthy of notice, that the divine will is neither necessary nor free (necessity and freedom being two imperfect perfections), but is a *transcendental perfection* which excludes both the imperfections inherent in the necessity of creatures and those inherent in their freedom, and comprises in a supereminent manner whatever goodness both the one and the other contain.

74. Freedom and Immutability of God.—Although God wills His works freely, He wills them once and for all, without ever revoking or modifying the free decree of His will.   God has no reason to cease from willing what He wills, or to will at the present time otherwise than He has already willed.   His

---

[85] ' Prima causa, proprie loquendo, nec est causa necessaria simpliciter, neque contingens, sed superior utraque. Nec habemus magis proprium vocabulum, quam ut dicatur quod est causa libera. Necessitas enim simpliciter repugnat libertati : contingentia vero imperfectionem in libertate importat, quia ponit mutabilitatem. Et idcirco divus Thomas in I Sent. dist. XXXVIII, praeveniens inepta modernorum vocabula, negat Deum causare contingenter. Cum enim regulare sit, quod superius praehabet in se unite quae in inferioribus sunt sparsa, consequens est ut causa prima, superior necessariis et contingentibus, praehabeat in se, non formaliter sed eminenter, naturam et modum causarum necessariarum et contingentium, et sit causa utrarumque, et co-operetur utrisque ad earum proprios effectus secundum modos earum.   Et propterea nos, quibus omnis causa videtur necessaria aut contingens, stupemus, non praevalentes videre quomodo una causa sit communis necessariis et contingentibus immediate.   Sed si elevemus mentis oculos in excellentius genus causae, eminentioremque causandi modum, cessat stupor, et omnia consonant ; quamvis remaneamus in caligine, non intuentes illum modum quo omnibus intrinsece illabens, cunctis juxta suos modos cooperatur.   Et hoc est valde attendendum in hujusmodi materiis.—Appellatur tamen Deus, vel ejus scientia causa necessaria, propter necessitatem non simpliciter, sed immutabilitatis quae in eo, etiam inquantum causa, formaliter salvatur '. CAJETAN, *Com. in Sum. Theol.*, I, q. 14, a. 13, n. 24.

will remains always, immutably, what it is; it is free, and therefore it always remains free.

75. Goodness, Justice, Liberality, Mercy of God.—After having studied the object of the divine will and the nature of the divine act of volition (*Summa*, I, q. 19), St. Thomas considers the divine will as united to its good, that is to say, God's *love* (*De amore Dei*, q. 20). This love, he observes, we call by different names according to the point of view in which we regard it when judging of its effects (q. 21). Hence we speak of the goodness, justice, liberality, mercy of God.

76. Omnipotence of God.—When a man has conceived a work and has judged good to carry it into execution, it may happen that the means for carrying out his design are not at hand. Now a want of this kind can find no place in God, not only for this general a priori reason that He is infinitely perfect, but also for this more special reason that His will is not dependent upon instrumental causes; such, e.g. as the bodily organs in man; in God will and the power to accomplish are identical. In other words, God is able freely to will all that His intellect judges good; in short, God is omnipotent.

This consideration leads us to the works of the divine omnipotence.

CHAPTER III

THE WORK OF GOD

77. The Works of God ' Ad Extra '.—Theologians explain, following the teaching of faith, that there is in God a fullness of life within Himself, the mystery of the personal Trinity in the Unity of nature. In contradistinction to this divine life *ad intra*, they speak of the operations and the works which by the light of reason we know belong to Him as the Creator of the world. The works of creation do not justify us in asserting that there are more persons than one in God ; they only lead us to recognize in God a supreme Cause endowed with intelligence, will and power. Of these divine operations thought and will are two immanent actions, and it is not essential to them that there should be any external resultant ; but the exercise of His power necessarily demands a terminus *ad extra*, outside Himself, for it is not immanent but *transitive*.

The power of God *created* the world (I), *preserves* it in being (II), and *governs* it (III).

I. CREATION

78. Meaning of Creation.—The agents which we see at work exercise their activity upon a given matter as subject ; whether they modify it accidentally or transform it substantially, they use it as necessary for their activity, for they are only able to work upon it. Now we may conceive an action which is freed from this dependence with regard to a presupposed matter.

Again, consider that when a man exercises an immanent activity, for example, when he thinks or loves, he puts his powers into exercise, and his activity brings about an interior perfection which these powers thereby acquire. This allows us to conceive an action which is not the putting into operation of perfectible powers, but which is the exercise of faculties that are no way potential but already in a state of actual perfection.

Creation means the act which excludes both the utilization of a pre-existing matter, and the actualization of the passive perfectible powers of the agent.   It is usually defined as ' productio ex nihilo sui et subjecti ' [86].   In positive terms, we may define it as ' the production of a substance according to the totality of its being '.   The creative act is opposed to the act which makes use of materials, or, to make use of the well-known phrase of the Scholastics, which draws upon the potentiality of matter, ' eductio e potentia materiae ', in the sense explained in *Cosmology*, **74.**

With this notion of creation to work upon, we have to show (i) that God created the world, (ii) which consequently is something distinct from Himself and not an emanation, and (iii) that He alone can create.

79. Theories concerning the Relation of God to the World.— The chief historical theories concerning the relationship of God to the world are : (1) *Atheistic materialism*, which, by doing away with God and suppressing one of the terms of the problem we are at present considering, is no real attempt at a solution.   (2) The *doctrine of creation*, in which the world is conceived as having been freely produced by God not only in its form but also in its very matter.   (3) Philosophical *dualism*, which allows to the world a necessary existence independent of God.   It has received its most complete expression in the doctrine of the Manicheans.   (4) *Pantheism* or, as it is more commonly known to-day, *monism*, a theory that God and the world are entirely one and the same substance.

The doctrine of creation can be proved *directly*, and *indirectly* by the refutation of dualism and pantheism.

The dualistic theory, which at one time enjoyed a great vogue, has now only an historical interest.   We have briefly given the reasons that make us reject it (**56**) [87].

Pantheism, on the other hand, is still full of vitality.   In the modern world it made its appearance in Italy with Giordano Bruno in the first days of the Renaissance.   In the seventeenth century it found a systematic expression in the ' geometric ' doctrine of Spinoza, and it thrives again to-day under the

---

[86] The preposition *ex* is not very felicitous ; *a* is better, for nothingness is not a source, *id ex quo*, but a point of departure, *terminus a quo*.   In the terminology of the Scholastics *subjectum* denotes the material cause, *subjecta materia* ; so that creation means production which does not presuppose any subject.

[87] For a more ample treatment see *Métaphysique générale*, cours supérieur, **125** and **126.**

influence of a renewed interest in his philosophy. It is the logical outcome of German idealistic philosophy of the last century. At the present time it has spread or is spreading, under the form of a *tone of thought* rather than a system, in the English-speaking world, in Italy, in Germany, in certain French philosophical circles, and it has succeeded in leaving a decided impress upon philosophy, history, natural science, art and literature. The limits of this elementary treatise do not permit us to dwell at length on this erroneous philosophical view of reality, but we wish to lay special emphasis on the little that we are able to say.

80. The World has been created by God. Refutation of Dualism.—1. *It is arbitrary to assert on a priori grounds that creation is not possible.* Some people triumphantly appeal to the old saying ' ex nihilo nihil fit ' in order to rule out of court any question of creation. But how do they prove that ' from nothing nothing can be made ' ? Is it by observation, by induction ? If so, the assertion ' ex nihilo nihil fit ' is an inductive inference and is tantamount to this : As far as my observations carry me I see that nothing appears which is not drawn from a subject prior to itself ; natural agents are clearly not creators. This we readily agree to ; nay more, we are willing even to allow that natural agents cannot be creators. Yet even so, is there any warrant for saying that creation is impossible to an agent which is not subject to the laws of material nature ? By what are we justified in asserting that it is not possible for God to create who is above all nature that we observe ? There is simply no justification for such an assertion. Indeed it may be evident that every effect demands an efficient cause, but it can never be proved that an effect demands a material cause. However true in fact it is that modifications and transformations of matter depend on a subjective cause, on a material substrate, and that an efficient cause producing accidental or substantial changes only makes one being succeed another ; nevertheless you cannot establish that it is impossible for some efficient cause to make some being come after no being, and this power of efficiency is all that is claimed for a creative cause. We conclude, therefore, that it is arbitrary to repudiate creation on a priori grounds.

2. *The creation of the world must be asserted* as a necessary alternative to maintaining the necessary existence of matter

and its co-eternity with God, which involves the contradiction of the proposition we have already established (**56**) concerning the essential unicity of the Divine Being.

Moreover, were matter self-subsistent it would be immutable and infinite. Yet bodies are manifestly contingent, changing and finite. Hence matter cannot be self-existent.

Note that the frequent expression ' eternal matter ' must not be the occasion of a pitfall. Matter as we read it in this phrase always means matter in general, matter in the abstract ; whereas actual matter is always in some body and all material bodies are subject to change and transformation.

It is along the lines of the arguments just indicated that we must refute Gnostic or Manichean dualism. It remains then to consider monism or pantheism.

81. The World is neither a Part nor an Emanation of the Divine Substance. Refutation of Monism.—Monism appears in the history of philosophy under two forms, the one idealistic, the other realistic.

1. *Idealistic monism* makes the origin of things to consist in an indeterminate being called the Absolute—which, on account of a law of its internal evolution, is ever progressively differentiating itself and ' becoming ' all things.

This doctrine (*a*) is due to a confusion of thought between being in general and the supreme Being. And (*b*), by making God subject to the law of becoming, it denies the real nature of God as the pure Actuality whose existence we claim to have demonstrated.

(*a*) Being in general, the object of the first conception of the mind, has a minimum of comprehension ; and it has, conversely, a maximum of potential extension, inasmuch as it is capable of being attributed to whatever exists or may exist. Being that is pure Actuality, on the contrary, connotes a maximum of positive perfection, whilst it has no extension, either actual or potential ; it is itself and it cannot be identified with anything else. Being in general is an abstract entity which, as such, cannot have an existence in nature : it exists only in the mind that thinks of it and puts it in relation to the individual subjects with which one by one it identifies it. Pure Actuality exists by itself, independently of our thought, or of that of any finite spirit whatsoever. To both, to indefinite being and to the Divine Being, we do in fact attribute a characteristic which we know by one and the same name, namely *simplicity ;* but predicated of the former it has a meaning entirely *negative,* it is an absence of composition which is due to the extreme poverty of abstract and universal being ; whilst in reference to the latter, to God, simplicity is something very positive, it stands for a plenitude of perfection such that, in its absolute indivisible unity, it surpasses all the accumulated perfections of created things.

(*b*) To confuse abstract and universal being with the divine Being is to deny the true nature of Him whose existence we have endeavoured to affirm and prove by arguments drawn from the spontaneous dictates of our individual conscience and of the general expression of feeling among the different races. If the result of our investigations must come to anything else than a mature reasoned conviction that a God exists who is at once pure Actuality, necessary and infinite Being, we may as well renounce all hope of being able to demonstrate the existence of God Himself which is the object of Theodicy (Θεοῦ δίκη).

2. *Realistic monism* is more directly opposed to the doctrine of creation we have just discussed. Monism, under this form, sees things to be so many parts or manifestations of the Divine Reality. Here we have not a theory which sets out from the minimum of reality in order to arrive by some illogical process at the maximum of it—from being in general to the Absolute ; but one which sets out from the Being which it supposes infinite and, in its endeavour to keep its infinity, asserts all reality to be substantially identical with it. With this aim it brings forward various considerations that are rather objections to the doctrine of creation than positive arguments : (i) the unscientific character of the idea of creation ; (ii) the impossibility of understanding efficient causality if action has to pass from an agent to an object that is substantially distinct from it ; (iii) the contradiction involved in supposing an infinite being which does not embrace the whole of reality.

Pantheism, whatever the form it assume, must necessarily fall foul of two facts : (*a*) the changes that take place in the universe, and (*b*) the consciousness of individual personality.

(*a*) A necessary being is necessarily what it is ; it can know no change. Yet the fact of change is manifest throughout the

universe.   Therefore the realities of nature are not phases
or modalities nor parts of the necessary Being.

God is independent, infinite.   The beings of this world are
dependent, finite.   Therefore they are not substantially
identical with God.

(b) Nothing in the world can persuade me that I am not
myself, or that I am the self-expression of somebody else.   The
very fact that I can use of myself the word *ego* in opposition
to whatever is *non-ego*, implies that I am myself, that my being
is incommunicable.   This personal consciousness that I am
distinct from what is not myself is the great stumbling-block
in the way of monism.

Furthermore, the considerations which monists bring forward have very little weight :—(i) The idea of creation contradicts a prejudice, it does not contradict reason.   On the
contrary, the notion of a perfect causality is identical with that
of creation.   As we have developed this thought already (**80**),
we will not repeat it here.

(ii) Causal action, indeed, raises an intricate problem of
general metaphysics.   But we may note that if there is a
difficulty in understanding how one substance acts upon
another, there is no less difficulty in understanding how a
substantial agent influences an accident really distinct from
itself or how one part can effectively act upon another part of
the same whole.   There are only two ways of escaping from
the difficulty : either to deny all efficient causality—this is
occasionalism—or to deny all real distinction between the
substance of the universe and its manifestations, which is
complete phenomenalism.   Yet monism refuses to recognize
either of these alternatives.

(iii) The existence of one or more beings which were
independent of the divine Being would certainly put a limit
to this Being's perfection, but He is not limited by the fact of
possessing the power to produce creatures that are dependent
on Himself.   Infinity, we must remember, is not a collection
of perfections and imperfections, it is a single reality which
contains in a supereminent manner all that is not itself.

82. God Alone can Create.—Here we embark upon what has
proved itself a thorny question.   Catholic tradition holds
that creation belongs only to God.   Further, Catholic philosophers are unanimous in saying that only God in point of

fact has created ; they are also of one mind in thinking that
no creature is capable of exercising the power of creating in
an independent way and as a principal cause.   They add that
were a creature to become, under the sovereign action of God,
an instrumental cause in a creative act, it would necessarily
have a limited sphere of action, if only for the reason that it
could not create itself.   But they question whether it is
impossible for a secondary cause to be an instrumental cause
of a creative act which makes a limited number of creatures
to come forth from nothingness.

St. Thomas is of the opinion that it is impossible, whilst
Suarez holds the opposite view.

There is often brought forward in favour of St. Thomas's
view this argument which does not seem conclusive : Between
non-entity and being there is an infinite distance ; and this only
an infinite power can bridge.—Against such an argument,
however, we may urge that the distance between non-entity
and being is not infinite ; it is measured by the finite reality
which is opposed to non-entity.

Kleutgen, in commentating upon St. Thomas, reasons thus :
God being infinite in all His perfections must have a mode of
causality proper to Himself, infinitely perfect.   This mode of
causality can only be the action which is independent of all
material cause, namely creation.   Therefore the creative act
belongs to God alone [88].

---

[88] St. Thomas presents his argument thus : ' Creare non potest esse propria
actio nisi solius Dei.   Oportet enim universaliores effectus in universaliores
et priores causas reducere.   Inter omnes autem effectus universalissimum est
ipsum esse.   Unde oportet quod sit proprius effectus primae et universalissimae
causae, quae est Deus.   Producere autem esse absolute, non inquantum est
hoc vel tale, pertinet ad rationem creationis.   Unde manifestum est quod
creatio est propria actio ipsius Dei.
' Contingit autem quod aliquid participet actionem propriam alicujus alterius,
non virtute propria, sed instrumentaliter, in quantum agit in virtute alterius. . . .
Causa autem secunda instrumentalis non participat actionem causae supe-
rioris, nisi in quantum per aliquid sibi proprium dispositive operatur ad effectum
principalis agentis. . . .
' Illud autem quod est proprius effectus Dei creantis, est illud quod praesupponitur omnibus aliis ; scilicet esse absolute.   Unde non potest aliquid
aliud operari dispositive et instrumentaliter ad hunc effectum, cum creatio
non sit ex aliquo praesupposito quod possit disponi per actionem instrumentalis agentis.   Sic igitur impossibile est quod alicui creaturae conveniat creare
neque virtute propria, neque instrumentaliter, sive per ministerium '.   Sum.
Theol., I, q. 45, a. 5.
Kleutgen sums up the thought of St. Thomas in this way : ' Things can
be the effect of secondary causes only in the respect that they are of this or
that particular kind ; but inasmuch as they have being they must be the effects

At first sight this argument appears insufficient. One who upholds the opinion of Suarez might rejoin that it is laid down as a principle that creation is a mode of action proper to God alone, when this is the very question at issue. Granted that God has a causal power that is proper to Himself, and even that only God can be a creative cause which is independent in its origin and universal in its object ; the question still remains whether a creative causality dependent on the sovereign action of God and limited in its action implies a contradiction or not.

Yet this objection of Suarez would appear superficial. A secondary cause which has the power of making a single object pass from non-being to being would have the intrinsic power of creating everything. For in respect of what we may call this creatability, that is to say, of their potentiality of passing from non-being to being, all objects are alike. An agent capable of producing one of them has in its nature the power of producing them all. And even Suarez recognizes that the power to create everything cannot, whether it be regarded as a principal cause or as a subordinate one, belong to a creature. Therefore it must be true that God alone can create [89].

The fundamental thought of St. Thomas is that a cause belongs to a higher order only on the condition that it has a mode of action which properly belongs to itself. The extent to which this cause is applicable is of secondary importance ; the essential point is the *nature* of its action. Now the mode of action proper to God can only be creation, for all exercise of activity other than creation presupposes it ; it alone does not presuppose any anterior causality. Therefore creation, being the most perfect possible operation, belongs properly

of the supreme Cause who produces all things. Now when a thing is created or produced from *nothing*, it is produced in respect of its *being*, not only in so far as it is this or that particular thing. Therefore its production is entirely the effect of the first Cause. Whence just as we conclude from the fact that God produces all things that He has the power to produce from nothing, so we may infer that what is produced from nothing can only be the effect of Him who produces all '. *Philos. Scholast., Diss. IX*, 1012.

[89] Palmieri very aptly expresses the argument thus : ' Facultas quaevis in ea omnia materialia objecta se potest extendere quae sub suo formali objecto continentur. Atqui formale objectum potestatis creativae est ens ut ens, est ens producibile, sive ens ex nihilo efficiendum ; quae causa ergo in id ferri potest, potest versari circa ea omnia, quae sunt ex nihilo producibilia : ideoque potest substantias omnes possibiles creare '. *Institutiones philosophicae*, Theologia, th. XXXVIII.

to the first Cause and cannot be shared by any being of a different nature from the divine Being [90].

II. Conservation

83. Meaning of Conservation.—By the act of creation being succeeds to non-being ; by conservation a being already existent perseveres in its existence. Conservation is the act by which created things persist in the existence which creation has conferred upon them. It is therefore known as ' continued creation '.

By annihilation we mean the total destruction of a thing ; it would come about as soon as God should cease to maintain a being in existence. Annihilation is thus seen to be no positive action : for it is impossible that a positive action should not have a real term, and to suppose a positive action of annihilation terminating in nothingness is an evident contradiction.

84. Everything created has Need of being conserved by God.—Things of this world are essentially contingent. The being which they have at the present moment is not, therefore, the sufficient reason of their persistence in being at the following moment. Everything is at every moment in dependence on the omnipotence of God. ' To will the essence of a being and to will that it should be is to create. To will that a being should persist in existence is to conserve. The act of conservation is the necessary prolongation of the act of creation. . . . It is the first effect of God's government ' [91].

III. The Divine Government

85. Providence and Government.—The conservation of beings is, says St. Thomas, the first effect of the divine government ; their being ordered towards the good is the second. ' Duo sunt effectus gubernationis, scilicet conservatio rerum in bono, et motio earum ad bonum ' [92].

[90] ' Ordo effectuum est secundum ordinem causarum. Primus autem effectus est ipsum esse, quod omnibus aliis effectibus praesupponitur et ipsum non praesupponit aliquem alium effectum ; et ideo oportet quod dare esse in quantum hujusmodi, sit effectus primae causae solius secundum propriam virtutem '. St. Thomas, *Qq. disput. De Pot.*, q. 3, a. 4.
[91] Monsabré, *Conférences de Notre-Dame*, 1876, 19 Conf.
[92] *Sum. Theol.*, I, q. 103, a. 4.

Providence is the design conceived by the divine intelligence which makes all things reach their end—' ratio ordinis rerum in finem in mente divina praeexistens proprie Providentia est ' [93].

Government is the realization in time of this scheme of divine providence.

The question is discussed whether providence is formally an act of God's intelligence alone or at once an act of intelligence and will. The two opinions are not so different from one another as would appear at first sight. When St. Thomas attributes the plan of providence to the divine intelligence, he presupposes a purpose in the divine will : God wills a supreme end for His work, and providence is the conception of the order which when made real will bring about this end. ' A world is not ', says Monsabré, ' an incoherent collection of substances without relation to one another, without direction towards a determined end. It is a single whole in which each thing has its own place and by working towards its own perfection concurs towards the perfection of the whole. To see the place of each thing, to assign to it its particular ends, to regulate all the particular ends towards a general end, to dispose, to decree, to apply the means by which all the ends are attained, —such is the act of providence : in short, it is to govern ' [94].

86. Universal Providence and Particular Providence.—We have already seen that God loves with a necessary love His essential goodness and that He enjoys freedom in the creation of creatures who receive, though imperfectly, a share in the effects of His infinite goodness.

God has no need of anything ; His own essential goodness is sufficient for Him. He does not create in order to increase His own goodness, but in order to communicate it. The communication of the divine goodness to creatures is therefore the *ultimate end* of creation, ' finis propter quem ' ; and in order to make it clear that by creation God receives no increase of intrinsic perfection, we speak of it as ' the *extrinsic* glory of God '.

To arrange all creatures with a view to the supreme end, to endow them with the means necessary to the realization of this end, is the object of *universal providence*.

[93] *Sum. Theol.*, I, q. 22, a. 1.
[94] *Loc. cit.*

Yet, intelligent creatures alone are able to understand the intentions of God's providence, to have a conscious appreciation of His goodness, to praise His perfections ; they are, then, in an *especial* way the end of the providential order, in this sense that it is established for their advantage—they are ' finis cui '.

87. The Providence and the Government of God are Universal.—*A priori proof :* God is infinitely good, wise, holy, and powerful. (*a*) Being infinitely good, He must necessarily wish to bring about in His work all the perfections that can belong to it, that is to say, to accomplish in it all the good that the elements of which it is made admit of. (*b*) Being infinitely wise, He sees how each element must co-operate towards the end of His work. (*c*) Being infinitely holy, He must will the order which His infinite wisdom has conceived. (*d*) Being omnipotent, He cannot execute a work which falls short of His ideal. And this is reasoning which applies to every bit of His created works, to each of the means they use in their activities, to each of their activities themselves ; it applies to individuals as well as to species, to parts as well as to the whole. To suppose a thing or a movement which does not contribute to the ultimate end of the universe, to suppose that there can be in the work of God any flaw either in the way of excess or defect, is to attribute to God either an evil intention or ignorance or lack of power [95].

A posteriori proof : It is impossible for a finite intelligence to show how each creature and each of its movements contribute in a positive way to the harmony of the universe. But if we consider all things together, we cannot but acknowledge that they furnish abundant evidence of a sovereign Designer. This is a proof we have already developed (**28**), and so we need here only summarize it in the following concise words of St. Thomas : ' We observe throughout the works of nature that, always or generally, that takes place which is better. Now this could not come about unless all beings were directed to an end, which is their good, by an action of providence ; this implies the governance of a ruler. Whence this order we see

[95] St. Thomas gives the argument very concisely in this form : ' Cum enim sit optimum optima producere, non convenit summae Dei bonitati quod res productas ad perfectum non perducat. Ultima autem perfectio uniuscujusque est in consecutione finis. Unde ad divinam bonitatem pertinet ut sicut produxit esse, ita etiam eas ad finem perducat, quod est gubernare '. *Sum. Theol.*, I, q. 103, a. 1.

manifest in nature clearly shows a government of the world, just as a well-arranged house manifests the design and action of one who has arranged it '[96].

Again, in the world of moral beings, where all seems to depend on the initiative of personal freedom and on the play of human passions, the sovereign dominion of God, although it is enshrouded in mystery, is still not without manifestations of its existence[97]. Man acts by himself and God leads him.

88. The Sovereignty of God and the Free-will of Creatures.— Whilst the governance exercised by God in His works needs be universal and sovereign, man is free, and this freedom makes him master of his own actions : how can we reconcile these two truths ?

We very much doubt—for reasons we have already given **(67, 68)**—of the possibility of being able to arrive at a fully satisfactory explanation which will positively reconcile them. God must know perfectly and infallibly what human actions will be. Each of His creatures forms a part of a whole in which every action, just as every being that exists, must be arranged with a view to a general end ; and for this it is necessary that all such activity should be known beforehand. Now, how can the action of a cause which is of its very nature indifferent, as indeed our free-will is, be known beforehand, if it is not determined by an influence absolutely dependent on Him who foreknows ?[98] God, who is infinitely wise, cannot wait for our decisions to be made in order to arrange the general plan of His work and His government[99].

Further, it is not sufficient that God should merely know what we shall do, it is necessary that He should have a sure way of

---

[96] 'Videmus enim in rebus naturalibus evenire quod melius est, aut semper aut in pluribus. Quod non contingeret, nisi per aliquam providentiam res naturales dirigerentur ad finem boni, quod est gubernare. Unde ipse ordo certus rerum manifeste demonstrat gubernationem mundi : sicut si quis intraret domum bene ordinatam, ex ipsa domus ordinatione ordinatoris rationem perpenderet '. *Sum. Theol.*, loc. cit.

[97] MONSABRÉ, *op. cit.*, 19e Conf.

[98] 'Quidam effectus futuri sunt, quorum causae indifferentes se habent ad utrumque : haec autem vocantur contingentia ad utrumlibet, ut sunt illa praecipue quae dependent ex libero arbitrio. Sed quia ex causa ad utrumlibet, cum sit quasi in potentia, non progreditur aliquis effectus. nisi per aliquam aliam causam determinatur magis ad unum quam ad aliud ; ideo hujusmodi effectus in causis quidem ad utrumlibet nullo modo cognosci possunt per se accepti '. *De verit.*, q. 8, a. 12.

[99] Cp. MONSABRÉ, *op. cit.*, 20e Conf., p. 83.

leading our acts to their ends. And can this be said to be anything else than a direct action of the divine will on the human will ?

To reconcile the freedom of man with the sovereignty of God's providence is the work of the theologian as well as of the philosopher, for it is intimately connected with the deep problem of predestination. We will here confine ourselves to a brief sketch of the principal attempts that have been made towards its solution.

Molina, followed by the majority of the theologians of the Society of Jesus, chiefly desirous of safeguarding the part of *human freedom* in the general economy of creation, attributes to God a concurrence, which he calls ' indifferent ', ' simultaneous '. The Thomist school defends a stricter theory, which they think indispensable for safeguarding *the absolute sovereignty of Providence* ; they attribute to God a motion anterior to the free determination of the created will, and this they name a ' pre-motion '.

(a) It is the opinion of the *Molinist school* that God co-operates with the creature in some general and indefinite way. This general co-operation becomes definite and particular by the action of each person, but in such a way that the action produced is *simultaneously* and *totally* both the act of God and the proper act of the created agent. Further, as an act of free-will has a priority of nature to the concurrence of providence, this concurrence, from the side of God, amounts to this : God wills from all eternity to accomplish in accordance with His creature's freedom those acts which the creature will himself freely perform.

To this the objection may be brought that if the initiative comes from the creature, if the proper part the creature plays is to make use of the indifferent concurrence of the divine will in this or that direction at its pleasure, we shall have to say that the creature makes the supreme action of God subject to its own decisions. How is the absolute sovereignty of providence to be safeguarded ?

Molinists meet this objection by urging that God has an eminent power of persuasion whereby He infallibly leads His creatures. Sometimes a man is so sure of his influence on his fellow-men that he acts with a kind of infallibility, without it being possible to say that he has over-ridden their freedom. If a man has so great a power of persuasion, does not this also belong to God, who knows most intimately all the different activities of our will and all the influences that may act upon it ?

To this we reply, however, that if we come to analyse the power of persuasion, we discover in it the composition of two distinct acts, and we cannot say that the first is the direct and efficacious cause of the second. It is I who yield to the persuasion, it is I who determine its efficaciousness. If God's sovereignty is nothing more than His power of persuasion, I am able to shake myself free from His action ; and, if I yield to it, since my determination is entirely my own act and the radical reason of the good that I may do and of the merits that I may acquire, this good and these merits cannot be ascribed to any supreme efficaciousness on the part of the first Cause.

(b) The *Thomist school* makes the absolute sovereignty of God consist in this, that He is, in the strictest way, the first Cause of all things, and He cannot be so, in this opinion, if He does not produce in us not only our being and our powers but also the very acts which result from the use of our powers. Hence in every created agent that acts God acts ; no being is able to accomplish its natural action unless by the influence of His divine power ; no cause, not even a spiritual one, however perfect we may suppose it to be, is able to act except it be moved by God. This motion that is always absolutely necessary to every created nature, is a motion imparted to the will. Unless such a motion is received by our will we cannot in truth say that God is the author of all that belongs to us, for, in the last analysis, every action of ours is something belonging to us.

In the well-known question, Q. 3, art. 7, of his opusculum *De Potentia*, St. Thomas sums up his views on the action of divine providence in the following words : ' Sic ergo Deus est causa actionis cujuslibet inquantum dat virtutem agendi, et inquantum conservat eam, et inquantum applicat actioni, et inquantum ejus virtute omnis alia virtus agit '. According to this teaching, the action of providence therefore comprises four elements : (a) God *creates*, and accordingly He is the author of every active power ; (b) God *conserves* the powers He has created ; (c) God ' *moves* to action ' these active powers ; (*d*) God is the *principal Cause* to which every secondary cause is subordinate as an instrumental one.

It seems clear that, according to the mind of the Angelic Doctor, the action of God has all the characteristics of what the Dominican commentators have called ' pre-motion ' or rather, in a less happy phrase, ' physical predetermination '.

But the idea of freedom seems quite inconsistent with a motion of this kind. What are we going to say to the man who assures us that he has dominion over his own acts and that we are transferring it to another cause ?

To this claim in favour of human liberty St. Thomas replies : ' Certainly a man has dominion over his acts, but not to 'the exclusion of the first Cause. Though it is necessary that the free-will should be the cause of its own movement, it is not at all necessary that it should be the first cause of it. God moves everything that is in the world, both natural causes and causes endowed with free-will ; and just as His motion does not stand in the way of the acts of natural causes being natural, so it does not stand in the way of free causes still being free. Indeed His pre-motion makes them to be so, because God works in each being according to its own nature. Not only does the divine will cause the being which It moves to perform an action, but It also causes it to do it in the manner appropriate to the nature of the secondary agent, in such a way that were there something repugnant to the divine pre-motion in the act which It causes our free will to accomplish, such an act would not be free '. In one word, the divine motion is *infallibly efficacious* but does not *necessitate*[100].

Once again the objection may be raised : Does not this doctrine make God share in our sinful acts ?—The answer lies in this : ' God is the first Cause of the whole reality our actions comprise, but evil is not a reality, it is a privation of reality.

---

[100] ' Cum aliqua causa efficax fuerit ad agendum, effectus sequitur causam, non tantum secundum id quod fit, sed *etiam secundum modum fiendi vel essendi.* . . . Cum igitur voluntas divina sit efficacissima, non solum sequitur quod fiant ea quae Deus vult fieri, sed et quod *eo modo fiant quo Deus ea fieri vult* '. *Sum. Theol.*, I, q. 19, a. 8.—' Deus movet quidem voluntatem *immutabiliter* propter *efficaciam virtutis moventis,* quae deficere non potest ; sed propter naturam voluntatis motae, quae indifferenter se habet ad diversa, *non inducitur necessitas,* sed *manet libertas ;* sicut etiam in omnibus providentia divina *infallibiliter* operatur ; et tamen a causis contingentibus proveniunt effectus contingenter, inquantum Deus omnia movet proportionabiliter, *unumquodque secundum suum modum* '. *De Malo,* q. 6, art. unico, ad 3. Cp. MONSABRÉ, *op. cit.,* 20e Conf.

This privation of being belongs to us who are defective causes, but to us alone ; it cannot be attributed to the first Cause which cannot be defective. Just as if I limp, it is not to my soul, the principle of my movement, but to my malformed limb that my failure to walk properly must be attributed ; so if I sin, it is not to God, the first and indefectible cause of my actions, but to the failure on the part of my free-will that my sin must be attributed. The whole responsibility belongs to me ; God is only responsible for the good there is in my material act of sin ' [101].

Both the Molinist and the Thomist theory raise difficulties to which, we must frankly avow, they do not give any answer that is completely satisfactory. And, we may add, that the prolonged contests these arguments have excited bear witness to their insufficiency. Bossuet is right in urging us to grasp firmly the two ends of the chain, although we do not see all the links of argument by which they are united. We hold in the one hand the truth of the sovereignty of God, in the other the truth of the free-will of man. If it should happen that the invisible link alluded to by Bossuet, which unites these two truths be badly constructed by human opinion, we may nevertheless rest assured that there is no flaw in the work of God.

After all, it is not astonishing that the relations of God to the world, of the essential Being to contingent subjects, of the Infinite and the finite, should be enveloped in obscurity. On reflection we must surely all recognize that it cannot be otherwise. A philosophy which should claim to solve all the mysteries of the divine nature and of its action on the world must stand condemned by its very claim.

89. The Government of God and the Presence of Evil in the World.—The working of the divine government is infallible and holy both in its end and in the choice of its means : how then can there be evil in the world ? Yet the existence of evil is a fact ; there are physical evils in the phenomena of nature, man is a victim to suffering, and moral evil defiles his conscience. How can we reconcile evil, under these three forms, with the necessary attributes of God's providence ?

---

[101] MONSABRÉ, *op. cit.*, 20ᵉ Conf.—The Thomistic view has been defended very ably against the attacks of Frs. Scheeman and Frins, S.J., by Dummermuth—*S. Thomas et Doctrina Praemotionis Physicae* (Paris, 1886), and *Defensio doctrinae S. Thomae de Praemotione Physica* (Louvain, 1895).

The answer lies in the following considerations :—

1. *Physical evil* is the privation of the perfection that is proper to a particular nature—' Malum non est aliquid, sed est privatio alicujus boni particularis ' ; ' Malum est privatio debitae perfectionis '[102]. Now these privations are the accidental effects of the clash of the laws of nature. Particular ends are accidentally sacrificed to the exigencies of the general order of nature. ' Who will deny that God can permit for the general order and the beauty of His work, that a being which is defective should give way, that an inferior good should be sacrificed to a higher good ? To do so would be to contradict wisdom '[103].

2. *Suffering*, moreover, is only a relative evil ; it can be and often is a good, if we take into consideration all the circumstances. If comfort were the supreme end of life, grief would be certainly out of place, but man has an end higher than earthly enjoyment, a moral and religious end. Consequently, it is a question of ascertaining whether grief furthers or retards these higher aims. If it is compatible with these aims, if even it furthers them, grief, far from being an evil, can be either a condition or a means of acquiring the real good of human nature. Yet experience bears witness that grief, whether it be a privation or endurance, detaches the heart from the trammels that bind it to a life of the senses, leaves free play to the moral aspirations, has a deep influence on the character and draws the soul to God. As Seneca says : It is not in life's luxuries that God looks for the man of good will— ' Bonum virum Deus in deliciis non habet ' ; but He proves him by severe tests and thus prepares him for Himself—' Experitur in dura, sibi illum praeparat '[104].

3. *Moral evil* cannot be attributed to God. As St. Thomas says, whatever is positive in the material act of sin must be referred to God as its first Cause ; but in so far as such an act is a falling away from what is right, it proceeds from the defect of our free-will ; thus it is that moral evil, which is a defect

---

[102] St. Thomas, *De Malo*, q. 1, a. 1, and a. 2.

[103] Monsabré, 22ᵉ Conf.—' Cum Deus sit universalis provisor totius entis, ad ipsius providentiam pertinet ut permittat quosdam defectus esse in aliquibus particularibus rebus, ne impediatur bonum universi perfectum. Si enim omnia mala impedirentur, multa bona deessent universo '. *Sum. Theol.*, I, q. 22, a. 2, ad 2.

[104] Seneca, *De Providentia*.

in the act of man, can never be attributed to God, the first
Cause of all good [105].   Moral evil exists not in virtue of a positive action on God's part, but of His permission, and this permission is a good—' Deus neque vult mala fieri, neque vult mala
non fieri, sed vult *permittere* mala fieri ; et hoc est bonum ' [106].

The free-will of man is the cause that is responsible for moral
evil, so that it would involve a contradiction to speak of an
immoral act which was produced without freedom.   God
cannot be obliged, for the sake of hindering man's abuse of his
free-will, to cease from or to suspend the exercise of His perfections.   He is holy, but He is free, omnipotent, wise, as well
as exceedingly bounteous.   Now all these attributes of God
are intimately connected with one another, and they must
attain their end, namely their legitimate manifestation.   God's
holiness, which wills the good, must will it before everything
else, before that good which would consist in our inability to
sin.

If God were obliged to prevent all moral evil, He would no
longer have the freedom to choose from all possible worlds the one
which it is His good pleasure to create, for the reason that there
would be only one possible, namely the world in which He sees
only beings that are perfect.   To expect that man's freedom
should necessarily never be abused, would be to demand
useless miracles of the divine omnipotence.   For it is the law
that every being acts according to its nature, and it is in the
nature of a defectible being that it should have the power to
fail.   And yet the objection we are considering demands that
God should have overruled this law of nature from all eternity.
Further, if the objection were sound, the possibility of evil
would make good impossible : every good would have to be
withheld lest, by the fault of him who receives it, evil would
necessarily follow.   And therefore God could not give men life
which is a good, intelligence which is a good, free-will which is
a good, His assistance which is a good, because some creatures
might abuse these divine gifts.

Finally, evil indeed may exist, yet the infallibility and the
holiness of God's government would only be compromised

---

[105] ' Quidquid est entitatis et actionis in actione mala reducitur in Deum
sicut in causam ; sed quod est ibi defectus non causatur a Deo, sed ex causa
secunda deficiente '.   *Sum. Theol.*, I, q. 49, a. 2, ad 2.
[106] *Id.*, I, q. 19, a. 9, ad 3.

if He permitted evil in the works of His creation to such an extent that evil should triumph over good. But this is not the case. God is sufficiently powerful, says St. Augustine, to make the evil which He permits serve the cause of the final good of creation. ' Ad providentiam Dei pertinuit ut ex libero arbitrio venientia mala voluntatis permitteret. Tanta quippe est omnipotentia ejus voluntatis, ut etiam de malis possit facere bona, sive ignoscendo, sive sanando, sive ad utilitatem piorum co-optando atque vertendo, sive etiam justissime puniendo ' [107].

However, whilst each of the answers we have considered has certainly some weight, none of them, we think, can give a *complete positive* solution. The relations between God and the world—the reconciliation of the divine immutability with the fact of creation, with the knowledge of things which come to pass in the course of time ; of His all-powerful sovereignty with the dominion of our free-will, and, consequently, of the infallibility of His foreknowledge with the contingent nature of our free acts ; of His perfect holiness and His perfect goodness with the existence of moral evil and its disastrous consequences for the guilty who bring down upon themselves irreparable loss—all these are necessarily mysteries to the limited understanding of man. Nor should we expect it to be otherwise, seeing that we have only *analogical* ideas of God's activity. The most we can do is to make ourselves thoroughly and rationally convinced of our present state of impotence where it is a question of knowing God's nature and of understanding in *positive* ideas the reason and manner of His action. The deepest knowledge of God convinces us, says St. Thomas, that, when left to the light of natural reason, we are necessarily ignorant of His nature and His dealings with men. Furthermore, in order to give ourselves a satisfactory explanation of His government of the world, we require to know the plan of providence in its entirety, whereas in fact we know only a small fraction of His work, and from this we cannot do more than make guesses at His design in creation. Is it, then, to be wondered at that in our laborious efforts to put together the detached fragments of the whole there should sometimes be a difficulty in seeing how part fits in with part ? When

[107] *De Continentia*, c. 6, n. 15.

we bear in mind that the entire universe such as it is known by the light of natural reason alone, forms but a part of God's work of creation, and that much more belonging to the realms of objective fact bears a supernatural character, then shall we be led to understand that an adequate solution of the many problems which confront us from real facts can never be found by investigation which is exclusively philosophical.

Conclusion

God is our First Beginning and our Supreme End ; from Him we receive our being, our faculties and our activity. For this reason we must direct to Him all the aspirations of our soul ; to Him we must devote our whole moral life. As Seneca has said : ' So oft as thou wishest to know what to flee or to find, fix thine eyes on the Sovereign Good, the end and purpose of thy whole life ' [108].

[108] ' Quoties quid fugiendum sit, aut quid petendum scire voles, ad summum bonum, et propositum totius vitae respice. Illi enim consentire debet quidquid agimus '. *Epistola* LXXI.

LOGIC

INTRODUCTION *

1. Definition of Logic.—Logic is *the reflex study of the order which needs to exist in our judgments, inferences and more elaborate reasoning processes for them to lead us to truth.* In this definition is laid down (1) what is the subject-matter of logic, the materials into which order must be introduced (material cause or object) ; (2) in what this orderliness, this elaboration of the materials consists (formal cause) ; and (3) the end towards which this elaboration aims—the attainment of truth (final cause).

2. Material Cause of Logic.—In a broad sense the materials of logic are the various acts of the mind—apprehension, judgment and reasoning. But to speak strictly, they are only acts of apprehension (**3** and **10**).

(1) By *apprehension* the mind represents to itself one or more things without affirming or denying anything about them. The concepts resulting from this act of conception, or apprehension, are expressed by *names* or *terms*. (2) The act of affirming or denying one thing of another is *judgment :* it consists in establishing between the objects of two concepts a relation of identity or non-identity, of agreement or disagreement. Its outward expression is the *proposition*. (3) *Reasoning* or inference is the combination of two or more judgments in such a way that a new judgment is formed. The *syllogism* is the common and complete expression of the simplest reasoning process.

3. Formal Cause of Logic.—The formal object of logic or the point of view from which logic regards acts of the mind

---

* Books for study or consultation—

Card. Mercier, *Logique* (5th ed., 1909, Institut supérieur de Philosophie Louvain).

P. Coffey, *The Science of Logic,* 2 vols. (Longmans, London, 1912).

JOYCE, *Principles of Logic* (Longmans, London, 1908).

JOSEPH, *An Introduction to Logic* (Clarendon Press, Oxford, 2nd ed., 1916).

WELTON, *A Manual of Logic,* 2 vols. (Tutorial Press, London, 2nd ed., 1904).

MELLONE, *An Introductory Text-book of Logic* (Blackwood, Edinburgh, 1902).

is their *suitability* or *adaptability* for being arranged in order
and gathered into bodies of truth, such as are the various
special sciences and the more fundamental science of Philosophy itself. Indeed the building up of our knowledge is a
progressive work : the mind has first to apprehend the manifold aspects of reality one by one before it can put its fragmentary explanations together and co-ordinate them in one
synthetic whole. The first elaboration of our simple ideas is
the work of judgment ; judgments in their turn supply the
materials for inference ; finally, since a single reasoning process
does not furnish a full knowledge of a thing, inferences become
the materials for the construction of a scientific system. This
building up of ideas by the mind, this introduction of order
into its own acts, this marshalling of its ideas with a view to
attaining truth, is what is meant by logical order, the order
with which logic deals : ' ordo quem ratio considerando facit
in proprio actu '.

4. Difference between Psychology and Logic.—Several sciences
may deal with the same object provided that each studies
different properties of it and so approaches it from a different
point of view. In such a case there is said to be one *common
material* (or indeterminate) object, whilst each has its *proper
formal* (or determinate) object.

Psychology also has the acts of the human mind as part of
its material object, but it does not claim to study them precisely as does logic (formal object). To psychology they are
vital acts whose nature and genetic principles have to be investigated. Logic, on the other hand, considers them only in so
far as they have a cognitional import, are *abstract and universal
representations of objects*, and furnish the materials for those
relations which the mind formulates in judgments and inferences and builds up into a scientific system. As in all the
other sciences that deal with the world of reality, in psychology
order is the *condition sine qua non* of the science ; in logic
it is an *object*, the very thing logic studies : since the proper
object of logic is the *form itself* which knowledge-building
requires.

5. Final Cause of Logic.—The ulterior *end* for which the
systematization of the results of our reasoning makes, is to
secure truth in our knowledge.

Before explaining how logic directs its acts *towards truth*, we must remember that truth and error are qualities of the judgment and not of the concept. As long as a man mentions only a single object (e.g. the sun, or some imaginative object) no one can say that he is right or wrong. Truth and error belong to the statement or *proposition* that the sun exists, that the Jabberwocky is real (*Criteriology*, 6).

Now as to the claim of logic to lead the mind ' to truth ', it must not be thought that the meaning is that logic, as one science, can take the place of all the special sciences. Obviously it cannot : each of the special sciences enlightens the mind in regard to the special object it contemplates, and so the man versed in them all is far better equipped for making a true judgment than the man who merely knows logic. There is, however, another way of getting at all truth than by means of the successive and collective study of the separate sciences, which is very different, namely, that way in which a more general science aids a less general one. Indeed, it is a law of our thought that the simple helps us to understand the complex (*Gen. Introduction*, 2) ; now in the matter of knowledge simplicity and universality always go together : therefore the most general sciences are those which have the simplest object, and so can throw light on any more complex—or particular—objects to which they can have application. In this sense it is that logic leads to truth, inasmuch as it is a general science because it regulates the content of all the other sciences, because they have all to be drawn up according to its laws. It has an object of the extremest simplicity and of the widest extension—' being of the mind ', *ens rationis*, as we will proceed to explain.

6. Difference between Metaphysics and Logic.—There is another science which has *all being* for its object, and therefore, since it touches all knowledge, also merits the name of a general science—namely metaphysics. Metaphysics and logic alike treat of all being, they have a common material object ; but they treat of it from different points of view, they have each their proper formal object. The former considers *real being, regarded formally as it is in itself* (ENS REALE) *and possessing real attributes.* Logic studies the same *being, formally considered as it is in the mind* (ENS RATIONIS), *as a logical entity, and possessing mental attributes bestowed on it by the mind and in virtue of its being subjected to the process of thought.*

Anything, whether existing or capable of existing, can be thought about. When it is thought about, as a concept in the mind, it necessarily becomes clothed with attributes which are the result of its being an object of intellectual thought ; as such, as a mental object, it is abstract and universal. Between abstract and universal objects it is possible to establish relations such as the concrete particularizing conditions of things as they are outside the mind do not allow of : one mental object becomes the *predicate* or attribute of another object of thought which, on account of its relation to the first, fulfils the rôle of *subject ;* the content and extension of ideas give rise to relations of identity or non-identity ; judgments are formed, reasoning processes ensue, and the material for all these various mental operations is throughout one and the same—namely, being : not real being, as it is in itself and independent of thought, but being-as-it-is-in-the-mind, *ens rationis*, i.e. under the aspect and with the attributes that attach to it as an object of thought.

We see, then, that whereas metaphysics is the universal science of *reality ;* logic is the universal science of our *knowledge* of reality[1].

7. Is Logic a Science or an Art ?—Is logic a *speculative* or a *practical* science ?—A speculative science is one which aims only at a knowledge of the nature of its object ; a practical one, on the other hand, furnishes a knowledge of its object with a view to action or to some ulterior purpose : ' finis speculativae, veritas ; finis operativae seu practicae, actio '. The logician does not contemplate the acts of his mind merely for the pleasure of knowing the relations they bear to one another, but with a view to using this scientific knowledge for the further direction of the operations of his mind.   In this sense, and not without reason, logic is said to be a *practical* science. But if a broader view is taken and the direction logic gives to the operations of the mind is considered as indeed but a step towards the knowledge of all truth, it may then be said to be a *speculative* science. This is the standpoint of St.

---

[1] The relations studied in logic are not the ontological relations on which the attention of the mind first of all falls, first or direct mental views ' primae intentiones ', objects of a first abstraction, but logical relations which arise from the juxtaposition of two abstract objects or ideas and which the mind learns of only upon reflecting, ' secundae intentiones ', objects of a second abstraction.

Thomas when he says : ' In speculativis alia rationalis scientia est dialectica . . . et alia scientia demonstrativa ' [2].

Logic is also an *art*, if thereby is meant a *collection of practical rules to direct action* [3]. But it is not an art according to the more restricted definition which requires the action in question to result in some *external* production.

8. Divisions of Logic.—1. It is not uncommon to-day to divide logic into two parts, *formal* logic and *real* logic. But the advisability of such a division is to be questioned :—(*a*) It owes its origin chiefly to some arbitrary presuppositions in Kantian philosophy (*Criteriology*, **42**). (*b*) Many of the questions discussed in real logic furnish for us the matter of a separate treatise following immediately after psychology, namely epistemology or criteriology, the scientific analysis of certitude.

2. *Formal logic* is generally divided into three parts, dealing respectively with apprehension, judgment and reasoning. Against such a division, excellent as it is inasmuch as it is based on the threefold nature of the object-matter of logic, we have nothing to say but that we prefer to adopt another division.

3. The other division we prefer, which is more in accord with the general division of all philosophical inquiry [4], is that suggested by the consideration of logical order through its four causes, *efficient, material, formal* and *final* (see *Gen. Metaphysics*, Part IV).

---

[2] *Sum. Theol.*, I-II, q. 51, art. 2, ad 3.

[3] ' Alia animalia, ait, quodam naturali instinctu ad suos actus aguntur, homo autem rationis judicio in suis operibus dirigitur. Et inde est, quod ad actus humanos faciliter et ordinate perficiendos diversae artes deserviunt. *Nihil enim aliud ars esse videtur, quam certa ordinatio rationis, qua per determinata media ad debitum finem actus humani perveniunt.* Ratio autem non solum dirigere potest inferiorum partium actus, sed etiam actus sui directiva est. Hoc enim est proprium intellectivae partis ut in seipsam reflectatur : nam intellectus intelligit seipsum, et similiter ratio de suo actu ratiocinari potest. Sicut igitur ex hoc quod ratio de actu manus ratiocinatur adinventa est ars aedificatoria vel fabrilis, per quas homo faciliter et ordinate hujusmodi actus exercere potest ; eadem ratione ars quaedam necessaria est, quae sit *directiva ipsius actus rationis, per quam scilicet homo in ipso actu rationis ordinate et faciliter et sine errore procedat.* Et haec est ars Logica, id est rationalis scientia. Quae non solum rationalis est ex hoc, quod est secundum rationem, quod est omnibus artibus commune ; sed etiam ex hoc, quod est circa ipsum actum rationis sicut circa propriam materiam. Et ideo videtur esse ars artium ; quia in actu rationis nos dirigit, a quo omnes artes procedunt '. St. Thomas, *I Post. Analyt.*, lect. 1.

[4] Cp. the introduction of a small treatise on logic among the works of St. Thomas : *De totius Logicae Aristotelis Summa.* Op. XLIV, Proemium. Ed. Parm.

The study of the efficient cause of logical order belongs strictly to the domain of psychology, yet here we shall make it the matter of a preliminary chapter (Chap. I). The first chapter of the treatise proper will deal with concepts and terms, the *material into which order* must be introduced ; in a word, with the *material cause* of this logical order (Chap. II). In Chapter III the order itself which has to be introduced into these materials will be investigated—the rules to be observed in the forming of judgments, the drawing of inferences, and the building up of scientific systems, if we wish to arrive at a knowledge of truth ; in a word, the *formal cause* of logical order. In a last chapter (IV) will be considered the utility to science and philosophy of this establishment of order in our mental operations, the *final cause* of logic [5].

 [5] Mention of the four causes of the order logic studies is made in our definition of logic (1) and in the text of St. Thomas quoted in the footnote on p. 139.
' [Logica] est directiva (formal cause) ipsius actus rationis (material cause)
per quam scilicet homo (efficient cause) in ipso actu rationis ordinate et faciliter
et sine errore procedit (final cause) '.

CHAPTER I

THE EFFICIENT CAUSE OF LOGICAL ORDER

9. Principles and Nature of Intellectual Acts.—The *remote* principle or source of our intellectual acts is the *human substance* made up of soul and body ; their *proximate* or immediate principle is the *intellectual faculty* (*Psychology*, **153**).

In psychology it is shown that all acts of the mind owe their beginning to some sense-experience. The object of sensation or sense-perception is always a *determinate* material thing, made of *this* matter and possessing *these* qualities ; the object of conception or of thought proper is abstract and universal, it is considered apart from the *particularizing* conditions with which it is really endowed when existing actually outside the mind (abstrahere, separatim considerare), and is consequently *universal* or applicable to any number of individual subjects. This bell, which I see and touch, which is made of brass and is round in shape and of a pleasing tone, occupies so much space on my table at this particular moment in time when I am looking at it. All this is quite determinate. But I can form a notion of a bell that abstracts from all these determining circumstances or particularizing attributes ; one by which I represent, at least in a general way, *all* bells whatsoever, no matter of what material they may be made, what particular qualities they may possess of shape or sound, or when or where they may exist.

10. Intellectual Acts, though Manifold, are Fundamentally Identical.—All the acts of the mind—apprehension, judgment, reasoning—are fundamentally the same kind of act, an intellectual intuition or understanding of what something is, quod quid est ; although they have certain different accidental features that it will be of interest to determine.

1. The first act—*apprehension* or *conception*—assumes different forms or modalities which have secured for it different names :—(*a*) When the mind considers an object independently

of the surrounding objects it is said to give *attention* to it.
(*b*) This attention may be directed either to one single attribute of the object independently of any others united with it,
or to its attributes taken as a whole, as they constitute the
essence of the object, but considered apart from those characteristics which individualize it in the world of reality : such
mental acts are called acts of *abstraction*.   (*c*) Abstraction is
the basis for *generalization*.   (*d*) Abstraction is also a work
of *analysis* or a mental process by which an object known is
decomposed into its several notes or attributes.   (*e*) The act
by which these notes, previously considered apart, are re-
united or gathered together by the mind is called a *synthesis*.
(*f*) When two objects are conceived successively by the mind and
a relation is perceived to exist between them, this apprehension,
or rather this double apprehension, is called a *comparison*.
(*g*) The direct perception of some existing reality is an *intuition*.   The words percept, *perception*, are used in the case of
existing realities, in contrast with concept, *conception*, which
refer to ideal objects of things considered apart from their
existence.   (*h*) When the mind has for its object acts of the
soul, especially its spiritual acts, apprehension is then termed
consciousness.   (*i*) Finally, the act by which the mind conceives that one object is not the same as another is known as
distinction (*Gen. Metaphysics*, **48**).   By ' object '—id quod
ob-jicitur cognoscenti—we understand whatsoever can be
matter for an act of thought.

2. The act of *judgment* consists in predicating one object
of another, in recognizing that two objects previously apprehended are in mutual agreement or disagreement.   It is an
act of apprehension having as its formal object the identity of
the terms of two previous apprehensions ; it is an *apprehensio
complexa* or *complexorum* as opposed to simple apprehension,
apprehensio incomplexa or *incomplexorum*.

3. *Reasoning, ratiocination,* or *inference,* is a series of judgments.   It is a process by which the *reason* compares two
extreme terms between which it does not yet perceive a relation
of identity to exist, with a third common term in order to discover by this comparison whether or not they are identical.

Apprehension in its manifold forms, judgment, and reasoning, are fundamentally one and the same kind of act, namely
an apprehension of or insight into *what a thing is*.   They are all

alike acts of one and the same faculty, be it called intellect, reason or understanding.

11. Judgment and Reasoning are made Possible by the Abstract Character of Concepts.—Every being existing in the actual order is itself and not another, it is individual, that is, possesses its own incommunicable individuality ; it is inconceivable that such a real being could be affirmed of another or in any way attributed to another. Socrates, for example, is himself and no one else ; this tree is this tree and not any other tree [6].

The question arises, then, how one thing can be affirmed of another when a judgment is made. The answer lies in the fact that the mind has the power of regarding beings apart from their individualizing notes, the power of *abstracting*. In consequence of this abstractive quality of apprehension the object of a mental concept is universal, that is, it is found or may be found realized in a multitude of other individuals, and in our judgments may be predicated of them (universale in praedicando). Hence it is that in virtue of this mental abstraction things may be affirmed or predicated of one another. In virtue of this same abstraction our ideas of things in nature can be attributed to an entire species or a whole genus ; they are representative of class-natures, of genera and species. Abstraction makes reasoning possible, inasmuch as the latter requires, as we shall see later, a universal middle term, and universality is the result of abstraction : *abstrahi ad quod sequitur intentio universalitatis.*

[6] See *General Metaphysics*, **26**. 'Non singularia de aliis sed alia de ipsis praedicantur'. ARISTOTLE, *Anal. pr.*, I, 27.

CHAPTER II

THE MATERIAL CAUSE OF LOGICAL ORDER

12. Object and Division of this Chapter.—By the materials or *material cause* of anything we understand *that out of which it is made* (id ex quo aliquid fit) : by the material cause of logic, then, that into which order has to be introduced, that which we are studying to arrange in order. The elementary materials consist in concepts (Art. I) and in terms (Art. II). Both of these articles alike allow of two subdivisions, dealing respectively with the content and qualities of the concept and term, and with the kinds of each.

ART. I. CONCEPTS

I. THE OBJECT AND QUALITIES OF THE CONCEPT

13. The Concept in Logic.—Since simple apprehension only supplies the materials for the act of judgment and inference is but a step forward to a new judgment, judgment appears as the chief act of the mind, and logic deals with concepts (4) only in so far as they are *elements of the judgment,* as they are capable of fulfilling the rôle of subject or predicate—*notio subjicibilis vel praedicabilis in enuntiatione.* For the business of logic is with mental acts in so far as the mind can direct them towards the attainment of truth, and truth and error appertain to the act of judgment, not to simple conception or apprehension (5) ; logic is concerned, then, with concepts precisely as they furnish the *materials for true judgments* and are *the occasion of erroneous ones.*

Concepts or ideas are then in logic the thought-object enunciated or predicated of another and the thought-object of which the predication is made. The nexus between them is expressed by the verb ' to be ', the *copula.* Together the *subject* (id quod est subjectum attributioni vel praedicationi) and the *predicate* or *attribute* (id quod praedicatur vel attribuitur) are known as the *terms* (termini) of a proposition, being indeed the extremes or limits of the assertion.

14. Logical Questions arising from the Act of Simple Apprehension.—The concept, we have just said, finds a place in logic only in so far as it acts as *subject* or *predicate*. Let us consider it then in these two rôles :—

1. The *subject* of a proposition is always ultimately, though in ultimate analysis only, an *individual*. Propositions may indeed have as their subject, and in fact often have, an abstract type, yet in such cases this abstract type is always itself the predicate of some other previous subject. This is so for two reasons : (a) because *psychologically* the first object of thought is drawn from sense-experience, and the senses can only grasp at what is concrete and individual ; and (b) because *ontologically* only an individual is a subject in the strict sense of the term—what Aristotle calls πρώτη οὐσία, first substance—since on the one hand it is attributable to no other, individuality being incommunicable to another, Socrates being identical with no one but himself (*Gen. Metaphysics*, 26), and on the other hand it is the subject of abstract, universal concepts which can be predicated of it on various titles [1].

Consider by way of illustration the proposition : ' Snow melts in the sun '. ' Snow ', a general or universal idea, is an abstract subject. But what does ' snow ' mean ? This something which I perceive to be white and falling to the ground in light flakes and I feel cold to my touch. *This* white, cold thing that falls in flakes is ' snow ' : this white, cold, flaky thing is a first subject ; and of this *first subject* ' snow ' is a predicate. The general or abstract idea ' snow ' next becomes the subject of a further predicate, of the attribute ' melts-in-the-sun '. This analysis of the terms of a proposition illustrates how there is always a first term which is originally an individual subject (τόδε τι) and to which the mind attributes all the predications it makes.

2. The *predicate* furnishes two special questions : (a) *What* does it mean or convey ; what does it state of the subject ?

---

[1] ' Omnium eorum, quae sunt, alia sunt ejusmodi, ut de nullo alio vere possint universe praedicari, velut Cleon et Callias, et res singularis et quod solis sensibus subjicitur, de ipsis autem alia praedicantur ; uterque enim illorum et homo est et animans '. Aristotle, *Anal. pr.*, I, 27.

And in answer we have the study of the *categories*, or the logical predicaments as the classification of predicates is sometimes called. (*b*) *How* does it belong to the subject, in what way must it be attributed to it ? This is a question of the *predicables* or ways of predicating.

15. The Categories or Logical Predicaments.—There is of course no question here of distinguishing in detail all the predicates of the immense variety of judgments the human mind is capable of making. What Aristotle attempted to do was to reduce them to a number of heads or *types of predication* (typus praedicationis) in order to see how many really different aspects of a subject might be indicated by means of predicates, each type constituting a *category* of ideas of the same kind. He discovered ten great headings, supreme genera, or types of predication, under one or other of which can be arranged every possible general notion we can conceivably use in interpreting or judging the individual things or subjects which come up for investigation in the course of our mental experience. They are as follows :—

1. *Substance*—that is to say, *abstract* or *second* substance. This something our senses perceive as white, cold and flaky is ' snow '. ' Snow ' is an abstract notion representative of the subject which our senses tell us has attached to it the accidental determinations expressed by the adjectives ' white ', ' cold ', ' flaky '. When the mind designates any concrete subject perceived by the senses—τόδε τι—by a concept signifying its substance or essence, it is applying to it a predicate of the *first category*, ἡ οὐσία, τι ἐστί.

By way of contrast to individual subject, πρώτη οὐσία, *prima substantia*, of which all predications are ultimately made (**14**), the category of substance is called δευτέρα οὐσία, *secunda substantia ;* for whilst it *can* serve as the subject of logical predicates or attributes, it yet itself presupposes a concrete subject to which it refers.

2. The other nine heads of predication represent *accidental determinations* [8]. Now some of these modes of being appertaining to substance are INTRINSIC to the individual subject to which they are attributed : two of them, *quantity* (e.g. two cubits in size) and *quality* (e.g. white, learned), are inherent

---

[8] For the difference between substantial essence and accidental essence we convey by our logical predicates, see *General Metaphysics*, 83 f.

in the subject considered in itself, absolutely ; a third, *relation* (e.g. double), is affirmable of the subject in virtue of some connexion with some thing or things other than itself. Some predicates, on the other hand, represent something EXTRINSIC to the subject : *place* (e.g. in the street) and *time* (e.g. yesterday) are respectively the measure of quantity and duration. *Action* and '*passion*' (i.e. being acted upon) are affirmable of a subject because it is the principle of the former and the object or end of the latter (e.g. he cuts a stone, a stone is cut). The exact meaning of the two remaining categories has provoked considerable discussion among commentators of Aristotle, but we think the philologist Max Müller has hit upon the right meaning by interpreting κεῖσθαι as *intransitive action* (e.g. I walk, I am afraid) and ἔχειν as the *passive intransitive state* (e.g. I am well) [9].

16. The Predicables.—Human thought has the two features of being *abstractive* and of *uniting* its ideas (*General Introduction*, **2**). It represents some reality of nature by means of a number of abstract notes that are potentially universal, i.e. are found to be universal upon reflection. Now the question arises how the mind unites these abstract notes or predicates in the single object which is the subject. What is the *relation* which exists between subject and predicate ? On what ground, with what justification, for what precise reason, can such and such an attribute be predicated of such and such a subject ? There is more than one answer : there are different relations or *predicables*, there are different ways or *modes in which things are predicable of other things.*

1. *Necessary, essential predicables.*—Certain qualities or notes constitute the essence or class-nature of a thing, are that which make the thing to be what it is (quod quid est, τὸ τί ἦν εἶναι), and without which it could not exist nor be conceived (e.g. the notes of animality and rationality in the case of man).

2. *Necessary, non-essential predicables.*—Other notes do not constitute the essence but are *necessarily* derived from it, and serve to reveal and develop the subject's essential perfection ; they are called its *properties* (proprium, ἴδιον).

3. *Contingent or accidental predicables.*—Lastly, there are other attributes that have only a contingent connexion with

---

[9] St. THOMAS, *In V Met.*, lect. 9.

the essence, which are called *contingent accidents* (contingit ut sint, συμβεβηκός) or simply *accidents* [10].

The first class, essential predicables, admit of a subdivision. For the object of the intellect is not the individual essence but the *specific* essence that it represents by a number of abstract, universal concepts. *Species* (εἶδος), then, designates the sum-total of the abstract, universal notes that together make up an essence as the human mind knows it [11]. Such of these notes constitutive of the species as are common also to other species form a *genus* (γένος), whilst the others, and therefore those peculiar to it, which differentiate it from all other species of the same genus, are the *specific difference* (differentia, διαφορά). Thus of essential predicables there are three distinct kinds— *species* and its two constitutive parts, *genus* and *differentia*.

To the three kinds of essential predicables must be added property and accident, and we find we have in all *five predicables*.

Properties are those determinations of a subject which though not of its essence are a necessary accompaniment of it, and in consequence can never exist apart from it. Indeed we say a thing is *proper*, or peculiar, to a specific type when it belongs *exclusively* to the species in question, is *universally* present whenever it is realized, and is *constant* throughout in every instance : ' proprium dicitur quod convenit *soli* alicui speciei, *omni* et *semper* '. Thus the faculty of learning to read and write is proper to man ; incorruptibility is proper to immaterial substances ; limitation is proper to creatures. In this, its strict acceptation, property and essence have the same exten-sion ; when one of the three conditions mentioned is not verified by a quality, it is not a true property, it is not conver-tible with the essence to which it attaches. The term property may however with reason be used in a less strict sense in this latter case, when a quality has one or two of the characteristics of the true property ; when, for instance, it belongs *exclu-sively* to a specific type, but is to be found neither universally

[10] There is opportunity here for confusing *ontological* accident (necessary or contingent) which is opposed to substance with *logical* accident which is immediately opposed to essence and to properties, and which is therefore relative to the subject of which it is predicated ; what is predicated as acci-dental of one subject may be predicated of another as essential.

[11] The student must be on his guard against confusing *logical species*, the meaning of which we have just defined, with the same term used in *natural science*. In the latter case it designates a group of individuals which are *inter se* fertile.

nor constantly in all beings representative of that type : thus to be a doctor or a mathematician is, in this sense, proper to man. Similarly a quality found in every individual of a species and found there always, yet not belonging to beings of that species only, can be called a property : in this sense does Porphyry say of man that it is proper to him to have two legs. So, too, may be called a property what is common to all the representatives of a species and to them only, but which belongs to them merely for a time ; for instance, according to Porphyry, it is proper to man to have white hair in old age.

The *common accidental quality*, or *accident* ($\sigma\upsilon\mu\beta\epsilon\beta\eta\kappa\acute{o}\varsigma$, opposed to $\H{\iota}\delta\iota\upsilon\nu$, *accidens commune* opposed to *proprium*), may best be defined negatively, as a quality that is not a property in the strict sense. As a positive definition Porphyry says that an accident is that quality to the absence or presence of which the essence of a subject is indifferent, ' accidens est id quod adest et abest praeter subjecti corruptionem '. He goes on to say that this accidental quality may be constant or not : an animal may at one time be sleeping and at another not ; a raven remains always black. Hence it must be noted that not every constant quality is a property. Mere observation is not sufficient to enable us to decide what is a property. As we shall see later, the discrimination between a property and what is accidental is the object of scientific induction and demands the employment of experimental methods.

17. Comprehension and Extension of Concepts.—Between the different predicables there exist certain relations of subordination for the right understanding of which it is necessary to notice two logical qualities of abstract concepts, namely their comprehension and extension.

The *comprehension* of an idea—or, as it is variously termed, its connotation, implication, intent or intension [12]—is its content, the sum-total of the characteristics or notes discovered to be contained in it. If we take as an instance the idea ' man ', its connotation or the notes it embodies are the various characteristics we have drawn by abstraction from individual man. The *extension*, denotation, or application of an idea, is its sphere or scope of application, the number of subjects to

[11] See Vol. I, p. 5, footnote.

which it is or can be applied or, in other words, to which it extends.

The abstract, universal concept is thus considered as a *metaphysical whole* and as a *logical whole*. The concept ' man ' viewed as to its comprehension—i.e. as comprising the notes of corporeity, life, sensibility and reason, is a metaphysical whole made up of so many metaphysical parts (*Gen. Metaphysics*, **46**). Viewed in its extension, i.e. as predicable of all men, past, present, future and merely possible, it forms a logical whole of which men taken distributively are the logical parts. The two Latin words ' *totus* ' and ' *omnis* ' correspond exactly to this distinction.

An idea is of greater or less comprehension in proportion to the number of notes it includes. It has a greater or less extension in proportion as it may be applied to a larger or smaller number of subjects. These two qualities of the concept vary inversely : *the greater the comprehension the less the extension, and vice versa.*

If we compare two or more ideas in respect of their extension and comprehension we shall discover that there are certain relations between the ideas.

18. Subordination of Ideas in Respect of their Extension.—As some ideas are more universal, i.e. are of wider application than others, among concepts referring to the same category there is a logical scale. At the bottom is *individual substance*, which is predicable of no subject and is the ultimate subject of all predication. Immediately above this comes the *species* asserted of the individual. Next the *genus* which is predicated both of the subaltern species and the individuals. Of genera there may be many, *proximate* or immediate, *subaltern* or intermediate, surmounted by the most general of all, the highest or *supreme genus*. The subjoined table, known as Porphyry's tree, shows the essential predicables of the category of substance and their mutual subordination.

19. Comparison of Ideas in Respect of their Comprehension. Relations of Identity and Opposition.—Two ideas are *identical* or *different* according as their contents are the same or different (e.g. the ideas of man and rational animal are identical ; not so those of man and animal).

Non-identical ideas are either *compatible* (e.g. those of liquid and sugar) or *incompatible* (e.g. those of liquid and solid).

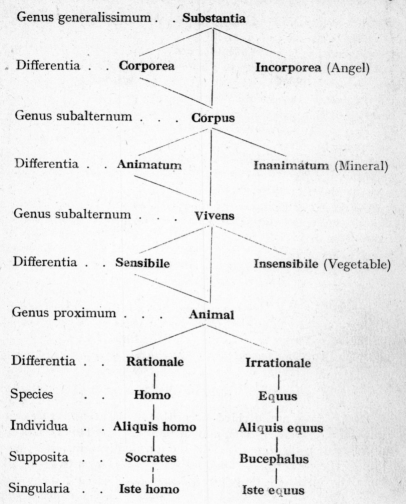

Genus generalissimum . . **Substantia**

Differentia . . **Corporea**   **Incorporea** (Angel)

Genus subalternum . . . **Corpus**

Differentia . . **Animatum**   **Inanimatum** (Mineral)

Genus subalternum . . . **Vivens**

Differentia . . **Sensibile**   **Insensibile** (Vegetable)

Genus proximum . . . **Animal**

Differentia . . **Rationale**   **Irrationale**

Species . . **Homo**   **Equus**

Individua . . **Aliquis homo**   **Aliquis equus**

Supposita . . **Socrates**   **Bucephalus**

Singularia . . **Iste homo**   **Iste equus**

Incompatibility of ideas or *opposition* is of four kinds: *contradictory*, *privative*, *contrary* and *relative*.

1. *Contradictory* opposition exists between two ideas when they have *nothing* in common, inasmuch as one of them is being and the other nothing, one is neither more nor less than the negation of the other (e.g. white and not-white, just and not-just).

2. *Privation* is the absence of a perfection in a subject

capable by its nature of possessing it, ' negatio alicujus formae in subjecto apto nato habere illam ' (e.g. blindness is the privation of sight, as is death of life). But it is not merely synonymous with negation or absence ; a mineral does not possess sight, but it cannot be said to be deprived of it.

3. *Contrary* opposition exists between the two extremes of a series of things belonging to the same genus. For instance, if degrees of light are mentally represented as a series, the two extremes, black and white, are contraries. Contrariety exists between things which cannot both exist at the same time in the same subject : health and sickness, justice and injustice, courage and cowardice, are all examples.

4. *Relation* or relative opposition exists when two ideas are dependent upon each other for their meaning ; e.g. the ideas of father and son, of double and half, of knowledge and that which is known.

II. Division of Concepts

20. Principles of Division.—Concepts or ideas may be divided (I) according to the *object* of the concept, i.e. the particular aspect, seized upon by the mind, of the knowable thing ; (II) according to the *manner of representing* the object known ; and (III) according to the *manner of their formation*. But these bases are such that the divisions are not mutually exclusive.

21. I. Ideas are divided according to Content.—1. *Transcendental, generic, specific* and *singular* ideas. This is a division based on the *degrees* of abstraction involved in the formation of the concept. If abstraction goes so far as to grasp all the determinations that an object is possessed of, including even those which constitute it an individual, the concept engendered is a *singular* one : e.g. the idea of Caesar, of Napoleon. If, however, the idea conveys a less determinate representation, embodying only such notes of an object as it possesses in common either with other individuals of the same species or with other species of the same genus, it is either a *specific* or *generic* idea ; and in both cases it is *universal*. Further, the content of an idea may be even less full ; the mind may conceive things under the aspect of those characteristics that they all share in common, that are possessed by all beings of the universe, in a word, its concept may be a *transcendental* one—'transcendit enim omne genus, omnem categoriam', its extension goes beyond all the categories. These transcendental notions are only six in number : *ens, res, unum, aliquid, verum, bonum* (*Gen. Metaphysics*, **37** ff.).

Note that when several individuals are considered as forming one whole, the idea representing them is called a *collective* idea ; such is the idea of ' people ', ' army '. But care must be taken not to confuse ' collective ' with ' universal ' idea.

2. *Adequate* and *inadequate* ideas. Of these the former embody all the characteristics of an object, or at least all those coming within the natural scope of the intellect. The latter are less full in their content ; they may be confused, indefinite and indistinct, so as to represent the object in a way that does not enable us to distinguish it from all others (e.g. ' fish ' as an animal which swims) ; or they may be clear and distinct, containing along with other notes common to other things some note peculiar to the thing represented and differentiating it from all others (e.g. ' fish ' as the animal which breathes only through its gills).

3. *Complex* and *simple* ideas. An idea is *complex* if it is made up of several elements each of which may stand as predicate ; thus ' just man ' is such an idea. But ' just ' and ' man ' are both *simple* ideas.

22. II. Ideas are divided according to their Manner of representing their Object, chiefly into *concrete* and *abstract, positive* and *negative, proper* and *analogous.*

1. There is no such thing really as a strictly *concrete* idea ; the term is improperly used to signify a note or quality *as existing in a subject :* for instance, the idea ' white ' represents a quality as belonging to some concrete subject. Whereas the so-called *abstract* idea (although all ideas are in reality abstract) represents a note *as if* it were something existing apart from a subject ; it is the result of the mind singling out or abstracting some note and disregarding that it is the note of a subject : e.g. ' whiteness ', ' animality '. Hence whilst the concrete idea is the result of one abstractive act, the abstract idea results from a double abstraction, is consequent upon reflection.

2. A *positive* idea is one which represents a thing by means of attributes that it really possesses : e.g. ' life ', ' light '. A

negative idea is one which gives us knowledge of a thing by emphasising the absence of a quality which does not belong to it : e.g. ' darkness ', ' death '.

3. A positive idea is *proper* when it connotes a property, that is, some quality which is distinctive of the being as it is positively in reality. An idea is *analogical* if it denotes an object that is beyond the grasp of the mind and requiring for its representation a comparison with something else known with proper knowledge : thus we form an analogous idea of life in God from our knowledge of created life, and of the presence of spirits from our idea of the presence of bodies in space.

23. III. Ideas are divided according to the Manner of their Formation into *immediate* and *mediate* ideas. Ideas are *immediate* or *intuitive* when the object of apprehension is itself united to the intellect or at least itself produces its own representation in it. When an object depends for its being known upon another object also being known, the apprehension or idea is said to be *mediate*. And in this case it is proper or analogical according as the object which serves to make the second known is of like or unlike nature to it. As distinct from intuitive knowledge, mediate is sometimes called *discursive* knowledge.

ART. II. TERMS

I. The Object and Qualities of the Term

24. The Object of the Term.—Terms or names are vocal signs expressive of objects as they are conceived by the mind ; they are not the expression of subjective concepts as such nor of things as they are in nature, in themselves ; but they stand for things *precisely as the mind conceives them*, they denote *objects known* : ' voces referuntur ad res significandas mediante conceptione intellectus ' [13]. The word ' sun ', for instance, does not stand for our idea of sun but for the sun itself ; and yet the word does not refer directly to the sun as it exists in the order of nature, since for ages the word connoted a body that revolved round our planet—which is evidently not true of the sun itself

---

[13] St. Thomas, *Sum. Theol.*, I, q. 13, a. 1.

but only of the sun as thought to be by men before the discovery of Galileo and Copernicus.

It belongs to psychology to study the nature and functions of language.

25. The Ten Parts of Speech.—Just as thought-objects admit of a tenfold division into the ten categories, so ten parts of speech are distinguished by grammarians corresponding to the ten categories of concepts. The correspondence between the categories and the parts of speech is however not quite adequate.

The first subject of every logical predication is that which the senses perceive in its concrete reality and which at the first mental contact, so to speak, is grasped only as something indeterminate, as ' this something—hoc aliquid '. Subsequently and gradually this indeterminate object is invested in the mind with formal determinations which the mind conceives by abstraction and which the terms of language express. The principal of these are expressed by the substantive, the adjective and the verb-predicate, which together constitute the essential materials of language.

1. Our first determination of a thing is by its essence or its very *substance*, and this we designate by the *noun* or *substantive*. The noun (or pronoun) is used to denote every object which is a substance or every quality considered as if it were a substance : e.g. man, horse, height, whiteness. The latter case grammarians speak of as an ' abstract noun ' : in reality all nouns are abstract, and so *common*, except when the word is used in a secondary sense and designates a substance further determined, i.e. individualized, when it is a *proper* noun.

2. The determinations which inhere in a subject, whether qualitative or quantitative, we express by the *adjective*.

3. The *verb-predicate* expresses action of or on a subject. The verb ' to be ', it must be noted, either expresses actual existence (e.g. I am = I exist) or is nothing else than a logical copula connecting subject and predicate, and is implied in every verb-predicate (e.g. I hear = I am hearing).

It is worthy of remark, moreover, that the results of philological research bear out what we have said of logical concepts, for just as predicates of judgments are abstract, so the primitive forms or roots of language are observed to express abstract ideas.

II. Division of Terms

26. Division of Terms.—Although the divisions we have noticed of concepts apply in general also to terms, a few remarks are called for.

1. Terms are either *common* or *singular*. Common terms are either *transcendental* or simply *general* and *universal ;* and if the latter, they are *generic* or *specific.*

Generic and specific terms are *univocal,* and transcendental ones *analogical,* according to a distinction based on the following division of terms.

2. Terms are *univocal* when by means of the same name they designate things which verify the same essential definition : the name ' animal ' is applied with identically the same meaning to man and cow, inasmuch as both comply with the definition of sentient living being. Terms are *equivocal* when by means of the same name they designate different things giving respectively different concepts : e.g. the name ' dog ' in its application to an animal and to a constellation. Terms are *analogical* when they stand for things which in the mind are represented by concepts that are only partly the same ; thus, when we say of material bodies and of spirits that they occupy space, the words ' occupy ' and ' space ' are not used in the same but in an analogous sense.

3. Terms, like concepts, are *simple* or *complex,* i.e. are single- or many-worded.

4. They are *concrete* or *abstract :* of the former ' white ' is an example, of the latter ' whiteness '.

5. They are *positive* or *negative :* e.g. ' death ', ' immortality '. Note that a positive term may be used to render a negative idea and vice versa.

6. Terms are *direct* or *reflex :* e.g. ' substance ', ' man ', are direct, ' genus ', ' species ' are reflex.

7. *Categorematic* terms are those which by themselves convey a complete meaning and thus are capable by themselves of fulfilling the rôle of subject or predicate (e.g. ' man ') ; *syncategorematic* terms are those which require to be used in conjunction with some other term (e.g. ' every ', ' none ').

CHAPTER III

THE FORMAL CAUSE OF LOGICAL ORDER

27. Introductory.—The introduction of order by the mind into its own acts, the arrangement of its ideas with a view to the acquisition of knowledge, is, as we have already said, a progressive work. The first step is judgment, when we formally attach a predicate to a subject. Next, by putting judgments together and comparing them we build up complex judgments and thus reason. Lastly, by a train of reasoning bearing upon one object we construct the more elaborate logical system of knowledge which we call a science.

Now this chapter will be divided into three main divisions corresponding to the threefold progressive formation of the order logic seeks to establish. The first main division (Art. I) in which judgment is studied falls into three subdivisions, dealing respectively with the nature of the judgment and the proposition (I), the various divisions of judgments and propositions (II), various relations existing between judgments and between propositions (III).

ART. I. THE JUDGMENT AND THE PROPOSITION

I. The Meaning of the Judgment and the Proposition

28. Definition.—The proposition, which is the verbal expression of the judgment, is an utterance announcing something about something else : ' propositio est oratio enunciativa ' ; ἀπόφανσις Aristotle calls it. Every utterance *signifies* something, ' omnis oratio est significativa ', φάσις φωνὴ σημαντική, but every utterance does not *announce* something. A term signifies something but it states nothing ; an imperative is not without signification, yet it makes no announcement ; likewise an entreaty [14]. ' An assertion may take an *affirmative* form or a

---

[14] Aristotle, *Perihermenias*, cc. IV and V.

negative form ; all more complex assertions are combinations
of these elemental enunciations '.   An assertion is made up of
two terms—subject and predicate, S and P—connected by
the verb ' to be '.   Looking then at only one feature of the
proposition, at a *property* disclosed by the mere analysis of
the notion, we may define a proposition as an utterance that
is true or false.

**29. The Place of the Judgment and the Proposition in
Thought.**—Not only is the judgment the chief act towards which
the progress of our thought converges, but in point of fact there
is no act of thought which does not terminate in an act of judgment.   Indeed whilst the mind seizes by successive acts of
simple apprehension the several attributes of some object
of knowledge—perhaps the sensible qualities of this tree I am
perceiving, the shape of its trunk and branches, the roughness
of its bark, the colour of its leaves and so forth,—there accompanies these acts a simultaneous apprehension of a something
subsisting, of a subject from which I have gathered my abstract
notes and to which I can refer them ; and my consideration
of these attributes apart—of external shape, roughness, and
colour—is really tantamount to attributing them in my mind
to this indeterminate subject which I am trying to describe,
to saying that they belong to it, to *judging* that a tree is what
they together connote.

The study of language supports and amplifies this testimony
of consciousness.   For the *invention of a name* is nothing but to
apply a concept, under the form of language, to some subject
which I denote in an indeterminate way by the demonstrative
pronoun ' this ' or ' that '.   As an instance in point, the etymology of the word ' wolf ', *lupus*, Sanskrit *Vrka*, shows it to mean
' that which tears in pieces ' ; to call the animal ' wolf ' therefore is nothing but to apply an abstract concept to something
otherwise indeterminate, to apply to this subject the attribute
of the act of lacerating.

II. Kinds of Judgments and Propositions

30. General Division of Propositions.—Some propositions
are *simple*, consisting only of subject, attribute and copula ;
others are *complex* or composed of several simple propositions
that are in some way connected.   Simple propositions allow

of a fourfold classification, namely, according to their matter (I), form (II), quantity (III), and quality (IV).

§ 1. *Classification of Simple Propositions*

31. I. Propositions are divided according to their Matter.— By the matter of a proposition is meant the terms mutually related as subject and predicate but considered previously to the formal assertion of this relation in the judgment. Now a proposition, to use the nomenclature of the Schoolmen, may be *in materia necessaria* or it may be *in materia contingenti*. It is the former, ' in necessary matter ', when the connexion between the two terms absolutely cannot be other than it is, and is apparent to the mind on the mere analysis of the terms, independently of all experience : e.g. $2 + 2 = 4$. A proposition is ' in contingent matter ' when the connexion between the two terms is such that it depends upon certain conditions in the order of contingent beings and consequently cannot be stated previously to the experience of it : e.g. water freezes at 32 deg. Fahrenheit. The contingent judgment of which logic takes cognizance must not be thought to be without the characteristic of necessity [15], but its necessity is a conditional one, whilst that of the judgment ' in necessary matter ' is an *absolute* necessity. Both judgments are necessary, but only the one kind is necessary in the sense of ' in necessary matter '.

The proposition ' in necessary matter ' is knowable by itself, ' propositio *per se nota* ' ; whereas the contingent proposition depends for its being known upon something else beyond the mere terms of the proposition, ' propositio *per aliud nota* '.

32. Two Kinds of Judgment in Necessary Matter.—1. In one class of judgments ' in necessary matter ' the connexion between the terms is necessary either because the subject, considered in its essential elements, is the *same term* as the predicate—which is a judgment of identity, as for instance that ' a square is an equilateral quadrangle', ' $2 = 1 + 1$ '— or because the subject *includes* the predicate inasmuch as the latter is some element in the essence of the subject, e.g. ' a square is a rectangle ', ' a man is intelligent '. In both cases

---

[15] The particular judgment ' in contingent matter' does not fall directly within the scope of science : *scientia non est de singularibus.*

the mere comparison of the two terms of the judgment is sufficient to make the *necessity* of their connexion evident.

2. In the second class the connexion is necessary because the predicate *necessarily involves* the subject, and in consequence cannot be defined without bringing it into its definition. This happens when the predicate is a *property* strictly so called of the subject, i.e. is not its essence but something necessarily resulting from it. Thus the definition of the predicate—be it simple or disjunctive—when juxtaposed with the essential notion of the subject shows up the necessary connexion of the two terms. Let us illustrate this :—(a) ' Five is a prime number ' is a proposition with a simple predicate. ' Prime number ' is by definition one which cannot be split up into groups each containing the same number of units [16]. Now in the elements of this definition is not to be found the number 5, nor is it the essential definition of 5 that it is a prime number ; but analyse the notion, split 5 up into groups so as to have $2 + 2 + 1$, and it immediately becomes evident that prime number cannot be defined without its necessarily agreeing with the number 5, inasmuch as it is a property of it. (b) ' Every number is either odd or even ' is a proposition with a disjunctive predicate. The attribute ' odd ' is not comprehended in the essential notion of number nor is it even a property ; the same may be said of attribute ' even '. But to be either odd or even, although it does not enter into the definition of number, is a necessary resultant of number ; for every number, unity excepted inasmuch as it is not reckoned a number, is divisible or not by two, is either odd or even.

The name for these two kinds of ' necessary ' propositions given by the Schoolmen, who herein followed Aristotle, was *duo modi dicendi* PER SE [17], καθ αὐτό, in contrast to the *modi dicendi* PER ACCIDENS, κατὰ συμβεβηκός.

---

[16] A prime number is generally defined as one divisible only by itself and unity.

[17] ' Per se dupliciter dicitur. Uno enim modo dicitur propositio per se, cujus praedicatum cadit in definitione subjecti sicut ista : Homo est animal ; animal enim cadit in definitione hominis. Et quia id quod est in definitione alicujus aliquo modo causa ejus, in his quae sunt per se, dicuntur praedicata esse causa subjecti. Alio modo dicitur propositio per se, cujus e contrario subjectum ponitur in definitione praedicati ; sicut si dicatur : Nasus est simus, vel numerus est par ; simum enim nihil aliud est quam nasus curvus, et par nihil aliud est quam numerus medietatem habens, et in istis subjectum est causa praedicati '. St. Thomas, *De anima*, lib. II, lect. 14.

It must be added that the necessity of the connexion is sometimes apparent *immediately*, sometimes *mediately*, according as the analysis of the terms is straightforward or difficult. But this is an entirely subjective matter and in no way affects the nature of the connexion.

33. Different Nomenclature for the Same Division.—Propositions in necessary matter are also called *absolute* or *metaphysical* propositions, as distinct from conditional or physical ones, seeing that their object is metaphysically necessary and independent of the conditions belonging to contingent beings.

They are also called *rational* or *pure* propositions by way of emphasising that reason by itself, pure reason, is capable of perceiving their truth ; contingent propositions are then experimental or empirical inasmuch as the knowledge of them depends upon an acquaintance with fact.

Lastly, since the days of Kant the two classes of propositions are respectively called *a priori* and *a posteriori*, or again, *analytic* and *synthetic*. It is very important to notice that these terms in Kantian and post-Kantian philosophy bear a different signification from that used in Scholastic philosophy [18]. The extent of this deep-rooted difference between the ' necessary ' and contingent judgments of Scholasticism and the analytic and synthetic judgments of Kantianism is a matter which engaged our attention in Criteriology (**40**).

34. II. Propositions are divided according to their Form.— *Form* here means the union of subject and predicate precisely as it is realized in the assertion of the judgment.

1. A proposition may be *affirmative* or *negative* [19], according as the mind declares that the predicate belongs, or does not

---

[18] JOYCE (*op. cit.*, p. 52, 53) thus succinctly contrasts :—

The Scholastic definitions—

An Analytic proposition is one in which either the predicate is contained in the intension of the subject, or the subject in the intension of the predicate.

A Synthetic proposition is one in which the connexion of subject and predicate is not involved in the intension of the terms.

The modern definitions—

An Analytic proposition is one in which the predicate is contained in the definition of the subject.

A Synthetic proposition is one in which the predicate is not contained in the notion of the subject.— TRS.

[19] A *negative* proposition may sometimes assume the appearance of an affirmative one : e.g. ' This man is lacking in generosity ' means ' is not generous ' ; similarly an apparently negative proposition may be really affirmative : e.g. ' Man is not infallible '. ' The world is not infinite '.

belong, to the subject, and accordingly must be united (compositio) or not united (divisio) with it [20].

2. Closely allied to form is the *modality* of judgments or the particular manner which qualifies the union of predicate and subject. On this score judgments may be divided into *apodeictic, empirical* or *assertoric,* and *problematic*—' omnis propositio eo continetur, ut aut inesse, aut necessario inesse, aut posse contingere ut insit, enuntiet ' [21].

The *apodeictic* proposition (which must not be confused with the proposition in necessary matter) asserts that the predicate either necessarily belongs to, or else is necessarily repugnant to, the subject : e.g. ' The world must have a first cause ', ' It is impossible for the world to exist by itself '.

The *assertoric* proposition declares that the predicate belongs to the subject as a matter of fact : e.g. ' Mr. X died yesterday '.

The *problematic* proposition, which is founded on simple possibility [22], is a tentative declaration of the occurrence or non-occurrence of some event that is not by nature connected with a determining cause : e.g. ' It is possible that Mr. X is appointed commander-in-chief '.

35. Import or Logical Value of the Predicate of a Proposition.—The intension and extension of the predicate depend upon the *form* of the proposition : in an affirmative proposition they are in inverse proportion to what they are in a negative one.

1. In an *affirmative* proposition the predicate is taken according to the whole of its comprehension, although this be less than the comprehension of the subject, and according to part only of its extension. All the notes of the predicate, taken together or separately, are applied to the subject, but the subject need not, and in fact does not, stand precisely in virtue of the enunciation for more than a part of the objects

---

[20] Every proposition announcing something (P) about a subject (S) effects a *mental* union (compositio) of S and P. The question is here concerning whether the predicate belongs *objectively* to the subject or not. St. Thomas, *In Periher.*, lect. III.

[21] Aristotle, *Analyt. pr.*, I, 2.

[22] By *possible* Aristotle does not mean here not-contradictory, but *contingent.* St. Thomas understands the same : ' Dicitur *necessarium* quod in sua natura determinatum est solum ad esse ; *impossibile* autem quod est determinatum solum ad non esse ; *possibile* autem quod ad neutrum est omnino determinatum, sive se habeat magis ad unum quam ad alterum, sive se habeat aequaliter ad utrumque, quod dicitur contingens ad utrumlibet '. *In Periher.*, lect. 14, n. 8.

included in the extension of the predicate : thus when I assert that ' the dog is a vertebrate ', I mean to declare that the dog has all the qualities, taken collectively and distributively, connoted by the idea ' vertebrate ' ; but I do not affirm that there are no other vertebrates besides the dog.

There is, however, one exception to be made, namely in the case of essential definitions : here the definition (P) and the thing defined (S) have the same extension and the same comprehension.

2. In a *negative* proposition the opposite is the case, the predicate is taken in the whole of its extension, yet only according to some indefinite portion of its comprehension : thus, that ' the mollusc is not a vertebrate ' means that the mollusc does not belong to the whole vertebrate class, inasmuch as, even though it may possess some note or other of the vertebrate class, it does not verify the whole definition of vertebrate ; I exclude all subjects to which the idea ' vertebrate ' may be applied, but I do not on this account exclude all the notes which this idea contains.

36. III. Propositions are divided according to their Quantity. —Propositions may be *universal, singular* or *particular, indefinite*.

A *universal* proposition is one which declares that an attribute belongs to *all* the subjects denoted by an idea or that it belongs to *none* of them : e.g. ' All men are mortal ', ' No man escapes death '.

A *singular* proposition is one which declares that an attribute belongs to *one* individual. Should the subject stand for a definite group of individuals, it is said to be a *collective* subject, but as far as logic is concerned it is not different from a singular one. Every proposition in which the subject is not universal is a *particular* proposition, no matter whether the subject be many individuals of the same class or simply one individual : e.g. ' Some men are wise ', ' The British nation is prosperous '.

An *indefinite* proposition is one in which the identity or non-identity of subject and predicate is expressed, yet so as to leave it ambiguous whether the subject is taken in the whole or a part of its extension : e.g. ' An old man is melancholy ', where the subject may be ' one ', ' all ' or ' some ' old men.

Attention need hardly be called to the superior importance

of the universal proposition over the particular, for inasmuch as the particular is contained in the universal a knowledge of the latter implies a virtual knowledge of the former, while the converse is not true.

37. IV. Propositions are divided according to their Quality.— Propositions are *true* or *false* according as the connexion declared between subject and predicate is in conformity or not with fact [23].

§ 2.   *Classification of Compound Propositions*

38. Division of Complex Propositions.—The *compound*, or better *complex*, proposition is really an assertion containing several simple propositions.   Of these the logicians of Port Royal enumerate six kinds in which it is immediately evident that there is more than one proposition and four where this is less evident.   Let us define and establish the conditions required for their truth.

1. The first six propositions are *copulative, disjunctive, conditional, causal, relative* and *adversative.*

(*a*) A *copulative* proposition is one in which there are several subjects or several predicates joined by the affirmative or negative conjunctions ' and ' or ' nor '.   This proposition is true only when each of its parts is true.   In the case where the conjunction is negative the proposition is also called a *remotive* proposition.

(*b*) A *disjunctive* proposition is one in which there are two incompatible predicates, one alone of which can be true : e.g. ' Every free action is morally good or bad '.   For such a proposition to be true the two members must be so opposed to each other as to admit of no middle proposition.

(*c*) A *conditional* proposition is one which contains two parts linked together by the conjunction ' if ' ; the first part containing the condition is termed the *antecedent*, the second the *consequent;* e.g. ' If the soul is spiritual, it is immortal '.   This kind of proposition is true when the *consequence* involved is true, even if the antecedent and consequent are false : e.g. ' If the animal soul were spiritual, it would be immortal '.

(*d*) A *causal* proposition is one made up of two parts joined

---

[23] By the *quality* of a proposition many authors understand what we have called *form*, i.e. whether it is affirmative or negative.   The question is one rather of words than of importance.

by a conjunction signifying a cause : e.g. ' Logic is studied because truth is sought '. To this class belongs the *reduplicative* proposition : e.g. ' Evil, as evil (or *qua* evil), is not attractive '. For all these propositions it is not sufficient that the two parts be true but also, and in particular, that one should be the real cause of the other.

(*e*) A *relative* proposition is one which expresses a relation, and on the accuracy of this depends the truth of the proposition : e.g. ' As a man lives, so does he die '.

(*f*) An *adversative* or *discretive* proposition is one which contains one or more different judgments separated by some adversative conjunction, ' but ', ' as ', ' nevertheless ', etc. : e.g. ' Happiness depends not upon riches but upon virtue '. For its truth such a proposition depends both on the truth of the parts and on the opposition set between them.

2. The four other kinds of propositions, called sometimes *exponible* propositions, which are in appearance simple but in reality compound, are *exclusive, exceptive, comparative* and *inceptive* or *desitive* propositions.

(*a*) An *exclusive* proposition is one which asserts that an attribute belongs to one subject only : e.g. ' God alone is to be loved for His own sake '.

(*b*) An *exceptive* proposition is one which affirms an attribute of a subject but with a restriction excluding part of its extension : e.g. ' All virtues admit of an excess except the love of God '.

(*c*) A *comparative* proposition is one which not only asserts that a thing possesses certain attributes but that it possesses them in a greater or less degree than some other thing : e.g. ' Wisdom is better than riches.'

(*d*) *Inceptive* and *desitive* are those which respectively assert that a certain thing has commenced or ceased to enjoy certain attributes : e.g. ' Slavery ceased in the British Dominions in 1834 '.

Each of these four propositions really contains two separate judgments and therefore is not true unless both parts are true.

III. Relations between Propositions

39. Relations between Propositions.—Propositions may bear different relations to one another which it is necessary to distinguish, namely of *equivalence, conversion, subordination* and *opposition*.

40. Equivalence of Propositions.—Those propositions are said to be *equivalent* which differ from one another in their expression whilst not in meaning and logical value. For example, ' All men are mortal ', ' No men are immortal ' [24].

41. Conversion of Propositions.—*Conversion* consists in so transposing the two terms of a proposition that the new proposition thus obtained is true if the original one is.

(*a*) A *universal negative* proposition is convertible since both its terms are universal : e.g. ' No mineral performs vital actions ' is as true as ' Any being performing vital actions is not a mineral '.

(*b*) A *particular affirmative* proposition is likewise convertible for the same reason that both terms are of equal extension : e.g. ' Some sensitive beings are endowed with reason ', ' Some beings endowed with reason are sensitive '. In both these cases the conversion is evident ; the two terms are clearly transposable. The question arises whether these are the only two cases. The answer would seem to be in the affirmative if we consider that—

(*c*) In the first place, the conversion of *singular* propositions is not real conversion since a concrete, or determined, individual term, which ultimately represents a ' first substance ', cannot serve as a basis of attribution. Thus, when I say that ' Peter is wise ' or ' One of the class of wise men is Peter ', the term ' Peter ' is in spite of the conversion still the subject.

(*d*) And in the second place, a *universal affirmative* proposition allows of conversion in the sense that subject and predicate may change places, but only *on the condition* that the predicate when made subject be limited in its extension. Thus ' All men are sensitive ' may become ' Some sensitive beings are men ', but the conversion is *imperfect* or, as it is otherwise called, *per accidens*, conversion *by limitation*. Among these propositions there is, however, one exception, namely that in which the predicate is an essential definition and thus subject and predicate are of equal extension. In other cases ' imperfect ' conversion is not true conversion, because instead of the two

---

[24] The term used by many Latin writers and adopted by Mill and Mansel is *equipollence*. The process of changing a proposition into its equivalent is commonly known as *obversion*, the new proposition being spoken of as the *obverse* of the original proposition, the *obvertend* (cp. *converse* and *convertend*).—TRS.

terms being simply substituted for each other, according to the definition of conversion, one term (P) is altered by having its extension restricted.

42. Relations of Opposition and Subordination.—These relations between propositions give rise to four different classes of propositions, namely *contradictory, contrary, subcontrary* and *subaltern.* The first two alone present the characteristic of true relative opposition.

(*a*) Two propositions are said to be *contradictories* if they are so opposed to each other as to exclude a middle proposition. They differ both in form and in quantity. Compare, e.g., ' All men are white ' with ' Some men are not white ' [25].

(*b*) Two propositions are said to be *contraries* which have the same universal quantity but differ in form, and are thus so opposed as to allow of a middle proposition being true. Compare ' All men are just ' and ' No men are just ' ; between these two extreme propositions a third or middle proposition may be true, that ' Some men are not just '.

(*c*) Propositions which differ in form only and are each particular in quantity, are *subcontraries :* e.g. ' Some men are just ', ' Some men are not just '.

(*d*) Propositions of the same form but of different quantities are *subalterns :* e.g. ' All men are just ', ' Some men are just ' ; or again, ' No man is just ', ' Some men are not just '.

It is the custom of logicians to make use of the conventional letters A E I O to symbolize propositions under their double aspect of quantity and form :—

A stands for a universal affirmative proposition.

E stands for a universal negative proposition.

I stands for a particular affirmative proposition.

O stands for a particular negative proposition.

The following diagram will serve to show the different modes of contradictory and contrary opposition [26] :—

---

[25] ARISTOTLE, *Periherm.*, c. VI.

[26] ' Universalis (propositio) affirmativa, et universalis negativa sunt contrariae, sicut *Omnis homo est justus, Nullus homo est justus ;* quia scilicet universalis negatio non solum removet universalem affirmationem, sed etiam designat extremam distantiam, in quantum negat totum, quod affirmatio ponit : et hoc pertinet ad rationem *contrarietatis,* et ideo particularis affirmativa et negativa se habent sicut medium inter contraria. . . . In *contradictoriis* negatio non plus facit, nisi quod removeat affirmationem '. ST. THOMAS, *In Periher.*, lect. 11.

43. Rules concerning the Truth and Falsity of Opposed Propositions.—1. *Contradictories cannot both be true nor both false*, since one is nothing more or less than the negation of the other. Hence if one is true, the other is false, and vice versa : if it is true that ' All men are just ', it cannot be true that ' Some men are not just '.

2. *Contraries cannot both be true, but both may be false.*—Contraries cannot both be true, for if they were the contradictories would both be true at the same time. If it is true that ' All men are just ', the contradictory ' Some men are not just ' is false. If it is false to say that ' Some men are not just, even one man ', still more is it false to say that ' Every man is not just ', or which comes to the same, ' No men are just '. The proposition ' No men are just ' is the contrary of the proposition ' All men are just '.

But the falsity of a proposition does not imply the truth of the contrary. It may be untrue that ' All men are just ' without its being true that ' No men are just ' ; there may be some men just, even though all men are not.

3. *Subcontraries may both be true, but both cannot be false.*— Both may be true : compare ' Some men are just ', ' Some men are not just ' ; justice may be found in one group of men without being the virtue of another group. But both cannot be false, for were they so the two contradictories would be false : if we suppose it untrue that ' Some men are just ', the contradictory ' No men are just ' must be true ; still more, then, must it be true that ' Some men are not just ', which is the subcontrary.

44. Rules concerning the Truth and Falsity of Subordinate Propositions.—The particular propositions I and O are respectively subordinate to their universals A and E. The truth of the universals implies that of the subalterns ; but the truth of the subalterns does not entail that of the universals. Again, if the particulars are false, so too are the universals ; but falsity of the universals does not imply the same of the particulars [27].

45. Immediate Inferences.—It will be seen presently that in a real inference the conclusion results from a comparison of three different terms, and that this comparison is made in two propositions or premisses of an argument. When, however, as is sometimes the case, it is permissible to draw a conclusion directly from a single assertion, the reasoning is called an *immediate inference* or *eduction*. Such inferences are obtainable through the *conversion*, *opposition*, and *subordination* of propositions. The rules we have just given are sufficient guide to show how these inferences may legitimately be made.

ART. II.　REASONING

46. Introductory.—In the present chapter we are considering the orderly arrangement of our knowledge or, as we have said, the formation of logical order. In the first article we saw how concepts are arranged in the judgment, and terms in the proposition. We then classified judgments before making a comparison of them. Judgments, however, are only elements in a still larger system of thought : from judgments that we already know we proceed to a new judgment by means of a discursive process called *reasoning* or inference. This process, whether expressed in words or in writing, is known as the *syllogism*. In this Article we have therefore to consider first (I) the nature of reasoning and of the syllogism, and next (II) the different forms they may assume.

---

[27] In the case of modal propositions the contradiction between affirmation and negation lies not with the attribute of the proposition but with the *verb*. The typical cases of opposition between modal propositions are best seen from the following square :—

S is necessarily P (S must be P)	CONTRADICTORIES	S is not necessarily P (S need not be P)
	CONTRARIES	
S is possibly P (S may be P)	CONTRADICTORIES	S is not possibly P (S cannot be P)

I. Nature of Reasoning and the Syllogism

47. Nature of Reasoning.—The end of all progress in knowledge is the attainment of truth. Now some truths are known *immediately*, others *mediately* through the medium of truths that have been immediately apprehended. Those of the one kind, which give rise to the second, are termed *principles ;* those of the other, *consequences* or *conclusions* flowing from principles. The passage from principles to a conclusion is *reasoning*.

As a conclusion is a proposition, it therefore asserts a predicate of a subject. When it is quite apparent that the predicate belongs to the subject, the proposition is *evident* (*Criteriology*, **52**). Evidence may be *immediate*, i.e. when the objective connexion between the predicate and the subject is immediately apprehended, and in this case the *certitude* engendered is also called immediate. Or, as is the case in most of our judgments, it may be *mediate ;* it may appear only after the mind has made use of one or more *middle terms*, i.e. common terms of comparison between the subject and predicate : such evidence furnishes *mediate certitude* or what is known as the certitude of *reasoning*. It is this kind of evidence which is characteristic of conclusions.

The reason why we have to proceed by means of comparisons is the disproportion existing between the complexity of knowable things and the relative feebleness of our mind striving to know them [28].

The power of reasoning or ratiocination is a perfection, yet such that metaphysicians call it a *mixed* perfection because it implies imperfection ; perfection, that is to say, because to be *able* to arrive at the truth is better than not to reason and to have to remain ignorant of it, and imperfection inasmuch as it is a circuitous and difficult way of attaining it.

48. The Syllogism and its Terminology.—Reasoning, then, consists in the comparison of two concepts—the S and P of a judgment to be established as conclusion—with a common

---

[28] 'Discursus rationis semper incipit ab intellectu et terminatur ad intellectum ; ratiocinamur enim procedendo ex quibusdam intellectis ; et tunc rationis discursus perficitur, quando ad hoc pervenimus ut intelligamus id quod prius erat ignotum. Quod ergo ratiocinamur, ex aliquo praecedenti intellectu procedit'. St. Thomas, *Sum. Theol.*, II., q. 8, a. 1, ad 2.

third or ' mean ' concept, in order thus to discover whether objectively the one includes or excludes the other. Its perfect and simplest type of expression is the *syllogism*. By Aristotle the syllogism is defined as ' a discourse in which certain things being posited something else necessarily follows simply from their being posited ' [29].

When the reason asserts that the predicate belongs objectively to the subject, the conclusion is affirmative ; when it sees that one only of the terms agrees with the middle term and that the second does not, the conclusion is negative.

The two terms of the conclusion are called *extreme terms,* or simply *extremes,* in contrast to the ' mean ' or *middle term (medius terminus)* with which they are both compared. The predicate is called the *major extreme,* the subject the *minor extreme.*

The two propositions from which the conclusion is drawn are called the *premisses* (praemittuntur conclusioni), and together they form the *antecedent.* The premisses are those judgments which, to use the phrase of Aristotle, once being posited or supposed as true, involve the conclusion. The conclusion is called the *consequent.* Often the proposition asserted first is spoken of as the *major* premiss and the one asserted second the *minor ;* but a more accurate use of the words is to call the *major* (or *propositio*) that proposition in which the major term is compared with the middle term and the *minor* (or *assumpta*) that one in which the minor term is so compared.

The premisses and conclusion, antecedent and consequent, constitute the *matter* of the syllogism. The *form* lies in the nexus existing between the antecedent and consequent ; it is summed up in the ' therefore ' expressing the consequence (*consequentia, consecutio*) of the syllogism.

In studying the nature of reasoning we inquire how it is that ' when certain things are posited, something else necessarily follows *simply from their being posited* '.

49. Nature and Logical Basis of the Syllogism.—The following argument is a specimen of a syllogism : ' Triangles which have two sides equal have two angles equal ; but this triangle

[29] *Anal. pr.,* I, 1.

ABC has two sides equal ; therefore this triangle ABC has two angles equal '.

Reasoning is the bringing of some definite subject under the extension of an abstract type in order to infer that something which is predicable of the abstract type as such is likewise predicable of this definite subject.

The major of the syllogism is a *necessary* proposition, asserting that the predicate of the conclusion (the quality of having two angles equal) is *necessarily* connected with an *abstract* middle term (triangle having two sides equal). As an *abstract* concept the middle term is not actually universal but capable of becoming universal, of being *universalized ;* that is to say, by a further act of reflection it may be recognized as predicable of one or of several or of all the subjects of a species or a genus. In the minor the mind preceives that the middle term extends to the subject of the minor (that this triangle has two sides equal). When therefore the mind puts major and minor together and regards them simultaneously, it perceives that the predicate of the conclusion (having two angles equal) which belongs necessarily to the middle term (triangle with two sides equal) belongs likewise to the subject of the conclusion which falls within the extension of the middle term ; thus does it perceive the necessary connexion between the subject and predicate of the conclusion, which is the advance of thought it set out to achieve.

The syllogism is essentially a *mental act of universalization.* The principle on which it is founded may be enunciated thus : *Whatever is necessarily predicable of an abstract subject—the middle term—is predicable also of every subject falling under the extension of the middle term.* From this it is clear that the connexion established in the syllogism between the extremes and the middle term depends at once on the comprehension and on the extension of the terms. In the major, one of the extremes, the predicate of the conclusion, is connected with the middle term in respect of *comprehension : quaecumque sunt eadem uni tertio sunt eadem inter se.* In the minor, the same middle term is considered from the point of view of its *extension,* and on this score related to the second extreme, the subject of the conclusion : *Quidquid affirmatur de subjecto abstractim considerato, affirmandum est de omnibus et singulis ejus inferioribus,* uno verbo, *universaliter.—Quidquid negatur de*

*subjecto abstractim considerato, negandum est de omnibus et
singulis inferioribus ejus,* uno verbo, *universaliter* [30].

Although the syllogism we have taken as an example leads
to an affirmative conclusion, the analysis may be easily applied
to one resulting in a negative conclusion [31].

50. The Nature of the Necessity of Syllogistic Principles.—
The general law stated in the major premiss and serving as the
foundation of a syllogism is sometimes *metaphysical* and
absolute in character (e.g. the example just analysed), sometimes it is *physical* or *natural* and consequently *dependent on
conditions* which must be empirically ascertained (e.g. the law
that water has its maximum density at 4° Centigrade).

In the first case the predicate attributed to the subject
of the conclusion connotes either the whole or part of the
essence of the middle term or else a necessary property of
that essence.   Here the necessity of applying this predicate
to the subject of the conclusion is *absolute*.

In the second case the attribute is predicated of the middle
term in virtue of a law which has had to be ascertained by
experience ;   accordingly its predication of the subject is
hypothetically necessary.   These laws empirically ascertained
we discover by the method of reasoning known as induction, as will be pointed out in a subsequent part of this
treatise.

51. Logical First Principles.—The syllogism, we have just
seen, derives its cogency or proving force from a necessary
proposition.   The question arises, Whence does this proposition itself derive its logical value ?   You may say from a
previous process of reasoning.   Yet, as we saw in *Criteriology*
(52-54), an infinite series of inferences is impossible, or we could
never be sure we have a certain conclusion.   There must then
be some propositions which serve as starting-points for our
reasoning processes, propositions which themselves do not
stand in need of demonstration.   These are called *logical
principles,* and they assert simple relations between first concepts.

[30] This view of the nature of the syllogism is explained more fully by Dr.
COFFEY, *The Science of Logic*, I, p. 301 f.—TRS.
[31] For an analysis of the objections made by J. S. Mill against the syllogism,
see large edition ;   also *Criteriology*, **58**.

There are two kinds of logical principles :—
1. The formative principles of each particular science ;
2. The regulative principles of all thought.

52. Figures and Moods of the Syllogism.—In Aristotle's terminology the *figures* (σχήματα) of the syllogism are the different forms which the syllogism may assume according to the relations the middle term bears to the two extremes :—

Fig. 1. The middle term is the subject of the major and predicate of the minor.

Fig. 2. The middle term is the predicate of both premisses.

Fig. 3. The middle term is the subject of both premisses.

The syllogisms which are possible in these different figures if we regard the quantity—universal or particular—and the form—affirmative or negative—of the proposition, are styled the *moods* of the syllogism. The number of such possible combinations, independent of their logical values, may be reckoned as 256 moods. But among this number there are only twenty-four in which a conclusion is derived, and of these five though valid are useless ; in all therefore there remain, as valid and useful, nineteen moods of the syllogism, viz. :

> 1st figure : AAA, AII, EAE, EIO
>   (indirect) AAI, EAE, AII, AEO, IEO
> 2nd figure : AEE, AOO, EAE, EIO
> 3rd figure : AAI, AII, EAO, EIO, IAI, OAO

53. Rules of the Syllogism.—Besides special rules for each figure, logicians usually give eight rules applying to the syllogism in general and expressing the nature of reasoning.

RULE 1. *Terminus esto triplex : medius, majorque, minorque.*— In the syllogism there must be three terms, neither more nor less. For reasoning is the comparison of two terms with a common third term in order to discover whether or how the first two terms are logically related to each other. This rule may be violated by defect, that is, if *only two* terms are used ; or by excess, should *more than three* be employed. (a) An instance of a syllogism of only two terms is that in which one of the premisses is tautological : e.g. ' Every effect has a cause. The universe is an effect. Therefore the universe has a cause '. Consequently this first rule is violated by all the fallacies known as Petitio Principii or Begging the Question. (b) A syllogism contains more than two terms when one of them is ambiguous, inasmuch as a term which can be used in two meanings is equivalent to two terms : e.g. ' Acts of thought have the brain for their organ. An act which has the brain for its organ is material. Therefore acts of thought are material '. Here the middle term, ' having the brain for organ ', is equivocal.

RULE 2. *Latius hoc (terminos extremos) quam praemissae conclusio non vult ;* or better : *Aeque ac praemissae extendat conclusio voces ;* the extremes must be the same in the conclusion as in the premisses. The conclusion expresses the result of the comparison made in the premisses. It cannot go beyond this. Were it to do so, it would pass from the terms compared in the premisses to some *other* and would thus violate Rule 1, the observance of which is indispensable for right reasoning.

RULE 3. *Aut semel aut iterum medius generaliter esto.*—The reason for this rule is easily understood after an analysis of the process of reasoning (49). The middle term must be taken universally at least once. If not, if it is used twice as particular, we should never be certain that the parts of the extension taken in each case were not different, and in consequence never certain that the syllogism had not four terms (Rule 1). E.g. ' All metals are heavy. This substance is heavy. Therefore this substance is a metal '—where ' heavy ' is not a universal in either of the premisses. This fallacy is often tersely expressed : *Ab uno disce omnes.*

RULE 4. *Nequaquam medium capiat conclusio fas est.*—The middle term must not appear in the conclusion. It belongs to the conclusion to apply to the *two* extremes the result of the comparison effected in the premisses between them and the middle term. Hence were the middle term brought into the conclusion the purpose of the reasoning would not be attained.

RULE 5. *Ambae affirmantes nequeunt generare negantem.*— From two affirmative premisses a negative conclusion can never be drawn. If two ideas agree with the same third, they cannot but agree with one another, all other rules being duly observed ; if there is an identity affirmed in the premisses, it cannot be denied in the conclusion.

RULE 6. *Utraque si praemissa neget, nil inde sequetur.*—Where both premisses are negative, there is no means of drawing a conclusion. The reason being that, if two extremes are both excluded from a middle term, they cannot be connected by reason of this exclusion with each other. Yet it may happen that the same two terms which are excluded from one middle term may by comparison with some other middle term be found on account of their agreement or disagreement to be definitely related or not to each other, and so a conclusion reached through the medium of this new middle term. Hence the mere fact that two extremes are excluded from a certain middle term gives us no warrant to affirm either that they are related or that they are not related to each other, to make any conclusion at all about them.

RULE 7. *Pejorem sequitur semper conclusio partem.*—The conclusion necessarily takes after the ' weaker ' premiss. The meaning of this may be expanded into :—

(1) *If one of the premisses is negative, the conclusion must be negative.* If A and B are two ideas of which A agrees with C and B does not, we can never assert positively and certainly that A agrees with B.

(2) *If one of the premisses is particular, the conclusion must be particular.* For, since both premisses cannot be negative (Rule 6), there are only two possible cases, viz. where both premisses are affirmative and where one is affirmative and one negative.   (a) If both premisses are affirmative, then their two predicates (**35**, 1) as well as one subject (by supposition) must be particular, and only one term is left to be universal. Now by Rule 3 we know that the middle term must be once universal. Therefore neither of the extremes can be universal in the premisses. And they cannot, therefore, be universal in the conclusion (Rule 2), i.e. the conclusion must be particular. (b) If one premiss is affirmative and one negative, the premisses will contain two universal terms, viz. the predicate of the negative premiss and the subject of the proposition which by supposition is universal. Further, the conclusion is negative, so that its predicate is universal. Now this term which when predicate in the conclusion is universal, is not the middle term (Rule 4) ; and therefore the other universal must be the middle term, and the extreme which becomes subject in the conclusion must be particular in the premisses and, in consequence, particular also in the conclusion : i.e. the conclusion has to be particular. Examples are : ' All men are material beings. A is not a material being. Therefore A is not a man '. The conclusion would be just the same if one only of the propositions

were both universal and negative : ' No men are pure spirits. A is a man. Therefore A is not a pure spirit '; or ' . . . B is a pure spirit. Therefore B is not a man '. In a word, when one premiss is particular, the conclusion is particular.

RULE 8. *Nil sequitur geminis ex particularibus unquam.*— From two particular premisses no conclusion can be drawn. Since both premisses cannot be negative (Rule 6), only two combinations, as above, are possible : either both premisses are affirmative, or one is affirmative and the other negative. (*a*) In the first case, all the terms are particular—the two predicates because they are predicates of affirmative propositions ; the two subjects by supposition. Hence there is no distributed middle term, it is not universal once ; there is a violation of Rule 3, and consequently no legitimate conclusion can be drawn. Take as an instance : ' Some men are rich. Some men are ignorant. Therefore some rich men are ignorant '. Were such a syllogism valid, one might prove in a similar way that some rich men are poor. (*b*) In the second case the premisses contain only one universal term, namely, the predicate of the negative premiss. But as the conclusion is negative, its predicate is universal, and if it is so in the conclusion, that term must also be so in the premisses. Hence the middle term —which is not the predicate of the conclusion (Rule 4)—is particular both times in the premisses, and Rule 3 is again violated to the prejudice of any conclusion. E.g. ' Some men are learned. Some men are not virtuous. Therefore some learned men are not virtuous '—which is obviously nonsense.

54. The Rules of the Syllogism and Truth.—The rules just laid down only safeguard the correctness of the inference and do not do more than ensure logical self-consistency. The *logical connexion* between antecedent and consequent is quite another thing from the *truth* of the consequent ; for the necessary connexion between the things posited and the thing necessarily following from their being posited throws no light upon the truth or falsity of the premisses in which those first things are posited. The truth or falsity of the conclusion is to be determined by the two following general rules :—

1. If the premisses are true, the conclusion will be true : *Ex vero non sequitur nisi verum.* The conclusion is nothing more than a statement of the relations perceived in the premisses ; what has been acknowledged to be true in the

premisses must be equally true when stated in the conclusion.

From the fact that true premisses cannot lead to a false
conclusion, it follows that it is a legitimate disproof of a doctrine
or theory to argue from the falsity of its consequences. Thus,
for example, atheism may justly be condemned by its consequences.

2. If one or both premisses are false the conclusion is
generally, but not necessarily, false : *Ex falso sequitur quidlibet.*
Aristotle gives the example : ' All men are minerals. All
minerals are animals. Therefore all men are animals '.
' All minerals are animals. No horse is an animal. Therefore
no horse is a mineral '. ' All horses are animals. No man is
an animal. Therefore no man is a horse '. Hence by the use
of a false premiss one may arrive at a correct conclusion, either
because the original statement is a mixture of truth and error
and the element of truth prevails, or because two falsehoods
may in the long run counteract each other.

Since a false antecedent may have a true consequent, it
is not enough for the proof of a doctrine or theory to show
that a certain number of its consequences are true : e.g. Newton drew many conclusions from his theory of emissions concerning the nature of light and verified them experimentally,
yet the theory itself was found to be a figment of his imagination. For an argument drawn from the consequences of a
theory to be conclusive it is necessary to show that all its consequences are true.   ,

II. Various Kinds of Syllogism.

55. Basis of Classification.—We may distinguish several
different kinds of syllogisms according as we consider the form
and the matter of syllogisms. The *form* of a syllogism is its
structure, its particular mode of arriving at a consequence, apart
from any consideration of the truth or falsity of the actual
premisses ; its *matter*, or the material aspect of the syllogism,
is the propositions it is made up of, which are either true or
false. In the two following subsections we shall consider in
turn both these two points of view, of *form* and of *truth*.

Scientific induction does not differ essentially from the
syllogism. *Analogy* and *example*, which logicians usually

connect with induction, may also therefore be brought under the method of the syllogism.   Hence all forms of real reasoning are, as we shall see as a general conclusion from this section, some phase or form of the syllogism.

§ 1. *Classification of Syllogisms according to their Form*

56. Regarded from the point of view of structure or form, the syllogism may be *categorical, hypothetical* or conditional, *conjunctive,* or *disjunctive.*   The last two kinds are reducible to the hypothetical syllogism, and two complex syllogisms—the *exclusive* syllogism and the *dilemma*—are respectively elaborations of the categorical and hypothetical forms.

57. Varieties of the Categorical Syllogism.—The syllogism we have hitherto spoken about is called the *categorical* syllogism, because it contains premisses which make straightforward, categorical statements.   It allows, however, of certain modifications in structure which give the various forms of reasoning called by logicians the *epicheirema, polysyllogism, sorites* and *enthymeme.*

The *epicheirema* (ἐπὶ χειρῶ, I take in hand) according to modern terminology [32] is a syllogism having one or both of its premisses immediately followed by a proof.   A *polysyllogism* is a series of syllogisms so connected that the conclusion of one serves as a premiss for the next.

In point of fact a polysyllogism is usually abridged into the form called *sorites* (σῶρος, a heap), where the predicate of the first proposition of the series becomes the subject of the second, and so forth, until finally the predicate of the last conclusion is linked up with the first subject.   Thus : ' The human soul forms abstract thoughts ; beings capable of forming abstract thoughts are spiritual ; spiritual beings are by their nature incorruptible ; beings which are by their nature incorruptible cannot be annihilated ; spiritual beings which cannot be annihilated are immortal ; therefore the human soul is immortal '.

An *enthymeme* is commonly put down as a disguised form of the syllogism inasmuch as it appears to lack one of its premisses, which is understood instead of being expressed.   In

---

[32] With Aristotle *epicheirema* means an attempted demonstration as distinguished from a real one.

reality this circumstance is not sufficient to warrant its having a special place as a distinct form of the syllogism. With Aristotle, however, it did mean something really different, namely a syllogism which has only a probable conclusion (**70, 1**).

58. Nature and Rules of the Hypothetical Syllogism.—A *hypothetical* syllogism is one in which the major is a conditional proposition. E.g. ' If the soul is simple, it is incorruptible ; but the soul is simple ; therefore it is incorruptible '.

The major simply affirms a necessary connexion between the condition (simplicity of the soul) and what is conditioned (incorruptibility). Granted this necessary connexion, the rest of the argument proceeds as an ordinary syllogism, of which the minor is the antecedent of the conditional proposition and the conclusion its consequent.

The important feature of the hypothetical syllogism is in the major. This premiss is equivalent to an absolute affirmative proposition : thus, ' If the soul is simple it is incorruptible ', is equivalent to ' All simple souls are incorruptible '. And as *a universal affirmative proposition is not convertible* (**41**), the two following rules for the hypothetical syllogism may be deduced : (1) Affirm the condition or antecedent and you must affirm the conditioned proposition or consequent—' If you are a Londoner, you are British. But you are a Londoner. Therefore you are British '. (2) Deny the conditioned proposition or consequent and you must deny the condition or antecedent —' If you are a Londoner, you are British. But you are not British. Therefore you are not a Londoner '. But in neither case is the converse true : you may affirm the conditioned proposition without having to affirm the condition, and deny the condition without having to deny the consequent.

Note that (*a*) it may happen, owing to the particular *matter* of the conditional proposition, that the truth of the consequent involves that of the antecedent. E.g. ' If a figure is a circle, its radii are equal '. (*b*) The conjunction ' if ' does not always express in the mind of the speaker a nexus of *necessary dependence* between antecedent and consequent. Not infrequently the ' if ' indicates that there is only a *partial*, or a contingent connexion between them, and in this case it expresses rather a *presumption* than a strict inference. E.g. ' If this man had been tried by ill-fortune, he would be of another opinion '.

59. Conjunctive and Disjunctive Syllogisms.—A *conjunctive* syllogism is one in which the major is a conjunctive proposition, i.e. one which posits an incompatibility between two cases, so that if one is affirmed the other is thereby denied. E.g. ' You could not be simultaneously in London and New York. You were in London. Therefore you could not have been in New York '. Such an argument is reducible to the hypothetical syllogism and is subject to the same laws.

A *disjunctive* syllogism has a disjunctive proposition for its major, i.e. a proposition that posits instead of a simple incompatibility, alternatives which are entirely exhaustive. Hence this form of syllogism requires the observance of the following rules :—(1) The disjunction posited in the major must be exhaustive. (2) When the minor affirms one of the members of the disjunction, the other member or members must be denied in the conclusion, and vice versa. For example : ' All free acts are morally good or bad. This act of swearing is not morally bad ; therefore it is morally good '. Or, ' It is bad ; therefore it is not good '. Or, ' It is good ; therefore it is not bad '. ' It is not good ; therefore it is bad '.

60. The Exclusive Syllogism is one in which *both* premisses are exclusive propositions. E.g. ' Only spiritual beings are free. Man alone is spiritual. Therefore man alone is free '. This syllogism may be split up into two propositions, one negative and one affirmative : ' Spiritual beings are free. Man is spiritual. Therefore man is free.—All free beings are spiritual. All beings other than men are not spiritual. Therefore they are not free '.

61. The Dilemma is a combination of a disjunctive proposition as major with two or more conditional propositions as minor. First the particular members of the disjunction are excluded by successive partial conclusions ; whereupon the general conclusion follows that the disjunctive proposition as a whole is inadmissible. It is a lively and effective form of argument : the adversary is left to choose one of two alternative propositions and whichever he chooses he is proved to be wrong. The validity of the argument requires the observance of the rules applying to disjunctive and to hypothetical syllogisms : (1) The members of the major must be such as to allow of no other possibility, they must be exhaustive or ' complete '. (2) The two hypothetical syllogisms which make up the minor must each lead to a conclusion and to one and the same conclusion.   A celebrated example of the dilemma is this : ' If we suppose that in spite of His own attestations Jesus Christ is not God, we are forced to accept one or other of the impossible conclusions that He was a fool or an impostor.   But if we suppose Him to have been a fool, how can we reconcile the penetrating wisdom displayed in His life and doctrine with the characteristics of a fool or madman ?   If He was an impostor, how reconcile His most ambitious claims with His humility and renunciation ?   Since both hypotheses are alike inadmissible, Jesus Christ is therefore the Messiah, the Son of the Living God'[33]. It can easily be shown that the above syllogisms are fundamentally reducible to the categorical or typical syllogism.

§ 2. *Classification of Syllogisms according to their Matter*

62. The Syllogism and its Truth-value.—From the point of view of matter, syllogisms are divided according to the relation their propositions bear to truth.   As judgments and propositions are certain, probable or erroneous, syllogisms are likewise demonstrative, probable or erroneous.

1. A judgment is *certain* when the mind firmly adheres to what it knows to be the truth : the syllogism leading to this certitude is a *demonstration*.

2. As long as the mind remains undecided between two opposite judgments without definitely adhering to either of them, it is in suspense or *doubt*.   When it is inclined towards one side, though without absolutely adopting it to the exclusion of the other, it has an *opinion :* the syllogism which results in an opinion is a *probable* one, and its probability varies in proportion to the cogency of the motives which solicit this partial adherence of the mind.

3. The opposite of truth, the disagreement of a judgment with the thing known, is error, and arguments producing it are called sophisms or *fallacies*.

The various kinds of *demonstration* and *probable arguments* as well as the more common *fallacies* call for closer attention.

---

[33] The dilemma must not be confused with a method of reasoning ' by successive parts,' which consists in enumerating all the species of a genus, pronouncing upon each of them in turn and then asserting of the whole genus the conclusion which was valid for each of the parts.

Different Kinds of Demonstration

63. I. Fundamental Division into Certain and Strictly Scientific Demonstration.—Demonstration is a process of reasoning by which from premises that are certain we arrive logically at a certain conclusion. In a stricter sense it is a syllogism which gives us to know that we know, i.e. ' to know the cause of a thing, to know that this cause is really the cause and that therefore the thing cannot be otherwise than we know it ' [34]. Our first distinction, then, must be between the demonstrative syllogism which leads to a *certain* conclusion and that which gives a *strictly scientific* conclusion.

64. Conditions for Scientific Demonstration.—In dealing with the nature of scientific demonstration Aristotle enumerates as the conditions, that the premises must be *true, ultimate, immediate, better known than,* and *prior to,* the conclusion, and the *cause* or *reason* of its truth.

1. *True :* although false premises may sometimes be followed by a true conclusion (**54**), their falsity, *as such,* can never be the cause of the truth in the conclusion. Since it is the aim of demonstration to arrive at a true conclusion from true premises, a valid demonstration will set out from true premises as a natural source for its true conclusion.

2. *Ultimate,* that is, partaking of the nature of first principles, not themselves demonstrable, in the sense that all the demonstrations of a science have to form as it were a single chain, the first link of which consists of premises that do not themselves admit of demonstration. These ultimate, or first, premises are, consequently, in relation to those which follow—

3. *Immediate,* of such a nature that they are *self-evident,* not requiring any proof.

4. The *cause* or *reason* [35] *of the conclusion,* not only in the *logical order* or the order of knowledge, but also in the *ontological order.*

5. *Prior to the conclusion,* since the premises must contain the cause or reason of the conclusion. The priority need be only a *priority of nature.*

6. *Better known than the conclusion,* because the aim of reasoning is to lead us from the better known to the less known

[34] Aristotle, *Anal. post.,* I, 2.
[35] For this distinction see *Gen. Metaphysics,* **165.**

or unknown.   Note that this theory of Aristotle's has reference
to the *ontological* order.   In the subjective order the fact of
experience is prior to the idea of its essence we form by abstraction from it ; we pass from the particular to the universal.
But in the world of reality the nature of a thing is prior to its
sensible manifestations, law controls what happens and is
necessary for its explanation.

65. Proof of Fact and Causal Demonstration.—Corresponding
to the fundamental distinction between the syllogism leading
to a certain conclusion and strictly scientific demonstration
is the Aristotelian division into proof of fact and causal demonstration.

The former, demonstration ὅτι, *demonstratio quia* or *quod*
(where ' quia ' signifies ' that ', not ' because '), is a *proof that*
something *is*, without any explanation how or why it is so.
The ' is ' Cajetan understands to have both a copulative and
existential signification.

Causal demonstration, διότι, *demonstratio propter quid*, on
the other hand, shows the immediate cause of the thing proved,
the *intrinsic reason* (ἀρχὴ οἰκεῖα) on account of which it is so ;
and it is therefore strictly scientific demonstration.

A proof which gives an *extrinsic* or a *general* reason to explain
the connexion between subject and predicate is not a real
demonstration διότι, propter quid, but belongs to the class of
proofs of fact.

66. II. A Priori and A Posteriori Proofs.—This distinction,
which modern logicians prefer to use in place of the one we
have just been considering, is not such a strict one, yet has a
foundation in nature.   An *a priori* argument is one in which
the middle term is prior *in reality* to the predicate of the conclusion, one which proceeds from the cause or reason (a causa
vel ratione quae in se est prior, a priori) to effect or result (ad
effectum vel rationatum).   In an *a posteriori* argument the
progress is just the reverse, being from effect to cause.   Examples
are : of the *a priori*—' An immaterial subject is incorruptible.
The human soul is immaterial.   Therefore it is incorruptible '.
Of the *a posteriori* argument—' Whatever commences to exist
demands a cause other than itself to account for its existence.
The universe is such that at some time it commenced to exist.
Therefore there is a cause accountable for the existence of the
universe '.

To this division some authors add what they term a *quasi a priori* proof or demonstration *a simultaneo*. They mean an argument which derives its conclusion about one thing from its connexion with another which is not distinct from it in reality, but is such that it cannot be conceived of in thought without involving the thought of the other.   An example is the argument St. Anselm made use of in endeavouring to prove the existence of God from the concept of the most perfect being.

67. III. Circular or Regressive Demonstration.—Reason ascends from effect to cause to descend again from cause to effect, in order to explain the latter by the former.   This process is known as circular or regressive proof, for the mind as it were completes a circle by coming back to the effect from whence it started its reasonings.   This argument, unlike the vicious circle (**75,** 2*b*), is perfectly valid; the undoubted existence of the phenomenon is the starting-point but its nature is as yet only known *confusedly ;* in the second part of the process the mind starts from the nature of the thing but only after it has acquired a more *distinct* notion of it ; the latter is then used to explain the effects observed at first.

68. IV. Other Accidental Forms of Demonstration.—1. *Direct* and *indirect* demonstration : This is a distinction due rather to extrinsic circumstances than to the nature of things.   Demonstration is *direct* (like all those yet enumerated) when it shows in a clear and straightforward way that the conclusion is virtually contained in the premisses.   It is *indirect* when subjective considerations are appealed to and positive assent is given to the truth of the conclusion on account of the necessity of rejecting its contradictory.   Free-will is thus indirectly proved from the absurd consequences of determinism.   This latter kind of demonstration is called *reductio per impossibile* or *reductio ad absurdum*.

2. *Absolute* demonstration is that which is adequate of itself to carry conviction and is true for everybody ; *relative* or *ad hominem* that which may be materially false but is sufficient to convince a particular opponent [36].

3. In contrast to scientific demonstration Aristotle mentions a *demonstratio a signo* or *per signum*, which is an *extrinsic*

---

[36] E.g. Our Lord's reply to those who censured Him for healing on the Sabbath by asking which of them would not rescue his ox or ass on the Sabbath.   For other examples see JOSEPH., *op. cit.*, p. 550.—TRS.

proof drawn from circumstances external to the thing to be proved. An example of this kind of extrinsic proof occurs below (71).

These accidental or secondary forms of demonstration can all be classified according to the fundamental distinction of demonstrations ὅτι and demonstrations διότι.

PROBABLE ARGUMENTS

69. Probable Arguments have for one or both premisses only probable propositions and a conclusion which in consequence is only as certain as the premisses. For a classification we may group under a first heading all that falls under the general term *arguments from analogy*—the *Aristotelian enthymeme, analogical induction, example,* and inferences drawn from the *calculus of probabilities;* under a second heading, *hypothesis;* under a third, *argument from authority.*

70. I. Arguments from Analogy.—1. The *enthymeme* according to Aristotle's definition is ' an argument drawn from probabilities or signs ' ; that is to say, from signs or symptoms which are not regarded as properties inevitably belonging to the subject to which they are attributed, but probably do belong. This kind of argument is extremely common in daily life. E.g. ' Most men act through self-interest. Therefore in this particular case Peter is acting through self-interest '.

2. *Analogical induction or analogy :* Scientific induction, as we shall see later (85-91), singles out some natural property from among the many various accidents a substance manifests, and from it infers with certainty that the property in question is the basis of a general law. Analogical induction or analogy is a similar method of argument, excepting that the conclusion is not certain but only probable. Thus we are making use of it when we argue from the knowledge that two objects or phenomena have actually certain qualities in common to the likelihood of their also possessing in common other qualities not yet known. This argument, it should be noted, is liable to abuse by resemblances between things being exaggerated, by differences being overlooked, or by metaphors being mistaken for valid grounds of inference.

3. *Example :* Both scientific and analogical induction work from an empirical fact to its natural sufficient reason, or its

law, and thence to the logical generalization that the law applies universally.   Example, on the other hand, is a form of argument which proceeds from a particular case to a particular case and never advances beyond a conjecture : e.g. ' Avarice has this effect in the case of A, therefore it will have it in that of B '.

4. *Inferences drawn from the calculation of probabilities*, and *Hypothesis* (II) are deferred for consideration later (**92**).

71. III. Argument from Authority.—In numberless cases in daily life we allow ourselves to be guided by the opinions and knowledge of other people ; in a word, we assent to arguments from authority.

A statement made by another whom we regard as having some degree of authority, whether it concern a fact or a doctrine, is in the scale of logical values a probability ; for it is not without reason that we incline to put faith in the accuracy and sincerity of the testimony of our fellow-men.   Yet confidence in such a statement, if we follow the laws of right reason, cannot be regarded as absolute.   Even one whom we esteem for his prudence and observation of facts may be caught napping at times, perhaps on this very occasion, or one of well-known sincerity may possibly on occasion be found untruthful and deceiving.   Whilst, then, the argument from authority has its value *according to the circumstances of each particular occasion*, human testimony of its very nature cannot beget a certainty which is absolute.

In matters bearing on doctrine St. Thomas does not hesitate to declare that the argument based on human authority is the weakest of all arguments : ' Locus ab auctoritate, quae fundatur super ratione humana, est infirmissimus '.

These words contain a valuable answer for those superficial minds who imagine that Scholasticism stands for the abdication of personal reasoning in favour of a blind following of authority.

ERRONEOUS ARGUMENTS AND FALLACIES

72. False Reasoning.—Error may be due to the grounds, or matter, of an argument or to its form.   It is due to the *grounds* when premisses that are false or doubtful are supposed as true and certain ; to the *form* when, consciously or unconsciously,

a conclusion is drawn from the premisses which does not logically follow from them.   In the former case the false reasoning
should be called *erroneous* argument, and in the latter a *fallacy*.
Further, a fallacy is a *paralogism* if the reasoner is deceiving
himself, and a *sophism*, in the present acceptation of the term,
when he is consciously reasoning falsely to deceive another.

73. Fallacies in General.—Following John Stuart Mill we
may classify fallacies into two main groups.

1. *Fallacies of simple inspection* or a priori fallacies : These
fallacies are popular maxims and generalizations which are
taken for granted, usually without discussion and therefore
without suspicion, and which are at least ambiguous if not
erroneous.   An example is the principle that ideas correspond
to things, the logical to the ontological order—a preconception
which becomes one of the chief supports of pantheism.   Again,
the fallacy by which rationalism endeavours to substantiate
its denial of revelation, namely, the a priori repudiation of one
or more methods of attaining knowledge along with the
simultaneous assertion that whatever is not known in an arbi-
trarily selected way is entirely unknowable.   Or, again, the
unqualified statement that man has the right to unrestrained
liberty.

2. *Fallacies of inference* or fallacies in the reasoning process
itself : These arrange themselves into fallacies of *induction*
and fallacies of *deduction*, the latter comprising *verbal* and
formal fallacies.

74. I. Fallacies of Induction.—Under this heading are to be
placed all fallacies occurring in inductive reasoning whether
they are concerned with the preliminaries of the argument
(fallacies of *observation*) or with the actual reasoning process
itself (fallacies of *generalization*, viz. of *interpretation* and of
illicit induction).

1. *Fallacies of observation* : For induction to be scientific it
must be the fruit of trustworthy and sustained observation
of facts ; very often it happens that the desire to reach a
conclusion leads to assertions which trespass beyond the limits
justified by observation.   Induction may be vitiated by *mal-
observation*, by seeing what is wished for, not what is as a matter
of reality : so Haeckel discovered his primary moners and
Huxley his famous Bathybius.   Or by *non-observation*, by the
failure to see what it would be inconvenient to see : thus false

biological theories see only what points to the identity of the cell in all kingdoms of life.

2. *Fallacies of interpretation :* These consist in a wrong interpretation of the facts observed. The observation is perfect, but through the influence of some preconceived theory an undue significance is attached to the facts. An instance in point is the inference, from the fact that forms of energy can be reckoned in terms of mechanical energy, that all material energies, including energies developed in a nervous subject as the accompaniment of sensation, emotion, or spontaneous movement, or of the thought processes and volition, are nothing but mechanical energies.

3. *Fallacies of illicit induction :* Example is abused when we pass on from a particular case under observation to another without first having taken care to discover by an inductive argument that they can be traced back to the same natural cause, ' Ab uno disce omnes '. In a similar way a false use may be made of analogy [37].

75. II. Fallacies of Deduction.—1. *Verbal fallacies.* These arise from the meaning of a word being altered from what it originally was or from words being used in different senses. The most important are :—

(*a*) *Equivocation or ambiguity of terms.* This fallacy is the use in a syllogism of a word which has a double meaning or the employment of some badly defined phrase in two different acceptations. Flagrant offenders are such words as ' liberty ', ' equality ', ' evolution ', ' rationalism ', ' liberalism ', ' socialism '. The ambiguity introduces a fourth term into the syllogism.

(*b*) *The fallacy of composition.* This consists in taking together in the conclusion what was not taken together in the premisses ; in other words, this consists in affirming of the whole what is true only of the parts taken distributively. Thus, when the Gospel records that ' The blind see, the lame walk, the deaf hear ', the statement is true only if the clauses are understood disjunctively, not if collectively.

(*c*) *The fallacy of division* is just the opposite of the preceding fallacy, and consists in predicating of things distributively what is true of them only when taken together. Thus I might argue,

---

[37] Some inductive fallacies can be ranged indifferently under several of the headings.

' Five is a single number.   But two and three are five.   Therefore two and three are a single number ' [38].

2. *Fallacies of ratiocination* : (*a*) *Begging the question* (*petitio
principii*).   This is a fallacy wherein something yet unproved
is implicitly assumed in the course of the argument as though it
were already proved.   It may take different forms : the very point
at issue may be taken for granted ; the whole may be assumed
whereas a part has to be proved ; or a part when the whole
requires proof ; or each of the parts of the whole to be proved ;
or it may be some point of doctrine necessarily connected with
the point at issue.

(*b*) *Vicious circle* is really the same fallacy, except that it not
only assumes what is to be proved but makes use of unproven
propositions for the proof of each other.   Thus did Descartes
prove the Divine Veracity by an appeal to self-evidence and
then justify self-evidence by the Divine Veracity.

(*c*) *Fallacy of accident* consists in confusing (*a*) what is *accidental*
with what is *essential*, or (*β*) what is *relatively* true with what is
absolutely true,—for instance, *absolutely* condemning a practice
because of the abuses to which it gives rise.

(*d*) *Fallacy of false cause.*   (*ā*) Here mere concomitance or
succession is mistaken for true causal relation : *cum* hoc, ergo
propter hoc, or *post* hoc, ergo *propter* hoc ; or again, concomitance
for identity : *cum* hoc, ergo *ipsum* hoc.   (*β*) Akin to this is the
fallacy of confusing *condition* and *cause*, or a *partial* cause and
the *total* cause.

(*e*) *Fallacy of many questions* is the combination of many
questions together as if only one answer would suffice, whereas
in reality more are required.   Thus if it is asked : ' Has the
honourable gentleman ceased beating his wife ? ' the question
implies an answer to a previous question : ' Has he been
beating his wife ? '

(*f*) *Evasion of the real question* (*ignoratio elenchi*).   This
fallacy may be of three kinds : the argument may prove *too
much, too little*, or something quite irrelevant and *beside* the
point [39].

---

[38] E.g. Heaven is for those who love their friends and forgive their enemies.
Caius loves his friends.   Therefore Caius will go to Heaven '.—Trs.

[39] To this list of common fallacies may be added the *paradox*.   Strictly
speaking it is a dictum contrary to received opinion (παρὰ δόξιαν), and in
itself may be either true or false.   There are accordingly two kinds of paradox,
the first of which alone strictly deserves the name.   Thus the statement

ART. III. SCIENTIFIC SYSTEMATIZATION

76. Knowledge is a System.—The construction of our knowledge is the work of a gradual process : concepts are united to form judgments ; judgments are marshalled into syllogisms ; syllogisms furnish new conclusions, fresh pieces of knowledge, fragments of a larger whole ; all the several inferences, subordinated and co-ordinated among themselves, together form a science. A science is, then, a whole body of propositions which stand together (σύστημα, a system) on one basis. Its unity belongs to it by reason of its having one formal object.

As soon as we have the definition of the essence or of the properties of a thing, we begin to make some simple, general propositions, known as principles (=beginnings) or axioms, and from these the mind proceeds to deduce various conclusions. These primary conclusions lead on to others, which are consequently either directly or indirectly dependent upon the principles, and so on, until we have a complete scientific edifice entirely constructed upon the principles first furnished by the analysis of the subject. This systematization of our knowledge is the supreme end or aim of logic.

77. Systematization of our Knowledge.—There are three factors which go to form a systematization of our knowledge, ' tres modi sciendi '—definition, demonstration and division.

Definition furnishes us with principles ; and *demonstration* carries us on to conclusions from them. As definition has to tell us what a thing is and to show us in what it differs from things of another species of the same genus, a differentiation or *division* is an indispensable aid or concomitant of definition.

We have already spoken sufficiently of one of these three factors, viz. demonstration. We have therefore to consider only the functions of definition and division and the conditions required for their lawful employment (I). After this we shall inquire how these factors or mental processes have an application in the several special sciences and in philosophy, i.e. we shall consider *method* in general and the different methods peculiar to different groups of sciences (II).

' All minds are equal ' (a statement of Helvetius) is a real paradox ; ' Far better to suffer evil than to do it ' is only *prima facie* a paradox, and not so in reality.—In a loose sense, which is of no importance here, paradox sometimes stands for a mere perversity of expression or a cynicism born of ill-humour.

I. Factors in the Systematization of Knowledge

78. I. Definition.—A definition of a thing is a statement of what it is. Definition has a twofold function inasmuch as, in the first place, it clears our ideas for us, it states the elements of which they are made up so that we can know things more accurately by them ; and, as its principal function, it provides a foundation or starting-point on which further knowledge can be built up.

Now just as not everything is demonstrable, so not everything is definable. Analysis is susceptible of further analysis and so on, but sooner or later we get down to notions which refuse to submit to analysis into simpler ideas : such, for instance, are the ideas of ' unity ', ' number ', the basic ideas of arithmetic. These ideas provide the materials for the definitions or first principles whereon the construction of the whole science rests for its foundation [40].

79. Kinds of Definition.—1. *Verbal definition* explains the meaning of a word either according to its etymology or according to its conventional use. Its purpose is to make us clear in our ideas and so avoid the possibility of ambiguity.

2. *Real definition* declares what a thing is, either according to its essence or some of its accidents or some of its natural properties.

(*a*) *Essential definition* gives a full statement of what a thing is inasmuch as it makes known its inner nature or essence. The essence of a particular thing, that whereby it is this thing and distinct from all others, is however individual, whilst our ideas are universal (*Psychology*, **89-91**) ; we can therefore never hope to know this essence, and must be content in our essential definitions with declaring the generic or specific essence of a thing.

(*b*) *Accidental definition :* As the generic, and still less the specific, essence of a thing is not evident to us at once, we take note first of its qualities, regardless of whether they are natural or accidental, and this general description may be called, though somewhat inaccurately, a ' *descriptive* definition '.

---

[40] ' The beginnings or principles of the sciences are unprovable definitions. Definition makes known what something is ; thus mathematics postulates as its starting-point a knowledge of what unity is, of what odd number means, and so on '.—ARISTOTLE, *Analyt. post.*, II, 3.

When it represents the thing by means of all the accidental notes which taken as a group belong only to it, it is called an accidental definition.

(c) *Natural definition :* From these qualities the mind can, by a process of induction, discover one or more which are necessary qualities, i.e. *properties ;* and the definition is then a natural definition.

The definitions used in chemistry, mineralogy, botany, zoology, etc., are for the most part descriptive, accidental definitions, or at the best natural definitions. Essential definition is rather an ideal to which in matter of fact we seldom attain. Yet really it is the only one which is strictly scientific and philosophical.

80. Definition is formed by Analysis or by Combined Analysis and Synthesis.—A science is rational or experimental according as its principles are furnished by pure reasoning or by induction from observation. In a rational science definition is obtained by a synthetic, deductive process, whilst in an experimental science the process is first of all analytic and then synthetic. Let us explain.

1. *The rational sciences :* From sensible data presented to us by general observation we abstract very simple ideas (decomposition), which we immediately proceed to put together (synthesis) and build into more and more complex ideas. The elementary ideas are wider in their extension than the notion in which they are all united by the act of synthesis, their sum is more restricted in its application than is each of them individually ; thus synthesis progressively restricts its object and provides it with a *definition* (ὅρος ὁρισμός, a boundary). Take, for example, the definition ' Three is the first odd number '. Each of the simple ideas belongs to other numbers besides ' three ', but the union of them narrows down their application to the number ' three ' and thus defines it. As the extension of a concept is restricted in proportion as its comprehension is fuller, synthesis or the binding together of many notes is therefore a direct process of definition, just as, we may remark incidentally, it is an indirect method of elimination or division. The attribute ' odd ' being the opposite of the attribute ' even ', excludes the number ' two '. The word ' first '—which may be taken in its double meaning of ' first ' and ' prime '—rules out all other numbers except'ng ' two ' and ' three '. Hence

when combined the attributes ' first odd ' exclude all numbers other than ' three ', they apply to it alone ; the compound concept is an adequate definition of it.

2. *The experimental sciences* or sciences of observation likewise employ synthesis as a final process but only after analysis. Before we can define life we have to observe the various kinds of being called ' living ', and to try to find out what that is in virtue of which the same attribute can be predicated of them all. We eliminate in thought whatever differences there may be among the operations which we term ' vital ' (nutrition, cognition and volition, whether sentient or intellectual) and we find ourselves left with their common characteristic—that they are all immanent operations (*Psychology*, **10**, **11**). Immanent activity is therefore the definition of life.

Division—the elimination of distinctive features—has enabled us to form a definition of the common element. Now, this definition will start another division from where the analysis began, and so the process is renewed. For instance, to continue the example, the common characteristic of life, viz. immanent action, is discovered to be specifically different in nutritive life, in cognitional and volitional life whether sentient or intellectual. Science legitimately passes again from the genus to the species.

This alternation of analysis and synthesis may be continued in other directions. Besides forms of immanent activity there are forms of transitive activity ; from these the mind abstracts (analysis) the common feature—activity ; this is the generic element, and immanence is a differentiating characteristic : the placing together (synthesis) of the two characteristics makes the definition, the combination of the two notions that are related as *genus* and *differentia*. In this way analysis tracks down through all these species a genus which becomes increasingly wide, and so a type that is more and more simple, until eventually elements are reached which defy further analysis, and which therefore are first definitions and the formative principles of all sciences.

The fundamental part played by definition in the scientific edifice is clear. In the sciences of observation no less than in the rational sciences definition consists in a decomposition of a thing through a grasping of its simplest attributes, together with their union or synthesis with which it is to be identified.

The attribute or determination which is the least comprehensive and in consequence the most extensive forms the *generic* element of the definition ; that which completes the generic element, which ' limits ' the concept, and is proper to the thing and specifies it, is the *specific difference.*

The building up of knowledge, scientific systematization, has always the same end in view, namely, to make the mind understand effects by their causes, and consequences in the light of their principles.

81. Rules for Definition.—The rules for definition may be arranged under two heads corresponding to the twofold function of definition mentioned above :

1. Since the essential function of definition is to furnish the first principles of the sciences, (*a*) a definition must proceed from an object which is prior to that defined : correlative terms, such as ' health ' and ' sickness ', may not therefore be used in the definition of each other, for the one is as much unknown as the other ; neither can the various members of a division be used in the definition of one another ; nor can a thing be defined by itself or by what is posterior to itself. (*b*) The genus made use of must be the proximate genus.

2. Since definition has as a secondary purpose to make us precise in our ideas, a definition must be clearer than the thing defined ; hence it must never repeat the name of the thing to be defined ; it must not be composed of metaphorical or of ambiguous and obscure words ; it must be concise and adequate in its expression.

82. II. Division, the Necessary Concomitant of Definition.— Definition and division are two mutually complementary logical processes. While definition informs us what a thing is, and by naming its genus and specific difference identifies it with the simple elements making up its essence, division makes clear how far, or to what special forms, the generic element of the definition extends. The genus of the definition is the foundation or ' reason ' of a division.

1. *In the rational sciences* reason starts with a generic notion and proceeds gradually to recount its species, at each step making a new division or subdivision of the genus into its different subordinate species. Thus the generic notion ' number ' is divided into the species ' odd ' and ' even.' The idea ' odd number ' is further subdivisible into ' factorizable ' and

' prime '. And the ' first odd number ' (' prime ' in both senses)
applies only to the number ' three '.

2. *In the positive sciences* the process is just the opposite, it
is first analytical : here division leads up to definition. For
instance, first of all the different activities of vegetable, animal
and human substances are observed, and the characteristic
common to these several divisions discerned, namely, immanent
activity. The two different kinds of activity are in their turn
analysed, and their common foundation or supreme genus is
discovered to be activity. Thus step by step reason passes
from the species to genera, from the members of a division
to the reason of their divisibility. When, however, the common
principle has been reached, the mind reverts again to the subjects analysed in order to obtain a complete synthetic view of
the formal division of the genus into its species.

Definition and division are, then, intimately bound up with
each other. In rational sciences division is subsequent to
definition ; in experimental ones there is first a superficial
division leading up to the formation of the essential definition,
and then this definition becomes ground for a stricter, formal
division than the provisional informal one with which the
analysis began.

83. Rules for Division.—Division, like definition, has to
serve a double purpose : its chief purpose is to help in establishing scientific orderliness in our knowledge, and its secondary
purpose to make clear thinking easier. From the first point
of view, to aid scientific arrangement, (1) division must be
complete, logically progressive and, as far as possible, *positive*.
And to be a real help to clear thinking, it needs to be (2) *complete, clear* and *methodical*[41].

II. METHOD

84. Diversity of Scientific Methods.—*Method* (μέθοδος)
means a ' road or way towards ' ; *scientific method* is the way
leading to scientific knowledge. It varies with the nature of
the science to which it leads and is accordingly sometimes
synthetic, sometimes *analytic*. Or rather we may say that the

---

[41] We may add, from the Port Royal logicians, that, ' it is as great a mistake
to make too few divisions as it is to make too many ; the one fault is to throw
too little light, whilst the other is to distract the mind '.

method of scientific knowledge is really a combination of both ; it is *analytico-synthetic* [42].

This section will treat of the different methods employed respectively in (I) the abstract sciences, (II) the experimental sciences, and (III) philosophy.

85. I. Synthetic Method.—The *rational* or *deductive* sciences, such as arithmetic and geometry, start with certain *principles in necessary matter*, and from these, taken in conjunction, deduce new truths and so define, as they advance, the various objects under consideration. The march of ideas is from simple to compound, from the more general to the less general ; in a word, the method is *synthetic*. The mental act which combines the elements expressed in the *definition* also at the same time effects the *division* of the object defined and is the chief factor in all deductive proof. As an example, let us suppose as already established that (*a*) the sum of the angles made on one side of a straight line by other straight lines is equal to two right angles ; (*b*) the internal alternate angles made with two parallel straight lines by a line cutting them are equal ; (*c*) a parallel straight line may be drawn to any given straight line : the *combination* of these three propositions furnishes the discovery of a new relation, the equality of the three angles of a triangle with two right angles.

86. II. Method of the Experimental Sciences.—The experimental or positive sciences start with the observation of concrete facts in order to formulate the laws which govern them. The progress here is from the complex to the simple, from the particular to the general : the method is *analytic*.

In spite of the numerous variations displayed in the phenomena of the natural world, it needs but a superficial observation to show that these variations are governed by certain constant general *laws*. It is the object of the empirical sciences to determine these *laws* of phenomena and the *nature* of the things observed. They commence with the observation of facts at once complex and variable, and end when they have discovered the simple elements of their composition and the stable laws governing their variability. This method of

[42] The analytico-synthetic methods are used in the building up of a science. We have nothing to do here with didactics or the methods of imparting science to others. See large edition, *Logique*, I, p. 378 f., and P. Coffey, *Science of Logic*, II, p. 14 f.

simplifying the complex, in other words, *analysis*, when considered in its completeness, is called *induction*. Hence these sciences are known as *inductive*, in contrast with those which are purely rational or deductive sciences.

87. Stages of the Inductive Process.—Induction is an argument from effects to their cause ; it consists first in determining the properties of the cause, and through them its nature, until finally the law of its action is understood. It includes four separate steps :—

1. *Observation* of certain facts which fall within the scope of the senses. For example, the chemist observes repeatedly and under varied circumstances that a fixed quantity of hydrogen (H) combines with another fixed quantity of chlorine (Cl) to form a definite compound, HCl.

2. *Hypothesis.* The scientist *supposes* that the observed phenomenon cannot be due to a constant repetition of purely fortuitous coincidences, and that therefore a *sufficient reason* must lie in the nature of the reacting bodies. Accordingly he makes a scientific hypothesis as a provisional explanation of the facts observed [43].

3. The *verification* of the hypothesis, which is the most important part of the inductive argument, is sometimes made by further observation, sometimes by the more decisive process of experiment. (*a*) By *observation :* he considers what would be the implications were his hypothesis true and looks to see if these results are actually present. (*b*) By *experiment :* the scientist does more than witness what happens ; he may bring an active influence to bear upon phenomena ; he may vary by artificial means the various agents concurring to produce a complex phenomenon, directing them in accordance with the preconceived idea which he set out to check.

4. *Deduction.* As soon as the mind recognizes the *property* possessed by H and Cl. of combining in the fixed proportions of 1 and 35·5, it goes further and, after verifying its observations, draws the *general conclusion* : Henceforth each time that H and Cl are mixed in the proportions 1 and 35·5 and subjected to the action of the sun's rays hydrochloric acid will be formed, accompanied by the disengagement of 22 calories the molecule-gramme.

---

[43] For a fuller treatment of hypothesis see the larger *Logique*, p. 345 f., and COFFEY, *op. cit.*

These various steps raise special points for consideration. (1) In reference to the observation of facts and their verification by experiment we must describe the *methods of induction.* (2) The generalization made from the facts obtained by observation and experiment leads us to ask : What are the *real grounds* of induction ? (3) The deduction which is the final stage of induction leads us to inquire into the *relations between* deduction and induction.

88. Methods of Induction.—Following J. S. Mill logicians usually enumerate the methods of *agreement*, of *difference*, of *concomitant variations*, of *residues*, and a *joint method*. The first three are the principal ones.

1. *Method of Agreement :* When the phenomenon the nature of which is in question occurs in different cases and each different case has only one circumstance in common, that circumstance is probably the sufficient reason of the phenomenon.

2. *Method of Difference :* When the phenomenon under investigation occurs in one of two cases and not in the other, and in both cases all the circumstances are identical save one which is present in the first and absent in the second, that circumstance is the total or partial sufficient reason of the phenomenon.

3. *Method of Residues :* This is a compound method made up of the two preceding ones slightly modified. When from a phenomenon that part is subtracted which is known by previous inductions to be the effect of certain antecedents, the residue of the phenomenon is caused by the remaining antecedents.

4. *Method of Concomitant Variations :* When the variations of a phenomenon correspond to the variations of a determinate antecedent, it is to be presumed that the phenomenon and antecedent are connected, immediately or mediately, as effect and cause. Mill observes that this method has its chief use in cases where the foregoing methods are of no avail, as indeed mostly happens when the cause of the phenomenon cannot be completely isolated.

5. *Joint Method :* This is a simultaneous use of some of the preceding methods.

89. Object of Induction.—The experiments which lead us to fix the law of some chemical combination deal with the *formal cause* of the body, for they reveal its *properties* and these are derived from the formal cause. They also determine what is the *material cause* of the chemical compound inasmuch as they fix the proportional quantities of the component elements. They may also regard the *final cause* of the combinations or the tendencies according to which the combinations take place.

Nevertheless whatever cause be the particular object of investigation the purpose of the train of observations is really one and the same, namely, to ascertain some *property* of a being and through this its *specific nature* and ultimately the *law* of its activity. Inductive research, then, aims at the discovery of causes (proof of fact, ὅτι) or at what lies deeper than this, the discovery of the laws of nature and the definition of natural types (demonstration διότι).

90. Logical Grounds of Induction.—The problem connected with induction may be stated thus : From particular facts induction formulates a general law ; we argue from *certain observed* instances to *all possible* instances yet to be observed : on what ground is such a procedure legitimate ? The solution is found in the consideration that where we find a considerable number of elements and forces that are variable always uniting to form a harmonious combination ever the same (a fact established by observation and experiment in all the particular cases), we are justified in arguing that there must be *a sufficient reason* for this union, and that this sufficient reason can be nothing else than a *natural tendency* on the part of the bodies which is to be found verified not in the particular cases only but always and everywhere as a general law [44].

91. Induction and the Syllogism.—Scientific induction [45] does not in reality differ from the syllogism. By means of the inductive methods we ascertain what is the cause of an observed phenomenon, and these inductive methods, being reducible to those of agreement and difference, are applications of the hypothetical syllogism. Again, when by the inductive methods we have established the fact that the presumed cause of a phenomenon is in truth its real cause (which is a demonstration ὅτι), we show that this is not an indifferent cause but one *determined by its nature* to manifest a certain *property*, to act according

---

[44] This argument has already been developed in *Criteriology*, **63**.
[45] There is no question here of *perfect* induction, or *induction of complete enumeration*, which is not a scientific method. Cp. *Logique*, 331 f., and COFFEY, *Science of Logic*, Vol. II, p. 48 f.

to a *law*. Such a demonstration may likewise be expressed in syllogisms.

92. Statistics and Induction.—The aim of scientific induction is to infer with certainty the existence of some fixed law of nature. Now frequently it may happen that we have before us a great multitude of facts which though obviously governed by certain laws are yet so complex that the mind cannot at once discern their various causes. As a step forward we may note down all the facts and the coincidences they display. In other words, we draw up *statistics*. Statistics form an inventory or list of a great number of facts wherein we tabulate them in classes according to their relative frequency or coincidence in the hope of discovering some indication of a natural connexion. A sufficient reason for the constant recurrence of these phenomena undoubtedly lies in the *nature* of the objects, but we may not be able to conjecture, much less know, which *natural properties* are the key to the law as yet undiscovered [46]. When the thoughtful observer is able to detect among this medley of facts which antecedents are constant (method of agreement), which exclusive (method of difference), and which the variants of intensity, he is then on the brink of knowledge : he is able to form a *scientific hypothesis*, and to verify this by the work of induction.

93. III. Analytico-Synthetic Method.—We usually distinguish two scientific methods, the synthetic of the rational sciences and the analytic of the experimental sciences. The distinction is valid in the sense that synthesis is the *dominant* feature of the first group and analysis of the second ; but neither method is employed exclusively in either group. The first self-evident principles on which the rational sciences are based necessarily presuppose some preliminary observations ; on the other hand, the results obtained in the positive sciences by analysis and induction prepare the way for later deductive or synthetic processes. All science indeed aims at the knowledge of things *through their causes*. Causal demonstration (propter quid)

---

[46] We find cases in which it is impossible to discover from the facts any constancy that indicates a law. You may use a die that is perfect—its faces with the usual markings 1 to 6—and of a dozen casts 3 and 5 will each turn up three times, 2 and 4 twice, 1 and 6 only once. The probability of the recurrence of *contingent* phenomena can be made the subject of calculation and yields interesting results. For the calculus of probabilities and its logical value, Bernouilli's theorem and Poisson's laws of numbers, see *Logique*, p. 352 f.

alone is strictly scientific. The particular sciences which
contemplate nature under one or other of its several aspects—
mechanics, chemistry, optics, etc.—aim at reducing their
conclusions to terms of mathematics and metaphysics. In
reality, then, there is one and one only scientific method, namely,
the analytico-synthetic, the combined inductive and deductive
method.

94. Method of Philosophy.—The same analytico-synthetic
method is that of all philosophical speculation. Philosophy
is the science of being in general, of *all being*, and therefore its
scope includes both the ideal order and the empirical order.
Both of them it traverses first *analytically* in order subsequently
to combine the results *synthetically* and thus offer a rational
explanation. In this sense is to be read Aristotle's definition
already quoted (*Gen. Introduction,* 4) : philosophy is the science
of things through their ultimate causes, or again, the science
founded on the universal order.

In each of its branches—physics, mathematics, metaphysics—philosophy avails itself of the inductive-deductive
method.

1. The physics of the ancients has been replaced to-day by
cosmology and psychology. Cosmology working from the
results of the physical, chemical and mineralogical sciences
arrives *inductivly* at the general conclusions that corporeal
substance is composed of matter and form and that it produces
certain distinctive activities. By these principles philosophy
explains *deductively* both the nature of corporeal activity
and the variety and stability of the laws which regulate it.
Similarly in psychology the observation of phenomena warrants
the *induction* that the first subject of human life is a material
compound informed by an immaterial soul ; and this conclusion, which forms the principle for the *synthetic* phase, enables
us to understand the proper object of the human intellect,
the complex character of man's life with the mutual dependence
of the activities of body and soul.

2. The philosophy of mathematics is bound up in practice,
and reasonably so, with the science of mathematics : no
mathematician ever separates his theorems from the axioms
from which they are deduced. Certain elementary *observations* are needed to suggest the axioms, and these in turn become
the principles of the *syntheses* from which are deduced the

sciences of number and quantity that eventually lead up to the more abstract speculations of pure geometry.

3. The several departments of the philosophical sciences lead the mind to objects *incapable of further analysis* and definition : physics to substance compounded of potentiality and actuality, of matter and form, to changes produced by an efficient cause in a passive subject under the influence of an intrinsic finality ; mathematics to unity, distinction, addition, number, etc., or to continuous quantity such as the line or the plain surface ; criteriology to truth ; ethics to the moral end, to the moral good ; logic to notional being, to the right ordering of the mind's objects. First philosophy or metaphysics gathers up the results of these philosophical branches, it contemplates these indefinable objects and their relations, and thus makes them principles of a general *synthesis* which constitutes ' rational wisdom ' (σοφία) or philosophy in the narrow, formal acceptation of the word.

The ideal aim of philosophy is to explain the universe with its elements and laws in the light of the most perfect synthetic knowledge man can attain of the First Cause, who has created all things by His almighty act and continues to govern by His infinite wisdom ; the comprehensive vision of the world in its First Cause is the culmination of the work of philosophy.

CHAPTER IV

THE FINAL CAUSE OF LOGICAL ORDER

95. Logic and the Attainment of Scientific Knowledge.—
The ordering or systematization of our judgments and reasonings that go to form a science is the intrinsic end of logic. Yet this orderly arrangement of our ideas is no guarantee of truth, which is the final object of man's intellect. The ultimate end of the logician therefore—though by contrast extrinsic—is certain knowledge of the truth. Such knowledge alone deserves the name of *scientia*, science, the understanding of what an object is.

96. Definition of Science.—We may define science as a body of propositions which are evident, certain, necessary and universal, as well as arranged systematically so as to form one whole, and which are drawn immediately or mediately from the nature of the subject and give the intrinsic reason of its properties and of the laws of its action.

We say these propositions which make up a science must be : (*a*) *Objectively evident*, that is, manifestly true. (*b*) *Certain :* scientific certitude is the fruit of reflective thought ; faith is concerned with objects formally lacking their own evidence and therefore cannot, as such, be the matter of scientific knowledge. (*c*) *Necessary, universal :* to collect particular facts is not the province of science, it is at most to prepare the way. The aim of the savant is to know what things are, apart from their contingent and variable circumstances, and what is the law of their action. 'Science deals only with the universal' is Aristotle's favourite dictum. (*d*) *Systematically arranged to form one whole.* Science is a unified body of propositions. The unity of science, considered *formally*, consists in this, that the first definitions furnish the principles whence all later propositions are synthetically deduced. These generating principles of a science are themselves founded on its formal object. This object is, if not the essence, at least a natural property of a real subject. Therefore the intimate reason of the unity of science is the *essence*, the *nature* (τὸ τί ἐστι) of the object.

Such unity is the *ideal of a perfect science*.

ETHICS

INTRODUCTION *

1. The Object of Ethics.—Ethical philosophy is a department of practical philosophy (*Gen. Introduction*, 7 and p. 20) ; it deals with the order to be realized in the free acts of the will. These acts of the will are its *material* object ; its *formal* object is the order that is to be established in these acts.

We may say, in other words, that it treats of human acts in relation to their ends. By human acts we mean those peculiar to man, i.e. those which are produced with a view to an end and are subject to the direction of reason and the control of free-will. These are also called moral acts.

2. General Ethics and Special Ethics.—Moral philosophy is divided into general ethics and special ethics. The former treats of the moral act in general and investigates the conditions under which it will conform to right order ; but it is not concerned with the various particular conditions relating to different moral acts. Special ethics, on the other hand, takes into consideration the variety of situations in which the moral agent may, and naturally does, find himself placed ; it examines the special requirements which flow from them when right order is to be brought about. According as special ethics considers the duties of man towards God, towards himself, or towards his fellow-men, it is called religious, personal, or social ethics.

---

* Books for study or consultation—
Cronin, *The Science of Ethics*, 2 vols. (Gill, Dublin, 1909-1917).
Jos. **Rickaby**, *Moral Philosophy* (Longmans, London, 3rd ed., 1900). *Aquinas Ethicus* (Burns and Oates, London, 1892).
Ryan, *A Living Wage* (ch. III, Basis and Justification of Rights) (Macmillan, London, 2nd ed., 1912).
Ming, *Data of Modern Ethics Examined* (Benziger, New York, 3rd ed., 1904).
Cathrein, *Socialism* (tr. Gettelman, Herder, St. Louis, 1904).
Plater, *A Primer of Peace and War* (*The Principles of International Morality*) (King, London, 1915).
Non-Scholastic—
Mackenzie, *A Manual of Ethics* (Clive, Tutorial Press, London, 5th ed., 1915).
Sidgwick, *Methods of Ethics* (Macmillan, London, 7th ed., 1907). *Outlines of the History of Ethics for English Readers* (Macmillan, London, 5th ed., 1902).

PART I

General Ethics : A Theory of Good and Evil

3. Division of General Ethics.—As the moral philosopher studies the order which should exist among acts of will and this order requires that acts should be appropriate to their ends, it will be necessary to give an account of *the end of human acts :* which will be the purpose of the first chapter. In the second we shall analyse the *psychological conditions* under which these human actions take place when there is question of subordinating them to the natural end of man. Next will arise the question, What is that moral order to which the acts of the will should conform ? This will form matter for the third chapter, which will treat of *moral order.* When we understand what is the moral order considered in itself, objectively, we shall then be in a position to give a final chapter to it in its subjective aspect, i.e. in as far as it is known and put into practice by the moral agent ; this final chapter will deal with the subjective aspect of the moral order, the human aspect of morality or as we specially designate it, *conscience.*

CHAPTER I

THE NATURAL END OF MAN

I. Preliminary Notions

4. Nature and Natural End : **The Good.**—None of the substances whose various manifestations come under our observation act in any sense aimlessly ; from the first moment of their existence they have a steady and continuous direction along one line, so that they make the many various forces at their disposal converge towards one supreme aim or end. The *end* is that for the sake of which anything comes to be done or made, *id cujus gratia aliquid fit*. The inherent inclination of a being towards its one end is called its natural tendency or, in one word, its *nature*. In its primary meaning, nature denotes the substance of a being in so far as it has within it a primary and internal principle of activity. This Aristotle defines as the intrinsic first principle of movement.

Nature, then, impresses upon the activity of a being a special direction, or tendency, towards a determinate end ; this end is also called the good of this being. The good is that which is in conformity with the natural tendency of any being : *Bonum est quod omnia appetunt*. It is a matter of indifference whether we say that the object towards which the natural activity of a being is attracted is its end or its good. We use one or the other term according as we consider either the direction of the activity towards its final aim or the relation of conformity between this end and the agent seeking it. *Finis et bonum, quamvis e suo conceptu formaliter distincta, objective tamen seu materialiter convertuntur* (*Gen. Metaphysics*, **66-75**).

Further, since the good is the source of all self-perfection, *bonum est perfectivum*, it is clear that a being perfects itself, or realizes itself to the full, by following the impulse of its nature. To strive after its natural good and to perfect itself are in reality one and the same thing.

5. Diversity of Natural Tendencies.—The inclination of any being towards its natural end may be exercised in two ways, namely, according as it enjoys the power of self-direction towards it or is passively directed.   In both cases the movement which proceeds from this fundamental tendency is different from a movement communicated by a cause that is wholly external ; and the reason of this is that the subject of the natural movement does itself contribute to its movement, whereas a body that is merely the subject of an extrinsic impulse does not contribute to it in any way.   The older philosophers called the first kind of movement natural, the second violent.

But natural movement itself is quite different according as it is or is not preceded by a knowledge of the end towards which it is tending ; the latter is simply natural, the former natural also, but in addition voluntary or spontaneous.

Man alone directs his actions in the full sense of the word, since he alone can freely order his will.   He knows the end which is assigned to him, he can freely direct himself towards it by suitable means, or, freely but culpably, turn himself from it.

6. Kinds of Ends.—The end is called proximate or immediate when it is subordinated to a higher end ; it is the last or supreme end when it is related to no ulterior end.   The last end may be the last subjectively, i.e. in the intention of the agent aiming at it, or the last in reality, in the ontological order of natural ends and means.   The latter is meant when we speak without qualification of the last end.

7. Kinds of Good.—We distinguish three kinds of good. 1. The will may be disposed towards an object considered as good in itself ; such an object is an *absolute* good.   It may also tend towards an object not as good in itself, but as leading towards an ulterior good ; such an object constitutes a *relative* good, *bonum utile,* a useful good.   The absolute good is an end for the will, the relative good is only a means.

2. By virtue of a psychological law, the attainment of the good is a source of pleasure to the conscious subject.   In striving after a good object the will may at the same time seek the pleasure which it will experience in the attainment of that object.   The good object itself is called the *objective* good ; the pleasure which its possession brings to the subject is *bonum delectabile*—the *agreeable* good.

3. The good object towards which the will under the guidance of right reason is inclined, is called *bonum honestum*.

When speaking of the natural tendency and of the end of a being, we are considering the being in the fullness of its nature. Thus while man certainly possesses many tendencies, so that we might even say that he has as many particular ends as he has faculties, yet when considered in the fullness of his being and activity, he has *one* fundamental tendency, one end only.

II. The Last End of Human Nature

In this section we shall show that man has one natural end and only one ; next we shall determine what that end is.

8. First Thesis : **Man has Subjectively and Really a Last Natural End.**—I. The human will is necessarily satisfied with an end which bears no further relation to a higher end. Human acts, by their very definition, are acts performed with a view to an end. Let us suppose one of these acts performed with a view to an end which we will call A. One of two results follows : either this end is a supreme end in which the will is at rest, or it is an end which the will refers to a higher end B. In the first hypothesis the thesis stands proved. In the second, the question is simply put further back, for we have to ask with regard to B what we have already asked respecting A : is it the last end of the will or is it subordinated to a further end C ? It may be that the end B is related to another end C, and C to D, but it is impossible that there should be no limit to this subordination of ends to a higher end. In a series of ends subordinated to one another, so that one does not act as an end except under the influence of another, the suppression of a last end, desirable in itself and capable of evoking the others, involves the abolition of every intermediate tendency and consequently the impossibility of any moral action. Hence there must exist a supreme end which possesses in itself the power of moving the will through the medium of the subordinated ends. ' If there were no last end, nothing would be desired, nor would any action have its term, nor would the intention of the agent be at rest ; while if there were no first thing among those that are ordained to the end, no one would begin to work at anything, and counsel would have no term, but would continue indefinitely ' [1].

II. ' There exists in reality a supreme natural end for human acts '.

Psychology teaches that man possesses a variety of faculties, each of which finds its expression in specifically different actions ; yet it also lays down, with no less emphasis, that man is a single substantial being, one nature, one person. In a word, there are in man many secondary principles of action, but all proceed from one primary principle. Now, every principle of action tends by its activity towards an end. Hence, the primary principle of action tends towards a primary end, and the secondary or derived principles of action can tend only towards an end subordinate to this primary end. This primary end is the natural end of man, his natural good, the cause (ratio) of all his progress towards perfection.

This may be more clearly seen from the fact that, were we to suppose human nature capable of being without an end, we should have to admit a disorder against which would have to be set the perfect order of the universe, especially the pre-eminent dignity of man, who is the crowning work of nature.

It is, moreover, impossible to suppose that an infinitely wise Being, the Creator of our nature, should have put in us a natural tendency which could never find its fulfilment.

9. Second Thesis : Man has only One Natural End.—' It is impossible for one man's will to be directed at the same time to diverse things, as last ends. The first reason is because, since everything desires its own perfection, a man desires for his ultimate end, that which he desires as his perfect and crowning good. It is therefore necessary for the last end so to fill man's appetite, that nothing is left beside it for man to desire. Which is not possible, if something else be required for his perfection. Consequently it is not possible for the appetite so to tend to two things, as though each were its perfect good ' [2].

---

[1] ' Si non esset ultimus finis, nihil appeteretur, nec aliqua actio terminaretur, nec etiam quiesceret intentio agentis. Si autem non esset primum in his quae sunt ad finem, nullus inciperet aliquid operari, nec terminaretur consilium, sed in infinitum procederet '. ST. THOMAS, *Sum. Theol.*, I-II, q. 1, a. 4.

[2] ' Impossibile est quod voluntas unius hominis simul se habeat ad diversa sicut ad ultimos fines. Prima ratio est, quia cum unumquodque appetat suam perfectionem, illud appetit aliquis ut ultimum finem quod appetit ut

The last end, St. Thomas tells us, must so fulfil all our desires that outside it there is nothing left as an object of further desire. Hence it follows that we cannot have two or more last ends. If one good satisfies our desires to the full, how could the will seek anything beyond ? And what purpose would a second good or a second end serve ?

10. Third Thesis : **The End of Human Nature, regarded Indeterminately and in the Abstract, is the Happiness of man.**—This is a conclusion rather than a thesis requiring proof. It is clear that the end of man gives full satisfaction to his natural tendency ; it is the complete good which excludes evil under all its forms and fulfils all the aspirations of human nature ; and this is the definition of happiness—' *Beatitudo, cum sit perfectum bonum, omne malum excludit et omne desiderium implet* '.

But in what does this complete and all-sufficing good in reality consist ? What is the object capable of providing man with perfect happiness ?

11. Fourth Thesis : **Regarded in the Concrete, the Objective End is in no Created Good ; it is in God.**—1. *Negative argument.*—The object capable of making us happy must completely satiate all our desires ; its possession must be secure and assured ; and this object must be attainable by all. But in no created good are all these conditions verified. Therefore no created good can be the adequate object of our happiness.

Proof of the minor : There are three kinds of goods : those of the body, those of the soul, and external goods. But all these goods have a threefold deficiency which renders them powerless to constitute man's beatitude : they are so incomplete that they have never satisfied anyone ; they are of so short duration and so unstable that no one can possess them without anxiety and fear of losing them ; they are so limited that they can be possessed only by a small number of people. No created good, then, can verify the conditions of man's objective beatitude. Furthermore, a union of all these different goods would be equally powerless to make man perfectly happy, for the insufficiency of each class is not due to the quantity but to the intrinsic quality of these goods.

bonum perfectum et completivum sui ipsius. Oportet igitur quod ultimus finis ita impleat totum hominis appetitum, quod nihil extra ipsum appetendum relinquatur ; quod esse non potest, si aliquid extraneum ad ipsius perfectionem requiratur. Unde non potest esse quod in duo sic tendat appetitus, ac si utrumque sit bonum perfectum ipsius '. *Id., Sum. Theol.,* I-II, q. 1, a. 5.

2. *Positive argument.*—The object in which our nature finds its absolute rest is none other than God Himself, the Uncreated Good. For an object can be the adequate cause of man's happiness only on condition that it realizes the whole perfection of which man is naturally capable ; and only in God is this condition verified.

Proof of the minor : Man's organic and sensitive powers are manifestly subservient to his intellect and will. The will in its turn comes into action only after the exercise of the intellect, under the attraction of the object which this latter presents to it. We must then conclude that the perfection of our nature is primarily connected with the perfection of the intellect. Now the perfection of the intellect demands the most perfect knowledge possible of its formal object, i.e. *the synthetic knowledge of the essences of all material things, through their supreme cause, of their properties and laws, together with the analogical knowledge of the supersensible realities that are connected with them.* Or more briefly, the complete development of the mind's activity is the knowledge of the First Cause, the principle of the order of the universe. Here, then, at length we have an object capable of making man happy.

How is he to come into possession of this object ? By what means will the objective beatitude communicate to him his subjective happiness ?

12. Fifth Thesis : Man enters into the Possession of his Happiness by an Act of his Intellect.—Human nature with its endowment of many faculties finds its highest perfection in the exercise of these faculties ; for action is the complement of the capacities of a subject.

The sense-faculties are subordinate to the intellectual faculties. It is evidently by the exercise of the latter that man's perfection must be attained.

Two faculties are man's highest endowment, viz. his intellect and his will. With which of these must the supreme happiness of man be connected ?

Philosophers are divided on this question. St. Bonaventure attributes happiness to both intellect and will, whilst St. Thomas and Duns Scotus argue for a single faculty—the former for the intellect, the latter for the will. The difference between these three is only one of standpoint. However this may be, we are of opinion that it is in the exercise of the intellect that the supreme end of human nature is formally realized.

Proof.—The exercise of the will cannot constitute the subjective end of human nature. Therefore this end must essentially be in an act of the intellect.

The act by which human nature enters formally into possession of its beatitude cannot be an act of the will. For we may distinguish two states in the activity of the will : the tendency of the will towards its end and the gratification of this tendency in its end. Now suppose the will at one moment to be in a state of tendency, of movement towards its end, and consider it again at a second moment when, having passed from its first state, it is in a state of repose. How has the passage from the first state to the second been brought about ? Clearly some change must have been produced in the disposition of the will with regard to its end ; and what could such a change be in the case of the will except its being brought into contact with its good by means of a representation made by the act of the intellect ? Hence the act by which human nature immediately enters into possession of its supreme end, the act by which the taking possession of the supreme end is actually brought about, is an act of intellect.

If it is true that the act which formally puts the human soul in possession of its end is an intellectual act, it remains to be inquired, as a last analysis, whether this is an act of the speculative or of the practical intellect.

13. Sixth Thesis : **Subjective Beatitude is realized by an Act of the Speculative Intellect.**—There are three considerations in support of this assertion : (1) God is not the object of the practical intellect. (2) Contemplation of the truth is sought for its own sake ; on the other hand, acts of the practical reason are considered with a view to the end for which the will pursues them and realizes them. (3) It is by the speculative intellect that man comes nearer to beings superior to himself.

14. Corollaries.—1. Two points are established : (*a*) God is the supreme objective end of human nature. (*b*) The means by which human nature attains its supreme objective end is the contemplation of God. This contemplation is, then, the subjective end of human nature ; yet, to speak strictly, it is only a subordinate end—'*finis sub fine*', as St. Thomas expresses it.

2. What is the part played by the will in the possession of
our end ?—The final love of God and the satisfaction which
this love affords the will does not constitute the essence of
beatitude.   The enjoyment of supreme happiness is the natural
consequence of obtaining our end, but it is only a consequence
of this.   For if this enjoyment is a good, it is because the
intellectual activity which has given rise to it is in reality the
supreme perfection of our rational nature.

15. Summary and Conclusion.—The end of a being is the most
perfect act of which its nature is capable.   In the case of man
this act is the contemplative knowledge of God.   This knowledge constitutes the end of man, his natural beatitude.

But the perfection of an act of knowledge, as indeed of any
action, involves three things : an object, a subject or principle
of action, and the delectation of which the action is the source.
With regard to the first, the perfection of our most perfect act
is God : He is then the perfection of the objective end of our
nature.   With regard to the second, the subjective end of our
nature is the exercise of our thought applied to its highest
object ; that is to say, it is the contemplation of God.   Finally,
with regard to the third, the complacency which results in the
will from the union of our nature with its supreme end also
forms part of our end.   However, as an action presupposes the
object towards which it tends, it is necessary to say that the
absolute last end is God, ' *finis ultimus* ' ; and the subjective
beatitude and the felicity which it brings are a subordinate
end, ' *finis sub fine* '.

16. A Difficulty.—This study of the end of man raises a
difficulty.   If every subordinate end borrows its influence from
the supreme end, it must be impossible for us to will anything
without God Himself being the first object of our knowledge and
love.   But our consciousness does not inform us that the
knowledge and love of God are the motive of all our acts of
volition.

It is true that man does not always represent his supreme
end to himself under the explicit concept of the Divine Being.
Hence we have from the first distinguished between two concepts of our last end, the one abstract and undetermined, the
other concrete and determined.   It is under the first concept
alone that the last end governs all our acts of will.   Further,
even under this undetermined form the end of man is not

always willed actually and consciously. What we have established is that every good for the will is either the perfect good itself, or else a particular good which can be the object of our will only inasmuch as it is related to the perfect good. It is in this sense that the desire of the Sovereign Good inspires, at any rate implicitly and virtually, each of our acts of volition,

17. Beatitude in the Present Life.—During his earthly life man does not experience that complete development of his being which allays all desire and want and endows the soul with the imperturbable repose of happiness. Beatitude in the full sense is possible only in a life to come. Nevertheless, in a restricted sense, happiness is not incompatible with the conditions of our earthly life. ' Some are said to be happy in this life, either on account of the hope of obtaining happiness in the life to come ; or on account of a certain participation of happiness, by reason of a kind of enjoyment of the Sovereign Good '. ' Men esteem that there is some kind of happiness to be had in this life, on account of a certain likeness to true happiness. And thus they do not fail altogether in their estimate ' [3].

18. Conditions for the Realization of Happiness.—Now that we have explained and proved the fundamental thesis concerning the essence of man's beatitude, it remains to consider what are the conditions on which happiness is to be realized.

1. A first condition is the rectitude of the will or sinlessness. The love that the will bears to its supreme end naturally includes the love of the means which conduce to it. But the love of the end and of the means relating to it will be rationally ordered only if the love of the means is subordinated to the love of the end ; and this subordination of the love of the means to that of the end is simply the rectitude of the will. Thus the rectitude of the will is one of the conditions of the state of beatitude.

2. Another condition of perfect happiness is security against its loss. Perfect happiness requires that the natural tendencies of the will shall be satisfied. But these aspirations are co-extensive with our intellectual knowledge, and this does not

[3] ' Beati dicuntur aliqui in hac vita vel propter spem beatitudinis adipiscendae in futura vita, vel propter aliquam participationem beatitudinis secundum aliqualem summi boni fruitionem.—Homines reputant in hac vita esse aliquam beatitudinem, propter aliquam similitudinem verae beatitudinis : et sic non ex toto in sua aestimatione deficiunt '. St. Thomas, *Sum. Theol.*, I-II, q. 5, a. 3, ad 1 and ad 3.

confine existence and happiness within a limited duration but abstracts from all time-limits. Thus the natural desire of existence and happiness cannot be satisfied if the happiness may be limited or lost.

Besides, the soul cannot enjoy a single moment's happiness which in other respects may be perfect, unless it is certain that its happiness must endure for ever.

3. Is the union of the soul and the body also a necessary condition of the state of perfect happiness ?   (a) It is certain that the body is not *essential* to the happiness of the soul. (b) On the other hand, since the union of soul and body is natural, we cannot admit that the reunion of the body with the soul after the dissolution of the compound can be an obstacle to perfect happiness.   (c) Indeed, it seems that the reunion of the soul and the body answers to the exigencies of human nature. If the human organism did not contribute its share to the perfection of the noblest faculties of the soul, we should be right in concluding that the union of the human compound is against nature (*Psychology*, **172**).

Here, however, we are met by a difficulty in the Thomistic explanation.

19. A Difficulty.—St. Thomas writes in the *Summa Contra Gentes :* ' The human soul becomes more perfect in proportion as it frees itself from the trammels of the body. For the highest knowledge consists in knowing whatever is most immaterial, and moral rectitude is measured by the ardour with which the will restrains the animal passions. It would seem, then, that the soul, far from being dissolved by its separation from the body, finds its perfection in this very separation '.

The first answer is that it is by no means inevitable that in every case the human body should impede the expansion of the higher activity of the soul ; these hindrances are an accidental consequence of the imperfections of the body which the spiritual soul has for the present at its service.

We must next distinguish carefully between the absolute and the relative perfection of a separated soul. It cannot be denied that a purely spiritual mode of knowledge is, absolutely speaking, superior to the psychological process which is dependent on the concurrence of bodily organs. But a process of cognition which is too elevated may be a relative imperfection for a soul that is not raised to so noble a state of perfection.

20. Accidental Qualities of Happiness.—The state of perfect happiness seems to demand certain qualities which are accidental and complementary. (a) After the general resurrection of the dead, which we suppose will be brought about by an almighty yet natural intervention of Divine Providence (*Psychology*, **172**), the sensitive faculties, no longer hampered by the countless infirmities of the present life, will exercise their activities in so far as this is compatible with the free play of the higher faculties. They will be subject to the empire of the will in such a way that the most perfect harmony will rule in all the manifestations of life ; the human body will receive from the beatified soul an increase of perfection, glory and joy. (b) Thus constituted in beatitude man will find a place of existence befitting his interior state. And (c) most probably will also find there the joys peculiar to him as a social being.

21. The End of Man is a Supernatural End.—If man had been made according to a state of pure nature (*Psychology*, **173**), and had he directed his aspirations towards the end then proposed to him, he would even so have been able to be the possessor of beatitude. But what might have been we know is not. From the moment of his creation God in matter of fact assigned to the first man, and to all his descendants, a *supernatural destiny*, that is to say, a destiny above the exigencies of all created nature and beyond its power of attainment. At the same time He gave them the supernatural means which were requisite for the realization of this end.

22. Does the Conception of a Natural Happiness involve a Contradiction ?—Our destiny is in point of fact a supernatural one ; such a destiny is intrinsically possible, since we know that it is actually a reality. May we, then, still speak of a happiness that is purely natural ? To be happy is to be in possession of a good which gives full satisfaction to the desires of the will, and if it is admitted that human nature is capable, by supernatural aid, of knowing God intuitively, it would seem that a discursive knowledge of God cannot suffice for man's happiness.

One attempt at solving this difficulty has been made by declaring that in the condition of pure nature—which the objection supposes—it would have been utterly impossible for man even to conceive the possibility of a supernatural intuitive vision of the Infinite. We doubt, however, whether this summary assertion has sufficient foundation.

It seems necessary here to make some distinctions : (1) Reason is in a position to establish with certainty that the vision of the Divine Essence surpasses the natural exigencies and capabilities of every creature. Man would not then have found in his nature any inclination (*appetitus innatus seu naturalis*) calling for the vision of the Divine Being as its final perfection. (2) Without the light of revelation man could not have convinced himself of the *positive* possibility of the vision of God nor of the essential capacity of a rational creature to bear such an intense felicity. On the contrary, he would surely have concluded that the vision of God was beyond the reach of created nature. It is reasonable to say that the will of man, in the condition of pure nature, is incapable of willing the vision of God with a categorical absolute will (*appetitus elicitus efficax*). (3) Nevertheless we are inclined to think that unaided natural reason might easily have conjectured the possibility of obtaining from the divine Omnipotence an intuitive knowledge of the Deity. From this would have followed a conditional desire (*appetitus elicitus inefficax*), a ' velleity ', a hope, rather than a categorical will, of the sight of God. But under the guidance of the wisdom proceeding from his reason, his will might have kept this desire within the limits ordained by the plan of Providence, and might have subordinated it to the higher absolute desire of maintaining the order of the universe which is the expression of the will of God. Hence it follows that the conception of a natural happiness is in no way a contradiction.

After these considerations the question of ascertaining whether the attainment of the natural end does or does not merit the name of happiness reduces itself to a matter of words. The happiness of a being consists in the possession of its supreme end. Now doubtless the supernatural end alone is, in the absolute sense of the word, the supreme end of an intelligent nature, in the real order of things in which we find ourselves placed. Yet the natural end, which in a possible order of things might have constituted the complete and exclusive end of man, is also, in a legitimate yet relative sense, a supreme end—that is to say, one not subordinated to a higher end. Thus there is nothing to prevent the attainment of the natural end being called happiness, though in a sense less complete than that of the supernatural end.

CHAPTER II

FREE-WILL

23. Object and Division of this Chapter.—The end of man's nature has been discussed. Later we shall see that the moral order consists in the subordination of the human act to this natural end. But the very existence of a moral order essentially distinct from the physical order rests on the presupposition that there is liberty in the subject. A chapter must, then, be devoted to the study of free-will. As the question of liberty has, however, already been treated in *Psychology* (**112-120**), it will suffice for us to recall in a preliminary section the various doctrines there established, and in a second to deal with moral philosophy, especially the influence of the passions on certain aspects of liberty that are of special importance in free-will.

I. MEANING AND PROOFS OF FREEDOM OF THE WILL

24. Meaning of Liberty.—The free act excludes all necessitating determination, no matter whether this determination comes from an exterior cause or from some internal law. The free act is such that, given all the antecedents necessary for its production, it depends upon the will to assent or to refuse assent. Liberty has its root in an indetermination of the judgment ; it resides formally in the will. Our abstract judgments, it is true, are always determined, but acts of free-will, since they have particular, individual facts for their object, can always be influenced by particular, contradictory and undetermined judgments of the mind. Consequently it belongs to the will and to it alone to put an end to the indetermination.

Moral liberty is the faculty of choice between different objects considered in their relation to the end of rational nature.   Indeed, it implies in man the faculty of choice between moral good and evil, but this power is a weakness and an imperfection of our free-will.

25. Proofs of Free-will.—Our consciousness informs us that we are free, and the study of the free act gives us the inner reason of this fact.   The universal good exercises an irresistible determining action upon us, since it corresponds adequately with the capacity of our will.   But with particular goods this is not the case.   These *may be* willed ; for they are means towards the attainment of the whole good (*summum bonum*) and on this account are real goods.   They *need not* be willed, since they are not *the* good.   Hence when the final determination is made, it does not proceed merely from the object but must depend on the will ; this faculty therefore controls its own volition (*Psychology*, **115**).

II. THE INFLUENCE OF THE PASSIONS ON FREE-WILL

26. Statement of the Question.—The exercise of liberty always involves a judgment on the part of the intellect and an act of desire on the part of the will.   Now although they are spiritual, the intellect and the will depend for the exercise of their action upon the sensitive faculties.   These latter are organic and therefore subordinate to the integrity and normal functioning of the organism.   Hence liberty depends in its exercise on the same material conditions.   This dependence is especially the case when the free act is not simply an act of the will (*actus elicitus*) but an act of an organic faculty resulting from a command of the will (*actus imperatus*).

27. Extent of the Influence of Man's Sensitive Nature and of Material Causes on Free-will.—That there are certain unfortunate individuals who owing to mental derangement are irresponsible, is beyond doubt and has never been disputed. That there are others who, whilst able to form correct judgments on speculative matters, are incapable of resisting solicitations to evil, does not contradict any point of our doctrine but seems rather to be established by experience.   It may not be even impossible that there exists, as Lombroso professed, ' a criminal type ', that is to say, monsters irresistibly given over to crime who can be recognized by certain anatomical, physiological and pathological characteristics. Such characteristics are to be found more or less numerous among most criminals. Further, we may also admit, though the experiments on which this assertion rests must be handled with caution, that a person may under the influence of hypnotic suggestion lose the use of his liberty. All these facts are not incompatible with the theory of free-will, as the exception does not disprove the rule.

Beyond these exceptions just mentioned, the passions or lower emotional states and external material agents do not generally do more than weaken moral liberty.

We are not concerned here with the passions which are consequent upon the free act, since so long as they are consequent upon it they cannot affect its nature : they are rather an indication of the intensity of the will's action and are subjects of its reaction. But of the *antecedent passions* the case is otherwise. Sometimes their action is in the same direction as that of the will, sometimes in opposition to it. When they act in the direction of the will, it would seem they ought to increase the liberty rather than weaken it ; but such is not the case. Self-control, the characteristic feature of freedom, is lost in proportion as sensible emotion increases. When the lower appetite pulls in opposition to the higher, liberty is thereby lessened, but it is not true to lay down as a general rule that it is made entirely to cease. Our consciousness clearly testifies that we have a real power of control over our passions ; one which if not absolute is none the less real because limited. We may exert it in different ways. Either indirectly, by diverting the soul's activity, through change of thought, through applying the will to other objects, even through exciting other passions. Or directly, by the will directly acting on the passions, to strengthen them or to repress them, at least to a certain extent. Or yet by a third way, perhaps the most effectual : by conjuring up in the imagination some appropriate object and retaining the sensitive appetite under its influence until the new passion neutralises what reason would have us combat.

The *organic or material conditions* of temperament and heredity, habits of life, climate and temperature, have all an immense influence on the functions of our sensitive nature and hence, indirectly, on the will ; but apart from certain anomalous and very rare cases their influence is not incompatible with liberty and responsibility [4].

28. Nature of the Influence of External Causes on the Will.— What is the influence which extrinsic causes, such as the sensitive appetite, the state of the bodily organs and material agencies, are able to exercise over the free will ?

1. First of all, no agent whatsoever, not even the action of God Almighty, can exercise violence in the strict sense upon the action of a human will. Violence may be done to our limbs, preventing by physical force a movement commanded by our will, but volition, the *actus elicitus* of our free-will, is by its nature proof against every directly constraining action [5].

2. No external agent, except God Himself, can have a necessitating influence over the determinations of the will.

3. The sensitive appetite influences the will directly and indirectly. Directly, either by strengthening it when it seeks the same object as the will, or by weakening it when it seeks a contrary object. In the latter case the loss of energy on the part of the will corresponds with the intensity of the lower appetite. Indirectly—and in a no less degree because the manner is indirect—by means of the passions affecting the cognitive faculties : they create a disturbance of the organism and in consequence upset the mind which is objectively dependent on the sensitive faculties. They also exercise a powerful influence over sensuous knowledge, for by reason of the attractions and repulsions which they foster within us they help to fix the imagination upon certain objects to the exclusion of others, a proceeding which cannot fail to exercise a bad influence on the rectitude of the judgment and on the uprightness and steadfastness of the will.

[4] ' Ex corpore aliquo modo voluntas inclinatur, non necessario, quia resistere potest, sicut cholerici ex naturali complexione inclinantur ad iram ; tamen aliquis cholericus potest resistere per voluntatem isti inclinationi '. St. Thomas, *De Veritate*, q. 22, a. 9, ad 2.

' Incontinens dicitur vinci a passionibus, non quasi ipsae passiones cogant vel immutent necessario voluntatem, sed in quantum earum impulsui voluntarie cedit '. *Ibid.*, ad 3.

[5] ' Deus potest immutare voluntatem de necessitate, non tamen potest eam cogere. Quantumcumque enim voluntas immutetur in aliquid, non dicitur cogi in illud. Cujus ratio est, quia ipsam velle aliquid est inclinari in illud ; coactio autem vel violentia est contraria inclinationi illius rei quae cogitur. Cum igitur Deus voluntatem immutat, facit ut praecedenti inclinationi succedat alia inclinatio, et ita quod prima auferatur et secunda maneat. Unde illud ad quod inducit voluntatem, non est contrarium inclinationi jam existenti, sed inclinationi quae prius inerat : unde non est violentia nec coactio '. *Ibid.*

4. The influence of the sensitive appetite upon our will leads us to understand how external agents and especially material agents are able to affect it. Their action is always indirect and remote since it must be exercised through the medium of the sensitive appetite.

We see, then, that between the fully free act—in the carrying out of which man has a clear view of the morality of his conduct and has complete control of his will—and the act entirely lacking responsibility and freedom, there are possible many intermediate states, in which the senses and the reason, the passions and the spiritual faculty of the will, each strive for their share in the determination of our activity.

CHAPTER III

THE MORAL ORDER

29. Object and Division of this Chapter.—The philosophy of the moral act comprises two parts : the one treats of human liberty, which is the psychological condition of morality ; the other, of the relations of the free act to good and evil. We have now to study this second part ; and we shall consider in order : (i) The distinction between good and evil ; (ii) The foundation of this distinction ; (iii) The moral law, which obliges us to choose certain goods ; (iv) The moral virtues, which arise from the observance of the moral law ; (v) Our knowledge of the moral law ; (vi) The sanction of the moral law ; (vii) Natural characteristics of the moral law.

I. Moral Good and Evil

30. There is a Real, Intrinsic Distinction between Moral Good and Moral Evil.—1. *Argument drawn from consciousness.*—Certain things come before our consciousness as good and right, other things as bad and wrong, and this distinction imposes itself upon us with irresistible evidence. Similarly there are certain judgments about good and evil, justice and injustice, virtue and vice, the truth of which it is impossible to contest with any sincerity.

2. *Inductive argument.*—Induction confirms the data of consciousness. The distinction between good and evil is always presented before us with such notes of necessity, universality and persistence—and this in spite of the contrary solicitations of passions and interests—that a sufficient reason for it can only be found in the objective manifestation of truth, or better, of compelling truths which are anterior to every code of merely human origin and independent of all contingent circumstances. Hence, short of denying the natural capacity of human reason to know the truth, and of

thus logically professing scepticism, we must admit that the distinction between moral good and evil is founded on the very nature of things.

No doubt the application of moral principles to particular facts allows of divergences and variations more or less considerable ; but the root ideas of good and evil, of just and unjust, of lawful and unlawful, are the same at all times and among all peoples.

3. *Deductive argument.*—Another argument may be drawn from the study of human nature itself. The good or right is by definition that which leads to the end of man's rational nature ; conversely, we call wrong whatever is in opposition to the end of human nature. Now there must be some objects suitable, others unsuitable to human nature [6]. Therefore between moral good and evil there must be a distinction which is founded on the nature of things.

31. The Distinction between the Goodness and Badness of Human Actions is not explained in its Ultimate Analysis by any Extrinsic or Positive Influence, whether Human or even Divine.—Many writers think that purely positive influences can account for this distinction, such as traditional prepossessions, social conventions or laws, or an absolutely free decree of God. Montaigne thought it enough to appeal to the prejudices created by education. Hobbes and Rousseau both made the civil law the foundation of morality. It would seem that Puffendorf, and before him Descartes, attributed to God's free will the power of creating the distinction made by us between moral good and evil.

In the first place, this distinction is not explained by any human influence. (*a*) The nature of good and evil, as presented to our consciousness and reproduced in the invincible convictions of the human race, has already shown that the distinction between the rightness and wrongness of certain actions is independent of all positive intervention or system of government. A cause that is local, particular and changing cannot explain an effect that is universal, general and constant. (*b*) It is useless to have recourse with Hobbes to the despotic commands of an absolute monarch, or with Rousseau to the exigencies of a social contract ; such commands or contracts do

---

[6] St. Thomas, *Cont. Gent.*, III, c. 129.

not themselves possess, *ex hypothesi*, an intrinsic goodness and consequently cannot communicate it to the acts which it is their purpose to regulate.

In the second place, this distinction does not rest on a free decree of the Divine Will. The opinion that makes the distinction between good and evil depend on the free will of God leads to inadmissible consequences : (*a*) God might then make blasphemy, perjury, violation of contracts and the like obligatory upon us. (*b*) Whatever is morally good would be obligatory, and even heroism would be a duty forced upon us. (*c*) If all moral law owed its origin to a free act of the sovereign will of God, a positive revelation would be necessary for us to discern the difference between good and evil. Such conclusions as these condemn the principle from which they logically follow.

II. The Foundation of the Distinction between Moral Good and Evil

32. The Distinction between Good and Evil is founded on the Natural Conformity or Non-conformity of our Acts with our Supreme End.—If the good is what answers to the natural tendency of a being, the moral good is what answers to the tendency of the rational nature of man and is that by which he perfects himself. Now the end of our rational nature is the knowledge and love of God together with the joy that results from this knowledge and love. Hence a morally good act is one which, whether directly or indirectly, helps us to know and love God, and in so doing contributes to the perfecting of our rational nature ; similarly, a thing is morally good which is the object of a morally good act.

Moral evil, on the other hand, is what is in opposition to the end of our rational nature ; it is the act which is prejudicial to the perfecting of our rational nature, or it is the object of this act ; in its ultimate analysis it is whatever withdraws us from the perfect knowledge and love of the Supreme Being and from the happiness which these acts should bring us.

What, as a matter of fact, is the criterion by which we judge of the intrinsic morality of an action ? Do we not always find it in the connexion of this action with the perfection of our nature or, what comes to the same, in its connexion with our

supreme end ?　We condemn drunkenness and licentiousness,
we look upon them as vices, because they degrade and disgrace
us.　We esteem temperance and chastity as true virtues,
because they ennoble us and answer to the demands of our
dignity as men.

33. Corollary.—Every good act is, at least implicitly or
virtually, an act which contributes to the glory of God, just as
every bad act is an offence against the majesty of God.　Hence,
St. Thomas teaches that every morally bad act, inasmuch as
it cannot be referred to God, the last end of creation, is blameworthy in His sight [7].

34. The Sources of Morality.—There are three things which
determine the goodness or badness of a human action, namely,
the formal object, the circumstances and the end.

1. The *formal object* is the first determinant of the goodness
or badness of a human action.　By formal object we mean not
the reality, considered absolutely, of a thing, but the reality
looked at in reference to the moral act, as bearing a relation of
conformity or want of conformity with the end of the
rational nature of the agent.　Thus a sum of money unjustly
acquired is the object of an act of theft, whereas the same
money bestowed freely on the poor becomes the object of an
act of almsgiving [8].

2. The objective *circumstances* of time, place and person
likewise contribute their share to the character of the moral
act.　Thus to steal five shillings from a poor man is a greater
wrong than to steal the same amount from a rich one.

3. Finally, the *extrinsic purpose* contributes to the perfection
or imperfection of an act.　Thus to give an alms from a religious
motive is an act which presents two distinct kinds of goodness,

---

[7] St. Thomas, *Sum. Theol.*, I-II, q. 21, a. 4.

[8] St. Thomas, *Sum. Theol.*, I-II, q. 18, a. 2.　' Bonum actionis, sicut et
caeterarum rerum, attenditur ex plenitudine essendi vel defectu ipsius.　Primum autem, quod ad plenitudinem essendi pertinere videtur, est id quod dat
rei speciem.　Sicut autem res naturalis habet speciem ex sua forma, ita actio
habet speciem ex objecto, sicut et motus ex termino.　Et ideo sicut prima
bonitas rei naturalis attenditur ex sua forma, quae dat speciem ei, ita et
prima bonitas actus moralis attenditur ex objecto convenienti : unde et a
quibusdam vocatur *bonum ex genere*, puta uti re sua.　Et sicut in rebus
naturalibus primum malum est, si res generata non consequitur formam
specificam, puta si non generetur homo, sed aliquid loco hominis, ita primum
malum in actionibus moralibus est quod est ex objecto, sicut accipere aliena,
et dicitur *malum ex genere*, genere pro specie accepto, eo modo loquendi quo
dicimus *humanum genus* totam humanam speciem '.

the one intrinsic to the act, that of succouring the needy, the other extrinsic, that of loving Christ in His suffering members.

For an act to be totally good, it must be so in itself, in its motives and in its circumstances. The absence of any one of these conditions is sufficient to make the act a bad one : ' Bonum ex integra causa, malum ex quocumque defectu '.

The question may well be raised here whether there is such a thing as an *indifferent or non-moral act :* is every human act necessarily either good or bad ? This is a subject of controversy among the theological schools. According to St. Thomas a human act that is really indifferent is impossible. Though there are human acts which, if we consider their object only, are neither good nor bad, yet taken in their concrete reality together with their end and the circumstances determining them they are necessarily either moral or immoral [9] **(61)**.

35. Neither Individual nor Social Well-being is the Measure of Moral Worth.—Hobbes and in general all the adherents of the modern positivist school consider man's well-being, that is, the pleasure of the present life, to be the sole motive-force of all our actions. In consequence, since the goodness of an action consists for everyone in its relation of conformity with his supreme end, pleasure and pain are the standard of right and wrong. Well-being thus becomes the ultimate criterion of morality.

The later positivists, such as Littré, Herbert Spencer, and Huxley, differ from Hobbes in this, that they have attempted to substitute the well-being of the community for the egoistic pleasure of the individual.

36. Criticism of Individualistic Utilitarianism.—1. We may notice first of all that it would involve a contradiction to maintain that pleasure is the first object of all volition. As a matter of fact, pleasure results from volition, which therefore naturally precedes the pleasure that it begets.

2. Pleasure is essentially relative to the individual person and

---

[9] Alexander VIII condemned as scandalous, rash, dangerous and erroneous the proposition : ' Peccatum philosophicum seu morale est actus humanus disconveniens naturae rationali et rectae rationi: theologicum vero et mortale est transgressio libera divinae legis. Philosophicum, quantumvis grave, in illo qui Deum vel ignorat vel de Deo actu non cogitat, est grave peccatum sed non est offensa Dei, neque peccatum mortale dissolvens amicitiam Dei neque aeterna poena dignum '. See DENZINGER, *Enchiridion Symbolorum*, ed. 1911, n. 1290 (Herder, London).

varies with the different circumstances of life. It cannot furnish a criterion by which we are enabled to distinguish one thing or action as objectively and intrinsically right from another as objectively and intrinsically wrong.

3. Moreover, pleasure considered simply as pleasure, if reason is left out of account and it is indulged in recklessly and without discrimination, is self-destructive, for experience teaches us that it is followed by pain or transforms itself into pain. This principle of moral hedonism or egoism is, then, self-contradictory and leads to logical suicide.

An attempt has been made to substitute utility for pleasure as the principle of morality. But the useful is not an end ; it is only a means in view of an end. Hence the question arises again : What is the end ? Is it pleasure ? Or is it some good different from pleasure, that is, the good considered in its relation of conformity or non-conformity with the end of our rational nature ? In the first case utilitarianism is really the same as hedonism ; in the second, pleasure is not the universal and fundamental criterion of good and evil.

37. Criticism of Social Utilitarianism.—According to this theory man must seek the welfare of the greatest number, the amelioration of humanity.

1. But if I am to make the happiness of another the principle of my happiness and the directing force of my conduct in life, is it not of the first importance that I should know in what the happiness of my neighbour consists ? The question of the nature of man's supreme end is accordingly deferred but not answered.

2. Whatever be the principle of happiness for humanity, we cannot acknowledge it to be the universal and primordial criterion of the distinction of moral good and evil. For, (a) such a criterion is not universal : for morality is anterior to the organization of any society. My conscience tells me that quite apart from any consideration of the happiness of the community there are certain things that are evidently good and others evidently bad. It is clear to everyone that intemperance, blasphemy, parricide, and the like, do not derive their malice from any social relations, and that even for the proverbial man on the desert island, or in the narrow circle of family life, these acts would retain their degrading or immoral character. (b) Such a criterion, even within the limits in

which it is applicable, is not fundamental : for what indeed is social happiness but the happiness of the individuals who make up society ? The distinction between good and evil for the community is accordingly subordinate to the distinction between good and evil for the individual.

38. The Evolutionist Theory of Herbert Spencer, far from putting Utilitarianism on the Scientific Basis which it lacks, logically leads to the Negation of Morality and of all Distinction between Right and Wrong.—Moral science, according to Herbert Spencer, is only a chapter in mechanics ; humanity is a part of the material universe. Now the universe is subject to two fundamental laws, the law of persistence of force and the law of evolution. The latter consists in the passing from ' the instability of the homogeneous ' to ' the stability of the heterogeneous ', and this stability results from the adaptation of a being to its environment. Hence, the moral end of man is nothing but the perfect adaptation of the individual to the conditions of social life. Cosmic evolution and the progress of humanity are subject to certain rhythmic oscillations ; nevertheless they must eventuate in a final state of equilibrium. For man this final equilibrium consists in the perfect adaptation of the individual to society and, reciprocally, of society to the individual. The egoist is a being ill adapted to his natural environment, which is society. He is therefore doomed to disappear. Only those individuals who are ruled by altruistic sentiments may expect themselves and their posterity to survive.

It belongs to the moral philosopher to investigate the means by which man's adaptation to his environment will be effected and to determine how and why certain modes of conduct are injurious whilst others are advantageous.

1. A complete refutation of Spencer's system of morality would involve the refutation of the mechanical conception of the universe. It is clear, however, that in such a system liberty can find no place and that the ideas of right and wrong no longer retain their proper meaning.

2. In order that ' the necessary laws of life ' might serve as a criterion of the distinction between moral good and evil, it would be required first that each individual should know what is to be the final state of humanity, and secondly that there should always be only one way of making an individual act

conduce to the realization of this supreme state, or if there are several that everybody should know the best. Now what could be more complicated than this final equilibrium of all the forces of the universe which is to constitute the ultimate phase of the cosmic evolution ? And suppose that there were in existence an intelligence sufficiently prodigious to put this final state of equilibrium in the form of equations and to solve them, each individual would still reserve to himself the right to submit these equations to the judgment of his conscience, either in order to assent to the conclusions which follow, or, perhaps, to reject them with a view to his own pleasure and interests. One is thus compelled always to come back to the variable criterion of pleasure and egoism, or else to the invariable criterion of the *rational* good, that is to say, to the good as conformable to the rational nature of man.

39. Sociological and Pragmatist Systems of Morality.— According to Levy-Bruhl, Durkheim and others of the sociological school of morality, our judgments on the value of human actions are the product of social environment and vary with it. This theory is erroneous, since our fundamental moral judgments are the same always and everywhere, and are therefore not affected by the vicissitudes of social life.

For pragmatists, as William James and Schiller, the moral ideal is lived in the collective consciousness by reason of the utility which it procures. As a moral system pragmatism falls under the weight of the same criticism as may be directed against every utilitarian system. Utility, howsoever regarded, varies with every individual. Consequently the pragmatist conception of morality cannot escape the condemnation of purely capricious subjectivism.

III. The Moral Law

40. Man is Subject to a Natural Law, that is, to an Inclination which habitually disposes him to know and will the End of his Rational Nature and what conduces to it, as well as to discern and reject what is contrary to it.—1. *Argument from analogy.*—Every being in this world has within it an inclination towards some end, and its law is to tend towards it. Man is no exception ; he is likewise set towards his end. This end directs human activity by influencing the reason and the will ;

and this influence exercised by the end upon the higher faculties of man is called the natural law. Therefore man is under a natural law.

2. *Argument from consciousness.*—Man is conscious that a higher attraction carries him on towards the good which his reason points out to him, and he yields to evil solicitation only by overcoming interior resistance and after self-reproach for his own weakness : hence the satisfaction that is given by the practice of virtue and the shame that follows an evil act.

3. *Argument drawn from Providence.*—Before creating the world by His free act, God must have set Himself some end in view and have chosen means adapted to its realization. Being infinitely wise, He could not be deceived with regard to the relation of proportion between a creature and its end ; being infinitely holy, He approved and willed this necessary relation ; being infinitely powerful, He was able to bring it into being according to the capacity of the respective natures of the agents He created. God has therefore given to created beings an impulse towards their ends, a principle which directs their activities in conformity with the eternal designs of His Providence ; in a word, He must have implanted in each created agent the natural law. Now this natural law must be in harmony with the constitution of the subject under its sway. The natural law implanted in man's nature, which is rational and free, cannot be, then, a fatalistic law ; on the contrary, it must consist in an intellectual tendency to form some principles of reason with certainty, and in an impulse which, without forcing or necessarily determining the will, inclines it towards the real good apprehended by the intellect.

41. The Eternal Law and the Natural Law.—By the *eternal law* is meant the destination, as conceived by Divine Wisdom, of all creatures to their respective ends, and the adaptation of their activities to them : ' Lex aeterna nihil aliud est quam ratio divinae sapientiae secundum quod est directiva omnium actuum et motionum ' [10].

The expression of this eternal law in the free rational creature is the *natural law :* ' Lex naturalis non est aliud quam lumen intellectus insitum a Deo, per quod cognoscimus quid agendum et quid vitandum. Hoc lumen et hanc legem dedit Deus homini in creatione '.

[10] St. Thomas, *Sum. Theol.*, I-II, q. 93, a. 1.

Regarded under its general form the natural law is summed up in this fundamental dictum : ' Bonum est faciendum et prosequendum, et malum vitandum '. It is the function of reason to draw from this first principle both immediate and more or less remote deductions that will serve to guide the will in its conduct through life.

With the notion of law there is bound up that of obligation and duty. It remains to examine the nature and origin of moral obligation.

42. Nature of Moral Obligation.—The idea of obligation contains also that of necessity. The necessity proper to duty (a) is not physical but moral ; (b) is not theoretical but practical ; (c) is not hypothetical but absolute.

Moral duty implies the practical, imperative necessity of freely doing what is morally good and of freely avoiding what is morally evil. How are we to reconcile such notions ?

43. Foundation of Moral Obligation.—In the opinion of most Christian moralists since the time of Kant, moral duty admits of only one possible explanation, namely the authority of God, the supreme Legislator of the moral order as He is of the physical. If there is a difference of opinion it is only on the question whether it is His essence, His intellect, His will, or His intellect and will combined, which gives the obligatory character to the moral law.

What are the arguments on which this interpretation of moral duty is based ?—There cannot be law, we are reminded, without a lawgiver, nor a command without a superior who has the power and right to issue commands to his subjects. Now God alone has the power and right to issue commands that have a universal and absolute value ; in God alone then do we find the principle of moral obligation. And secondly, the theological interpretation of moral duty is the only one which separates us from the theories of ' the autonomy of reason ' and ' independent morality ' as put forward by the rationalistic schools.

However, it would seem to us, this necessity of choosing between the theological morality, as explained above, and autonomous morality is in no way forced upon us. Consequently we prefer to follow unreservedly the opinion of St. Thomas which makes the moral obligation rest on a double foundation—immediately, upon human nature ; remotely, upon the intelligence of God who rules all things by His Providence.

44. Moral Obligation has its Explanation and Foundation in Human Nature.—The moral necessity of obligation has three elements : (1) the physical necessity of willing our good, our complete good, and, as a correlative, the physical impossibility of willing what is not or does not appear to be our good (*Psychology*, **110**) ; (2) the physical necessity of discovering sooner or later and repeatedly, both (*a*) by the attention of the mind and (*b*) by the spontaneous application of the principle of causality to our actions and to our dependent and finite nature, that as our real good can only be completely found in the possession of God, the realization of the happiness which we necessarily pursue demands the entire employment of our nature in the service of God.   (3) The physical liberty of fulfilling our duty.   Although there is an evident objective connexion between the complete happiness we necessarily will and our performance of the moral good and of the service of God, nevertheless our performance of the moral good and the service of God is not subject to that necessitating law which obliges us to seek our own happiness.   From this it follows that the imperativeness of duty is consistent with liberty in its performance.   For in the conditions of this present life the performance of the good and especially of the service of God is attended by obscurity for the intellect and by fear, toil, and privations for the will, so that this latter faculty, of which the adequate object is the total good, may not always will what is its true good.

Hence it is the physical necessity of willing our good and of seeing in what it will be realized in the life to come, combined with the liberty of choosing the concrete object wherein it is in fact found realized, which gives to the duty of man that complexity of attributes included under the name ' moral necessity ' or ' moral obligation '.

This moral necessity obliges our will in particular to seek after our true moral end, but also as a consequence to use the means leading to the same.   We have a special natural facility disposing us to know the means which lead us to our end, a facility or ' habit ' which the Scholastics called ' habitus principiorum rationis practicae ' or, more briefly, ' *synteresis* '.

We can therefore say that human nature is a law unto itself, that it bears within itself the obligation of doing good and avoiding evil, inasmuch as the soul's own tendency towards its complete good puts upon the will, enlightened by the practical judgments of the reason, the moral necessity of willing the good that is upright and, in its final analysis, the supreme good in which its complete good and perfection is realized.

45. The Ultimate Reason of the Distinction between Good and Evil, and consequently of Moral Obligation and Law, is found in God ; it is formally in the Practical Reason of Him who has destined Beings to a Necessary Last End or, more briefly, in the Practical Reason of Providence.—God knows His own essence. He knows Himself as a necessary good. He accordingly knows how the beings He has power to create are related to His essential goodness, and sees that every created being must of necessity have for its end the Divine Being, who alone is the necessary and infinite good.

If God wills creatures to exist distinct from Himself, it is impossible that He should not perceive by His practical reason the necessary relations of subordination which must exist between these creatures and the essential goodness of the Divine Being. These relations as conceived by the Divine Mind are ' the eternal law '. Such is the ultimate foundation of the distinction between good and evil, and of the natural law and of moral obligation.

IV. Moral Virtues

46. Moral Virtue.—As regard for the moral law consists in the performance of good acts dictated by the end of man's rational nature, we may say with St. Thomas that the direct and immediate effect of the law is to make him who observes it a good man. The habitual qualities that result from the observance of the moral law are called moral virtues. ' The proper effect of law is to lead its subjects to their proper virtue : and since virtue is *that which makes its subject good*, it follows that the proper effect of law is to make those to whom it is given, good '[11]. A virtue is an habitual disposition,

---

[11] ' Hoc est proprium legis, inducere subjectos ad propriam ipsorum virtutem. Cum igitur virtus sit quae facit bonum habentem, sequitur quod proprius effectus legis est bonos facere eos quibus datur '. *Sum. Theol.*, I-II, q. 92, a. 1.

either received from God (*infused* virtue) or acquired by the individual (*acquired* virtue), which is added to the natural powers of the rational soul and makes the normal exercise of its activity easier. Some virtues perfect the intellect, others the will. The latter are moral virtues.

47. Principal Moral Virtues.—It is readily admitted that the moral virtues hinge upon four fundamental or cardinal virtues : prudence, justice, fortitude and temperance.

V. THE SUBJECTIVE CRITERION OF MORALITY

48. We distinguish between Moral Good and Evil, between the Commands and the Prohibitions of the Natural Law, by Judgments of our Practical Reason.—The practical reason passes judgments on the conformity or non-conformity of an act with a determined end. The uprightness of an act lies objectively in the relation of subordination which this act has to the end of our rational nature. Therefore the judgment which estimates this relation must be the subjective criterion of the goodness or badness of moral acts.

49. There is no Need to suppose in Human Nature a ' Moral Instinct ' or a ' Moral Sense ' distinct from the Intellect to account for our Knowledge of the Moral Order. The Evolutionist Theory that the Principles of Morality owe their Origin to ' the Experiences of Utility, gathered and consolidated in the Course of Human History, which by arousing in us Corresponding Nervous Modifications have made us into Beings Organically Moral ' is at once Insufficient and Erroneous.—This thesis comprises two parts. The first is concerned with those theories which attribute the origin of our moral ideas and our attraction towards the good either to some kind of instinct overruling our cognitive and appetitive faculties, or to an affective power of the soul, or again to a special faculty, *sui generis*, termed the ' moral sense '. The second part deals with the theory of ' organic morality '.

Proof of the first part. The theory of Moral Sentiment breaks down before an introspective analysis of the testimony of conscience. For when we analyse a moral sentiment we learn that ultimately it is always subject to the practical judgment of the mind, which either condemns or approves it according as its object agrees or disagrees with man's natural end. Moreover the arguments brought forward by the adherents of this theory—the spontaneity, universality and persistent energy of the moral conscience—undoubtedly establish the fact that we have a natural and constant disposition towards moral good, but they prove nothing more.

Proof of the second part. The theory of ' organic morality ' is insufficient and erroneous.

1. It is insufficient : an instinctive impulse is not a principle. We have to ask then whether this organic impulse or disposition is a true manifestation of the good and of our duty, or if it puts us in the state of those deluded persons who are a prey to hallucinations. If the first case is true, the theory of the English evolutionists reduces itself eventually to our own ; if the second, it is necessary to explain the origin of these hallucinations in our ancestors, and their universality and persistence as they obsess and deceive us. It would be interesting, moreover, to know how the evolutionist theory is not self-destructive when it affirms that the moral conscience is simply an illusion.

2. It is erroneous : apart from its fundamental error of identifying a nervous disposition, or the structure of an organ, with an animal instinct, or again this instinct itself with a spiritual faculty or habit, the evolution of moral ideas and sentiments, invented by the English Naturalists, is in manifest opposition to experience. (*a*) If our moral ideas and propensities are due solely to the hereditary dispositions of the organism, how does it come about that morality so often imposes a duty upon us, and that the will has the power of acting contrary to the instincts which our nature has inherited ? (*b*) Man's reason is constantly discovering new relations in the moral order, more complex applications of the laws of right conduct. By what right can we deny to our ancestors this same faculty of judging right and wrong, duty and prohibition, which we find daily exercised by ourselves ?

50. The First Principle of the Practical Reason, and consequently the First Commandment of the Natural Law, is that Good must be done and Evil avoided. ' Bonum est faciendum et prosequendum, et Malum vitandum '.—The intellect has to discriminate between good and evil, between what is prescribed and what is prohibited by the natural law. It is, then, of importance to know what is the first principle of the practical reason, what is that judgment which is at the base of all others so as to be the norm or ultimate criterion for them.

In the speculative order, where the notion of ' being ' is the first of all notions, the first principle is that we should be able to affirm that a being is or is not ; so in the practical order, where the first notion is that of ' good '—since every agent acts for an end and wills a good—the first principle is that which affirms that good must be sought and evil avoided. ' The precepts of the natural law are to the practical reason what the first principles of demonstration are to the speculative reason ; because both are self-evident principles. . . . Now a certain order is to be found in those things that are apprehended universally. For that which, before aught else, falls under apprehension, is *being*, the notion of which is included in all things whatsoever a man apprehends. Wherefore the first indemonstrable principle is that *the same thing cannot be affirmed and denied at the same time*, which is based on the notion of *being* and *not being :* and on this principle all others are based. . . . Now as *being* is the first thing that falls under the apprehension simply, so *good* is the first thing that falls under the apprehension of the practical reason, which is directed to action : since every agent acts for an end under the aspect of good. Consequently the first principle in the practical reason is one founded on the notion of good, viz., that *good is that which all things seek after.* Hence this is the first precept of law, that *good is to be done and ensued, and evil is to be avoided.* All other precepts of the natural law are based upon this : so that whatever the practical reason naturally apprehends as man's good (or evil) belongs to the precepts of the natural law as something to be done or avoided ' [12].

[12] ' Praecepta legis naturae hoc modo se habent ad rationem practicam, sicut principia prima demonstrationum se habent ad rationem speculativam ; utraque enim sunt quaedam principia per se nota. . . . In his autem quae in apprehensione hominum cadunt quidam ordo invenitur. Nam illud quod primo cadit sub apprehensione est ens, cujus intellectus includitur in omnibus quaecumque quis apprehendit. Et ideo primum principium indemonstrabile est, quod non est simul affirmare et negare, quod fundatur supra rationem entis et non entis ; et super hoc principio omnia alia fundantur. . . . Sicut autem ens est primum quod cadit in apprehensione simpliciter, ita bonum est primum quod cadit in apprehensione practicae rationis, quae ordinatur ad opus. Omne enim agens agit propter finem, qui habet rationem boni. Et ideo primum principium in ratione practica est quod fundatur supra rationem boni, quae est : *Bonum est quod omnia appetunt.* Hoc est ergo primum praeceptum legis, quod bonum est faciendum et prosequendum, et malum vitandum ; et super hoc fundantur omnia alia praecepta legis naturae, ut scilicet

VI. The Sanction of the Moral Law

51. The Moral Law demands a Sanction.—Considered objectively, the sanction of a law consists of all the rewards and punishments attached to the performance or to the violation of it ; considered formally, the sanction is the promulgation of this system of rewards and punishments reserved for those who observe or transgress the law.

The moral law, by its very definition, is concerned with actions to be performed ; it is a collection of practical judgments. Now man can perform an action only under the aspect of its being a good, and can reasonably will no good but what is his good in reality. But all the particular goods that are the object of his desires are such really only in virtue of being subordinated to his supreme good. Whence it follows that it would have been inconsistent with the wisdom of God had there not been established an indissoluble connexion between man's happiness or misery on the one hand and the practice or violation of the moral law on the other. In other words, Divine Providence, in imposing the moral law upon man, must also have assured happiness to him as a reward if he observed it, and have reserved unhappiness for him in punishment if he violated it.

52. During the Present Life there is a Sanction for the Moral Law, but it is Insufficient.—As far as the present life is concerned, four kinds of sanction are usually distinguished : (a) The *natural* sanction, which consists of the natural consequences of our actions ; health, comfort and success, generally follow temperance and diligence, whilst weakness and disease, both in mind and in body, are the normal result of vice. (b) The *interior* sanction of the voice of conscience, or the satisfaction which results from the fulfilment of duty, the remorse consequent upon an unworthy act ; the sense of honour or of shame, self-approval or self-condemnation ; the joy of being united to God by love, the misery of being separated from Him by grave sin. (c) The *legal* sanction, or the system of rewards and penalties established by positive laws. (d) The public or *social* sanction of praise or blame from others, of esteem or

---

omnia illa facienda vel vitanda pertineant ad praecepta legis naturae, quae ratio practica naturaliter apprehendit esse bona humana '. St. Thomas, *Sum. Theol.*, I-II, q. 94, a. 2.

discredit, glory or infamy which attaches in different degrees to our external actions.

That the moral law is not without its sanctions during the present life is proved by the daily facts that goodness is seldom without its reward and wrongdoing its chastisement, and that man's conduct is arraigned before the different sanctions we have mentioned.

Yet these present sanctions are insufficient. For, to be truly adequate, a sanction requires to be (a) *universal*, that is, it must leave no good action without its reward, no bad one without its chastisement ; (b) *proportionate*, it must exactly meet the merit or demerit of the agent ; and (c) *efficacious*, that is, it must have sufficient influence upon man's free-will to guarantee in general the maintenance of the fundamental principles of the moral order. Now none of the sanctions offered in this present life verifies all these conditions. A sanction, then, to be adequate must be found elsewhere, in a future life.

53. After a Time of Trial, the Length of which we do not know, the Virtuous will be eternally rewarded in a Future Life and the Wicked will be deprived for ever of their Happiness.—We have already remarked in *Psychology* (**171**) upon what reason by itself can tell us about the length of our time of trial ; and we shall presently interrogate the same source about the joys and pains of the body in the other life. Here, we have particularly in view supreme or eternal happiness and misery. But the question is really only about eternal misery, since, as we have already pointed out, happiness cannot be complete except on the condition that it is eternal.

With regard to the proposition before us, philosophy can establish two points : (i) The idea of eternal punishment is not contrary to reason ; God *can* inflict on man for certain grave or mortal delinquencies a supreme eternal damnation. (ii) If we consider the exigencies of the providential order of the universe, God *must* give a sanction to the moral law by inflicting on the guilty a supreme eternal punishment. If, therefore, He can and must punish grave transgressions with an eternal chastisement, it is a logical conclusion that the guilty will in fact be for ever unhappy.

Proof that God can visit the guilty with a supreme eternal punishment.—The essence of the sin we term mortal, of sin in the strict sense, lies in the repudiation of God who is our ' summum bonum ', our ultimate end.   By this sin, then, man freely puts himself into a state contrary to that of right order, namely, into one of the repudiation of his last end.   And if a man of his own free choice persists in such a state until the very end of his life of trial, he becomes himself the cause of his privation of his end and of the happiness which flows naturally from it. Hence it follows that if God allows events to take their course, the man who dies in a state of mortal sin will be for ever in a state of unhappiness.

' Sin incurs a debt of punishment through disturbing an order.   But the effect remains so long as the cause remains. Wherefore so long as the disturbance of the order remains the debt of punishment must needs remain also.   Now disturbance of an order is sometimes reparable, sometimes irreparable : because a defect which destroys the principle is irreparable, whereas if the principle be saved, defects can be repaired by virtue of that principle.   For instance, if the principle of sight be destroyed, sight cannot be restored except by divine power ; whereas, if the principle of sight be preserved, while there arise certain impediments to the use of sight, these can be remedied by nature or by art.   Now in every order there is a principle whereby one takes part in that order.   Consequently if a sin destroys the principle of the order whereby man's will is subject to God, the disorder will be such as to be considered in itself, irreparable, although it is possible to repair it by the power of God.   Now the principle of this order is the last end, to which man adheres by charity.   Therefore whatever sins turn man away from God, so as to destroy charity, considered in themselves, incur a debt of eternal punishment ' [13].

[13] ' Peccatum ex hoc inducit rationem poenae, quod pervertit aliquem ordinem.   Manente autem causa, manet effectus : unde quamdiu perversitas ordinis remanet, necesse est quod remaneat reatus poenae.   Pervertit autem aliquis ordinem quandoque quidem reparabiliter, quandoque autem irreparabiliter.   Semper enim defectus, quo subtrahitur principium, irreparabilis est ; si autem salvatur principium, ejus virtute alii defectus reparari possunt, sicut si corrumpatur principium visivum, non potest fieri visionis reparatio nisi sola virtute divina ; si vero salvo principio visivo, aliqua impedimenta adveniunt visioni, reparari possunt per naturam vel per artem.   Cujuslibet autem ordinis est aliquod principium per quod aliquis fit particeps illius ordinis.   Et ideo si per peccatum corrumpatur principium ordinis quo voluntas subditur Deo erit inordinatio, quantum est de se, irreparabilis, etsi reparari possit virtute divina.   Principium autem hujus ordinis est ultimus finis cui homo inhaeret per charitatem.   Et ideo quaecumque peccata avertunt a Deo, charitatem auferentia quantum est de se, inducunt reatum aeternae poenae '.   St. Thomas, *Sum. Theol.*, I-II, q. 87, a. 3.—*De malo*, q. 7, a. 1.

Proof that the order of God's Providence demands that the guilty should be eternally deprived of happiness.—Liberty is only a property of the human will. The human will is not its own end ; it is subordinate to an end higher than itself. Hence its liberty too has, and must normally maintain, the character of being a means to our end. But if Divine Providence did not attach the possession or the privation of our end to the proper use or the abuse of our liberty, this liberty would lose its character of being a means, since then the proper use or the abuse of moral liberty would bear no real influence on our final destiny. Therefore Divine Providence must vouchsafe happiness to the good as a recompense for virtue and deny it to the bad as a punishment for crime.

The above argument is corroborated by the consideration that eternal reward and eternal punishment are necessary if the observance of the fundamental laws of morality is to be made really efficacious.

54. The Christian Teaching that the Sinner who freely turns from his Last End must in addition to the Eternal Loss of Happiness suffer the Infliction of Positive Pain is not opposed to Reason.—Punishment must fit the crime. Now by mortal sin man not only turns away from God but also adheres to creatures as his end. It is reasonable, then, not only that he should be deprived of his real end, which is God, but also that creatures should be a source of positive punishment for him.

Secondly, the purpose of punishment is to deter man from sin. But no one fears to lose that for which he has no desire. The man who deliberately turns from his last end has no distress in losing it. Chastisement will then deserve the name only if it includes the infliction of positive punishment [14].

55. Outline of the Kantian Doctrine of Moral Duty.—The moral obligation, Kant observes, is universal, absolute and necessary. What is universal, absolute and necessary cannot derive its origin from the things of experience. Moral obligation is therefore due to some principle anterior to all experience, to an ' a priori ' form.

What is this pure form which has no empirical connexions and in consequence is alone capable of being universal and

[14] St. Thomas, *Cont. Gent.*, III, c. 145.

necessary ? It is the principle : ' Act as if the maxim from which you act were to become through your will a universal law of nature ', or : ' Act in accordance with a maxim which can serve as a universal law '. This is the well-known absolute or *categorical imperative,* so called in contradistinction to an hypothetical imperative which, according to Kant, though regarding a real object is subordinate to a contingent condition : ' If you will this or that, then you must proceed thus or so '.

The perfection of the will consists in not allowing itself to be influenced by any other motive except the absolute imperative itself. This independence of the will with regard to any real motive of action, this power of submitting itself to none but the categorical imperative, is what Kant calls ' the autonomy of practical reason ', the pure self-determination of the rational will, or, in a word, ' freedom ', which is the exclusive source of morality, understanding thereby of good and virtue.

According to this principle, it is contradictory to wish to make the moral law efficacious by the incentive of reward or by the fear of punishment. Likewise the legal sanction cannot touch the conscience, which has its play in an interior province aloof from all influence of civil power, so that there is a radical and essential separation between moral law and right [15].

But this does not mean to say that Kant regarded the moral law to be without sanction : for although he says that it is a contradiction that there should be a moral act which is performed in view of a recompense or through fear of a punishment, or in more general terms in view of happiness, yet it is no less true that ' virtue is worthy of happiness '.

By combining this principle with the fact that in the present life virtue is not always rewarded, Kant is brought to the necessity of postulating a future life where the law of justice reigns, and where consequently a sovereign legislator and judge will establish an indissoluble connexion between virtue and happiness.

Thus did Kant endeavour, by means of an analysis of moral duty, to justify the fundamental laws of that spiritualism the validity of which he had impugned in his speculative philosophy.

---

[15] Kant makes a difference between voluntary obedience to the moral law, which is a matter of disposition, and conformity of external action to the demands of positive law, which is regardless of disposition.—TRS.

56. The Categorical Imperative is no Moral Standard by which Good and Evil may be distinguished, nor is it a True Moral Law. Moreover the Principles on which Kant bases his Argument are False.—*Proof of the first part:* By its definition a moral rule is a practical judgment, and therefore a judgment concerning the relation of an act with its end. But the Kantian theory of a moral act does away with the idea of any real end. Consequently it makes any relation of an act to an end impossible and therefore rules out any true norm of morality.

Proof of the second part: Obligation, which is the essential note of a law, is a certain necessity, put upon the will, of freely acting in a determined way. But it is inconceivable that the will should be drawn to act except by a final cause, that is, by the representation of a good to be willed. Hence the categorical imperative which claims to exclude all real final causes from the sphere of the moral will cannot produce any real obligation and consequently is not a law in the proper sense.

Proof of the third part: It is not true that the notes of universality and necessity that are characteristic of the moral law cannot derive their origin from the data of experience when these are put to the service of the spiritual faculties of man's soul (*Psychology,* **89-92**).

It is not true that human nature is or can be its own end, and that in consequence the perfection of the practical reason consists or can consist in an absolute autonomy.

Finally, it is not true that reason forbids us to follow the natural attraction we experience towards the enjoyment of our happiness ; it is only necessary that the desire of this enjoyment should be rightly directed, in order to make it compatible with the highest standard of morality of which human nature is capable. Our love when perfectly ordered seeks God, our objective end, *primarily* and above all things, and *secondarily* that subjective happiness which results from the possession of God.

VII. NATURAL CHARACTERISTICS OF THE MORAL ORDER

57. Characteristics of the Moral Law.—The moral law has the distinctive characteristics of being immutable and universally known.

1. When we say that the moral law is *immutable* we do not mean that the matter which the moral obligation regards never changes ; but that in so far as this matter remains the same, the precepts of the moral law which concern it cannot be subject to any modification. From this it follows that the application of the moral law is general, independent of the circumstances of time and place, and in this sense is eternal and common to all ; it binds every man in possession of his natural reason no matter at what time he may live or where he may dwell.

Being immutable, it does not admit of exceptions. Yet we must be careful not to identify the objective law itself with certain abstract formulae of which we make use for the purpose of giving it as accurate an expression as possible, and which, being enunciated to meet the generality of cases, allow of additions and restrictions for particular cases [16].

2. The moral law is *universally known* ; it is sufficiently promulgated that no man who has come to the use of reason can be ignorant of it without being responsible for his ignorance. Indeed this is a truism. For ' the age of reason ' does not denote the age at which a child is capable of using his reason ; he reasons well enough before the years at which we grant that he has come to the age of reason : but it signifies the time when he has it in his power to reflect and is capable of perceiving the subordination his actions should have in regard to their moral end, and the time at which he has become a moral agent.

A general distinction is made between first principles, derived principles or immediate conclusions of the moral law, and remote conclusions [17]. The natural possibility of error or of invincible ignorance applies only to remote conclusions.

The universality of the promulgation and of the knowledge of the moral law has been proved above.

---

[16] Cp. SUAREZ, *De legibus*, II, c. 13, n. 6-10.

[17] In the same strain St. Thomas writes : ' Quaedam sunt, quae statim per se ratio naturalis cujuslibet hominis dijudicat esse facienda vel non facienda ; sicut : Honora patrem tuum et matrem, et : Non occides ; Non furtum facies. . . . Quaedam autem sunt quae subtiliori consideratione rationis a sapientibus judicantur esse observanda ; et ista sic sunt de lege naturae, ut tamen indigeant disciplina, qua minores a sapientibus instruantur, sicut illud : Coram cano capite consurge, et honora personam senis ; et alia hujusmodi '. *Sum. Theol.*, I-II, q. 100, a. 1.

58. Characteristics of the Moral Act.—The moral act has three natural characteristics :

1. It bears the stamp either of moral rectitude or of sinfulness, which is a deflection from it [18].

2. It is imputable to the agent who performs it, and this we express by saying that the act is deserving of praise or blame. To bear these epithets, an act must be free and proceed from a responsible agent.

3. It earns merit or demerit before God, even if not always before men.

59. Notion of Merit.—The idea of merit is a relative one ; we merit a thing from somebody else. How do we merit ? By an act which is morally good, done for the advantage of another. Conversely, we deserve condemnation by any morally bad act, done with the design of injuring another.

Merit, then, is the characteristic of a morally good act done with a view to its usefulness to *another*, in virtue of which it *demands a recompense* from him in return. ' Meritum et demeritum dicuntur in ordine ad retributionem, quae fit secundum justitiam. Retributio autem secundum justitiam fit alicui ex eo quod agit in profectum vel nocumentum alterius ' [19].

Hence it follows that the *power* of meriting requires two conditions : (*a*) That of being in a state to receive a recompense ; for one who is in possession of all that his nature could desire would no longer be in a position to merit ; and (*b*) that of being master of one's actions : ' Unde naturalis facultas liberi arbitrii requiritur ad merendum '. Whilst to merit *in matter of fact* requires the further conditions : (*c*) that an action be performed which is morally good ; (*d*) that it be performed in view of another's good ; and (*e*) that it either actually be, or at least be considered to be, an action advantageous to the person on whose behalf it is done and accordingly accepted by him.

Our actions may have merit, or demerit, in the eyes of another individual, or of the community, or finally of God [20].

60. Basis of Merit.—Merit *demands*, or at least justifies, the

---

[18] ' Actus bonus vel malus habet rationem laudabilis vel culpabilis, secundum quod est in potestate voluntatis ; nihil enim est aliud laudari vel culpari, quam imputari alicui malitiam vel bonitatem sui actus '. *Ibid.*, q. 21, a. 2.

[19] *Ibid.*, q. 21, a. 3.

[20] St. Thomas, *De veritate*, q. 29, a. 6.

giving of a recompense on the part of him before whom a person has merited. What is the foundation of this title? How is it that the right order exacts that a good action done to another should be requited by the bestowal of something equivalently or proportionally good, and that an evil one be punished with an evil return? Several answers have been suggested.

That God who providentially arranges for the observance of the primary laws of morality should direct our conduct by means of a system of rewards and punishments, is easily understood, and it is on these grounds that we base our proof of the necessity and, consequently, of the reality of the sanction of the moral law (**51** ff.). But however valid this first answer may be, does it sufficiently account for the intrinsic nature of merit and demerit? Must there be recompenses and chastisements in morality *in order that* the law may be kept, or do recompenses and chastisements exist *because* the law has been kept or violated?

By pushing his theory of disinterested morality to excess, Paul Janet goes so far as to deny that the hope of a recompense or the fear of a punishment can be a legitimate motive of action. This is of course an exaggeration. Reward can be a legitimate motive, the final cause of a moral act. It must, however, be acknowledged that, in the order of finality, merit is anterior to recompense, and that it must be considered in a certain sense the cause of the recompense since it demands it.

According to Taparelli, the recognition of merit is an application of the laws of symmetry, proportion and unity [21]. But this is transferring to the order of aesthetics a problem which belongs to morals. Certainly the moral order, too, has its laws, its harmony and its beauty; but the question we must ask is how precisely would this beauty be disregarded if the person to whom a good action is done failed to reckon its 'merit' at its proper value.

The following consideration will perhaps help towards a solution. All the good accruing to an act must, it would seem, by right redound to the author of the act. When therefore out of a benevolent intention he turns his good action to the

---

[21] *Saggio teoretico di diritto naturale*, I, c. 6. Liberatore also takes the same view, *Instit. eth. et juris nat.*, c. 2, n. 56.

profit of his neighbour, he is really depriving himself of something that is his own ; and instead, the person to whom the service is done, without his own personal contribution to the good effect, acquires a good which is not his own. Whereas justice strictly so-called effectively restores with a mathematical precision the equality of strict rights, the recognition of merit is the approximate estimate of an exchange of goods and profits which could hardly be estimated in terms of strict justice. The person benefited confesses and acknowledges that the equality of things has been altered in his favour : accordingly he will be anxious that it should be restored on behalf of his benefactor, since such is the natural order of things. Should it be impossible for him to do anything towards effectively restoring this equality, he will at least, unless he wishes to be guilty of miserable ingratitude, acknowledge in his mind the good action by which he has been benefited. Merit and the recognition and reward of it are therefore really an application of justice in the wide meaning of the term.

These explanations help us to understand how man has not, if we speak precisely, any merit before God. For, ' What hast thou that thou hast not received ? ' The faculties by which we perform our virtuous actions are gifts from the hand of God, and consequently the good works themselves which are their fruit are, by their principal title, also the gifts of God.

61. Are any Acts Morally Indifferent ?—We hold with St. Thomas that although certain acts considered only in relation to their specific object are neither good nor bad, yet if taken in their concrete reality, with the end and circumstances determining them, all acts are necessarily moral or immoral (**34**). ' It may happen that the object of an action does not include something pertaining to the order of reason ; for instance, to pick up a straw from the ground, to walk in the fields, and the like : and such actions are indifferent according to their species '. ' Since it belongs to the reason to direct ; if an action that proceeds from deliberate reason be not directed to the due end, it is, by that fact alone, repugnant to reason, and is specifically evil. But if it be directed to a due end it is in accord with reason ; wherefore it is specifically good. Now it must needs be either directed or not directed to a due end. Consequently every human action that proceeds from deliberate reason, if it be considered in the individual, must be good or bad '[22].

62. ' Good ' and ' Duty '.—Many writers—amongst others Janet [23] and Tiberghien [24]—make duty and the good co-extensive. What view should we take of this ?

The moral good and duty occupy the same field if moral goodness is taken in the generic or formal acceptation of the word, inasmuch as it means what is conformable to the practical judgments of reason ; for man is bound never to do anything which is contrary to these rules of conduct, and every time he does act he must act in accordance with them. But man is not bound actually to do everything that is specifically, or rather, materially good ; he has to do what is materially good only when such an act is *necessary* for the realization of the proper end of the moral order [25].

63. The Good and the Supreme End.—As good, rightness, the moral law, are words which have a meaning only in respect of our supreme end, it follows that every right act is *implicitly* and *virtually* an act that contributes to the glory of God. But it would be illegitimate to conclude that every human act cannot be morally good unless inspired by the *actual* or *express* intention of giving glory to God [26].

Can the glory of God be the supreme object of our will ? Is it not physically necessary that we should subordinate this to the desire of our own happiness ? No ; it is not necessary. A will rightly ordered embraces at once what is objective—the supreme end which rules it being none other than the objective glory of God—and the subjective happiness which is the natural concomitant of the possession of this objective end. Nor must we forget that the moral act is free, and that being

---

[22] ' Contingit quod objectum actus non includit aliquid pertinens ad ordinem rationis, sicut levare festucam de terra, ire ad campum etc. . . et tales actus secundum speciem suam sunt indifferentes '. *Sum. Theol.*, I-II, q. 18, a. 8. ' Cum rationis sit ordinare, actus a ratione deliberativa procedens, si non sit ad debitum finem ordinatus, ex hoc ipso repugnat rationi, et habet rationem mali ; si vero ordinetur ad debitum finem, convenit cum ordine rationis, unde habet rationem boni. Necesse est autem quod vel ordinetur vel non ordinetur ad debitum finem. Unde necesse est omnem actum hominis a deliberativa ratione procedentem, in individuo consideratum, bonum esse vel malum '. *Ibid.*, a. 9.

[23] *La Morale*, II, ch. II.

[24] *Les commandements de l'humanité*, 11e comm., p. 128.

[25] *Sum. Theol.*, I-II, q. 94, a. 3.

[26] *Ibid.*, q. 60, a. 1.

free it is the result of reflection. Now reflection leads a man to see that he himself, together with all that he is and has, is essentially subordinate to the giving of glory to God. When he wills that this essential subordination should be maintained, he wills the right order of things, and a man capable of reflecting is certainly capable of willing this [27].

64. Degrees of Goodness or Wickedness in Human Acts.—It is evident that both good and evil admit of degrees. To estimate them we must have recourse to the various principles both objective and subjective which we have already shown to constitute moral rectitude (34). After having laid down the proposition : ' Neque omnia bona opera, neque omnia peccata sunt paria ', St. Thomas shows that for determining the degree of goodness or malice of an act we must take into account its subject, its conformity with the judgment of reason, the degree of intensity of the will, and the perfection of the virtue which inspires the act [28].

65. Pessimistic Morality.—The philosophy of Schopenhauer and von Hartmann is a congeries of arbitrary hypotheses, often mutually contradictory, some borrowed from the theory of materialistic evolution, others from pantheism.

The principle which is the key of the universe is a *will*, absolute, unconscious, and free. The ultimate reality is the unconscious One-All ; the individual is an illusion. (Mere assertions without proof.)

The manifestation of the absolute will is effort (an hypothesis) which is relative and fatalistic (a contradiction—a moment ago it was free) and has for its sole end pleasure (mere hypothesis, for how can it know of this if it is unconscious ?). But the effort of will is pain, the ache of the ' not-yet-satisfied ' (a confusion of ideas). Hence the end of effort cannot be attained ; effort is illusory. Whence it follows that we must arrive at the negation or denial of the will itself. The world, then, is only a will that is striving painfully to search for an impossible happiness (gratuitous and contradictory).

As for moral duty, it lies in willing the good of others through motives of sympathy and altruism and in ceasing to will one's own good. This renunciation of one's own good will bring

---

[27] *Sum. Theol.*, I-II, q. 23, a. 1 and 7.
[28] *Cont. Gent.*, III, c. 140.

about a universal brotherhood and lead all men to absolute unity.

From these theories it would seem that we must logically conclude that suicide is a moral obligation binding upon all ; but to avoid such a universal annihilation Schopenhauer adduces a phrase, though it is not an answer : ' Suicide is the negation only of life, not of the will-to-live '. Von Hartmann, the most energetic of Schopenhauer's disciples, argues to the necessity, for the annihilation of the will-to-live, of a collective evolution towards *cosmic suicide*.

66. Independent Morality.—This term may stand for any theory of morality, whether deistic or rationalistic, which is independent of all positive religion. Catholic doctrine merely sums up accurately the lessons taught by experience when it proclaims the universal and constant inferiority both in the knowledge and practice of the moral law among those peoples who are without the supernatural aid of revelation and grace. The doctrine of the relative necessity of Revelation—which finds its application equally in the moral as in the purely speculative order—is briefly summed up in the following extract from the Council of the Vatican : ' To this divine Revelation it is indeed to be attributed that those things which, in matters divine, are not of themselves beyond reason can be known, even in the present condition of the human race, *by all men, without difficulty, with firm certainty* and *with no admixture of error* ' [29].

To-day, however, the term *Independent Morality* is more generally used for the attempt to build up a system of ethics, both in regard to the knowledge of the moral law and its performance, which is purely philosophic, and entirely independent of God.

Now a moral system without God is as erroneous as it is impracticable.

In the first place there is no justification for the moral imperative in an atheistic conception of life. Take away, as the ultimate term of our volitions, an *absolute*, that is to say, an end which subsists of itself, and all our aspirations towards good and all our deliberate volitions cease to have any

---

[29] ' Huic divinae revelationi tribuendum quidem est, ut ea quae in rebus divinis humanae rationi per se impervia non sunt, in praesenti quoque generis humani conditione *ab omnibus expedite, firma certitudine* et *nullo admixto errore* cognosci possint'. DENZINGER, *Enchiridion Symbolorum*, ed. 1911, n. 1786.

final object. We cannot conceive the absolute obligation to will what is morally good—in other words, duty—unless there be, beyond all contingent goods that I may or may not will, a good which is not contingent, which is an end in itself, namely God.

Secondly, the study of natural theology shows us that there exists, in the ontological order, an absolute fact on which the whole of the moral order depends, namely the fact that God loves Himself with a necessary love [30], so that only in view of Himself can He love those beings who are capable of sharing, though in a way far different from Himself, His infinite Perfection or His infinite Goodness [31].

Finally, it is a vain hope to expect the moral law to be observed without recourse to the idea of God. For how is the observance of the moral law to be sufficiently guaranteed if man has no certitude that a just and powerful God will sooner or later establish an eternal harmony between virtue and happiness on the one hand, and between vice and misery on the other ? (**51** ff.).

67. Secular or Lay Morality.—Independent Morality, in the second meaning of the word, is called by preference to-day *Lay Morality*. Aiming at the suppression of God, it claims to have found a substitute for God. The principal forms which it has assumed during the last few years may be summarized under three heads.

1. The *Theory of Solidarity* puts forward the idea of contract and debt as the basis of the moral volition : by the mere fact of his birth man is bound by both these ties alike with society in general which puts at his disposal an immense capital accumulated by generations of his ancestors, and with his immediate neighbours whose services he is continually receiving. This, however, offers no foundation for the moral obligation, as in point of fact there is no such contract. A

---

[30] St. Thomas, *I Dist.*, 45, a. 1.
[31] ' Sicut Deus cognoscendo essentiam suam cognoscit omnia quae sunt ab eo inquantum sunt similitudo quaedam veritatis ejus ; ita etiam volendo vel amando essentiam suam, vult omnia quae sunt ab eo, inquantum habent similitudinem bonitatis ejus. Unde id quod est volitum primo ab eo est bonitas sua tantum. Alia autem vult in ordine ad bonitatem suam. . . . Non quidem ordinat Deus creaturas in finem bonitatis suae, quasi per eas bonitatem suam assequatur, sed ut ipsae creaturae divina operatione similitudinem aliquam divinae bonitatis acquirant, quod esse non posset, nisi eo volente et faciente '. *Ibid.*, a. 2.

contract can only exist and bind when it is entered into freely. No engagement of this nature has been contracted by the individual. And furthermore, the inheritance represented by the discoveries of generations of forebears has no natural heirs : it belongs to everybody and anybody, and in the use we make of it we are not incurring any debt properly so-called.

2. The *Sociological Theory* claims to see the origin of duty in the idea of society, which it regards as a moral person distinct from its members, superior to them, and with a right of command.

But society is not a person nor is it a *real* being distinct from the individuals composing it. Moreover, it has no end in itself ; it exists for the good of the individual, not the individual for it. If the individual obeys it, this is not because it has the absolute right to command simply, but because it has the right to command in what conduces to the individual's welfare, and on this ground only do laws find their ultimate justification.

3. The ' *Nature* ' *Theory* of morality looks for the foundation of the moral imperative in the idea of man's submission to his nature. Our end, it is said, is to realize ourselves, to maintain and develop ourselves, first as individuals, and then as members of society to which we belong.

What is this human ' nature ' which is to serve as the standard of our conduct ? Do not moralists interpret it in contradictory ways ? And are not the instincts we endeavour to repress in order to further the harmony of our nature given equally by nature with those we strive to foster ? Like all the other forms of Independent Morality this too seems doomed to failure.

CHAPTER IV

CONSCIENCE

68. Meaning of Conscience.—Every complete judgment of the practical reason concerning the rectitude or obligation of a concrete act is the conclusion of a syllogism one of whose premisses is general and the other particular. The general premiss is formulated by the mind through an habitual disposition which was called by the Scholastics *synteresis* (**44**). The act by which the reason applies a universal principle of morality to some particular case is what we understand by *conscience* : ' Conscientia nihil aliud est quam applicatio scientiae ad aliquem actum ' [32].

69. Directive and Obligatory Power of Conscience.—Whilst the principles of morality are immutable and several amongst them are so easily perceived by the human mind that no one can be without the knowledge of them (**57**), the *application of these principles* to the conduct of actual life varies with particular cases and allows of a measure of ignorance and error ; and as every moral act which man has to perform is necessarily concrete, the true, immediate and decisive rule which has to direct human conduct is not one of the abstract principles of synteresis but a concrete judgment of *conscience*. How, we have then to ask, is man justified in relying upon his conscience ? Several different solutions have suggested themselves :

1. When an act comes before the conscience as good or bad, as lawful or unlawful, bearing all the guarantees of certitude that are possible where the matter of a moral act is contingent

---

[32] *Sum. Theol.*, I-II, q. 19, a. 5.—' Secundum enim quod applicatur scientia ad actum ut dirigens ipsum, secundum hoc dicitur conscientia instigare, vel inducere, vel ligare ; secundum vero quod applicatur scientia ad actum per modum examinationis eorum quae jam acta sunt, sic dicitur conscientia accusare vel remordere, quando id quod factum est invenitur discordare a scientia ad quam examinatur, defendere autem vel excusare, quando invenitur id quod factum est processisse secundum formam scientiae '. *De verit.*, q. 17, a. 1.

and variable, we can readily understand that the will follows the
direction of conscience.   Where the matter is of such a character it would even be unreasonable to expect all the clear
marks of mathematical evidence [33].

2. But what is to be done when the reason is in doubt
whether an act is good or bad, lawful or unlawful ?   To do an
act when in doubt whether it is good or bad would be to will good
or evil indifferently ; and to hold the will indifferent to good or
evil is to do evil, since the will must choose good alone and must
eschew evil. No man, therefore, may act when doubtful whether
the act in question is good or bad.   The immediate conclusion of
this is that he who happens to be so placed must endeavour
to solve his doubt and must exert himself to arrive at certain
knowledge that the act is good and that he is able or bound to do
it, or else that the act is bad and that it is his duty to abstain
from it.   (a) If he succeeds in his efforts, we are brought back
to the first hypothesis.   (b) If his efforts do not succeed in
resolving the doubt, they will nevertheless lead to an important
result, namely, to the conviction that the case is *invincibly
doubtful*, that is to say, to the certitude that the moral character
of the act, its goodness or badness, is doubtful.   What then
must be done ?   Must I abstain from action ?   This would be
an expedient, but no solution.   May not the doubt bear
precisely on the question of my knowing whether it is lawful or
unlawful, in this particular case, for me to abstain from
acting ?

Since it is to reason that has fallen the duty of directing my
moral conduct, it goes without saying that I must when in
doubt take the most reasonable side.   Which is this ?   Is it
the safest course, the one in which there is least danger of sin ?
Yet the safest course may be the least probable, that is, the
least conformable to the manifestation of truth ; it may even
happen that the safest course is improbable ; shall we say that
it is reasonable to adopt definitely one side without taking into
account the objective manifestation of the truth, under the
pretext that this manifestation is incomplete ?   Reason can

[33] 'Certitudo non est semper quaerenda in omni materia : in actibus enim
humanis, super quibus constituuntur judicia et exiguntur testimonia, non
potest haberi certitudo demonstrationis, eo quod sint circa contingentia et
variabilia, et ideo sufficit probabilis certitudo quae ut in pluribus veritatem
attingat, etsi in paucioribus a veritate deficiat'. *Sum. Theol.*, I-II, q. 70,
a. 2.   Cp. I-II, q. 96, a. 1, ad 3.

by an indirect process or, to use an accepted expression, by a reflex principle get rid of the doubt it knows to be incapable of a direct solution, and thus arrive at a conscience that is practically or definitely certain. We may put this process in the form of a syllogism :—

A man does not sin formally when he prudently judges that he is doing a lawful action. Now when, after a serious effort, he is not convinced that an act is unlawful, he can prudently regard it as lawful. Hence when the direct doubt concerning the moral character of an act is invincible, a man can indirectly form a deliberate and certain conscience that the act is right and lawful.

The whole difficulty consists in knowing when a judgment on the moral character of an act is really prudent. Two points are controvertible : (i) that a judgment favourable to the goodness of an act is prudent when it has against it only an apparent or a futile reason, and (ii) on the other hand that it is imprudent when the reasons which rise up in favour of a law to which it is opposed show a very high degree of probability. The ' rigorist ' school reject the one and the ' lax ' school the other. Between these two extremes there are various shades of opinion, the chief of which are represented by the ' Probabilists ', the ' Equi-probabilists ' and the ' Probabiliorists '.

The common opinion of the present-day moralists who are known by the name of pure Probabilists is that an act is formally lawful the moment that the moral agent can rest the lawfulness of his act on a seriously probable reason, even supposing that there are equal reasons, or even higher ones, against it. The Probabiliorists hold that a probable opinion ceases to be prudent when the contradictory reason appears to have a higher or even a simply equal probability, with the result that, according to them, in the case of a conflict of opinions of this kind the more probable or safer must in practice prevail. Finally, the Equi-probabilists, taking a midway position between the Probabilists and the Probabiliorists, maintain with the first that a probable reason remains sufficient for a prudent judgment in spite of a contrary opinion which rests only on a less or even equal probability, and concede to the latter that it ought to give way, in the name of prudence, to a contradictory judgment that rests upon a higher probability.

Without entering into a discussion of these different systems we will confine ourselves to a difficulty which is common to them all : Any opinion whatever, be it probable or more probable, may be in disagreement with the truth, so that a judgment of conscience formed on a simple opinion may be erroneous. Now is it permissible to maintain that an erroneous judgment is or ever can be matter of obligation ? ' Utrum conscientia erronea liget ? ' St. Thomas replies to this question in the affirmative, and sums up his mind in these precise terms : ' Although an erroneous conscience may dictate something not in accordance with the law of God, the person in error nevertheless accepts it as the real law of God ; and so, strictly speaking, if he depart from this he will depart from the law of God. . . . The erroneous conscience does not bind simply and in all cases, but it binds only whilst it lasts ' [34].

[34] ' Quamvis id quod dictat conscientia erronea non consonum sit legi Dei, tamen accipitur ab errante ut ipsa lex Dei ; et ideo, per se loquendo, si ab hoc recedat, recedet a lege Dei. . . . Conscientia erronea non ligat simpliciter et in omnem eventum, sed ligat dum manet '. *De veritate*, q. 17, a. 4.

PART II

Special Ethics : A Theory of Right and Duty

INTRODUCTION

70. Definition of Natural Law.—In its wide sense Natural Law or Right comprises all the rules of conduct which are logically deduced from the moral law, and which form the basis of our rights and duties both with regard to our neighbour and society in general. Thus understood Natural Law is the same as Social Morality. But in a more restricted sense the term ' Natural Law ' stands for that part of social morality which treats of our duties arising from justice. It therefore designates all the rules of conduct which are logically derived from the moral law and whose execution, if need be, may be enforced by coercive measures.

71. Distinctive Character of the Natural Law.—It is commonly said that the Natural Law is distinguished from Positive Law by its universality and its immutability. Its precepts are ever the same in all times and among all peoples.

This statement provokes an objection we must needs answer here,—an objection drawn from the evolution of moral ideas among different nations. The conception of justice, it is said, varies according to different races, countries and ages.

We reply that the natural law in itself, such as it would present itself to a perfectly illumined and upright conscience, must not be confused with men's opinions. The conscience of peoples as well as of individuals may become obscured. The human race does not become possessed of all moral truths at once. Yet variations in opinions, just as much in morality as in science, are no prejudice to the constancy of natural laws. Certain acts are of their very essence in conformity with our rational nature and others are opposed to it. There are a number of relations derived from the very essence of the acts and the agent which are independent of time and space. In this sense the Natural Law, which formulates them, is immutable and universal.

Furthermore, although it may happen that certain acts or institutions are not condemned absolutely by the moral law but only under certain conditions, this does not militate against the uniformity of the moral law and prove it self-contradictory : in identically the same circumstances it invariably sanctions or condemns the same things.

72. Relation of Natural Law to Positive Law.—Our obedience is due to positive laws because such obedience is a condition of social life in its full development. Social life is demanded by our nature. Hence nature or, what comes to the same, natural law, enjoins a respect for the commands of a human legislator. The will of a legislator, since it is of a kind no different from our own, cannot of itself constitute the source of a true obligation for us ; but the natural law, being dictated by God, does possess sovereign claims to our obedience.

73. Corollary.—An important conclusion follows : No one must obey a positive law that clearly contradicts the fundamental principles of the moral law. In such circumstances the inalienable rights of the individual conscience must be resolutely vindicated against the claims of any form of absolutism.

Such a declaration may be thought by some to be a dangerous application. This objection, however, only furnishes a reason for not making a light use of its application and for carefully gauging its extent, not for repudiating it. Moreover there is no question here of the right to rebel or to refuse obedience to a law we may consider prejudicial to our interests. Nor is there question of ranking our own opinions above submission to law. But, unless we are prepared to subscribe to absolute scepticism in morality, we must grant that the fundamental principles of the natural law are sufficiently clear to the right conscience of the normal individual. As a matter of fact we see these principles admitted by the generality of men. What, therefore, we lay down is that if, after a serious, impartial and sincere examination, anyone arrives at the conclusion, no matter whether true or false, that a positive law bids him do what is reprehensible by the moral law, he is bound not to obey it. In the case where a doubt exists concerning the morality of a law, the question should be decided in favour of authority, seeing that its special function is to interpret the natural law. But the refusal of obedience is a duty incumbent upon anyone who is convinced of the immorality of what is commanded by authority. It is useless to invoke the imprescriptible rights of the ' powers that be ' and the higher claims of society. What is more sacred than the authority of the father over his children ? Yet if a father were to bid his son to do what is criminal, the latter would have the right to disobey. If the moral law imposes restrictions on paternal authority, how much more on the authority of the State ?

Any doctrine which bases the authority of the civil law on the will of one man or on a body of men is destructive of the rights of the individual. There is a higher law than human laws, one ' written on the tables of the heart ', in the name of which the individual always has the right to protest against the tyranny of rulers. In vindication of this right the martyrs shed their blood.

74. Origin of Rights.—1. *Are rights derived from a priori principles of the individual reason ?*—The will, we are told by Kant, must conform itself to the imperatives of the practical reason. These imperatives, just like the judgments of the speculative reason, arise from the constitution of the mind (55). Reason bids us respect the human person, whose one perfection is his liberty. Hence this is the imperative judgment that, according to Kant, summarizes all our juridical obligations : ' Act externally in such a manner that the free exercise of thy will may be able to co-exist with the freedom of all others, according to a universal law ' [35].

Surely, however, there is nothing more vague than this formula. If the autonomy of the human person is in a true sense absolute, I shall respect this autonomy in myself only by exercising my liberty as fully as possible ; my right then will know no limit but my might. And everyone else may say the same of himself. Hence an inevitable conflict will arise between the activity of individuals, each of whom will try to extend his rights indefinitely. Two hypotheses, consequently, are possible : either the strongest will impose his will on the weakest, and the liberty of the human person, by its triumph in one, will suffer violation in the other ; or else a compact will be entered into between the individuals for the purpose of fixing

---

[35] HASTIE, *The Philosophy of Law*, p. 46 (Clark, Edinburgh, 1887).

the sphere of activity for each one. Thus the theory in question is reducible either to the sanctioning of a reign of force or to a social contract as the ultimate basis of law. In either case the existence of natural rights is denied. As a matter of fact, the Kantian conception of the human person is anti-social. If a man cannot without prejudice to his own dignity, make himself subservient somehow to the claims of humanity, which social life implies, the use of the individual's powers on behalf of all is obviously impossible.

If, on the other hand, it is a question of respecting a liberty which is in some way limited, these limits require definition : it is not enough to lay down that the liberty of each must be reconciled with the liberty of all. The principles which will bring about this reconciliation must be stated as well. Thus Kant's formula is, to say the least, too vague [36].

2. *Are rights derived from the impersonal reason as identified with the State ?*—This theory, held by Hegel, Schelling and their disciples, solves the problem of the origin of rights by the use of pantheistic principles. The Absolute is one with the substance of the Universe, and this substance is mind. The State is only a mode or aspect of the absolute or divine reason. The will of the State, not as arbitrary but as regulated according to the immutable principles of reason, creates rights.

This theory is open to all the arguments that may be brought against pantheism in general. It is a denial of the individual and, consequently, of his rights ; it even elevates civil law to an absolute sovereignty.

3. *Do rights originate in any hedonistic principle ? Utilitarian theories.*—The egoistic seeking for self-satisfaction or for well-being is, according to Hobbes, the supreme law of our actions. The state of nature that was prior to all social organization was a state of warfare. Men hearkening to the voice of their own interests agreed to make reciprocal concessions. By common consent they set up an authority with the purpose of regulating each one's sphere of action and thus of avoiding conflicts. The edicts decreed for this end constitute Law. Law and rights, therefore, have their immediate foundation in the will of a

---

[36] Kant does also say : ' Act in accordance with a maxim which can serve as a universal law ' ; but no action bears this character unless it is done with due respect to the liberty of everybody else. Yet what is due to another ? What is liberty ?

legislator and in the social contract.   But, in their last analysis, they rest on utilitarian considerations.

This is likewise the idea of Bentham and John Stuart Mill. Yet they cease to consider simply the individual's welfare and look rather to that of the race. Bentham's formula is as follows : The just man is he who endeavours to procure the greatest happiness of the greatest number.

Bentham once more makes appeal to the egoistic sentiments of the individual ; he tries to persuade himself that man's highest interest is to work for the good of his neighbour. Mill preaches the doctrine of pure altruism, of disinterested love. He hopes that among men of the future this altruism will spontaneously spring up under the influence of certain psychological forces. Both of these, like Hobbes, make no distinction between right and utility.

4. *Mixed system of Rousseau : Rights the resultant of free acts of will.*—Rousseau is a utilitarian inasmuch as he teaches that our ancestors were obliged to combine in order to resist inimical forces from without. But his doctrine resembles that of Kant by reason of the emphasis he lays on the rights of the human person. Hobbes is a materialist who considers man's nature in so far as it is capable of pleasure and is determined only by the need of it ; on this sensualistic conception he endeavours to establish a system of morality and a theory of rights. Rousseau, on the other hand, is a spiritualist, imbued with a high idea of human personality. The former sees in man nothing beyond egoistic instincts ; the latter knows him as a free being, and one among other free beings. Yet Rousseau differs from Kant in an essential point. Liberty, according to Kant, consists in the emancipation of the will from sensual pleasures together with its submission to the imperatives of reason. For Rousseau liberty means that the individual is emancipated from all laws, or at least is bound only by those laws which he has agreed with others to establish. For this reason the author of the ' Social Contract ' looks for the origin of rights in the free combination of individual wills.

5. *Rights the product of biological factors.*—This is the system of the Synthetic Philosophy, of which Herbert Spencer is the chief exponent. Society is an organism subject, like all other organisms, to the general law of evolution. Right is the expression of the needs of the social organism. The juridical

relations which obtain among individuals and constitute them as a society do not differ essentially from the biological laws which bind cells together into one living body. The theory of the social organism, as thus expounded, is a development of the materialistic conception of the individual through its application to a collective being. The same criticism may therefore be raised against it. We shall have occasion later to examine its political consequences.

6. *Rights are founded immediately on the moral law inasmuch as this is the expression of the intrinsic exigencies of our nature, and mediately on the Divine Will.*—This is the explanation which we adopt. With Kant we believe that it is the moral law which is the source of rights. Yet this law, we maintain, does not resolve itself into a priori judgments arising from the constitution of the mind and without any objective validity. The principles of our reason are the expression of essential relations which exist between things ; our reason is not determined in the formation of its judgments by any blind necessity (e.g. by a priori forms) but by the force of objective evidence (*Criteriology*, **24-40**). Hence when it prescribes certain rules of conduct in our dealings with other men, it does but formulate an order of relations which are derived from our very nature. Man is by nature a social being. The moral law therefore teaches him to live in accordance with that social nature. From this there result a number of practical judgments or imperatives which constitute the Natural Law. The function of Positive Law is to interpret what is enjoined by the Natural Law, to develop its consequences, to enforce its execution and to check its violation. Thus the entire system of laws is based, we maintain, on the moral law as being the expression of the inherent exigencies of our nature and of the relations which arise from it. But as our nature, and consequently the moral law, have their origin from God, it must be the Divine Will, acting under the guidance of the Divine Reason, which is the metaphysical source of the Natural Law.

75. Kinds of Rights.—Rights are distinguished into those of the individual, those of the family and those of the community. *Individual Right* determines the relations that exist or may exist between individuals as such, without any consideration being made of ties of kindred or political ties. *Family Right* regulates the relations of justice which exist between the

parties living in the conjugal state and between members of
the family group. *Public Right* concerns the relations between
subjects and rulers, between different states considered as so
many moral units. We shall study in turn each of these
principal divisions of Right by examining them from the point
of view of the Natural Law.

CHAPTER I

RIGHTS OF THE INDIVIDUAL

Individual Right, we have said, indicates the obligations of justice which a man must fulfil with regard to his neighbour, obligations which are independent of any family or political ties. Justice binds us to respect the well-being of others, especially in the matters of life, liberty and property. In the present chapter we shall treat of these three rights.

I. RESPECT OF HUMAN LIFE

76. Foundation of the Right to Live.—In General Ethics it has been shown that man is created for an end which in excellence surpasses every other end, inasmuch as it consists in the possession of the Absolute Good by contemplation and love. This end implies the full and complete functioning of our highest faculties, and consequently our perfection; it implies the satisfaction of the deepest aspirations of our soul, and consequently our happiness. Since man is created for this state of perfection and happiness, he must tend towards it during his life. He has therefore the right to work out his perfection, the right to act and to live. He is much more than a means towards the welfare of his fellow-men. We may not, then, dispose of the life of another as we may that of an animal. The human personality is the ground of the right to live. Only higher moral motives can justify the sacrifice of human life.

77. Lawful Self-defence.—By the right of lawful self-defence we mean that of resisting an unjust aggressor by such force as is needful for safeguarding the right assailed. The application of the principles of lawful self-defence to two particular cases forms the subject of controversy, as we shall now briefly explain.

1. May the defence of one's possessions ever justify homicide? The theory upheld by some Penal Codes and adopted by

many writers gives a negative solution. In this particular case, it is argued, there is a conflict between two rights : the right of the owner to his property and the right of the aggressor to his life. Now the second far outweighs the first. One may not therefore in defence of property sacrifice the life even of an unjust aggressor, for the reason that no proportion exists between the two things. At the same time, however, those who maintain this opinion grant that the owner need not stand by and let himself be despoiled : assault upon property very closely resembles assault upon the person when it is accompanied with threats or grave acts of violence against the owner, or even when it is a question of goods indispensable for his subsistence.

According to the other opinion, held by the famous Spanish moralist De Lugo, it is allowable to kill a thief if there is no other means of defending one's possessions ; provided, however, that the goods are not a matter of very little consequence, for motives of charity as well as the higher interests of social order justify this exception. The ground for his opinion is this : in the case at issue it is not a question of inflicting upon the aggressor a punishment proportionate to the evil of his intentions, but rather of preventing him from committing an injury. The aggressor is in the wrong. It is he who constrains us to make an attempt upon his life, if we wish to protect our property. We cannot allow our right which he threatens to remain without defence. The man who attacks us unjustly puts himself outside his rights. Inasmuch as he is an aggressor, he is no more than brute force, against which we ought to be able to react according to the measure and manner necessary. The defence of a right must not be stopped by the fact that a criminal forces us to do him a greater injury than that with which he threatens us. An example will make clear the fallacy of the reasoning on which the opposite opinion relies. Must an innocent traveller, whose life is demanded by a highwayman, refuse to defend himself rather than kill his adversary ? Certainly not, and all are agreed on this point ; and this even though by killing the aggressor at the moment when he is yielding to his criminal impulse, he may be exposing his soul to eternal damnation. And yet to a believer in the next world the preservation of this earthly life is of far less consequence than the salvation of a soul.

2. A man has decided to kill me and there is no doubt whatever that he has made up his mind. He has made all his plans to attack me unawares. He is always lying in wait for me. At any moment he may make an attempt on my life before I have time to defend myself. Only yesterday he was lying in ambush with revolver cocked ; a chance circumstance alone caused me to turn out of my way. It is quite certain he will kill me some day if I do not take the offensive. In this case may my state be called one of lawful defence ?

Most authors reply in the negative ; for the aggression has not yet commenced. But De Lugo has another opinion : I can lawfully be on the defensive from the moment that my right becomes gravely menaced. In the hypothesis this is already so. My life is exposed to certain and imminent danger. One expedient alone is open to me, to slay instead of being slain. He is already an aggressor against me who resolves to kill me and has for this purpose taken steps which amount to a commencement of actually doing the deed, and he may at any moment take me by surprise.

II. Respect of Liberty

The duty of preserving and developing his life confers on man the right of putting his faculties to an external use, provided that in doing so he acts in accordance with the moral law and the just precepts of public authority. A man is infringing his neighbour's liberty when he prevents him from doing an act which is lawful for him, or when he forces him to do an act which he has the right of not doing.

78. The Right to Work.—Man has the right to labour, that is, to apply his activity to external things and to make a general use of the energies of his being, either for his own advantage or for that of others. Such a right is evident.

But it is necessary not to confuse this right to work, in the sense above, with the pretended right to be given work, which would put on the State the obligation of providing a scope for the activities of each. The State has, of course, to protect the rights of the individual against any coercion ; it has even to provide in general the conditions favourable to their exercise. But it cannot be said that it is part of its duty as universal protector to see that in every particular case such conditions shall be supplied. It falls on the individual to bring about these conditions, and this must be the work of personal initiative and effort. The State cannot set itself to be a particular providence for each. Should it do so, it would run the risk of crushing all private enterprise besides taking upon itself an impossible task.

79. Liberty to choose a Profession.—Man has the right not only to make use of his natural activity but also to do so in the way most suitable to his natural capabilities. Now our nascent aptitudes generally manifest themselves through tendencies and tastes, that is, by inner experiences that escape all external observation. Hence the individual is the only one who is ultimately able to judge of what direction his activity should take, since he alone is conscious of his own inclinations. Very often these will disclose to him his natural avocation; although, of course, there is always the possibility of mistake. Some people think they have natural qualifications which they have not, and consequently turn out not only useless to the community but perhaps even a burden. But far more serious would be the consequences if a regime existed which denied to individuals the free choice of their own career. This choice belongs to us as rational and free beings. By endowing us with this quality nature has empowered us to choose our own walk in life. It is for us to decide what are the best means of developing our faculties. The work of individual perfection must first and foremost devolve on the individual himself. This principle is the ground for the liberty of choice of occupation in life. Yet, it may be objected, this freedom has not always been recognized as the right of the worker : for centuries slavery was the lot of the majority of men.

To understand the institution of slavery from the point of view of Natural Right, we must note the difference between absolute slavery and mitigated slavery or serfdom. By the first the slave is accounted as a chattel, destitute of the essential rights of a human person, without the rights to live, to create a family, to acquire property, etc. All modern authors condemn this form of slavery without qualification. Of old it called forth the denunciations of the Stoics : ' Whom thou callest slave ', wrote Seneca, ' is born of the same seed as thyself, he enjoyeth the same sky, breatheth the same air, liveth and dieth as thou thyself '. And Epictetus : ' There is no slave by nature, save the being devoid of reason ; not of men, but of beasts only, is this true '. But these late and solitary protests wrought no appreciable change in the conditions of slaves throughout the pagan world. We know, on the other hand, that Aristotle sets himself to justify slavery by the needs of the social order : ' Not having risen to the conception of natural rights,' writes A. Fouillée, ' Aristotle is led to separate men into two classes, those whose occupation should be chiefly intellectual, and those who should devote themselves to manual work : to the former alone does he allow civil and political rights, the latter he condemns to slavery '. Still Aristotle admits elsewhere that the slave does ' partake of reason '.

It needed the enduring influence of Christian ideas to effect the gradual change from slavery to serfdom, and so to prepare the way for perfect freedom. Though the influence of Christianity was no doubt seconded by certain economic forces, it remains true that it was the preponderating motive power in bringing about the change. To fail to recognize this would be supremely unjust. The slavery of the ancient world received its death-blow the day when slave and patrician met in the depths of the catacombs to partake of the Mystic Banquet.

Serfdom is a mitigated form of slavery, or rather it is radically different from it. The personality of the slave becomes recognized ; he is acknowledged to possess inalienable rights in virtue of his nature. He is no longer part of his master's goods, able to be sold or even put to death ; he has the right to marry, to take part in religious worship, to receive a wage for his labour. Only is he denied the right to choose his occupation, he is bound all his life to the service of a master and to the working of the soil. Yet such a position procures for him certain advantages ; it ensures his having work and the means of subsistence, and frees him from anxiety with regard to the future. What view are we to take of the morality of this mitigated form of slavery ?

Some authors condemn it outright. Others would allow it, provided that it is grounded on a free contract between the villein and his lord. There is no reason, they say, why a worker should not let out his services for life in order to put himself and his family beyond the reach of the uncertainties of the future. By doing so it is true he gives up once and for all a part of his liberty, he renounces his right of taking up a different career or of offering his services to anyone else ; but there seems no reason why the right he would thus relinquish is essentially inalienable, and the serf does not relinquish it lightly but only for the sake of a serious compensation.

Whatever may be said of the hiring out of one's service for an unlimited time, it is forbidden by many modern legislations on account of the abuses that would inevitably arise.

There is a third opinion, according to which a system of serfdom, even on an hereditary basis, can be justified by certain pressing necessities. Peoples, like individuals, must gradually grow accustomed to the enjoyment of their liberty. Too often an immediate emancipation of slaves without any transitional stage has been the reverse of a blessing. It has offered an easy path to idleness and immorality. After being habituated to a rule of absolute slavery or to the wild independence of barbarism, a man is not likely to conform to the great law of work except under some form of compulsion. A mitigated slavery that respects the dignity and the fundamental rights of human personality can then, it would seem, be justified, not indeed as a definitive institution but as a provisional state of affairs. Here will be found the explanation of the attitude of infant Christianity and later of the Church—as previously that of Judaism—towards an institution which could not pass away until a profound reform in ideas and customs had eventually been accomplished.

80. Liberty of Opinion.—We must make a distinction in the matter of free choice of opinions : there is the choice which is free from physical restraint, because it takes place in a man's inner consciousness ; and there is the external manifestation of such opinions in speech, writing or action.

1. *Choice of opinion.*—Man does not escape the law which binds every thinking being of searching for the truth. His fancies, his interests, his passions have no claim when there is a question of the higher rights of truth. When after serious and earnest reflection we are convinced that a given opinion is true, or at least morally certain, we are bound to give assent to it ; and this duty becomes more strictly obligatory when doctrines are in question which regard the ordering of our life and our supreme destiny.

Kant was fully aware of the attitude dictated to us by conscience with respect to religious and moral ideas. After raising his voice—though with too little logic—against the claims of metaphysic, he was no less emphatic in proclaiming the duty of every man to assent to certain beliefs that are indispensable for morality. ' In the case of *moral belief* ', he says, ' action is absolutely necessary, that is, I must obey the moral law on all points. The end is here firmly established, and, according to all we know, one only condition is possible under which that end could agree with all other ends, and thus acquire practical validity, namely, the existence of God and of a future life. I also know for certain that no one is cognisant of other conditions which could lead to the same unity of ends under the moral law. As, then, the moral precept is at the same time my maxim, reason commanding that it should be so, I shall inevitably believe in the existence of God, and in a future life, and I feel certain that nothing can shake this belief, because all my moral principles would be overthrown at the same time, and I cannot surrender them without becoming hateful in my own eyes ' [37].

Freedom of opinion, then, does not mean the right to be indifferent to religious and moral questions. As in other fields, so even more emphatically here, eagerness for the truth must be the ruling principle in the whole of man's mental progress. To use Kant's forcible expression, I cannot surrender the principles and beliefs that my reason declares to be of sovereign importance from the moral point of view without incurring thereby my own self-condemnation. Religious indifference, therefore, far from being a natural right, is the violation of the most sacred of duties.

May we, then, in this age of intellectual anarchy, hurl our anathemas against whosoever happens not to hold the same doctrine as ourselves, or may we resort to force to make them prevail over others ? Certainly not. We say that it is undoubtedly the duty of every intelligent being to assent to the truth according to his opportunities of knowing it. But it is quite possible that under the prejudices of education or by other influences a man may in good faith adopt what is false. The assent of the mind to doctrine is not always determined by mere evidence. It is generally the highly complex resultant of subjective conditions that entirely escape the observation of others. The tribunal of a man's conscience is a sanctuary into

[37] *Critique of Pure Reason*, tr. F. Max Müller, II, p. 710 (London, 1881).

which no one may enter. To form an estimate of the sincerity of another's opinions is a matter of the utmost delicacy. God alone searches the reins and the heart. We have no right, therefore, to condemn anyone as soon as he thinks differently from ourselves. Still less may we use coercive measures. To resort to persecution would be not only odious but absurd. Not by force but by persuasion are ideas propagated. Christ did not send His disciples to conquer the world by the sword, as did Mohammed ; His only injunction to them was to go and teach.

Respect for the opinions of another consists in presuming his good faith when we think him to be in error, and in using no constraint to make him either repudiate what he believes to be true or approve what he believes to be false. But this respect for opinions is inspired by no such idea as that all doctrines are of the same metaphysical value, and that man is allowed to look upon them all with the eye of indifference or to please himself which he will accept. As rational beings the duty is incumbent upon us of seeking the truth with sincerity. Only such a duty is a matter wholly between the individual conscience and God. It does not constitute a juridical obligation, that is to say, one which falls within the scope of public Authority.

2. *Manifestation of opinions.*—The publication of opinions through speech, writing or action should be under the control of legislation, but only in the measure that this is necessary for the public good.

In the first place, every true or doubtful opinion ought to be allowed free expression. For to influence thought is as much the sphere of a man's activity as to control things. Social life does not mean simply the interchange of economic productions, but also of views and ideas. Since man is by nature rational and social and is endowed with the faculty of speech, he has the right to communicate to the minds of his fellow-men the truths he possesses and thus to give them the benefit of his own intellectual fruit. He should, moreover, be free to give expression to his doubtful judgments, in order that they may be checked by discussion. The State must therefore recognize the rights of its citizens to manifest their ideas and views. As it is not the depositary of absolute truth, it has not the sovereign power of silencing discussion. The supreme direction of man's mind does not belong to the State.

With the question we are here treating is closely connected that of the liberty of training the young. The right to teach is only another form of the right to express one's ideas. The State cannot claim a monopoly of teaching. Private enterprise is a great factor in progress, alike in the intellectual as in the economic sphere. The action of the State must be limited to protecting, encouraging and, where necessary, seconding the initiative of others ; never must it supplant it. The State has no right to mould all its citizens in one type, or to oblige them all to think alike, on the pretext of bringing about perfect unity in the body politic. It was this idea which led Plato, with all his genius, into the worst absurdities. The right of teaching, like that of thinking, is derived from human personality and has no direct connexion with the mission of the State.

Yet freedom to diffuse one's opinions has some limitations. In the public Authority, which is the interpreter of the natural law and the guardian of social order, must be recognized the right to repress the diffusion of opinions which are clearly inimical to the general peace. Intervention in the matter of opinions has been allowed as a final resource by even the most liberal legislations. Examples of abuse are not wanting ; but this only means that liberty requires serious safeguards. However, between a dogmatism or a sectarianism that is intolerant and persecuting, and a liberalism that authorizes the diffusion of the most subversive ideas, there is surely a just mean. This mean can scarcely be determined theoretically, but common sense will not have much difficulty in fixing it in practice. Here, as in many other questions, we may defer to the discretionary power of those who are appointed to see to the welfare of society.

81. Liberty of Conscience.—By liberty of conscience we mean the right every man possesses of acting in accordance with the dictates of his own conscience.

This right is injured (a) by inciting another to do wrong by example, counsel or threat ; (b) by forcing him to do something which he believes to be forbidden ; (c) by preventing him from doing what he believes must be done.

Is the right of acting in accordance with one's conscience an absolute right ? It is, when the voice of conscience is clear and right. If, however, it is a question of interfering with a false conscience, it is certainly legitimate to oppose any of its manifestations which would damage lawful rights and interests or would be directly subversive of public order. If a religion were to prescribe human sacrifices or other immoral practices, Authority would be evidently right in taking active steps in spite of respect for the liberty of conscience ; it would have to endeavour to put an end to such practices, no matter how strong the good faith of those who should adopt them. Hence liberty of conscience may be restricted in the case of a false conscience.

But on no account may recourse be had to persecution or other coercive measures in order to obtain a person's external adherence to a doctrine which he internally repudiates, nor to make him repudiate a belief which he feels bound by conscience to accept. For, to repeat what we have already said, it is by persuasion, not by violence, that truth extends its dominion [38].

III. Respect of Property

82. Definition.—Property, as synonymous with ownership, is the right to use and to dispose of an animal or thing for a legitimate end without the interference of any other person.

The right of use, as distinguished from the right of disposal, is the power recognized in law of putting a thing to any use that does not involve its transfer, or destruction, or radical transformation. Any of these effects shows that the right of disposal has been exercised. They are actions characteristic of the sovereign power of ownership.

83. Limits of Ownership.—Jurists and economists have conceived the right of ownership as the right of absolute disposal. According to this opinion, an owner may do whatsoever he chooses with a thing so long as he observes established laws and does no injury to the rights of another. This is how ownership is regarded from the point of view of positive law.

---

[38] When it is said that St. Thomas Aquinas maintains the repression of heresy to be lawful, it must be added that he looked upon the heretic as a rebel not only against God but also against society, based as it was at that time entirely on Christianity. To him the heretic was one who committed a sin which had anti-social effects. In this fact alone lies his reason for justifying civil measures of repression ; for he expressly recognizes that some of our obligations are matters for the individual conscience alone, notably such as duties to God. Moreover, he proscribes every measure of constraint in the case of those who are strangers to the true faith, on the ground that no one is bound to give an enforced assent to dogma. On this question see CASTELEIN, *Droit Naturel ;* CRAHAY, *La Politique de Saint Thomas.*

But the moral law lays important restrictions on the power of an owner. The positive law does not deny the existence of these restrictions ; it merely omits to consider them for reasons of the public good. It could not reasonably be expected that regulations should be made concerning the administration of private wealth or concerning the enjoyment of goods in particular cases. Such interference would give rise to the worst abuses. Yet certain acts which the positive law refuses to punish may still be infringements of the moral law.

The limitations of the right of ownership arise partly from the nature of the goods committed to our dominion, and partly from our own nature, which is that of a rational and social being.

In the first place, we must not disregard the design of divine Providence concerning each thing. To destroy a thing out of mere caprice, with no purpose in view for oneself or for others, is certainly to disregard its end ; still more so, if we make it serve to gratify illicit desires. The same principle must regulate our treatment of animals. For they, more than inanimate things, show forth the power of the Creator, and on this account deserve a greater respect. We may not inflict upon them unnecessary suffering, for the reason that animal suffering has never been willed by the Creator as an end in itself but only as a necessary condition or an unavoidable consequence of some good. It is worthy of remark that kindness to animals, so marked out for praise in these days, is much more consistent with the principles of the old spiritualistic philosophy than it is with the principles of evolutionary materialism. Whilst the first certainly will not recognize the animal as of our own kith and kin, nevertheless it sees in it a creature made by God. If the materialist should regard the animal as one of his own, yet belonging to a lower race, it is proper that it should be subdued, even if not destroyed, in accordance with that great law of nature which decrees the struggle for existence and the non-survival of the weaker.

Secondly, the moral law forbids us to use our possessions for purely selfish motives. Man is a social being and must behave as such. But this does not mean that ownership has an exclusively social function, as some would suppose. Since the individual has his personal life to consider, he can aim at furthering his own development and his own happiness by the disposal of his goods ; only he must never forget that he is a social being as well. By doing this, he will not play a merely selfish part. If he possesses a superfluity, he will share with those who are in want of the bare necessaries of life. His position as a person of wealth will put at his dispoal a means of exercising a great moral influence over others.

84. Basis of the Right of Ownership.—A distinction must be made between the concrete right or the right of a definite person to a definite thing and the right in the abstract, the general power every man has of becoming an owner. By the basis of ownership is meant the principles from which the abstract right is derived. The question is therefore : Can a man legitimately claim dominion over things, and why ? Various answers are given. Some base the right on social conventions and laws, others on labour ; others again, and with these we associate ourselves, consider that it is derived from the very nature of man, inasmuch as he is a person.

85. Ownership founded on Social Conventions and on Legislation.—Everything, it is argued, was originally common property. By a social compact men set up a legislator whose mission it should be to apportion the wealth of the earth. In this way was ownership established. Its foundation is therefore in the social contract and in the laws established for its execution.

Whatever may be the value of this theory from the point of view of history, it is quite certain that it does not solve the problem proposed. The ultimate foundation of ownership cannot lie in the social contract. Men could never have set out to divide goods, if they had not previously the right to dispose of them, that is to say, the right of ownership, at least the abstract right ; they could not agree to share goods over which they had no right. Ownership must therefore logically precede the social compact ; instead of being derived from it, it must furnish the basis for the contract. An agreement may effect the transference of a right, or regulate its use, but never can it create one.

86. Ownership founded on Labour.—This is a conception very widespread to-day, and one that is very often made to do duty as an argument against the present order of things ; for all legitimate ownership, it is said, must depend upon labour and must be the reward of a man's effort. Labour, however, cannot

be shown to be the ultimate basis of this right. Labour
transforms things so as to adapt them to our needs or to make
them useful towards further production. In this respect it is
what we have called above an act of disposal, which is a way of
asserting our sovereign control over the things. Hence labour
is not the foundation of ownership ; it is an exercise of it and
presupposes the general right to dispose of the goods of the earth.
I cannot claim to transform anything by my labour if I do not
first of all possess the right of making it serve my purpose, that
is, the right of disposing of it. Again, would anyone forbid me
to eat wild fruit which I found to hand and happened to
pluck without effort ? Would anyone deny that if I picked
up an uncut diamond on my path it was my property from
the moment that I found it ? Could anyone deprive me of it on
the sole ground that it had not yet been worked upon by my
industry ? Labour, it must be confessed, is not the ultimate
source of ownership. A thing does not become mine because I
have put forth my labour upon it, but rather because it answers
to certain exigencies of my nature and I have been able to
obtain possession of it before anyone else. This is the reason why
I may eat the wild fruit I have plucked without effort and why I
may appropriate the uncut diamond I have simply picked up.

Furthermore, the theory we are combating finds its refutation in the very consequences that would follow from it. It is
stated that a man may legitimately own only what his personal
labour has produced. What, then, about land and natural
wealth ? My labour never created the land ; I cannot therefore
dispose of it, nor reclaim it and cultivate it, since that too is a
way of disposing of it. For a similar reason I may not transform by my labour any of the raw materials that are indispensable for the production of every object that is made.
This argument is equally true of a collective body : the earth
and raw materials were no more created by a body than by an
individual. Thus every kind of ownership is found to be
proscribed, of personal as well as landed property, collective as
well as individual. The human race must simply perish
through inanition, if deference is to be paid to the principle
which disallows man the ownership of everything he has not
produced by his labour.

87. The Right of Ownership derived from Man's Nature.—
The earth and its wealth were made for the use of man. This

statement cannot seriously be disputed. Man has the right to use and to dispose of things and of animals, because, as we have already said, he is a person. As such he has the right both to provide for his own preservation and to make use of his natural powers. Hence he may establish his dominion over things, since this is a necessary condition both for his existence and for his development. And it is clear that this dominion must not only look to the satisfaction of his present needs. Man is not condemned to live from hand to mouth, the existence of the savage. As a rational and free being capable of foreseeing the future and of restraining his appetites, which are the perennial spring of new desires, he acts in conformity with his nature when he regulates his conduct with a view to his future needs. As the head of a family he is bound to some extent to provide for the future of those whom Providence has entrusted to his care. For these reasons he may claim the right of acquiring a capital which beyond supplying the needs of the day will produce for the morrow. Thus, freed from material cares, he will be in a position to employ his faculties in higher spheres and exercise a beneficent influence on those around him. Subordinated to these ends, the possession of wealth is certainly legitimate. It is necessary for the full development of human personality.

But a special question presents itself here. Granted that the human race may use and, consequently, appropriate the earth and its riches, still it would seem, on a priori considerations, that there are two possible forms of appropriation, namely by the individual and by the community. The question arises : Is the first form as legitimate as the second ? This must be examined, if our argument is to be established.

The considerations we have been developing establish the legitimacy of individual ownership quite as much as that by the community. For we have seen that man has the right to dispose of the earth and its riches by reason of the fact that he is a human person. But what is due to man by virtue of his humanity does not belong simply to the race as a whole but to each individual member of it. Hence it confers on each the same essential rights, and in particular the right of appropriating things. Individual ownership is therefore legitimate. This truth, however, is not accepted by two schools of thought, the communist and the collectivist.

88. Outline of the Doctrine of Communism.—Communists assert that all men have the same right to live and to work for their perfection, and therefore they have the same right to the goods of this world. By natural law, then, the earth and its wealth is the common patrimony of the whole race. At first, by a joint ownership, they belonged to everybody. According to the theory of Hobbes, such a state of affairs would beget incessant warfare ; with a view to what was obviously their common interest, they exchanged, by means of a social contract, the regime of communism for one of private ownership.

89. Criticism of the Doctrine of Communism.—1. *This theory is based on a false conception of the nature of the goods of the world.*—They are not meant to be possessed promiscuously by all men. Surely this is a common-sense truth which no one would dream of doubting in practice. In addition, we have just seen that Hobbes himself was alive to the necessity of putting an end to the state of joint ownership which he imagined originally obtained.

Articles for personal use and consumption, and also instruments of production, have but a limited utility ; they cannot, therefore, be used by everybody. And the land itself will only yield its wealth to the man who makes it fertile by the sweat of his brow. Now cultivation of the soil evidently implies appropriation, at least by the community, if not by the individual. If the whole of the earth belonged to everybody in common, who, pray, would care to devote his capital and his labour to the exploitation of property which somebody else could immediately after come and possess ? If to individuals, singly or together, we allow the right of establishing a permanent abode on a given estate and of building a settlement and putting it under cultivation, we are at the same time admitting that a real and true ownership is legitimate. By the very act by which a man exchanges a nomad life for a settled one, he of necessity also takes possession of the soil. The ground then occupied or put under cultivation ceases henceforth to be at the disposal of anyone else.

Thus land, no less than instruments of production and articles of consumption, is matter for individual possession. Such ownership is conformable with the designs of Providence, since the very nature of the things themselves demands it. Hence it can in no way be admitted that the natural law is the basis of, or even sanctions, a state of common ownership which is repugnant to the nature of things. Hobbes and the communists forget this elementary truth when they proclaim the primordial right of every man to everything.

2. *The pretended community of goods has never existed as an historical fact.*—There was no doubt a time when vast unexplored tracts of land lay free for the first occupier. In this sense they were common, but entirely in a negative way, in so far as they belonged to nobody. But the earth was never, in a positive sense, possessed by all men. Appropriation of land by families or tribes dates from the dawn of history. A hunting or a pastoral tribe has already taken possession of a piece of land as soon as it prevents a neighbouring tribe from trespassing upon it.

Private ownership of land would seem to be simply the usurpation of the patrimony of the tribe as a whole. Whilst the bulk of the tribe would prefer the nomad state, living by the chase or the rearing of flocks, a family would settle down on some relatively very small part of the common land, and rely on the produce of its cultivation for their means of subsistence [39]. Such a settlement would in no way injure the rights of the community ; it would be done with tacit if not expressed consent and for its greater advantage. For by settling itself in one spot a family would relinquish in favour of the community its rights to hunting and to pasturage over a very much larger area than the particular plot of which it claimed to be the exclusive owner. Beyond this, it would furnish a very fruitful example : for owing to its initiative being followed by other groups, the land would be cleared and reclaimed and thus become capable of providing for a very much larger population.

3. *The reasoning of the communists would lead logically to the denial of all ownership, collective as well as individual.*—If the earth belongs to everybody, an individual cannot call the very smallest part of it his own without violating the rights of others. This statement is equally true of the family, of the tribe, and even of the nation. Any appropriation whatsoever is privative in so far as what is appropriated is withdrawn from

---

[39] See LEROY-BEAULIEU, *Collectivism*, tr. and abbrev. by Sir A. Clay (Murray, London, 1908).

the use of others. It matters little whether the reservation of
the goods be made in favour of one individual or of many.
Accordingly communists are violating the most elementary
logic when they allow national ownership after denying the
right to the individual because of the pretended primordial
right of every man to everything.

4. *Communism makes the natural law self-contradictory.*—The
natural law would be self-contradictory if it gave us a right
that would necessarily involve by its use the violation of the
right of another. It would also be self-contradictory if at one
and the same time as it confers a right it bids us renounce it,
either entirely or in part. Now this case would be verified here
if we granted that a positive right of ownership is conferred by
nature on all men and that it extends to all goods. Since
everybody would be entitled equally with everyone else to own
each article, he would have the same right to dispose of it, yet
at the same time would not be able to do so without violating
the right of his neighbour. Under these conditions the natural
law would either have to allow this violation, or absolutely
forbid the exercise of man's right, or at least demand that he
should partially remove it by some kind of transaction. Each
of these solutions implies an *essential opposition* of rights, and
consequently a fundamental contradiction in the natural law.

Once again. It is admitted that universal community of
goods—and especially of the earth—would be an utter impossibility. Hobbes saw therein the source of incessant conflicts. But how could the state of nature be one such as to
prevent the resources of nature from being developed ? Is it
conceivable that the moral law should give individuals rights
which by their use must assuredly lead to a state of warfare ?
To be true to his theory, Hobbes had to deny that man is by
nature sociable. But if his sociability is a fact, it is clear that
a state of things which is destructive of all social life could not
be founded on nature itself. Hence, we conclude, nature does
not give to all men the same effective or positive right to all
things.

90. Conclusion.—From the above considerations it is clear
that the right of ownership which every man has in virtue of
his human personality is not a concrete or positive right to
dominion over everything ; but it is the abstract right of
property, that is to say, the power of becoming an owner of

things not yet belonging to anyone or freely ceded by their legitimate possessors.

Our proof, however, is not yet complete. Certainly it may be granted without much difficulty that Robinson Crusoe may clear and cultivate his desert island for his own advantage without doing an injury to the rights of the human race. But there are some natural rights which were at first exercised by the individual and subsequently became a function of Public Authority. Such, for instance, as the right of procuring reparation for an unjust injury. Now may not the right of property be numbered among such rights as these ? Is not the individual to-day merged in the community, in this advanced stage in the economic development of nations ? This is the question that now demands our attention.

In saying that the basis of ownership lies in the very nature of man, we have shown that appropriation of the soil can be made for the benefit of the individual ; but it may be made equally for the good of a corporate body of individuals. In fact we know that collective ownership of land was anterior in more regions than one to private ownership. In the case of a civilized people ought not the first form to be substituted again for the second ? This is the question which remains to be examined.

91. Outline of the Doctrine of Collectivism.—The theory in question is sketched by Schäffle in his booklet entitled *The Quintessence of Socialism* [40]. Its programme is summed up in the three following items : the nationalization of land and all the means of production, the refusal to allow any individual to own any productive capital, and the administration by the state of all economic concerns. Such a system we maintain would be contrary to the rights of man, and this for many reasons which we will develop in turn.

92. Criticism of Collectivism.—I. *Collectivism is incompatible, both theoretically and practically, with the liberty and dignity of the human person.*—Man, we have already said, has the right to realize to the full his own personality, and to use for this end the goods which Providence has put at his disposal. Now how can he perfect himself except by the exercise of his faculties ? The development of the individual is therefore a

---

[40] (Allen, London, 9th ed., 1906.) A supplement to this was published in 1911, entitled *The Impossibility of Social Democracy.*

work which is personal to himself. He is the only one who knows exactly his own wants and tendencies. With him, then, must the ultimate decision lie of the path along which his activity will be best directed, and it is his business likewise to determine his own wants. God has given him reason that he may conduct himself towards his true end, by freely choosing such means as appear the best suited for the fulfilment of his end. Hence it follows that the individual is not for society but society for the individual. It must provide an environment favourable for his development. Far from paralyzing his initiative, it must protect it and secure him a sphere of action as wide as possible.

Can it be maintained that a collectivist regime would further this end ? One would be led to think so from the statements of certain collectivists who are loud in their protestations of respect for the personal rights of man. But it remains to be seen whether their attitude is a logical one. To require the State to be owner of all land and capital, to have the entire management of the production and the distribution of wealth, to preside over all functions of social life, like the brain over organic life, is surely, if logic is to count for anything, to desire that the individual should abdicate his own will and submit himself as completely as possible to the ruling of the State. Such a power and part cannot be given to the State without lessening in a proportionate degree the liberty of the citizen. Every collectivist who follows out his opinions to their logical conclusion must desire the effacement of the individual before the superior unit which is the community. If the State is the brain of the body politic, the individual is no more than a cell. A contradiction therefore exists between the collectivist ideal and the full ideal of liberty.

Yet suppose we admit for the sake of argument that collectivism is not inconsistent with the personal liberty of the individual in theory, in practice their harmonious alliance would nevertheless be found to be impossible. The orderly and permanent working of machinery so complicated as that of the collectivist State would require nothing short of a discipline of iron. The officials appointed to organize the national production would have to be given absolute powers. The assessment of the wants to be satisfied, and accordingly of the things to be made, the allotment of labour, the distribution of products, would all have to depend on the supreme will of the State.

We are reminded that this will, though supreme, need not necessarily be arbitrary ; but the whole point is whether it would be so in practice. In estimating requirements, the State would make it its duty, we are told, to consult the consumers and consider their needs. But would it do so ? What guarantee is there to this effect ? In brief, the practical difficulties would be found to be very numerous and weighty. We are further informed that the collectivist regime would not interfere in any way with a man's liberty of profession. But here again we have no assurance that this liberty, which is valued above every-thing, would be effectually safeguarded against an absolute authority. If the State were going to organize the national production, would it not previously have to determine the number of hands to be employed in each branch of industry ? To-day, although the individual is free in theory to choose his occupation, he very often meets with obstacles that make a choice impossible. He can overcome them only by persevering effort and if he is really qualified by nature with the necessary gifts. In a word, a man's calling in life is generally well tested. Thus, in the existing state of society, force of circumstances correct any caprice on the part of private liberty. But, under the proposed regime, there would be nothing except the ruling of authority to prevent persons from changing their occupation at will. The division of labour, being freely arranged, would necessarily be unstable. Man has a strong dislike for uni-formity ; he is pleased with variety ; he is ever ready to fancy that the lot of others is preferable to his own. Thus the staff of workers would be exposed to incessant variations. How, pray, in such conditions could the collectivist State fulfil its task ?

The question has been appositely put by an apologist for socialism [41] : ' How is the army of workers to be regulated so as to be neither too great nor too small ? ' He answers as follows : ' In what are called the liberal professions it will be enough to raise the standard of knowledge required, to intro-duce a more severe test in selection that would lessen the number and force those less capable to fall back on other

---

[41] RENARD, *Etude sur le socialisme.*

occupations '. In the case of other occupations the State would pay a higher remuneration in those that are less popular.

But is not this equivalent to admitting that the State would adopt multifarious indirect methods for procuring a distribution of labour according as it decides best ? So that the choice of occupation, no less than the fixing of the individual's requirements, would ultimately depend on the good-will of a certain number of State officials. No one would be able to engage in any employment unless he fulfilled the conditions set by the State. But who would be the judge in the matter of deciding whether this person is fitted or not for any given career ? The State or, what comes to the same, a committee made up of persons appointed by the State. What guarantee would there be in such a regime for the choice of one's occupation ? It is true that even to-day the State lays down the conditions of admission to the liberal professions and to certain posts that are State appointments. But in countries where freedom of education is allowed, this power of the State is really of small moment. People intending to take up a liberal profession have the choice between several examinations, some of which are independent of all government influence. Then again, there are very many professions that as such do not come under the cognizance of the law of the land at all. And it must be acknowledged that even in the present system State intervention in this matter is attended with not a few abuses : partiality and favouritism too often determine appointments. How very much more numerous would such abuses be under a system which has as a principle that no one shall engage in any occupation at all without the consent of the public authority !

The supremacy of the State would be even more formidable in the domain of thought. Here it would not only have the monopoly of education, but also every literary production would have to be submitted to its control, since for its publication recourse would have to be had to the State press. For the printing-house along with all the other instruments of production would be under the management of the State.

Thus, not only the economic life but also the intellectual life of the whole nation would be under the sovereign direction of the public authorities.

Now who or what, indeed, is the State that it should be granted such absolute powers ?

It is too often forgotten that the State is not a sort of divinity, infallible in what concerns its mission. It is nothing but a body of men influenced, as other men are, by prejudices, passions and self-interest, and the more liable to abuse their authority according as it is the more absolute. We have shown that the power of these men, under the collectivist regime, would be unrestricted. In the existing society the power of the State is limited in a thousand ways. Private interests and free associations exercise a check upon it. The freedom of the press submits all the actions of the government to the control of public opinion. What would become of this liberty and this control if a system prevailed that would put into the hands of the State the machinery necessary for the propagation of ideas ? There is no need to ask what would become of the influence of private interests and free associations which to-day so happily counterbalance the power of the State. By owning all wealth the State would possess paramount influence ; it would be like a huge tree that kills all vegetation around and stands alone in its glory.

It is useless to expect that universal suffrage would supply a remedy against any abuse of power. How guarantee a free expression of opinion and independence at the poll amongst a nation of officials ? Officialdom as it exists to-day is too often a scandal in the electoral system. Unhappy the lot of dissentients under a regime that compels all its citizens to seek the necessaries of life from the hands of the State.

Yet let us suppose that the people retain the sovereign power, that notwithstanding all we have said they maintain their complete independence in voting, and can overthrow a government at will as soon as it ceases to please them. The consequences of such a state of affairs are immediately evident. Such criticism of the actions of the public authority would mean the speedy ruin of all discipline. Party rivalry would grow keener as the stakes became greater ; dissatisfaction and mutual recriminations the more frequent as the governing power endeavoured to settle more widespread interests. All these circumstances would keep the government necessarily unsettled and make it constantly pass into different hands. In such conditions how would the collectivist State perform the very complex and difficult duties which this theory entrusts to it ? Above all, how could it obtain success in industrial and

commercial enterprises which require habits of regularity and
unity of direction in the highest degree ? Imagine some
anonymous society, composed of a great number of shareholders none of whom have any direct interest in the success of
the business, formed for many enterprises which must all be
undertaken at once, managed by a *personnel* necessarily ever
changing and whose nomination is determined by the votes of
a crowd swayed by all kinds of political views. What folly it
would be to invest one's capital in such a concern ! Yet this is
a picture of the collectivist State. It is quite evident that
rivalry of parties and fluctuations in public opinion would have
a most baneful effect upon the economic life of the society.
There would only be one way of preventing disorder and
anarchy, namely, by crushing the citizens under the yoke of an
iron discipline.

Thus the collectivist regime, by putting the individual under
the absolute guardianship of the State and indeed robbing
him of all the liberties he enjoys to-day, would be nothing less
than a disparagement of his human personality ; and this is one
of the reasons why such a system would be contrary to the
natural law.

2. *The establishment of any such regime, far from furthering
social progress, would be a great obstacle to it.*—That the system of
individual ownership is superior to a collectivist regime such as
we have described is demonstrated by arguments both from
history and psychology.

(a) *Argument from history.*—Collective ownership has existed
in many places and everywhere it has always evolved into
private property. A system of allotments has followed that of
the working and enjoyment of common land, periodic redistributions have tended to become less and less frequent, and
perpetual possession or ownership has eventually replaced
temporary possession or usufruct. Now this evolution was
parallel in time with the progress made in land cultivation. It
became necessary, as a population grew more numerous, to
abandon the wide-area cultivation of former times. This fact
shows the necessity of allowing the worker an increasingly
longer, and eventually a perpetual, ownership. The inconveniences of the village community explain its disappearance.
But these inconveniences were not accidental ; on the contrary, they belonged to the very essence of such a system. As

the cultivation of the soil required more capital and greater labour, the incentive of personal ownership became indispensable. In the village community it very often happened that the worker on the soil would neglect the cultivation of his allotment as the time for redistribution drew near ; the new possessor was in consequence obliged to devote a more or less lengthy period of time to getting the exhausted land back to a fit condition. Hence, under such a system, there was a considerable loss of time and energy. It was precisely to remedy this evil that the periods between the redistributions became longer, until eventually mere usufruct gave place to perpetual ownership. This evil consequence which was always found in the village community would be very much more aggravated under a collectivist regime. Not only would the cultivator not own the soil which he worked, but the result of his labour would not be to his personal profit. For the produce would be gathered into the granaries of the State and apportioned to the citizens in exchange for other proceeds of labour.

(*b*) *Psychological argument.*—If we look into the nature of man it is easy to understand why a system of collective ownership is not to be preferred to that of private property. For most men to obey the great law of work there is needed the stimulus of personal interest, the hope of self-aggrandisement and of provision for the future of the family. Those men are few who can dispense with these motives and take to their work solely from a sense of duty or for the good of others. Such will always be men of an exceptional nature. Now, need we say that individual ownership provides far more potent incentives to work than would be given by collective ownership ? Far, then, from being a help to social progress, the establishment of collectivism would be a great drawback. It would be simply a return to an elementary form of economic arrangement which has disappeared under the development of cultivation.

To attain its maximum of productiveness human labour must be free, and, as a rule, be undertaken in the interests of the worker himself, or at least in the interests of those endeared to him. By this we do not mean that selfish motives are the only ones which man obeys, but that we agree with Hobbes in acknowledging that the part they play in human conduct is very great. A man is in earnest over what he does of his own initiative and over what it is his interest to make a success.

Work which is not done under the stimulus of self-interest or by natural taste but simply under the goad of constraint will in most cases be much less productive. The man who works under compulsion will, if opportunity allows, be a mere eye-server, and will put forth the minimum of effort. The work of one who is an owner has an advantage over that of the wage-earner or the slave. The slavery of times past affords a singularly instructive example in this matter. When the quality of the work done by slaves became very poor, their masters had recourse to stimulating them with the offer of personal gain; they were allowed then to put by their savings with a view eventually to purchasing their own liberty. Collectivism would exactly reverse this in replacing voluntary labour by compulsory labour, and would thus rob the worker of the mainspring of his energy.

In the first place, competition among private producers would give way in every branch of human activity to State monopoly. Yet competition, notwithstanding certain drawbacks, is recognized by all to be one of the most powerful factors in economic progress. History proves that the most fruitful inventions and greatest undertakings are due not to public action but rather to private management and initiative, which is ever kept on the alert by the stimulus of competition.

Secondly, whilst private producers in their rivalry with one another naturally strive to vary their productions and invent more effective and more economical methods of manufacture, an opposite course would be the policy of a collectivist State, namely, to introduce as far as possible uniformity in all requirements, and never to improve upon the methods already in use. And as a matter of fact, what immense difficulties would arise every time a new invention of any importance should make it necessary for the State to reorganize its system of labour.

Furthermore, besides suppressing all competition, the proposed regime would deprive the individual of any hope of enriching either himself or his relations. It would be strictly forbidden for him to acquire any of the means of production, and to work them for his own profit or pass them on to his heirs. Yet it cannot be denied that the desire to build up a fortune, if not for himself at least for his children, is in a very great number of cases the mainspring of a man's activity.

No matter what may be said to the contrary, the idlers of

the community are relatively a small class. How many parents lead a life of toil with no thought of satisfying their own wants but because they are looking to the future of those dependent upon them. How many people does not this one thought keep from taking the pleasant path of ease. When at length they have made their mark in life, they still work on to make secure the position that has cost them so much. In his struggle for the manifold necessities of life, obliged to provide a means of livelihood for himself and his family, harassed with anxiety for the future, every man has a powerful incentive to work. Quite otherwise, however, would be his position under the collectivist system : his business would not be his own, and he would have no prospect of bequeathing it to anyone. Indeed, he would be working less for himself than for the community ; that is to say, personal interest would give place to a mere general interest, the influence of which upon the worker is admittedly very much less powerful. The State, as the owner of all wealth, would of course be able to compel everybody to work in order to live ; but this enforced labour, lacking in natural incentives, would not be likely to produce better results than that of the slaves in previous ages.

3. *Collectivism would impose upon the State a task beyond its powers, and one in no way in accordance with its natural mission.* —It is easy enough to form an a priori conception of the working of the collectivist machinery, but the aspect of things changes very considerably when looked at from a practical point of view. Difficulties immediately arise which in theory were not contemplated. We will examine briefly the chief economic functions which the new regime would lay upon the State.

(1) First of all, it would be the duty of the State to determine *what things* would have to be made. The first question that presents itself is how to make a distinction between necessary objects and objects of luxury. This, it will be admitted, is no easy matter, especially when there is the question of reconciling it with each man's liberty to settle his own requirements. These requirements are constantly varying and become more numerous in proportion as man becomes more highly civilized. Things which to-day are articles of common use were originally objects of luxury. The State would have to reckon with this fact if it is not to hinder all economic progress. It would not

be sufficient to make out, once and for all, a list of the things to
be produced, and to divide them into the two classes of necessary articles and articles of luxury.   Such a classification would
have to be subjected to constant revision according as demands
varied ; and for this an army of officials would be required.
Even then its purpose would scarcely be attained.   ' No person ', says George Renard, ' is competent to draw a line of
division between what is necessary and what is merely useful,
for such a line must change according as society grows richer
and more cultured ' [42].   Since no one is competent in this
matter, this socialist writer asserts ' the necessity of submitting
it to the judgment of everybody '.   He means that there should
be an understanding among all the parties concerned to fix
the minimum standard of living which the community would
engage to provide for each individual.   This, he adds, would
be laid down in the Constitution that would be drawn up
by the whole community.   It would be a kind of declaration
of the citizen's economic rights.   Thus, in order that the
bicycle, which a few years ago was a luxury, might come into
use as the errand-boy's tool or the artisan's convenience to get
to his work, a revision of the Constitution would be necessary !
Further, what would be the issue of this referendum introduced for the purpose of settling the economic rights of man ?
What is there that would not be demanded by the masses,
impatient for the oft-promised reign of the age of gold ?   Each
and all would clamour for the choicest delicacies in food and
the greatest comfort in clothing.

(2) The State would have to determine not only the kind but
also *the quantity* of the things to be produced.   To do this, it
would naturally have recourse to the powerful aid of statistics.
But think for a moment what are the immense difficulties of
the commissariat of an army in the field.   Imagine the calculations to be made, the details to be foreseen !   Here there
is not a question of an army, but of immense cities, nay, of a
whole nation, to be provided with rations, and that too
every day.   ' London's millions ', wrote Leroy-Beaulieu, ' can
sleep in peace without either the individual or the public
administration having the least anxiety about the arrival of
victuals for the morrow. . . . People who know nothing of

[42] *Op. cit.*

political economy and never give a thought to the general welfare, still continue to produce each day all of the various articles that Paris consumes in the twenty-four hours. Yet, on the other hand, we notice that when the State has to transfer a few thousands of men, a brigade or a division, for instance, for the sake of manœuvres, it has, in spite of all its conscious foresight, no easy task in providing for their needs ' [43]. What to-day happens spontaneously through the joint action—in no way concerted yet none the less effective—of innumerable individuals each guided by personal interest, would have to be undertaken by committees formed for the purpose of attending to the various departments of economic life. What a responsibility to assume ! What practical difficulties to be overcome ! And what disastrous consequences the least error in calculation would entail !

(3) But the undertaking of the collectivist State would remain yet unaccomplished. After the catalogue of articles to be produced had been drawn up, a *method of production* would have to be organized. A sufficient number of hands would have to be provided in each single industry, and yet, we must remember, the State must allow everybody to follow what he considers to be his natural calling. For we have already agreed that freedom of choice of occupation would be just as much then as now a condition of progress ; and the difficulty which the collectivist organization would meet with here we have noticed above. A uniform system of training for all would produce everywhere the same ambitions ; everybody would prefer literary or office work, and there would be a dearth of willing hands for the rougher toil on the land or in the mines. The State would be obliged to resort to coercive measures, either direct or indirect. Yet this could not even be attempted without arousing ill-feeling and resistance. To overcome these it would certainly be necessary in the end to establish an iron discipline that would annihilate individual personality.

(4) Once the workers have been drafted into the several industries, the State has to supervise what is being done by each person in order to see that he is fulfilling the task assigned to him. For this purpose it would be *necessary to create an army of officials*. The workers would then find realized, under

[43] *Op. cit.*

a form they had little expected, the much-vaunted ideal of
equality. To-day, at least in the majority of cases, work proceeds without any need of interference, for there is the spur of
personal interest to keep the worker at work. But in the collectivist regime we have seen that this would have ceased to exist.

(5) Again, the State would have to undertake *the distribution
of wealth* for the community. On this point especially socialistic writers display the greatest variety of opinions. Several
formulae have been suggested. Among socialistic theorists,
some say ' to each according to his needs ' ; others ' to each
according to his labour ' ; whilst others again would combine
both these principles, without, however, showing how this is to
be carried out in practice. Lastly, there are some who speak of
giving the same remuneration to all workers.

The formula ' to each according to his needs ' is essentially
vague. Man's needs are well-nigh infinite, and they become
more definite as well as more numerous with the progress of
civilization. Again, what would have to be considered as
needs ? The State would have to step in to settle this question.
And would all needs be reckoned as equal ? Then, as Schäffle
admits, socialism would be the enemy of all progress and all
liberty. Perhaps the State would order each citizen to draw up
a list of all his wants ? It is not difficult to guess what would
be the result of such an inquiry. And then, if each did receive
according to his needs, where would be, no matter what the
task he had to fulfil, the stimulants to labour ?

Equally vague is the second formula, ' to each according to
his labour '. How could the value of labour be determined ?
According to the effort and the moral merit of the worker ?
If so, how is the merit in each individual case to be estimated ?
Here all would be arbitrary, with free scope for favouritism.
In this connexion the socialist G. Renard frankly writes :
' It may be that experiment will show that, since it is impossible to reckon directly in terms of effort, it may be necessary
to base the calculation on its visible and tangible results, that is
to say, on the work accomplished ' [44]. But by doing this we
renounce the principle of giving ' to each according to his
labour ', for the visible and tangible results by no means
always correspond to the effort of the worker. They largely

[44] *Op cit.*

depend on a variety of circumstances that have nothing to do with moral merit. After so repeatedly reproaching capitalism with its failure to give to each the reward of his effort, this is the way that socialism declares by the pen of one of its exponents ' that it will be necessary to give up the idea of taking into account the intrinsic merit of the individual '. Wherefore we must conclude that each would see his work repaid according to the value of the things he has produced.

But a new question now presents itself : According to what standards is the value of different commodities to be fixed ? Marx would have had them rated according to the average length of labour-time required for the production of each of them : ' That which determines the magnitude of the value of any article is the amount of labour socially necessary, or the labour-time socially necessary for its production ' [45]. But to determine this amount is not so easy a matter as one would be led to suppose. ' For example ', says Maisonabe, ' a man has just brought a bushel of wheat to the national granary. In order to fix the value of the labour-time which this bushel represents, a great number of elements must be taken into consideration : not only the time spent in manuring the ground, in sowing the seed, in harrowing, in threshing the grain, but also the time spent in tending the oxen that have helped the labourer, plus the time spent in making or repairing the implements, waggons, sacks, etc. '. We are given an example here of how many inquiries and calculations would have to be made by the officials appointed to settle the value of commodities according to the Marxian principle.

Moreover, this principle gives an erroneous meaning to the word ' value '. A consumer cannot be made to pay more for a thing than he would otherwise do simply on the ground that its production took a longer time. Would it do, for instance, for wheat grown on steep hillsides or in more barren districts to be assessed more highly than that produced in the fertile parts of the plain ? Marx forgets that the same number of hours of labour done under different conditions would vary in their power of production.

Moreover, this leader of scientific socialism fails to attain the object he proposes, namely, to procure a more equitable system

[45] MARX, *Capital*, ed. Engels, p. 6 (Sonnenschein, London, 12th ed., 1908).

of remuneration for human effort. Effort is no more proportionate to the length of labour-time than it is to the result obtained. The quantity of coal extracted in the same space of time is greater or less according as the seam is more easily accessible or not. In the first case the amount of labour expended was considerably less.

Some examples will show that the Marxian principle cannot be easily reconciled with the claims of socialism to remunerate labour more equitably. Take the example of two bushels of wheat grown respectively in the barren hilly district and in the fertile lowlands. Let the figures 10 and 5 stand for the amount of labour required in the two cases. The average will be 7½ hours. Since this average is to settle the rate of wages in both the regions, it is abundantly evident that all the advantage is with the growers in the fertile plains. Their competitors, in their struggle against greater difficulties, will have worked twice as hard ; and yet they will not receive higher pay. As a second example take two industrial labourers engaged on different kinds of work. The work of one is done under very trying conditions and therefore will require a greater intensity, and precisely on this account takes a much less time. Must he, in spite of this fact, content himself with less reward because his effort took less time ? Yet this would be the logical consequence of the principle of Marx. The shepherd watching his flock in sweet idleness from dawn till evening would receive a greater recompense than the glass-blower whose health is quickly ruined.

Then, again, how is Marx's principle to be applied when it is a question of mental labour, which is more exhausting and cannot be endured so long as some kinds of physical labour at a low tension ? Would the mechanic who watches over a machine receive a higher wage than the engineer, the artist, the man of letters, etc. ?

These consequences might lead one to look rather to the social value of the articles produced or to the needs of the consumer as a basis for the distribution of wealth, but to do so would be in the first place to go contrary to the very essence of the collectivist doctrines, that part company with the present regime precisely because prices are regulated not by work value but by the law of supply and demand ; and secondly would leave the difficulties unremoved which the masses would make against the acceptance of rises and falls in wages settled by ministerial decisions.

Such considerations as these show that collectivism would impose upon the State a task beyond its powers. And this task would not be at all consistent with the function of public authority. Its action must not supersede that of the individual, but, on the contrary, should facilitate and safeguard as far as possible private initiative—necessarily and always the essential factor in social progress.

(6) Finally, we need hardly say, collectivism could never be established except by a flagrant *violation of existing rights*. The working of the soil and mines, the making of implements and machinery, and in general the progress achieved in the various branches of human industry, are the work not of the State but of private enterprise. They are due to personal initiative, to individual skill and effort. By what right could the State assert itself the master of all this wealth that it has in no way itself produced ? Would it be in the higher claims of the community ? Yet we have already shown that the community would gain nothing by the establishment of a regime which would deprive labour of all its incentives and would lead in a short time to a decrease in the general wealth. Should the objection be raised that the existing titles of ownership are nullified by the undeniable cases of usurpation of wealth, it may be rejoined that surely prescription with the labour of generations superadded is not an empty plea in justification of the existing state of things. And if you reject prescription, then the same fundamental flaw must ever vitiate national as it does individual ownership. For we must not forget that the putting of the land under cultivation and the subsequent improvements that have gradually increased its value represent the accumulated efforts of generations, and these generations were made up of individual persons who acted without any inducement from the State. Why should not we be the rightful heirs of those who have gone before us ?

This particular piece of land was left me by my ancestors, or else again some other party sold it to me for a price which included the increased value he had given to it ; I, in my turn, expend my capital and labour upon it. The cherished hope of leaving it some day to my children has given zest to my

efforts. It was the same resolve that had urged on my predecessors. Who will deny that such a property is rightfully
owned? Yet the State steps in and numbers it among its
possessions! Could a more flagrant violation be imagined of
rights most firmly established?

Yet some, it is true, talk about indemnifying the expropriated owners. The State should pay a rent during their
lifetime, or else should gradually buy them out of their
possessions. But have the financial difficulties such a transaction would entail ever been considered? Where, pray,
will the State raise the necessary funds? From the tax-
payer—that is to say, from the pockets of those who are to be
indemnified! Besides, the sums paid to the expropriated
owners would be of no avail except for the purchase of articles
of consumption or use. In such conditions, then, they would
not be getting any compensation at all. In fact, it would be a
confiscation, not an indemnification; in other words, the
collectivist regime would have to be established in defiance of
all existing rights.

**93. Reply to Objections brought against the Capitalistic
Regime.**—*First objection:* The capitalistic regime is unjust,
because by it some are allowed to work the land and the
natural sources of wealth to their own selfish advantage. But
these things were meant to furnish the means of subsistence
for the whole human race; and further, they are not the
product of the labour of the individual. No individual, therefore, may be the exclusive owner of them.

Reply: It is true that the land has to provide nourishment
for everybody. But, precisely for this reason, it is of importance that the system should prevail which secures its being
as productive as possible. That system is the one which is
founded on private property. For under any other regime the
worker is without the motives that will stimulate him to make
the soil productive. Of course he is the first to reap the benefit
of his labour, as is only just; but the whole community too
shares in the fruit of it.

Again, if the individual himself may not possess land because
it is not the fruit of his labour, as much may be said about
the community.

Thirdly, collectivism would not guarantee to everybody an
actual possession of the soil, any more than the prevailing

system does. The landowners and farmers of to-day would simply be replaced by a number of public officials.

Finally, in a country with a dense population where the system of a division of labour prevailed, how could all have an actual possession of the land ? The most one could hope for is that the community should reap the greatest possible profit from its exploitation. Such is the case under a regime of private property : it affords greater incitements to work, and therefore the productiveness of the soil will be increased and with it the wealth of the community.

Second objection : The capitalistic regime is unjust, because instead of being true to the maxim ' to each according to his labour ', it makes the acquisition of riches depend on the mere chance of circumstances. This argument is to be found developed at length in the writings of Lassalle.

Reply : Certainly it is desirable that everybody should receive the reward of his merit and efforts as far as is possible in this world. But the dominant principle governing the distribution of wealth is that of commutative justice. It may be formulated in the words ' to each according to the services he renders to others '. A labourer new to his work who by very reason of his inexperience gives more time and more effort than another in making an object, has manifestly no claim to a greater wage from his employer. The clever inventor who has made his fortune has very properly received his deserts. Nevertheless the difficult and strenuous life of the ordinary manual labourer is perhaps more meritorious. Will it be said that the State is guilty of an injustice in giving a higher reward to the man of talent ?

For ownership to be legitimate it need not necessarily be the reward of moral merit : a service rendered may still be a service even though due merely to fortuitous circumstances. To make use of chance is censurable only in the case of the man who trusts solely to it alone for making his position in life and who in this way endeavours to exempt himself from Nature's law of labour. It is not right to say that every reward received must depend simply and solely on the recipient's merit. Where in this case would matters end ? Good fortune and bad fortune play their part in every human enterprise. Is it not by chance that one man is gifted by nature with talents above his fellows ?

And again, how often does it not happen that some entirely fortuitous circumstance puts a man of genius on his way to a great discovery ? Is he not to be allowed to turn his talents to his own account, whilst he is enriching the whole of society by his discovery? No work done by a man is the exclusive product of his own efforts ; a number of factors always come into play that are quite independent of the human will.

If the intervention of chance vitiates a man's title to property, then the acquisition of riches by a corporation must be condemned equally with that by an individual. Is it not merely the good fortune of a people that the soil is good for vine-growing ? Is it to be said, then, that a nation commits an injustice because it draws a profit from the special fertility of the land it occupies ?

Furthermore, Lassalle clearly exaggerates the part played by chance in economics. For when indeed did industry and economy, professional skill, etc., become matters of in-difference to the success of an enterprise ? We have to notice later the means of safeguarding ourselves in this world against the chances of misfortune.

Third objection : Capitalism by striving to divorce labour and capital puts one man at the mercy of another. For some men get all the means of production into their hands and thus are in a position to lay down the law to their fellow-men.

Reply : First of all, is it unjust for capital not to belong to labour or, in other words, for one man to be benefited by the labour of another ? An affirmative answer is given but we do not find any proof of it.

I allow you the usufruct of my land in consideration of a certain charge, or again, I invite you to co-operate with me in its cultivation. This co-operation is freely given by you in exchange for certain emoluments agreed upon. What right is here violated ? Where is the injustice ? If I may not reap any advantage whatever from the labour of another, I must, then, myself set about making everything that I require. For just like the capitalist producer, every consumer profits by his neighbour's efforts, with the aggravating circumstance that he does so to satisfy his purely personal needs, whilst the capitalist sets afloat other concerns that in the long run further the interests of the whole community. In both cases an advan-tage is taken by one man of the efforts of another man. Are we to be logical and decry every kind of division of labour, every exchange of services and material advantages ?

The divorce of capital and labour would become an actual reality under the collectivist regime, whilst at present this is not always the case. Under the proposed system the workman who cultivates the field would have always to avail himself of the implements belonging to the State. It is true he would be a joint-owner of such things, but only in an infinitesimal degree, as a starving beggar is the proud owner of the public commons. Such a right is a purely theoretical one. In practice his position would be that of a mere wage-earner.

We hear it said that where capitalism reigns the man who possesses the means of production holds sway over the rest of men. But would not all those paid by the State be subject to the rule of the supervising officials, from whom they would have to beg the daily necessaries of life ? Such a dependence would be even more direct. To-day when so many industries are in private hands, the oppressed worker may at least seek another employer. But he would cease to enjoy this opportunity as soon as the State became sole manufacturer and sole merchant.

This separation of capital and labour would then be an absolute one ; for it is indeed the root-principle of the new system. But to-day capital and labour are often in the same hands ; nor is their combination merely a matter of theory, but a matter of fact : a great amount of land is cultivated by its owners ; the farmer has a right to the harvest, and the agricultural implements are his own capital. Even the workmen themselves may become capitalists by the formation of co-operative societies. It is lawful for them conjointly to acquire by their savings the means of production and to use them to their common profit. They may also become shareholders of societies already existing.

The present system does not exclude any of these combinations. What is the reason why work-people most frequently prefer to live under a system in which capital and labour are separated ? Why does the thrifty artisan seldom embark on capitalistic enterprises ? Why does he prefer to look for other investments ? Undoubtedly because he judges them to be safer.

Fourth objection : The capitalistic system makes it possible for some to enrich themselves by levying a percentage on the fruit of the labour of others.

This argument is very closely allied to the one we have just answered. It represents the sum of Marx's objections. We have seen above that Marx measures the exchange-value of commodities by the normal labour-time required for their production. According to him, it is the only means of finding a common measure of things, and so of fulfilling the requirements of commutative justice, by which everyone should receive in exact proportion as he gives. For looked at from the standpoint of their use-value, i.e. their fitness to satisfy the needs of the consumer, commodities have no standard of comparison, they do not admit of being reduced to any common measure. Marx therefore makes the price of an article higher or lower according as the labour-time required for its production shall be greater or less. It is accordingly easy to see whence the capitalist derives his wealth. The capitalist is a man who with his ready money purchases goods in their raw state and then sells them at a higher price. In this way he uses his money to produce more money. And how does he manage this? By the labour of his operatives who work up the raw material into articles of use. Suppose, says Marx, it requires six hours of labour to produce an article equal in value to that of the necessaries of life for one day. What does the capitalist do? He makes his employee work six hours extra, and puts into his own pocket the surplus-value which they produce. Thus we see that the wealth of the capitalist is accumulated from what belongs to his employee.

Reply: We have already reviewed Marx's theory of value. The question is one in which it is impossible to leave out of account the utility of things. Commutative justice does not exact a mathematical equality between the things exchanged. None of its principles are violated so long as each of the parties, acting with full liberty and knowledge of the matter in hand, considers that he has received a compensation for the advantages he has ceded to the other. Hence account must be taken of use-value.

Marx keeps in view merely one of the factors of wealth, namely labour, and that the labour of the employee. But as a matter of fact the commercial value of things is the extremely complex result of a number of factors: the labour of the operatives, the work of the machines, the quality of the raw materials, the needs of the consumer, the fluctuations of the market according to the law of supply and demand, good business management, etc., etc. The labour of the artisan is certainly a productive force, but it is useless by itself. It can effect nothing unless certain conditions are present. Now it is the capitalist who provides these conditions, who builds the factory, who sets up the machinery and buys the raw material, and in person directs the concern. If the objection be raised that a number of capitalists merely give financial support to an enterprise but do not contribute anything personal, we must remember that the principle which should govern the economic world is not one of distributive justice, ' to each according to his efforts and merits '.

94. Titles to Property : I. Occupancy.—Occupancy is an external act by which a man really takes possession of a thing with the intention of making it his own.

For occupancy to be a title to property the following things are necessary : (1) a ' res nullius ' ; (2) a thing capable of being appropriated ; (3) an external act performed in regard to this object and in some way bringing it under the agent's power ; (4) a clear manifestation of his intention to possess it permanently and exclusively.

That occupancy under these conditions can be a legitimate title to property is easily understood. To take possession of a thing which has no owner, with a view to making it mine and using it to meet my legitimate wants or for any other upright purpose, is in no way in itself opposed to the natural law. For I do not injure any pre-existing right by taking possession of a ' res nullius '. And if I am allowed to appropriate such a thing, no one without injustice can prevent me from doing so ; it becomes therefore my possession.

We do not think that the external act which occupancy involves necessarily represents labour in the economic sense of the word ; that is to say, that there must take place some improvement in the object. In the case of movable property, labour is always consequent upon possession. Here possession is effected by a mere act of taking, provided that this act evidences the intention on the part of the occupier to become the owner. In the case of a piece of ground, occupancy may be effected, it is true, by reclaiming it and cultivating it, but also by setting up an enclosure or marking out its boundaries. Whatever method be used, it is essential that the exact portion of land which one desires to possess should be clearly determined by the very nature of the work done.

95. II. Prescription.—By prescription (*usucapio*) is meant the transfer of property or of any other real right by possession which fulfils certain conditions fixed by civil law. Sometimes it is immediate, and sometimes it requires a possession extending over a definite period of time.

What is the rational basis of prescription ? The question may be looked at from the point of view of the authority who legalizes prescription ; or from the point of view of the beneficiary, that is, of the one who has entered into possession.

1. How is the action of the legislator justifiable who prevents an owner or claimant from asserting his rights after a certain lapse of time ?

(a) *Presumption of abandonment.*—An owner who allows considerable time to elapse without reclaiming his property when he might easily have done so, is presumed to have renounced his right to it. At a given time he ceased to consider it as his. From that moment it became a ' res nullius ' and therefore liable to be the property of the first occupier ; that is, in the case at issue, of its present possessor.

(b) *Presumption of negligence.*—A man is allowed by civil law to employ measures that may lead eventually to his recovering his own rights ; but it requires that private individuals should look after their own interests. This requirement is seen to be not unreasonable when we consider that a too lengthy delay would complicate the task of the public authority and perhaps endanger other rights that ought to be respected. An owner, therefore, who does not take proceedings within the available time, though he knows that he is empowered to do so and is aware of the legal consequences of his attitude, may be justly presumed to have abandoned his claim to his right. If this has not been his intention we can at least understand that his negligence deprives him of the right to summon the aid of the law.

(c) *Argument from equity.*—The possessor in good faith who retains an article for several years and who has devoted his money and labour to preserve and improve it, who has reckoned it as part of his fortune and regulated his expenses accordingly, might perhaps suffer serious loss if he were obliged to restitution.

The law considers that the careless owner ought to suffer the penalty of his neglect. Why should injury be sustained by the possessor in good faith who is in no way blameworthy ?

(d) *Argument from public utility.*—Positive legislation in the matter of usucaption and prescription is also justifiable on grounds of public utility. (i) Such legislation tends to further *efficient administration* of property, for, in the first place, as we have said, it encourages vigilance on the part of owners. In the second place, it gives security, after a certain time, to anyone who has acquired an article in good faith and in the ordinary way of transfer. Such security is clearly a necessary condition for the good administration of property. For it is a matter of no small importance that those who hold property should not always have to be reckoning with the possibility of proceedings being brought against them by others, thus abruptly disturbing the peace of their possession and robbing them of the fruit of their labour. Lastly, it prevents articles that have been lost and whose owner continues to be unknown, from remaining indefinitely neglected, without anyone being able to make use of them. (ii) It facilitates *commercial transactions.* A purchaser cannot always be inquiring into the previous history of objects exhibited for sale. Yet the man who purchases an article in normal circumstances ought to be able to rely on the value of his title as purchaser. Consequently regulations in the matter of prescription are made by the law for the purpose of promoting such transactions. After three years [46] the owner of what has been stolen or lost may no longer take action for the recovery of his property. Such action, if taken within the available period, obliges the possessor in good faith simply to restore. But consistently with its purpose, the law makes this exception that if a man has bought a stolen or lost object in an open market or in the ordinary course of business where objects of the like nature are sold, he is bound to restitution only on being paid by the owner the price which he paid. (iii) Many *lawsuits* would be prevented that would often be occasioned, should a long-standing claim be allowed of a thing that had passed from hand to hand. (iv) Finally, in some special circumstances,

---

[46] This is the period laid down by canon law for movable articles possessed with a ' colorable ' or supposed title, such as sale in an open market.—Trs.

prescription makes for social peace so indispensable for the *re-establishment of public order*.   For example, after a revolution it may happen that a great deal of property has been usurped and, after a lapse of several years, there is no way of restoring to the rightful owners.   The dispossessed families are perhaps not to be found ; the titles to ownership have been destroyed ; what was originally usurped has in the course of time passed through the hands of a series of possessors in good faith, who have each in turn acquired it through the ordinary channels of conveyance, and have perhaps largely increased its value by their labour and money.   In such a state of affairs it behoves the public authority to give a legal recognition to a situation the origin of which was due to violence and usurpation.   Here prescription is a method of settlement made necessary by the force of circumstances.   The need of recognizing some such method becomes even more apparent if we remember that most of the land now occupied was at one time taken by violence from the primitive peoples who dwelt on it.   All trace of them has been lost long ago ; the injustice, however, of which they were the victims does not keep such lands from ever being made use of by future generations.   Eventually there arises the necessity of creating new rights to supersede the old ones, and the basis for them is to be found in the duration of occupancy.

2. Prescription from the point of view of the possessor.

(*a*) The *possessor in bad faith* and his residuary heir are not in conscience free from the duty of restoring the possession of another, even if the owner has no legal means to enforce his right.   The law is not made to help the possessor in bad faith. In such a case it would be without any justification whatever. If, by acts of limitation, it forbids the rightful owner to sue for lost or stolen property after an appointed time, the reason, as we have seen, is that commercial transactions demand this—it is not to abet the possessor in bad faith in enriching himself at the expense of another.   No possessor in bad faith, then, can in conscience claim the aid of the civil law as a title to his possession [47].

(*b*) With regard to the *possessor in good faith*, moralists generally allow that he may avail himself of prescription,

---

[47] English law apparently does not expressly require good faith as a condition for prescription.—Trs.

provided that his good faith has lasted beyond the expiration of the legal period. This was granted by the ancient canon law. If, as may be, civil law require good faith only at the time that possession is taken, we think a distinction should be made between two cases : (i) It may happen that the owner has not claimed his goods within the appointed time, although he had the opportunity of doing so. His negligence is quite evident. Presumption of renunciation is fully justified, as we have shown. The owner is aware that his attitude is tantamount in practice to a renunciation of his right. He had the intention, we may say, to renounce it. It follows, then, as a consequence that the possessor in good faith may avail himself of prescription. (ii) It may happen that the owner does not know who is the present possessor of his goods. This is the reason why he has allowed the stated time to elapse without taking action. Here no presumption of renunciation exists. Is the possessor in good faith who comes to know, after the expiration of the legal time, that he holds what belongs to another, bound to restitution ? It would seem that he is not if by restoring he would suffer some injury. Why, we may ask, should the possessor in good faith suffer by reason of a situation that has arisen from some negligence on the part of the real owner ? It is the latter who has been wanting in vigilance by allowing himself to be robbed or his goods to be lost. Nevertheless the possessor is bound to restitution, we think, if this would involve no injury to himself ; for if not, he would merely be enriching himself at the expense of the owner, as, for instance, in the case of stolen goods which their present possessor has acquired gratuitously.

96. III. The Right to make a Will.—The right to make a will is the right to dispose of one's goods in view of the time after one's death. This right is not a simple creation of the civil law, but is a natural right derived from human personality, just as the right of ownership of which it is an aspect.

Man, endowed as he is with reason, has the right to look forward into the future, the right to act with a view towards some purpose that will not be realized until after his death. He may, accordingly, take steps to secure its eventual realization. By so doing he will be acting as a rational being. For a rational creature is not made to live simply in the present and for himself alone ; but he must have an eye to the future, and not to his own future alone, but to that of those who are to follow him, especially of those whom Providence has entrusted to his care. If the end is legitimate, the act of will which would secure it is legitimate. It must be respected by all, and the death of its author furnishes no reason why its sacred character should be violated. In brief, man may make disposal of his goods for a time when he shall himself have passed away, since it is part of his nature to look to the future, and the limit of his personal existence is not co-terminous with that of his desires and intentions. As Taine says, ' The dead have rights in the society of the living. They have moulded the character of this society. We enjoy the heritage they have left, only on the condition that we carry out their testament '.

We may consider certain objections : 1. Every conveyance of goods, it is argued, presupposes the mutual consent of the parties. This cannot be said to exist in the case we are considering. At the time that the testator expresses his desire to bequeath, the act of acceptance on the part of the legatee has not yet been made. When the latter makes his acceptance, the former is no longer living. There is, then, no mutual consent, and consequently no conveyance of the goods takes place.

To this we answer, that the objection supposes, in quite an arbitrary manner, that a simultaneous consent of the two parties is essential. It is enough if the action of one follows that of the other. The wish of the testator continues to hold good, supposing no subsequent retraction take place, until the last moment of his life. It becomes irrevocably fixed by his demise, and from that moment it furnishes a right of acceptance which the legatee may claim. Mutual consent, then, exists, the legatee by his acceptance giving his consent to the wishes of the testator. We have only to notice that the action of the parties has not been simultaneous. But that it needs to be simultaneous for a transfer of property to be legitimate must be proved.

2. Another objection may be urged : that since a will has no force until the testator is dead, he is in reality intending to dispose of his goods at a time when he has ceased to exist. But a man has no power to do this, for the things of this world are for the use of the living and cannot be controlled by the dead.

A last will and testament is an act of disposition made by a person who has complete control over himself and his property.

We may grant that the effects of this act do not take place until after his death ; but, as we have just said, we are not justified in denying a man the right of providing for a time when he has ceased to be, and of ordering his affairs with a view to any end which, though he will not live to see it realized, is an honest one. As a matter of fact, any act by which a person disposes of his goods will produce effects that will continue long after his own lifetime. If I sell some of my property and die immediately afterwards, the law will consider that it has changed hands definitely and for ever, independently of the fact that I who made the bargain have already passed away. The new owner could appeal in support of his right to the voluntary action of him who is now deceased. A man's death does not nullify the legal validity of the acts of his lifetime. These effects continue in virtue of the intention of one who is now dead. Because his purpose was upright and legitimate, whatever he intended and whatever that intention necessarily involved, has acquired an inviolable character ; and this character continues to exist equally with the reasons on which it is based. The right I have given you by leaving you my property continues to be yours after my death. We conclude, then, that a real right is conferred by a man's last will and testament.

3. The further objection may be raised, that the property of the testator does not belong to him after his demise nor does it yet belong to a legatee who, we may suppose, is ignorant of the will. The gift bequeathed is, then, a *res nullius* until such time as he accepts it. The State takes possession of it and hands it on to the legatee. He, therefore, holds his rights from the State.

We answer that the will confers on the legatee the right of accepting the offer that has been made to him. This right has been assigned exclusively to him by the testator when acting in the full possession of his faculties. It follows, then, that the property is not at all at the mercy of the first chance comer, nor at the disposal of the State. It is already definitely ear-marked in favour of the legatee. Unquestionably he does not yet enjoy the right of actual ownership or the right of property in the strict sense of the word, but rather a potential right of ownership ; or more strictly, as we have shown, he has the right of accepting the offer that has been made him. This right is bound to be respected by all others and is a bar to the property being classed as *res nullius*.

The value of a will in the eyes of the law is that, whereas it does not effect a transfer of property in the strict sense of the word since it is a unilateral act, yet it confers the right of acceptance on the legatee.

97. IV. The Right of Inheritance.—The right of inheritance is that which anyone enjoys of having a share in the patrimony of another to whom he is united by the ties of kinship.

Two theories exist concerning the foundation of this right.

The first makes the right of inheritance rest solely on the presumed intention of the deceased person. It presupposes that it was his wish to leave his patrimony to his children, or, failing them, to the next of kin. This presumption is fully justified by the mutual affection which is generally to be found among members of the same family. The right of inheritance is, then, directly connected with the right to make a will.

The second theory asserts that the father of the family is not the sole owner of the family patrimony. These possessions are intended to serve the ends of a society whose members are both parents and children, and not the parents only. Thus, the father is not able, although he is the administrator of the property, to dispose of it in his own interests alone ; he cannot divert it from its end, which has a social character ; he has the duty of administering it in the interests of the community of which he is at once the head and protector. The property, in consequence, is not his exclusive possession ; it is a joint possession belonging to all the members of the group. And therefore the children already have a certain right to it during the lifetime of the parents. But this right is suspended while the parents are alive. Both of them, but especially the father, have the duty of the sovereign management of the interests of the community they represent. On the death of the parents the right of the children comes, *ipso facto*, into effect ; and this is the right of inheritance.

From this theory important consequences follow : the father is found wanting in his duty as administrator of the family patrimony if he dissipates his fortune, and in this case the children ought to be allowed to claim the protection of the law. There is another consequence of no less importance : that a father has not an absolute liberty, which leaves him without any responsibility when he makes his will. He is free only within the limits imposed by the interests of the community that is under his guardianship. The father who dissipates the family patrimony injures the rights of his children and does not fulfil the duties of protector to which he is bound by the law of nature.

CHAPTER II

RIGHTS OF THE MEMBERS OF THE FAMILY

98. We have defined the right pertaining to the family as the sum-total of those relations in justice which exist between husband and wife on the one hand, and between parents and children on the other. The family in its wide meaning comprises two societies : the one, arising from wedlock, formed by the partners in life ; the other, arising from ties of consanguinity, formed by the parents with their children. The relationships which constitute the first are derived from a free contract, yet one which, as we shall see, cannot be annulled. Those which constitute the second have their origin in the very fact of the procreation of children.

I. Purpose of the Institution of Marriage

The family, in the wide sense, comprising both the conjugal and the parental society, has been instituted for a double end : the good of the married couple and the good of the children.

99. First End of the Family : The Good of the Spouses.—When man and wife are united by the bonds of marriage, they have each in view their own individual well-being and their own perfection as well as that of their partner in life. This is the reason why they give themselves to one another, each being the complement, as it were, of the other by sharing in common the physical, intellectual and moral resources of their individual natures.

The satisfaction of human instincts, besides being designed by nature as a means for securing the perpetuity of the race, is an element of happiness legitimately sought by those in wedlock. It is in their case an element in their perfection inasmuch as it accompanies the fulfilment of one of the most important functions of human life, and tends to allay in some measure the importunities of passion. However, this element must not have a preponderating influence. Sensual gratification must always be subordinated to a higher motive, for if this is sought as an exclusive end, the worst excesses may result. The union of marriage is not that of merely material organisms but of persons with spiritual natures. To be of one flesh is but a means to a closer union of soul. This the dignity of human personality requires.

100. Second End of the Family : The Procreation of Children and their Education.—The family is instituted also partly in the interest of the child. It must provide the conditions for his maintenance and development so long as he is unable to take care of himself ; for only gradually does the human being attain to the possession of his faculties. In infancy and in adolescence he requires a constant protection. The period of youth must be one of guidance.

To parents above all others falls the duty of being the protectors and educators of their child. This is not difficult to understand. Together they have been instrumental in bringing into being a human person like to themselves, possessing the same imprescriptible right both to life and perfection and yet incapable of providing for himself. To whom should such a one turn to obtain the assistance to which he has a right unless to those who are the authors of his being ? To their instrumentality his life is due ; by bringing him into being they have taken upon themselves the duty of providing the means for his preservation and his full development. Such is what right order would require. An undertaking once begun must not be relinquished before it is completed. A child is not given life that he may be at once abandoned to his natural weakness and devoted to a premature death. The education of a child follows naturally and logically from his procreation. As the parents were in fact responsible for the latter, they cannot shirk the responsibility of the former. This is the dictate of logic, and is not the natural law the law of reason ?

Furthermore in this we see the clearest manifestation of the intention of Nature. Not without a great purpose has she implanted in the heart of the father, and still more in that of the mother, deeply rooted instincts impelling them to seek before all else the welfare of their offspring. To parents has been given the vocation of nurturing the children, because they can understand them better than any other, they love them more than any other and receive in their turn reciprocated affection from them. Who, indeed, will bring a greater solicitude to such a task? Who, more than father and mother, is capable of entering into the soul of the child, of divining its nascent aspirations and of directing their course? Indeed, do not children inherit the very character of their parents—are they not flesh of their flesh? No doubt very frequently parents require the assistance of others; but even then it devolves on them primarily to continue to be the educators of their children. To the parents belongs the responsibility of choosing those as masters who are the most reliable as well as the most proficient; to the masters that of remembering that they are but the delegates of an authority higher than their own, whose opinions they are bound to respect.

But what precisely does the work of education comprise?

101. Education is Physical, Intellectual, Moral and Religious. —Education, in the wide sense of the term, consists in directing and furthering the development of a child's natural faculties. According to the nature of these faculties we may regard education as physical, intellectual and æsthetic, moral and religious.

Physical education looks to the health of the body. It must provide a healthy environment and a wisely chosen method of exercising the body, with a view to strengthening any weaknesses of constitution and so furthering the harmonious and normal development of its various parts.

Physical exercises do not contribute simply to the health of the body. They have a reaction also on the intellectual and moral life. Whilst affording a relaxation to the mind, they strengthen at the same time the power of the will by teaching it to fight against inclinations to laziness, and they lessen the incentives to passion.

Intellectual education is concerned with the development of those faculties that have for their object the true and the beautiful. It is its function to give and to foster æsthetic tastes and to help in the acquisition of knowledge. Regarded in this latter aspect education is called instruction.

The co-operation of many faculties is required for the acquisition of truth: on the one hand the senses and the memory, on the other the intelligence. The first supply the data upon which the latter exercises its activity. The first, then, have a subordinate place, and the teacher must recognize an order of dependence in the faculties. Whilst not neglecting the education of the senses or the training of the memory, he will look principally to the development of the intelligence. For this reason he does not consider that he has fulfilled his duty by giving his teaching an encyclopedic character. On the contrary, his first care is to avoid overburdening his pupil with a multiplicity of facts and studies which would make it impossible for his ideas to develop. Development is a slow process and requires quietude of mind. Reflection takes place normally in inverse ratio to the amount of matter put forward by the teacher. Human life is short and the field of knowledge is immense. To try to learn everything is to court the risk of knowing nothing ; the memory would be enriched for the moment but the mind would not be formed for judgment. The primary purpose of education is not to stock the mind with erudition but to make it capable of thought. Accordingly among the branches of human knowledge preference is given to those which necessitate the effort of reflection, due account being paid, of course, to the capacities of the pupil.

Are we then to understand that any utilitarian point of view is to be left out of education ? By no means. The formation of habits of thought is not the sole end of intellectual education. It must enable each one to follow some day the career to which his natural abilities and inclinations and the circumstances of his position in life lead him. The schooling that is given must not be identical for all and each ; it will vary in different cases, and especially according as the pupil is destined or not for one of the liberal professions.

Nevertheless all must possess certain rudiments which form the basis of all intellectual culture and are one of the conditions for sharing the life of a civilized society. This constitutes the minimum which parents are in duty bound to procure for their children. And it would seem that public authority has here the right to interfere in the last resort in order to safeguard the right of the child against any remissness or selfishness on the part of the parent. In theory scarcely anyone would be found to deny this. But it remains to inquire whether as a matter of fact, the spirit and the tendencies of the modern State being such as they are, the principle of compulsory education, as it is imposed by law, does not imperil certain higher rights and interests. In such a case resistance would seem to be lawful that a greater evil might be avoided. Whatever answer may be given, the education enforced by the State can only deal with that minimum of knowledge that is strictly indispensable. Beyond this the intellectual education of each one must be suited to the avocation he is likely to follow. The right which each person has of choosing a career best suited to his tastes and abilities stands opposed to any legal compulsion in this delicate matter.

Lastly, the heart of man is the well-spring of *religious* and *moral* aspirations. Education must then develop this side of his nature which is indeed the highest of all. As morality is meaningless if divorced from the idea of the Absolute—the proper object of religion—the moral upbringing of anyone must have religious education as its foundation. By the first he will be shown the law which must govern his conduct, he will be taught how to conform to it, and for this end his will-power will be strengthened against the allurements of the senses; by the second he will be shown the august origin of this law and the sovereign sanctions on which it rests. Parents owe to their children this moral and religious education, and this both because the latter have an inviolable right to attain to their supernatural destiny, and because society at large has an interest in the preservation of beliefs which, to use the words of Taine, lend the strongest support to the social instinct.

102. Corollary.—It follows from the above that parental authority has been instituted for the good of the children. It is not, therefore, absolute ; there are restrictions upon it arising from its very end. That end is to make it possible for the rights and capacities of the child to attain their full development. With this obligation upon them, the parents will not put any obstacle in the way of the natural calling in life of their child provided that this vocation has been clearly indicated and wisely tested. A young man and a young woman must be allowed a free choice of their own career ; if they feel called to the marriage state, they must be free in the choice of a partner who is to share the fortunes of their life. Undoubtedly parents may quite rightly interfere in such matters, but only as counsellors. Only under the stress of higher reasons may they put an absolute veto on the choice of their children. They must not allow motives of vanity or self-interest to stand in the way of his lifelong happiness.   Far from thwarting the child in the exercise of his rights, parents must make his way easy. And hence the father has the duty of administering the family patrimony, not for the satisfaction of his own selfish caprices, but to the end that the future of those whom Divine Providence has entrusted to his guardianship may be provided for.

The duty of parents towards their children implies as its counterpart the rights to obedience, respect and affection from the latter towards them.

II. Perpetuity of the Marriage Bond

103. Principle.—Marriage is an indissoluble contract, because it is founded upon love, not indeed upon love that is merely sensual, but upon a love that is rational, which alone is worthy of the dignity of man.   Such love is not superficial ; being under the sway of reason it is not content with outward qualities that are by their nature fleeting, but it has the grasp of a substance that is enduring.   Its very nature is that it should last.   It demands a self-surrender without reserve, without condition ; it is a sovereign love.   These are precisely the sentiments that animate a young couple when with a sincere mutual devotion, as is fitting, they plight their troth to one another.   The idea of a possible rupture at some future date never crosses their minds.   As they make their mutual vows, they would regard the very entertaining of a thought, however vague, of some future union, as dallying with treason.

The perpetuity of the conjugal tie becomes more manifest still if we consider the second end of family life : the pro-creation and the upbringing of children.   The rearing of a child requires an active and constant co-operation on the part of the father and of the mother.   This joint labour of theirs extends over a period of many years, even during the whole of their mature life, however few may be the new births at different intervals in the family.   Children, although arrived at the age of emancipation, are not on that account freed from all lawful ties that bind them to their parents.   The claims of gratitude may put upon them imperious obligations binding in strict justice.   Hence the parental society constituted by the be-getting of children is necessarily perpetual.   Hence too the

conjugal society which is the basis of the former must be
perpetual as well. The dissolution of the latter would shake
the very foundations of the economy of the former.

104. Divorce.—The principle of the perpetuity of the conjugal
bond having been thus established, is it permissible, we must
ask, to disturb it under certain given circumstances? Many
legislators have thought so.

We distinguish between divorce by mutual consent, divorce
for incompatibility of temper, and again divorce for adultery,
cruelty and ill-treatment. It is evident that *divorce by mutual
consent*, or for mere incompatibility of temperament, notwithstanding the legal formalities that accompany it, is nothing
short of a direct negation of the whole principle of the perpetuity of the marriage tie. For matrimony would then
resemble, entirely or certainly in part, any other contract that
is rescindable at will. To treat it as such would be to expose
society to the most baneful consequences. It would encourage to the greatest possible extent engagements lightly
contracted, and from that very fact ill-suited unions. Aware
of the possibility of a separation later on, those intending to
engage in wedlock would have less fear of the deceptions of love.
Reason would play a lesser part in their decision, the blindness
of passion would be predominant. A marriage once entered
upon under such conditions would assuredly stand considerably less chances of endurance. As soon as the burdens of
conjugal life began to weigh heavily the thought of freedom
would be quick to suggest itself ; and the means of obtaining it
would be at hand. It would be easy for the one desirous of a
new union to make the life of the other intolerable, to offer
opposition in a thousand ways, perhaps even to force acts of
violence or other misdemeanours that could be urged as a plea
for divorce. And again how would the desire to contract a
new marriage be reprehensible when it was aiming merely to
bring about a situation that was perfectly regular and sanctioned by the law? If both parties could reserve to themselves the power of going back on their word in the event of
their failure to find the happiness they had anticipated, we
should have to recognize that they have the right to entertain
such a possibility and to dream of some happier partnership in
the future. Thus the wicked thought could find a free entrance
into their minds, nothing would prevent it lingering there and

becoming an object of complacency, until it would become gradually a passion ruling the heart and will, and finally make the dissolution of the marriage an accomplished fact.

As to the plea for *divorce on account of adultery* or some other grave crime, one is inclined at first sight to admit it. For certainly the innocent party, condemned to live a solitary life under the hard law of continence, has a claim on our sympathy. But it is not the interest of this one person alone that is here at stake. Divorce is admitted by everyone to be always an evil ; but in the case in point we may inquire whether it is not the lesser of two evils. The Catholic Church has decided in the negative. She has absolutely prohibited divorce in the name of the higher interests of morality and social order. And the experience of centuries has clearly justified her action. We are well aware that when divorce is once sanctioned by law it slowly but surely becomes a practice in all classes of society. It works as a germ bringing social dissolution and death. In vain does legislation attempt to restrain the growth of the evil. The time comes when the restrictions thought to be capable of opposing further developments are swept away by the impulse of passion. So great is the violence of human passions, so inconstant is the heart of man, that in these matters there is need for absolute principles, based not on the unstable decrees of civil legislation but on the authority of divine laws. It was for this reason that the Founder of Christianity laid down the principle, ' what God hath joined together let no man put asunder '.

Furthermore, though divorce may bring some alleviation in the case of the innocent sufferer, it enables the guilty party to reap the benefit of his crime. It grants the realization of his desires. The criminal union surreptitiously entered into in violation of his plighted troth is raised to the dignity of a marriage. The guilty party henceforth enjoys in peace what he could gain only by his crime. And a most baneful example, only too easily followed, is put before all who feel within their breast the conflict between duty and passion.

III. The Family and the State

105. Relations between the Family and the State.—Since the family is bound to civil society by many juridical relations, society has a certain claim on the family for obedience to its laws. Nevertheless the institution of the family is not the result of legislation, nor are the rights and duties of its members created by it.

This follows from what we have considered above. Marriage, we said, is a contract resting on the mutual love of man and wife. Freedom is of the essence of love. Love acts spontaneously, not by command. Although, then, the civil law may ordain certain formalities in order that the marriage may be recognized as public, make provision for pecuniary settlements in connexion with it, and sanction the mutual obligations of the contracting parties, yet it is not in any way the foundation or cause of these obligations. They have their origin in the free engagements of the contracting parties themselves.

Still less do the juridical relations existing between parents and their children have their origin in positive law. These relations are derived from the very fact of the generation of offspring. As the relationship of father and son is not due to the law, so also the rights and the duties arising from this mutual relationship are quite independent of it. Hence the State must respect the autonomy of the family, nor must it endeavour to substitute its authority for that of the parents. It must not, then, lay claim to be the sole teacher of the child. As we have said, it is the office of the parents to bring up their children, and they have the right to choose those who shall assist them. This right is overridden if officialdom arrogates to itself a monopoly of education.

CHAPTER III

THE RIGHTS OF THE STATE

I. General Notions

106. Definition and Division.—The Rights of the State are constituted by all those juridical relations which unite the governed to the governing power in the civil society.

What is the origin, nature and end of this society ? What accordingly are the functions of the public authority ? What form should it assume in view of these functions ? What are the rights and the duties of the citizens with regard to the State ? What principles should guide international relations ? What are the relations of the civil society to the religious society ?

All these questions, inasmuch as they not only concern this or that particular state but are of a general import, belong to the sphere of the philosophy of Natural Law. Various solutions have been offered. Some regard the State as an aspect of the Absolute, which is to be identified with the substance of beings. Others regard it, if not as God, at least as directly instituted by Him, making the political regime to be of divine positive law. Others again, on the contrary, assign it a purely human origin, regarding the State as the result of individual wills freely united by contract. A fourth view sees in the civil society a real organism, the product of an evolution which embraces the whole of nature. Whilst, finally, others recognize it as an institution at once natural, human and divine. We shall now examine each of these theories in turn.

II. Pantheistic Theory of the State

107. The Spirit-State.—This pantheistic idea coloured the political philosophy of the old world. Plato in ancient and Hegel in modern times are its chief exponents.

The philosophy of Plato borders on pantheism in more

respects than one. He teaches that the different parts of the universe are informed with a kind of psychic principle, and of this the soul of the individual is but an emanation. And he also teaches that to the universal ideas there correspond universal essences. Thus a germ of pantheism is contained in the theories he holds concerning the objective reality of ideas and the constitution of human beings. The theories put forward in *The Republic* are but a logical development of this germ. Every philosophy with pantheistic tendencies is bound to lead, in the sphere of politics, to the absorption of the individual by the State. Indeed, pantheism is by its very definition the negation of human personality.

Plato is led to this theory of State absolutism by another train of thought, namely, his conception of the moral ideal. Justice is synonymous with harmony and unity. It is found in the individual when the reason holds a sovereign control over all the other faculties ; it is found in the city-state when the wills of all and each of the citizens are in absolute subordination to that of the State. The aim of the State is precisely this subordination. Thus it is seen that the State is, as it were, a superior being with an end of its own, namely, the cohesion and unity of the social body. Hence the aim of Plato's political theory is to efface as completely as possible the personality of the individual. The existence of autonomous families within the city-state, he says, breaks up its unity, as also does private property which is the source of inequality and conflict. Consequently he is led to abolish the family and private property, and to substitute for them community of wives and of goods. In keeping with this conception, he would make the State supreme in all matters of education as well as of conscience, in order that with all the citizens thinking alike the unity of the city-state may be as perfect as possible.

Such is the ideal of Plato's absolute State. He really does nothing more than emphasize the principles that were embodied in the customs and institutions of Greece and Rome. He does not, however, identify the State with the deity of the universe ; his object is to bring it as far as possible into harmony with the divine being whose chief characteristic, according to him, is unity.

With Hegel, who here follows Schelling and Fichte, the case is otherwise. Inindivualistic at first, in his later writings he professed the completest pantheism. ' The State ', he says, ' is the social substance that has arrived at self-consciousness. . . . It is the *rationnel* of itself and for itself . . . it is a terrestrial divinity ' [48]. Here we find the State has become an aspect of the Absolute which, according to Hegel, is the common substrate of all things, the universal substance, of which individual beings are but so many modes or determinations. The different forms which the State has assumed in the course of time are so many different manifestations of the divine life. Each of these forms had necessarily to come into being at that precise period. Yet the latest, namely, constitutional monarchy, appears as the best. Hegel thus represents the life of the Absolute as a progress towards what is better.

The State thus blended with the eternal substance of the universe is not, therefore, a human institution, such as Rousseau would have it. It is anterior to individuals. Far from being founded by them it is the very principle of their subsistence.

Since the State is identical with the divine essence, it has its own end superexalted above all other ends. Without its own self-destruction it cannot use its authority to subserve the interests of individuals. Yet is not its function to protect their liberty and their goods ? Hegel's answer is that the State must be viewed as an organic and living unity having its own subsistence as its one end.

Again, since it is the divine being, its will must be the sovereign law, the source of all rights and all duties. Therefore against its decisions no individual right founded on nature can be of any avail.

All these logical consequences of pantheism, already developed by Plato, are expressly referred by Hegel to their metaphysical principle. The theory of the Spirit-State was given by this disciple of Schelling its radical formula. It falls to the ground on account of the same criticisms that are brought against pantheism in general. If the Absolute is not the real substance of beings, if human personality is more than a mere appearance, it becomes manifest that the will of the State is not the supreme law nor, consequently, the source of our rights.

[48] Hegel, *Philosophy of Right*, trans. by Dyde (Bell, London, 1896) .

III. THE STATE AS AN INSTITUTION OF POSITIVE DIVINE RIGHT

108. This theory comes from the jurisprudence of the seventeenth century. Especially in its logical implications is it closely allied to the theory we have just noticed. The ruler impersonates the State, whilst he himself holds his office by direct divine right. He is then responsible directly to God alone and need give no account to his subjects for his government. The political interest of the monarch, namely, the consolidation and extension of his power, dominates all other interests. He is known as the ' *raison d'Etat* '. Before his superior claims the rights of the individual must yield.

The conception that the State, existing under the form of an absolute monarchy, is a divine institution recalls the ancient theocracies of the East. Its origin is not Christian. It is incorrect to appeal in its behalf to the words of St. Paul, ' All power cometh from God ', because, as we shall see later, these words have quite another signification. The truth which they posit is not an historical but a philosophical one : they do not pretend to teach how in the first instance public authority was established, but what are its claims to our obedience.

IV. THE THEORY OF SOCIAL CONTRACT

109. Interpretations of the Contract-Theory.—According to this theory civil society owes its rights to a contract, either expressed or tacit, that has been freely entered into by its members. It has been explained in many different senses. Some interpret it in favour of an absolute monarchy, others in favour of an absolute democracy, others again in favour of individualism.

Hobbes devoted himself to the development of the first of these interpretations ; the other two come from the writings of Rousseau. Owing to the great confusion of thought displayed in his works, the author of the *Social Contract* is at once the originator of the individualistic ideas of the liberal school and also of the absolutist tendencies of certain democratic theories of that time.

110. First Interpretation of the Contract-Theory.—Absolute monarchy was viewed by the legists of the seventeenth century as a divine institution. Hobbes made it a human institution, founded on an original contract, and he justified it on utilitarian grounds. As we have said, he started with the principle that man is at bottom an egoist. The state of nature was a state of warfare, which made all progress impossible. The primeval right of every man to all things involved an incessant conflict. To put an end to this reign of anarchy men agreed by a free contract to found a commonwealth. But nevertheless selfish instincts remained in spite of all in the human breast and were a permanent menace to society. To repress them a strong Power was required, a Power resting in the hands of a single and irresponsible sovereign. Absolute monarchy thus appeared as the norm or type of government. No doubt it had its drawbacks ; the ruler might abuse his authority. Yet even so, complete submission must be given to him, for, let revolution once gain the upper hand, you have a return to a state of warfare, which is the worst of all evils. Far better, all things considered, to have the abuse of authority than the re-establishment of the original anarchy.

111. Second Interpretation.—Under the influence of rationalistic philosophy the idea that society is due to a primordial contract received a new interpretation, this time in favour of liberty and individualism. Rationalism had laid down the principle in philosophy that the individual is autonomous. It appeared as an attempt to emancipate the human mind from all authority alike in matters of thought and morality. From the spheres of religion and philosophy the individualistic conception passed into that of political science. There it fostered liberalism, and drew conclusions from the theory of the social contract which were directly opposed to those of Hobbes.

Since man is born free, the social state with the manifold obligations it imposes upon us cannot be considered as a state of nature. In this theory the state of nature is represented as a state of felicity which men were compelled to give up in order to offer a common front against the evils that threatened them from without ; a state to which they may lawfully return whenever they judge it expedient. Such at least is the reasoning of Fichte (1762-1814), who developed all the consequences in political science that arose from the rationalistic idea.

Rousseau (1712-1778) had already represented primitive man as perfectly happy and completely free to follow his natural instincts, for in them there was no trace of evil. But with the advent of society came mutual jealousies and the conflicts of self-interest and every species of human vice. Humanity became corrupted by the very fact of social education. State authority, by opposing in countless ways the instincts of our nature, has vitiated our whole being.

Nevertheless the social state is indispensable. Left to himself man cannot struggle against the forces of destruction which expose his life to constant peril. It follows that the commonwealth is an evil, but an evil to which humanity must submit if it is to survive. It is a burdensome necessity without doubt, yet one that is inevitable. But although the primitive conditions of our race can no longer obtain, none the less they remain as an ideal to which the political state should as far as possible conform. And this is the reason why government is founded on freedom and must assure its exercise to all.

From this the liberal school has deduced two principles, one in reference to the juridical basis of public authority, the other in reference to its purpose.

The first may be expressed thus : ' The free consent of individuals is the one and only source of all lawful authority '. If man is by nature independent, if it is contrary to his nature to submit to the authority of another, laws have no obligatory force except by his own consent. In no other way can the rights of power be reconciled with those of liberty. Since the political regime is the result of a contract freely consented to by all the citizens, in obeying its behests they are in reality only obeying themselves.

The second principle concerns the function of the public authority. Since Nature has made man independent, and absolute master of his thoughts and acts, the public power must guarantee to everyone the greatest possible freedom. As it is contrary to the principle of rationalism to accept any guidance from constituted authority alike in matters intellectual as well as moral, so it is consistent to assert that the function of the State is not in any way to direct the action of individuals as regards any ideal whatever, but simply to safeguard them from obstacles that would hinder their free development. Accordingly the function of the State is not to civilize, but only to guarantee that the rights and liberty of the citizens shall be protected. This is the train of thought in the writings of Kant.

As an advocate of the principle of the autonomy of reason, he gives us the conception of the State as the mere guardian of the rights of the individual.

112. Third Interpretation.—We have already remarked that the contradictions which abound in the writings of Rousseau justify us in considering him as the founder of two opposite schools of thought, the one favouring liberty, the other favouring the absolutism of the democratic state. He teaches, it is true, that the political state must be based on the liberty of the individual and must guarantee its exercise ; but the conditions of this liberty will be realized whenever the law expresses the General Will, since then every citizen will be deemed to be obeying himself. And to this general will, which is in reality the will of the majority, he attributes an absolute sovereignty. The sovereignty of the people, he tells us, is not only inalienable and, consequently, incompatible with a representative regime ; it is also incorruptible. Whilst Montesquieu suggests that those in power are men easily influenced by prejudice and passion, and that therefore guarantees are required against the possible abuse of authority—guarantees which he thought would be found in a distribution of authority—Rousseau expressly formulates another view : the will of the ' sovereign people ' is indefectible ; it must of necessity tend to its end. Just as a person must necessarily will his own good, so the general will, which is expressed by the majority of the votes of the people, cannot deviate from the good of the community. Accordingly this will is infallibly right and just. How, indeed, can it stand in opposition to right, since it is the source of all right ? Rousseau makes the juridical order to spring entirely from the political order. The individual becomes a being with rights and duties only by his taking part in society. From this moment he renounces in their fullness the prerogatives nature has conferred upon him by leaving it to the State to define what power shall be his. In virtue of these being defined by the law they acquire a juridical character. Liberty exercised within the limits prescribed by the civil law becomes Right. It is therefore the law or, more accurately, the will of the majority, that creates rights, and especially the right of property. In the state of nature the individual was at liberty to dispose of his earthly possessions regardless of any law ; but he renounced this power by the social compact the clauses of which, Rousseau says, ' reduce themselves to one, namely, the total transfer of each associate, with all his rights, to the community '. Hence the community acquires the supreme dominion over everything ; it becomes the dispenser, the citizens merely the holders of all goods. In all this we find a case already made out for all the pretensions of the collectivist State and, in general, for all attempts of public powers against the principle of private property.

By becoming a citizen a man has even lost his own individual existence. For Rousseau informs us that ' the mission of the legislator is to transform each individual, who by himself is a solitary unit, into a part of a larger whole from which this individual in a certain measure receives his life and his being '. The pantheistic conception of the ancient state seems to have inspired these lines. But there is even more to be said. Christianity in asserting the independence of religious from civil authority had liberated the human conscience from the yoke of the State. Rousseau would replace that yoke. Imbued like the philosophers of old with the idea of unity, he even conceived the notion of an official belief which the State ought to impose upon everybody under the penalty of death. Surely it would be difficult to find a more complete conception of the absolutism of the State.

Criticism : In attempting to reconcile the natural liberty of the individual, supposed to be unlimited, with the authority possessed by the State, Rousseau utterly failed in two points. First, by misconceiving the social nature of man, he made all his rights dependent upon the body politic. If man is not naturally social, the relations arising from the mutual rights which bind citizen to citizen have no foundation in nature but in the human conventions that are formulated by the civil laws. Consequently there is no such thing as natural right ; the civil law reigns supreme. In fact, as we have seen, this is just the conclusion that Rousseau himself draws.

In the second place, another line of argument in the teaching of the ' Social Contract ' logically leads to anarchy. He makes the sovereignty possessed by the laws rest on the free will of the individual. I am bound to obey the laws simply because I have willed it. But why can I not change that act of will ? Why, if I cease to will in any particular case, should my present state of mind be any less effective than my former one ? If some higher principle of authority is appealed to which obliges me to abide by the engagements I have contracted, then it is no longer my good-will that creates my obligations. Their source must be elsewhere, in some transcendent principle. Rousseau quite failed to see that no obligation is possible where he who binds is but binding himself. Fichte, who was the *enfant terrible* of individualism before he became a pantheist, accepted this conclusion of Rousseau's teaching. He allowed also that everybody has the right of returning to the state of nature. Kant, without relinquishing the idea of the social contract, recognized that if anarchical consequences are to be avoided all individual rights as well as the contract itself must be based on the immutable principles of reason. It was reason that caused the individuals to make the contract in order to guarantee protection for their rights ; it was reason that demanded from each the faithful execution of its terms. Yet had Kant the right to speak of a social order founded on nature, after having set up the absolute autonomy of human personality ? It is certainly questionable.

V. Theory of the Social Organism

113. Statement and Criticism.—The idea that society is an organism is not altogether a novel one. That Plato was influenced by it we see by his distinguishing in the State, as in the individual, the functions of nutrition, defence and control. Later it appeared again in the teachings of the Physiocrats, and in Hegel and his disciples ; but in our own time, under the influence of certain scientific theories, it has been more clearly put forward and elaborated in all its details, especially in the writings of Lilienfeld, Schäffle and Herbert Spencer.

We are told by Spencer that all phenomena are governed by a law of evolution. Under its force the primitive nebula became consolidated to form the planets, the first combinations of life arose spontaneously from inorganic matter, and elemental types gradually gave birth to all others. Now under this same law of evolution individuals are brought together to form social organisms. And these expressions of Spencer have, we may well believe, much more than a mere figurative meaning. For he viewed the life of a society as not essentially different from the organic life of a man, proceeding from the same factors, developing itself according to the same laws, and presenting the same essential functions.

It is easy to see how in accordance with this theory the mutual relations between the individual and society should be stated. The theory of the social organism reduces the individual to a mere unit in an aggregate ; it is simply a restatement of the old-world materialism. We see that materialism, no less than pantheism, implies the denial of human personality : the individual is no more than an atom lost in the social whole, he being to society just what the cell is in the organic body, his rights in regard to the State no more than those of the cell in regard to the organism. Spencer would no doubt protest against such a conclusion as unfair ; still, logic is inexorable. If we are assured that progress consists in the aggregation and concentration of units which were at first isolated, that social life in the course of its development passes through the same phases as the life of the individual, then must we not conclude that the absorption of the individual by the State is the goal of political evolution ? In the earliest stages of organic life, the cell constitutes the whole substance of the being, it is a complete individual by itself. This is exemplified in the case of primordial and unicellular types, and in fact in any cell until embryonic development begins. But in the higher organic forms of life, when development is complete, the cells are so aggregated that instead of each being an autonomous whole they are but the lowest element in the living substance. If, then, the individual stands to society as the cell to the whole organism, social progress will be measured in inverse proportion to the development of individual liberty. We thus see how ill-suited are Spencer's conceptions of liberalism and of society as an organism. Schäffle, starting from the same premises, arrives, and quite logically, at collectivism. As nothing can be performed in the organism except through the action of the nervous system, so nothing can be accomplished in society except under the action of the State. As the centre of control it will preside over even the least functions of the social body, in the same way as the brain presides over the least functions of the human body.

The discussion of this theory really depends on opinions belonging to psychology. The whole question is whether the individual, who is also the social unit, is not something more than a mere aggregation of cells, such as materialists would have us believe.   It will suffice here to notice that their denial of any further principle leads, when applied to political science, to the most radical absolutism.   Liberty and the traditional philosophy of man's spiritual nature stand or fall together.

VI. THE CHRISTIAN CONCEPTION OF THE STATE

114. Nature of the Individual.—The individual is by nature a personal and social being.

Man is a personal being : He has been created for an end which excels every other end, since it is identical with God Himself, inasmuch as He is the object of the knowledge and love of mankind.   Such an end implies the perfection and the happiness of the rational creature : his perfection, because the knowledge of God is the highest to which we can attain, and the love which this inspires is the most noble of all ; his happiness, because the possession of this object appears as the goal of the deepest aspirations of the human soul.   We see, then, how the idea of the personality of man is logically bound up with one of the essential dogmas of the Christian religion, namely, the dogma of his supernatural destiny.   Being children of the same Father who is in heaven, redeemed by the same Saviour, called to the same celestial inheritance, men are all brethren and possessors of the same essential rights.   In this we have the true idea of human personality.

Man is likewise a social being: This is the teaching of all the Doctors of the Church, here in accord not only with Aristotle and Plato but also with the essential doctrine of Christianity.   For by its visible organization, by its precepts of justice and of charity, by its dogmas of the divine Fatherhood, original justice, redemption and communion of saints, the Christian religion proclaims the solidarity and, consequently, the sociability of all mankind.

115. Nature and Foundation of Civil Society.—Civil society or the State is not a superior being, some transcendental reality having an end of its own [49].   It is constituted by the personal members who unite to form it ; but yet it is not exclusively the product of their individual wills.   Its foundation is indeed in

---

[49] See the encyclicals of Pope Leo XIII, especially *Rerum Novarum*, trans. *The Pope and the People*.   C.T.S., London.

nature. It partakes of the objective reality of nature, for in the first place the rights and duties which it implies find in their last analysis their support and their supreme sanctions in the moral law ; and secondly, civil society responds to the needs of human nature. Nevertheless nature does not determine the form it shall take ; it leaves that to circumstances and to the will of man. It fosters needs and instincts in men, and by following these they coalesce into a social organization. But, finally, the natural foundation of society presupposes another, more august than nature. For the exigencies of nature necessarily disclose the designs of the Author of nature. The State, then, because demanded by nature, organized by man, willed by God, is at one and the same time an institution natural, human and divine.

116. Origin of Authority.—Society exists by the will of God, and therefore obedience of subjects to its authority is by the will of God, for this obedience is a necessary condition of its existence. Yet He does not intervene in any special way to determine what form authority shall assume. It is for men to settle in accordance with particular circumstances. Any form of government is lawful so long as it is properly adapted to fulfil the mission of the State.

117. Rôle of Public Authority.—Civil society exists for the sake of the individuals composing it. It furnishes that environment which is indispensable to them if they are to look to the various needs of their existence on the earth and to develop their faculties and personality to the full. To provide the general conditions for our happiness and for our perfect development, conditions which we cannot establish and maintain by isolated effort, is the end of civil society, namely, the common weal. Hence the rôle of the public authority in the society is none other than to direct it towards its end. As the public good implies the reign of peace and concord and consequently a mutual respect of rights, the first function of authority is to secure that our rights are respected. But it has a further duty to discharge as part of its mission : the common weal consists not only in the absence of injustice, but it also presupposes a state of affairs such as will favour the full exercise of the individual's rights and further the proper development of his faculties. To bring this about is the duty incumbent on the public authority and in proportion as its power is greater than all private initiative. This is what is meant when the State is described as having ' civilization ' as its mission.

118. Limits of Sovereignty.—Christianity opposes the pretensions of absolutism by its insistence on the rights of the individual, of the family and of religious society.

The will of the State is supreme and its commands obligatory only in so far as they are in conformity with the natural law, which is the expression of the divine Will. It is better to obey God rather than men. As, then, the natural law is the foundation of the rights possessed by the individual and the family, it follows that these rights must be respected by the public power, seeing that this power is instituted for the very purpose of guaranteeing their exercise. In virtue of this higher law, which in reality is the divine Will, the individual has the right of pursuing his own personal destiny which involves his happiness and his perfection. He has therefore the right to act and to make use of his natural powers. From this may be judged what are the limits of the ' civilizing mission ' of the State. Man's self-development is essentially his own work, for, as it implies the full play of his personal powers, his own initiative must guide them and his own effort put them forth. Thus a proper sphere of action must be left to him. Far from trying to suppress private action, the State must encourage and foster it in every way. We thus see how Christianity, with its fundamental doctrine of a higher destiny for man, is opposed to the ideal of the collectivist.

The rights possessed by the members of the family are likewise not created by the State. Marriage according to the Christian conception is a free contract giving rise to certain inviolable engagements that have the sanction of divine positive law ; and the relations between parents and their children are also in the highest sense natural. Founded on this basis the family enjoys a juridical existence that is independent of the civil law. It has its own end proper to itself, and therefore its own rights. The State has no power to dissolve it and usurp its place. The Christian State makes no claim to mould the character and destiny of men, as Aristotle and Plato prescribed that it should do. It respects the natural vocation of the parents and leaves to them the education of their children.

There is a third restriction laid by Christianity on the power of the State. In pre-Christian times religious authority and civil power rested in the same hands. Christianity, however, has clearly defined their respective spheres and entrusted their exercise to two distinct bodies, the State on the one hand and the Church on the other. In this way the conscience of the individual is freed from the yoke of the secular power. Certainly it brings it under another power, but this a spiritual one, whose influence is essentially not one of constraint but of persuasion. By proclaiming the incompetence of the State in the governance of the soul and the essentially voluntary character of the act of faith, Christianity has laid the foundations of true liberty of conscience.

The separation of this twofold jurisdiction and the voluntary nature of the act of faith come from the Founder of the Christian religion. In the Scriptures we read how Jesus said, ' Render to Caesar the things that are Caesar's and to God the things that are God's ', and that He sent His apostles to conquer the world not by the sword but by the preaching of the word : ' Go and teach '.

OUTLINES OF THE HISTORY
OF PHILOSOPHY

INTRODUCTION *

1. Introductory.—It is obviously a matter of no little difficulty to present in the form of a summary the history of the very varied teachings of different philosophers and systems. The following pages are intended to be only an outline to be filled in by oral instruction and on this account a critical examination of the various doctrines has been designedly omitted[1]. Reference should be made to the treatises in the Manual where a particular view is further developed or criticized or brought into relation with Scholastic doctrine.

2. Meaning and Utility of the History of Philosophy.—By the History of Philosophy we mean a statement and analysis of the genesis of the different philosophical systems which have been put forward. This inquiry into their logical antecedents and mutual connexions is useful and necessary (*a*) if we wish to obtain a thoroughly complete grasp of what the great minds of

---

* Books for study or consultation :—

W. TURNER, *History of Philosophy* (Ginn, Boston, 1903). A concise manual for the whole of the history.

WINDELBAND, *A History of Philosophy* (trs. Tufts, Macmillan, London, 1901). A larger work.

BURNET, *Greek Philosophy*, 2 vols. (Macmillan, London, 1914) ; or his shorter work, *Early Greek Philosophy* (London and Edinburgh, 1908). For the special epochs of Greek philosophy, see also Zeller's works, various volumes, translated.

DE WULF, *History of Medieval Philosophy* (trs. Coffey, Longmans, London, 1909).

HÖFFDING, *History of Modern Philosophy*, 2 vols. (trs. Meyer, Macmillan, London, 1900), *Modern Philosophers* (trs. Mason, Macmillan, London, 1915). MERZ, *History of European Thought in the Nineteenth Century*, 4 vols. already published (Edinburgh, 1904, etc.).

[1] Most of the statements given in the following outlines of the history of philosophy have been developed and justified in the author's larger works, especially in the one mentioned above. In this Manual he has added as footnotes the most important philosophical works of the different writers. The translators have made some additions to the list with regard to the English philosophers ; and they hold themselves responsible for indicating the English sources for the further study of various systems and writers. In some cases they are indebted to Dr. Turner's *History of Philosophy*, as they are also for some ideas incorporated, and approved by the author of these Outlines, in paragraph 164.—TRS.

the world have thought on any special question or on philosophy as a whole, seeing that the historical setting of a doctrine is a great aid to an appreciation of it. (*b*) It allows us to sift out the elements of truth contained in each philosophical system. (*c*) It is a means which will help us to set side by side with neo-Scholasticism views of reality which contradict it, and thus by comparison with rival systems we shall be in a better position to judge its doctrinal value. (*d*) Finally, it enables us better to understand modern works on philosophy, which in an ever increasing degree are attaching importance to history.

3. Division of the Treatise.—Following the historical succession of different philosophical cycles we may distinguish four periods in the history of philosophy, and accordingly this treatise will fall into four main Parts : I. Indian and Chinese Philosophy ; II. Greek and Latin Philosophy ; III. Patristic and Mediaeval Philosophy ; IV. Modern Philosophy. A brief summary of the general features of philosophy at the present day and mention of the chief systems in vogue will form an Appendix.

PART I

The Philosophy of India and China

4. Indian Philosophy.—The dominant form of all Indian philosophy[2] is *pantheism*. The writings which express it may be distinguished under three periods : (1) The period of the hymns of the Rigveda, B.C. 1500-1000 ; (2) Period of the Brahmanas, B.C. 1000-500 ; (3) Later Sanskrit or Hindu Period, B.C. 500 to the present day.

5. Hymns of the Rigveda.—The Veda is the collection of sacred writings looked upon by orthodox Indians as of divine origin and authority. The Rigveda, which forms the first part of it and is the most ancient monument of the Indo-Germanic civilization, develops a cosmic pantheism according to which a single being manifests itself under the numberless various forms which the manifold phenomena of the universe present.

6. The Philosophy of the Brahmanas and of the Upanishads.— In the Brahmanas and later on in the Upanishads, two other parts of the Veda, pantheism takes a *psychological* form : fundamentally what constitutes our individuality (âtman) and that of all things is absolutely identical with Brahman, the eternal being who is above all time, space, multitude and becoming. Brahman is the source of all things and in him are they all absorbed. Atman or monistic consciousness is present in the elements, the earth, and the plants, until it reaches down to man ; so that the whole of nature is endowed with soul. To arrive at âtman it is not sufficient to be in contact with empirical reality which is multiple, finite and alone knowable ; it is necessary to pierce through the envelope with which the one and infinite âtman or self is clothed and to unite oneself to its ineffable essence by sloughing selfhood and identifying the individual ego with the infinite.

[2] See MAX MÜLLER, *The Six Systems of Indian Philosophy* (London, 1899) ; BOSE, *Hindu Philosophy* (Funk, New York, 1884), *Hindu Heterodoxy* (Calcutta, 1887) ; DE LA VALLÊE POUSSIN, *The Way to Nirvana* (University Press, Cambridge, 1917).

7. The Systems of the Hindu Period.—Amongst the numerous systems which were developed in conformity with the spirit of the Vedic books, and for this reason are called *orthodox* (Mimâmsâ, Vedânta, Nyâya, Vaiseshika, Sânkhya, Yoga), the most important is the Vedânta. The philosophy of this is that the phenomena which inferior science knows are merely illusions ; in reality âtman or Brahman in which all things are confounded is unknowable and without attributes. The end of life is the higher knowledge of our identity with Brahman. This knowledge is obtained by mystical revelations and alone can free us from the transmigration of souls.

Alongside these orthodox theories we meet a number of heterodox systems which set aside the teaching of the Vedas, and of these the most widespread is Buddhism. This doctrine, which is connected with the name of Sâkya-Muni, reduces itself to a moral pessimism ; it teaches that in order to get free from the miseries of life and also from metempsychosis we have to look for happiness in an impersonal repose. This repose, which is the dream of all Oriental philosophies, does not consist, as in the case of Brahminism, in the absorption of the soul in God, but in what is vaguely called Nirvâna or extinction, and which consists according to one view in annihilation of personality, and according to another in some state of positive happiness.

8. The Philosophy of China.—We find in China three principal philosophical systems :

1. The doctrine of Lao-Tse (born in B.C. 604), who recognized a first, intelligent Being from whom the world emanates. His teaching is completed by a moral theory of irreproachable purity.

2. The doctrine of Confucius (born in B.C. 551), an incoherent collection of moral dicta which contain little that is remarkable.

3. Buddhism, which was banned from India and introduced into China at the beginning of our era and into Tibet in the seventh century A.D., and which constitutes the fundamental thought of the mysticism of the lamas.

The philosophies of Eastern Asia have remained uninfluenced by outside contact. Those which are to be met with there to-day are an unbroken and pure tradition from times of the greatest antiquity.

PART II

Greek Philosophy

9. Periods of Greek Philosophy.—The period of Greek Philosophy comprises the six centuries before and the six centuries after Christ, and may be subdivided into the four following periods on the basis of the successive dominant points of view :

1. From Thales of Miletus to Socrates (seventh to fifth century), being mainly cosmological.

2. Socrates, Plato and Aristotle (fifth and fourth centuries), mainly psychological.

3. From the death of Aristotle to the rise of the neo-Platonic School (from the end of the fourth century B.C. to the third A.D.), when the tendencies were ethical.

4. The neo-Platonic School (from the third century A.D., or including the systems leading up to neo-Platonism, from the end of the first century B.C., to the end of Greek Philosophy in the sixth century A.D.), marked by tendencies to mysticism.

CHAPTER I

PRE-SOCRATIC PHILOSOPHY

(From Thales to Socrates, seventh to fifth century B.C.)

10. Characteristics and Subdivision.—The earliest Greek philosophers [3] confined their attention to the external world, the non-ego, and did not enter upon the psychological aspect of the questions raised. Their chief concern was to investigate *changes* or the succession of beings, and to attempt to discover what was the *constant* element among them. Here there are two questions; it was the second which chiefly engrossed attention during the seventh and sixth centuries, B.C.; only later was particular notice taken of the manifest succession of things. Heraclitus was the one who shifted the view-point (fifth century). Hence we find two groups of schools : the first comprising the old Ionians up to the time of Heraclitus, the Pythagorean School and the Eleatic School ; the second, the Atomist School.

11. First Group of Pre-Socratic Schools.—The ancient Ionians looked for the foundation of things in a concrete principle. Water for THALES OF MILETUS (about 624-548 B.C.), infinite matter (ἄπειρον) for ANAXIMANDER OF MILETUS (about 611-547), air for ANAXIMENES OF MILETUS (about 588-524), air endowed with intelligence for DIOGENES OF APOLLONIA, were the respective cosmic elements, the fluidity and mobility of which were thought to be capable of explaining the genesis of all things.

12. Pythagoras (about 580 or 570 to end of the century) went from Samos to Italy. The story of his numerous travels and notably his sojourn in Egypt are not established facts. His doctrine marks the transition from the teaching of the Ionians to that of the Eleatics. All things can be reduced to

---

[3] See BURNET, *Early Greek Philosophy* (London and Edinburgh, 1892), or his larger work, *Greek Philosophy*, vol. I, Thales to Plato (1914).

numbers ; number is the very *substance* of things and all things are born of it, inasmuch as each being is nothing but a determined *harmony* or fixed mixture of odd and even, of indeterminate and determinate.

Pythagoras founded a school, and his disciples, in addition to being philosophers and men of science, were moralists and mystics initiated into secret rites.

13. The School of Elea identified reality with being in the abstract, being that is universal and endowed with the logical attributes of unity, eternity and immobility. Changing phenomena are but an illusion of the senses. This very decisive conception of the world makes its appearance with PARMENIDES[4] (born about 544 or 540). Everything *is*, nothing becomes or ceases to be ; being has neither past nor future ; all is full and a vacuum does not exist, for it would introduce division in being.

ZENO OF ELEA (about 490-430) is the apologist of the School. He defended the theory by showing the contradictions of those who abandon themselves to the testimony of common sense. His arguments against plurality, and above all against the possibility of movement, are famous for all time.

14. Second Group of Pre-Socratic Schools.—This includes : (1) The *Ionian dynamism*, or the theories defended by the new Ionian School after the time of Heraclitus ; (2) the *mechanistic* theories (*a*) of Empedocles, (*b*) of the Atomist School, (*c*) of Anaxagoras [5].

The system of HERACLITUS [6] (about 535-475) was an original blending of *phenomenalism*, *dynamism* and *pantheism*. Parmenides had asserted that nothing changed ; Heraclitus now declared that everything was continually changing (πάντα ῥεῖ), and he saw a symbol of this perpetual flux in that mutable element par excellence—fire. A principle of internal activity animates the incessant flow of the ' fire ' phenomena ; whatever ' becomes ' is itself the principle of its appearance and development. Moreover, this primordial element is endowed with unity and intelligence, and regulates its own evolution.

EMPEDOCLES OF AGRIGENTUM (about 495-435) gathered

---

[4] Περὶ φύσεως.
[5] See *Cosmology* concerning dynamism and mechanism in general.
[6] Περὶ φύσεως.

together in his system of physics [7] the organic ideas of mechanism, but this was adequately treated only in the school of Abdera, the founder of which was LEUCIPPUS and its most authoritative exponent DEMOCRITUS [8] (about 460-370). The whole of matter is composed of an innumerable multitude of corpuscles or atoms which are qualitatively homogeneous, but differentiated by their form and size, and by their combination account for the whole of cosmic becoming. Atomic movement is that of a ' whirling motion ', and results from the existence of empty space and the action of gravity. The psychology of Democritus is merely a chapter of this physical mechanism. The soul of man, like his body, is an aggregation of atoms, but more subtle and lighter. Sensation and thought are only atomic vibrations, provoked by certain material emanations from the objects perceived which travel through the exterior medium and enter into the sense-organs (theory of atomic images or *species*, εἴδωλα).

ANAXAGORAS [9] (500-428), another adherent of mechanism, considered matter as an original conglomeration of particles which are made up of all the different substances of the universe. ' There are parts of all in all things '. Aristotle has called these minute particles *homœomeries*. The moving and guiding agency which determines the diverse combinations of matter, corresponding to the different bodies of the universe, is an immaterial, intelligent being.

15. The Sophists.—The nature-philosophers had concentrated their attention exclusively on the external world, without taking into account the knowing subject. A group of controversialists seized on this popular physical philosophy and showed that it leads to the destruction of all knowledge ; they became known as *Sophists*. Their scepticism has no independent or absolute value, since it is inspired only by the philosophy of Heraclitus or that of Parmenides. The chief of the sophists were PROTAGORAS (born at Abdera, about 480) and GORGIAS (480-375).

---

[7] Περὶ φύσεως ; Καθαρμοί.
[8] Μέγας καὶ μικρὸς διάκοσμος.
[9] Περὶ φύσεως.

CHAPTER II

GREEK PHILOSOPHY FROM SOCRATES TO ARISTOTLE

(*Fifth and fourth centuries B.C.*)

I. SOCRATES

16. Characteristics of Greek Philosophy during this Period.
—The Greek genius reached its maturity in the fifth and fourth centuries. Hitherto philosophers had studied only the external world, the non-ego. Henceforth their investigations were concerned primarily with man, and they studied the external world as dependent on the faculties of the knowing subject.

17. Philosophy of Socrates.—SOCRATES [10] (born about 470) lived at the time when Athens was rising to the zenith of its glory under Pericles. We know little or nothing of his life. He presents the figure of a moralist inspired from on high (the Socratic Δαίμων), and he never ceased to be the ' gad-fly ', denouncing the vices of Athenian society. In 399 he was condemned to drink the hemlock.

Socrates taught under the form of *dialogue*. His method rests on what is known as the *Socratic induction :* the cardinal point of all science is the forming of general intellectual representations of things, and this can be attained by observation of concrete experiences of our ordinary daily life. His philosophy is above all a system of morality, and the fundamental principle of his ethical teaching is the reduction of virtue to knowledge : *to possess science, i.e. universal notions, is to act morally.* To know is not only, as Plato and Aristotle taught, the *condition* which must precede all moral conduct ; but the possession of genuine universal ideas itself actually constitutes the morality of our conduct.

[10] ZELLER, *Socrates and the Socratic Schools* (trs. Reichel, London, 1885).

The great influence of Socrates is the result of his original conception of knowledge. From this conception Plato and Aristotle elaborated new philosophical syntheses.

II. PLATO

18. Life.—At the death of his master Socrates, PLATO (427-347) went first to Megara, then sailed for Egypt and later for Cyrene. After remaining eight years at Athens, he went to reside in Italy (388), where he encountered the disciples of Pythagoras ; thence he went to Sicily, to the court of Dionysius the Elder. On his return to Athens, Plato founded a school in the gymnasium of the Academy.

In the philosophy of his master Aristotle distinguished dialectics, ethics and physics. This form of classification is not explicitly found in Plato, but it corresponds with his thought [11]. The keystone of the Platonic philosophy is the Idea : dialectic studies the Idea in itself ; physics, ethics and aesthetics consider its applications to nature, to human conduct and to artistic productions.

19. Dialectic or Theory of the Ideas.—Dialectic—the word is Plato's—is the science of objective reality, and this itself is called the Idea (εἶδος, ἰδέα). This reality, which is apprehended by our abstract, universal, necessary and immutable representations, is not able to exist in the world known to our senses where everything is particularized, contingent and unstable (Heraclitus). It exists *outside and above the sensible world.* The Idea exists by itself ; it is necessary, one, immutable (Parmenides). This theory of the Idea is an extreme application of *exaggerated realism,* which invests real being with the attributes of being as it is in the mind : to each of our abstract representations there corresponds an Idea-being.

The real world being thus modelled after the world of thought, the Ideas are hierarchically arranged like our representations of them. At the apex of the ascending scale of essences, is enthroned the Idea of the Good, ' the sun of the ideal life ', which is the final cause and the formal cause of all things.

[11] Plato has left thirty-five dialogues. His principal works are : the *Timaeus,* the *Phaedo,* the *Republic,* the *Laws,* the *Politics,* the *Philebus,* the *Gorgias,* the *Theœtetus,* the *Sophist,* the *Parmenides.* See ZELLER, *Plato and the Older Academy* (trs. Alleyne, London, 1888) ; JOWETT, *Translation of the Dialogues* (London and New York, 1892).

The relations of the sovereign Idea, the Idea of the Good, to God, the personal and intelligent Demiurge who directs the world, such as Plato describes Him in the *Timaeus*, present one of the most obscure problems of Platonism. It seems preferable to maintain with Hermann the co-existence of the Idea of the Good and of God, the diarchy of two independent sovereigns, both alike free from the laws of change ; and that whilst the former is the final and formal cause of all things, the latter is regarded as the provident ruler of the visible world.

20. Physics.—1. *The Ideas and the sensible world.* Plato gives a monopoly of reality to the Ideas ; sense-perceived things, the objects of opinion, are only partial and incomplete manifestations of the Ideas. He explains things by matter and world-soul. *Matter* or non-being (μὴ ὄν), which is the ' shapeless and invisible ' element, the receptacle in whose bosom sensible phenomena are evolved, is space, or *place devoid of all content* [12]. The *Soul of the world* is an alloy of two elements which he calls the *one* and the *other* (ταὐτόν and θάτερον), probably the Idea and Matter, and is the connecting link between the sensible and the supersensible. He thus makes the world a kind of huge animal (ζῶον) composed of a visible body and invisible soul, which latter sets it in motion by a circular movement, the symbol of the perfect among the ancients, and is endowed with intelligence.

2. *Structure of the corporeal world.* Corporeal substances consist of configurations of simple bodies (water, air, fire, earth), which are not to be considered as small material masses but as pure regular geometrical figures ; and so these surfaces are pure sections of space and do not form the boundaries of material mass. The phenomena of nature are the outcome of differences in arrangement of simple bodies, and the motion which determines their groupings is extrinsic to them and must come from the world-soul. In this Plato shows himself a mechanist.

21. Psychology.—The teaching of Plato on man may be said to centre round a theory of intellectual cognition, inspired throughout by his dialectic of the Ideas.

1. *Theory of knowledge.* Since the Ideas are not immanent in the sense-world, the consideration of phenomenal things can

[12] Historians are not agreed as to the proper interpretation of the term ' matter ' in Plato's philosophy.

never lead us to a knowledge of immutable reality. But as we have a knowledge of this reality, Plato infers that we have contemplated the world of Ideas face to face in a previous existence ; and he regards sensible perceptions as serving only to re-awaken dormant, previous knowledge and as exercising no causality properly so called on the acts of our intelligence.

2. *Nature of the soul.* The body is a hindrance to the free contemplation of the Idea. The soul here below suffers a state of violence contrary to its nature and is ever striving to set itself free. Man may thus be likened to the charioteer who drives a team of two horses, or again to a monster composed of different natures. In spite of this antinomy, Plato endeavoured to explain the reciprocal interaction of body and soul by dividing the soul into two parts, the one intelligent and immortal (νοῦς), and the other unintelligent and perishable, and in its turn made up of a noble part (the will, θυμός) and a lower or less noble part (all purely organic activities).

22. Ethics and Aesthetics.—The end of man consists in the contemplation of the pure Ideas by the soul in a state of separation from the body. Plato leaves in the background the ethics of the individual and the family, but on the other hand he compiles a complete code of politics or public ethics (*Republic*) in which the individual is sacrificed to the State.

The beautiful resides in order and in the elements which form it. It is the same as the Good, inasmuch as it is one of its aspects. Works of art are imitations of sensible things, and consequently but the shadow of a shadow (*Ethics,* **107**).

III. ARISTOTLE

23. Life.—ARISTOTLE[13] was born at Stagira (whence the name *Stagirite*) in B.C. 384, and for twenty years studied philosophy at the school of Plato. The second important fact of his life is his sojourn at the court of Macedonia, whither he was

---

[13] See ZELLER, *Aristotle and the Earlier Peripatetics,* 2 vols. (trs. Costelloe and Muirhead, London, 1897). His chief works are : I. Logic, collected later under the name of the *Organon ;* the *Categories ;* the treatise *On Interpretation ;* the two *Analytics ;* the *Topics ; Sophistical Reasonings.*—II. Philosophy of nature and the natural sciences : the *Physics ;* the *Book on the Heavens ;* the *Book on Generation and Corruption ;* the *Meteorology ;* the *History of Animals ;* the treatise *On the Soul.*—III. Metaphysics : the *Metaphysics.*—IV. Ethics : the *Nicomachean Ethics,* the *Politics,* the *Athenian Constitution.* The *Greater Ethics* and the *Eudemian Ethics* are probably the work of his pupils. See various translations.

summoned in 342 to direct the education of Alexander the Great. It was only in 335 or 334 that he opened at Athens the Peripatetic School. He was forced to take flight after the death of Alexander, and died at Chalcis in the year 322.

24. General Character and Division of his Philosophy.— Aristotle gave to *speculative knowledge* its full value, and elaborated a *complete philosophical system*, based on the two-fold method of analysis and synthesis. The method of proceeding by observation, inaugurated by Socrates and timidly applied by Plato, was established on a scientific basis by Aristotle. In fact, after having gathered those immense stores of materials which made him the first scholar of antiquity, he constructed so vast a general synthesis, capable of explaining the whole of reality, that he earned for himself the right to be known as the prince of ancient philosophy. Everything that is, is the object of Philosophy, or science in the higher sense that he gives this word.

Philosophy, or science par excellence, is the investigation of the principles and causes of things (*Metaph.*, I, i, 981). It includes (1) the *theoretical sciences : physics*, or the study of corporeal things, subject to change ; *mathematics*, or the study of extension ; *metaphysics*, called *theology* or *first philosophy*, or the study of being conceived of as incorporeal and unchangeable. (2) The *practical sciences : ethics, economics* and *politics*, the second often running into the third. And (3) the *productive* or *poetic sciences*. *Logic*, the vestibule of philosophy, to which he devoted special attention, must also be added.

25. Logic.—Aristotle was the creator of logic or, as he called it, the ' analytic ' of the mind, for he was the first to make out *a whole system of the laws which the human mind must follow in order to acquire scientific knowledge. Scientific demonstration,* and the *syllogism* which is its basis, teach us to discover the essence of things and their causes : they constitute the main topic of Aristotle's logic. But both these processes of the mind presuppose a study of the more elementary operations into which they are resolvable, namely, conception and judgment. The syllogism enables us to see whether the predicate of the conclusion is contained in the comprehension of a third idea, which includes in its extension the subject of the conclusion (*Logic*, **49**). To join ideas by deducing the particular from the general, to co-ordinate and to subordinate conclusions according to the degree of their universality, is the mental process whereby we come upon scientific knowledge.

26. Metaphysics.—Metaphysics is the *science of being, considered as such* (τὸ ὄν, ᾗ ὄν). In real being there is an element which is stable (Parmenides) and an element of becoming (Heraclitus), and the ' real ' of Plato he conceives not as existing apart but as immanent in individual and sensible objects.

Aristotle classifies beings in ten categories or highest classes, of which the two fundamental are *substance* (οὐσία) and *accident :* e.g. Socrates is a substance ; the virtue of Socrates is an accident. An accident belongs to different categories : quality, quantity, relation, place, time, posture (κεῖσθαι), possession resulting from change (ἔχειν, *habitus*) [14], activity and passivity implied in change (ποιειν καὶ πάσχειν). In order to understand the scope of the Peripatetic metaphysics, it is necessary to set side by side with this division, which is of the static order, the classification of actuality and potentiality based on the *becoming* of being. Every change implies the passage from one state to another state. Suppose the case of a being B, passing from the state *a* to the state *b*. The analysis of this passage requires that B already possesses in *a* the *real principle* of its change to *b* ; before being *b*, it was capable of becoming *b*. *Actuality*, or ' act ', is then its present perfection, the degree of being (ἐντελέχεια, τὸ ἐντελὲς ἔχειν). *Potentiality*, potency or power, is the aptitude to receive perfection (δύναμις). The actualization or passage from a potential state to an actual state is called *motion* or *movement* (*Gen. Metaphysics,* 112 ff.).

Three important theses of the Peripatetic metaphysics follow from the distinction between actuality and potentiality : the composition of matter and form (**28**), the composition of universal and individual, the theory of the four causes.

1. The theory of *matter and form*, although it belonged originally to physics, takes a metaphysical sense inasmuch as it is an explanation of change as such. Movement, or change, requires an amorphous or undetermined substrate (matter) which receives some determination (form). The first of these elements is the principle of all that is potential ; the second, of

---

[14] Concerning κεῖσθαι and ἔχειν see *Logic,* **15**.

all the actual perfections in a being and especially of its unity. Movement is eternal, and matter is in consequence also eternal.

2. The *universal* is not anything existing by itself ; but it is immanent in individual things and is multiplied in all the representatives of a class. Herein Aristotle differs from Plato. Its independent form, its universality or aloofness from individuals, it gets only by means of the subjective consideration of our minds (**29**).

3. A *cause* is whatever exercises a real and positive influence on the actuality of a being, in every one of the stages of its becoming. Aristotle distinguishes four causes. The *material* and *formal* causes are the constitutive elements of a being. The *efficient* or motor cause is the principle of its becoming or its passage from potentiality to actuality ; the series of efficient causes has never commenced and will never end ; generation is eternal and matter which is its subject is also eternal, and Aristotle does not account for its existence. The fourth cause, the *final* cause, explains the co-ordination of the activities of a being towards an immanent end ; it is the attraction by which the efficient cause is drawn in a given direction ; without purpose and finality the regular recurrence of natural phonomena would be inexplicable.

27. Pure Actuality.—Over and above all beings subject to change, which are admixtures of actuality and potency, there reigns supreme one immutable Being, the purely Actual (τὸ τί ἦν εἶναι τὸ πρῶτον).

The principal proof of the existence of God is drawn from the existence of movement. A first motor-cause or mover is necessary. Since nothing can be raised from potentiality to actuality save by the action of a mover, were there no single first mover, itself not subject to any becoming, an infinite series of motor-causes would be necessary in order to explain any change whatsoever, and this would be equivalent to declaring that movement is impossible. Pure actuality is eternally quiescent ; it is substantial and indivisible thought. God has no dealings with the world of changing beings, except that He draws them to Himself with an irresistible attraction of finality, i.e. by His desirability.

28. Physics, according to Aristotle, is concerned with the study of natural bodies in so far as they are subject to movement.

There are four kinds of movement : genesis and disappearance of substantial compounds, qualitative change or alteration, quantitative change of growth and decay, and local movement. Since terrestrial substances owe their generation and disappearance to their transformation into one another, it is necessary that there should be in them a permanent substratum, namely *first* or *primary matter* (ἡ πρώτη ὕλη), identical throughout the various stages of the process, and another principle peculiar to each one of these stages, namely *substantial form* (εἶδος). The becoming of forms in matter is regulated by an inevitable purpose, which nature unceasingly tends to realize, but of the final terminus of which Aristotle has no clear conception.

Of substances there are two classes, celestial and terrestrial, and the nature of these is different. More perfect than terrestrial bodies, *celestial* substances (fixed stars and planets) are swayed by a circular movement (the most perfect according to the ancients) ; they are immutable and not subject to generation or corruption. The special natural element of which they are constituted is ether, a substance which is purely topical in its nature (*Metaph.*, VIII, iv, 1044b.), and therefore cannot be classed as a fifth element. Earth, water, air and fire are the four elements whose transformation and admixture explain every production of *terrestrial* bodies, and these productions are accounted for by the agency of the celestial bodies. The world is finite, single and eternal.

Among sublunary bodies, organisms and man in particular occupy a special place, and thus we are led to Aristotle's psychology.

29. Psychology.—Psychology owes its origin as a science to Aristotle. To him the soul appeared as the first actuality (entelechy) of a natural body potentially possessed of life (ἡ ψυχή ἐστι ἐντελέχεια ἡ πρώτη σώματος φυσικοῦ. *De Anima*, II, i) ; it is the substantial form of the living being, as the body is the first matter of the latter.

Though radically one, the soul finds its expression through faculties of various kinds, which are the principles of all specific vital phenomena : *nutrition, sensitive* and *rational knowledge, appetition,* and *locomotion.*

All knowledge, whether sensitive or intellectual, requires the concurrence of an object and the subject, the first exercising a determinating influence on the second. This double phase of knowledge—the *action* of the object on the human faculty, and the *re-action* of the latter—is something of the *psychical* order. Sense-knowledge—whatever be its form, whether through the external senses, the common sense, the memory, or the sensible imagination—presents to us the particular and contingent properties of things ; whilst the intelligence, by a process of abstraction, perceives their reality apart from their individual characteristics and the limits imposed by time and space upon them. This is the reason why, along with the *passive understanding* which receives a stimulus from without, there is an *active intellect* which in concurrence with the sense-knowledge engenders this stimulus, the final resultant of which is in the passive understanding an abstract knowledge of what exists outside in concrete form. The active intellect is im-passible and alone is imperishable. Aristotle's theory of the two intellects presents many obscure points and is full of difficulties.

The definition of the soul states exactly its relations with the body ; since the soul is the form of the body, it is its intrinsic determining principle. To Aristotle psychology is not the study of the soul (as to Plato), but of man as composed of body and soul.

By reason of the functions which it performs without the intrinsic and immediate concurrence of the organism, the intelligence (νοῦς) is spiritual ; and its immateriality involves its *immortality*. The theory of immortality has raised amongst the commentators of Aristotle endless controversies ; the difficulties which it presents arise from the complete separation he makes between the passive intellect and the active intellect. The latter alone is imperishable, and consequently a doubt shrouds the question of the personal nature of immortality.

30. Ethics.—Practical philosophy makes knowledge sub-ordinate to the direction of conduct. The subject-matter of ethics is the acts of the individual in their relationship to his last end, and the latter consists *adequately* in the harmonious exercise of all the faculties (including the sensitive faculties) and *formally* in the development of the highest activities, namely those of the intellect.

Aristotle gives a twofold series of virtues, the dianoetic or intellectual virtues which depend on the speculative or theoretic reason, and the moral virtues which depend on the practical reason. Wealth and pleasure he does not exclude from being elements of happiness, but he gives them a secondary place. This ethical system is a rational eudaemonism.

His Politics is the study of social activity. Man is by nature a sociable being (φύσει πολιτικόν ζῶον), and the perfect form of society is the State.

GREEK PHILOSOPHY FROM THE DEATH OF ARISTOTLE TO THE RISE OF THE NEO-PLATONIC SCHOOL

(From the end of the fourth century B.C. to the third century A.D.)

31. General Characteristics and Division.—The predominance of *moral* speculation is the fundamental feature of philosophy after the death of Aristotle, and this deals chiefly with questions of *personal conduct*, theoretical speculations thus taking a subordinate place.

The beginning of the third century B.C. shows us four great schools in existence : the Peripatetic School, the Stoic School, the Epicurean School, and the New Academy which perpetuated the Platonic tradition. For a century and a half these different schools ran side by side, each following out its own ideal in complete independence. But after the second half of the second century B.C. the disciples departed from the absolute purity of doctrine professed by the founders of the respective schools. We may say in general that they were *Eclectics*. Eclecticism was above all the fruit of the scepticism of the New Academy ; in its turn it gave rise, during the last years of the first century B.C., to a new form of scepticism, which for two centuries enjoyed a parallel development with eclecticism.

32. The Philosophical Schools of the Third and Second Centuries B.C. [15]**.—I. The Stoic School.**—ZENO OF CITIUM (about 342-270), the founder of the school, CLEANTHES, his immediate successor (about 331-251), CHRYSIPPUS (about 281-208), who popularized and systematized Stoic thought, were all principally moralists, although they advocated the study of physics in so far as it is related to ethics.

The physics of the Stoa is *materialistic, dynamistic, pantheistic, deterministic.* Material bodies are the only real

---

[15] See ZELLER, *Stoics, Epicureans and Sceptics ;* and *Eclectics.*

beings (materialism) : and by bodies we must understand not only substances, but the properties, cognitions, etc., which affect them, so that the Stoics admit interpenetration of bodies in the same place (κρᾶτις δι' ὅλων). A principle of internal force inheres in matter (dynamism), namely, warm air or atmospheric currents (πνεῦμα) ; and the different degrees of tension (τόνοι) of this heat explain the different changes of bodies. This πνεῦμα is one throughout its manifold activities (monism) ; it is the supreme plastic force (λόγος σπερματικός), and its generative action produces in the world a closed system of necessarily connected phenomena, each of which is representative of a certain stage of a fatalistic evolution (determinism).

Sensation is the source of all our cognitions, thought being nothing but an elaborated or collective sensation. The criterion of certitude is the convincing force or power (καταληπτικόν) which a representation possesses of winning our firm adherence.

Human acts, just as all other cosmic events, are fatally determined. The human soul is an ephemeral emanation of the divine πνεῦμα, and is material.

Man has knowledge of the laws of the universe to which fate compels him to submit himself. Virtue is a self-determination of the will to act in conformity with our knowledge of the true without regard to any other motive. The only evil is to will contrary to reason. Between good and evil there is a radical opposition, which does not admit of degrees, and the passage from the one to the other is instantaneous. Virtue is obligatory, for since it is the natural form of the activity of man, it has a cosmic significance. The wise man professes an absolute indifference for every motive that has not its source in the reason ; he suppresses his passions and becomes apathetic, i.e. passionless.

33. II. The Epicurean School.—EPICURUS (342-270) opened a school of philosophy at Athens. Although it exercised an influence over a period of more than six centuries, Epicureanism preserved unchanged the form that it had received from its founder. At the end of the second century B.C. it gained favour alike in the Greek and the Roman world. The poet LUCRETIUS [16] (94-54) was a disciple of Epicurus. Still a

[16] *De Rerum Natura.*

flourishing school in the third century A.D., its popularity began to wane in the fourth. Several of its theories survived even after its disappearance, and fragments of its teachings were brought to light again in the Middle Ages.

Epicurus only studied nature in order to free man from the fear which superstitious beliefs in God and death bring upon him. His physics is a revival of the materialistic mechanism of Democritus. And yet the movement of atoms is not caused exclusively by the action of their weight. He was influenced by the need of explaining the freedom of man and conferred on the atom a discretionary power of turning aside—the *clinamen* of Lucretius—owing to which it swerves slightly according to its whim, from the vertical direction which is given to it by the action of gravity. All knowledge both in its origin and its nature is sensible, and the very existence of sensation is a sure criterion of its object, for its object is not the exterior thing, but the representation this thing produces in us. Will is a mechanical movement of the soul, and it is free. Unlike the Stoic determinist morality, the Epicurean ethics is a defence of individualism and egoistic well-being. Yet this individual pleasure, which is the supreme good, consists rather in repose of mind and the absence of pain than in any positive satiation of the soul. Thus Stoicism and Epicureanism, so different in their principles, arrive at one and the same definition of happiness.

III., IV. The Peripatetic School of this period continued the teaching of Aristotle and dealt especially with logic, ethics and physics (STRATO OF LAMPSACUS). **The Sceptic Schools**—the school of PYRRHO OF ELIS (about 360-270), the *Second or Middle Academy*, formed by ARCESILAUS OF PITANE (315-240) ; and the *Third or New Academy*, formed a century later by CAR-NEADES OF CYRENE (213-129)—are of secondary importance.

34. Eclecticism. (*From the latter half of the second century B.C. to the third century A.D.*)—The Stoic, Peripatetic and Sceptic schools developed side by side with Athens as their centre, until eventually their teachings coalesced. The result was a body of eclectic doctrines whose authors may be classified, according to their main tenets and in spite of mutual infiltrations, with one or other of the four principal tendencies of post-Aristotelian philosophy. In the selection of their theories the Eclectics of this period were guided by the convergence of them towards the practical ends of life ; and for them the supreme criterion of this convergence is *our immediate consciousness* of it, the instinctive conviction we have of it independently of all real objectivity of knowledge. An interior voice makes itself heard, and its dictates are peremptory commands. This is subjectivism ; and in this again eclecticism reminds us of scepticism.

With the different forms of eclecticism we may associate some prominent names : with that of the Stoics, the philosophy of SENECA (d. 65 A.D.), an admixture of Stoicism and Platonism [17] ; with that of the Academy, CICERO (106-43 B.C.), who, without having any originality, had a talent for accommodating Greek thought to the Latin mind [18] ; to that of the Peripatetics, a group of commentators on Aristotle, such as ANDRONICUS OF RHODES, the leader of the Athenian school from 60 to 40 B.C., who published in collaboration with the grammarian Tyrannio a complete edition of the works of the master, and above all ALEXANDER OF APHRODISIAS (about 200 A.D.), whom posterity has called *the second Aristotle,* although he dissociates himself on some important points from Aristotelianism and leans towards materialism.

35. The Scepticism of the neo-Pyrrhonic School.—At the end of the first century B.C. scepticism reappeared with AENESIDEMUS [19], who professed in express terms a real and universal doubt. All his objections against the possibility of certitude circle round the idea that, since our representations are only relative, we can have no criterion of truth. Consequently, we must necessarily abstain from forming a judgment. At the end of the second century A.D., SEXTUS EMPIRICUS gathered together in some long treatises [20] the complex work of the sceptic school ; they form a repertory, detailed but ill arranged, of arguments against all forms of dogmatism.

---

[17] *Letters to Lucilius, Quaestiones naturales, De ira, De consolatione, De animi tranquillitate, De clementia.*

[18] *Academica, De natura deorum, De divinatione, De finibus bonorum et malorum, De officiis, De republica, De legibus.*

[19] Πυῤῥώνειοι λόγοι.

[20] *Phyrrhonii Hypotyposes.*

CHAPTER IV

NEO-PLATONISM AND THE SYSTEMS LEADING TO IT

(From the end of the first century B.C. to the sixth century A.D.)

36. General Character and Division.—Philosophy now becomes *theurgic and religious.* On the one hand it places God in heights inaccessible to human reason ; on the other it admits a *direct communication* of this inscrutable God with the human soul. This communication is brought about by means of ecstatic and mystic intuitions and by the intermediary agency of numerous new beings who take their rank between man and God. Under the influence of these tendencies the thinkers of this period conceived an infatuation for teaching of a religious character, especially for the oriental religions which had taken up their permanent abode at Alexandria, the great metropolis of thought at this time. These traits gained their full power in neo-Platonism, which dominated the last three centuries of Greek philosophy ; but we find them in germ in a group of systems which led up to it, at the end of the first century B.C.

37. Systems leading up to neo-Platonism.—Before the advent of neo-Platonism two currents of philosophy developed, mainly at Alexandria : the one a current of Greek philosophy, the fruit of a revival of Pythagorean ideas, which comprised neo-Pythagoreanism and Pythagorean Platonism ; the other a current of Graeco-Judaic philosophy. There was also in the last years of the second century and still more in the third a *Christian philosophy* which for the trend of its thought should be grouped with the Patristic philosophy (**42**).

The neo-Pythagoreans, like the eclectic Platonists, produced a blending of doctrines that remind us of Platonic, Stoic and Peripatetic traditions, combined with theurgic and religious speculation. Among the eclectic Platonists we must mention

PLUTARCH OF CHERONEA (48-125 A.D.), the author of the well-known biographies and of numerous minor works, MAXIMUS, APULEIUS OF MADAURA, ALBINUS, whose lectures Galen attended at Smyrna in 151/2, CELSUS, NUMENIUS (about 160), and the authors of a series of works dating from the end of the third century, which have been handed down under the name of HERMES TRISMEGISTUS.

The complete fusion of Judaic theology and Greek philosophy was the work of PHILO the Jew (30 B.C.-50 A.D.) [21]. He proclaimed the absolute infallibility of the Holy Scriptures, the subordination of philosophy to theology, and the dualism of the infinite God and the finite world.

God's action on the world takes place through the agency of a series of intermediary powers (δυνάμεις), proceeding from the Divine λόγος, which he identified with the angels of the Judaic religion and the daemons of the Greek religion. The religious mysticism of Philo is very definite and full ; the trammels of the body prevent us from knowing God except in the manifestations of Himself, but ecstatic illuminations and prophetic states may enable us to see God such as He is in Himself.

38. Neo-Platonism. Plotinus.—The dominant idea of neo-Platonism is *religious mysticism*. Man must withdraw from and conquer the world of sense, and approach God by a series of stages. From this mystical conception he developed a complete system of metaphysics, which is a kind of *emanationism*. At the same time neo-Platonism is an original syncretism or mixture of the various systems of Greek philosophy, since it interprets in a mystico-religious sense all the theories which preceded it.

PLOTINUS (205-270 A.D.) was the founder and the most brilliant representative of neo-Platonism. An Egyptian by birth, he directed a philosophical circle at Rome. His works, after having undergone a previous recension at the hands of his disciple Eustachius, were published by Porphyry under the name of *Enneads*. The philosophy of Plotinus evolved gradually. Considered in its most synthetic form we may sum it up in two fundamental ideas.

1. *The intelligible and sensible world is formed by an eternal process of emanation* from a supreme principle, the source of

---

[21] *Commentaries on the Old Testament.*

all reality. The degrees in the descending scale of emanations are The One, Intelligence, The World-Soul, Matter.

(a) At the summit of all reality reigns The One or the Supreme Essence. Transcendent in its nature, it possesses all perfections to an ineffable degree (positive theology) ; but on the other hand, since all the notes we attribute to The One are analogical, we may say, from this second point of view, that The One is indeterminate and without any attribute (negative theology). The One consciously sheds around itself Intelligence, not by diffusing its substance and so diminishing its own being, but by permeating, it would seem, by its activity that to which it gives birth. The nature of this generation is one of the obscure points in his teaching. (b) *Intelligence* is that by which the One Primary Being knows itself. This νοῦς, being less perfect than The One by virtue of the progressive decadence, cannot absorb in a single act of knowledge the energy communicated to it ; this energy is dispersed into a multitude of *ideas*. The νοῦς or second principle necessarily produces (c) the *World-Soul*, which is of a hybrid nature, possessed of ideas and containing also wavelets of the universal life or ' plastic forces ' which are scattered forth in the sensible world. Indeed, it is the World-Soul that generates (d) *Matter*, which is merely the place where its plastic forces appear. Matter is non-being, μὴ ὄν, as Plato held. The divine generation reaches a stage when it is weakened by the successive emissions, and its limit or final necessary stage is this non-being or exhaustion of reality, that beyond which there cannot be anything less real.

If we inquire whether this philosophy is a form of pantheism, we may say that it is so if Intelligence which the One voluntarily begets is regarded as one of its energies : in any case the rest of reality is a necessary effusion from Intelligence and hangs upon the Mind's thought.

2. *The mystic return of the soul to God* by the perfect exercise of intellectual activity. The mind gradually mounts the ascending degrees of metaphysical reality. First of all it sees only the world of phenomena, then it attains to contemplation of the νοῦς, and finally rests in ecstatic and unconscious union with The One. The perfection of knowledge is proportionate to its purification (κάθαρσις) from the world of the senses, and the fullness of knowledge brings about supreme

happiness. Plotinus firmly insists upon the personality of man. Religion, since it is the means of bringing about the ecstatic union more easily, occupies a place in the mysticism of Plotinus that his successors continued more and more to enlarge. Religion and philosophy became one and the same.

39. Porphyry.—Among the immediate disciples of Plotinus PORPHYRY (232/3-304) is the most remarkable. He popularized the teaching of his master [22], and emphasized its religious and ascetical character by establishing between man and The One a series of intermediary deities. He also emphasized the confusion we have spoken of between philosophy and religion which was a neo-Platonic survival for many centuries. He was the first of a long line of neo-Platonic commentators on Aristotle : his introduction to the Categories of Aristotle [23] acquired a great celebrity. Neo-Platonism, indeed, regarded the study of the *Organon* of Aristotle as an introduction to the philosophy of Plato.

40. End of Greek Philosophy.—Porphyry's successors retained nothing of neo-Platonism but a mystic craving after the supernatural. The Syrian Jamblichus, for example, built on the foundations of neo-Platonism an international pantheon of pagan deities. Later neo-Platonism took an encyclopedic character and confined its attention to the commentaries of Aristotle.

The philosophers of the last centuries gathered together in the three chief centres of the Eastern empire : Constantinople, Athens, Alexandria. THEMISTIUS, in the second half of the fourth century, is the only personality worthy of note in the school of Constantinople. At the school of Athens the most brilliant thinkers were PROCLUS [24] (410-485), who systematized the philosophy of Plotinus and emphasized his monistic and mystic teachings, and SIMPLICIUS, a commentator on Aristotle, who when the school of Athens was closed by Justinian in 529 migrated to Persia. The most celebrated philosopher at Alexandria was AMMONIUS, a disciple of Proclus. After him, under the influence of JOHN PHILOPONUS, at the beginning of the sixth century, the school of Alexandria underwent an evolution towards Christianity.

---

[22] Ἀφορμαὶ πρὸς τὰ νοητά.
[23] Εἰσαγωγὴ εἰς τὰς Ἀριστοτέλους κατηγορίας, called also περὶ τῶν πέντε φωνῶν.
[24] Στοιχείωσις θεολογική.

The influence of Greek philosophy may be seen throughout mediaeval philosophy, in which it showed itself in three principal directions—in the Byzantine philosophy, in the Asiatic and in the Western. Accordingly we find it in the philosophy of the Fathers of the Church which marks the transitional period between the Greek philosophy and the philosophy of the Middle Ages.

PART III

Patristic Philosophy

41. General Features and Division.—The philosophical speculations of the Fathers of the Church [25], incidental and fragmentary as they were, owed their origin to the religious controversies which they were called upon to maintain, and they served no other purpose, in their eyes, than to establish and defend dogmatic truth ; hence their want of unity and fullness. The patristic period in this way accentuated the tendency inherited from neo-Platonism to confound philosophy with the speculative aspect of religious questions. The philosophy of the Fathers of the Church was essentially *a religious philosophy* subservient to dogma. In other respects, since they lived in a civilization permeated with Greek ideas and were influenced by them, their manner of thought kept the colouring of the ancients.

We may divide Patristic philosophy into two periods, basing our division on the religious controversies which gave rise to speculative discussions. The first period, which included the first three centuries (from the foundation of the Church to the Council of Nicea in 325), was the period in which the fundamental dogmas of the faith became fixed. The second period extended from the fourth to the seventh century, from the Council of Nicea to the Trullan Council (692), and was the era of doctrinal development.

42. Patristic Philosophy during the First Three Centuries.— Gnosticism, which was the principal heresy of the early Christian centuries, was a syncretic alloy of the Greek ideas current at the time. The essential dualism of God, the principle of good, and of matter, the principle of evil ; the evolution of God producing by way of emanation a series of

---

[25] See SCHMID, *Manual of Patrology* (trs. Schobel, St. Louis, 1899) ; BARDENHEWER, *Lives and Works of the Fathers of the Church* (trs. Shahan, Herder, St. Louis, 1908).

Eons less and less perfect ; the mixture of the divine and the material elements in the world : such are the principal theories of the Gnostic metaphysic and cosmogony.

In the third century Gnosticism was violently opposed by the Christian school of Alexandria, of which the leaders were CLEMENT OF ALEXANDRIA (died prior to 216) [26] and ORIGEN (185-254) [27]. The former directed his vigorous mind chiefly to working out a system of natural theology, anthropology and ethics, in agreement with Christian dogma. He established the transcendent nature of God and defended the theory of creation, the spirituality of the soul and the moral freedom of man.

43. St. Augustine.—To the second period of Patristic philosophy belong the names of ST. GREGORY OF NYSSA (331-394), ST. GREGORY OF NAZIANZUS (329-390), ST. AMBROSE [28] (about 340-397) and above all that of ST. AUGUSTINE.

St. Augustine is not only one of the most celebrated Fathers of the Church, but he also stands out as the greatest philosopher of the Patristic period. Born in 354, he was converted to Catholicism by St. Ambrose of Milan, who baptized him in 387. We find him again later at Hippo (395), where he held the episcopal office with great renown until his death in 430 [29].

St. Augustine gathered together and reduced to a concise form the intellectual treasures of antiquity, and he is one of the chief media by which these treasures were destined to be passed down to the modern world. He was well acquainted with neo-Platonism, and to it he owed his psychology, his method of investigation by the human consciousness, his excessive distinction between the sensible and the supersensible and a great number of his teachings concerning God.

Before reaching its complete form the philosophy of Augustine, as he himself tells us, underwent a progressive

---

[26] Λόγος προτρεπτικὸς πρὸς Ἕλληνας ; Παιδαγωγός ; Στρωματεῖς.

[27] Περὶ ἀρχῶν.

[28] *Hexaemeron, De officiis ministrorum.*

[29] His principal works from a philosophical point of view are : *Confessionum libri XIII*, his autobiography (about 400 A.D.) ; *Retractationum libri II ; Contra Academicos*, directed against the neo-sceptics, whose doubts he had at one time shared ; *Soliloquiorum libri II ; Liber de immortalitate animae ; De quantitate animae ; De magistro ; De libero arbitrio ; De anima et ejus origine ; De Civitate Dei* and *De Trinitate.* Nearly all the works of St. Augustine have been translated (ed. Schaff, Buffalo, 1886-92 ; Library of the Fathers, Oxford, 1844-47 ; etc.).

development. In its final form it took a character in which the religious point of view was very much emphasized; it was a fusion of intellectualism and mysticism with the study of God as its essential thought. Augustine proved the existence of God by a series of a posteriori proofs and above all by the analysis of our ideas. He studied the divine nature, taking the various Alexandrine themes and putting them in an anti-pantheistic sense. His analysis of the divine knowledge, which is one of the problems to which he devoted the greatest attention, led him to his theory of exemplarism, which is so intimately associated with his name. In the same way as a workman before he constructs an arch must make a conception of it in his mind, so God conceived the wonderful plan of the universe before He put it into execution. For each thing that exists there is the *idea corresponding* in the mind of God, and this is the standard or norm of its reality and the ultimate foundation of its intelligibility.

In the physics of St. Augustine we find the theory of matter and form. But matter is described sometimes in the Aristotelian sense, sometimes as a chaotic mass brought forth from nothing by the act of the Creator. In matter God has placed a hidden treasure of active forces, which St. Augustine calls *rationes seminales ;* and to the gradual development of these germs or seminal principles must be ascribed the different species of corporeal things.

St. Augustine was also a great psychologist. The human soul is spiritual and immortal; but concerning its origin he was unable to decide between traducianism and creationism. The soul and the body each independently preserve their own substantial nature (Plato). The soul manifests itself by various activities that are not really distinct from its substance, and amongst these the principal ones are those of intellect and will.

With regard to knowledge he insists that whilst we cannot be certain of our transitory, variable sensible perceptions (Plato), we can be so of our mental acts, especially of the states of our own consciousness, of first principles and of our intellectual representations of the exterior world. The ultimate foundation of certitude lies in the resemblance of our ideas to the divine ideas and therefore to objective reality ; and it is in this sense that we must understand many of the texts in which St. Augustine speaks of the Divine illumination of our souls. There are passages, however, where this irradiation of the divine light within us, which is the point of departure for many celebrated and endless controversies, must be taken to refer to other elements of St. Augustine's teaching, notably to his theory of the origin of ideas. For ideas are drawn from the inmost depths of the soul ; God implants them in us as the seal leaves its impress in wax, and the senses are only the occasion of their genesis (Plato).

The will plays a more predominating rôle in our psychic life than the intellect, inasmuch as purity of its desires is a condition of knowledge, and because in the case of some truths the mind's assent can be secured only by the will's intervention. The will is morally free. Evil is not a real element existing side by side with the good (Manicheism), but is the privation of the good.

St. Augustine's manner of reconciling the freedom of the human will with the divine government of man by grace, which is the subject of some very difficult texts, has given rise to ardent controversy.

44. Writers of the Fifth Century. Nemesius. The Pseudo-Dionysius.—Nemesius, Bishop of Emesa, wrote at the end of the fourth century or at the beginning of the fifth a popular treatise entitled περὶ φύσεως ἀνθρώπου, which is an adaptation to dogma of an eclectic psychology and a Grecian mode of thought.

From the point of view of his influence on the future, the most important writer of the fifth century is the author falsely known by the name of St. Dionysius the Areopagite, the disciple of St. Paul. Long controversies have been waged concerning the real identity of this writer. It seems that we must place his writings at the end of the fifth or at the beginning of the sixth century. They did not appear before the time of the great religious conference at Constantinople. The treatises of the PSEUDO-DIONYSIUS on *The Divine Names, Mystical Theology, The Celestial Hierarchy, The Ecclesiastical Hierarchy*, largely inspired mysticism and scholasticism down to the time of the Renaissance. The philosophy which we find in these writings centres around the thought of God and of mystical union with Him. Neo-Platonic influences are manifest not only in a great number of particular teachings, both philosophical and mystical, but also in his terminology and formulae. Nevertheless the author rejects pantheism, and his mysticism, based on grace, is Christian. The veiled terms in which the Pseudo-Dionysius had written caused confusion among the thinkers of the Middle Ages who sometimes interpret them in an orthodox, sometimes in a heterodox, sense.

The philosophers later than the fifth century, both on account of their race, their mode of thought and their influence, belong to mediaeval times.

PART IV

Mediaeval Philosophy

45. General Remarks on the Philosophy of the Middle Ages and Scholastic Philosophy.—Concerning the philosophy of the Middle Ages and Scholastic philosophy [30] there exists a very large number of misconceptions and prejudices which are due to unfortunate confusions. We may mention the chief ones which need dispelling.

1. Confusion between *mediaeval* philosophy and *Scholastic* philosophy.—The historical works which have recently been published in great numbers have shown that in the Middle Ages there were many philosophical systems, some closely interrelated, others of a very different character, and this not only in the West but also at Byzantium and in the East. Though indeed Scholasticism was the dominant philosophy in the West and that with which we may associate the greatest names, that also which was the best systematized and destined to have the most glorious future, it was none the less only one out of many philosophical systems belonging to the Middle Ages. This is so true that throughout the course of the Middle Ages, at whatever stage of its development we consider it, whether at the height of its glory or in its decadence, Scholasticism had to deal with philosophical systems that were opposed to it, whose teaching was *anti-Scholastic* or, if you prefer, *non-Scholastic*. This is true if we consider the West alone, but we must also remember that Byzantium and the East also produced in the Middle Ages systems which had nothing at all in common with Scholasticism. To confuse Scholasticism with the philosophy of the Middle Ages is the mistake of confusing a part with the whole.

2. Confusion of Scholastic *philosophy* and Scholastic

---

[30] The new view of Scholasticism outlined in the following pages is discussed at length in DE WULF, *History of Medieval Philosophy*, trs. Coffey ; cp. also by the same authors, *Scholasticism Old and New*. Enlarged editions of the *History* appeared in 1913 in Italian and German.

theology.—The princes of the Scholasticism of the thirteenth century have clearly marked the distinction between philosophy and theology. Their *philosophy*, like every philosophy, is a study by the light of human reason of the whole or of part of the problems which are presented by an endeavour to explain the order of the universe through its ultimate causes. Their *theology*, in so far as it is dogmatic, is a body of teachings made known by a positive revelation of God. It is certain that these two notions, though ill-defined at the beginning of the Middle Ages, were very clearly distinguished well since the twelfth century.

What has had the greatest share in perpetuating among historians of the present day the misleading conception which makes Scholastic philosophy but a department of the history of religions, is the misunderstanding of the mediaeval principle that philosophy holds a position subordinate to that of theology. This has led some to define Scholastic philosophy as that philosophy which is under the direction of the dogmatic teaching of the Catholic Church, *philosophia ancilla theologiae*, and others to call Scholastic all philosophy subject to any dogma whatsoever [31]. We certainly admit that in the Middle Ages philosophy had some relations with theology : not only relations of common origin and of methods of instruction which were in vogue in a civilization very different from our own, but also relations of co-ordination and of subordination. Of *co-ordination*, inasmuch as philosophical arguments were made use of in theology for apologetical purposes, and on this account philosophy, although it existed as an autonomous science, contributed in theology to form what is known as the dialectic method or, as it was called in the twelfth century, the method of *rationes*, as distinguished from the use of *auctoritates* or the scripture method. Of *subordination*, since philosophy, whilst having no concern with the positive demonstration of a dogma, might never negatively contradict any dogma : a thing which the regulations of the University of Paris expressed by forbidding any master of philosophy to ' determinare *contra* fidem.' Nevertheless, these connexions between theology and philosophy do not at all detract from the real specific difference in the nature of the two sciences, and in order to bring home

[31] Thus it is that we hear of a Jewish Scholasticism (Zeller), of an Arabian Scholasticism (Carra de Vaux) and of a Protestant Scholasticism.

to ourselves how far it is incorrect to introduce the idea of a primacy of theology into the definition of Scholastic philosophy, it will be sufficient to notice on the one hand that a great many of the tenets of mediaeval Scholasticism have no direct concern with the truths of faith, as is evident if we but glance at their Aristotelian origin ; and on the other hand that all philosophical systems in the Middle Ages, even those that were opposed to Scholasticism, endeavoured to establish their agreement with dogmatic truth.

3. Confusion between *Scholastic* philosophy and *an ancient* philosophical system.—The prejudice that would make Scholasticism a mere servile counterpart of Aristotelianism has now been finally dissipated. The influence of Aristotle was very real ; but that of St. Augustine was no less so, especially before the time of St. Thomas Aquinas. St. Augustine served as the channel by which neo-Platonic tendencies of thought were passed on. Not to mention Pythagoreanism, the mechanism of Democritus and especially Platonism both show traces of their influence. Scholasticism made use of all the traditional teachings to the great benefit of its own characteristic systematization.

4. Confusion between *Scholastic philosophy* and its *didactic methods*—its formal procedure, its use of the syllogism and of the Latin tongue, etc.[32].

These false or one-sided views date from the Renaissance, which put down as scholastic all the theologians and all the philosophers of the Middle Ages *such as it knew them at the time*, or *as it thought it knew them*. The epithet ' scholastic ', which was held in honour at the beginning of the Middle Ages (from *schola*, school), came to have a contemptuous meaning at the end of the fifteenth century and to signify in some vague way *any* philosopher-theologian, whose language people sneered at and of whose teaching they knew nothing. The same happened in architecture with the epithet ' gothic '. But owing to recent historical works these long-standing prejudices which were so unjust to the philosophy of the Middle Ages are now fortunately all but dissipated.

[32] One might as well define Grecian Philosophy as the philosophy taught in Greek, or Kantianism as the philosophy that can be studied only with the aid of a certain specially compiled glossary, as conceive such a definition for Scholasticism.

46. Division of the Philosophy of the Middle Ages.—The philosophy of the Middle Ages developed simultaneously in the West, at Byzantium and in numerous centres in the East ; but of these three philosophies, Western, Byzantine, and Oriental, the first is by far the most important ; and in Western philosophy Scholasticism is that most representative of the ideas of the age. Therefore by taking into account this central position of *Scholasticism* we are the better able to trace out, in the different phases of its development, the divisions of all philosophy in general of the Mediaeval Period. From this point of view the scientific renaissance of the thirteenth century marked an epoch ; the period which preceded it may briefly be called one of long and painful elaboration : in the thirteenth century Scholasticism unfolded all the riches of its genius ; but the time of its glory was not of long duration. Already in the fourteenth century there were signs of the decadence which came about in the fifteenth. From the middle of the fifteenth until the seventeenth Scholasticism languished, and the more so because it was assailed on all sides by new systems which were the forerunners of Modern Philosophy. Some distinguished minds tried in the sixteenth century to regain for it the predominance it had lost, but their efforts were without success.

From the above it is clear that the mediaeval philosophy falls into four periods : (1) period of formation (from the ninth to the end of the twelfth century) ; (2) period of its glory (thirteenth century) ; (3) period of decadence (fourteenth and first half of fifteenth century) ; (4) period of transition from mediaeval philosophy to modern philosophy (second half of the fifteenth to seventeenth century).

With these divisions of Western philosophy we shall connect the history of philosophic thought at Byzantium and in the East.

CHAPTER I

FIRST PERIOD OF MEDIAEVAL PHILOSOPHY

(To the end of the twelfth century)

ART. I. WESTERN PHILOSOPHY

I. GENERAL VIEW

47. Main Characteristics of Scholasticism during this Period.—1. *Gradual demarcation of the scope of philosophy.*— The Celtic and the Gallo-Franks and the other neo-Latin races (and in a minor degree the Teutons), now called upon to create the new civilization of the Middle Ages, gathered together the relics of a great heritage left by the Roman world. At the outset their work was neither original nor constructive, but encyclopedic. In the great collectanea of ISIDORE OF SEVILLE (560-636) [33], of GREGORY THE GREAT (about 540-604), of VENERABLE BEDE (673-735) [34] and RHABANUS MAURUS (784-856) [35] philosophy stands for knowledge in all its very various branches. By the ninth century there was no definite demarcation between philosophy and theology, nor again between philosophy and the liberal arts. This demarcation only came about as the result of a slow process of specialization during the following centuries.

2. *Gradual formulation of the problems.*—The commencement of the Middle Ages showed an altogether undue esteem for *dialectic,* which alone was taught as such as a branch of the liberal arts ; but simultaneously there were debated many problems of cosmology, natural theology, ontology, and, after the eleventh century, of psychology.

3. *Absence of systematic arrangement.*—The solutions given to these different problems were wanting in that convergence of view which is characteristic of the synthesis of the thirteenth

---

[33] *Originum seu Etymologiarum, Libri XX.*
[34] *De natura rerum.*
[35] *De universo.*

century. We must look for the principal cause of this in-coherence in the very varied influences which were brought to bear upon Scholasticism : a preponderating group of Platonic-Augustinian ideas together with a group of Aristotelian ideas. And further, mingled with these two groups we find the influence, less important but very real, of various other theories—Pythagorean, Epicurean, Stoic, neo-Platonic, Arabian. We may say of the philosophy of this period that it resembled a crucible in which materials of very varied kinds were fused together.

48. Organization of Philosophical Schools.—Far back in the Middle Ages there were two or even three types of schools [36], and in these the teaching of philosophy took a prominent place along with the teaching of the other sciences. These were (1) the *monastic schools,* each comprising the *schola interior* or *claustri,* reserved for the monks, and the *schola exterior,* open to lay students ; (2) the *episcopal, cathedral* or *capitular schools ;* (3) the *court* or *palace schools, scholae palatinae* or *palatii,* of which the most celebrated was the Palatine court of the Frankish kings. The celebrity of these schools dates from Charlemagne, who encouraged their erection, and from ALCUIN (735-804), who organized them.

Amongst the most famous schools we may mention those of York (England), of Liége, Tournai (the Low Countries), of Fulda (Germany), of Rheims, Tours, Laon, Compiègne, Chartres and Paris (France), of Monte Cassino (Italy).

In these schools there were taught (1) the liberal arts, comprising the *trivium* (grammar, rhetoric, dialectic or logic) and the *quadrivium* (arithmetic, geometry, astronomy, music) ; (2) the natural and historical sciences ; (3) philosophy ; (4) theology.

The commentary (*lectio*) or expounding of the text of an author was the first and natural form of teaching, and it was based on the works we shall mention below. The *disputatio,* or the exchange of views between master and pupils, made its appearance in the twelfth century. We also find at an early date attempts at a systematic instruction on particular questions. This systematization became a dominant feature from the time of Abelard. And we must note how philosophical

---

[36] Cp. Mullinger, *Schools of Charles the Great* (London, 1877).

arguments and questions are intermingled with those which belong to theology.

49. Philosophical Literature.—Of Aristotle's works only the *Organon* was known, and this in its entirety not until the twelfth century; and about this time we have evidence of his *Physics*. Plato was known only by his *Timaeus*. On the other hand there were in circulation numerous commentaries upon Aristotle and Plato by Porphyry (the *Isagoge*), by Boëthius, Marius Victorinus, etc. The Greek authors were read only in Latin translations. Works or parts of works of Cicero, Seneca and Lucretius were considerably used, and amongst the Fathers of the Church the Pseudo-Dionysius and especially St. Augustine had the greatest renown. Three writers of a new line may be considered as directing the philosophical thought of the Middle Ages—MARTIANUS CAPELLA of Carthage (middle of the fifth century) [37], CASSIODORUS (470-570) [38] and BOETHIUS (480-525) [39], the last two being ministers of Theodoric, king of the Goths.

50. Division of this Period.—The twelfth century being the golden age of the schools of philosophy, the present period may be subdivided into two parts : the one, Western philosophy in the ninth, tenth and eleventh centuries (I) ; the other, Western philosophy in the twelfth (II).

To this division according to a chronological order we shall add another division according to the ideas contained in the systems of philosophy ; in each of these two periods we shall make a distinction between the theories that are Scholastic and those that are not. This classification will be based on the objective conformity or want of conformity that the theories of a philosophy have with the fundamental tendencies of the Scholasticism of the thirteenth century, when the teachings handed down from the early Middle Ages were completed and crystallized [40].

[37] *Satyricon ; De nuptiis Mercurii et Philologiae.*

[38] *De artibus ac disciplinis liberalium litterarum ; De institutione divinarum litterarum.*

[39] Translations of the *Isagoge* of Porphyry and of various works of Aristotle, notably the *Organon ;* commentaries on the *Isagoge*, the *Categories* and the *De interpretatione* of Aristotle, the *Topics* of Cicero ; original treatises on categorical and hypothetical syllogisms, division, definition, topical differences ; *De consolatione philosophiae.*

[40] For the justification of this criterion see the author's *History of Medieval Philosophy*, p. 146 f.

II. Western Philosophy of the Ninth, Tenth and Eleventh Centuries

§ 1. Scholastic Philosophy

51. The Question of Universals.—The first stages of Scholastic thought were the outcome of discussion of the problem of universals. We can follow step by step the gradual expansion of the different controversies, the development of a psychology and with it the slow elaboration of a solution of the main problem which reached its final form in the twelfth century. The early Scholastics did not clearly see the many aspects that this question involved. The problem did not spring up spontaneously in the Middle Ages, but was forced upon the attention of philosophers by an obscure text of the *Isagoge* of Porphyry, the meaning of which was made still more obscure by the vague and scarcely consistent commentaries of Boëthius. The question Porphyry asked was : Do *genera* and *species* exist as things in the world of reality, or are they mere products of the mind (*sive subsistant, sive in nudis intellectibus posita sint*)? The Scholastics took up the discussion as it stood just in these terms, that is to say, they looked merely at the objective aspect of the question and neglected the *psychological* point of view ; they asked simply, Do the objects of our concepts, that is to say, species and genus, exist in nature (*subsistentia*), or are they merely abstractions of the mind (*nuda intellecta*)? Simply : *Are they, or are they not, things?* Those who replied in the affirmative received the name of *realists ;* the other party were known as *anti-realists.*

The principal realists were FREDEGIS (ninth century) [41], REMIGIUS OF AUXERRE (ninth century) [42], GERBERT (tenth century) [43], who was remarkable in his time as a logician, a man of learning and a humanist, and ODO OF TOURNAI (eleventh century) [44]. They established a strict parallelism between being and thought, and attributed to each species and to each genus a universal essence (*subsistentia*), shared by all the subordinate individuals.

[41] *De nihilo et tenebris.*
[42] Commentaries on Donatus and Martianus Capella.
[43] Letters ; *De rationali et ratione uti.*
[44] *De peccato originali.*

By anti-realists we mean those who opposed realism, those who followed commonsense and agreed with Aristotle in maintaining that universals are not things and that the individual alone exists. The anti-realists of this period— RHABANUS MAURUS, ERIC OF AUXERRE (ninth century) [45], or ROSCELIN (born about 1050), the originator of the *sententia vocum*—did not get beyond the simple negative reply to the incomplete dilemma propounded by Porphyry. The last named in particular did not solve the problem of the relation between the universal and the thought in the precise sense that we now understand by the word *nominalism*. We do not find this question broached in the texts of his which we possess.

The quarrels among dialecticians gave rise in some quarters to argumentations at once superficial and degrading to reason. Men like ANSELM OF BESATE (eleventh century) [46] must be regarded as sophists rather than philosophers.

Extreme realism considered only the *real* element in our concepts and attributed to it an actual universality ; anti-realism on the other hand, under its first forms, may be summed up in the negative thesis that essences do not exist in a universal state. Each of these theories gave only an imperfect solution of the problem of universals ; but whilst the former was vitiated by a radical flaw, the latter was the expression of a truth which was destined to become clear and full as more adequate formulae were found to clothe it.

52. St. Anselm (1033-1109), Abbot of Bec and afterwards Archbishop of Canterbury, was the first to make an attempt, in his well-known works [47], to combine the truths so far reached in philosophy. He expressed in Augustinian terms, exact but incomplete, the relations between faith and reason (crede ut intelligas, intellige ut credas), and, on a metaphysical basis, he formed a system of theodicy which embraced all the problems of philosophy. The name of St. Anselm is inseparably connected with one special argument for the existence of God : the famous ontological argument examined in Natural Theology (**17**). Following the thought of St. Augustine, Anselm treated of the simplicity, immutability and eternity

---

[45] Commentaries on dialectical problems.
[46] *Rhetorimachia*.
[47] *Monologium, Proslogium, Liber apologeticus ad insipientem, De fide Trinitatis* (against Roscelin), *De incarnatione Verbi, Dialogus de grammatico, De veritate, De libero arbitrio, Cur Deus homo ?* (on redemption and atonement).

of God, of exemplarism, and of divine truth and knowledge ; and these theories became the treasured patrimony of the Scholastics. He was frankly realistic in his tone of mind. In psychology he recognized the essential distinction between sensation and thought, and he dealt with many of the questions concerning the genesis of ideas along the same lines as St. Augustine.

§ 2. *Non-Scholastic Philosophy*

53. John Scotus Eriugena (800/15-877), of Irish birth (Eriugena), must be regarded as the father of the anti-Scholasticism of this period. His main work *De Divisione Naturae* contains indeed the principles of a pantheistic philosophy such as we find in neo-Platonism.

1. His metaphysical teaching may be summarized thus : There is only one being, God, from whom all things proceed by a series of *substantial* emanations (participationes). In this process of emanation there are four stages : (*a*) Nature neither created nor creating, i.e. God as the origin of all things, as He exists unknown even to Himself ; (*b*) Nature uncreated and creating, i.e. God as He knows within Himself the primordial causes of all things that are to appear as phenomenal or visible existences ; (*c*) Nature created but not creating, i.e. the externalization of God in genera, species and individuals—the world of phenomena—all contingent things, corporeal or incorporeal, being only *theophanies* or unfolding of the divine substance ; (*d*) Nature neither creating nor created, i.e. God as the ultimate term of the Universe.

2. In his psychology he regards man as a projection of God ; and in addition to his ordinary method of cognition, man has an *intuitus gnosticus* in which for the acquisition of knowledge the reason follows a process parallel to the evolutionary stages of the divine substance.

Scotus Eriugena, by confusing religion and philosophy, interpreted the Scriptures and dogmas of the Church in a symbolic and naturalistic sense. His philosophy exercised a profound influence on the development of Western thought in the Middle Ages. By his pantheism he was anti-Scholastic, inasmuch as the substantial distinction between God and His creatures is one of the fundamental principles of Scholasticism.

Other indications of anti-Scholastic teachings are to be found in the *De Constitutione Mundi* of the Pseudo-Bede, who refuted a form of human monopsychism upheld by some of his contemporaries.

§ 3. *Philosophy and Theological Controversies*

54. Their Bearing on Philosophy.—The discussion of several philosophical questions was the natural outcome of the theological controversies on predestination, transubstantiation and the dogma of the Trinity. The endeavour of certain dialecticians, such as Berengarius of Tours and Roscelin, to place dialectic beyond all authority provoked a reaction on the part of a group of theologians—Peter Damian, Otloh of St. Emmeram, Manegold of Lautenbach (eleventh century)—who declared themselves more or less hostile to all philosophy. Peter Damian notably would not tolerate philosophy except as subserving the cause of dogma, and it was he who popularized the much-abused principle *philosophia ancilla theologiae*. Yet it was with Lanfranc, the champion against Berengarius, that we find developing a more accommodating tendency in theology which was destined to issue in what became known as the dialectic method. He was ready to admit the value of profane studies, but always required philosophy to be the handmaid of theology.

III. WESTERN PHILOSOPHY IN THE TWELFTH CENTURY

§ 1. *Scholastic Philosophy*

55. Realism.—The twelfth century stamped a well-defined character on mediaeval thought, fixing the religious, social and artistic outlook of the West and moulding the national features of peoples which were now to take the predominant place in political life.

The schools of Chartres and Paris were centres of stirring intellectual tournaments. In the first half of the twelfth century Chartres was the focus of culture, but its fame was gradually eclipsed by that of the schools of Paris, which became by the end of the century the first university of the Middle Ages.

The time was one of extraordinary activity in philosophic

thought, which displayed itself in very complex and quite dissimilar movements. Scholasticism took up with vigour the problem of the universals, and the discovery of the new books of Aristotle on logic fomented the discussions.

During the first half of the twelfth century we witness a revival of extreme realism : WILLIAM OF CHAMPEAUX [48] (1070-1120), however much he may have been inconsistent in his terms, taught, at Paris, that universals are contained in each individual thing, the essence of which is identical in all and universal in character. At Chartres, which was a stronghold of realism, BERNARD OF CHARTRES [49] (died about 1125) professed a realism very akin to the ancient Platonism, by attributing a real universal existence to genera and species. His disciple, THEODERIC OF CHARTRES [50] (died 1155), the soul of the humanist movement for which Chartres was famous, regarded God as the *existential act* of every creature. WILLIAM OF CONCHES [51] (about 1080-1154) for some time followed the lines of his teachers, but later applied himself to the study of physiology, cosmology and ethics.

56. Anti-Realist Formulae.—Under this term we group many solutions of the problem of universals which were brought forward in the first half of the twelfth century and which, faithful to the mind of Boëthius, set out from the principle that genera and species are nothing but the individual subject *as regarded under different aspects ;* such is the theory of the *respectus* of ADELARD OF BATH [52], that of the *status* of WALTER OF MORTAGNE, or those known as the *indifference* theory and the *collection* theory. All alike attack extreme realism ; despite their shades of difference, they were steps towards a final solution of the question ; their lack of greater precision will be understood when once they are placed in their proper historical setting [53]. The one who gave extreme realism its death-blow was Peter Abelard.

57. Abelard (1079-1142), as a critic of more than ordinary

---

[48] *Liber sententiarum*, treatises on dialectics.
[49] *De expositione Porphyrii.*
[50] *Eptateuchon, De inventione rhetorica ad Herennium.*
[51] *Magna de naturis philosophia, Dragmaticon philosophiae, Summa moralium philosophorum.*
[52] *De eodem et diverso, Quaestiones naturales.*
[53] See *History of Medieval Philosophy* by the author for further developments on this subject, p. 187 ff.

power [54], heaped ridicule on the realism of William of Champeaux and on the nominalism of Roscelin. Yet his anti-realism marks no very great advance on the theories of his contemporaries : his position is that the universal is not a mere mental idea, not *vox* (Roscelin) but *sermo*, i.e. that which is capable of being predicated of several, *natum praedicari de pluribus*. Between philosophy and theology he established a system of theoretical relations, scholastic in spirit, but he went wrong in the practical application of these principles to the dogmas of religion. By his *Sic et Non*, in which he presented the pros and cons of each question, he did much to popularize a new didactic method.

58. The Dawn of Moderate Realism.—GILBERT DE LA PORRÉE [55] (1076-1154) caused a decisive advance in the problem of universals by maintaining that there is in things an objective ' fundamentum ' for the universality of our concepts : the mind compares and gathers together (colligit) the essential determinations (diversae subsistentiae) realized in a number of individual beings and it makes a *mental union* of the realities in them that are alike, and it is this element of likeness, of mutual conformity (cum-forma, having the same form) which we call genus or species. His distinct contribution towards the solution of the problem is the teaching that it is the similarity of the essences which furnishes the ground for the universalizing abstraction on the part of the mind. The chronicler OTTO OF FREISING [56] (about 1115-1158), one of Gilbert's disciples, taught the same, and the theory and its importance in the question of universals was fully emphasized in an anonymous treatise *De Intellectibus* of the second half of the twelfth century.

59. John of Salisbury attempted to co-ordinate the various teachings. A well-known figure in the schools of Paris from 1136, the confidant of English kings and of popes, and Bishop of Chartres from 1176 till his death in 1180, he showed himself in

[54] *Tractatus de unitate et trinitate divina ; Theologia christiana ; Introductio ad theologiam*, which is the first part of the Theologia ; the *Sic et non ; Scito teipsum seu Ethica ; Dialogus inter philosophum judaeum et christianum ;* commentaries on Aristotle, Porphyry and Boëthius ; *Dialectica ; Historia calamitatum* (his autobiography).
[55] *Liber sex principorum ;* commentaries on Boëthius.
[56] Chronicles; *Gesta Frederici*.

two remarkable works [57] as the leader of the humanism of Chartres and the most elegant writer of the twelfth century. He inveighed against a group of cavilling grammarians and obscurantists who aimed at the destruction of all learning (the Cornificians) ; but beyond this he was the first to undertake a history of the philosophical thought of his times, and he furnished an exact solution of the question of universals, in treating which, he said, ' the world had grown old, taking more time to solve it than the Caesars took to conquer and govern the earth '. He also took up the study of psychological questions, especially that of the faculties and acts of the soul. Though we find in his psychology certain Aristotelian principles, it is substantially that of St. Augustine.

The work in which the Platonic-Augustinian psychology appears in its purest and most didactic form is the *Liber de Spiritu et Anima* of ALCHER OF CLAIRVAUX, which we may regard as the manual of psychology for this first mediaeval period.

60. Alan of Lille [58] (about 1128-1202) was, like John of Salisbury, a subtle dialectician, who collected and fused together Platonic, Aristotelian and neo-Pythagorean elements, but transformed the whole by a Christian conception. He clothed all his ideas in a poetical garb, and his style, elegant in its imagery, is often allegorical and ill-adapted to express his thought clearly. His attacks against the Cathari in defence of the immateriality and immortality of the soul form the most important part of his work. His psychology is drawn entirely from St. Augustine.

61. Hugh of St.-Victor (1096-1141) presents to us a personality which is at once philosopher, dogmatic theologian and mystic. His *Didascalicon* is a sort of encyclopedic review of all the known sciences and formed the model for numerous imitators. His exegesis of the Pseudo-Dionysius corrected in an individualistic sense the monistic formulae of J. Scotus Eriugena. His proofs of the existence of God open out a new phase in the history of Scholastic theodicy, inasmuch as he renounces a priori methods and takes his stand upon experience. His psychology also is Augustinian.

[57] *Entheticus de dogmate philosophorum, de septem Septenis*, and especially the *Polycraticus* and the *Metalogicus*.

[58] *Tractatus contra hereticos, ars catholicae fidei, theologicae regulae, anti-claudianus, de planctu naturae.* He was also a mystic.

§ 2. *Non-Scholastic Philosophies*

62. Various Forms of Non-Scholastic Philosophy.—Every theory which denies the spirituality of the soul, the personality of man, or the essential distinction between God and the creature is subversive of the fundamental principles of Scholasticism, and must be referred to some other philosophical system. Hence we cannot classify among the Scholastics anyone who professes materialism, transmigration of souls, atheism or pantheism.

Materialistic Epicureanism manifests itself in certain of the teachings of the Cathari and the Albigenses, especially in their denial of the after-life of the soul ; but the principal forms of anti-Scholasticism belong to the pantheism which was due to the influence of J. Scotus Eriugena. Namely : (1) The pantheism of the school of Chartres, represented by BERNARD OF TOURS [59]. (2) The pantheism of AMALRIC OF BÈNE and the Amauritian Sect—that all that exists is one and God is immanent in all things. Amalric of Bène died in 1204, but his ideas survived him, and we find certain sects having recourse to his theories to deify humanity—theories which have more than one point of contact with similar errors expounded by Joachim de Floris and by the author of the *Evangelium Aeternum*. (3) The pantheism of DAVID OF DINANT (closing years of the twelfth century), which is the most absolute materialism—God is the primary matter identical in all things. His work, *De Tomis, id est de Divisionibus*, was proscribed for schools by various councils and is now lost.

§ 3. *The Theological Movement of the Twelfth Century*

63. Schools of Scholastic Theology.—In the twelfth century Scholastic theology stands clearly distinct from Scholastic philosophy, and the two queens of mediaeval wisdom enjoy an absolute autonomy as two distinct sciences. Theology rose to a very notable position ; great schools developed, and progress was made in two important respects—the codification of materials under the form of *Sentences* (sententiae, libri sententiarum) and the introduction of the ' dialectic method ', used side by side with what may be called the scriptural

[59] *De mundi universitate.*

method, but subsidiary to it. The object of the dialectic method was to find out the rational character of every dogma, so that the authority of the Scriptures, *auctoritates*, might have the support of a true apologetic, *rationes*. The distinction between these two terms appeared first in the writings of Peter of Poitiers and later in those of Thomas Aquinas; it is of considerable importance.

The application of the dialectic method to theology gave rise to some ardent controversies and served to divide theologians into distinct parties. Whilst a certain group of *rigorist theologians* entirely opposed its introduction into the realm of theology (**54**), the majority allowed it, although in strict subordination to the method of scriptural interpretation. These latter in their turn may be classed in two groups : the one, who regarded philosophy as merely being useful for bringing out the rational element in the dogmas of the Church, merit the name of *practical theologians* (e.g. Peter Lombard, known as the Master of the Sentences, and his disciple Peter of Poitiers) ; the other, who fully recognized the value of philosophical study in itself and cultivated it for its own sake, may be called *academical theologians*. It was these who were the true representatives of the Scholastic genius and were the forerunners of the great minds of the thirteenth century. We may group them round the three schools of Abelard (whose disciple was Roland Bandinelli, the future Alexander III), of St.-Victor at Paris (Hugh and Richard, and Robert of Melun), and of Gilbert de la Porrée (disciple : Radulfus Ardens).

64. Mystic Schools.—The aim of mysticism as a speculative science is to give an account of the relations brought about by the *direct* communication between the soul and God and to explain the universal order of things by the union thus effected.

If the Scholastics were not to lay themselves open to the charge of being illogical, they could not admit a mysticism that was of the natural order ; for according to their theory of ideas the reason is able to know God and the will to love Him only through the medium of sensible experience. But such an analogical knowledge of the Infinite does not constitute a direct communication with Him, which is the central phenomenon of the mystical life. For this reason Catholic mysticism belongs in the eyes of theologians to the supernatural order. Whilst mysticism is distinct from Scholastic philosophy, it is not incompatible with it.   In fact, we find that the great Scholastic philosophers of the Middle Ages were at the same time philosophers, dogmatic theologians and mystic theologians.   In the twelfth century the centre of mysticism was the School of St.-Victor, where Abbots HUGH and RICHARD were conspicuous leaders.

ART. II.   BYZANTINE AND ORIENTAL PHILOSOPHY

65. Byzantine Philosophy.—Banished from Athens in 529 by the decree of Justinian, Greek philosophy found a home in the capital of the Eastern Empire during the whole of the Middle Ages.   But the work of this Byzantine philosophy was not very fruitful ; its character was chiefly encyclopedic and its representatives borrowed from Plato (such as Arethas in the tenth, Michael Psellus in the eleventh century) or from Aristotle (such as Photius in the ninth, Joannes Italus in the eleventh century), and it had no marked individuality of its own.

The Greek schism (858), the source of endless misunderstandings, separated the East from the West, and the contact between the two civilizations during this period was merely superficial, until the crusades and the taking of Constantinople in 1204 put an end to the intellectual isolation of the East.

66. Philosophy among the Armenians, Persians and Syrians. —In Armenia, we meet the name of a celebrated translator of Aristotle, DAVID THE ARMENIAN (about 500 A.D.).

In Persia, the court of Chosroes Anoshervan gathered together the last representatives of the Greek philosophy, the Syrian DAMASCIUS, SIMPLICIUS, and a number of neo-Platonists driven from Athens, but the philosophical movement created by these Greek scholars was destined to be short-lived.

The Syrians had a direct inheritance of philosophical thought from Greece, and a number of translators (of the schools of Edessa, Resaïna and Chalcis) handed on to the Arabians, and indirectly to the Jews, various works of Aristotle, Porphyry, Galen, etc.

67. Philosophy among the Arabians and Jews.—The Arabians for three and a half centuries had a philosophy of their own, a blend of the philosophy of Aristotle, for whom they had an unbounded admiration, and neo-Platonic teachings.   Their theories about the emanation of the spheres and the extra-human existence of man's intelligence gave a specific colouring to their explanation of the universe. Most of the Arabian philosophers were concerned chiefly in harmonizing philosophy with Mussulman dogma.

ALKINDI († about 873), ALFARABI [60] († 950), and above all AVICENNA [61] (Ibn Sina, 980-1036), are the chief representatives of those who have a claim to be called Oriental philosophers. The *procession* of the spheres as understood by Avicenna tends to give a monistic signification to his philosophy, and he makes the active intellect the last to be formed in the series of generations ; yet he counterbalanced these pantheistic tendencies by a psychology that is individualistic and he distinctly taught a personal immortality.

In the West, the name of AVERROËS [62] (Ibn Roshd, 1126-1198) eclipsed all others. His admiration of Aristotle amounted almost to worship. The intelligence of the spheres, the eternity and potentiality of matter, the monism of the human intellect (both active and passive) and the denial of personal immortality, are the chief characteristics of his teaching. He made his philosophy accord with the Koran by giving an allegorical interpretation of its texts.

Jewish philosophy developed chiefly under the influence of the Arabians. The most notable personality was AVICEBRON (Ibn Gebirol, about 1020-1070), the author of a treatise *Fons Vitae*, greatly valued by the Scholastics of the thirteenth century, in which he expounds a system of pantheistic emanations inspired by neo-Platonism. From God the One and supreme Being, who is the source of all reality, a cosmic spirit composed of matter and form is derived ; from the unchangeable generative power of these two principles of matter and form there spring, by a series of intermediaries, all the beings of the universe, each having in itself, besides the common cosmic matter and form, its own derived matter and form, and these are the constituents of the specific perfection of each individual thing. With the name of Avicebron we may associate that of MOSES MAIMONIDES [63] (1135-1204), the last great representative of Jewish philosophy.

[60] Commentaries on the Posterior Analytics ; *De ortu scientiarum, De intellectu et intelligibili.*
[61] *Shifâ* (called by the Scholastics *Sufficientiae*), Metaphysics, *Najât*, Book of Theorems, Guide to Wisdom.
[62] *Destructio destructionis, Quaesita in libros logicae Aristotelis, de substantia orbis.*
[63] *Guide of the Doubting.*

CHAPTER II

MEDIAEVAL PHILOSOPHY IN THE THIRTEENTH CENTURY

ART. I. GENERAL

68. General Survey.—The thirteenth century was the golden age of mediaeval philosophy and its greatest splendour was seen in the West. As in the preceding century, France held the hegemony in philosophy, as well as in art and literature. Towards the end of the twelfth century Western philosophy came into contact with the Arabian, Jewish and Byzantine philosophies and entirely to its own advantage. The historical part played by the Arabians concluded ; the Jewish writers, such as Samuel Ben Tibbon [64], Falaquera, Gerson Ben Salomon [65], were content to repeat Averroës ; whilst the Byzantine genius lay dormant until the Renaissance and produced only compilations (Nicephorus Blemmides and George Pachymeres).

In the West Scholasticism did not triumph without a struggle ; it had to battle against powerful rival theories. This chapter will deal with (1) Scholastic philosophy (Art. II) ; (2) non-Scholastic philosophies (Art. III) ; (3) some minor philosophical currents (Art. IV). First, a word about the scientific and philosophical renaissance of the thirteenth century.

69. Causes of this Renaissance.—This rapid and wide-spread movement which appeared with such brilliance in the first years of the thirteenth century in the West may be attributed to three causes :—

1. The introduction into the West, through the medium of Latin translations from the Greek or from the Arabic and Hebrew, of a great number of philosophical works, notably the most important treatises of Aristotle (Physics, Metaphysics and the treatise on the Soul), the Greek scientific works, the

---

[64] *The Opinions of Philosophers.*
[65] *Gate of the Heavens.*

philosophical treatises of Avicenna, Averroës, Avicebron and a number of pseudo-Aristotelian productions, apocryphal but evidently of Alexandrine origin. The translations made directly from the Greek are the most perfect. Robert Grosseteste, Henry of Brabant, Bartholomew of Messina and especially William de Moerbeke († 1286), among many other translators, deserve special mention. The translations made from the Arabic or Hebrew are much less trustworthy. The bulk of them were the work of a celebrated college of translators, organized by Raymond, Archbishop of Toledo (1126-1151), the best known amongst them being DOMINICUS GUNDISSALINUS or GUNDISALVI. Gerard of Cremona and, later, Michael Scot and Herman the German should also be mentioned.

2. The creation of the universities, particularly those of Paris, Oxford and Cambridge, which gave philosophical studies the place of honour [66]. Though at the beginning of the thirteenth century the writings of Aristotle were several times prohibited by ecclesiastical authority, little by little these censures came to be overlooked and from 1255 the faculty of arts admitted Aristotle into the course of teaching. Thus in this faculty the scholar studied philosophy, and after being progressively *baccalaureatus*, *licentiatus* and *magister*, proceeded to his course in the faculty of theology.

3. The foundation of the two great Mendicant Orders, the Dominicans and the Franciscans, which compelled their members to study the sciences and established themselves at the universities. The prominent philosophers of the thirteenth century belonged to these religious bodies. Following the lead given by the Dominicans and Franciscans, and perhaps to counterbalance their influence, great colleges were shortly afterwards established for the secular clergy, the most celebrated of which was the Sorbonne in Paris (1253).

ART. II. SCHOLASTIC PHILOSOPHIES

I. GENERAL VIEW

70. General Characteristics and Division.—Scholastic philosophy, which was gradually built up by the collaboration of thinkers in various countries, reached its culmination in the

---

[66] See RASHDALL, *Universities of Europe in the Middle Ages* (Oxford, 1895) ; DRANE, *Christian Schools and Scholars* (London, 2nd ed., 1881).

thirteenth century. Dealing in its wide purview with all the problems which fall within the scope of a complete philosophy, it gave to each one its own solution whilst reducing it into the harmony of a complete synthesis. The teachings which formed an organic part of the whole system were generally accepted, but the individual personality of each philosopher was at the same time strongly marked. Scholasticism was thus systematized in many signal forms according as the several exponents were guided by their own genius in putting into concrete form the abstract, common synthesis. These systems of the thirteenth century may be classified into different groups which succeed one another both in order of time and logical sequence.

1. *The older Scholasticism of the thirteenth century, embracing the pre-Thomistic systems.*—The first Scholastics of the thirteenth century, while accepting the structural ideas of the Peripatetic system handed down in the translations of Aristotle, held a large number of the doctrines inherited from their predecessors, even though several of them were incompatible with Peripateticism : for example, the pre-eminence of the good over the true and, analogously, of the will over the intellect ; the necessity of an immediate action on the part of God giving light for the accomplishment of certain mental activities ; the positive actuality of primary matter, independently of any substantial form ; the doctrine of ' rationes seminales ' in bodies ; the hylomorphic composition of spiritual substances ; the plurality of forms in organic beings ; the identity of the soul and its faculties ; the impossibility of the creation of the world *ab aeterno*. Consequently we find in their systems a certain number of doctrinal incoherences.

The body of doctrines irreconcilable with Peripateticism has been known as *Augustinianism*, and the group of philosophers who held to them known as the Augustinian party of Scholasticism in contradistinction to the Peripatetic party. There is no doubt that several of these teachings did come from an Augustinian source, e.g. the theory of ' rationes seminales ' ; yet since many others, e.g. plurality of forms, special illumination of the mind, are alien or even opposed to the philosophy of St. Augustine, we prefer the wider designation of ' the older Scholastic school ' to that of ' the Augustinian school '. However, we must notice, the weakening and discordant elements of these systems became less as time went on, and the great Scholastics steadily eliminated from their teaching all inconsistent opinions.

2. *The Peripateticism of the Albertino-Thomistic School.*—A new movement, more frankly Peripatetic in character, was introduced by the philosophy of Albert the Great. This St. Thomas developed into a fixed and magnificent form, at the same time overthrowing many of the theories hitherto held in honour in the schools.

3. *Conflict of Thomism with the older Scholasticism.*—Thomism at once necessarily encountered the opposition of the older Scholasticism, for it rejected many of the current promiscuous theories as inconsistent with its own principles. The struggle issued in the formation of three groups : the irreconcilable opponents of Thomism, the loyal and whole-hearted supporters of Thomism, and finally a group of eclectic thinkers, Thomists on some points, adherents of traditional views on others, themselves innovators in various ways.

4. *The Peripateticism of Duns Scotus and the Franciscan School.*—Duns Scotus, in the last years of the thirteenth century, formulated a system of philosophy which was founded on Peripateticism, yet deviated both from St. Thomas's thought and from the lines of the older Scholasticism.

5. *A group of logicians and grammarians.*

71. The Scholastic Synthesis.—Above all the matters of disagreement among the multitude of Scholastic doctors of the thirteenth century there was a common tone of mind, shared in varying degrees by all alike, and there reigned a tacit agreement about a number of the cardinal doctrines ; the *sum-total* of these we call the Scholastic synthesis, which we have already spoken of in its abstract character and its gradual formation. This synthesis reached its full expression in the thirteenth century. It will suffice here to outline its principal doctrines.

Human knowledge is now systematized in all its stages, the particular sciences as the foundation, theology at the summit, philosophy holding an intermediate place. The distinction between philosophy and theology, which we have already spoken of, involves their mutual independence and the autonomy of the elements proper to each ; yet this recognized distinction still allows the subordination of philosophy to theology. The philosophical sciences still follow the Aristotelian classification. The Stagirite is still regarded as the undisputed master of logic, and the special favour with which logic is regarded in the thirteenth century explains how dialectic pervades the study of the science of grammar which henceforth becomes speculative in character.

Metaphysics is given the place of honour in the Scholastic curriculum. Eminently deductive, it studies not only the substance of sensible beings, but being as such, investigating it at once in its static reality and in its becoming. The theory of the actual and the potential occupies a central position, closely connected with which are the questions of the composition of substance and accidents, of matter and form, of universal and individual, of essence and existence ; the individual alone exists, and the universal character of the mental concept is due to the action of the mind.

The science of natural theology is closely associated with metaphysics. Reason proves the existence of God from the imperfection of being as manifested in the contingent world of things. God is pure actuality, and the absolute subordination of the finite to the Infinite is made clear by the theories of exemplarism, creation and providence.

Physics investigates the movement or change of bodies and its divisions. The appearance and disappearance of substances are explained by their composition of matter (indeterminate element) amd form (determining element) ; a rhythmic evolution governs the becoming of forms and directs the cosmos towards a final end, known by God, which is none other than His external glory. The world is neither infinite nor eternal, and God was able to create the universe more perfect than it is.

Psychology is regarded as a subdivision of physics. Man, composed of body (matter) and soul (form), excels all other beings by his privilege of the possession of the higher activities of intellect and will. His knowledge of extra-mental reality is sensible or intellectual, for man knows not only the concrete and individual by means of his senses (*this* oak) but also the abstract and universal by means of his intellect (*the* oak). All our abstract ideas have their origin in the sensible—' nihil est in intellectu quod prius non fuerit in sensu '—but we possess besides our faculty of understanding (passive intellect) a faculty of abstracting (active intellect) by the power of which a sensible object (*this* oak) engenders a representation (e.g. height, life, etc.), the content of which is stripped of all the individual and concrete determinations that are found in the existing real thing. This character of the idea constitutes its immateriality and serves as the chief argument for the survival and immortality of the soul.

The act of will follows upon that of the intellect—' nihil volitum nisi praecognitum '—and appetition is sentient or intellectual according as it follows sensation or thought. Rational appetition is, under certain conditions, free and this freedom makes man master of his destiny. Indeed, like every natural being we have an end, namely, our true good, which we are morally obliged to strive after, although it is in our power to turn from it.

Man's natural happiness must be the result of the full development of his higher activities—knowledge and will ; it was God's design that man should know and love Him in His works through the possession of a perfect knowledge of sensible nature and its forces ; but this possibility has not been realized ; the Creator has designed to elevate man's nature by grace and therefore will replace the happiness, which would have resulted from the work of abstraction, by a direct intuition of the divine Essence. Thus moral philosophy is regarded in the thirteenth century as the avenue to moral theology, though still distinct from it.

The doctrines we have briefly sketched are only an abstract epitome, a skeleton, as it were, which was clothed with flesh and life by each concrete system, yet they portray the essential features of a conception of the world which was peculiar to the Middle Ages.

Descriptive definition of Scholasticism.—First of all Scholasticism is a *pluralistic* philosophy, not a monistic system. The substantial distinction between God, who is pure Actuality, and creatures, which are a composition of actuality and potentiality, makes it the uncompromising enemy of pantheism. We cannot emphasize too much the great care the Scholastics took to eradicate every pantheistic tendency from the tenets borrowed from the Arabian philosophers. The composition of matter and form, of the individual and the universal, the substantial distinction between the subject knowing and the object known, between the beatified soul and God who satiates all its faculties, are so many Scholastic teachings absolutely incompatible with monism and are rather express declarations of individualism ; of an individualism which came into direct conflict with the monopsychism of Averroës, especially on account of the many lines of argument the Scholastics used for establishing man's sovereignty in the cosmos. In metaphysics the Scholastics professed the doctrine of *substance*, which is very far removed from exaggerated relativism, since each being is itself, distinct from every other, and it is accidental to its nature that it be known by us. Their metaphysical standpoint as regards contingent being is a *moderate dynamism* (actuality and potency, matter and form, essence and existence), and this dynamism regulates the appearance and disappearance of natural substances. From another point of view they give the world of matter an *evolutionary* and *teleological* interpretation : but their evolutionism is only of a mitigated form and does not extend to the formation of specific essences ; the doctrine of innate purpose reconciles the immanent tendency of beings towards their ends with the providential government of God. Theodicy is *creationist* and *personalist ;* God is shown to be infinite, the first beginning and last end, the controller and judge of each, the principal efficient cause of all things, and notably the co-operator with man in his acts of thought. In psychology this telic conception explains the epistemological *optimism* of the Scholastics : man's intellect, since it was made for the truth, attains to the knowledge of things such as they are in themselves, though in an imperfect manner ; in fact it could not be otherwise when they regard his mind as a spark, as it were, from the unfailing light which is God. Sensations, too, are not less infallible, when they present before us their proper object. The whole Scholastic theory of ideas is *objectivist*, and if we turn from the critical point of view to the genetic point of view we see that it is *experimental* or empiricist, not innatist nor idealist. It is, above all, *spiritualist,* since the supersensible character of our intellectual representations is based on mental abstraction ; and again we observe their standpoint to be that of *moderate realism* inasmuch as it reconciles the individual nature of extra-mental beings with the universal nature of our concepts which correspond to them. The ideological spiritualism of the Scholastics is reflected in their theories of the nature of the soul and its origin and immortality, and in such matters as these they are absolutely opposed to materialistic philosophy. Their logic, based as it is on their psychological and metaphysical teachings, places great value upon the *analytico-synthetic* method. Their ethical philosophy is *libertarian*, and its optimism is expressed in their *eudaemonistic* tenet that the end of man is attained through the highest activities of his higher faculties.

All these characteristics are mutually complementary and are inseparably bound up with one another, for the doctrinal departments which they severally portray form one whole like the members of an organism. Few are the historical systems of philosophy which can claim to be such a studied endeavour to obtain harmony or make such a bid for *unity*, which indeed is the source of quietude to the human mind. To attain this, Scholasticism looked for the golden mean between extremes in all the problems it strove to solve ; and this *moderation* found its expression in their realism, their dynamism, their evolutionism, their ideology, their theory of the union of body and soul, of the compatibility between duty and happiness, and their conception, at once objective and subjective, of the beautiful.

If we can appreciate the fact that the Scholasticism of the thirteenth century took the central place in the evolution of ideas in the Middle Ages, that it unified, completed and consolidated the teachings handed down from previous centuries, that it was even the inspiration of the philosophy of succeeding centuries, and represents the zenith of the glory of mediaeval Scholasticism, we shall easily understand that this system deserves par excellence to bear the name of ' Scholasticism '.

II. THE OLDER SCHOLASTICISM

72. Its Precursors.—DOMINICUS GUNDISSALINUS, whom we have already mentioned, was an eclectic compiler [67] whose Aristotelianism, especially in metaphysics and psychology, was tainted with neo-Platonism. His classification of the sciences was the starting-point of a genuine onward movement alike

[67] *De divisione philosophiae, De immortalitate animae, De processione mundi, De unitate, De anima.*

didactic and scientific, and led to the more exact division of the branches of philosophical study such as we find it in Albert the Great and Thomas Aquinas.

WILLIAM OF AUVERGNE [68] († 1249) should be coupled with him as representing the elaboration of the new Peripatetic teachings ; but his work lacks cohesion. He accepted the theory of actuality and potentiality but made certain concessions to the emanation theory. He adhered to the Augustinian school of psychology ; he gave up the active intellect which he thought useless and had recourse to a special illumination of God for our knowledge of the principles of demonstration.

73. Alexander of Hales, a Franciscan († 1245), may be regarded as the first great Scholastic. His *Summa Theologica* was a synthesis at once theological and philosophical, which made use of nearly all the philosophical thought of Aristotle and the Arabians, yet was wanting in that unity and harmony of teaching which characterizes every really great work. In his metaphysics we find the two important theories known later as the Franciscan theories, namely the composition of matter and form of all contingent beings, even of spiritual substances (Avicebron), and the plurality of substantial forms. His psychology represents a vigorous but fruitless endeavour to harmonize the traditional doctrine of St. Augustine concerning human nature and its faculties with the definition of man as in Aristotle and the new theory of ideas which sprang from it.

JOHN DE LA ROCHELLE [69] (born about 1200) was the most renowned of the numerous disciples of Alexander of Hales, and was also in touch with ROBERT GROSSETESTE [70], the organizer of the Franciscan school at Oxford. The latter held an important place in the progress of thought owing to his translations, commentaries and numerous opuscula on physics, metaphysics and psychology.

74. St. Bonaventure (1221-1274) was the most brilliant representative of the older Franciscan school, taking his mastership in theology at the same time as his friend St. Thomas (1257), and afterwards becoming General of his Order and Cardinal. Whilst upholding the old traditional teachings of

---

[68] *De trinitate, De universo, De immortalitate animae, De anima.*
[69] *De anima.*
[70] See DE MARTIGNE, *La Scholastique et les traditions Franciscaines* (Paris, 1888) ; STEVENSON, *Robert Grosseteste, Bp. of Lincoln* (London, 1899).

St. Augustine and being in agreement with the leading thinkers of his time concerning many important Peripatetic theories, he gave them an interpretation of his own [71]. He held the two great metaphysical doctrines of Alexander of Hales and harmonized them more closely with the distinction between actuality and potentiality. His proofs of the existence of God have an Augustinian touch, but on some other points he was nearer to the mind of St. Thomas ; he upheld the theory of exemplarism without sharing the strange views of those who account for our synthetic knowledge of God by recourse to a special illumination of the mind. He held to the creation of the world *in tempore*, and explained its evolution by the theory of *rationes seminales*. His psychology is Aristotelian except that his views on the nature of man are coloured by the Franciscan tendencies of his metaphysics. St. Bonaventure was, in addition, one of the great lights of the school of contemplative mystics, and it is as such that he has been held in great veneration by posterity.

The influence of St. Bonaventure outlived him, and of his immediate successors MATTHEW OF AQUASPARTA [72] (1235 or 1240-1301), JOHN PECCHAM [73] and, later, RICHARD OF MIDDLE-TOWN [74] are the best known. As belonging to the old Scholastic tendency of thought we may add the names of the first Masters of the Dominican school, notably ROBERT KILWARDBY [75] Archbishop of Canterbury, and PETER OF TARANTAISE [76]. And finally to this same intellectual tendency belongs the Franciscan PETER JOHN OLIVI [77], whose doctrines were condemned at the Council of Vienne in 1311, when it drew up the well-known definition of the union of soul and body 'anima rationalis seu intellectiva est forma corporis humani per se et essentialiter'.

---

[71] *Commentarii in IV lib. sententiarum P. Lombardi ; Quaestiones disputatae* (especially *De paupertate*) ; *Breviloquium ; Itinerarium mentis ac Deum ; De reductione artium ad theologiam.*

[72] Commentaries on the Sentences ; *Quodlibet, Quaestiones disputatae.*

[73] *Quodlibet, Quaestiones disputatae.*

[74] *Quodlibet, Quaestiones disputatae.*

[75] *De ortu et divisione philosophiae.*

[76] *De unitate formae, De materia caeli, De aeternitate mundi, De intellectu et voluntate.*

[77] *Quodlibet.*

III. The Peripateticism of Albert the Great and St. Thomas

The Dominican Scholasticism, inaugurated by Albert of Bollstädt and definitely constituted by Thomas Aquinas, ushered much that was new into the teaching of the Friars Preachers and in general into the schools of the thirteenth century, the master and his disciple collaborating in many respects. It differed from all systems hitherto in vogue by its more thoroughly Peripatetic basis and by its superior doctrinal consistency. Its chief inspiration came no longer from St. Augustine, still less from Plotinus, but from Aristotle. As the result of St. Thomas's labour, Mediaeval Europe came into possession of one of its finest monuments of constructive speculative thought.

75. Albert the Great (about 1193-1280).—After a long career consecrated to teaching, principally at Cologne where St. Thomas was among his pupils, Albert became Provincial of the Dominicans in Germany and later Bishop of Ratisbon. The favour with which Aristotle was received in the West was due chiefly to him, and he was held in renown not only for his prodigious erudition [78] but also as one of the most remarkable men of science of his age. ' Albert's claim to renown lies less in the construction of an original system of philosophy than in the genius and industry he showed in bringing within reach of the mediaeval world of letters all the previously acquired treasures of human knowledge, in starting a new and vigorous and fertile intellectual movement in his lifetime, and in winning over to Aristotle the best intellects of the Middle Ages ' [79]. Whilst Albert continued to hold many of the theories of the older Scholasticism, at the same time he accepted some

---

[78] Paraphrases : *De praedicabilibus, De praedicamentis, De sex principiis, Perihermenias, Analytica, Topica, Libri elenchorum ; Physica, De caelo et mundo, De natura locorum, De proprietatibus elementorum, De generatione et corruptione, De meteoris, De mineralibus, De anima, De sensu et sensato, De memoria et reminiscentia, De intellectu et intelligibili, De somno et vigilia, De spiritu et respiratione, De motibus animalium, De morte et vita, De vegetabilibus, De animalibus ; Metaphysica ; Ethica, politica.*—More original treatises: *De unitate intellectus contra Averroïstas, quindecim problemata contra Averroïstas, De causis de processu universitatis ; Summa philosophiae naturalis,* or *Philosophia pauperum ; Summa Theologiae, Summa de creaturis ;* Commentaries on the Sentences of Peter Lombard.

[79] Mandonnet, *Dict. Théol.,* I, col. 672.

neo-Platonic (Arabian) and Aristotelian doctrines, yet without successfully creating a complete fusion of these disparate elements. If we except St. Thomas Aquinas, the most notable of his disciples was ULRIC OF STRASSBURG [80].

76. St. Thomas Aquinas (1225/27-1274), the prince alike of Scholastic philosophy and theology [81], entered the Dominican Order in 1243 and in 1258 began his public teaching at Paris, having taken his mastership in theology in 1257. He went to Italy in 1260, and then returned in 1268 or 1269 to Paris, which he left finally in 1272. He died at the age of forty-eight, on his way to Lyons, whither Gregory X had summoned him to assist by his great talents at the work of the General Council.

His brilliant talent for exposition that drew round his chair crowds of seculars and regulars alike is particularly apparent in his larger works. His language is always clear and simple, and rigidly precise ; his method systematic and free from glosses and digressions ; his explanations are short and to the point ; minor considerations receive only the attention they deserve, so that his thought can travel straight and steadfastly towards its end, and to this end he makes everything else converge.

The essential tenets of St. Thomas's synthesis have been treated in their proper place in the course of the Manual of Philosophy, and it would therefore be superfluous to repeat them here.

The most noteworthy feature of the Thomistic synthesis consists in the harmony and unification of the several doctrines,

---

[80] *De Summo bono ; Summa theologica.*

[81] *Summa theologica ; Summa philosophica contra Gentiles ; Quaestiones disputatae, Quodlibeta ;* Commentaries on several Aristotelian treatises : *De interpretatione, Analyt. poster., Physic., De caelo et mundo, De Generat. et corrupt., Meteorum, De anima, Parva naturalia, Metaphysic., Ethic., Politic. ;* Commentaries on the Book of Causes, on the Four Books of Sentences, on Boëthius *De hebdomadibus* and *De Trinitate ;* Opuscula : *De ente et essentia, De aeternitate mundi, De substantiis separatis, De spiritual. creaturis, De unitate intellectus contra Averroïstas, De principio naturae, De motu cordis, De mixtione elementorum, De natura materiae, De principio individuationis ; De regimine principum.*

See VAUGHAN, *Life and Labours of S. Thomas of Aquin.* (The original work in 2 vols., Longmans, London, 1871 ; or in abridged form, Burns & Oates, London, 1890, and Catholic Publication Society, New York.) Also Life of S. Thomas, by Père Sertillanges in the series Les Grands Philosophes ; also *La philosophie morale de Saint Thomas d'Aquin* (Paris, 1916).

in the masterly co-ordination of the dominant ideas, in the complete correlation of all the parts. What we may call scholasticity is here more fully realized than in any other philosophical system ; and this is precisely the reason why Thomism is one of the most signal products of mediaeval thought. This solidarity of doctrine is secured by a deep understanding of the common fundamental theories of Scholasticism and their fusion with new elements calculated to strengthen the cohesion of the system. By introducing these new theories St. Thomas breaks with the tradition of the old Scholasticism : he emphasizes the close relations of philosophy and theology ; he combats plurality of forms by unity of the substantial principle ; to the hylomorphic composition of spiritual substances he opposes the doctrine of subsisting forms and the Peripatetic conception of matter ; for the theory of *rationes seminales* he substitutes the passive evolution of matter ; against St. Augustine's theory of the identity of the substance of the soul with its faculties he advocates that of their real distinction, and against his voluntarism an intellectualist conception of the psychic life. And we might mention many other questions as well. He is bold and thorough in his innovations, sure of his ground, fearless to follow to logical consequences no matter whither they may lead. In this he rises above both Albert his master and Bonaventure his friend. At the same time he is moderate and tolerant, and in his scientific relations with others he never tries to propagate his views by sharp and imperious controversy but always by calm persuasion ; such adversaries as Peccham bear testimony to his pacific and dignified bearing in the midst of the most ardent controversies. Although personal in his choice of new doctrines and eclectic in his details and illustrations, the genius of the Angelic Doctor is most akin to that of Aristotle. But so far is he from following the Averroïsts in their servile abdication of personal thought that he proclaims the argument from human authority to be the last and weakest of all arguments (locus ab auctoritate . . . est infirmissimus). He enlarged the scope of the Peripatetic tradition and developed its teachings in the direction of a very pronounced individualism. In fine, he succeeded in welding the main tenets of Aristotelianism and the most important doctrines given to us by St. Augustine.

IV. THE CONFLICT BETWEEN THOMISM AND THE OLDER
SCHOLASTICISM

77. Adversaries and Supporters of Thomism.—The innovations introduced by St. Thomas aroused a strong opposition on the part of the masters brought up in the older
Scholasticism, and in particular his teaching on the unity of
substantial form occasioned a violent storm of tracts. The
Correptorium Fratris Thomae of WILLIAM DE LA MARE is a
veritable manifesto against Thomism. This opposition culminated in official censures, notably those of the year 1277.
For at Paris (March 7) STEPHEN TEMPLIER condemned his theory
of individuation along with the principal errors of the Averroïsts, thus associating by an unworthy manœuvre the name of
St. Thomas with his adversary Siger of Brabant in a common
condemnation. And at Oxford (March 18) Robert Kilwardby
and then John Peccham (in 1284), both Archbishops of Canterbury, used their influence to urge the masters to censure a
number of his teachings.

This uncompromising opposition called forth numerous and
resolute advocates of St. Thomas's cause ; notably from 1278
the whole Dominican Order espoused the Thomistic philosophy.
In the same year GILES OF LESSINES wrote a treatise entitled
De unitate Formae to defend him against the attacks of Kilwardby and the Oxford masters. The prohibitions of his
teachings gradually failed in their force or were withdrawn, and
the prestige of Thomism steadily grew, until by the close of the
thirteenth century Aquinas was honoured with the title of
Doctor Communis.

78. Eclectics of Paris University.—During the years from the
death of St. Thomas to the commencement of the teaching of
Duns Scotus many of the masters of the University of Paris,
notably Henry of Ghent [82] (died 1293), Godfrey of Fontaines [83]
(died after 1303) and Giles of Rome [84] (died 1316), were
eclectic philosophers. Of these, the one most in sympathy
with Thomism was GODFREY OF FONTAINES, who emphasized
intellectualism, even more than St. Thomas, but parted

---

[82] *Summa theologica ; Quodlibet.* See DE WULF, *Etudes sur Henri de Gand*
(Louvain, 1894).
[83] *Quodlibeta.*
[84] *Quodlibeta, De ente et essentia, De regimine principum, De partibus
philosophiae essentialibus.*

company with him on the question of the distinction between essence and existence, although he did not subscribe to any of the Augustinian theories. The most original was HENRY OF GHENT, who maintained that in man the body itself has a form besides the spiritual soul, though in all other substances he held to the unity of form as did St. Thomas ; that certain truths are known by divine illumination ; that essence and existence are not really distinct ; and that the will is the sovereign faculty in the life of the soul. GILES OF ROME professes an eclectic Thomism ; his attachment to certain Augustinian theses disfigures his teaching with doubts and inconsistencies.

V. JOHN DUNS SCOTUS

79. John Duns Scotus [85] (1266 or 1274-1308), a native of the British Isles and a professor at Oxford (1294), at Paris (1304) and at Cologne (1308), became the leader of a powerful school and traced out a new line of thought in which for some centuries the whole Franciscan Order became entangled. He brought into fashion a Peripateticism that was *sui generis ;* his personal genius gave an original stamp even to the earlier Scholastic theories which survived in his philosophy.

Endowed with a very great critical acumen, Scotus employed his power in demolishing other systems. The positive, constructive side of his philosophy is less developed than the negative, critical side. He laid extreme emphasis on the distinction between theology and philosophy. Taking from Avicebron, to whom he openly appealed, a theory which his predecessors attributed to St. Augustine, he considered every created being to be composed of matter and form ; and matter, as the common indeterminate element of contingent beings (*materia primo prima*), to be endowed with a real unity though not numerically one, since every being has its own matter (against Avicebron). He also admitted a plurality of forms in the same being : of forms, that is to say, subordinated to one another, constituting one and the same thing, but according to irreducible ' formalities ', which differ by a *distinctio formalis a parte rei*—a distinction that is neither simply logical nor real but partly both. This celebrated distinction of Scotus points,

---

[85] Commentaries on Aristotle, *Opus Oxoniense, De rerum prinoipio, Theoremata, Reportata Parisiensia, Quodlibet.*

in one and the same individual substance, to the objective forms or formalities that are realized in it, and really in it, independently of any act of the mind [86].   In real nature the individual alone appears or disappears, and in it the formalities are united in such a way that the one constitutes a *unity of individuation* together with all the others, ' in the same way that the specific form of white thing is only one with the nature of colour '. This ' formal distinction in the object itself ' he introduces also into his natural theology.   In psychology he admits in addition to our abstract and universal knowledge of things an antecedent, intuitive knowledge which reveals to us in a confused manner the concrete, singular being ; he asserts the superiority of the will over the intellect.   He considers that there is in man, besides his intellective soul, a *forma corporeitatis* which gives the body its organic perfection ; and regards it as impossible to demonstrate the immortality of the soul by the Peripatetic arguments.

The characteristic and original element in the philosophy of Duns Scotus, and the key for the understanding of his system, is its ' formalism ', which colours his Peripatetic teachings and impregnates his whole system.   By it he took up a position not only against St. Thomas but also against the representatives of the older Franciscan school.   The metaphysic of Scotus is mainly a subtle analysis of the individual being, and the position he takes with regard to the plurality of objective principles or realities is an endeavour to interpret what is real in the singular being.   Despite certain differences, Scotus and Aquinas are much allied in thought in this and also in many other questions concerning which the divergency of teachings in these two princes of mediaeval Scholasticism has hitherto been much exaggerated.

VI. LOGICIANS AND GRAMMARIANS

80. Petrus Hispanus and the Speculative Grammarians.— A number of philosophers of the thirteenth century devoted their attention to *logic*, which occupied a place outside the arena of the great controversies.   The most celebrated of these was PETRUS HISPANUS.   This curious invasion of grammar by logic

[86] Cp. *Opus Oxon.*, I, 81 ; I, 170.

is worthy of notice. Towards the end of the century it produced at Paris real philosophies of language. Some of the speculative grammarians like Siger of Courtrai and Michael of Morbaix went beyond reason, but the treatise entitled *Grammatica Speculativa* of Duns Scotus and others of the kind are certainly achievements not to be passed without notice.

ART. III.   NON-SCHOLASTIC PHILOSOPHERS

81. Latin Averroism.—The most complete and important system in the thirteenth century opposed to Scholastic philosophy was Averroïsm. Those who thought that they could find the true mind of Aristotle in the commentaries of the Arabian philosopher defended a group of doctrines that were distinctly anti-Scholastic. The chief of these were as follows : (1) The unity of the human intellect and monopsychism : a doctrine incompatible with the Scholastic theory of ideas, of the intrinsic union of body and soul, and of personality. (2) The denial of personal immortality. (3) The production of the world by a series of intermediary beings and, consequently, the denial of divine Providence in the government of men and things ; for the first cause, being immaterial and simple, can produce immediately only a single being, an intelligence, and this produces another, and so on. The world of sense is the product of the last celestial intelligence ; wherefore God has no concern for a world that is not immediately dependent on Him. These theories are destructive of the Scholastic doctrine of creation, providence, the preservation of things in being, the concurrence of the first cause with the action of secondary causes. (4) All these productions are necessary and co-eternal with God. This is a denial of the contingent nature of the world and also of the freedom of the creative act of God. (5) A cosmic and psychological determinism, and denial of moral responsibility. For the phenomena of the heavens and the conjunctions of the planets govern the events that succeed one another on the earth and the destinies of the human race ; there is an endless repetition of civilizations and religions, including the Christian religion, governed by the recurrence of the stellar cycles. This psychological determinism overthrows the ethical system of Scholasticism. (6) The theory of ' the

two truths ', by which they divorced reason from faith, asserting that what is true in philosophy may be false in theology, and
vice versa. This theory is tantamount to a denial of the
principle of contradiction, as well as of the Scholastic view of the
mutual relations of philosophy and theology ; the Averroïsts
introduced it in order to make their philosophy accord with the
Catholic faith which they held.

82. Siger of Brabant († before 1300) was the leader of the
Latin Averroïsm about 1270, and was followed by Boëthius
the Dacian and Bernier of Nivelles and several masters of the
faculty of arts at Paris. The soul of the agitations in the
schools and a brilliant pleader of the cause of Averroïsm [87],
he directed his attacks ' contra praecipuos viros in philosophia
Albertum et Thomam '. The rivalry between the two pro-
tagonists is conspicuous in Aquinas's *De Unitate Intellectus* and
Siger's *De Anima Intellectiva*. The latter's philosophy was not
merely anti-Thomistic but anti-Scholastic ; and both aca-
demic and ecclesiastical authority was moved by the progress of
Averroïsm so that it was condemned in 1270 and 1277, and all
the Scholastics bestirred themselves to refute it. Nevertheless
it survived the thirteenth century, and we shall find its re-
appearance later.

ART. IV. MINOR PHILOSOPHICAL CURRENTS

83. Neo-Platonic Direction.—The philosophers who represent
this current of ideas admit the doctrines of the earlier Scholasticism into their conception of the world as well as Thomistic and
Aristotelian elements, but all alike were moulded in a neo-
Platonic setting and made to harmonize more or less with
certain Alexandrian theories. Yet there is a great difference,
as we have already said, between the ancient neo-Platonism
and that of mediaeval times : the monist theory, which is the
essence of Proclus's writings, is not only absent from, but
expressly combated in, the works of the thirteenth century neo-
Platonists ; hence we may not regard their philosophy as
positively opposed to individualism. The Dominican THEO-
DERIC OF FREIBURG, a master at Paris about 1297, has left a
series of works [88] which reveal him as both scientist and

---

[87] *De anima intellectiva, De aeternitate mundi, Quaestiones naturales.*
[88] *De luce et ejus origine, De intelligentiis et motoribis caelorum, De cognitione
entium separatorum.*

philosopher. Whilst vigorously defending the teachings newly introduced by Thomism, he systematizes all in a neo-Platonic sense, the setting of which he takes from Proclus : beings are produced by intermediaries ; in our soul all is activity and its principle is the *intellectus agens*, produced by God, multiplied in individual men (against Averroës), knowing in God, its producer, the reasons of all things (divine illumination). Further, we find neo-Platonic theories, given in the mode of the Schoolmen, in a Silesian philosopher of the middle of the twelfth century, named WITELO, the author of some remarkable books on optics [89], and most probably also of a treatise *De Intelligentiis*.

84. Experimental Direction ; Roger Bacon.—This celebrated Franciscan (about 1210/15-1292/94), who devoted his life to study and is remarkable for the boldness of expression displayed in his writings [90], belongs in his general philosophical outlook to the earlier Scholasticism, but by pushing certain traditional doctrines to extremes and by introducing some fundamental ideas of his own he built up a system *sui generis*. When we bear in mind that he knew the experimental sciences better and was a more acute observer of natural phenomena than any of his contemporaries, and that he brought about a real appreciation of the method of observation, we shall understand that he was one of the best known personalities of the thirteenth century.

From the essential unity of all knowledge and the essential primacy of theology, Bacon infers that both philosophy and the sciences have no other place or scope but that of explaining what is contained in sacred Scripture. Moreover, he introduced what is a veritable *traditionalism :* God alone can have taught men to philosophize, by revealing the truth to them, and it is God who is the only *intellectus agens* of our souls, illuminating them with His truth. This illumination, the idea of which he borrowed from the older Scholasticism, he regarded as one of the forms of ' internal experience '. But by endowing each individual with a proper *intellectus possibilis* of his own—a theory similar in general to that of a fellow English Franciscan, Roger Marston—he took care to free his philosophy from the

---

[89] *Perspectiva.*
[90] *Opus majus, Opus minus, Opus tertium, Communia naturalium, Compendium studii philosophiae, De multiplicatione specierum.* See *Roger Bacon : Commemorative Essays,* ed. Little (Clarendon Press, Oxford, 1914) ; FLEMING, *Ruggero Bacone e la Scolastica* (reprint from *Rivista di Filosofia Neoscolastica,* Firenze, Florence, 1914).

charge of Averroïsm ; yet on the other hand intellectual, as well as sensible, cognition is *intuitive*, for the universal elements existing in individual extra-mental objects produce directly in our minds universal determinations (*species*). No other philosopher of the thirteenth century dared to approve of this return to the old realism.

Bacon aimed at originality, and his mentality is profoundly different from that of the other Schoolmen, for his intuitionism, his solution of the question of universals, his theory of the active intellect, and his traditionalism, coloured his Scholasticism with a character entirely personal. He reduced philosophy to an apologetic, and in spite of his professed respect for Aristotle, he never imbibed the true spirit of his philosophy or assimilated any of its fundamental tenets. In spite of all that has been written in his favour, we must recognize that both the philosophy and the theology of Bacon lagged behind the intellectual movement of his time.

With the scientific works of Roger Bacon may be grouped those of Peter of Maricourt, of Henry Bate, and of the aforesaid English Franciscan Roger Marston, whose work presents many similarities.

85. Raymond Lully [91] (1235-1315), another Franciscan, elaborated a system of theosophy in which, the better to refute the Averroïst theory of the ' two truths ', he maintained that the whole content of faith being rational, reason can and should *demonstrate* everything, even the mysteries of religion. The other original element in his philosophical work is the planning of the *Ars Magna :* to the analytic method which sets out from sensible observation and rises to a knowledge of the supersensible world (*ascensus*), he wished to add as the complement to knowledge a synthetic method (*descensus*) ; by combining all these deductions one would then have a foundation for the solution of any question whatsoever. The *Ars Magna* was intended not only to aid the memory but also to yield new positive knowledge ; in this it differs essentially from the analytico-synthetic method of Scholasticism, which *guides* us in the pursuit of knowledge but makes no pretensions to *create* knowledge.

---

[91] *Declaratio per modum dialogi contra aliquorum philosophorum et eorum sequacium opiniones ; Ars magna.*

MEDIAEVAL PHILOSOPHY DURING THE FOURTEENTH AND FIRST HALF OF THE FIFTEENTH CENTURY

86. General Outline.—Byzantine philosophy throughout the fourteenth century and until in the fall of the Greek Empire in 1453 settled down into a lethargic condition. Devoid of all originality, it went on commentating the two great philosophers who furnished it with all its inspirations. The principal writers were GREGORY PALAMAS [92] (about 1347), NICEPHORUS GREGORAS, the Emperor JOHN VI CANTACUZENUS and NICHOLAS CABASILAS [93]. The Jews living in the south of France continued their work of translating Averroës from Hebrew to Latin, notably LEVI BEN GERSON (born about 1288).

It is in the Western philosophy that progress of thought continued to be conspicuous. As in the former period we may examine in turn : Scholasticism (I) ; Non-Scholastic systems (II) ; some secondary lines of philosophical thought (III).

I. THE SCHOLASTIC PHILOSOPHY

87. Decline of Scholastic Philosophy.—The period of decline followed closely on that of its greatest glory. Several causes combined to undermine its influence : (1) The incompetence of the Schoolmen of these times, who lacked originality, departed from or did not understand the synthesis they had inherited, abused methods of teaching and technical language, and did nothing to check the growth of an excessive attention to dialectic. It was the age of compendiums ; schools multiplied in number, but they were deficient in original thinkers. (2) The decay of the spirit of study both in the universities and in the religious orders. At Paris the course was shortened and every

---

[92] Προσωποποιία.
[93] A refutation of the *Hypotyposes Pyrrhonienses*.

facility granted for taking degrees. The rise of other universities dissipated the current of philosophic thought so that Scholasticism, whose development was intimately bound up with that of the university of Paris, was involved in its fall. (3) The gradual encroachment of new systems which assumed an aggressive attitude towards the philosophy of the Schoolmen.

At the beginning of the fourteenth century the Thomist and Scotist schools monopolized attention, but a third school was soon to rival both—the Terminist School.

88. The Terminist School ; William of Ockham.—As a reaction against the excessive formalism of the Scotists, this new philosophy aimed at complete simplification, and treating all metaphysical speculations as useless, it devoted its particular attention to logical problems and exaggerated the importance of dialectic ; and by considerably limiting the number of truths considered as capable of demonstration by reason, it came dangerously near to scepticism.

WILLIAM OF OCKHAM, a conspicuous figure at Paris about 1320, was the real founder [94] of the terminist school, although the way for this new theory was prepared by Durandus of St. Pourcain and Petrus Aureolus. Faithful to the spirit of Duns Scotus, Ockham made philosophy and theology departments of study quite separate from one another, regarding a number of questions hitherto considered as belonging to both (e.g. the existence of God) as the exclusive province of the latter. He denied the distinction between the universal and the individual ; the latter alone, he said, exists, and the universal is a purely mental form to which no reality whatever corresponds in nature. The mind elaborates abstract concepts but these have no *real* value outside us ; the universal merely holds the place (supponere), in the mind, of the multitude of things to which we attribute it ; this is conceptualism. Yet the mind has an intuitive knowledge of things existing apart from us, and this direct concept, as in the case of the sensation, puts us in touch with the extra-mental world. Every cognitive representation is a sign or *term* (terminism) which, as such, takes the place of the object signified. All willing, even spontaneous activity, is free, and the will is identical with the essence of the soul which is not distinct from its faculties. The immateriality

[94] *Super quatuor libros sententiarum, Quodlibeta,* Commentaries on Aristotle (*Expositio aurea super totam artem veterem*), *Tractatus logices.*

and spirituality of the soul cannot be demonstrated by reason alone.   He gave logic a renewal of popularity, adopting all the prolix divisions of the *Summulae* of Petrus Hispanus, and thus prepared the way for the extravagant dialectic of his successors.

In brief, the characteristic features of Ockham's philosophy consist in his conceptualist terminism, his theory of the sign and the excessive emphasis he laid on logic, the *scientia rationalis.*

89. The Ockhamists.—As a novelty and a reaction Ockham's teachings obtained a success in the Paris schools of the four-teenth and fifteenth centuries which all official prohibitions were powerless to withstand.   The tenor of these prohibitions (1339-1346) make it clear to what an extent the disciples had gone beyond their master, and especially what extravagancies they had introduced into dialectic which even he would not have countenanced.   The dangerous and anti-Scholastic ten-dencies to which this philosophy gave birth (**95**) gives the explanation of these censures.

The chief Ockhamists at Paris were JOHN BURIDAN [95] (died after 1359), who advocated a determinist psychology which suggests the later teaching of Leibniz ; MARSILIUS OF INGHEN [96] (died 1396), who became the first rector of the university of Heidelberg ; the mystic PETER D'AILLY [97] (1350-1425).   With this school of thought we must also associate ALBERT OF SAXONY, who wrote a commentary on Ockham's logic but is noteworthy chiefly as the author of numerous works on physics and mechanics.

90. The Scotist School.—Duns Scotus became the official teacher in the Franciscan Order, but his disciples of the four-teenth and fifteenth centuries, particularly Francis of Mayron, accentuated his formalism and multiplied his abstractions. At the same time their language became cumbersome and confusing, like their method, and they contributed, no less than the terminists, to the decadence of Scholastic teaching.

91. Thomism.—This school continued during the fourteenth and fifteenth centuries the best traditions of Scholasticism. The Cistercians, Carmelites and especially the Dominicans brought it many followers.   HERVÉ OF NEDELLEC [98], JOHN

---

[95] *Summa de dialectica, Compendium logicae*, Commentaries on Aristotle.
[96] *Quaestiones supra quatuor libros sententiarum.*
[97] Commentary on the Sentences, *Tractatus de anima.*
[98] Commentary on the Sentences, *Quodlibet.*

CAPREOLUS [99] (about 1380-1444), called *Princeps Thomistarum*, ST. ANTONINUS OF FLORENCE [100] (1389-1459), DENIS THE CARTHUSIAN (1402-1471) and GERSON [1] (1364-1429) were philosophers of real merit. The two last also took a part in the great revival of mysticism which took place in the fourteenth and fifteenth centuries. The *Libri Defensionum* of Capreolus is a monumental repertory of all the teachings of Thomism brought into comparison with Scotism and Ockhamism, but unfortunately it is not free from certain defects of method which mar the Scholasticism of the decadence. St. Antoninus applied the principles of Thomism to various social questions that had recently arisen, and his work contains valuable data for the history of the economic and social theories of the fourteenth and fifteenth centuries.

92. The Aegidian School.—As an offshoot of Thomism, there arose in the fourteenth century an Aegidian school proper, which faithfully perpetuated the traditional teachings of Giles of Rome. Gregory of Rimini (died 1358) caused a doctrinal schism by striking out a line towards Ockhamism. He had a following, but about the middle of the fifteenth century unity was restored among the members of the Augustinian Order by a return to the teaching of Giles of Rome.

93. Mysticism of the Fourteenth and Fifteenth Centuries.—This was the epoch of a vigorous awakening of mystic life and teaching. The best known among the orthodox mystics are Bl. John Ruysbroeck (1293-1381), and Gerson, Peter D'Ailly and Denis the Carthusian, mentioned above.

II. NON-SCHOLASTIC PHILOSOPHIES

94. Latin Averroism.—Averroïsm continued to be the most formidable rival of Scholasticism throughout the fourteenth and fifteenth centuries, and despite the censures of authority and the opposition of each succeeding generation of doctors, it steadily gained a growing number of supporters. At Paris the

---

[99] *Libri defensionum.*

[100] Commentary on the Sentences and on the *De consolatione* of Boëthius, *Summa fidei catholicae, Compendium philosophicum* and *theologicum, Dialogon de fide catholica.*

[1] *Centilogium de conceptibus, De modis significandi, De concordantia metaphysicae cum logica.*

undisputed leader of Averroïsm in the fourteenth century was
JOHN OF JANDUN or John of Ghent (*de Genundo, de Ganduno*),
who in his numerous works [2] expounded its theories, especially
that of the two truths, with undisturbed frankness. He
declares himself the ape of Aristotle and Averroës, the imperfect
imitator of their perfect work ; he professes a blind ipsedixitism
and makes no pretence of being original. From the end of
the fourteenth century—and indeed until the seventeenth—
the north of Italy, and especially the university of Padua,
remained a hotbed of Averroïsm. It adopted the teaching of
John of Jandun, and frankly acknowledged its indebtedness to
him. Pietro D'Abano (died 1316), a physician, was the founder
of this school.

95. Development of Ockhamism.—The philosophy of Ockham
contained in germ many anti-Scholastic doctrines which were
never formulated by him but were seized upon and developed
by others. Thus his terminist theory of the sign served as a
pretext for the development of a most radical subjectivism,
which asserted that we know only the mental sign or term and
not the thing signified. Such teachings as these show us the
reason why Ockhamism was proscribed by various censures from
1339 to 1346. Many heterogeneous elements were, moreover,
admitted into this school of thought.

The most important system was the theistic determinism
of THOMAS BRADWARDINE [3] (1290-1349), a professor at Oxford,
who taught that the free-will of God is the sovereign norm of
man's nature and the necessitating cause of all our actions ;
thus he destroyed human liberty by reducing freedom to
spontaneous volition.

NICHOLAS OF AUTRECOURT, a master of arts at Paris in 1340
and the promoter of an anti-Scholastic movement which was
condemned in 1346, openly professed the most radical subjectivism. The Cistercian JOHN OF MIRECOURT, condemned in
1347, starting from the determinism of Bradwardine, arrived at
the conclusion that God is even the author of sin. A certain
Guido (Aegidius of Medonta) professed an explicit pantheism.

---

[2] Commentaries on divers treatises of Aristotle and Averroës.
[3] *De causa Dei contra Pelagium et de virtute causarum, ad suos Mertonenses*
(between 1338 and 1346), Treatises on mathematics, Commentaries on the
Sentences, a *Summa theologica* or *Summa scientiarum.*

III. Minor Currents of Philosophy

Systems of secondary importance, which, whilst retaining a large number of Scholastic doctrines, assimilated various principles foreign to it, may be classed in three groups : (1) the German mysticism of Master Eckhart and his school ; (2) the theosophic mysticism of Nicholas of Cusa ; (3) the theosophy of Raymond of Sabunde.

96. Master Eckhart and German Mysticism.—MASTER ECKHART of Hocheim (about 1260-1327), a Dominican of Cologne, propounded a metaphysic and a mysticism which it is difficult to free from the reproach of pantheism, however much its author strove to deny the allegation [4]. He distinguishes essence and existence in contingent beings, but in place of saying that God gives their existence he maintains that God is their very existential act. Master Eckhart was, moreover, the promoter of a popular mysticism, known as the ' German Mysticism ', with which we may associate such men as TAULER (1290-1361) and Bl. HENRY SUSO (about 1300-1366).

97. Nicholas of Cusa (1401-1464), whose work [5] almost foreshadowed the coming break-up of the world of speculation, invented a farrago of mysticism, theosophy and quasi-pantheism. The Infinite is inaccessible to human reason, and this consciousness of our own ignorance constitutes true wisdom, *Docta Ignorantia*. God is the source of all reality, and all contradictions will be found to merge and coincide in Him (*coincidentia oppositorum*). The universe contains *explicitly* what God contains *implicitly*, all things being divine ' theophanies '. He strenuously defends himself against the charge of pantheism, but certainly his orthodoxy is only preserved at the expense of his logic.

RAYMOND OF SABUNDE (died 1432), the author of a *Theologia Naturalis*, takes up again the theosophy of Lully, a rationalism belonging strictly to the Middle Ages, which is a product of an exaggerated view of the Christian faith ; an attempt to decipher by reason not only the book of Nature but also the book of Scripture.

---

[4] A great number of **sermons** in German, and an important Latin work *Opus tripartitum* (comprising the *Liber propositionum*).
[5] *De docta ignorantia, Apologia doctae ignorantiae, De conjecturis.*

CHAPTER IV

PHILOSOPHIES OF THE RENAISSANCE PERIOD

(Second half of fifteenth century to seventeenth century)

98. General Sketch [6].—The capture of Constantinople by the Turks in 1453 is generally looked upon as the close of the Middle Ages in the strict sense of the word. In reality, the breaking up of the Byzantine Empire was but an episode in the period of deep and far-reaching upheavals which compassed the ruin of mediaeval civilization and led to the formation of modern society. The second half of the fifteenth century and the whole of the sixteenth witnessed a universal transformation as various nationalities were building up. The Renaissance considered under its three aspects of art, philosophy and science put out of date all that the Middle Ages had dearly prized.

Almost contemporaneous with the great intellectual revolution of the Renaissance was the great religious revolution known as the Reformation. Not only did Protestantism set up against the ecclesiastical organization of the Catholic Church various new forms of government peculiar to each national church, but it seriously modified Catholic dogma in several essential points ; and, as we might expect, the religious teachings of Protestantism were not without an indirect influence upon philosophy.

These new factors were in travail with the future, but from another point of view they were a product of the past. This remark applies to all the various branches of human activity, but is especially true in respect of philosophy. Traditional theories did not suddenly disappear as soon as fresh systems of thought arose ; often those of a dying school pervaded the early thought of the ensuing period. Thus it was with the transitional systems of the second half of the fifteenth

---

[6] See HÖFFDING, *op. cit.*, for the philosophy of the Renaissance.

century and the sixteenth : viewed in relation with what was coming, they prepared the way for modern philosophy ; considered in connexion with what preceded, they are a continuation of mediaeval philosophy. We shall study in turn (I) the new systems of the Renaissance, and (II) the different forms of Scholasticism during this period.

I. New Philosophies of the Renaissance

99. General Features and Division.—A yearning for independence governed almost all the systems to which the Renaissance gave birth, and all declared a furious war against Scholastic philosophy. Except for this purely negative point of contact, there was no link between these schools, which developed in the most varied directions.

At first, under the impetus of the blind admiration for Antiquity which the Renaissance introduced, there were attempts to revive the philosophies of Greece and Rome under their archaic forms. But besides this return to the past, there almost immediately developed new lines of work which made Nature and Social Right their chief object of study. At the same time other systems set up a close connexion between religion and philosophy with, however, reason as the sole arbiter of religious beliefs. Scepticism came at length as a final phase in this long and painful parturition of Renaissance ideas.

100. Revival of the Systems of Antiquity.—The leading forms in which an attempt was made to bring out a direct restoration of the systems of Greece and Rome were as follows :—

1. *Cult of Classical Philology.*—The representatives of the Renaissance who called themselves ' humanists ', enamoured of the beauty of classical Latin, delivered the first and most crushing attack on the Scholastics, who henceforth were dubbed ' Peripatetics ' ; confusing the substance and form of Scholasticism in a common reprobation, they judged that men who were unable to write were also, in consequence, unable to think. The humanists aimed at replacing ' scholastic ' by ' dialectic ', which for them meant rhetoric ; looked at from a constructive point of view their work is valueless. The chief philologists amongst the humanists were Lorenzo Valla [7]

---

[7] *Dialecticae disputationes contra Aristotelicos.*

(1407-1459), RUDOLPH AGRICOLA [8] (1442-1485) and LOUIS VIVÈS [9] (1492-1540) ; and the most influential, PETER DE LA RAMÉE [10] (Petrus Ramus, 1515-1572).

2. *Platonism.*—From 1450 to 1550 Italy became enthusiastic in its admiration for Plato. GEORGIOS GEMISTOS, later known as PLETHO [11] (1355-1450), inspired Cosmo de' Medici to found a Platonic Academy at Florence, where later MARSILIO FICINO [12] (1433-1499) became a brilliant figure. But this Platonism which the numerous disciples of these two so pertinaciously opposed to Aristotle was generally only a badly devised neo-Platonism. Cardinal Bessarion [13] (1403-1472) looked for a means of reconciling the differences between Aristotelians and Platonists by urging that the great Greek masters differed from each other by the method rather than by the substance of their teaching : an idea which has often been defended since that time.

3. *Aristotelianism.*—Against Plato another party pitted Aristotle, not indeed the Aristotle of the Scholastics which they considered a mere travesty, but the true Aristotle : in reality, they gave only an interpretation of Aristotle's teaching. And further, they split themselves into two groups, one interpreting him according to Averroës, the other according to Alexander of Aphrodisias. The question of the immortality of the soul provided the chief bone of contention, the former who were upholders of monopsychism (**81**) advocating an impersonal immortality, the latter the view that the human soul entirely perishes with the body, as a form disappears on the dissolution of a compound (**34**) ; they all denied Providence as well as the freedom of the human will. The Averroïst school at Padua at the beginning of the sixteenth century was represented chiefly by ALEXANDER ACHILLINI [14] (1463-1518), ZIMARA († 1532) and NIFO [15] (Niphus, 1473-1546). The last carried on a very ardent controversy with POMPONAZZI [16] (1462-1524), the leader of the Alexandrists whose centre was at Bologna.

[8] *De inventione dialectica.*
[9] *De causis corruptarum artium.*
[10] *Dialecticae institutiones.*
[11] *De Platonicae atque Aristotelicae philos. differentia.*
[12] *Theologia Platonica de animarum immortalitate.*
[13] *In calumniatorem Platonis.*
[14] *De intelligentiis, De orbibus.*
[15] *De intellectu et demonibus, De immortalitate animae.* He also edited the works of Averroës.
[16] *Tractatus de immortalitate animae, Defensorium.*

4. *Stoicism*.—This in its ancient form was advocated by JUSTUS LIPSIUS [17] (Joest Lips, 1547-1606), who was followed by many representatives of theism.

5. *Atomism*.—The theories of Democritus and Epicurus were resuscitated in the works of PETER GASSENDI [18] (1562-1655)

101. The Naturalistic Movement.—A form of naturalism was a special product of the Renaissance. It displayed three chief characteristics : the observation of natural phenomena which amounted to a cult ; the high praise given to occult sciences which should supply what was wanting in the simple observation of nature ; the tendency towards pantheism which by excessively exalting nature came to deify it. These features were common to the movement, though manifested in varying degrees by its devotees, whom we may group in three classes according as they gave prominence to one or other of them.

In a class apart, however, stands the striking personality of LEONARDO DA VINCI (1452-1519), who, besides being a genius as an artist and a savant, led the way towards the modern science of mechanics and physics. More than one of his scientific conceptions he borrowed from Albert of Saxony († 1390). His philosophical ideas are set down casually rather than in the form of an elaborate system.

1. The *empirical* character of the naturalistic movement was best represented by Telesio and Campanella. TELESIO [19] (1508-1588), who was an original thinker and may justly be called the founder of the naturalism of the Renaissance, maintained that two mutually exclusive immaterial forces, cold and heat, make up the totality of passive matter, the earth being the centre of cold, the heavens that of heat, and that all particular beings, man included, owe their origin to the contact of these two. And further, each element, having in itself a tendency to self-preservation, is endowed with a faculty of feeling by which it wards off the destructive influence of the element opposed to it : thus he made sensation a cosmic phenomenon. In accordance with this theory that each individual thing is a compound of heat and cold, he

---

[17] *Manuductio ad stoicam philosophiam.*
[18] *Exercitationes paradoxicae adversus Aristotelicos ; De vita et moribus Epicurii ; Disquisitiones anticartesianae.*
[19] *De natura rerum juxta propria principia.*

regarded the principle of animal and human life as a breath of warm air (*spiritus*, animal spirit) which circulates in the body.

CAMPANELLA [20] (1568-1639) took over this vitalism and amplified it into a metaphysic, by attributing to being as such the triple properties (*primalitates*) of life, feeling and desire. He also outlined an ideal scheme of political government.

2. The practice of the *occult sciences*—cabalistic theosophy, astrology, magic, alchemy—enabled a group of medical scientists, such as PARACELSUS [21] (1493-1541) and CARDANUS [22] (1501-1576), to develop a system of speculative thought.

3. The *pantheistic* tendency of naturalism is exemplified in PATRIZZI [23] (1529-1597), who made the creature a continuation of the being of the Creator, a divine ' becoming *ad extra* ' parallel with the Blessed Trinity which is a ' becoming *ad intra* '. At the same time he developed the thought of Telesio, regarding all individual beings as owing their origin to the action of light and heat. This became a complete pantheism in GIORDANO BRUNO [24] (1548-1600), who made God entirely immanent in the universe, and fell back on a theory of a world-soul for an explanation of the diversity found among the various beings, which he regarded as ' accidents ' of this one and only substance.

102. Natural and Social Law.—The awakening of the spirit of nationality, the study of the political institutions of Rome and Greece, the kindling of the sense of patriotism within the different states, gave a stimulus to the growth of the philosophy of national and social law, based on the study of the human person.

In *Il Principe* of MACHIAVELLI (1469-1527) and his even more noteworthy *Discorsi*, the mediaeval theory that the State was not an end in itself but an institution affording men the conditions which would enable them to secure happiness in a future life, encountered severe criticism. In its place the author sketched a theory, borrowed from antiquity, that the State is itself an end ; that the prince, in consequence, is not bound in his ruling by any considerations of honour,

---

[20] *Prodromus philosophiae instaurandae, Realis philosophiae partes quatuor, Philosophiae rationalis partes quinque, Universalis philosophiae seu metaphysicarum rerum juxta propria principia partes tres.*

[21] *Opus paramirum, De natura rerum.*

[22] *De varietate rerum, De subtilitate.*

[23] *Nova de universis philosophia.*

[24] *De monade, numero, et figura ; Dell' infinito, universo e dei mondi.*

cruelty or injustice, if the good of the State can be furthered ; that morality and religion should be subservient to politics. Machiavelli had in his immediate vision actual events, especially in the state of Florence, so that the issues which he raised were rather political than general and philosophical.

The real initiator of the new theory of social right was BL. THOMAS MORE (1480-1535) ; his *Utopia* [25], an imaginary ideal republic, whilst being imbued with the ideas of Italian Platonism, exactly reflects the new aspirations of his age—the mutual independence of Church and State, and a neutral attitude on the part of the State towards the Churches.

GROTIUS [26] (Hugo de Groot, 1583-1645), born in Holland, where the religious wars had led to indifference, thoroughly developed these principles and reduced them to system, so that he may be regarded as the great Renaissance legislator of the natural and social law. He laid emphasis on natural right (*jus naturale*) or what reason recognizes as agreeing with man's social nature ; he placed the origin of society in the *social contract* or the deliberate agreement of individuals to create the State for their own welfare ; he recognized that the people have the right to delegate to a representative their sovereign power, with the prerogative, according to one interpretation, of being able to withdraw it—which is the theory of revolution in germ,—but according to another the delegation is irrevocable. He made a complete distinction between human right based on reason, and divine right based on revelation, and thus advocated religious indifference on the part of the State.

103. Protestant Philosophy and Mysticism.—The theological discussions brought about by the Reformation had their counterpart in the domain of philosophy. The principle underlying Protestant theology was private judgment in interpreting the Scriptures and in determining religious dogma. If then each one considered himself free to devise a system of dogma for himself, we might expect that he would try to bring it into harmony with a philosophy, in which he had a still greater liberty of thought. Hence the philosophical systems of early Protestantism were multifarious and often contradictory—neo-Platonism, Stoicism, Aristotelianism, pantheistic mysticism.

---

[25] *De optimo rei publicae statu sive de nova insula Utopia.*
[26] *De jure belli et pacis.*

Luther (1483-1546) was no philosopher, but his dogmatic teaching presupposed a philosophy. Certain of his disciples sought to establish a harmony between reason and the reformed scheme of dogma. The chief were Zwingli and Melanchthon. ZWINGLI (1484-1531), the great Swiss reformer, was an ardent humanist. To support his religious conceptions, particularly his theory of justification and sanctification, he had recourse to the neo-Platonic and Stoic philosophy, both of which suggested pantheistic immanence and the deification of man when regenerated by the sovereign good. MELANCHTHON (1497-1560) was not a creative genius but an adapter of Aristotle to the service of Protestant theology, an Aristotle very much interspersed with Platonic and Stoic elements, and the manuals he compiled from his Logic, Physics and Ethics, remarkable for their order and clearness, earned for him the title of *Praeceptor Germaniae*.

The pantheistic conception, already brought forward by Zwingli, dominated the mystic anthropology of Sebastian Franck [27] (1500-1542), and especially the thought of Böhme. JACOB BÖHME [28] (1575-1624), brought up without books or any humanistic influence, conceived a mystical philosophy, the originality of which consists in a metaphysical explanation of the co-existence of good and evil in the world : there is an eternal dualism in God, proper to His nature and therefore necessary. The human soul is an appearance of God (pantheism), and being endowed with free-will may turn to good or evil, which are primordial qualities of its being.

104. Theism, or the Philosophy of Religion.—The religious conflicts born of the Reformation inspired a certain group of writers to attempt to bring about a reconciliation between the various churches, for it became their conviction that all forms of religion have in reality the same essential truths concerning God, that their content is identical notwithstanding the diversity of their dogmatic expression. Theism was, too, in agreement with the independent spirit of the Renaissance, for it was nothing more than naturalism applied to religion. Just as an inspection of human nature had given rise to a systematic philosophy of Natural Law, so reason alone was used for the

---

[27] *Paradoxa, De arbore scientiae boni et mali.*
[28] *Aurora* (1610), *Vierzig Fragen von der Seele, Mysterium magnum, Von der Gnadenwahl.*

unfolding of all ideas on religious matters. Thus it was that theism gathered a vast number of followers, not only among Protestants, but in general amongst all engaged in the Renaissance movement. ERASMUS of Rotterdam (1467-1536) propagated the theory that the teaching of Christ if purified from its accretions is identical with the religion of Plato, Cicero and Seneca. COORNHERT (b. 1522) in Holland reduced all the dogmas of Christianity to elements common to all religion. A crowd of names might be mentioned of those whom this theism seduced.

105. Scepticism.—The multitude of contradictions in religious, philosophical and scientific questions led men to doubt of the capacity of the mind to discover truth. This scepticism of the Renaissance period was not a thorough and positive criticism of the possibility of attaining certitude, but rather a practical conclusion against the sufficiency of all existing systems of thought. It marked the stage of transition between the Middle Ages and the development of modern philosophy ; and in this it had many points of similarity with the sophism of the Greeks, for both prepared the way for new constructive thought. The best known sceptics of this time were MONTAIGNE [29] (1533-1592) and CHARRON [30] (1541-1603). The bankruptcy of the Renaissance philosophies affords some explanation of the rapid spread of the ideas of Descartes and Francis Bacon.

II. SCHOLASTIC PHILOSOPHY

106. General.—Except by a few brilliant minds, Scholasticism became less and less represented, and ignorance of the system reached its lowest depth at the end of the seventeenth century. For this the Scholastics themselves were largely responsible by their attitude towards their opponents. When attacked in all their positions by the allied systems of the Renaissance, they offered no defence, principally because they made the double mistake of ignoring both the history of contemporary philosophy and the progress of the particular sciences.

107. Ancient Scholastic Schools.—The Thomist, Terminist and Scotist schools still continued. Among the first, FRANCIS

---

[29] Essays (trs. Cotton and Florio).
[30] *De la sagesse.*

A Sylvestris [31] (Ferrariensis, 1474-1528) has left a masterly commentary on the *Summa contra Gentiles*, and Cajetan [32] (Thomas de Vio, 1469-1534) on the *Summa Theologica*. The Ockhamists in the fifteenth century held the supremacy in most of the old universities, where they were known as *moderni*, *nominales* and their teaching as *via modernorum*, in contradistinction to the Thomists and Scotists who represented the *via antiqua*. The subtlety of the Ockhamists at Paris provoked a humanistic reaction on the part of Jacques Lefèvre (Faber Stapulensis) and his disciple Josse Clichtove (1472-1543). Scotism continued to be the favourite teaching of the Franciscans and underwent a revival in the seventeenth century.

108. Spanish Scholasticism.—The sixteenth century witnessed a brilliant restoration of the theology and philosophy of the Scholastics in Spain. This was marked by a renewed love for the clear expression and systematizations of the thirteenth century, more especially for the Thomistic, and by an original interpretation of the basic doctrines, together with the incorporation of certain new elements, several of which were inspired by the New Learning. For these reasons Spanish Scholasticism bore a character entirely its own. The centre of this movement was in Spain and Portugal, with ramifications in Italy. The revival was promoted in the Dominican Order—Francis of Vittoria (1480-1566), Melchior Cano (1509-1560), Bañez [33] (1528-1604), John of St. Thomas [34] (1589-1644)—and in the Society of Jesus. The most celebrated among the Jesuits was Suarez [35] (1548-1617). His philosophy is a remarkable interpretation of the Scholastic synthesis, constructed mainly of Thomistic materials but embodying other elements : for instance, he rejects the real distinction between essence and existence, admits the possibility of the separate existence of first matter, and accords to the intellect the power of forming a direct concept of the individual. In his *De Legibus* he treats especially of the question, then very much discussed, of the origin of civil power,

[31] Commentaries on St. Thomas's *Summa contra Gentiles*, and on his writings on Aristotle's *Post. Analyt., Physic.* and *De Anima*.
[32] Commentaries on various works of St. Thomas, *De ente et essentia, De predicam., Post. Analyt., De Anima, Sum. theol.*
[33] Commentaries on St. Thomas's *Sum. theol.*, I and II-II.
[34] *Cursus philosophicus ad exactam, veram et genuinam Aristotelis et doctoris angelici mentem.*
[35] *Disputationes metaphysicae ; De legibus.*

maintaining boldly against the theory of immediate divine right [36] that the free consent of the people constitutes the original title of authority.   Under the direction of P. FONSECA the Jesuits at Coïmbra carried to a successful issue an immense commentary on the philosophy of Aristotle, known as the *Collegium Conimbricense* or *Cursus Conimbricensium*.   In Italy we meet with the names of VASQUEZ [37] (1551-1604), ALAMANNI [38] (1559-1634) and SILVESTER MAURUS [39] (1619-1687).

The Spanish restoration worked a profound change, which was a testimony to the vitality of Scholastic philosophy when handled by capable men.   Unhappily this revival was neither widespread nor enduring.   And other groups of Scholastics continued to compromise the good name of Scholasticism by an ignorance of scientific questions, which gave rise to lamentable misunderstandings.

109. Misunderstanding between Scholastics and Scientists in the Seventeenth Century.—The great discoveries of Copernicus, Galileo, Kepler, Newton, Torricelli, and Lavoisier revolutionized physical and mechanical astronomy, physics, chemistry and biology ; whilst at the same time Descartes, Newton and Leibniz reconstructed mathematics on a new basis.   All this meant the destruction of the scientific theories concerning celestial and terrestrial physics which in the Middle Ages were part and parcel of the accepted conception of the universe. When Copernicus and Galileo substituted the heliocentric for the geocentric system of astronomy, and the telescope revealed such discoveries as the spots of the sun, the phases of Venus and the existence of new stars, the old conceptions that the heavens are solid, the stars immutable and ' ingenerabilia et incorruptibilia ', passed away for ever.   Such theories as these had by long-standing tradition become interwoven, albeit artificially and loosely, with the fundamental principles of general metaphysics and cosmology.   To some it seemed that they were necessarily so bound up together that to throw over the old scientific conceptions meant the abandonment of the ancient philosophy.   Such, however, was not the necessary

---

[36] Such as James I of England had supported by theological arguments. —TRS.

[37] *Disputationes metaphysicae.*

[38] *Summa philosophica.*

[39] *Quaestionum philosophicarum libri IV.*

consequence, for in the midst of the ruins of the mediaeval science there still stood unimpaired a solid groundwork of observation sufficient to sustain the great constitutional doctrines of its philosophy. All that was necessary was to make a clear distinction between its organic principles and the many quite arbitrary applications of these principles in questions relating to particular sciences, and to show a zeal in maintaining the everlasting validity of the former and a readiness to renounce the latter. Instead of this, these ardent followers of Aristotle persisted in attempting to defend in its entirety the Aristotelian conception of the cosmos, as if it were a sacred monument, to remove a stone of which would involve the complete downfall of the whole edifice. We cannot be surprised, then, that they brought upon themselves the ridicule of the new scientists, who threw the responsibility of all the aberrations of the mediaeval science on the Scholastic philosophy, since its adherents declared that both must stand or fall together. Thus the misunderstanding between the men of science and the Scholastics became inevitable and proved to be irresistible ; in metaphor, the former tried to fell the giant oak because it had some rotten branches on its crown, whilst the latter fought to keep all hands off on the foolish pretence that to remove a withered twig might deprive it of its life. Eventually it fell not through want of vitality but through default of defenders.

PART V

Modern Philosophy

110. General Character and Division.—Whilst the leading feature of the philosophical work of the Renaissance was that it was negative, modern philosophy is marked chiefly by its constructive thought. Numerous systems have been developed, the majority asserting an independence from dogmatic control. Many of them had great influence and were strongly constructed. They varied much in character, for it is a mark of the modern mentality to pride itself on original thought. This individualistic tendency was especially favoured by the growth of national spirit and diversity of language.

A predominant place has been given to psychology and epistemology. The epistemological problem focusing the chief attention, the question of the origin and validity of knowledge, which the Scholastics solved by a metaphysical theory of finality, has been treated by modern philosophy from an analytical and psychological standpoint. Since Kant has given a new orientation to the study of epistemology and has exercised a decisive influence, we may best divide Modern Philosophy into three periods : the pre-Kantian (Chap. I), the philosophy of Kant (Chap. II), and the post-Kantian (Chap. III). We add a few words also on the philosophy of the present day.

CHAPTER I

MODERN PHILOSOPHY BEFORE KANT

(Seventeenth and eighteenth centuries)

111. Outline.—The founders of Modern Philosophy were Descartes and Francis Bacon (I). The former gave the impetus to the rationalistic movement by emphasizing the rights of reason (*ratio*) in the acquisition and in the subsequent use of human knowledge ; the latter inaugurated the empirical tendency (ἐμπειρία, observation, experiment), and made sensation the only source of knowledge. The two aimed at the same purpose, namely, the discovery of a *new method*, fundamentally different from the traditional Scholasticism, of attaining to certitude (*Discours de la méthode ; Novum Organon*). The philosophy of the seventeenth century is saturated with the thought of Descartes, not by way of a direct descent from him, but through the influence of several original systems to which the Cartesian spirit gave rise (II). The empiricism which quickly developed from the elementary doctrines of Bacon, spread in England (III) and in France (IV) in the seventeenth and eighteenth centuries. And we find it, although not quite so clearly marked, in Germany, where the system of Leibniz, which is an indirect offshoot from that of Descartes, had the predominant influence (V).

I. DESCARTES AND FRANCIS BACON

112. René Descartes [40] (1596-1650) was in very close touch with the scientists of his time, not only at Paris but also in the Low Countries, where his teaching met with a very warm reception.

---

[40] *Discours de la méthode, Meditationes de prima philosophia, Principia philosophiae, Traité des passions de l'âme*. Consult MAHAFFY, *Descartes* (Edinburgh and London, 1884) ; CUNNINGHAM, *Influence of Descartes on Metaphysical Speculations in England* (London, 1876). Trans. of *Meditations* and *Objections*, Haldane and Ross (Cambridge, 1912). For criticism of Descartes' method, see *Criteriology*, **15, 17**.

In 1649, at the invitation of Queen Christina of Sweden, he went to Stockholm, where he died.

Descartes set out to discover a new method of attaining to all knowable truth, and on this he proceeded to build up his entire philosophy.

1. *His new method.*—Descartes sought to base all knowledge on a single principle, from which it would be possible to deduce *more geometrico* one entire system of truths. To discover this principle he used the method of calling into doubt (universal methodic doubt) all acts of human knowledge, alike of internal consciousness, of external sensations, of first principles, etc. ; and he even went so far as to throw doubt upon the very capability of the faculties, which he said some ' evil genius ' might vitiate. Yet, most illogically, he made one exception in this universal doubt ; the certitude of his own existence he asserted was known by intuition in his act of thought ; ' Cogito, ergo sum ' he made the first application of his new method, and in this he found his criterion of certitude, namely, that a clear and distinct intuition of a thing involves the existence of that thing (realism, rationalism), and, he went on, every act of consciousness which appears to me as clear and distinct as the fact of my existence gives me absolute certainty. All he had to do, then, to construct his system of philosophy was to gather together and arrange these clear and distinct ideas.

2. *The construction of his system.*—These clear and distinct intuitions assured him, in the first place, of the *existence* of himself, of God, and of the external world. I am certain, he argued, of my own existence : ' Cogito, ergo sum '. I am certain of God's existence, for I have the idea of the infinitely perfect, and I see that this idea, which is prior to that of imperfection, must have been given to me by God Himself. I am certain of the existence of the world, for I have the idea of this external world, and God who has given me this idea could not have deceived me. Furthermore, all clear and distinct ideas are true since they have God for their author, and error can come only from the will, not from the intellect. In the second place, these intuitions informed him of the *nature* of God, of the world and of himself. God alone can, strictly speaking, be called a substance, which he defined as that which so exists as to need nothing else for its existence ; created beings can be called substances only inasmuch as they are

independent of any other being besides God. Corporeal reality is not made up of the sensible qualities (secondary qualities) we attribute to them, but consists in extension (the primary quality) ; it is something essentially extended, infinitely divisible and continuous (evidence of his mathematical bent) ; and since the notion of movement is not contained in that of body, movement is extrinsic to body (cosmic mechanism, vortex theory). In dealing with psychology he defines man or the ego as a *res cogitans ;* the essence of the ego is thought or, which for him is synonymous with it, the conscious act. Between extension and thought there is an absolute incompatibility ; the union of soul or ego, a *res cogitans* with body, a *res extensa*, is a purely mechanical one. Hence Descartes displays a tendency to reduce all psychic phenomena to states of consciousness and to lessen the part played by the will (supremacy of the intellect over the will) ; and this involves him in the necessity of regarding all non-conscious activities as extended and mechanical phenomena (theory of animal spirits, animal automatism, theory concerning the passions).

113. Francis Bacon (1561-1626), after being raised to a high political position under Elizabeth and James I, fell into disgrace and devoted his life of solitude to the elaboration of two chief works [41], in which, like Descartes, he looked for a new method on which to base the certitude of science.

1. His *new method* consisted, first of all, in regarding as certain only what falls within the scope of sensible experience, by which he understood not ordinary experience but that which excluded all phantoms or ' idols ', the sources of common error. Next, by applying scientific induction to the data of experience stripped of appearances, he proceeded to interpret corporeal nature. His work must be judged not by the content of his system of thought but by the accurate and precise formulation of inductive methods, which we may note in passing were not unknown to the Scholastics. To these methods he gave the names of *tabulae praesentiae, absentiae, graduum.*

2. In the *construction of his philosophy* Bacon laid down the principles of a materialistic naturalism, in which physics, psychology and social philosophy alike show the domination of a mechanical necessity which excludes any teleological

---

[41] *De dignitate et augmentis scientiarum ; Novum organon scientiarum.* See Introduction to the edition by FOWLER (Oxford, 1889).

conception. Bacon's successors developed the scientific method that he had advocated.

II. Cartesianism of the Seventeenth Century

114. The Earlier Disciples of Descartes.—Cartesian thought was quick to permeate the philosophy of France and the Low Countries. In France, among his personal friends Descartes counted Mersenne, Claude Clerselier, and Pascal ; the Jansenists of Port Royal ranked among his first admirers, and the *Port Royal Logic* was published in 1662 by A. Arnauld (1612-1694) and Pierre Nicole (1625-1695), who were much influenced by the mathematical thought of the modern philosophy. Bossuet and Fénelon were also subject to Cartesian influence, and also Huet, the fideist. The universities of the Low Countries witnessed a contest with many interesting episodes between his partisans and the advocates of Aristotelian thought. Louvain, Utrecht and Leyden counted such men as Geulincx, Reneri and Heydanus among their staunch Cartesians, and censures from the Southern Province in 1662 and from the Northern Province in 1642 were powerless to arrest the spread of the movement.

115. Occasionalism.—Nicole Malebranche [42] (1638-1715), a member of the congregation of the Oratory at Paris, and well known for his friendship with Bossuet and his correspondence with Arnauld, was the professed defender of occasionalism, although it had already been expressly contained in the writings of Geulincx (1625-1669). This system held fast to the strict principles of Descartes, and pushed them to their logical consequences, especially in the field of psychology. Since there is nothing in common between extension, the attribute of matter, and thought, the attribute of mind, there cannot be any real interaction between the soul and the body of man ; their mutual influences are nothing more than the simultaneous occurrence of actions that are mutually independent ; the production of the one is the *occasion* of the production of the other, and their harmonious correspondence is arranged and governed by God. Further, even the *idea* of body comes not from the body itself but must be given us by God ; so that we

---

[42] *Recherche de la vérité.* Consult Joly, *Malebranche* (*Grands Philosophes* series, Paris, 1901).

cannot see material things in themselves but only in God,
' the universal Reason ', ' the place of minds '.

116. Mysticism.—The foregoing theory that knowledge
comes directly from God is found also in BLAISE PASCAL [43]
(1623-1662), who, starting from Cartesian principles, convinced
himself that reason is incapable of arriving at the complete
truth and therefore the criterion of truth must lie in sentiment
or faith : ' the heart has reasons of which the mind itself knows
nothing '. We find a similar tendency in POIRET (1640-1719).
But religious mysticism met with no great favour in France.
Occasionalism, too, had but little following. The most
striking development of Cartesianism was due to a fusion with
it of other elements by Spinoza and Leibniz.

117. Baruch Spinoza [44] (1632-1677) belonged by birth to a
colony of Portuguese Jews at Amsterdam and studied in turn
the Talmud and the Cabbala, Descartes, Giordano Bruno, Francis
Bacon and Hobbes. Excommunicated by his co-religionists
for his heterodox views, he led a wandering life and settled
finally at the Hague, where he died.

In order to overcome the antinomy between extension and
thought, Spinoza thought the solution lay in considering both
these attributes to belong to a *single substance*, God. Here he
took Descartes' definition of substance in its most rigorous
meaning, and herein showed himself a pantheist. Then from
the idea of God he deduced *more geometrico* a complete system
of thought concerning the universe.

God, considered in Himself and as infinite, is the substance
absolutely devoid of determination (*natura naturans*). But He
can exist only as assuming *attributes* that are necessary to Him ;
these attributes are very numerous, but we know only two of
them, namely, extension and thought, which appear side by
side though in varying degrees in all things, which are thus
expressions of God or *divine modes*. God as so determined to
an infinity of modes of being (*natura naturata*) unfolds Himself
according to an absolute mechanical necessity, and in this
theory Spinoza finds no place for the concept of finality, for
finality involves prevision, and so destroys the necessary
parallelism of the extension-mode and the thought-mode. In

---

[43] *Lettres provinciales ; Pensées.*
[44] *Ethica more geometrico demonstrata ; Tractatus politicus ; De intellectus
emendatione* (unfinished) : part trs. by Elwes, Hale White, Wolf. Consult
POLLOCK, *Spinoza, his Life and Philosophy* (2nd ed., London, 1899) ; and
CAIRD, *Spinoza* (London, 1903).

this system man is no longer an anomaly in nature, for our mental states are regarded as following one another with a blind necessity, parallel with the modes of objects represented but without any causal efficiency ; and in the same way our actions take place not freely but fatally, and moral activities are explained just as if they were ' geometrical propositions of lines, surfaces and bodies '. This view applied to morality leads to the denial of all liberty, and in natural right admits of no distinction between virtue and brute force. With Hobbes, Spinoza regards the selfishness of the individual as responsible for the warfare of the passions, and with Grotius the establishment of civil society as a means of ending this. The reward and crown of a moral life consists in a ' mystical intuition '.

Spinoza's philosophy contains many inconsistencies and is open to different interpretations ; it was not understood by his contemporaries and came into favour only in the following century.

118. Leibniz [45] (1646-1716), who was an original thinker and has been called the founder of philosophy in Germany, marks a return towards the individualistic tendency of Descartes. But he was conversant not only with the philosophy of Descartes and his contemporaries, but also with that of Plato and Aristotle, and with the Scholastic system, which he spoke of in terms of high praise. Further, he was by no means ignorant of the science of his day, and is distinguished as the discoverer of the differential calculus, which he applied to mechanics. At the same time he was actively engaged in political life, and put before himself as the ideal of his diplomatic career the dream of bringing together all the various churches. In 1700 he founded the Academy of Sciences at Berlin.

The leading idea of Leibniz's monadology is a dynamic conception of the universe : substance is a force, and extension and thought are but forms of its activity ; the world is an aggregate of monads or forces ; the series of mechanical movements is ruled by a final purpose.

1. *The monad in itself* or force-substance is immaterial and indestructible, and each monad is with reference to the rest a

[45] *De scientia universali seu calculo philosophico ; Système nouveau de la nature ; Monadology* (trs. Latta) ; *Essais de Theodicée sur la bonté de Dieu et l'origine du mal ; New Essays* (trs. Langley). Consult RUSSELL, *Critical Exposition of the Philosophy of Leibnitz* (Cambridge, 1900). See *Psych.*, **117, 151**; *Gen. Met.*, **85**; *Nat. Theol.*, **18, 36**.

perfectly independent being, for the monads, as he expressed it, ' have no windows ' by which they can experience or exercise influence ; the monad is impenetrable ; it is endowed both with a power of resistance within the limits of its being (*vis resistendi*, matter) by virtue of which it is, or rather appears to be, extended, and also with a purely internal power by virtue of which it develops its own individual nature (form, soul, entelechy). Its activity is essentially *representation ;* each state of the monadic life is in itself expressive of all preceding and succeeding states. Because these representations succeed one another without any break of continuity, they have an organic bond and all are regulated by a pre-established harmony, in such a way that the end of the monad is attained ; the monad goes on its course following its ' innate dream '.

Monads differ from one another according to their power of representation, which admits of varying degrees of clearness proportionate to the perfection of the monad, from obscure or totally unconscious representation to clear and distinct representation that is fully conscious. But conscious and unconscious states differ not in nature but only in degrees of clearness, and in this Leibniz departs from the view of Descartes who identified representation with consciousness. Man has unconscious or less conscious perceptions and distinct perceptions or ideas ; from the first he insensibly passes to the second, for there is nothing in our distinct ideas ' which has not previously been dreamt of in the obscure regions of the soul '. Thus, whilst Leibniz allows that we have an empirical and experimental knowledge (truth of facts) by the side of rational and deductive knowledge (eternal truth), he considers the second as the gradual development of the first.

2. *The order which exists between the monads* is accounted for by (1) the law of continuity, by which there is an uninterrupted graded series from ' lower ' monads to souls and minds, each being differing from the next by a very small difference (influence of the infinitesimal calculus), according to the axiom ' natura non facit saltum ' ; (2) the pre-established harmony, or divine arrangement by which the activities of the monads are so adapted to one another that, whilst they exercise no causal efficiency, the changes in one are parallel to, or correspond with, the changes in every other, and there results a perfect harmony in the cosmic system ; (3) their activity in representing, by virtue

of which each monadic state is a ' living mirror ' of the whole universe.

3. Leibniz applied these general principles to the study of all different beings and particularly to man. Body and soul have no direct influx on each other, but are adjusted as two clocks which keep perfectly in time (Geulincx, Malebranche). Besides ' petites perceptions ', which in the language of to-day would be called subconscious mental states, man has distinct ideas, and in this he is superior to all simple monads. To act morally is to follow intellectual representations ; these follow necessarily a pre-established harmony, and therefore Leibniz upholds a psychological determinism. The beautiful he regards as a ' dull ' and less conscious perception of the order of the universe.

4. There must exist a supreme monad, God, since his non-existence is inconceivable (which was Descartes' plea). He has created the best possible world (cosmological optimism). Leibniz also endeavoured to harmonize the positive religions of the various churches with natural religion.

The whole philosophy of Leibniz displays a powerful unity of conception, which makes it worthy of a place among the great systems in the history of modern philosophy. The trend of thought amongst the German philosophers of the eighteenth century was deeply affected by his system.

III. English Philosophy in the Seventeenth and Eighteenth Centuries

119. General Sketch [46].—English philosophy was influenced by several currents of thought, but most of all by the empiricism of Francis Bacon, which with Hobbes took the name of sensualism. This term, together with its synonyms sensism or sensationalism, has reference to the origin of human knowledge, and in this connexion appeared in two forms, objectivist sensualism (called also materialism) and subjectivist, according as sense-perception, which this theory held to be the only source of knowledge, was regarded as establishing or not establishing the real existence of things outside the subject

[46] See Leslie Stephen, *English Thought in the Eighteenth Century* (1876

perceiving. It developed in England under both forms, displaying a vast variety of shades, as two stages of the same logical evolution. Subjectivist sensualism brought about a very strong reaction, especially on the part of Reid and the Scottish school. Besides these theories dealing with questions of epistemology, we must notice also various theories on moral and religious questions which were the natural outcome of the sensualist philosophy.

|120. **Thomas Hobbes** [47] (1588-1679), who was the friend of Bacon, Gassendi, and Campanella, and was also acquainted with Mersenne and other Cartesians at Paris, endeavoured to bring out clearly and develop the fundamental ideas of Bacon's naturalism.

1. *Theory of knowledge.* All knowledge is derived from experience (empiricism), and this has its source in sensation (sensualism). Sensible qualities, and even representations in time and space, possess no objective reality ; logically this should have led him to subjectivism, but he reverted instead to the materialism of Bacon.

2. *Materialism.* Philosophy, by his definition, is the science of bodies, and physics the study of the movement of atoms—a movement regulated by mathematical and necessary laws (Descartes) without any intervention of final causes. He considered psychology as dealing with the human body and its movements, which he divided into two classes, the theoretical (sensations) and the practical (volitional acts). The will he regarded as passive and dependent upon knowledge (cp. Descartes' supremacy of knowledge, **112**) ; and in this shows himself as a moral determinist. The instinct of self-preservation alone guides our actions ; but men agreed for the sake of putting an end to the clash of individual self-interests to unite in a civil society (Grotius), and have accordingly invested state officials with autocratic powers. Before this sovereign authority the individual must forego all his own rights, even to the extent of renouncing his religious convictions, except where the government does not impose a state religion.

---

[47] *On Human Nature ; De corpore politico ; Leviathan, or the Matter, Form and Power of a Commonwealth, Ecclesiastical and Civil.* Consult LESLIE STEPHEN, *Hobbes* (1904) ; JOS. RICKABY, *Free Will and Four English Philosophers* (Hobbes, Locke, Hume, and Mill) (London, 1906).

121. John Locke [48] (1632-1704) had a scientific education at Oxford and studied Bacon and Descartes. To escape the turmoil of political affairs, he betook himself to Holland, where he wrote his chief works and returned to England in 1689 in the suite of William of Orange. He must be regarded as the founder of the sensist philosophy. To him it appeared necessary, before attempting the solution of any other philosophical problem, to determine what is the origin and what the validity of human knowledge.

1. *The origin of knowledge.* Locke devoted the first book of his *Essay* to proving that ' there are no innate principles in the mind ' [49]. The mind of the new-born child resembles a clean sheet of paper (*tabula rasa* of Aristotle). All knowledge is derived from experience, which he teaches is twofold : external, namely sensation or the perception of the external phenomena by means of the senses, and internal, namely reflection or the consciousness of the activity discernible in sensation. This internal experience comprises several activities which tend to combine simple representations together, and so ' make ' complex ideas by ' reflecting, comparing and combining ' (association-theory in germ).

2. *Validity of knowledge.* After having laid it down as a principle that neither sensations, nor reflections, including complex representations, teach us anything about the external world, Locke introduced into this subjectivism a twofold modification (Descartes) : he affirmed the real existence of the primary qualities of bodies, such as extension, etc. **(112)** ; and he admitted the existence of substances, as objects of some complex representations, although we remain ignorant of their nature.

These inconsistencies gave Locke's system a transitional character : this objectivist sensism tended towards subjectivism, which Berkeley and Hume erected into a system.

122. The Associationist School.—The association of ' ideas ', or the transformation of simple representations into complex

---

[48] *Essay concerning Human Understanding ; The Reasonableness of Christianity ; The Conduct of the Understanding ; Two Treatises on Government.* Consult BASTIDE, *John Locke; ses théories politiques et leur influence en Angleterre* (Paris, 1907).

[49] According to the terminology of seventeenth and eighteenth centuries, ' idea ' is a synonym for ' knowledge ' ; hence the name ' idéologue ' for some of the French materialists and ' idéaliste ' for sensationalists.

ones, of which traces are to be found in Locke and others, soon came to be the object of special studies. These at first were confined to the investigation of the origin of our consciousness. PETER BROWN († 1735) made a study of the formation of representations and JOHN GAY of that of volitional acts. DAVID HARTLEY [50] (1704-1757), who was the founder of the associationist school of psychology in England, worked out these conceptions, and found a constant correspondence between physiological antecedents and psychological consequences, albeit the two sets of facts he asserted to be irreducible. JOSEPH PRIESTLEY [51] (1733-1804) gave a materialistic interpretation of Hartley's psychology by his teaching that the psychological state does not differ in nature from the physiological, and that consequently psychology is merely the physics of the nerves. He tried to reconcile these theories and his religious beliefs by having recourse to the doctrine that what is true in theology may be false in philosophy, and vice versa (cp. the two truths of Averroës, 81).

123. George Berkeley [52] (1685-1753), Anglican bishop of Cloyne, set out from Locke's principle that our knowledge extends to ideas only and arrived at a subjectivism peculiarly his own : he maintained that all things are ideas and the external world or the qualities we attribute to matter, primary as well as secondary, are nothing more than clusters or aggregates of mental representations which we call 'things'; mind-phenomena alone exist—*esse est percipi*. But whilst matter does not exist, spirits which are the subjects of these representations have an existence, and especially God ; and because He exists and has given all the representations that come before us, and has arranged them in order, these must be true (cp. Malebranche, 115).

124. David Hume [53] (1711-1776), who was born at Edinburgh and there wrote several of his works, did not succeed at first in attracting attention ; his treatise on Human Nature, he tells

---

[50] *De motu, sensus et idearum generatione.*

[51] *Hartley's Theory of Human Mind on the Principles of Association of Ideas.*

[52] *Treatise concerning the Principles of Human Knowledge ; New Theory of Vision ; Dialogues.* Consult FRASER, *Berkeley* (Edinburgh and Philadelphia ; 1894), and *Selections from Berkeley* (London, 1891).

[53] *Treatise on Human Nature,* which later he recast into *Enquiry concerning Human Understanding, Dissertation on the Passions, Enquiry concerning the Principles of Morals. Essays, Moral, Political, and Literary.* Consult LESLIE STEPHEN, *op. cit.,* and RICKABY, *op. cit.*

us, ' fell dead-born from the press '. But in the course of time his words struck root in England and France, and a visit to Paris in 1763, where he formed the acquaintance of Rousseau, culminated in a triumph for himself and his philosophy.

Hume divided perceptions or states of consciousness into impressions, or the more lively perceptions experienced in seeing, loving, etc., and ideas or thoughts which are faint images of impressions. Both are purely psychical phenomena, and whilst giving certainty of their existence within us, teach us nothing at all about extramental reality. These states of consciousness are associated together according to a threefold natural law, namely the law of contiguity in space and time, the law of resemblance and contrast, and the law of causality. In dealing with his laws he arrived at the denial of all substance, even including that of the human mind, and of the principle of causality. Thus not only with Berkeley did he reduce external substance to a bundle of impressions, but even the ego or the mind itself [54], and he further regarded the existence of God as incapable of proof. Hume accordingly condemned all metaphysics ; Locke had reasoned away all but primary qualities of bodies and the unknowable substance in which they inhere ; Berkeley had disposed of substance and primary qualities ; Hume, more logically, left nothing but our mental states. The baneful consequences of his teaching in matters of moral, natural and social law and religion laid his system open to the charge of scepticism and atheism. This resulted in a reaction.

125. Reaction against Sensationalism. The Scottish School.—The sensist philosophy was destined to meet with a very keen opposition in England [55] on the part of a mystical and Platonic school at Cambridge, represented especially by SAMUEL PARKER († 1688) and RALPH CUDWORTH (1617-1688), who asserted that moral principles and ethical ideals come not from experience but from ' the ideas which necessarily exist

---

[54] Hume's denial of the substantiality of the mind is his most distinctive contribution to psychology : what we call mind is simply ' a heap or collection of different perceptions united together by certain relations, and supposed, though falsely, to be endowed with simplicity and identity '. Cp. *Works* (Green and Grosse's edition, 1890), I, 534.—TRS.

[55] See SELBY-BIGGE, *British Moralists*, 2 vols. (Oxford, 2nd ed., 1913), being extracts from all the writers of this class. Also McCOSH, *The Scottish Philosophy* (London, 1875).

in the mind of God and are universally and immutably present in the human mind '.

More far-reaching in its effects was the reaction on the part of the Scottish school. This was directed chiefly against the ideological conceptions of Berkeley and Hume. In place of subjectivist sensationalism this school professed a theory of innate ideas which permitted the attainment of dogmatic truth : we have inborn within us *instinctive judgments*, which together form the truths of common sense and which have a real objective import ; as Reid expressed it, ' All knowledge and all science must be built upon principles that are self-evident ; and of such principles every man who has common sense is a competent judge '. These judgments come into play chiefly in questions of morality, social life and religion. The founder and chief representative of this school was THOMAS REID [56] (1710-1796), and there also belonged to it ADAM FERGUSON (1724-1816), JAMES OSWALD (1727-1793), and especially DUGALD STEWART [57] (1753-1828), whose doctrines found great favour, particularly in America and France, with the spiritualistic eclectics.

126. Ethics and Natural Law.—The study of psychological problems naturally had its counterpart in questions dealing with ethics and natural law. There were a number of distinguished writers known as the BRITISH MORALISTS, some of whom attacked the sensism of Hobbes whilst others improved upon it.

1. *Reaction against Hobbes*, whose ' selfish system ' (120) was very strenuously opposed. The Cambridge school vindicated the existence of an innate moral law, based at once on the altruistic and egoistic inclinations of man ; and a group of adherents to the theory of moral sentiment made the good to be the object of an innate sentiment and one to be willed for its own sake. SHAFTESBURY [58] (1671-1713) identified this sentiment of the good with aesthetic enjoyment ; BUTLER [59] (1692-1752) called it conscience ; and FRANCIS HUTCHESON [60] (1694-1747)

---

[56] *An Inquiry into the Human Mind on the Principles of Common Sense ; Essays on the Intellectual Powers of Man ; Essays on the Active Powers of Man.*
[57] *Elements of the Philosophy of the Human Mind.*
[58] *Characteristicks of Men, Manners, Opinions and Times.*
[59] *Analogy of Religion.*
[60] *Inquiry into the Original of our Ideas of Beauty and Virtue, System of Moral Philosophy.*

an aesthetic taste. Parallel in their development with these aesthetic moralists were several aesthetic sensists, such as Henry Home (1696-1782) and Edmund Burke (1730-1797), who reduced the beautiful to an agreeable sensation. Hobbes's morality of pleasure met also with lively opposition from SAMUEL CLARKE [61] (1675-1729)—well known for his controversy with Leibniz—who sought for the basis of goodness in the correspondence of our actions with the nature of things.

2. *Sensism applied to ethics* found its first expression in a theory of egoistic utilitarianism. MANDEVILLE [62] (1670-1733) found individual self-interest to be the source of all activity, whether personal or social ; JEREMY BENTHAM [63] (1748-1832) formulated the principle that the end of morality is ' the greatest happiness of the greatest number ' and that ' every virtuous action results in the balance of pleasure ' ; but he maintained that each one's primary care should be for his own welfare. Sensism in its second form became an altruistic utilitarianism which brings into consideration sympathy or a power of participating in the joys and sorrows of others ADAM SMITH [64] (1723-1790) was its chief representative. These two currents of utilitarianism continued to develop in the English ethical conceptions of the nineteenth century, particularly in James Mill and John Stuart Mill (**162** and **163**). It may be added that Smith and Bentham are reckoned amongst the founders of political economy.

127. Deism.—English deism, or free-thought, went further than the Renaissance, which left men indifferent and tolerant in matters of religion (**104**), and made an attack on all positive religion, in place of which it substituted, according to its view of an inborn religious sense, a universal naturalism or philosophical religion. This consists in personal speculation about God's existence and the immortality of the soul. The leader of this movement was Lord HERBERT OF CHERBURY (1581-1648) ; and JOHN TOLAND [65] (1670-1722), MATTHEW TINDAL [66] (1656-1733), Lord BOLINGBROKE (1672-1751) and others represented

---

[61] *A Demonstration of the Being and Attributes of God.*
[62] *The Fable of the Bees, or Private Vices made Public Benefits.*
[63] *Introduction to the Principles of Morals and Legislation ; Deontology.* For the modern English utilitarianism founded by Bentham consult LESLIE STEPHEN, *English Utilitarians*, 3 vols. (London, 1900).
[64] *Theory of Moral Sentiments ; The Wealth of Nations.*
[65] *Christianity not Mysterious.*
[66] *Christianity as old as the Creation.*

the deistic side in a great controversy with the upholders of orthodoxy.

With deism we must associate some noteworthy attempts made in the eighteenth century to reconcile the teleological conception of the universe, which all theists favoured, with the mechanical view very commonly held after the time of Galileo and Kepler alike by the followers of Descartes and the English empirical school. Newton, who had given a great impetus to the mechanistic theory by his formulation of the universal law of gravitation, was nevertheless an advocate of a cosmic theology, and in this he stood side by side with Leibniz ; thus we see the two greatest geniuses of the seventeenth century allied as the foes of the excessive claims of the mechanical conception of the universe.

IV. French Philosophy in the Eighteenth Century

128. General Sketch.—Cartesianism, which as we have seen (II) underwent many profound changes, is no longer to be found as an entire system in France in the eighteenth century ; some of its tenets lingered, and the one to survive the longest and to enjoy the most considerable influence was that of universal mechanism. On the other hand, the philosophy of France became in many other respects permeated with English empiricism, especially after Voltaire had taken upon himself to popularize it. This French sensism appeared not only in its speculative forms, especially in materialism, but also it became a popular philosophy spread throughout the masses and, by being applied to religion on the one hand and to morality and social life on the other, it quickly dechristianized the people and prepared the way for the Revolution of 1789.

129. Speculative Sensism.—Before developing into an absolute materialism, the sensist philosophy showed itself in many forms, between the two extremes of subjectivism that denied all reality, and dogmatism that postulated that knowledge could be attained by the use of the faculties.

1. *Non-materialistic sensism* was represented by Condillac[67] (1715-1780). He reduced all knowledge to external sensation, and regarded consciousness, even in its most complex states, as nothing more than transformed sensation ; for this purpose he instituted his classical comparison of the statue. His view of

_____
[67] *Essai sur l'origine de la connaisance humaine ; Traité des sensations.*

the cognitional value of sensation is a strange blending of subjectivist sensism, inasmuch as he regards sensible qualities as having no reality, with dogmatism, for he admits the objective reality of spatial determinations ; and he even includes spiritualism by recognizing the immaterial nature of the soul. We find similar contradictions in the theory of CHARLES BONNET [68] (1720-1793).

2. *Materialistic sensism,* which was dominant in France in the eighteenth century, is the doctrine that there is no knowledge but sensuous and no reality but material. These principles are to be found with all their various implications (1) in the striking book *L'homme machine* of LA METTRIE (1709-1751), in which he teaches that nothing exists except matter endowed with movement ; that psychic phenomena are nothing more than the higher functioning of the nervous system ; and that all man's activities are governed by necessary mechanical laws. Such so-called spiritual entities as the soul, human liberty and God, are a delusion ; religion is an evil ; the atheistic State advocated by Bayle (**130**) is the ideal of society ; the purpose of life is egoistic pleasure which we should hasten to enjoy before it is too late and the ' comedy of life is at an end '. (2) In a great number of articles in the famous ' Encyclopedia ' (*Dictionnaire Raisonné des Sciences, des Arts et des Métiers*) which was published in Paris between the years 1752-1772 under the direction first of D'ALEMBERT [69] (1717-1783), then of DIDEROT [70] (1713-1784). The encyclopedists arrogated to themselves the title of ' philosophers '. (3) In the work entitled *Système de la nature* which was published under the pseudonym of Mirabaud in 1770, but was chiefly from the pen of D'HOLBACH (1723-1789), and may be called the bible of the materialists of the end of the eighteenth century. (4) In the mechanistic theories of many scientists such as FONTENELLE [71] (1657-1756), BUFFON [72] (1708-1788) and ROBINET (1735-1820). The opposition between those who held a mechanistic view of the universe and those who held a teleological view, ' cause-finaliers ', to use Voltaire's expression, underlies all the controversies of this period both in learned and

[68] *Essai de psychologie ; Palingénésies philosophiques.*
[69] *Discours préliminaire.*
[70] *Pensées philosophiques ; Pensées sur l'interpretation de la nature ; Entretien de d'Alembert et de Diderot* (posthumous).
[71] *Entretien sur la pluralité des mondes.*
[72] *Histoire naturelle générale et particulière.*

unlearned circles, and is an evidence of the enthusiastic cult of naturalism which is the characteristic of the whole of the eighteenth century.

130. Religious Philosophy.—The French philosophy of this century assimilated and accentuated the rationalistic criticism that the English sensualist philosophers had brought against all positive religions ; and this accounts for the widespread hatred of Catholicism which became the dominant note in all forms of religious philosophy.

1. *Religious scepticism.* PIERRE BAYLE (1647-1706), the author of the *Dictionnaire historique et critique,* laid it down as a principle that all religion, not only revealed dogma but even every teaching in favour of natural religion, is as a matter of fact and by its nature incompatible with reason. Yet he professed himself a believer, and sought to reconcile the inconsistency of his position by the theory of the two truths, namely that what is true in philosophy may be false in theology and vice versa. His influence was most pernicious, for many of his followers paid attention first and foremost to the absurdity of all religious belief which he had put before their minds. He was largely instrumental in completely divorcing religion and reason ; and in consequence, religion being absurd, morality was made to rest on a rationalistic basis and an atheistic State became possible.

2. *Theism.* VOLTAIRE [73] (1694-1778), although a very versatile and often a very superficial writer, takes his place in the history of philosophy as a representative of theism. He popularized the views of Locke, and whilst he agreed in more than one point with the materialistic view, he did not hesitate to oppose it on many others. After having taken upon himself to demolish all positive religion and Catholicism in particular, he elaborated an incoherent theory about God which varied in his different works. He was a believer in God's existence, but he sometimes spoke of Him as Nature, sometimes as the Architect of the world, sometimes as the motive for honest conduct and the foundation of social order, and necessary as a deterrent for men in the same way as law-courts and police : ' If God did not exist, we should be under the necessity of inventing a God '.

---

[73] *Lettres sur les Anglais ; Éléments de la philosophie de Newton mis à la portée de tout le monde ; Candide ou sur l'optimisme ; Dictionnaire philosophique* (1764), which he wrote after having quarrelled with the other authors of the famous *Encyclopedia.*

3. *Atheism.* The theories advocated by La Mettrie, d'Holbach, etc., raised atheism to the standard of a demonstrated thesis which it is idle to dispute, and belief in God came to be regarded not only by the educated but also by the masses as a thing unworthy and harmful.

131. Ethics.—The ethical deductions of the sensualist psychology appear in the writings of HELVÉTIUS [74] (1715-1771), who carried egoism to its extreme consequences ; at the same time he endeavoured to reconcile the selfishness of the individual with the welfare of the many by an appeal to the ' sentiment of French honour '. The ethical aspect of materialism appealed mostly to the lower classes, where its only effect was to aggravate the growing discontent with the political and social state of affairs at the time.

132. Natural Law.—The movement to establish the individualistic point of view which MONTESQUIEU [75] (1689-1755) had treated in its application to political philosophy, JEAN JACQUES ROUSSEAU [76] (1712-1778) developed in its bearing on Natural Right and social philosophy. The state of nature, in which man is naturally good, consists in a solitary life ; the social state, based on a mutual contract, has led to the division of labour, individual ownership, inequality of station in life, etc., and has put an end to this happiness. A return to the state of nature is now impossible, but men may approach to it as far as possible by abandoning artificial culture and society conventions, and by ensuring that each shall possess the inalienable rights and freedom with which nature has endowed him, so that without let or hindrance he may develop his personality to the full. On natural sentiment Rousseau built up an ethical system and a philosophy of religion. During his lifetime his ideas permeated the masses and hastened the coming of the Revolution.

V. GERMAN PHILOSOPHY IN THE EIGHTEENTH CENTURY
(LEIBNIZ TO KANT)

133. General Sketch.—The German philosophy of the eighteenth century lacked both originality and depth. (1) In the first place, most of its systems were derived from Leibniz's

[74] *De l'esprit.*
[75] *Lettres Persanes ; De l'esprit des lois.*
[76] *La nouvelle Héloïse ; De contrat social ; Émile ou sur l'éducation.* See *Ethics,* **74, 111** f.

theory of monads ; thus the school of Wolff, the aesthetic and sentimental school, the advocates of the philosophy of history and certain eclectic writers developed isolated, and sometimes secondary, theories from Leibniz. No one revived his system in its entirety. (2) On the other hand, a reactionary movement against certain exaggerated principles in Leibniz's philosophy encouraged the development of an empirical philosophy which was due to the influence of the English schools. (3) German philosophy formed an early alliance with literature, and received a considerable impetus from a sudden awakening of artistic feeling and assumed a popular form.

134. The School of Wolff.—CHRISTIAN WOLFF [77] (1679-1754), who was a professor at Halle University (1706), where he fell into disgrace under William I of Prussia and was later reinstated, was an ardent admirer of Leibniz's philosophy and endeavoured to give a systematic exposition of it. He started with Leibniz's division of truths of fact and eternal truths, but departed from him by asserting a distinction of nature between them; he maintained that every object can be known empirically and by way of pure deduction. We find a similar conception in TSCHIRNHAUSEN [78] (1651-1708), who perhaps influenced him. This parallelism concerning the sources of knowledge he made to be the basis of a new classification of the philosophical sciences, which in great part is still admitted to-day. According to this, the theoretical sciences comprise general metaphysics or ontology, and special metaphysics ; this latter admitting of subdivision into natural theology or theodicy and teleology, deductive and empirical psychology, rational cosmology and the natural sciences. This attempt at classification constitutes the most noteworthy feature in his contribution to philosophy, which in itself is a marshalling of Leibniz's ideas after a method that is oftentimes pedantic.

Wolff founded a school and may be called the professor of philosophy to all Germany in the eighteenth century. The most individual among his disciples was Baumgarten.

135. The Aesthetic School.—In the human consciousness Leibniz had placed the aesthetic impression as midway between

---

[77] *Logica, ontologia, cosmologia, psychologia rationalis, theologia naturalis, philosophia practica universalis, jus naturae, jus gentium; Vernünftige Gedanken.*
[78] *Medicina mentis.*

the clear concept and the confused sensation (118), describing it as ' the confused perception of the order and harmony of the universe '. Taking this idea, BAUMGARTEN (1714-1762) considered aesthetics as a study of the *sensation* of order (αἰσθάνομαι), and regarded this new science as the younger stepsister of logic. He wrote the first treatise on the beautiful [79], and this is his chief title to celebrity. The cosmological optimism of Leibniz led him to regard the imitation of nature as the ideal of art ; and several of his contemporaries, such as Eschenburg, Meier, Sulzer and Mendelssohn carried on his work. Meier showed that beauty vanishes on the analysis of an object ; Sulzer thought that the feeling of the beautiful is connected with obscurity of representation, and Mendelssohn regarded it as an endowment of lower natures alone.

136. The Philosophy of Sentiment.—As an outgrowth from Leibniz's theory of ' dim ' perceptions flourished a literature of autobiographies. The theory started also a psychology of feeling, and led indirectly to a new tripartite division of the human faculties—cognition, feeling, conation. These ' dim ' perceptions were regarded rather as a state of the soul—of pleasure or of displeasure—than as representations or volitional acts, and the sentiment of the beautiful was ranged as one of the numerous feelings of the soul. This threefold division of faculties was popularized by TETENS [80] (1736-1805), the predecessor of Kant, and replaced among very many modern philosophers the old twofold division into intellect and will. Subsequently the novelty was carried so far as to despoil intelligence of its rights in order to allow individual sentiment the primacy as sole source of knowledge. Here was a new triumph for the theory of the indistinct perceptions of Leibniz. HAMANN (1730-1788), surnamed the Wizard of the North, and JACOBI (1743-1819) are the representatives of this tendency in epistemological studies. Kant found his first opponents among these advocates of the philosophy of feeling, inasmuch he restored clear representations to their place of primacy and honour.

137. The Philosophy of History.—The historical conception of the development of the monads had been neglected by the first disciples of Leibniz. A return to the teleological view

---

[79] *Aesthetica.*
[80] *Philosophische Versuche über die menschliche Natur und ihre Entwicklung*

which interprets history from the standpoint of the organic unity of the human race was effected by Lessing and Herder, who besides being philosophers were also intimately associated with the intellectual culture of Germany in the eighteenth century. LESSING [81] (1729-1781) applied this theory of historical evolution to the study of religions, regarding all the religions in the history of the world as so many successive and more perfect phases of one and the same religious life. HERDER [82] (1744-1803) extended this view to the whole of the history of the human race, and endeavoured to show that by a necessary evolution the past was what it had to be [83].

138. Reaction against Leibniz and Wolff.—A protest was raised by the immediate disciples of Wolff against the determinism of Leibniz and the pedantic formalism of Wolff's philosophical teaching. RÜDIGER (1673-1731) and CRUSIUS (1712-1776) took the lead in judging and condemning the exaggerated use of the deductive method, as incapable of affording an explanation of the world of reality if the experimental method is ignored. This departure from the system of Leibniz created, under the influence of the English and French philosophies, a current of empirical ideas, which was hardly original and confined chiefly to descriptive psychology. The English philosophy also had an influence on a series of religious disputes, which however were less philosophical in their nature than in England, because in Germany men were less able to throw off their adherence to the various creeds. It was in these controversies that we can trace the beginnings of biblical criticism.

139. Philosophy in Popular Form.—To complete this sketch of German philosophy it is necessary to add that THOMASIUS (1655-1728), who is considered the first of the German 'Enlighteners', became the apostle of a popular and practical philosophy based on an appeal to 'middle-class common sense'. His influence made itself felt on all classes of minds, notably on artists and writers, and was thus instrumental in

---

[81] Translation of the New Essays of Leibniz ; *Erziehung des Menschen geschlects ; Theologische Streitschriften.*

[82] *Auch eine Philosophie der Geschichte der Menschheit; Philosophy of the History of Mankind* (trs: Churchill).

[83] Similar ideas had already been put forward by the Italian philosopher Vico (1668-1744). In the middle of the eighteenth century there also appeared, in Germany, the first historians of philosophy—Brucker (1697-1770) and Tiedemann (1748-1803)

giving the philosophical veneer that was characteristic of the intellectual productions of the period. At the awakening of the German romanticism the works of the great literary scholars Schiller (1759-1805) and Goethe (1749-1832) further cemented the alliance between poetry and philosophy, giving to the latter the popularity which the works of these great men of genius enjoyed.

Compared with Leibniz all other German philosophers in the eighteenth century pale into insignificance, and all were eclipsed by the giant personality of Kant.

CHAPTER II

THE PHILOSOPHY OF KANT

140. Critical Philosophy.—Kant was born in 1724 at Königsberg, where he applied himself to the study of theology, philosophy and the natural sciences. During the first part of his philosophical career he set himself to assimilate, and even adopted as his own, the principal theories of modern thought, especially those of Leibniz, Wolff and Crusius, and later on those of Locke and Hume, and Rousseau. The second stage was when, in the midst of all these conflicting influences, the traits of his own originality developed [84]; after thirty years' personal reflection this appeared before the world in 1770, in which year he was given a public chair of philosophy at Königsberg. This he held until 1797. He died in 1804.

The new philosophy of Kant was given by himself the name of Critical Philosophy; it is also known as transcendental criticism. By the analysis of the *concept* of knowledge he claimed to find out what must be the structure of the cognitional faculty, what the conditions in the undisturbed faculty which precede knowledge, and finally what the limits of certitude. Adhering to the new tripartite division of faculties **(136)**, he made in turn a critique of the speculative or theoretic reason, of the practical reason or will, and of the faculty of sentiment or, as he termed it, of ' judgment ' (Urtheilskraft).

141. The Critique of Pure Reason.—1. This first part of Kant's critical philosophy deals with a theory of scientific knowledge. Such knowledge consists of a body of universal,

---

[84] Chief works of the second—the ' critical '—period of Kant's career: *Critique of Pure Reason* (trs. Max Müller; also Meiklejohn), *Fundamental Principles of the Metaphysic of Morals* and *Critique of Practical Reason* (trs. Abbott); *Critique of Judgment* (trs. Bernard). Consult WATSON, *The Philosophy of Kant Explained* (MacLehose, Glasgow, 1908); CAIRD, *The Critical Philosophy of Kant*, 2 vols. (MacLehose, Glasgow, 1889). We pass over here the dogmatic philosophy of Kant and the writings of the first period of his life. See *Crit.* **27, 32, 39** f.; *Log.*, **33**; *Gen. Met.*, **109**; *Ethics*, **55** f., **74, 80, 111** f.; *Nat. Theol.*, **5, 9.**

necessary judgments. The first question, then, to present itself was concerning the nature of a necessary, universal judgment.

The ' analytic ' judgment, according to Kant, is one in which the predicate can be asserted of the subject upon the mere analysis of the latter ; and this he regarded as having no strictly scientific value (against Leibniz). Similarly what he termed the ' synthetic a posteriori ' judgment, which bases the union of predicate and subject upon some sensible experience, though without the latter containing the former, he considered to be also unscientific, since experience is by its nature contingent and variable, and cannot be the foundation of knowledge which is formed by laws, that is, of necessary and immutable judgments (against Hume). Only the ' synthetic a priori ' judgment has a scientific value and is capable of regulating universally and necessarily the world of experience : it is, in fact, a judgment wherein the mode of our joining subject and predicate is a priori, that is to say, determined by the structure of our faculties and not by experience.

A second question consequently arises concerning the nature of our faculties of knowledge and of the certitude to which they may attain. Kant distinguished between sensibility, understanding and reason.

2. *The faculty of sense-knowledge.* The impression of our senses, both external and internal, in Kant's system, makes the *matter* of all knowledge. This is elaborated in us; and this first elaboration is due to two a priori *forms* or determinations which belong to the structure of the faculty, namely time and space, the external senses representing all objects as extended in space, and the internal senses all conscious states as succeeding one another in time. Space and time are thus the a priori conditions of sensation : they are ' pure forms of our intuition ' (reine Anschauungen), moulds, so to speak, into which the impressions of our internal and external senses are received. A sensation of an object is an impression formed in space and time.

These *forms* of sense-perception, inasmuch as they are universal and necessary, are objective, that is to say, in every man every sensible impression appears necessarily in space and time ; yet, as these forms belong entirely to the structure of the faculty, their value is only phenomenal; in other words, we have no right to apply to things themselves the properties in accordance with which they appear before us.

The *matter* or content thus elaborated, or the impression, is incapable of teaching us anything at all of the inner nature of the extramental world, since every impression, as it is in us, is 'informed'. The thing-in-itself or the noumenon, by contrast with the thing such as it appears to us or the phenomenon, must always remain an unknown and unknowable *x* ; and Kant does not delay to investigate thoroughly the origin of this impression and its sufficient reason.

3. *The understanding* (Verstand). The intuitions of sensibility which furnish us with sensations in space and time (matter) are elaborated in their turn by forms or *categories* of the understanding which establish manifold relations between these sense-experiences. Hence a second kind of elaboration. Judgments of the Transcendental Analytic, or inquiry into the a priori elements of thought as distinguished from sensation, are the expression of these relations or syntheses and constitute science, the only rational knowledge of the sensible world. The types of the relations necessarily established by every human intelligence, independently of any experience (hence *a priori*), between the sensible intuitions and governing them all are twelve in number, namely : unity, plurality, totality (referring to the quantity of judgments and corresponding to universal, particular and singular judgments) ; reality, negation, limitation (referring to the quality of judgments and corresponding to affirmative, negative and infinite judgments) ; subsistence and inherence, causality and dependence, reciprocity (referring to the kind of relation between subject and predicate and corresponding to categorical, hypothetical and disjunctive judgments) ; possibility and impossibility, existence and non-existence, necessity and contingency (referring to the modality of judgments and corresponding to problematic, assertoric and apodeictic judgments).

Mathematics and the natural sciences are the only human sciences: in mathematics our intuitions do not result from some direct experience, but from some imagined experience, *e.g.* I imagine points and lines in space ; in the natural sciences, the intuition is direct, is related to things. Mathematics and the natural sciences build up sensible intuitions according to *categories*, and their judgments are a priori laws.

One of the most important of these categories is that of causality by which is meant that between an antecedent phenomenon and a consequent phenomenon we construct a relation of dependence and judge the one to be the cause of the other.

Since the categories are determinations of the pure understanding, we cannot apply them to things, and thus scientific knowledge of the world is the product of our mental organization; of things-in-themselves the mind can know nothing. Accordingly the problem of the nature of reality is insoluble.

When Kant speaks of the *objectivity* of a judgment we must bear in mind that he means the necessity and universality with which it imposes itself on all minds and extends to all the possible cases of experience. The condition of this objectivity he declares to be the 'transcendental apperception of the ego', that is to say, that over and above the empirical consciousness, which is variable and individual, there must be a super-individual consciousness, which is the same in all men, a priori and unknowable in itself, and of which the intuitions of sensibility and the categories of the understanding are but the functions.

4. *Reason* (Vernunft). Since scientific knowledge extends only to the sensible world, the super-sensible is unknowable. Yet we are obliged to *conceive* it, since we experience within ourselves the need of bringing conditioned and relative phenomena that are the objects of our cognitions into relation with some unconditioned and absolute realities. Thus the *world* and the *soul*, unconditioned wholes with which we bring into relation the phenomena of the external and internal senses respectively, and, above these, *God*, whom we conceive as the supreme cause of these two, are the three pure ideas or a priori forms of the pure reason. These ideas no longer apply to anything material that is the object of experience and they have only a subjective value.

To sum up : scientific knowledge stops at the threshold of super-sensible reality. But this occupies no mean part in the Kantian system, seeing that theoretic life is dominated by moral life, as his second *Critique* will show us.

142. The Critique of Practical Reason.—Knowledge or theoretic experience has nothing in common with our actual moral experience ; the direction of our conduct forms a domain apart. In his first *Critique* Kant analyses thought ; in the second he analyses action, and to determine the laws which regulate moral conduct he proceeds, on the same lines as in the first treatise, to get a clear meaning of the idea of morality and then to determine the conditions which it presupposes.

1. *Idea of moral obligation.* That there exists an obligation our conscience attests, but in analysing it Kant finds that it does not consist in a precept, applying in a particular case, nor in a hypothetical imperative, which means that *if* I wish to obtain a certain good known by experience I must act thus or so. The moral law is a *categorical imperative*, that is to say, a command independent of any utilitarian motive and universally valid for all men and in all cases, one which gives no external reason for its commands and exacts unconditional obedience. He expresses this formal imperative thus : ' Act according to the law because it is the law ' ; ' Act out of reverence for thine own worth as man ' ; ' Act as if the maxim from which thou actest were to become through thy will a universal law of nature ' (cp. *Stoicism*, **32**).

2. *The postulates of Practical Reason.* The existence of the moral law involves as a corollary the reality of certain conditions without which moral conduct, as so defined, would no be possible. These guarantees, which we cannot prove but must postulate, resting them on the consciousness that ' thou canst, for thou oughtest ', are demanded by the practical reason, and are threefold. (1) *Freedom*, or the autonomy of the practical reason, the pure self-determination of the rational will. This does not follow any empirically given impulse, but acts according to the moral law because such is the law. The theoretic reason, before which every phenomenon appears as conditioned by an antecedent phenomenon (category of efficient causality), ignores human freedom and the conception of finality. (2) *Immortality of the soul.* A second postulate is the conception of the highest good. Virtue or the observance of duty is not the same as happiness, but virtue is worthy of happiness and the moral consciousness demands it. Since the present life does not fulfil this demand, we must postulate the reality of a future life, and this involves a third postulate : (3) *God*, for an authoritative voice implies a law-giver and reward for moral conduct a rewarder.

Kant conceived the morality of an act to rest in the intention and not in external conduct, and thus natural law, which is concerned with the latter, he regards as independent of morality.

3. *Primacy of Practical Reason.* Freedom, immortality and God are certain truths, for the simple reason that were they not so the problem of morality would be insoluble. Their certainty is based on the exigencies of the will or the practical reason. There stand, as certainties, before the practical reason, a number of super-sensible realities or things-in-themselves that are unknowable by the theoretic reason. This ' supreme antinomy ' or apparent contradiction Kant solves by declaring the primacy of the practical reason ; that is to say, the rational will dominates the theoretic reason and completes the knowledge it gives us. This theory of Kant has had important developments in later philosophy.

143. Critique of the Faculty of Judgment or Sentiment (Urtheilskraft).—In his third *Critique* Kant designs to show wherein the two preceding ones are closely connected. The notion of finality is foreign to scientific knowledge and comes to us from the consideration of moral conduct. Feeling or sentiment, says Kant, is a distinct idea from both knowledge and will, and by this third faculty we are made aware that sensible nature possesses a purposiveness ; by it we contemplate sensible phenomena that are the objects of theoretic reason by applying to them an a priori form of the practical reason. Finality is not a category of the understanding and therefore not an object of knowledge, and since all phenomena are regulated from the standpoint of knowledge by the category of efficient causality, purpose cannot be known but only contemplated or felt ; in other words, can only be the object of the faculty of judgment or sentiment. Moreover, this feeling, sentiment or contemplation of purpose is universal and necessary (objective) and belongs to the structure of the faculty. There are two kinds of judgment regarding finality, both synthetic a priori.

1. *The teleological judgment* is concerned with *objective* finality. By it we apprehend the phenomena of the sensible world in their relation to an end assigned to them by the supreme intelligence of God. Of course this finality does not regulate the world-in-itself but only the world as the object of contemplation.

2. *The aesthetic judgment* is concerned with *subjective* finality.

By it we apprehend phenomena in their relation to the sentiment of harmony which it is their nature to procure for all our
faculties. The beautiful and the sublime are attributes not of
things but of our representative states. The sentiment of the
beautiful is calm and serene ; it is the free play of the faculty,
a disinterested satisfaction. This satisfaction which the
beautiful gives is an indication of a finality, for the object is
made to please ; but the beautiful does not give the concept of
definite design, for if this were known aesthetic satisfaction
would vanish. The sublime gives rise not to a calm sentiment,
for it is complex ; at first it gives a ' humiliating ' impression
when the faculty is face to face with what is great beyond all
comparison ; but ultimately it gives a sense of the exalted
nature of our understanding [85].

[85] Besides the remarkable influence of Kant on philosophical thought, with
which we deal in the following chapter, it is not difficult to see in his assertion
of the supremacy of the moral law the origin of the tendency to regard
Christianity more as a system of ethics than as one of dogmatic truth. He
had, too, an unparalleled influence on German literature, and through his
English exponents, especially Coleridge (1772-1834), Wordsworth (1770-1850)
and Carlyle (1795-1881), on the literature of the English-speaking world.—TRS.

CHAPTER III

POST-KANTIAN PHILOSOPHY

(*Nineteenth Century*)

I. German Philosophy during the First Half of the Nineteenth Century

144. General Sketch.—The influence of Kant upon the philosophy of the nineteenth century can scarcely be exaggerated. It took some time before it was felt outside Germany, but there it was immediate and gave birth during the first three decades of the century to several original systems, and as its result German genius rose to a height unknown before. This was the time also of a great development of romanticism, which had much in common with the philosophic movement.

The various disputes ranged chiefly about two points in Kant's teaching, the noumenon and the transcendental apperception (**141**), concerning which we have many new attempts to formulate a critical philosophy. (1) Kant made the a priori forms of knowledge to belong to the structure of the mind, but not the experimental matter which these forms elaborate ; to him the production of sensible impressions remained an enigma, since things-in-themselves which are necessary to provide them are unknowable. Kant's successors set themselves to solve this problem by taking a new attitude towards the world-in-itself. The Critical Idealists made experimental matter to be as much the product of the mind as the form-in-itself, and thereby denied the existence of noumena ; the Critical Realists referred sensible impressions to things-in-themselves and so affirmed their real existence. (2) The transcendental apperception or super-individual consciousness the same for all men, to which Kant had devoted little attention, was given a preponderating place in the thought of his German disciples. Most of them transformed his doctrine by interpreting the transcendental apperception in a *monistic* sense, regarding it as identical for all men, the universal Ego or Spirit.

In classifying the German philosophies derived from Kant, if we leave aside his immediate disciples and opponents, we may consider the *critical idealism* represented by Fichte, Schelling and Hegel as the first and greatest transformation of Kantianism. As a reaction, in some respects, against this idealism was the *critical realism* of Schopenhauer and Herbart. Lastly, there was a group of psychologists who endeavoured to vindicate against the exaggerations of this metaphysical criticism the rights of individual experience, but even so their conclusions showed unmistakable evidence of a Kantian impress.

145. The Immediate Disciples and Opponents of Kant.—The new system of Kant was too original to be fully comprehended by his first disciples. They first of all formed a school at the university of Jena, whence it was called the second home of Kantianism, and in a short time spread into the other universities of Germany. Tinged with other doctrines, the new philosophy infiltrated into the theory of natural law (FEUER-BACH), of history (SCHLOSSER) and the history of philosophy (TENEMANN and BUHLE). The most notable among Kant's first followers were REINHOLD [86] (1758-1823) and the poet SCHILLER [87] (1759-1805). The former developed several ideas of the Critique of Pure Reason, but abandoned Kant's position with regard to the noumenon, maintaining that things-in-themselves are necessary in order to explain the origin of our experimental impressions. The latter took from Kant only his aesthetic theories. The impression of the beautiful, according to Schiller, resides in the contemplation of sensible appearances when we pass by with perfect unconcern their scientific elaboration and make them an object of disinterested pleasure as if all were a ' play ' ; and this is not a mere passing phase but occupies a very large place in the psychic life : ' man is only truly man when at play '.

On the other hand, Kant met with a very lively opposition

[86] *Versuch einer neuen Theorie des menschlichen Vorstellungsvermögens ; Das Fundament des philosophischen Wissens.*
[87] *On the Sublime ; Letters upon the Aesthetical Education of Man :* (trs. Bohn Library).

and several reviews were started with the object of combating him. Hamann and Herder criticized the minute divisions into which he divided up psychic life. Jacobi pointed out the contradictions which lay hidden in his theory of the noumenon (136, 137). The reasonableness of Jacobi's criticisms was implicitly recognized by Reinhold and forcibly substantiated by the attacks of SCHULZE [88] (1761-1823) and SALOMON MAIMON [89] (1754-1800), of whom Kant could say that, of all his adversaries, none understood him so well.

146. Critical Idealism.—Two principles sum up critical idealism : (1) The world of things-in-themselves is the product of our faculties of representation just as is the phenomenal world ; the matter of our cognitions equally with their form is derived from the structure of the representing ego, who creates for himself an object of knowledge. (2) All psychic functions are the self-development of a principle (which corresponds to the transcendental apperception of Kant), but there exists only one psychic principle for the whole of humanity, and thus this principle, or Mind, is the only existing reality (monism).

147. Fichte (1762-1814) became acquainted with the Kantian philosophy at Leipzig, and knew the Master at Königsberg. He succeeded Reinhold in the chair of philosophy at Jena, and there from 1794 to 1799 elaborated an original system to which he gave the name of *Wissenschaftslehre* [90] (literally ' doctrine of science ') ; this he modified in subsequent works [91]. He became the first rector of Berlin University, which was founded in 1810.

1. The *Wissenschaftslehre* or idealism of activity. The absolute and universal Ego is a tendency to act, infinite and unbroken activity, acting for itself and through itself (das Thun des Thuns), and in acting it converts its own states into objects of knowledge and by reflection becomes self-consciousness. The process of becoming self-conscious covers three stages : (1) *thesis*—the ego ' posits itself ', i.e. it knows itself as existing and as identical with itself (Ich = Ich) ; (2) *antithesis*—it

---

[88] *Aenesidemus* (anonymous).

[89] *Versuch einer Transcendentalphilosophie ; Versuch einer neuen Logik.*

[90] *Grundlage der gesammten Wissenschaftslehre ; Grundriss der eigenthümlichen Wissenschaftslehre ; Erste und zweite Einleitung in die Wissenschaftslehre ; Das System der Sittenlehre :* (part trs. Kroeger, *The Science of Knowledge*).

[91] *Die Grundzüge des gegenwärtigen Zeitalters* (trs. Smith, *Fichte's Popular Works*) ; *Reden an die deutsche Nation.*

posits within itself the non-ego, i.e. it creates the world, not the world-in-itself (which would be absurd) but the world as an object of representation ; (3) *synthesis*—the ego (and it must be borne in mind that the Fichtean ' I ' means not the individual but the universal self-consciousness) becomes aware that it is limited and determined by the non-ego, i.e. the object represented in and before the Mind (theoretic or representative ego), and that the non-ego is limited and determined by the ego (practical ego). Hence we have a division of the *Wissenschaftslehre* into two parts : (*a*) The Theoretical, which studies the development of knowledge. As every conscious act, according to Fichte, entails reflection on a previous act, the first acts of the mind cannot be conscious ones, and thus Fichte maintains that the generation of experimental material is the fruit of an *unconscious* self-determination of the ego. These sensible impressions are then elaborated according to all the apparatus of the a priori forms of the pure reason of Kant. (*b*) The Practical, which shows that if the ego is incessantly creating to itself objects of representation this is because it is a *tendency to act*, and without resistance or an object opposed to it, it would not act ; the ego is theoretic or knowing precisely because it is practical or acting, that is to say, it represents a non-ego in order to act upon it. The ultimate foundation of the incessant impulse of the intelligence to be knowing is the absolute need of the ego to act, and this absolute need is duty.

Such is the new sense which Fichte gave to the Kantian doctrine of the primacy of the practical reason. It is precisely in this autonomy or self-determination of the ego, impelled to activity for activity's sake, that *morality* lies. Nature as represented has no value of its own other than as material which serves for the accomplishment of duty. The individual —which is a ' positing ' of the absolute and universal Ego—acts morally when he draws from the insufficiency of every action a motive for further activity.

2. The second idealist system of Fichte introduced the idea of an absolute Being, God. Since reflection or the fundamental activity of the Ego is by its very definition a turning back upon something anterior to itself, it follows that, to explain its possibility, there must be at the beginning an absolute and immutable principle ; this is not a mere form of reflection, but

God. Conscious knowing or reflection is nothing else but a necessary and phenomenal continuation of the Absolute.

Without actually founding a school, Fichte greatly influenced the thought of Schelling and Hegel.

148. Schelling (1775-1854) was a professor at Jena from 1798, and at first taught side by side with his master Fichte, but he soon broke with him. Later he had Hegel as a disciple and colleague, until he also became an opponent. From Jena he went to different universities, and finally to Berlin (1841), where he met with no great success. His philosophic work is marred by its want of unity, for it comprised at least five systems.

1. *Physical idealism* [92] (1797-1799) is only a development of one part of the Fichtean 'Doctrine of Science', namely that nature is spirit, as it is a psychical product of mind representation. It is an account of unconscious Spirit passing, according to a rhythm of absolute evolution and a purposiveness, through the various stages which constitute the different kingdoms of nature. Thus nature did not possess, as with Fichte, merely a moral value ; Schelling advocated the recognition of it as a product of spiritual activity and the study of it for its own sake. His philosophy had a considerable influence, the more so because the theories of the absolute evolution and unity of the cosmic life were held in high esteem by the scientists of his time. It succeeded in gaining over the romantic schools, with which he was in close touch. And further, it benefited from the revival of Spinoza's teaching which resulted from the polemical writings of Lessing. The conception that the cosmos is endowed with one vital principle is found in the teaching of his immediate disciples and in OKEN (1779-1851), GOETHE (1749-1832) and NOVALIS (1772-1801).

2. *Transcendental or aesthetic idealism* [93] (1800-1801), conceived under the influence of German romanticism, was the second form which Schelling's philosophy took. It is marked by a complete fusion of romanticist and idealist teachings [94] :

---

[92] *Ideen zu einer Philosophie der Natur ; Von der Weltseele ; Erster Entwurf eines Systems der Naturphilosophie.*

[93] *Der transcendentale Idealismus ; Vorlesungen über die Philosophie der Kunst.*

[94] This had already been begun by Novalis and especially by Schlegel (1772-1829).

the aesthetic production of the absolute Ego is the principle of all its activities, the basic function which reduces to unity the operations of both the theoretic and the practical ego ; and hence the work of art is the ego producing itself most perfectly. Certain romanticists, such as SCHLEGEL and SOLGER, known as the ' humorists ' or ' ironists ', drew the conclusion that the *romantic ego* of the poet, invested with the prerogatives of the absolute Ego, produces for the sake of production itself, without any concern for the content of the work of art or public judgment.

This second system of Schelling gives an account of the conscious ego, as the first did of the non-ego. Later he united both in a third system.

3. *Absolute idealism* or *the philosophy of identity* [95] (1801-1804). Schelling gradually modified the subjective idealism of Fichte by giving nature a real value independent of consciousness or spirit ; he then sought for some common ground or principle anterior to both nature and consciousness from which he could deduce both ; this he called the Absolute and defined it as the identity of the real and the ideal. One of his contemporaries, Oken, symbolized it by the symbol $+$ o. The Absolute develops itself in a twofold seriation, the real and the ideal, and the points of similarity between Schelling and the neo-Spinozism become more marked.

Later the philosophy of identity assumed a slightly new form by the Absolute being regarded as not indifferent but endowed with Intelligence and Ideas. KRAUSE (1782-1832) was one of his many followers who adopted this system, and put it in an original form as ' panentheism ' in which he tried to fuse pantheism and divine personality. The identity of being and thought was very effectively taken up by Hegel and Schleiermacher, the former giving it a logical and the latter a religious direction. SCHLEIERMACHER (1768-1834) acknowledged that whilst we cannot attain to any direct knowledge of God we have a feeling that we are interpenetrated by the Absolute, and it is this religious sentiment which keeps the balance of all the faculties and is the foundation of morality.

4. *The philosophy of freedom* [96] (1804-1813). In this system

---

[95] *Darstellung meines Systems der Philosophie.*
[96] *Philosophie und Religion ; Untersuchungen über das Wesen der menschlichen Freiheit.*

Schelling seeks to discover how the divine Ideas transform themselves in finite reality, and he finds that this ' becoming ' of the Absolute constitutes an original, incomprehensible fact, a fact without rational ground, and in this sense he considers it as a ' free ' fact, one of the free acts of the Ego which has no rationale. He accounts for the origin of the world as a ' falling away ' of the Ideas from God. Yet the finite world must return to the infinite, and this return in the case of man is brought about by mysticism and religion. BAADER (1765-1841) developed this theory from the Catholic standpoint as Scheiermacher did from the Protestant.

5. *Philosophy of mythology and Revelation.* This last phase of Schelling's thought is only of secondary importance.

149. Hegel and Logical Idealism.—HEGEL [97] (1770-1831) commenced his professional career at Jena by the side of his master Schelling ; later he went to Heidelberg (1816) and then to Berlin, where he immediately gained an unrivalled celebrity, which continued as long as he lived, and imbued a whole generation with his philosophy.

His style is as obscure and complicated as Schelling's is clear and precise, but his system is marked by its completeness and the rigorous unity which runs throughout it. He set out to show that Spirit or Idea in its becoming develops itself in conformity with an irresistible necessity which is of the conceptual or *dialectical* order : ' All being is reason, and the rational alone is real '. This development is regulated by the triadism of thesis, antithesis and synthesis, for we may consider the universal and absolute spirit in-itself (an sich)—logic—out-of-self, as exteriorized before itself (fürsich, in seinen Anders-sein)—philosophy of Nature—and for-itself, coming back to itself in consciousness (an-und-fürsich)—philosophy of Mind or Spirit. (1) *Logic* studies the categories or the forms of the becoming of Being, developing itself by a movement of ' immanent and incessant dialectic ' towards self-consciousness. (2) The *philosophy of Nature* describes the various stages which Spirit passes through in its state of otherness and self-estrangement or externalization ; hence we have mechanics (matter and space), physics (body) and

[97] *Phenomenologie des Geistes ; Wissenschaft der Logik* (part trs. H. Stirling, *Secret of Hegel*) ; *Encyclopädie der philosophischen Wissenschaften* (part trs. Wallace, *Hegel's Philosophy of Mind*) ; *Grundlinien der Philosophie des Rechts* (trs. Dyde).

organics (life). (3) The *philosophy of Spirit or Mind* (Geist) studies the conscious return of the Idea upon itself in humanity. This is the most original part of Hegel's thought. The philosophy of Spirit comprises three parts : (*a*) Psychology, or the study of *Subjective Spirit*, traces the stages of knowledge through which the individual spirit, through multifold contradictions of thesis, antithesis and synthesis, gains a consciousness of its identity with the universal and absolute Spirit. (*b*) The science of *Objective Spirit*, or of humanity, reviews the many and various manifestations of social life and the development of these. The highest realization of objective mind is the State, by which he means not any determined state, but the gradual evolution of civil society. (*c*) The science of *Absolute Spirit* considers mind as it becomes in art (contemplation of mind), in religion (representation of mind), and in philosophy (the concept of mind).

Hegel regarded the world as necessarily being what it is, since Spirit can exist only in its becoming, and this becoming evolves according to a logical necessity. Thus we see how the historical conception dominates all his thought and colours every detail in his whole study of man and humanity, which is the supreme becoming of the Idea.

150. The Hegelians.—Hegel had many followers, and they were faithful adherents to his thought, except on the special problem of God and the personal nature of the human soul, over which they divided into two camps. The so-called 'right wing', to which belonged GOSCHEL (1784-1861) and BAUER (1809-1882), admitted the personality of God and the personal immortality of the human soul, whilst others, such as RUGE (1802-1880) and FEUERBACH (1804-1872; in later life became a materialist), maintained that God is a universal substance and impersonal. Many others, WEISSE (1801-1866), the younger FICHTE (1797-1879) and ULRICI (1806-1884), followed Hegel for the most part, but differed from him on sundry points and affirmed the personality of God [98].

151. Critical Realism.—Critical idealism as elaborated in its various forms made concessions in the direction of allowing the extramental objectivity of reality. Critical realism claimed to

[98] The dualism worked out by Günther, a personal God and monistic creature, and the theories of Hermes, both condemned by the Church, were derived from Hegelian teaching.

be a return to Kantian principles by conceding real existence to things-in-themselves. Monism, which is not Kantian, was adopted by Schopenhauer, but not by Herbart, whilst others inaugurated a psychological movement.

152. Schopenhauer (1788-1860) obtained his doctorate at Jena, and went to live at Dresden and at Weimar (where he knew Goethe) until he joined the professorial staff at Berlin (1820). He retired to Frankfort in 1831, where he remained till his death.

An elegant writer and a mordent critic, he undertook in his chief work *The World as Will and Idea* [99] a violent attack on idealism, and at the same time, working on material supplied by Kant, he elaborated an original cosmic synthesis. The world is representation and thing-in-itself. In treating of the *world as representation* or as it appears to us, he shows that representation, the primordial fact of consciousness, is dependent on the a priori forms belonging to the structure of the faculties, namely, time, space and causality. In treating of the *world as reality* he maintains the existence of a thing-in-itself and identifies this with will. Of the nature of will we can know nothing except by opposition to phenomena. Therefore it must be said that, since representation is dependent on time and space, the will is independent of the forms of time and space, it is not subject to multiplication but is one (monism); and since it is unhampered by the laws of efficient causality and thus acts without bounds or cessation, it is free; it is blind and infinite activity (Wille zum Leben). Therefore, too, phenomena are not the effect of will but its objectivization, and the relation of effect and cause does not extend to things-in-themselves.

These principles laid down, Schopenhauer proceeds to their application (*a*) in nature, including man, every part of which, in its higher or lower order, he sees to be only different types of will; (*b*) in aesthetics, where he shows that the beautiful realizes in a higher way the 'volitive energies' of matter, and that the 'intuition of genius' is able to put us in direct contact with the world-in itself [100]; (*c*) in morality, where he bases a doctrine of pessimism on restlessness in the will, and looks for

---

[99] *Die Welt als Wille und Vorstellung* (trs. Haldane and Kemp).
[100] Especially is this achieved in music. An effort to translate in his musical compositions this insatiable self-expression of will, the thing-in-itself, was made by Richard Wagner (1813-1883).

nirvana or the cessation of sorrow in the negation of every act of will.

Chief among the disciples of Schopenhauer was VON HART-MANN (1842-1906), who, in his *Philosophy of the Unconscious* and voluminous works written later, assigned a part to reason whilst maintaining the primacy of will, and expressed himself less pessimistic by foreseeing salvation not in mere personal asceticism but in collective social effort.

153. Herbart[1] (1776-1841), a professor at Göttingen, admitted, against Fichte and Hegel, the existence of things-in-themselves (Realen) for the reason that ' if the world were not, it would not appear '. But he did not consider that things-in-themselves are such as they appear ; they are immutable and always keep their identity, and they are not affected by any of the contradictions involved in extension, causality, etc. ; in fact, inherence and succession are nothing more than relations which we set up between things and which do not affect things themselves. He abandoned the monistic conception of Schopenhauer and the majority of the German criticists by maintaining the multiple character of realities (Realen).

In applying these principles to psychology he conceived the soul as a simple real essence, and its faculties and acts as pure relations between the soul and other *Realen*. He rejected the theory of a plurality of faculties and regarded representation as the fundamental function of the soul. The theory of education, of which Herbart was one of the creators, shows that education can influence the way in which representations unfold themselves and are associated.

The disciples of Herbart later on became an important group, among which we may mention DROBISCH, STEINTHAL and ZIMMERMANN, and LAZARUS, who inaugurated the so-called *Volkerpsychologie*, Comparative or Folk-Psychology.

154. The Psychological School.—In addition to the two main metaphysical currents of post-Kantian philosophy there was a group of psychologists who asserted the claims of individual experience and of descriptive psychology, and emphasized the value of Kant's first researches. FRIES[2] (1773-1843) was the chief one, and he maintained that internal experience informs us

---

[1] *Hauptpunkte der Metaphysik ; Lehrbuch zur Psychologie* (trs. Smith); *Psychologie als Wissenschaft.*

System der Philosophie als evidente Wissenschaft, Neue Kritik der Vernunft.

very directly of the a priori forms which regulate our elaboration of the world, and this same conscious feeling teaches us the existence of things-in-themselves. Others, such as BENEKE [3] (1798-1854), failed to detect in the data of consciousness the presence of a priori elements of knowledge.

II. FRENCH PHILOSOPHY FROM THE REVOLUTION TO THE MIDDLE OF THE NINETEENTH CENTURY

155. General Sketch.—Until the French Revolution a materialistic sensualism was the dominant philosophy in France. This soon met with a reaction on the part of an eclectic spiritualism which blended theories of the Scottish school with elements of Cartesianism, and in some cases showed signs of a superficial influence of German philosophy. In course of time this eclecticism witnessed the growth of rival systems in traditionalism and ontologism, which received the full attention of certain Catholic philosophers of this period. Later still the sensist line of thought reappeared under a seductive form in positivism, which was destined to meet with very great success.

156. Materialistic Sensualism.—This school of thought predominated in France at the end of the eighteenth century through the writings of such partisans of the Revolution as DE CONDORCET [4] (1743-1794), DE VOLNEY [5] (1757-1820) and DE SAINT-LAMBERT (1716-1803), who applied the principles of materialism to natural law and political life. CABANIS [6] (1757-1808) extended them to the field of epistemology, whilst GALL (1758-1828) and BROUSSAIS (1772-1832) thought that they had discovered in phrenology an experimental proof of their materialistic psychology. On the other hand, we have the first signs of a reaction in certain other physiologists, notably in the Schools of Medicine at Paris and Montpellier, represented by BICHAT (1711-1802) and BUCHEZ (1734-1806) ; and at the same time DESTUTT DE TRACY (1754-1836), a disciple of Condillac, and DEGÉRANDO corrected the exaggerated view of the physiological sensists, that the origin of our psychic

[3] *Lehrbuch der Psychologie als Naturwissenschaft.*
[4] *Esquisse d'un tableau historique du progrès de l'esprit humain.*
[5] *La loi naturelle ou principes physiques de la morale, déduits de l'organisme de l'homme et de l'univers ou catéchisme du citoyen français.*
[6] *Les rapports de physique et du moral de l'homme.*

states lies purely in sensation, by a system of ideological sensism and so prepared the way for Maine de Biran.

157. Spiritualism of the Eclectic School.—Maine de Biran is commonly considered as the first representative of the French psychologico-spiritualistic school, of which Victor Cousin became the unrivalled leader. This school, to which Cousin gave the name of *eclecticism*, made a vigorous attack on sensualism. Although its adherents did not all follow any uniform system, they were at one in asserting that intellectual knowledge cannot be reduced to sensation, that immaterial substances, notably the human soul and God, do exist, and that morality has a spiritual basis. Psychological introspection was the chief method employed in this spiritualistic philosophy.

MAINE DE BIRAN [7] (1766-1824) emphasized the activity of the will as the fundamental function of our being and personality, and herein found the boundary between psychical and physiological life. He regarded the will as giving us a consciousness not only of our own activity but also of a resistance coming from without, and it is this awareness of voluntary effort which brings before us the notions of causality and substance, and the other elements of a metaphysic. AMPÈRE (1775-1836) confined this attention chiefly to the capacity for classification which the intelligence enjoys [8]. ROYER-COLLARD (1763-1845), the immediate precursor of Cousin, completed the views of Maine de Biran and Ampère by introducing the psychological teaching of the Scottish school, and inaugurated in France a philosophy of common sense which prevailed against the sensist school.

VICTOR COUSIN [9] (1792-1867), the leader of the spiritualistic school, was enabled by lecture courses at the Sorbonne (1815-1820) and influence subsequently gained in academical and political life to secure the triumph of his eclectic system during the first half of the nineteenth century. His design was to consolidate into one system truths scattered up and down in various systems. For this reason he attached great importance to the history of philosophy, wherein he opened out new paths, and with Degérando may be considered as the initiator of this study in France. He meant his philosophy to

[7] *Nouvelles considérations sur les rapports du physique et du moral.*
[8] *Essai sur la philosophie des sciences.*
[9] *Cours de l'histoire de la philosophie moderne ; Du vrai, du beau et du bien.*

be eclectic, but in reality it was not and could not be ; it came more and more to be a particular system, and it is apparent that even in his classification of historical systems into sensualism, mysticism, scepticism and idealism he gave a preference to idealism. Next he took up the ideas of Royer-Collard, later on the teachings of Hegel, and finally he arrived at a spiritualistic system of his own, which, as a vague combination of the theories of the Scottish school, Descartes and Royer-Collard, makes the observation of the phenomena of consciousness the starting-point of all philosophy ; the soul, God, the beautiful, the true, the good, space and time, are all made known to man by a kind of mysterious revelation which is an inexplicable work of the reason.

Of the numerous disciples of Cousin the best known is THEODORE JOUFFROY [10] (1796-1842), who still further accentuated the Cartesian tendencies of the school and its psychological method. The same exclusive method was that of DAMIRON [11] (1794-1862), GARNIER [12] (1801-1864), SAISSET [13] (1814-1863), JUL. SIMON (1814-1896) and BARTHÉLEMY SAINT-HILAIRE (1805-1895).

158. Traditionalism and Ontologism.—There was a reaction on the part of the French Catholics against materialism and rationalism during the first half of the nineteenth century, but the systems embodying it unduly depreciated the power of our intellectual faculties.

Traditionalism was the first and most powerful form in which it appeared, being at the same time a reaction against eclectic spiritualism. DE BONALD (1754-1840), the founder of the traditionalist school, lived during the period of the Revolution, and opposed not only its excesses but its theory of the origin and mission of social power by putting forward the Catholic position [14]. In his theory of philosophy he showed his originality mostly in regard to the genesis of ideas. Before the human reason could attain to any truth there was needed, as a prerequisite condition, a primitive revelation from God. Moreover, even language itself, as well as these fundamental

[10] *Les sentiments du beau et du sublime ; Cours de droit naturel.*
[11] *Essai sur l'histoire de la philosophie en France au XIXe s.*
[12] *Traité des facultés de l'âme.*
[13] *Essai de Philosophie religieuse.*
[14] *La législation primitive ; Recherches philosophiques sur les premiers objets des connaissances morales.* See *Psych.,* **98**; *Crit.,* **24**; *Nat. Theol.,* **12.**

truths, must have been revealed to man. They have been transmitted down by the medium of tradition through society, the origin of which de Bonald maintained, in opposition to Rousseau's theory of social contract, to be primordial and natural.

JOSEPH DE MAISTRE [15] (1754-1821) followed up the political thought of de Bonald. DE LA MENNAIS [16] (1782-1854) subscribed rather to the epistemological principles of traditionalism by proclaiming the Catholic Church as the sole depositary of every tradition, which the individual left to himself is incapable of knowing. After being regarded for a long time as the leader of the Catholic party in France, and well known for his personal friendship with Lacordaire, Montalembert, Gerbet, etc., he at length broke with his friends and refused to submit to the decisions of the Church ; the final phase of his philosophy, as developed in his *Esquisse d'une philosophie*, showed evidence of pantheistic tendencies. The principles of the traditionalist teaching were carried on by BALLANCHE (1776-1847), BAUTAIN (1796-1867), and BONNETTY (1798-1879), who in 1830 started the *Annales de philosophie chrétienne*.

Ontologism was another form of reaction. Its characteristic doctrine was that we see the object of our ideas directly in God. It was a theory which was broached in France by such men as Fabre d'Envieu, but found its best defenders in Italy in the person of Gioberti (1801-1852) and in Belgium in that of Ubaghs. It was broken, together with traditionalism, by different censures of the Holy See.

159. Positivism.—Sensualism passed from the extravagant form it had assumed during the period of the French Revolution into a more seductive form as a solution to epistemological problems : in this new appearance it was known as positivism.

AUGUSTE COMTE (1798-1857) was the founder of positivism. An enthusiastic advocate of the social teachings of SAINT-SIMON (1760-1825), with whom, however, he subsequently quarrelled, he opened at Paris in 1826 a *Cours de philosophie positive* [17], published 1830-1842. Only what is positive, i.e. only facts which are accessible to observation by the external senses, can, according to Comte, be the object of scientific

[15] *Soirées de Saint-Pétersbourg.*
[16] *Essai sur l'indifférence en matière de religion.*
[17] Abbrev. trs. Harriet Martineau, *The Positive Philosophy of A. Comte.* See *Natural Theology,* 11

investigation. There is a stage in our knowledge when we give a ' theological ' explanation of things by assigning them to a supernatural agency ; we next find ' metaphysical ' explanations by causes, essence and ' occult ' qualities, and finally arrive at a ' positive ' explanation, whereby we associate phenomena together according to laws : this is Comte's famous ' Law of the Three Stages '. Comte also made a classification of the sciences, and at the head of his six positive sciences he placed sociology or the experimental study of the phenomena which result from the action of the various elements in society.

From the year 1842, Comte's ideas underwent a peculiar evolution. He became prepossessed with a mystical tendency, and aimed at making positivism a new religion, the religion of Humanity, of which he proclaimed himself the first pontiff [18].

Of his immediate disciples, if we leave out of count those who followed his religious philosophy (such as Lafitte, 1823-1893, his successor as so-called High Priest of Humanity), LITTRÉ [19] (1801-1881) was the most noteworthy. He adhered to the fundamental principle of positivism, but introduced several important modifications, especially by departing from Comte's denial of reality to whatever is not directly observable by the external senses, and by waiving all questions concerning the first origin, the nature and ultimate destiny of beings. This agnostic attitude has become one of the salient features of present-day positivism.

160. New Phases of Positivism.—The spirit of Comte's philosophy survived him, but both in France and in England it developed under various new forms. The most significant of these developments appeared in the work of TAINE [20] (1828-1893), a distinguished critic and writer of great talent, who did much to popularize in France the tenets of positivism. The object of science is to observe facts by the external and internal senses, to determine the laws or connexions existing between them and to simplify more and more these laws, yet without ever attaining to the one universal reality of which they are the expression (monism). His thought is dominated throughout by

[18] To this period belong *Système de politique positive* (trs. Bridges and others) ; *Catéchisme positiviste* (trs. Congreve) ; *Synthèse positiviste*.

[19] *Paroles de philosophie positive*.

[20] *Les philosophes français du XIX siècle ; Le positivisme anglais ; De l'intelligence ; Histoire de la littérature anglaise* (trs. Van Laun) ; *Philosophie de l'art.*

his psychology. In his study of the individual he endeavours to show that nervous activity and consciousness are nothing more than two aspects of the same phenomenon, and that psychic life is one continual flow of sensations necessarily connected with one another. As regards social life, as it manifests itself in literature, art and politics, he explains the appearance and interconnexion of social facts by the influence of the three co-efficients of race, environment and time. All this is in reality a form of determinism. These same principles he also applies to the study of history. In working out his theory he shows a colossal erudition and a wonderful talent for observation, yet his observations are not always complete and he sometimes shows himself the victim of his own preconceptions.

III. ENGLISH PHILOSOPHY IN THE NINETEENTH CENTURY

161. General Sketch.—At the beginning of the nineteenth century there were two rival schools of philosophy, the Scottish school and the Associationist school. The former soon admitted alien elements, and the latter became submerged in the vaster conceptions of positivism which constituted the dominant philosophy.

162. The Scottish School ; Associationism.—Of the numerous followers of Dugald Stewart some were unable to maintain the brilliance of the Scottish school, others fell under the influence of French eclecticism or German criticism. Amongst the latter the most conspicuous was SIR WILLIAM HAMILTON [21] (1788-1856), who combined the teachings of Reid and of Kant in an original system of his own. With Reid, he agreed that inner experience is the only source of certain knowledge, and that this testimony of consciousness points out in particular the existence of the external world ; with Kant, that consciousness also reveals the limits of our knowledge, and proves the inability of the human mind to think anything except under the conditions of time and space : science, therefore, has no knowledge of the 'unconditioned' Infinite and Absolute. MANSEL [22]

[21] *Discussions on Philosophy, Literature and Education ; Lectures on Metaphysics ; Lectures on Logic.* Consult J. S. MILL, *Examination of Sir William Hamilton's Philosophy* (5th ed., London, 1878).

[22] *Psychology ; Metaphysics or the Philosophy of Consciousness ; Philosophy of the Conditioned ; Limits of Religious Thought.* Sir James Mackintosh (1765-1832) must also be mentioned here as adhering in certain respects to the Scottish School. His principal philosophical works : *Dissertation on the Progress of Ethical Philosophy ; Discourse on the Law of Nature and Nations.*

(1820-1871), the best known of his disciples, brought this agnosticism into the service of revealed theology, making a still stronger and more sceptical employment of Kant's theory of knowledge. This unknowableness of the Absolute was destined to play an important part in other philosophical tendencies in England, e.g. in the system of Herbert Spencer (164).

Associationism was brought again into favour by THOMAS BROWN [23] (1778-1820), who was with Dugald Stewart at Edinburgh, but parted company with the Scottish school inasmuch as he gave a larger scope to association in our universal and necessary beliefs. Still more influential in this direction was JAMES MILL [24] (1773-1836), who was the most important of Bentham's collaborators. In psychology he neglected the physiological aspect and made the association of our conscious states, a process in which we play no active part, account for the whole of our psychic life ; outside the succession of internal and external phenomena nothing exists. In ethics he reasserted Bentham's doctrine that moral value is identical with utility.

With J. S. Mill, brought up in his father's school of thought, associationism enlarged its horizon.

163. English Positivism.—England is the second home of positivism. Its advocates here extended the teachings of Comte by combining with them associationist theories and accentuating the epistemological side : the existence of any supersensible reality which Comte had definitely denied was no longer ruled out of court, although unknowable, but declared possible if not actual.

JOHN STUART MILL [25] (1806-1873) was the most influential in spreading positivism in England. In psychology he found the laws of association of succession, contiguity and similarity sufficient to account for the formation of our psychic states. He maintained that experience is the sole source of knowledge and rejected all a priori or intuitive knowledge, and was thus obliged to reduce body to ' the permanent possibility of sensations ' and mind to ' the series of actual and possible states '. The supersensible is possible but unknowable : a position for

[23] *Inquiry into the Relation of Cause and Effect ; Lectures on the Philosophy of the Human Mind.*

[24] *Analysis of the Phenomena of the Human Mind.*

[25] *A System of Logic ; Examination of Sir William Hamilton's Philosophy ; Utilitarianism* (13th edition, 1897). See DOUGLAS, *J. S. Mill* (1895), *Ethics of J. S. Mill* (1897) ; RICHABY, *op. cit.* Also *Criteriology*, **58**; *Logic*, **88** *Ethics*, **74**.

which Huxley, followed by American positivists, coined the word 'agnosticism'. In keeping with his main thought Mill created a positivist logic. He held that the fundamental axioms of logic and mathematics are merely generalizations from experience ; that causation is nothing but 'invariable and unconditional sequence' ; that all knowledge deals with particulars, and judgment is only an association of sensations ; he recognized only one kind of inference, from particulars to particulars, and taught that the syllogism is not a valid form of proof. His really important contribution to logic was his formulation of the rules and methods of experimental inquiry. In ethics he adhered to the Benthamite principle of the greatest happiness of the greatest number, but was more genuinely altruistic in his interpretation and laid greater stress on the qualitative than on Bentham's quantitative factor in moral calculation.

As another representative of the same school, and in many respects a follower of Mill, must be mentioned ALEXANDER BAIN [26] (1818-1903), who as a psychologist is known chiefly for availing himself of current physiological science and as the originator of the theory of psycho-physical parallelism.

164. Evolutionism.—The idea of development from simple to complex was applied to history by Herder, to astronomy by Laplace, to zoology by Buffon and Lamarck, to anatomy and embryology by von Baer and to geology by Lyell. The history of evolution in the more restricted meaning which the word bears to-day begins with the name of CHARLES DARWIN (1809-1882), who deserves mention in the history of philosophy because of the new point of view which his discoveries established. His provisional hypothesis of the 'struggle for existence' became known to the world in his *Origin of Species* (1859) ; and in the *Descent of Man* he applied the evolutionary theory to the origin of the human species. He did not profess to account for the origin of life, nor did he dogmatize about the first beginning of variation. Darwin laid the foundation of modern evolutionistic ethics by referring the moral feeling to natural selection or the struggle for existence. A. R. WALLACE (1822-1913) was more diffident of including the higher powers of the human mind in the general process of

[26] *The Senses and the Intellect ; The Emotions and the Will ; Manual of Mental and Moral Science.* See *Psychology,* **56.**

development, and he allowed more scope to a teleological principle. JOHN TYNDALL (1820-1893), GEORGE ROMANES (1848-1894) and THOMAS HUXLEY (1825-1895) and others applied Darwin's theory to the different departments of natural science.

It remained for HERBERT SPENCER (1820-1904) to attempt to make a philosophical application embracing all the human sciences ; this was the aim of his *Synthetic Philosophy*, the plan of which he announced in 1860 :—

1. *General principles*. What cannot be apprehended by the external and internal senses is unknowable. This unknowable, which he is fain also to call force, exists, although we do not know in what it consists, since we can know only the modes in which it appears. These knowable modes are the ego and the non-ego, and they are reducible to unity in virtue of two principles running through the whole of Spencerian thought— the persistence of force, or the persistence of the relations of its manifestations, and the transformation of these manifestations into one another, or the evolution of force, which is not a process limited, as in the Darwinian theory, to living beings but extends to all reality. The law of evolution Spencer announces as ' an integration of matter and concomitant dissipation of motion, during which the matter passes from an indefinite incoherent homogeneity to a definite coherent heterogeneity, and during which the retained motion undergoes a parallel transformation ' (*First Principles*, § 144).

2. *Application of these principles*. Spencer applied his colossal erudition to the working out of these laws in the various departments of human knowledge : first in the in-organic world, then in the organic, which is only a necessary further development of the former, and finally in man, who is the most perfect birth of nature's travail. In his psychology of the individual he investigated the genesis of psychical life, the transformation of nervous phenomena into conscious states, and their association. The conscious state is noticed sensation. It corresponds to a double manifestation of the unknown force—the strong aggregate composed of external sensations, and the weak aggregate composed of concepts and volitions, the latter being the result of the evolution of the former. Between the external fact and the internal there is a certain correlation (transformed realism). In sociology he

studied the social nature of man, and traced evolution through the phenomena of religion, of the family and of politics. In ethics, or the science regulating conduct, he discovered that the moral sense is itself a product of evolution following the general development of life, and is progressive, i.e. from egoism to altruism. The highest conduct is that which conducts to ' the greatest breadth, length and completeness of life '. ' Sub-human ' justice requires that each individual should receive his share of the goods and evils which are the consequence of his structure and conduct. Spencer's system is a monument of erudition, but it is rather a work of art than a system of truth.

St. George Mivart (1805-1900) held a unique position as a defender of theistic evolution inasmuch as he sought to reconcile the evolutionistic hypothesis with the essential doctrines of Christian philosophy. Another staunch theist and opponent of utilitarian ethics was James Martineau [27] (1805-1900), who defended what is known as the preferential theory of ethics, that the virtue of an action consists in its motives.

IV. Philosophy in Italy and Spain

165. Italy.—Hegelianism was for a long time the leading tendency in philosophical thought among the official circles. Vera [28] (1813-1885) and d'Ercole were the chief leaders.

A place apart must be assigned to Gioberti [29] (1801-1852), who was a recognized representative of ontologism ; and to Rosmini [30] (1797-1855), who created an original system derived from ontologism, remarkable especially in its theory of ideas.

More recently positivism has been systematically taught, and has a considerable following in Italy.

166. Spain.—In the middle of the nineteenth century there was a large Krausist school represented especially by Del Rio [31] († 1869) and Salmeron. But the most distinguished name in modern Spain is that of Balmès [32] (1810-1848), an original thinker whose doctrines have many points of contact with Scholasticism.

---

[27] *Types of Ethical Theory.*
[28] *Essai de philosophie hégélienne.*
[29] *Introduzione allo studio della filosofia ; Del bello ; Del buono.*
[30] *Nuovo saggio sull' origine delle idee ; Theodicy* (trs. Signini). Consult Palhoriès, *Rosmini* (Alcan, Paris, 1908).
[31] *Sistema de la filosofia.*
[32] *Fundamental Philosophy* (trs. Brownson).

APPENDIX

Contemporary Philosophy

167. Favourite Problems.—It may be said that the chief philosophical interest of to-day centres round psychological questions, and, among these, in particular round the question of certitude. Kant, indeed, has left a prevailing influence, not only because he was the originator of critical formalism, but especially because he demonstrated to all who have come after him the urgency of first settling the fundamental question of the limits of human knowledge.

Moreover, modern experimental research into psychical states upon ground where the scientist joins hands with the philosopher has led to the creation of a new branch of study, physiological-psychology. This now finds a place in the syllabus of nearly every modern university. It originated at Leipzig, with the school of Wundt, and Würzburg, and has rapidly been taken up all over Europe and in America.

The great favour shown to psychology has accentuated the subjective side of aesthetics, the objective and metaphysical element of which many of our contemporaries refuse to recognize. Among theories in vogue we must first of all note the Kantian, or the theory that aesthetic judgment is only formed in accordance with the functions of our mind, and even more particularly the aesthetic of ' sympathetic feeling ' or of *Einfühlung* (literally ' feeling oneself into '). This is the theory, supported by Lipps, Volkelt, Vernon Lee and others, that the beautiful consists in the projection of our own feelings into a natural object or a work of art ; after we have invested it with this new meaning, we then take pleasure in beholding it. There is also a theory, put forward in France by Lalo, which from sociological premises conducts by another path to the conclusion that the beautiful is a psychical impression. Benedetto Croce in Italy likewise arrives at aesthetic subjectivism.

The same excessive attention to psychology has had, too, a detrimental influence on other branches of philosophy. In the first place it has led to the unjust ostracism of metaphysics. And similarly it has invaded the domain of logic, where beside the ancient logic or dialectic there has risen a mathematical or symbolic logic (Peano, Pierce, Mitchell, etc.), and still more recently a genetic logic, which purposes to study no longer the fixed laws of thought but the changing process of mental life and its genesis (Mark Baldwin).

In the field of ethics new life has appeared, especially in connexion with social questions, the principles of which are matter for the moral philosopher. The sociological school claims that only the social side of human conduct is worthy of attention ; that the old-fashioned moral theory with its static notions of duty and virtue must give place to empirical laws that are subject to social evolution, and the whole validity of which is derived from the approbation they receive in a community (Sidgwick, Huxley, Leslie Stephen, Durkheim, Levy-Bruhl) : just as the sociological aesthetic reduces judgments concerning the beautiful to judgments which vary from age to age and from one social group to another.

As for the history of philosophy, not only have very extensive specialized studies been made, but it daily finds a larger place in the treatment of any philosophical question. This may be accounted for chiefly by the impulse given by the schools of Cousin and Hegel, by the progress in historical study in general, and also by the confusion arising from the clash of the multitude of doctrines and the distrust which this confusion has bred. Notable works have been produced by Deussen, on Indian and Oriental philosophy ; by Zeller, on the Greek ; by Denifle, Hauréau, Bäumker, Mandonnet, on the mediaeval ; by Windelband, Kuno Fischer, Boutroux, Delbos, Höffding, on that of modern times—to mention but a few names.

168. Tendencies and Systems.—It is no easy matter to segregate philosophies at the beginning of the twentieth century into well-defined groups. Positivism and neo-Kantianism are the easiest to recognize, but they are marked by the personal contributions of their individual exponents. It might be safe to say in general that positivism and neo-Kantianism have produced a prevailing atmosphere of phenomenalism, which is no doubt due to the fact that positivism and neo-Kantianism agree on the same important doctrine, that knowledge and certitude are only possible within the limits of the phenomenal world which is the immediate object of experience. Positivism by insisting on the exclusive rights of sensory experience, and Kantian criticism by appealing to the structure of our faculties of knowledge, alike maintain that what we can know extends only to appearances : outside and beyond is the absolute, an abyss of obscurity, the existence of which, however, is being less and less called into doubt, although no hope yet prevails of sounding it.

1. *Positivism*, under one or other of its various forms, has been recently supported in England, for example, by the disciples of Herbert Spencer, by Huxley, G. H. Lewes, J. Tyndall, F. Harrison, Congreve, Beesly, J. Bridges and Grant Allen ; by Arthur Balfour, who at the same time advocates, in a way of his own, the principle of authority and makes a return to fideism. From England positivism passed over to America, where in a short time it undermined the influence of the Scottish doctrines, which had been put forward by Carus. Elsewhere the best-known representatives of it are de Roberty in Russia ; Ribot and Durkheim in France ; Ferrari, Ardigo and Morselli in Italy ; Laas and Riehl in Germany.

By totally ignoring supersensible reality, positivism is less brutal than materialism which denies its existence, but it contains the radical flaw of identifying the knowable with the sensible. Vain is the attempt to reduce the general idea to a collective image and to dispose of its abstract, universal character ; vain the refusal to recognize that logical first principles, on which all scientific knowledge turns, have something more than a mere empirical value, and vain the hope of ever succeeding in the attempt to demonstrate that the certitude of such judgments as $2 + 2 = 4$ will ever increase the oftener we may add up numbers of oxen or of coins.

Vogt, Büchner, Haeckel and Moleschott gave materialism an ephemeral vogue, but it has now been carried out of fashion by a powerful reaction towards Kantianism.

2. *Kantianism* was forgotten in Germany for a period of some thirty years, but ' the return to Kant ' (Rückkehr zu Kant), which is due largely to Lange's *History of Materialism*, is traceable from the year 1860, and almost all contemporary German philosophy may be said to be impregnated with

Kantian doctrines (Otto Liebmann, von Hartmann, Paulsen, Remke, Dilthey, Natorp, Eucken, the immanentists and the empirico-criticists).

French neo-criticism, represented by Renouvier, bore a close affinity to the second Critique of Kant, and brought in a special form of voluntarism. Vacherot, Secrétan, Lachelier, Boutroux and Fouillée are all in greater or lesser degrees indebted to Kant. Ravaisson follows Maine de Biran. Paul Janet, who with Bouillier and Caro was one of the last heirs to the spiritualism of Cousin, professes in his *Testament philosophique* adherence to a monism drawn from Kantian sources. Kantianism has been welcomed by many professors in official centres of education.

Many of those who side with Kant and the positivists in proclaiming the ' bankruptcy of science ' look for the foundation of certitude in an imperative demand of the will. This voluntarism is inadequate to provide firm bases for the theoretic sciences either of ethics or social philosophy, since sooner or later reflection is brought to bear on the worth of this need of living and of willing and, in so far, reason again becomes the supreme arbiter of certitude.

From Germany and France Kantian philosophy has spread over the whole world. In England it has given birth to a critical idealism, connected with which the most prominent names are those of T. H. Green and Bradley. In America Emerson, Harris, Everett and Royce have helped to spread idealism. On the other hand, Shadworth Hodgson, as also Adamson, have returned to a form of realism ; and James Ward gives prominence to the function of the will. In Italy, with Benedetto Croce and Gentile a neo-Hegelian movement has been manifest for some years.

3. *Monism* is discernible as a substratum in the critical philosophy of a great many Kantians who regard the thing-in-itself as numerically one. And the same tendencies are to be observed in some evolutionary positivists, such as W. K. Clifford, G. Romanes and G. T. Ladd.

The monistic conception is also to be found in the philosophy of Lotze (1817-1881), the thought of whom is as changeable, and at times as obscure, as that of Fichte. After laying stress on the mechanical value of the phenomena of nature, he reduces atoms to spiritual realities and absorbs their multiplicity in the unity of a single substance or thought, which is God.

4. *Pragmatism*, which William James of Harvard has brought to the fore, makes the criterion of the truth of any theory, to whatever domain it belongs, to consist in the practicableness of its consequences. Schiller has recently advocated much the same at Oxford under the name of *humanism*. Inasmuch as pragmatism makes out the true to be something relative and changeable, it falls under the weight of the same criticism as may be directed against all utilitarian philosophy.

5. Under the general name of *neo-realism* the years immediately preceding the war have witnessed the rise and rapid growth of a philosophy which confesses to the existence of ' realities ' which in themselves are ' neutral ', and become in certain relations the exterior world and in others the knowledge of that world (Bertrand Russell in England, Perry in America). These systems represent a reaction against the excesses of positivist phenomenalism and neo-Kantianism in so far as they admit the real existence of things outside of us. In more than one respect they mark an approach to neo-Scholasticism.

6. A special place requires to be assigned to two philosophers —*Nietzsche* and *Bergson*.

Nietzsche (1844-1900) is a moralist whose writing has had a wide influence for evil, principally in Germany. His theory starts with a supposed distinction that there is one moral code practised by men of war and the strong, and another code by the servile herd which is dictated by weakness and pity and self-abnegation. The so-called ' slave ' morality has prevailed owing to Christianity ; but Nietzsche would have it replaced by the ' master ' morality, which according to him is the end towards which we must tend. The ' over-man ' who reckons naught of either pity or pain will create new judgments of value, and will enforce their acceptance by violence and the frightfulness of war.

Bergson has the great merit of combating Kantianism in France by giving to external reality its true value. He endeavours to explain the world by a ' creative evolution ', of which the human mind is a product, but only a very imperfect one, and the immediate data of consciousness yield us a higher kind of knowledge or ' intuition '. MM. Wilbois and Le Roy are his well-known supporters.

169. Neo-Scholastic Philosophy.—Although Scholastic philosophy has never been abandoned, it received new vigour about the last quarter of the nineteenth century (from Liberatore, Taparelli, Cornoldi, etc.) [33], and acquired a new impetus from the pontificate of Pope Leo XIII. It is from this time that we can speak of it as Neo- or Modern Scholastic Philosophy, since it began from this time to accommodate itself to the thought of our own day. This it has been able to do owing chiefly to two characteristic orientations ; namely, in the first place, by its contact with the natural sciences and its care to provide an explanation of the material and moral world by studying the facts in their entirety ; and, secondly, by its contact with all other contemporary philosophies and the comparison of its own solutions with theirs by attention to the history of philosophy.

Modern Scholastic philosophy is an *objectivist* and not a subjectivist philosophy, because it makes a place for realities which are not pure creations of our mind, although it recognizes the limitations and imperfections of our manner of knowing. It lays down that if the *real* exists, it belongs to us to find out under what aspects it reveals itself to us. Yet it does not maintain that we can have an *adequate* knowledge of it, least of all of substances and causes. The reproaches of critics against neo-Scholasticism are aimed at its metaphysics and arise from a misapprehension of it.

It is also an *intellectualist* philosophy, by which we mean to say that knowledge is the fundamental and most perfect activity of psychical life.

Lastly, it is worthy of remark that neo-Scholasticism tends to become ever more and more the philosophy of Catholics. Indeed, it has replaced the systems of Ontologism, Traditionalism and Cartesian spiritualism which have all been weighed

---

[33] See PERRIER, *The Revival of Scholastic Philosophy in the Nineteenth Century* (New York, 1909) ; BESSE, *Deux centres du mouvement thomiste, Rome et Louvain* (Louvain, 1902) ; COFFEY, *Philosophy and the Sciences at Louvain ;* Appendix to De Wulf's *Scholasticism Old and New ;* PACE, *St. Thomas and Modern Thought* in *Cath. Univ. Bulletin* (1896).—Kleutgen, S.J., had previously rendered the greatest service to the cause of Scholastic philosophy in Germany. Prominent among those who have contributed to the success of the neo-Scholastic movement are Zigliara, O.P., Lepidi, O.P., De Maria, S.J., De Mandato, S.J., Satolli, Lorenzelli, etc. ; in Germany, Pesch, S.J., and in France the Sulpician M. Farges, Sertellanges, O.P., etc. In England Scholasticism has been developed notably by Jesuit writers, and in America especially by the professors of the Catholic University.

and found wanting. Yet it must not be thought that its appeal to Catholics lies in their Catholicism ; on the contrary, its conception of the world and of human life is such that it cannot but interest every loyal and unprejudiced mind, quite independently of religious beliefs : the theories of this neo-Scholasticism, because they are philosophic, are of just that much worth as reason can convince us they possess. Even those who do not subscribe to the rejuvenated and more fully completed syntheses of neo-Scholasticism consider them worthy of serious discussion.

Let us add that the first home of the neo-Scholastic movement has been at the *Institut de Philosophie* at Louvain, an establishment founded and directed by Mgr. Mercier, the present Cardinal Primate of Belgium. It has now spread through Europe and into America [34].

[34] NOTE ON THE PUBLICATIONS OF THE INSTITUT DE PHILOSOPHIE. Besides the *Grand Cours de Philosophie*, and this Manual, the Institute has been publishing a quarterly *Revue néo-Scholastique de Philosophie*. The same topics, it is interesting to note, have found expression in France in the *Revue de Philosophie*, the *Revue Thomiste* and the *Revue des Sciences philosophiques et théologiques*, in Germany in the *Jahrbuch für Philosophie und spekulative Theologie* and the *Philosophisches Jahrbuch*, in Spain in the *Ciencia Tomista*, and in Italy in the *Rivista di filosofia neo-scolastica*. The Louvain review was founded by Mgr. Mercier and personally edited by him until his elevation to the see of Malines. It then passed to the hands of the present editor, Prof. de Wulf, and was on the point of publishing its 83rd number (August, 1914) when the war broke out.

In 1901 the Institute undertook to publish or edit a series of studies or texts on the *Philosophy of the Middle Ages*, under the direction of Prof. de Wulf. Nine volumes have so far appeared, consisting of the works of Gilles de Lessines (de Wulf), Godefroid de Fontaines (de Wulf and Pelzer), Siger de Brabant (Mandonnet), Siger de Courtrai (Wallerand), Guibert de Tournai (de Poorter).

Two other series were also started three or four years ago : the *Annales de l'Institut*, under the editorship of Mgr. Deploige and M. Noël, and a translation, with commentary and notes, of Aristotle. Of the latter have appeared the first book of the Metaphysics by G. Colle and an introduction to the Physics by A. Mansion. To mention a few other individual works, besides *Les Origines de la Psychologie contemporaine* of the Cardinal, which is perhaps the best-known of his almost numberless publications, there are psychological works by MM. Thiéry and Michotte, especially dealing with its experimental side ; works by Mgr. Deploige and MM. Defourny and Harmignie on present-day problems of natural law and social philosophy ; by M. Noël on epistemology ; by M. Balthasar on metaphysics ; and M. de Wulf announces a book on the philosophy of art as already in the press, whilst M. Nys has revised his Cosmology and accommodated it to the new requirements of physics. The Institute was enjoying a period of great and fruitful activity when the storm-cloud of war burst over it. Fortunately, as we learn, the material property has not been swept away, so that all sincere devotees of the truth must hope that it will soon be once again the busy centre of philosophical research.—TRS.

SYNOPSIS

IN THE FORM OF THESES STATING THE
PRINCIPAL DOCTRINES MAINTAINED IN THE
MANUAL

I

Cosmology

I. There are two kinds of atomism : one a metaphysical theory, called philosophic atomism or mechanism ; the other purely scientific, called chemical atomism (**9-11**).

II. The theory of mechanism cannot be reconciled with the facts of chemistry—notably with the constancy of atomic weights, affinity, valency, the phenomena accompanying chemical combination, and the recurrence of the same simple and compound species (**12-21**).

III. Mechanism is incompatible with the ascertained results of crystallography (**22, 23**).

IV. The mechanical explanation of gravity and the qualities of gaseous bodies is inadequate (**25-27**).

V. Local movement is not a force, nor is it a cause capable of producing a mechanical effect ; it is neither transmissible nor transformable (**30-34**).

VI. The composition of bodies into matter and form involves no contradiction (**38-48**).

VII. Every substantial form intrinsically dependent upon matter is divisible (**49**).

VIII. Every being has only one substantial form (**48**).

IX. A real distinction may be made between material substance and its quantity (**57**).

X. All the parts of an extended thing are themselves extended and in consequence divisible indefinitely (**58**).

XI. The parts of a whole are not actual but potential parts (**59**).

XII. The forces or powers of a material being afford grounds for various specific distinctions being made among them (**67-71**).

XIII. The essential unity of a chemical compound is a fundamental tenet of the Scholastic theory (**80-82**).

XIV. The Scholastic theory is in harmony with all the facts of chemistry and physics (**83-95**).

XV. The order of the universe and the unity of living beings furnish a cogent proof of the Scholastic theory (**96-101**).

XVI. The arguments drawn from the specific diversity of properties and from the opposition that appears to exist between certain properties of matter furnish only incomplete proofs of the Scholastic theory (**106**).

XVII. Dynamic atomism is irreconcilable with several ascertained facts (**108, 109**).

XVIII. There is formal extension in the material world (**113-116**).

XIX. The essence of a body is not force nor a collection of forces (**117, 118**).

XX. *Actio in distans* is a physical impossibility (**121**).

XXI. ' *Tempus est numerus motus secundum prius et posterius* ' (**132, 133**).

XXII. Real space is a relation of distance in three dimensions (**144, 145**).

II

Psychology

I. Vital acts differ from the actions of inorganic matter inasmuch as they are immanent whilst the latter are transitive (**10**).

The first subject of organic life is a material nature (**13**).

II. Sense-perception is a hyper-physical operation ; that is to say, it is of a higher nature than any of which inorganic bodies or organic substances of the vegetable kingdom are capable. Nevertheless it is essentially in a material organ as its subject (**50, 51**).

III. Sensuous appetency is of a higher order than the natural tendencies of brute bodies and of vegetables. Nevertheless it is an organic faculty (**68, 69**).

IV. As the animal puts forth spontaneous movements, i.e.

movements the determining reason of which is of a psychical nature, so likewise does man in the exercise of his sensuous life (**75**).

V. The first subject of sensibility is a single substance, which is material. It is of a higher nature than that of the vegetable (**78-81**).

VI. The common formal object of the intellect is being. Its proper object is derived from sensible things, but is abstract and capable of becoming a universal notion (**88-92**).

VII. The intelligence is a passive faculty—potential intellect —which has to be determined to intellection by some extrinsic action (**96**).

The determination of the intellective power to intellection is effected by a double efficient cause, namely, by the imagination and an immaterial abstracting force, or active intellect (**101**).

As soon as the intellective faculty is presented with a conceptual determinant effected by the double cause, it passes from power to act ; it knows, that is, expresses to itself what a thing is (**103**).

The intellect knows first and directly the quiddities of sensible things, and its own nature secondly and through reflection (**104**).

VIII. The soul knows its own existence through its own acts ; it knows its own nature through reflection upon its acts (**107**). It knows God indirectly, that is, by the process of composition, negation and transcendence (**108**).

IX. The will is a principle of necessary acts (**110**). It is also a principle of free acts (**111-115**).

X. Pleasure is the resultant of every conscious activity that is subjectively and objectively perfect (**121**). There is no special faculty of emotion or feeling, but such states appertain to the appetitive faculty (**122**).

XI. Man alone has abstract, universal ideas, whilst animals have no such ideas ; consequently there is a difference of nature between man and animal (**125-127**).

XII. Man's various acts have an influence upon one another (**137**). His free will has a really efficient though not absolute control over the other activities of his soul (**138**).

XIII. The ego is one substance (**141**).

XIV. The human soul is spiritual, although its highest

exalted activity, which is intellectual and free, depends extrinsically upon matter (**143, 144, 148**).

XV. The human soul is simple, i.e. it is composed neither of quantitative nor of constitutive parts (**145-147**).

XVI. The body and rational soul together form one single substance, one nature or person (**150-153**). The rational soul is the substantial form of this single substance (**154, 155**).

XVII. The human soul is not begotten by the parents but created by God (**162**).

XVIII. The human soul is by its nature immortal ; in point of fact it will survive the body, and will live for ever (**167-169**).

XIX. If a purely natural end had been appointed for man, it would have consisted in a synthetic knowledge of the order of the universe through its supreme Cause and in the love of God considered as the beginning and end of all things (**170**). For its perfect happiness the soul requires its reunion with the body (**172**).

XX. The supernatural end of the human soul is a direct intuitive knowledge of God, which is the Beatific Vision (**173**).

III

Criteriology

I. The truth of a thing or ontological truth is a relation of conformity of that thing with the ideal type of its nature (**4-5**).

II. The truth of knowledge or logical truth is that of the judgment and consists in its conformity with ontological truth (**6**).

III. Certitude is the firm assent of the mind to a truth after reflection and determined by the mind's perception of the identity or agreement of two terms (**8**).

IV. The question to be answered in criteriology may be stated in very general terms as whether the assents we make spontaneously are justifiable upon reflection (**9**).

V. The Cartesian statement of the question considered in criteriology is not only incomplete but contradictory (**10**).

VI. The question considered in criteriology is really twofold : (1) Is the bond which unites subject and predicate in our judgments subjective or objective ? (2) What value have the terms of our judgments ? (**11**).

VII. The initial state of the mind when embarking upon the

question of certitude is not the universal doubt of the sceptic, who suspects a priori and without reason the mind's ability to know truth (16) ; nor the universal doubt of Descartes, which not only does not open the way to any kind of certainty, but wrongly extends to some propositions of which it is impossible to have any doubt, and rests upon reasons which are quite without value (17).

VIII. The theory of 'three primary truths' is useless as a refutation of scepticism, since the 'three primary truths' are not fundamental premises of all our demonstrations (18-19).

IX. The legitimate state of the mind when attacking the problem of knowledge consists in not affirming a priori either its ability or its inability to know the truth, but in examining by reflection the value of our cognitive acts and, accordingly, of our cognitive faculty (20).

X. As soon as we begin to examine our knowledge, we find there are some *immediate* propositions which cannot be proved yet compel our assent (22).

XI. The criterion of truth for our immediate judgments of the ideal order must not be extrinsic, nor subjective, nor mediate, but it must be intrinsic, objective and immediate (23).

XII. In those certain judgments which are immediate we attribute the predicate to the subject because it is apparent that the predicate objectively belongs to the subject, and not exclusively because the natural constitution of our cognitive faculty compels us to do so (33).

XIII. Against the positivists it must be asserted that truths of the ideal order have a universal value (36-38) ; and against Kant firstly that analytic judgments convey information, and secondly that the fundamental principles of the sciences are not synthetic a priori judgments (40).

XIV. The intelligible forms which furnish our predicates and which we attribute to the subjects of our judgments are endowed with objective reality (43-45).

XV. We assert against Kant that the ideas of space and time are not a priori forms but are notions abstracted from the data of experience (47, 48).

XVI. Principles do not require to be demonstrated, as they are self-evident (53).

XVII. Truths of consciousness admit of no proof, but it would be unreasonable to call them in question (55).

XVIII. The value of deductive reasoning employed in the rational sciences is not undermined by the criticism of John Stuart Mill (**58**).

XIX. We can attain certain knowledge of the *existence* of the external world (**60**).

XX. The logical foundation of induction is the natural tendency substances have on account of which they demand definite properties (**63**).

XXI. By their own power the senses are, strictly speaking, incapable of attaining certitude (**64**).

XXII. The reason is able by inductive argument to obtain certain knowledge with regard to the permanent properties of sensible objects (**65**).

XXIII. The motive of historical certitude is one which is indirect but evident (**67**).

XXIV. The motive of the certitude of faith is one which is extrinsic and not evident, namely, the authority of a witness (**68**).

XXV. The certitude of the act of supernatural faith is compatible with its freedom, inasmuch as the act remains free on account of the intrinsic obscurity of its object (**69**).

XXVI. There are two distinct kinds of certitude : certitude arising from evidence and certitude of faith (**70**).

XXVII. Immediate evidence is the first and fundamental criterion of truth (**71**).

IV

General Metaphysics

I. The object of metaphysics is the substance of sensible things (**7**).

II. Two elements need to be distinguished in substance the *thing* itself and that *in virtue of which* it exists, or, essence and existence (**13**). Existence is that which actualizes essence (**14**).

The essence of a thing is that which constitutes it what it is ; in relation to existence it is an indeterminate subject which receives its ultimate determination from existence (**15**).

III. Possible being is an essence considered as not existing in nature but capable of so existing (**18**).

IV. There are two kinds of possibility : *intrinsic* and

extrinsic. The former is the absence of contradiction in the constitutive notes of an essence ; the latter implies the existence of another being as sufficient reason for the existence of an essence which is intrinsically possible (**18**).

V. The ultimate basis of a being's *extrinsic* possibility is the existence of God (**19**).

The basis of an essence's *intrinsic* possibility is to be found in the sensible world considered abstractly and analysed by the intelligence (**20, 21**).

VI. The individual is principally known by its dimensions in space (**25**).

VII. The formal reason of the individuality of a being is its own entity (**26**).

VIII. The principle of individuation is primary matter as the foundation of quantity (**29**).

IX. There is a real distinction between essence and existence (**32, 33**).

X. There are six transcendental properties of being : essence, thing, unity, distinction, truth and goodness—*ens, res, unum, aliquid, verum, bonum* (**38**).

XI. The ideas of non-being, distinction and indefinite plurality arise from the different impressions we receive from two or more objects (**40**).

XII. Unity is the undividedness of a being (**41**).

XIII. The notion of unity is antecedent to that of definite plurality (**43**).

XIV. Metaphysical composition and physical composition are not incompatible with the substantial unity of a being (**50, 51**).

XV. *Transcendental* unity is to be distinguished from *predicamental* unity (**55**).

XVI. Ontological truth is a relation of conformity with an ideal type abstracted from sensible reality (**61**).

XVII. The good has two aspects : it is what serves as the object of some natural tendency (**67**) and it is the adaptation of a being to its end (**68**).

XVIII. In the ontological order a thing is the object of a natural tendency because it is good ; and it is good because it is adapted to its end. In the logical order the ' desirable ' is prior to the ' suitable ' (**69**).

XIX. Good things are suited to the nature of a being because they are so many means whereby it can realize its end, and consequently their goodness is derived from the good end they make it possible for the nature to attain. Hence the only way to explain the goodness of things is by referring them as relative goods to one or more absolute goods (**70**).

XX. The end is the principle of perfection for the nature which tends towards it : it is the first principle of actuation of its passive powers (**71**).

XXI. Evil is essentially relative, inasmuch as it is the privation of a good (**75**).

XXII. Between being and its transcendental properties there is an *incomplete virtual* distinction (**76**).

XXIII. The mind obtains its first principles from a comparison of the transcendental notions (**78**).

XXIV. There are three first principles : the *principle of identity*, the *principle of contradiction* and the *principle of excluded middle* (**79**).

XXV. There are substances (**83**).

A substance exists in itself and is the subject of accidents (**84**).

XXVI. Substance, considered as complete in itself for existence and action, is called a *suppositum*, or *hypostasis* ; when endowed with intelligence, it is called a *person*. The characteristic perfection of an hypostasis is called *subsistence* (**88-91**).

XXVII. An accident is a being which does not subsist in itself but presupposes a subject in which it exists (**92**).

XXVIII. It is preferable to hold that an accident has the same actuality of existence as the substance which it determines (**93**).

XXIX. A real distinction exists between substance and some of its accidents (**94-95**).

XXX. There is a real distinction between substance and its powers of action (**104**).

XXXI. The foundation for the classification of faculties is to be found in the adequate distinction of their formal objects (**105**).

XXXII. There are real relations (**109**).

XXXIII. The principles of change or movement, considered in the abstract without reference to any material determinations, are actuality and potentiality (**112, 113**). By movement in metaphysics is to be understood ' the actuality of a subject that is formally potential ' (**115**).

XXXIV. Every movement requires a mover distinct from the thing moved (**116**).

XXXV. Both the Latin words *potentia* and *actus* have a double meaning : *potentia passiva, subjectiva,* or potentiality, must be distinguished from *potentia operativa,* power of action or faculty, corresponding to the difference between *actus,* meaning actuality or an intrinsic principle of perfection, and *actus,* meaning action, the exercise of a faculty (**119**).

XXXVI. The various kinds of being studied by metaphysics have in common a certain analogousness (**126**).

XXXVII. The material cause receives the substantial form, and by its union with it constitutes a new compound substance (**133**).

XXXVIII. The formal cause is intrinsically communicated to the matter, and by its union with it constitutes a substance of a determinate kind (**135**).

XXXIX. The efficient cause is the extrinsic, active principle of movement (**139**).

XL. The action of a created agent is in the patient (**144**).

XLI. The concept of ' movement ' is applicable to immanent action, with the restriction that such action does not react upon the stimulus evoking it (**146**).

XLII. The action of created agents has the becoming of something as its formal resultant (**148**).

XLIII. Understood in a metaphysical sense the principle of causality may be stated thus : The existent thing to which existence is not essential exists in virtue of some action external to it (**151**).

XLIV. Besides formal, material and efficient causes, ' movement ' also entails final causality (**152**).

XLV. There is intrinsic finality in nature (**152**).

XLVI. The final cause may be defined as that for the sake of which something is done or made (**153**).

XLVII. The causality of the final cause consists in an attraction which the end exercises upon the appetitive power and in the consequent tendency in that power towards it (**154**).

XLVIII. Nature is a substance considered precisely as the intrinsic first principle of the operations proper to the being which produces or undergoes them (**155**).

XLIX. Law is the internal, fundamental determination in

virtue of which a substance, as first principle of action, tends to realize a determinate end (**156**).

L. Natural causes and effects must be distinguished from accidental causes and effects (**157**).

LI. The exemplary cause is the mental type which an intelligent efficient cause follows in producing his effect (**162**).

LII. The exemplary cause is at once an efficient and final cause and an extrinsic formal cause. Its peculiar causality consists in its being an extrinsic formal cause (**163**).

LIII. Among the four causes there is only an analogical resemblance (**164**).

LIV. Ontological principles and causes are the same things ; elements are material causes ; principles, causes and elements are the reasons of things (**165**).

LV. Order has been defined as the exact adaptation of things to their ends (**168**). Order is understood in two senses : teleological order and aesthetic order, or, in other words, order of subordination and order of co-ordination (**169**).

LVI. The order in the universe proves the existence of final causes (**170**).

LVII. Perfection means everything that befits the nature of a being (**173**).

LVIII. There are three objective conditions of the beautiful, namely, integrity or perfection, due order, and splendour (**178**).

LIX. Beauty is that quality of a work whereby, on account of a happy co-ordination of its various parts, an ideal type to which it is related is given intense expression and made to excite admiration (**179**).

LX. Art need not be used as an instrument for moral or religious purposes ; but it is not beyond the pale of the moral law (**180**).

LXI. The internal finality of things is the foundation of the relative finality of the universe ; this constitutes its order (**181**).

LXII. The immanent relative end of the universe should be distinguished from the transcendent relative end (**182, 183**).

V

Natural Theology

I. The idea of God is that of an absolutely simple perfection. It is sufficient and necessary for providing natural theology with its proper object (**5**).

II. Our knowledge of the absolutely simple perfections of the Divine essence we acquire by means of the triple process of attribution, elimination and transcendence (**6**). This is a method of procedure which is neither misleading nor useless (**7**).

III. The existence of God *can* be proved.

(*a*) Agnosticism is based on a principle which is not self-evident (**10**).

(*b*) Comte's ' Law of the Three Stages ' finds no support in the history of science or of philosophy, and it is not verified in the mental development of the individual ; it is without any logical proof (**11**).

(*c*) The natural sciences owe their progress to the experimental method, and not to the positive method extolled by Comte (**11**).

(*d*) The failures of some minds to arrive at the existence of God does not prove, as the theory of traditionalism maintained, our incapacity to demonstrate it (**12**).

IV. The existence of God *must* be proved.

(*a*) Ontologism is based on a false theory of ideas, and it is contradicted by experience (**13**).

(*b*) The ' New Philosophy ' is powerless to establish the affirmation of the true God (**14**).

(*c*) Mere subjective sentiment is no foundation for real religion (**15**).

V. The only valid proof of the existence of God is an a posteriori one (**16**). The ontological argument of St. Anselm involves the fallacy of Begging the Question (**17, 18**).

VI. St. Augustine's argument from our knowledge of possible essences is not an immediate proof of the existence of God (**19**).

VII. An analysis of metaphysical movement furnishes a proof of the existence of God (**21**).

VIII. An analysis of the efficient causality of natural agents furnishes a proof of the existence of God (**23**).

IX. An analysis of the contingency of beings furnishes a proof of the existence of God (**24**).

X. An analysis of the degrees of perfection manifested in beings furnishes a proof of the existence of God (**27**).

XI. An analysis of the order of the universe furnishes a proof of the existence of God (**28**).

XII. The scientific proofs of the existence of God are not

valid unless completed by the introduction of certain philosophical considerations (**31**).

XIII. The argument from the common consent of mankind is valid if not pressed too far (**32**).

XIV. The proof from the higher aspirations of human nature does not exceed probability (**33**).

XV. The moral obligation can be explained without recourse to a divine Legislator ; it is therefore not an immediate proof of His existence, but inasmuch as it is an indication of contingency it does furnish a proof of a necessary Being (**34**).

XVI. The metaphysical essence of God is His self-subsistence (**36**).

XVII. God is absolutely simple (**41**).

XVIII. God is perfect (**44, 45**).

XIX. God unites in Himself all the perfections belonging to His works (**46**).

XX. God is infinite in perfection (**48, 49**).

XXI. The activity of God is substantial (**57**).

XXII. Thought may, and must, be attributed to God (**58**).

XXIII. The knowledge of God considered subjectively is a single act of adequate comprehension (**60, 61**).

XXIV. The knowledge of God, from the point of view of content, has for object in the first place the nature of God and then all things actual and possible (**61**).

XXV. The divine ideas are infinite in number, and yet are identical in reality with the divine essence considered as the supreme archetype of all things (**62**).

XXVI. God possesses a knowledge of possible things (**64**).

XXVII. God possesses the so-called ' knowledge of vision ' (**65**).

XXVIII. The object of His ' knowledge of simple intelligence ' God sees in His essence (**66**).

XXIX. The future effects of necessary causes God knows in the decrees of His will (**67**).

XXX. There seems reason to distinguish with the Molinist school an ' intermediate ' sort of knowledge in God different from His knowledge of simple intelligence and that of vision (**67**).

XXXI. The divine foreknowledge of free future acts is not incompatible with the freedom of the latter (**68**).

XXXII. In God there is a will (**69, 70**).

XXXIII. The primary formal object of God's will is the goodness of His own essence (**71**).

XXXIV. For its secondary material object the will of God may have whatever partakes of the divine goodness (**72**).

XXXV. God loves the goodness of His Essence necessarily, and freely the goodness He has communicated to created beings (**73**).

XXXVI. God never changes the free decree of His will (**74**). Inasmuch as His will remains attached to its good, it is called by us *love* (**75**). The divine will is omnipotent (**76**).

XXXVII. The world has been created by God (**80-81**).

XXXVIII. God alone can create (**82**).

XXXIX. The world has need of being conserved by God in being (**84**).

XL. The world is subject to the action of divine providence (**85, 86**).

XLI. The providence and government of God are universal (**87**).

XLII. The sovereignty of God and the free-will of creatures are equally certain facts ; but none of the theories yet advanced to show how they are mutually compatible is entirely satisfactory (**88**).

XLIII. The existence of evil in the world is not irreconcilable with God's providence and government (**89**).

VI

Logic

I. Logic is the reflex study of the order which needs to exist in our judgments, inferences and more elaborate reasoning processes for them to lead us to truth (**1**).

II. Considered as the materials of knowledge, concepts are predicates that fall within one or other of the ten categories of thought (**14-15**).

III. Judgment is the attribution of a predicate to a subject (**28**).

Judgments are either in necessary matter or in contingent matter, according as the predicate attaches to the subject by a necessary or a contingent bond, i.e. by one which is independent or not of experience and of the existence of things.

The former kind of judgment is the basis of the rational sciences, and the latter of the experimental sciences (**31-33**).

IV. Reasoning is a process whereby the mind passes from immediate judgments or *principles* to a mediate judgment or *conclusion*. The logical form it assumes is the syllogism or ' discourse in which certain things being posited (in the premisses) something else necessarily follows (in the conclusion) simply from their being posited ' (ARISTOTLE, *Anal.*, *Pr.* I,1) (**47, 48**).

V. The objective foundation of the syllogism may be enunciated as follows : Reasoning is the bringing of some definite subject under the extension of an abstract type in order to infer that something which is predicable of the abstract type as such is likewise predicable of this definite subject (**49**).

VI. The necessity of the laws that serve as principles of the syllogism is sometimes *metaphysical* and *absolute*, sometimes *physical* and *natural* and so depending on conditions that have to be empirically ascertained (**50**).

VII. Every science has as its starting points certain first principles, or first judgments, which are immediately evident, necessary and indemonstrable (**51**).

VIII. First principles enunciating the simple relations of being and non-being direct and control not only every science but every judgment of the mind (**51**).

IX. Scientific demonstration is a reasoning process which sets out from premises that are certain and leads to a logically certain conclusion. The premises on which it rests must be true, ultimate, immediate, better known than the conclusion, prior to it, and the cause or reason of its truth (**63, 64**).

X. Essential definition, which states what something is, is the foundation of science (**79, 80**).

XI. Deduction or the synthetic method of reasoning, which is that employed in the rational sciences, is one which begins with certain principles in necessary matter, and enables one by a process of combination to deduce new relations and thus define what is progressively presented for explanation (**85**).

XII. Induction or the analytic method of reasoning, which is that employed in the experimental sciences, is one which begins with concrete facts furnished by observation and ends with the formulation of laws (**86**). Scientific induction is a process which ascends from facts to the nature of the things of which these facts are the manifestation (**90**).

XIII. The method of philosophy is combined induction and deduction (**94**).

XIV. Science is a body of propositions which are evident, certain, necessary, and universal, as well as arranged systematically so as to form one whole, and which are drawn immediately or mediately from the nature of the subject and furnish the intrinsic reason of its properties and of the laws of its action (**96**).

VII

Ethics

I. Man has subjectively and really one last natural end (**8, 9**).

II. Regarded in the abstract and indeterminately the end of human nature consists in happiness (**10**).

III. Regarded in the concrete and definitely the objective end of man is not in any created good but in God (**11**).

IV. The action of the senses and of external causes can affect without destroying free-will and responsibility (**27, 28**).

V. The distinction between moral good and evil is real and intrinsic (**30**).

VI. The distinction between good and evil is founded on the conformity or want of conformity of our action with our supreme end (**32**).

VII. The morality of a human act is determined by its formal object, the circumstances and the end for which it is done (**34**).

VIII. Neither individual nor social well-being is the measure of moral value (**35-37**).

IX. The evolutionist theory of Herbert Spencer leads logically to the negation alike of morality and of all distinction between right and wrong (**38**).

X. Man is subject to a natural law, that is, to an inclination which habitually disposes him to know and will the end of his rational nature and what leads to it, as well as to discern and reject what is contrary to it (**40**).

XI. The moral obligation has its explanation and foundation in human nature (**44**).

XII. The ultimate reason of the distinction between good and evil, and consequently of moral obligation and law, is found in God; formally it is in the practical reason of Providence (**45**).

XIII. There is no need to suppose in human nature a 'moral instinct' or a 'moral sense' distinct from the intellect to account for our knowledge of the moral order (**49**).

XIV. The first commandment of the natural law is that good must be done and evil avoided (**50**).

XV. During the present life there is a sanction for the moral law, but it is insufficient (**52**).

XVI. After a time of trial, the length of which we cannot determine, the virtuous will be eternally rewarded in a future life and the wicked will be deprived for ever of their happiness (**53**).

XVII. The Christian doctrine that the sinner who freely turns from his last end must in addition to the eternal loss of happiness suffer the infliction of positive pain is not opposed to reason (**54**).

XVIII. The categorical imperative of Kant is no moral standard by which moral good and evil may be distinguished, nor is it a true moral law (**56**).

XIX. The moral law is immutable and is known to all (**57**).

XX. Theories of Secular or Independent Morality are not true, and lead logically to impracticable conclusions (**66, 67**).

XXI. By the natural law the individual possesses in justice certain rights and duties in respect of his neighbour independently of any natural or political relationship (**70-74**).

XXII. One is bound in justice to respect the good of another, particularly in respect of his life, his liberty and his property (**76-77**).

XXIII. Liberty implies the right to work (i.e. to follow some profession), to have one's own opinions, and to act according to one's conscience (**78-81**).

XXIV. The right of property is derived from human nature (**87**).

XXV. The theory of communism is based on a misunderstanding of the nature of the goods of this world and would make the natural law self-contradictory (**88, 90**).

XXVI. The theory of collectivism is inconsistent with the dignity and freedom of man; and its realization would hinder social progress and impose upon the State a task beyond its capacities and incompatible with its natural function (**91, 92**).

XXVII. The titles to property are occupancy, prescription, the right of testament and of inheritance (**94-97**).

XXVIII. The purpose of the institution of marriage is the good of the spouses and of the children (**99, 100**).

XXIX. The perpetuity of the marriage bond rests on the rational love of the spouses and on the requirements called for in the education of the children (**101-104**).

XXX. The theory of the Spirit-State is an aspect of pantheism and is subject to the same criticism as the system to which it belongs (**107**).

XXXI. The theory which places the juridical basis of society in a free contract, either explicit or understood, is patient of several interpretations, all of which lead to inadmissible conclusions (**109-112**).

XXXII. According to the Christian conception civil society is constituted by the union of individual persons and has no reality of its own. Its foundation is in the nature of man, and this draws its origin from the designs of God (**114, 115**).

XXXIII. As God wills the existence of society, He also wills the existence of authority which is a condition of its existence ; but He leaves the form of authority undetermined (**116**).

XXXIV. Since civil society is instituted for the good of the individuals composing it, it follows that the rôle of authority is to ensure respect of rights and to provide opportunity for the development of its members (**117**).

XXXV. The State may not take the place of individual activity, nor may it take the place of parents in their duty of education, nor interfere in the religion of its members (**118**).

GLOSSARY OF PHILOSOPHIC TERMS

THIS Glossary was intended in the French edition, which lacks an Index, partly to save the student the trouble of unearthing the meaning of technical words explained up and down the Manual ; but chiefly to give him a useful, though not exhaustive, series of essential definitions as an aid to memory, and as a test by means of which he can revise his work and discover if he understands fully the principal ideas he has read in a more diffuse form. The addition of Latin definitions, chosen from the works of St. Thomas or, when stated, from one or other of his authentic interpreters, has been adopted in accordance with the ideas developed in the Preface, in order to initiate the student into the use of Latin and into the mediaeval terminology. Let it be added that the Index will often prove helpful where this necessarily incomplete Glossary proves deficient.—TRS.

Absolute : As a substantive, a being which is self-sufficient in its existence (*Nat. Theol.*, **36**). As an adjective, that which exists (metaphysical sense), or is known (logical sense) without requiring to be connected with something else or with something already known ; in this sense it is the same as unconditional and is the opposite of *relative* (*Gen. Met.*, **111**). 'Absolutum est non dependens ab alio ' (*In IV Metaph.*, l. 19).

Abstraction : An operation by which the intellect expresses to itself the essence of a thing whilst ignoring those determinations of it which make it such and such a particular thing (*Introd.*, **2, 17** ; *Psych.*, **89, 91, 101** ; *Criter.*, **44** ; *Log.*, **9**). 'Abstrahere speciem intelligibilem a phantasmatibus est considerare naturam speciei absque consideratione individualium principiorum quae per phantasmata repraesentantur ' (*Sum. Theol.*, I, q. 85, a. 1, ad 1).

Accident : That which cannot exist and which cannot be conceived of except as dependent upon some presupposed being (*Gen. Met.*, **82**).

An *ontological accident* is a reality whose natural mode of existing is in another being (*Gen. Met.*, **92**). 'Accidens est res cui debetur esse in alio ' (*In IV Sent.*, dist. 12, q. 1, a. 1, sol. 1, ad 2). Ontological accidents are either *contingent* or *necessary* (*Cos.*, **52**).

505

Action at a distance. Con. (I) p. 135.

A *logical accident,* one of the predicables, is the contingent mode in which a predicate is related to a subject (*Log.,* **16,** 3). ' Accidens est quod contingit eidem inesse et non inesse praeter subjecti corruptionem ' (*Sum. Log.,* T. I, c. viii).

Act, Action : Regarded as a result, action is a change or movement produced in a being (*Gen. Met.,* **144**). ' Actio et passio conveniunt in una substantia motus, differunt tamen secundum habitudines diversas ' (*Sum. Theol.,* I, q. 28, a. 3). See *passion.*

Regarded as related to the principle from which it proceeds, action is the actuation or putting into use of the power to do something ; it is what makes something to become something which previously it was not (virtus) (*Gen. Met.,* **118, 119, 148**). ' Potentiae activae respondet operatio vel actio in qua completur potentia activa ' (*In I Sent.,* dist. 42, q. 1, a. 1, ad 1).

Immanent action is action which has its final result in the agent itself ; *transitive* action is that which is terminated in some being other than the agent (*Psych.,* **10** ; *Gen. Met.,* **145**).

Actuality, ' Act ' : The *intrinsic* principle on account of which a thing possesses a certain degree of perfection ; or, another definition : the perfection which fulfils the capacity of a perfectible being. Actuality is opposed to potentiality, to receptive potency or ' power ' (*Gen. Met.,* **114**). ' Omnis actus, perfectio quaedam est ' (*Sum. Theol.,* I, q. 5, a. 3).

Pure actuality is what is perfection simply, a being whose perfection is limited by no potentiality (*Nat. Theol.,* **2, 36, 45**). In the terminology of the Middle Ages *actus purus,* being that is purely actual, is expressed as *esse irreceptum, esse imparticipatum, esse subsistens* (*Gen. Met.,* **117, 126** ; *History,* **27**).

Actuality is termed *first* or *second actuality* according as it is the first determination of a potential subject, or a subsequent, accessory determination of a subject already relatively determined (*Gen. Met.,* **117** ff.).

Aesthetics : The philosophy of the beautiful (*Introd.,* **8** ; *Gen. Met.,* **176** f.).

Alteration : A change of quality, and therefore an accidental change, that does not affect the substance of a being. ' Motus qui est in qualitate, vocatur alteratio ' (*In V Physic.,* l. 4).

Analogical, Analogous : Analogical knowledge is knowledge of something through a proper knowledge of something else which is by its nature different from it but because of certain resemblances is capable of representing it (*Log.,* **22** ; *Psych.,* **87** ; *Gen. Met.,* **126**). A term which expresses an analogical idea is also called analogical, or analogous (*Log.,* **26**). ' Analoga sunt quae deficiunt ab unitate seu convenientia absoluta et solum habent convenientiam modo relativo, id est, juxta proportionem seu commensurationem ' (JOHN OF ST. THOMAS, *Log.,* II, q. 13, a. 3).

Analogy : A likeness in one or more respects between two things which are otherwise different (*Log.*, **22, 26**). ' Analogia est media inter puram aequivocationem et univocationem, eo quod res significata nec est omnino eadem, neque omnino diversa, sed in se quidem diversa, proportionaliter autem et secundum habitudinem una ' (JOHN OF ST. THOMAS, *Log.*, II, q. 13, a. 3).

Analysis : The resolution of a compound thing into the elements of which it is made up. In logic, analysis or rather the analytical method is the method of starting with an examination of facts in order to discover their causes and to formulate their laws (*Log.*, **80, 86** ; *Gen. Met.*, **1**, and cp. *Induction*).

Analytical judgment : A judgment the truth of which is known to us through the mere analysis of the terms contained in it. Formerly it was with reason called a *judgment in necessary matter* to point out the necessary connexion of the two objects represented by the terms of the judgment, and a *judgment per se notum* because a knowledge of the two terms of the judgment sufficed to make the judgment known (*Crit.*, **36** ; *Log.*, **31** f.). ' Aliqua propositio est per se nota, quod praedicatum includitur in ratione subjecti ' (*Sum. Theol.*, I, q. 2, a. 1).

In Kantian terminology analytical judgment is a term restricted to that judgment alone wherein an analysis of the subject reveals the predicate (*Crit.*, **39** ; *Log.*, **33**).

Apperception : A term used first by Leibniz to express a reflex knowledge of an internal state, consciousness (*q.v.*).

Appetite : The faculty of appetition. According as appetition ensues from sensuous or intellectual knowledge, appetite is called sensible appetite, or supersensible, rational appetite or will. In a modern restricted sense appetite signifies an organic craving (*Psych.*, **64, 137**).

Appetition : The tendency or inclination of a knowing subject towards what it perceives as good (*Psych.*, **64. 137**). ' Appetere nihil aliud est quam aliquid petere, quasi tendere in aliquid ad ipsum ordinatum. Appetere est speciale animalibus in quantum in eis invenitur appetitus et movens appetitum ; ipsum bonum apprehensum est movens appetitum. Vis appetitiva appetit quodcumque bonum apprehensum ' (*De Veritate*, q. 22, a. 1 and 2).

Apprehension : The act of the intellect whereby it represents to itself what something is, without affirming or denying anything about it (*Psych.*, **105** ; *Log.*, **2, 10**).

Attribute : Anything which determines a thing. A logical attribute, or predicate, is that term in a judgment which is referred to another term that is called the subject (*Log.*, **28**).

Categories, Predicaments: Attributes to which can be reduced whatever the mind can predicate of a subject ; these attributes are the categories in the primary sense of the word ; in a secondary sense the categories are the ten groups or heads of predication under one or other of which these attributes may be placed—these are the *logical* categories. The *ontological* categories are the ten classes of being into which reality may be divided and which correspond to the logical categories *(Gen. Met.,* **97** ; *Log.,* **15)**. 'Oportet quod ens contrahitur ad diversa genera secundum modum diversum praedicandi qui consequitur diversum modum essendi. Dicuntur praedicamenta quia distinguuntur secundum diversum modum praedicandi' *(In V Metaph.,* l. 9).

According to Kantian philosophy the categories are forms of the understanding which with the matter of knowledge constitute intelligible objects *(Crit.,* **42)**.

Cause : Whatever something depends upon, either for its being or for its becoming *(Gen. Met.,* **165)**. 'Illud est proprie causa alicujus sine quo esse non potest' *(Sum. Theol.,* III, q. 86, a. 6).

There are four kinds of cause. By the *efficient* cause a thing comes to be what it is : '*id a quo* aliquid fit' *(Gen. Met.,* **139)**. By the *final* cause the efficient cause is drawn to action ; for the sake of it something is done or is made, '*id cujus gratia* aliquid fit' *(Gen. Met.,* **152-3)**. The material and formal causes combine as constituents of a material being : the *formal* cause is the intrinsic principle of its perfection, that by reason of which it is what it is, '*id quo* ens est id quod est' *(Gen. Met.,* **135)** ; the *material* cause, or subjective cause, is the subject receptive of the formal cause, it is that out of which a thing is made, '*id ex quo* aliquid fit et in quo forma existit' *(Gen. Met.,* **133** ; *Introd.,* **5)**.

Certitude : The firm adherence of the mind to one proposition : 'Certitudo non est aliud quam determinatio seu adhaesio intellectus ad unum' (JOHN OF ST. THOMAS, *Log.,* II, q. 26, a. 4). Or more explicitly and in connexion with the solution of the criteriological problem certitude may be defined as the firm adherence of the mind to an evident truth after reflection and because a relation of identity or conformity between the two terms is perceived *(Crit.,* **8)**. 'Certitudo proprie dicitur firmitas adhaesionis virtutis cognitivae in suum cognoscibile' *(In III Sent.,* dist. 26, q. 2, a. 4).

The *certitude of faith* and *historical certitude* are respectively assents to non-evident propositions through the extrinsic motive of another's authority or of a coincidence of facts and testimonies *(Crit.,* **67** ; see *evidence, faith*).

Compound : The resultant, possessing substantial unity and proper qualities, of a combination of simple indecomposable elements *(Cos.,* **89)**. 'Quando est mixtio utrumlibet miscibilium convertitur in unum tertium' *(Contra impugn. Dei cult. et relig.,* 12). 'Quandocumque fit mixtio aliquorum differentium . . . mixtione completa, non retinet unumquodque qualitatem propriam' *(In II Sent.,* dist. 30, q. 2, a. 1).

Comprehension : The sum-total of constitutive notes discovered by analysis in the concept of a thing (*Log.*, **17**).

Concept : The result of an act of simple apprehension (*Psych.*, **105** ; *Log.*, **21**). ' Quandocumque intellectus actu intelligit, quoddam intelligibile format, quod est quaedam proles ipsius, unde et mentis conceptus nominatur ' (*Declaratio contra Græcos*, c. 3).

Condition : That which without lending a positive influence is required for the efficient cause to produce its effect (*Gen. Met.*, **140**).

Conscience : The definitive judgment of the practical reason concerning the rectitude or obligation of an act here and now to be performed or omitted, or of an act already performed (*Ethics*, **68**). ' Conscientia nihil aliud est quam applicatio scientiae ad aliquem actum ut dirigens ipsum vel per modum examinationis eorum quae jam acta sunt ' (*Sum. Theol.*, I-II, q. 19, a. 5 ; *De Verit.*, q. 17, a. 1).

Consciousness : In general a name for an awareness of one's internal states, whether of a sensuous or supersensuous character. ' Conscientia est actus quo scientiam nostram ad ea quae agimus applicamus ' (*Sum. Theol.*, I, q. 79, a. 13). What to-day we should call sense-consciousness the Schoolmen called internal sense, and they kept the term consciousness for a knowledge of an intellectual internal state. In this strictest sense, of the mind's knowledge of itself, self-consciousness, it is synomymous with the modern word apperception (*Psych.*, **30-50**).

Contingent : That which has not in its essence the sufficient reason of its existence ; what may be but need not be. ' Contingens est quod potest esse et non esse ' (*Sum. Theol.*, I, q. 86, a. 3).

Continuum : The property of matter in virtue of which the parts of a given quantity are such that the boundary of one is identical with that of another (*Cos.*, **52. 122**). ' Continuum est, cujus partes ad unum terminum communem copulantur ' (*In III Physic.*, l. 1).

Contradictory : Opposition between two terms which are so opposed that they have nothing in common (*Log.*, **19**). Contradictory propositions are so opposed as to exclude any middle proposition (*Log.*, **42**). ' Universalis et particularis propositio, si opponantur, opponuntur secundum contradictionem ' (*Sum. Theol.*, I-II, q. 77, a. 2, obj. 3). ' Enuntiatio quae significat universale opponitur contradictorie ei quae non significat universaliter sed particulariter, si una earum sit affirmativa, altera vero sit negativa ' (*In I Perih.*, l. 19).

Contraries : Opposition between two extremes of a series of things belonging to the same genus (*Log.*, **19**). Propositions are contrary when they are both universal and the one affirms what the other denies of the same subject. 'Universalis affirmativa et universalis negativa sunt contrarie quia universalis negativa non solum removet universalem affirmativam sed etiam designat extremam distantiam in quantum negat totum quod affirmatio ponit et hoc pertinet ad notionem contrarietatis, et ideo particularis affirmativa et negativa se haberit sicut medium inter contraria' (*In I Perih.*, l. 11). When the subject in the two opposed propositions is particular, they are called *sub-contrary* propositions (*Log.*, **42**).

Conversion : The interchange of the terms of a proposition in such a way that the new proposition is true if the original proposition was true (*Log.*, **41**). 'Convertuntur quae aequaliter de se invicem praedicantur' (cp. *In I Post. Anal.*, l. 31).

Corruption : Substantial change considered as the disappearance of one substantial form that is replaced by another (*Cos.*, **72**). 'Corruptio est proprie compositi transmutatio de esse in non esse' (*In II Sent.*, dist. 19, q. 1, a. 1, ad 2). Corruption is the correlative of substantial generation (*q.v.*).

Creation : The production of a substance in its entirety (*Gen. Met.*, **147**). 'Creatio est productio alicujus rei secundum totam suam substantiam, nullo praesupposito' (*Sum. Theol.*, I, q. 65, a. 3).

Criteriom : A standard by which to distinguish truth from error (*Crit.*, **1**, **23** f.).

Deduction : A process of knowledge which starts from certain principles in necessary matter and by their combination enables one to discover new relations between them and to form scientific definitions (*Log.*, **85** ; *Introd.*, **16**). See *synthesis*.

Definition : *Verbal* definition expresses what this is which the *word* defined designates. *Essential* definition gives a full statement of what a thing is, inasmuch as it declares its inner nature (*Log.*, **79**). 'Definitio est oratio indicans quid est res' (*In IV Physic.*, l. 5). 'Definitio est oratio naturam rei aut termini significationem exponens' (JOHN OF ST. THOMAS, *Log.*, I, c. 3). *Descriptive* definition, which is improperly called definition, is the designation of a thing by a number of qualities which allow us to recognize it without giving an insight into its nature (*Log.*, **79**).

Demonstration : A syllogism which engenders true knowledge. 'Demonstratio est syllogismus faciens scire' (*In I Post. Anal.*, l. 4).

Causal demonstration, διότι, leads to the knowledge of a particular thing by indicating its immediate cause. *Demonstration*, ὅτι, or *proof of fact*, supplies a remote extrinsic reason for our having to admit that something *is* (*Log.*, **65** ; *Introd.*, **16**).

A priori demonstration deduces the existence and nature of an effect from a knowledge of its cause ; *a posteriori demonstration* proceeds to a knowledge of a cause from that of its effect (*Log.*,

66). ' Demonstratio per causam dicitur propter quid : haec est per priora simpliciter. Demonstratio per effectum dicitur demonstratio quia, et haec est per ea quae sunt priora quoad nos ' (*Sum. Theol.*, I, q. 2, a. 2).

Circular demonstration is the combined employment of a posteriori and a priori proofs : from the existence of the effect that of the cause is reached, and then from the knowledge of the cause a deeper knowledge of the effect is obtained (*Logic*, **67**). It is also called the *analytico-synthetic method* (*Logic*, **93**).

Discursive method : A mental process which consists of a succession of cognitive acts representing the various notes of a thing and their unification through relations being established between them (*Log.*, **3** ; *Nat. Theol.*, **61**). ' Discursus intellectus attenditur secundum hoc quod unum per aliud cognoscitur ' (*Sum. Theol.*, I, q. 58, a. 3, obj. 1). ' Adhuc tunc rationativa vel discursiva est nostra consideratio quando ab uno considerato in aliud transimus ' (*Cont. Gen.*, I, c. 57). For an opposite process, see *intuition*.

Distinction : Opposition between things, objects or acts of knowledge. In a narrower sense it means the act whereby this opposition is perceived, and may be defined as that act of knowledge by which the mind opposes two or more things or two or more concepts of the same thing (*Gen. Met.*, **43**). ' Distincta sunt, quorum unum, non est aliud ' (*Cont. Gen.*, I, c. 71).

Real distinction is that which exists between different objects independently of our knowledge, either because they exist separately or because they are the physical parts of a whole.

Logical distinction is that which the mind conceives in one and the same thing owing to its having different concepts whereby to represent it. It is *virtual* or *founded on reality* (cum fundamento in re) if the difference of the concepts is justified by the very nature of their objects ; but it is *purely logical,* or purely the result of reasoning, if it is entirely the work of the mind (*Gen. Met.*, **48** ; *Nat. Theol.*, **7**). ' Distinctio *realis* est remotio identitatis, quae datur a parte rei sine apprehensione seu fictione intellectus. Distinctio vero *rationis* quae beneficio intellectus fit et in re non datur. Dividi solet haec distinctio rationis in distinctionem rationis *ratiocinantis* et rationis *ratiocinatae.* Illa prima dici solet distinctio quae fingitur ab intellectu sine fundamento in re et ita solum est distinctio quoad modum significandi et intelligendi ; secunda vero dicitur formata ab intellectu cum fundamento in re ' (John of St. Thomas, *Log.*, II, q. 2, a. 3).

Distributive : Expressing that the predicate of a universal proposition applies to each and all of the individuals denoted by the universal subject. It is opposed to *collective*.

Doubt : A state of suspense when the mind does not perceive clearly the relation of identity or non-identity of two terms

(*Crit.*, 8). It is said to be a *negative* doubt when there are no motives in favour of a decision either way ; and a *positive* doubt when the motives in favour of each side are of equal value.
 Dubitatio principaliter significat motum supra utramque partem contradictionis cum formidine determinandi ' (*In III Sent.*, dist. 17, q. 1, a. 4).

Eminently (*eminenter*) :   The manner in which a higher perfection contains an analogous lower perfection (*Nat. Theol.*, **5, 6**).   To predicate a perfection in a supereminent way of a thing— ' praedicare per eminentiam ' (*De Pot.*, q. 9, a. 7, obj. 2)—means to identify it with that thing, because it possesses some higher perfection that includes the one attributed to it.   This attribution of perfections is known as the process of *transcendence*.

Emotion :   An organic modification that is agreeable or disagreeable to the subject and perceived as such (*Psych.*, **66, 122**). See *passion*.

End :   See final *cause*.

Equivocal :   A term is equivocal when it designates things which have nothing in common but the name by which they are called (*Log.*, **26** ;   *Gen. Met.*, **126**).   ' Aequivocarum est omnino ratio diversa ' (*Sum. Theol.*, I, q. 13, a. 10).

Essence :   That whereby a thing is constituted this kind of thing and not that '(*Gen. Met.*, **15**).   ' Essentia proprie est id quod significatur per definitionem ' (*Sum. Theol.*, I, q. 29, a. 2).   ' Quando variatur aliquid de essentia rei, non est eadem res ' (*In IV Sent.*, dist. 22, q. 2, a. 3).

Evidence :   A quality of those propositions the truth of which is apparent to the intellect (*Crit.*, **8**).   ' Illa videri dicuntur quae per seipsa movent intellectum nostrum ad sui cognitionem ' (*Sum. Theol.*, I-II, q. 1, a. 4).   It is *immediate* or *mediate* according as the truth of the proposition is apparent as soon as the terms comprising it are known or is apparent only after they have been compared with other intermediary terms (*Crit.*, **51** f.).

Extension of an idea :   The number of subjects to which it can be applied (*Log.*, **17**).

Faith :   Assent determined by an act of will to a proposition that is formally not evident (*Crit.*, **68**).   ' Intellectus assentit alicui per quamdam electionem voluntarie declinans in unam partem magis quam in aliam, et si sit cum certitudine absque formidine alterius partis, erit fides ' (*Sum. Theol.*, II-II, q. 1, a. 4).   See *certitude*.

Finality :   The immediate effect of the final cause, the tendency of a thing towards its end.   It is *intrinsic* or *immanent* when it arises from the nature of the thing that tends to realize its end ; it is *extrinsic* when it comes not from the nature of a thing but from some other thing really distinct from it (*Gen. Met.*, **152** f.)

Form :   An intrinsic determining, perfective principle (*Gen. Met.*, **113**). ' Per formam significatur perfectio uniuscujusque rei ' (*De Ente et Ess.*, c. 7).   ' Est actus dans esse rei ' (JOHN OF ST. THOMAS, *Nat. Phil.*, I, q. 4, a. 1).   See formal *cause.*

A *substantial form* is one of the constitutive elements of a substance, namely that which makes it a specific being and differentiates it from all other substances (*Introd.*, **5** ;   *Cos.*, **44**). ' Forma substantialis facit esse simpliciter ' (*Sum. Theol.*, I, q. 77, a. 6).   It is the correlative of primary matter.

An *accidental form* is one determining a substance already constituted (*Introd.*, **5** ; *Gen. Met.*, **113**). ' Forma accidentalis non facit esse simpliciter sed esse tale aut tantum aut aliquo modo se habens ' (*Sum. Theol.*, I, q. 77, a. 6).

An *informing form* is one which requires for its natural existence to exist in conjunction with matter.   It is synonymous with substantial form but opposed to separated form.

A *separated form* is one which need not be united to another principle in order to be able to receive actual existence (cp. *Sum. Theol.*, I, q. 7, a. 2 ; *Gen. Met.*, **117**).   The informing form and the separated form are called respectively *incomplete* and *complete* forms.

Formally :   In a determinate manner ;   opposed to materially. See formal *cause*, formal *object, reduplicative.*

Generation :   The appearance of a new substantial form in the process of a substantial change (*Cos.*, **74**).   ' Quando (aliquid) est transmutatum ita quod materia accipiat aliam formam substantialem, erit simplex generatio et corruptio ' (*De Generat.*, I, l. 5).

Genus :   The sum of constitutive notes which are common to several different species (*Log.*, **16**).   ' Genus logicum est id quod praedicatur de pluribus specie differentibus in eo quod quid ' (JOHN OF ST. THOMAS, *Log.*, II, q. 7, a. 1).

Good :   The object of a being's natural tendency ;   what corresponds to the exigencies of its nature (*Gen. Met.*, **67**, f. ; *Ethics*, **4** ; for different kinds see *Psych.*, **109**).   ' Bonum est id quod omnia appetunt ' (*In I Nic. Eth.*, l. 7).

Habit :   A permanent quality belonging to the nature or to the spiritual faculties of a subject and disposing it favourably or unfavourably in respect of its end (*Gen. Met.*, **101**).   ' Habitus dicitur dispositio difficile mobilis secundum quam bene vel male disponitur dispositum aut secundum se aut in ordine ad aliud ' (ARISTOTLE, *Met.*, V, c. 20 ; *Categ.*, c. 6).

Hypostasis :   A first substance that is complete in itself and part of no other being (*Gen. Met.*, **88**).   ' Hoc nomen hypostasis significat substantiam individuam, id est quae non potest de pluribus praedicari ' (*De Pot.*, q. 8, a. 3).

Hypothesis : A provisional explanation of facts observed (*Log.*, **87**). ' Hypothetica enunciatio non continet absolutam veritatem, cujus cognitio requiritur in demonstratione sed significat aliquid verum esse ex suppositione ' (*In I Periherm*, l. 1).

Idealism : A word designating two different systems that are in some respects contradictory of each other. In general, the philosophic doctrine that the human mind can know only ideas. Idealism is objective if ideas are regarded as Platonic ideas or universal essences (*Platonic* or *realist idealism*). It is subjective if ideas are subjective forms resulting from the very constitution of the mind (*modern* or *subjective idealism*) (*Psych.*, **97** ; *History*, **19** ; *Crit.*, **42-59**).

Idea : As synonymous with exemplary cause, the mental type after which an intelligent efficient cause realizes some effect (*Gen. Met.*, **162**). ' Idea est forma quam aliquis imitatur ex intentione agentis determinante sibi finem ' (*De Verit.*, q. 3, a. 1).

As synonymous with concept (*q.v.*), the mental representation of a thing.

Image : See *phantasm*.

Immanent : See immanent *action*.

Immaterial : Independent of matter. Considered in itself an immaterial or spiritual being contains neither constitutive nor integrant, quantitative parts (*Psych.*, **143**).

Imperative (Categorical) : The absolute, necessary and universal law which, in Kant's system, serves as the foundation of the moral obligation and indirectly justifies the fundamental truths of ethics and religion (*Crit.*, **27** ; *Ethics*, **55** ; *History*, **142**).

Indefinite : Indeterminate (*Gen. Met.*, **43**).

Individual : A subsisting being that is complete in itself and incommunicable to another (*Psych.*, **158** ; *Gen. Met.*, **27, 89**). ' Individuum est quod est in se indistinctum, ab aliis vero distinctum ' (*Sum. Theol.*, I, q. 29, a. 4).

Individuation (principle of) : That which constitutes a nature an individual, i.e. complete in itself and incommunicable, and, in the case of material beings, makes it possible for it to be realized in a number of beings that are really distinct whilst specifically the same (*Gen. Met.*, **28** f.). ' Formae quae sunt receptibiles in materia, individuantur per materiam ; quae autem non est receptibilis in materia, individuatur per seipsam ' (*Sum. Theol.*, I, q. 3, a. 2, ad 3 and 4).

Induction : A process of knowledge which starts with the observation of the many different accidents exhibited by a substance and discovers which of them are invariably connected and reveal the presence of a property (*Crit.*, **61** ; *Log.*, **86** f.). This is *scientific induction* as distinguished from complete induction. ' In syllogismo accipitur cognitio alicujus universalibus notis ; in inductione autem concluditur universale ex singularibus quae sunt manifesta ' (*In I Post. Anal.*, l. 1).

Infinite : See *perfection*.

Intellect : Synonymous with intelligence. In a more restricted sense it means the active intellectual faculty, as distinguished from the passive intellect or understanding (*q.v.*), and may be defined as the power of abstraction whereby the sensible object of human knowledge is disengaged from its individual conditions and rendered intelligible (*Psych.*, **101, 104**). ' Necesse est quod sit intellectus ad hoc quod possit omnia intellibilia facere actu, qui vocatur agens ' (*De III Anima*, l. 10).

Intension : The same as *comprehension* (*Log.*, **17**).

Intention : A sort of ' intellectual view '. In ideology it is synonymous with cognitive act, but denotes in particular the direction taken by the intellect to fix one of the aspects of the object known. ' In omnibus intentionibus hoc communiter verum est quod intentiones ipsae non sunt in rebus sed in anima tantum, sed habent aliquid in re respondens scilicet naturam ' (*In I Sent.*, dist. 33, q. 1, ad 3).

An intellectual act is one of ' first intention ' when it is directly concerned with some real object ; it is one of a ' second intention ' when it is concerned not with the object known itself but with the special form it assumes in the mind by the act of knowledge (*Log.*, **6,** note). ' Nomina primae intentionis sunt quae rebus sunt imposita absolute, mediante conceptione, qua fertur intellectus super ipsam rem in se ; nomina autem secundae intentionis sunt illa quae imponuntur rebus non secundum quod in se sunt sed secundum quod subsunt intentioni quam intellectus facit de eis ' (*De Nat. Gen.*, c. 12).

Intuition : In a wide sense, an act of immediate knowledge. In a narrower sense and as opposed to discursive (*q.v.*) reasoning, the peculiar manner pure spirits have of knowing by a single act all that they can know of a thing (*Nat. Theol.*, **63**). ' Intuitio erit, si intellectus in ipso principio inspiceret conclusionem uno intuitu apprehendens utrumque ' (*Sum. Theol.*, I, q. 19, a. 5).

According to Kant a priori intuitions are natural dispositions of the mind by which it elaborates sensible impressions to put them in space and time (*Crit.*, **42**).

Judgment : An act by which we predicate one thing of another (*Log.*, **10, 29** f.) ; by it the mind unites or disunites the objects represented by two concepts : whence the Latin names for it *compositio* and *divisio*. ' Enuntiatio significat compositionem et divisionem intellectus ' (*Sum. Theol.*, I, q. 85, a. 4, ad 3). ' Compositionem propositionis anima adinvenit conjungens praedicatum subjecto ' (*Sum. Theol.*, I, q. 3, a. 4, ad 2).

Law : Considered as in the being itself that is subject to it, law is the internal fundamental determination in virtue of which a substance tends to produce an effect that is proper to it ; it is

akin to the word ' proprium ' of the Schoolmen (*Gen. Met.*, **156**).
Considered as a scientific conclusion, it is the expression of the
constant and invariable way in which a thing acts or exists.

The *eternal law* is the destination, as conceived by divine
Wisdom, of all creatures to their respective ends, and the adaptation of their activities to them. ' Lex aeterna nihil aliud est
quam ratio divinae sapientiae, secundum quod est directiva
omnium actuum et motionum ' (*Sum. Theol.*, I-II, q. 93, a. 1).
The *natural law* is the expression in the free rational creature of
this eternal law (*Ethics*, **41**). ' Lex naturalis non est aliud quam
lumen intellectus insitum nobis a Deo per quod cognovimus
quid agendum et quid vitandum '.

The *moral law*, in general, is the norm according to which a
man ought to conduct himself to attain his purpose in being. In
a more restricted sense, it is an ordinance promulgated for the
common good by one who is responsible for the good order of some
society (*Ethics*, **50**). ' Quaedam rationis ordinatio ad bonum
commune, ab eo, qui curam communitatis habet, promulgata '
(*Sum. Theol.*, I-II, q. 90, a. 4).

Liberty : A quality in virtue of which the will can choose between
several concrete goods that the reason puts before it and judges
to realize partially the universal, complete good towards which
the will is necessarily inclined (*Psych.*, **111** f.).

Moral liberty is freedom exercised in respect of moral acts ; it
is therefore the faculty of choosing between different objects
considered in relation to the end of man's rational nature (*Psych.*,
119 ; *Ethics*, **24**).

Materialism : A system that is a denial on principle of the existence
of anything which is not purely and simply material (*Psych.*, **95**).

Mathematics : The science which has quantity as its formal
object, a property common to all material beings (*Introd.*, **9** ;
Gen. Met., **1**).

Mathematical abstraction prescinds from sensible changes that
take place in material things and fixes the mind on intelligible
quantity, a property common to them all. ' Mathematica
abstrahunt a materia sensibili, sed non a materia intelligibili, in
quantum in intellectu remanet continua quantitas abstracta a
sensibili quantitate ' (*De III Anima*, l. 8).

Matter : See material *cause*.

Primary matter : one of the two constituent elements of a
material substance, being the one which is of itself entirely
without any specific determination and receives it from the
substantial form ; or in short, an indeterminate, perfectible
subject (*Cos.*, **38** ; *Gen. Met.*, **113, 132**). ' Id materia prima
nominatur quod est in genere substantiae ut potentia quaedam
intellecta praeter omnem speciem et formam et etiam praeter
privationem, quae tamen est susceptiva et formarum et pri-
vationum ' (*De Spirit. Creat.*, q. 1, a. 1).

Second matter, or sensible body : a completely constituted material substance that is naturally endowed with quantitative parts can be matter for determination by accidental forms, but by such forms only (*Introd.*, **5**, 2 ; *Gen. Met.*, **132**). ' Materia sensibilis dicitur materia corporalis, secundum quod subjacet qualitatibus sensibilibus, scilicet calido et frigido, duro et molli et hujusmodi ' (*Sum. Theol.*, I, q. 85, a. 1, ad 2).

Metaphysics : The science which has for its formal object being that is positively or negatively immaterial (*Introd.*, **9** ; *Gen. Met.*, **1, 3**). ' Philosophus in metaphysica determinat de ente in communi et de primo ente quod est a materia separatum ' (*De Gener. et Corrupt.*, Proaem.).

Method : Means of attaining scientific knowledge (*Log.*, **84** f.). See *Analytic, synthetic, circular demonstration*.

Monism : See *pantheism*.

Morality : The quality characterizing moral acts and the object of moral philosophy, namely, the relation of conformity of a human act with the end of man (*Ethics*, **1, 2, 32, 34**). ' Moralis philosophia habet hoc proprium, scilicet considerare operationes humanas ut ordinantur ad invicem et ad finem ' (*In I Eth.*, l. 1).

Movement : The actuality of a subject that is formally potential (*Gen. Met.*, **115**). ' Motus dicitur actus imperfecti, id est existentis in potentia ' (*Sum. Theol.*, I, q. 18, a. 1).

There are three kinds—' Motus est solum in istis tribus generibus, scilicet, qualitate, quantite et ubi ' (*In V Physic.*, l. 4) : *local movement* or successive and continuous reception of new positions in space (*Cos.*, **26**) ; *movement in quality* or *alteration* (*q.v.*), which consists in receiving new qualities ; *movement in quantity*, or *increase* and *diminution*, the acquisition or loss of a certain amount of matter, ' Motus qui est in quantitate nominatur secundum suas species quae sunt augmentum et decrementum ' (*In V Physic.*, l. 4).

Natural : That which corresponds to the exigencies of a nature and to its proper manner of action. ' Aliquid dicitur naturale ex eo quod naturae convenit ' (*Sum. Theol.*, I-II, q. 34, a. 1).

Nature : Synonym for substance considered as a principle of action ; or, more precisely, the intrinsic, first principle of the operations that are proper to the being which produces or undergoes them (*Gen. Met.*, **87, 155**). ' Nomen naturae significat essentiam rei secundum quod habet ordinem vel ordinationem ad propriam operationem rei ' (*De Ente et Ess.*, c. 1).

Noumenon : In Kantian philosophy the opposite to phenomenon : the thing in itself, which the understanding cannot attain to nor represent (*Crit.*, **42**).

Object (of a faculty) : That to which the exercise of a faculty is applied. ' Objectum non est materia ex qua, sed materia *circa quam* et habet quodammodo rationem formae in quantum dat speciem ' (*Sum. Theol.*, I-II, q. 18, a. 2, ad 2).

The *object of knowledge* is that wherein the act of knowledge rests and by which it is completed (*Log.*, **10**). ' Objectum operationis terminat et perficit ipsam et est finis ejus ' (*In I Sent.*, dist. 1, q. 2, a. 1, ad 2).

The *material* object is something of which the special point of view for consideration is not determined ; whilst the *formal* object is that special point of view from which a thing is dealt with by a faculty (*Introd.*, **4**, note 10).

The *proper* object of a faculty is what falls immediately within its range and for the attainment of which it is made ; the *improper* object is something it cannot attain to except through the medium of the proper object. ' Proprium (id est formale) objectum alicujus potentiae est illud sub cujus ratione omnia referuntur ad potentiam ' (*Sum. Theol.*, I, q. 1, a. 7).

Objectivity (real) : The relation of conformity between an object of knowledge and some reality independent of mental representation (*Crit.*, **22** f., **41** f. ; *Psych.*, **45**).

Obligation (moral) : The practical imperative necessity of freely doing what is morally good and of freely avoiding what is morally evil (*Ethics*, **41**).

Occasion : A circumstance or combination of circumstances favourable to the action of a free cause (*Gen. Met.*, **141**). ' Quaedam causa per accidens est quae aliquid operatur, non tamen pertingit ejus operatio usque ad effectum conjunctum . . . et talis causa dicitur proprie occasio ' (*In I Sent.*, dist. 46, q. 1, a. 2, ad 3). ' Occasio nominat causam per se insufficientem . . . sed inducentem ' (*In IV Sent.*, dist. 38, q. 2, a. 1, ad 4).

Occasionalism : The theory that God is the one and only efficient cause and that creatures simply afford God occasions for acting (*Gen. Met.*, **149** ; *History*, **115**). ' Quidam erraverunt putantes quod nulla creatura habet aliquam actionem in productione effectuum naturalium, sed quod Deus causat hos effectos, ita scilicet, quod creatura non agit, sed Deus causat effectum, praesente creatura (id est occasione praesentiae creaturae) ' (*Cont. Gent.*, III, c. 69).

Operation : Synonymous with action (virtus). Preferably used for the action of an immaterial faculty. ' Operatio dicitur quilibet actus rei, etiamsi exterius non transeat sicut intelligere est operatio intellectus ' (*In II Sent.*, dist. 12, in fine).

Opinion : Assent to a probable proposition, or the state of the mind when it inclines to one of two contradictory propositions, but without definitely excluding the other. ' Opinio significat actum intellectus qui fertur in unam partem contradictionis cum formidine alterius ' (*Sum. Theol.*, I, q. 79, a. 9, ad 4).

Pantheism : The metaphysical and cosmological doctrine that there is only one substance and the phenomena of the world are parts of it (substantialist pantheism) or manifestations of it (dynamic pantheism) or subjective representations of the spirit taken as the one and only substance (idealist pantheism). Inasmuch as the one substance comprising all reality is God, this system is called *pantheism ;* it is also called *monism* by reason of its fundamental principle that this substance is one.

Paralogism : Erroneous reasoning (*Log.*, **72**). See *sophism.* ' Ille qui peccat in forma non est syllogismus sed paralogismus, id est apparens syllogismus ' (*In I Post. Anal.*, l. 22).

Participation : See pure *Actuality.* ' Quod non totaliter est aliquid, habens aliquid aliud adjunctum, proprie participare dicitur ' (*In I Metaph.*, l. 10).

Passion : From the viewpoint of *efficiency,* passion is the result of the efficient cause considered in the being acted upon (*Gen. Met.*, **119, 144**). ' Actus passivi vocatur passio ' (*In III Physic.*, l. 5). ' Passio est effectus agentis in patiente ' (*Sum. Theol.*, I-II, q. 26, a. 2). See *action.*

From the *metaphysical* viewpoint, passion is the third kind of quality, and denotes every quality which modifies a subject by some material change (*Gen. Met.*, **106**). ' Passio sumitur pro qualitate secundum quam fit alteratio ' (*In V Metaph.*, l. 20).

In *psychology,* passion denotes an intense inclination of the sensible appetite accompanied by organic modifications ; a synonym for what is now commonly called emotion (*Psych.*, **66**). ' Passiones proprie dicuntur operationes appetitus sensitivi quae sunt secundum transmutationem organi corporalis ' (*In II Eth.*, l. 5).

In *ethics,* passion means an intense inclination of the sensible appetite, preceding a decision of the free-will and lessening the power of the will in the performance of a moral act (*Ethics*, **27**). ' Dicitur passio (perfecta) quando passio sensitivae partis pertingit usque ad immutandam rationem ut . . . non habeat liberum arbitrium super eam ' (*Sum. Theol.*, q. 46, a. 7, ad 3).

Perfection : The possession of whatever is suitable to a being: *Absolute perfection* is that which contains all perfections in a supereminent way (*Gen. Met.*, **173, 174** ; *Nat. Theol.*, **43** f.). ' Dicitur universaliter perfectus, (cui) non deest aliqua nobilitas quae inveniatur in aliquo genere ' (*Sum. Theol.*, I, q. 4, a. 2). *Infinite perfection* is that which has no bounds (*Nat. Theol.*, **48**). ' Infinitum dicitur aliquid ex eo quod non est finitum ' (*Sum. Theol.*, I, q. 7, a. 1). ' Esse infinitum est non limitatum ad aliquod genus entis sed praehabens in se totius esse perfectionem ' (*Sum. Theol.*, I, q. 25, a. 23).

Person : An individual substance of a rational nature (*Gen. Met.*, **88**). ' Persona est rationalis naturae individua substantia ' (*Sum. Theol.*, I, q. 29, a. 1, obj. et passim).

Petitio principii : The fallacy of 'begging the question,' of supposing at the beginning the point to be proved (*Log.*, **75**).

Phantasm : A sense-representation, or image of the imagination, of some material thing already perceived and no longer actually present (*Psych.*, **55**, **93**). 'Phantasma est similitudo rei particularis' (*Sum. Theol.*, I, q. 84, a. 7, ad 2). 'Phantasma per actum imaginationis repraesentatur' (*In I Sent.*, dist. 3, q. 4, a. 3).

Phenomenalism : The theory that there is no such thing as substance supporting and distinct from phenomena perceived in external things, and that all that is real is the existence of these transitory appearances (*Gen. Met.*, **83** ; *Crit.*, **42**).

Phenomenon : A comparatively modern word arising from idealism, denoting the accidental aspect under which a substance manifests itself and 'appears' to the one who has knowledge of it (*Crit.*, **42**).

Physics : According to the *ancient* classification of the sciences, the science which has for its formal object the properties of material things and, in general, any kind of movement (*Introd.*, **9** ; *Gen. Met.*, **1**). 'Physicus . . . est de corpore mobili' (*In I Post. Anal.*, l. 14).

According to the *modern* classification, the experimental science which has for its formal object the superficial properties common to matter (*Cos.*, **3**).

Positivism : A system which does not explicitly deny the existence of supersensuous reality, but on principle waives the question of its existence and limits the field of knowledge to sensible phenomena, or facts that are simultaneous or successive (*Psych.*, **95** ; *Crit.*, **28**, **38**).

Possible : A thing is *intrinsically* possible the constituent notes of which do not involve a contradiction. A thing is *extrinsically* possible when the intrinsic possibility of it can be made actual by virtue of some other existing being capable of making it exist (*Gen. Met.*, **18** ; *Nat. Theol.*, **18**). 'Possibile dicitur dupliciter : uno modo per respectum ad aliquam potentiam . . . alio modo absolute propter ipsam habitudinem terminorum' (*Sum. Theol.*, I, q. 25, a. 3).

Potentiality : Perfectibility, capacity for being perfected by some form (see formal *cause ; Gen. Met.*, **114**, **117**, **118**). It is consequently a relative imperfection. 'Purus actus non habet aliquid de potentialitate' (*Sum. Theol.*, I, q. 3, a. 2).

Power : Oftentimes synonymous with *potentiality* (*q.v.*), potency ; and is *passive* or *receptive* power. 'Potentia passiva est principium patiendi ab alio' (*Sum. Theol.*, I, q. 25, a. 1).

An *operative power* or power of action is an immediate principle of action, and synonymous with faculty (*Gen. Met.*, **118**).

' Potentia activa est principium agendi in aliud ' (*Sum. Theol.*, I,
q. 25, a. 1). This may be *active* or *passive* according as the
faculty has need or not of receiving some intrinsic complement
before it can come into exercise (*Gen. Met.*, **117** ; *Cos.*, **68**).

Predicables : The ways in which the predicate can be attached to
the subject (*Log.*, **16**).

Predicaments : Synonymous with *categories* (*q.v.*).

Predicate : Synonymous with *attribute* (*q.v.*).

Principle : That in virtue of which something exists or is done or
is known. In the last sense it is called *logical principle ;* in the
two former, *ontological principle* (*Gen. Met.*, **165** ; *Log.*, **51**).
' Principium est id quo aliqui d est, fit, vel cognoscitur '
(ARISTOTLE, *Metaph.*, *IV*, c. 1).

Privation : In general, the absence in a subject of a perfection
which should naturally belong to it (*Gen. Met.*, **75**). ' Privatio
est negatio debiti inesse alicui subjecto '. In cosmology, the
absence of the determinate form which primary matter can
naturally receive (*Cos.*, **74**). ' Privatio nihil aliud est quam
absentia formae quae est nata inesse ' (*Coel.*, I, l. 6).

Property : An accident which is necessarily and invariably bound
up with a substance, and by means of which the substance
displays its nature (*Cos.*, **52**). One of the five predicables (*Log.*,
16). ' Proprium non est de essentia rei sed ex principiis essentialibus speciei causatur, unde medium est inter essentiam et
accidens sic dictum ' (*Sum. Theol.*, I, q. 77, a. 1, ad 5).

Proposition : The verbal expression of a *judgment* (*q.v.* ; *Log.*,
29). ' Propositio est oratio enuntiativa '.

Quiddity : That which answers the question *Quid est ?* what-a-
thing-is, τό τι ἐστι ; synonym for essence (*Psych.*, **89** ; *Gen.
Met.*, **15**). ' Quia illud per quod res constituitur in proprio genere
vel specie est quod significamus per definitionem indicantem quid
est res, inde est quod nomen essentiae a philosophis in nomen
quidditatis mutatur ' (*De Ente et Ess.*, c. 1).

Realism : The theory of knowledge according to which the object
of knowledge is real, in the sense of something extramental.
According to *exaggerated* realism the external object is just as it is
represented in our mind, with all the notes of abstraction, universality, etc., that it assumes in the act of knowledge (*History*,
52, 56 ; see Platonic *Idealism*). According to *moderate* realism
the object in the real world is the correlative of the object of
knowledge, but the modes in which it appears before the intellect
are the work of the act of knowledge itself (*Crit.*, **44, 45, 60, 65**).

Reason : As a *faculty*, synonym for intelligence and denotes the
knowing faculty as proceeding by a *discursive* (*q.v.*) process.
As an *object* of knowledge, that which the mind grasps in a
thing and which is the foundation of its properties ; synonymous
here with the nature of the thing (*Nat. Theol.*, **62**).

In *logic*, that which corresponds to the question, *Why ?* what explains some thing, occurrence or truth known (*Introd.*, 5 ; *Gen. Met.*, **165**). ' Ex nomine rationis intelliguntur, primo quaedam cognoscitiva virtus. Alio modo ponitur pro causa ut cum dicitur : qua ratione hoc fecisti. Tertio modo . . . dicitur ratio aliquid simplex a multis abstractum sicut dicitur ratio hominis naturam pertinens ' (*Comment. in lib. de div. nom.*, c. 7, l. 5).

Reasoning : A logical act by which the reason compares the two terms of a judgment not yet evident with the same middle term to see if objectively the one includes or excludes the other (*Log.*, **46** f.). See *discursive*.

Reduplicative : Laying stress upon an idea. The reduplicative sense is usually expressed by such phrases as ' as such ', ' inasmuch as ', ' formally ', ' *qua* ' (*Log.*, **38** *d*). ' Id quod in aliqua propositione reduplicatur est illud per quod praedicatum convenit subjecto ' (*In III Sent.*, dist. 1, q. 1, a. 3).

Reflection : A deliberate turning back of the mind either to the object of a previous thought or to the act of thought itself. (*Psych.*, **144, 2**). In the first case it may be called *ontological* or objective reflection, and in the latter *psychological* or subjective. ' Sunt duo modi reflexionis animae, quarum altera cognoscit se et quae a parte sua sunt, altera vero quae sunt a parte objecti sui ' (*De Princ. Indiv.*).

Reflex : In physiology, reflex movement is that made in response to peripheral stimulation, without the intervention of any conscious effort (*Psych.*, **74**).

In psychology, reflex knowledge is that which is obtained through the influence of the free-will on the intellect, making it to think again upon what has already been an object of thought, or to bend back upon itself and think of its own act ; see *reflection*.

Relation : In general, a connexion between two or more distinct things, whether realities or concepts (*Gen. Met.*, **108**). ' Ratio propria relationis non accipitur secundum comparationem ad illud in quo est sed secundum comparationem ad aliquid extra ' (*Sum. Theol.*, I, q. 28, a. 2).

A relation may be *real* or *logical* according as it follows from the very nature of the things connected or from the knowledge that we form of them (*Gen. Met.*, **109**). ' Sicut realis relatio consistit in ordine rei ad rem, ita relatio rationis consistit in ordine intellectuum ' (*De Potent.*, q. 7, a. 11).

Relative : Unable either to exist or to be conceived of except in connexion with some other being, which is its *correlative* (*Gen. Met.*, **108** ; see *absolute*).

Relativism : The theory which denies that we can perceive the absolute, that is, any immutable and necessary truth.

Science : A body of propositions which are evident, certain, necessary and universal, as well as arranged systematically so as to form one whole, and which are drawn immediately or mediately from the nature of the subject and furnish the intrinsic reason of its properties and of the laws of its action (*Log.*, **96**). ' Omnis scientia habetur per aliqua principia per se nota et per consequens visa ' (*Sum. Theol.*, II, q. 1, a. 5).

A *rational* or *deductive* science is one which starts with certain principles in necessary matter and combines them to deduce new truths and to form definitions of those objects the knowledge of which it has to develop. A *positive* or *experimental* science is one which starts with the observation of concrete facts in order to formulate the laws which govern them (*Log.*, **85, 86** ; see *deduction, induction, synthesis, analysis*).

Sentiment : Often used to-day to denote higher emotional feelings principally connected with the rational appetite or higher affective life (*Psych.*, **66, 122**).

Simplicity : The quality in virtue of which a substance has neither constitutive nor quantitative parts (*Psych.*, **145** ; *Gen. Met.*, **52**).

Sophism : Fallacious reasoning transgressing the laws of logic (*Log.*, **72**).

Species : In zoology, a *natural* species is a series of living beings descended from a common stock and indefinitely fertile *inter se* (*Psych,.* **83**).

In logic, the *predicable* species denotes the sum-total of abstract notes which make up an essence (*Log.*, **16**). ' Unumquodque constituitur in specie secundum quod determinatur ad aliquem specialem gradum in entibus ' (*Sum. Theol.*, I, q. 50, a. 2, ad 1). ' Species constituitur ex genere et differentia ' (*Sum. Theol.*, I, q. 3, a. 5).

In psychology, *species intentionalis*, literally ' mental image ', is the Schoolmen's phrase for what we have denominated cognitional determinant : the complement of the cognitive faculty, the natural determining cause of an act of cognition. It may be intellectual or sensible according as it determines intellectual or sensuous knowledge (*Psych.*, **38, 49**). ' Species quae est principium intellectualis (seu cognitivae) operationis ut forma, est similitudo rei quae cognoscitur ' (*Cont. Gent.*, I, c. 53).

Spirituality : The property of being able to exist and to act without depending intrinsically upon matter (*Psych.*, **143**). ' Substantiae spirituales secundum esse suum non dependent a corpore ' (*In IV Sent.*, dist. 45, q. 1, a. 1).

Spontaneous : Necessary, spontaneous *activity* is determined by appetition, which in turn is evoked by some representation. Spontaneous acts are opposed, on the one hand, to reflex acts (in the physiological sense), and, on the other, to acts consequent upon reflection.

Spontaneous *movement* is a movement of the locomotive organs determined by some sensuous appetition (*Psych.*, **74**). ' Proprio motu et sponte agunt, ita quod a nullo exteriori moventur ' (*In III Nic. Eth.*, l. 4).

Subject : In logic, that of the two terms in a proposition of which the predication is made (*Log.*, **13**). ' Dicitur subjectum, de quo alia praedicantur ' (*In VII Metaph.*, l. 2).

In metaphysics, that to which accidental determinations belong ; synonym for substance. ' Soli substantiae convenit proprie ratio subjecti ' (*In I Post. Anal.*, l. 34).

In psychology and criteriology, a being capable of knowledge and appetition and consequently capable of entering into relation with things which, by way of distinction, are called objects (*Gen. Met.*, **114,** note).

Subjective : In psychology and criteriology, pertaining to the subject thinking.

In metaphysics, pertaining to the subject of accidental determinations, i.e. to substance (*Gen. Met.*, **114,** note). ' Soli substantiae convenit proprie ratio subjecti ' (*In I Post. Anal.*, l. 34).

Subsistence : Formerly synonym for *substance* (*q.v.*). Now used to express that perfection in virtue of which a thing is self-sufficient alike for existence and action.

Substance : That which has the reason of its reality in itself and not in something else (*Gen. Met.*, **84, 85**). ' Ens in se, per se stans '. To emphasize the trait of existence-in-self, it was formerly called *subsistentia :* ' Secundum quod per se existit et non in alio vocatur subsistentia ' (*Sum. Theol.*, I, q. 29, a. 2). To express its rôle of serving as a support of accidents, which it underlies (sub-stat), it is called *substance :* ' Secundum quod supponitur accidentibus dicitur substantia ' (*Sum. Theol.*, I, q. 29, a. 2).

First or *individual substance* is that which has the first claim to be called substance, inasmuch as it contains within itself the reason of its reality and, as such, is, from the logical point of view, in ultimate analysis the subject of predication, and, from the ontological point of view, the real support of all that makes up the being of a thing (*Log.*, **14**). ' Dicitur substantia ipsum subjectum ultimum quod non praedicatur de alio et hoc est particulare in genere substantiae ' (*De Pot.*, q. 9, a. 1).

Second substance is substance considered in an abstract way, namely, as the generic or specific essence ; it serves as a subject for accidental predications, but may itself be predicated of a first substance or concrete subject, in which alone it has reality (*Gen. Met.*, **86** ; *Log.*, **15**). ' Substantia prima est quae proprie et principaliter et maxime dicitur. Hujusmodi enim secundum se omnibus aliis substant, sc. speciebus et generibus et acciden- tibus. Substantiae vero secundae id est genera et species sub- stant solum accidentibus et hoc etiam non habent nisi ratione primarum' (*In VII Metaph.*, 2 et sq.). 'Substantia secunda significat naturam generis secundum se absolutam ; prima vero substantia significat eam ut individualiter subsistentem' (*De Pot.*, q. 9, a. 2, ad 6).

Substance is *complete* or *incomplete* according as it is sufficient in itself to exist or requires the concurrence of another sub- stantial element similarly incomplete (*Gen. Met.*, **117**, note ; see informing *form*, separated *form*). A complete substance which results from the union of two incomplete substances is termed a *compound ;* and is opposed to a *simple* substance.

Suppositum : Same as *hypostasis*.

Syllogism : The complete, typical expression of a reasoning process ; see *reasoning*.

Synteresis : A natural facility of the mind to have an habitual knowledge of moral first principles (*Ethics*, **44**). 'Synderesis dicitur lex intellectus nostri, in quantum est habitus continens praecepta legis naturalis quae sunt prima operum humanorum' (*Sum. Theol.*, I-II, q. 94, a. 1, ad 2).

Synthesis : A mental gathering together or union into one whole of elements or notes which by a previous analysis have been considered separately (*Log.*, **10** *e*).

As a logical method, synthesis is to proceed from principles, or axioms, in order to deduce consequences or conclusion (*Log.*, **85**).

Synthetic judgment : A judgment in which the union of the predicate and subject depends upon experience. It was called by the Schoolmen a judgment in contingent matter (*Log.*, **31, 33**).

The Kantian synthetic a priori judgment is a judgment of the ideal order (i.e. independent of experience) in which the necessary connexion of predicate and subject does not follow from the necessary connexion of what the predicate represents with that which the subject represents, but is merely the inevitable result of the laws of our understanding (*Log.*, **33** ; *Crit.*, **39**).

Teleology : The study of the final cause (*Gen. Met.*, **156** f.).

Theodicy : Synonym for natural theology or the study of positively immaterial being (*Gen. Met.*, **1, 3**). 'Dicitur scientia divina sive theologia in quantum substantias quae nunquam in materia esse possunt, sicut Deus et intellectuales substantiae, considerat' (*In Metaph.*, Prolog.).

Sometimes used in the sense of a vindication of the justice of God in permitting evil.

Thought : A word used to-day sometimes to designate the in- tellectual concept, sometimes the work of the mind by which it is elaborated ; sometimes in a more particular sense, to express the concept as the product of the combined work of the senses and the intellect or the work of this production itself (*Psych.*, **148**).

Transcendence : See *eminently.*

Transcendental or metaphysical property : An attribute belonging to being as such, and therefore verified in all beings (*Gen. Met.*, **37**).

In modern philosophy that knowledge is called transcendental which surpasses sense-experience.

Transformation : For complete or substantial transformation, see *corruption.*

Truth : The truth of a being is the conformity of this being actually considered with its nature as already supposed to be known (*Gen. Met.*, **60**). ' Denominantur res verae a veritate quae est in ipsa re (quae nihil est aliud quam intellectui adaequata, vel intellectum sibi adaequans) sicut a forma inhaerente, sicut cibus denominatur sanus a qualitate sua, a qua sanus dicitur ' (*De Ver.*, q. 1, a. 4). *Ontological* truth is the relation of identity of nature between a thing presented to the mind and an ideal type previously known there : ' Veritas est adaequatio vel conformitas rei et intellectus ' (*Crit.*, **5** ; *Gen. Met.*, **61**). *Logical* truth is that attributed to knowledge ; it is the quality of a judgment in which the connexion between subject and predicate is in conformity with fact (*Crit.*, **6**).

Ubication : The localizing accident in virtue of which a body takes possession of a definite place (*Cos.*, **139**).

Understanding : Synonym for intelligence or intellect. More precisely and in connexion with the Scholastic theory of the idea, it may be defined as the passive power which, on receiving the conceptual determinant produced by the active intellect, accomplishes the act of knowledge. Called by the Schoolmen *intellectus possibilis*, and also passive, as opposed to the active intellect or power of abstraction (*Psych.*, **96, 103, 104**). ' Intellectus possibilis est in quo possint omnia intelligilia fieri ' (*De III Anima*, l. 10).

Unity : The state of a being which is undivided (*Gen. Met.*, **41**). ' Unum nihil aliud significat quam ens indivisum ' (*Sum. Theol.*, I, q. 11, a. 1).

Universal : Capable of being referred or attributed in the same way to an indefinite number of concrete subjects (*Psych.*, **92** ; *Log.*, **9** ; see *abstraction*). ' Hoc enim dicitur universale quod natum est multis inesse et de pluribus praedicari ' (*In VII Metaph.*, l. 13).

Universals : Universal concepts considered in their relation to the ndividual things of which they are predicated (*Crit.*, **44** ; *History*, **51**).

Univocal : Terms are said to be univocal when they are applied to things which verify the same essential definition (*Log.*, **26**). ' Quidquid dicitur de pluribus univoce dicitur de eis secundum unam rationem communem ' (*Sum. Theol.*, I, q. 68, a. 4, obj. 3).

Virtually : The manner in which a cause contains the perfection of its effect.

Virtue : Moral virtue is an habitual disposition, either received from God or personally acquired, which is added to the natural powers of the rational soul to make the normal exercise of its activity easier (*Ethics*, **46**). ' Omnis habitus qui facit rectam electionem, potest dici virtus proprie loquendo ' (*In IV Sent.*, dist. 14, q. 1, a. 1).

Volition : An act of the rational will—or, as sometimes used less accurately, of the other appetitive faculties by which the agent moves himself towards something (*Psych.*, **64**, 137 f.).

Voluntary : That which is due to the action of the will under the influence of intellectual knowledge. It is not the same as the object of a volition or *volitum*, which is presented by intellectual knowledge and constitutes the object of an act of volition, no matter whether or not the volition has any influence on its realization. ' Ad rationem voluntarii requiritur quod principium actus sit intra cum aliqua cognitione finis ' (*Sum. Theol.*, I-II, q. 6, a. 2). The word is to-day used also in a wider sense (*Psych.*, **64**, note).

INDEX

APPENDIX TO THE COSMOLOGY
OF M. NYS

By PROF. ALFRED RAHILLY, M.A., B.Sc.

The *Manual* here translated was written in 1905 and presumably stereotyped. Some footnotes were added as late as 1913 (*e.g.*, on pp. 54, 139, by M. Nys), and a few were inserted by the translators (*e.g.*, pp. 75, 85). Owing to the present abnormal circumstances it became impossible, after the inception of the translation, to communicate freely with M. Nys. The section on Cosmology appears, therefore, without any revision which recent scientific research might suggest. Of course it is a moot point whether in an elementary text-book such as the present it is desirable to introduce a discussion of the latest, and perhaps disputable, conclusions of science. It is certain, however, that the author, could he have been directly consulted, would have modified some of his statements and perhaps recast some of his arguments. But as no *essential* change seemed to be necessitated, the translators decided not to withhold the publication until the end of the War—a decision justified by the almost immediate exhaustion of the English edition of the first volume. The issue of the present volume has been delayed until an expression of the views of M. Nys has been possible. Unfortunately they appear only in the briefest form (translated below) in a short letter to Cardinal Mercier. At the beginning of the War the author had in the press a new and revised edition of his larger *Cosmologie*. In the last number of the *Revue Néo-Scolastique* (May, 1914), he published an article on the ' Constitution of Matter according to Modern Physicists ', but deferred to a subsequent issue the consideration of its philosophical implications. Under these circumstances the translators have asked the present writer to add a note to the section on Cosmology. It must be understood that Dr. Nys is in no way responsible for this note, and, should another edition be called for, it is to be hoped that he will be able to revise his section and thus render this note unnecessary.

From the philosophical standpoint the outstanding feature of physico-chemical science is its advocacy of mechanism, the theory that (as M. Nys puts it, p. 53) ' two factors alone are needed to explain the world—homogeneous mass and communicated local motion '. The world is to be reduced to spatial configurations and motions, no longer of a hundred different kinds of atoms, but of absolutely identical electrons and *perhaps* of another set of similar entities (nuclei of positive electricity). Against this later form of mechanism the arguments of M. Nys lose none of their force, and only require refurbishing. It is well, at the outset, to assert explicitly that in combating ' the theory adopted by the majority of modern scientists ', Scholastic philosophy makes no attempt to deny facts or to shirk difficulties. Perfect loyalty to facts is quite compatible with the denial that current scientific constructions are an adequate representation of reality. This is perhaps most evident in the case of biology, wherein the facts of heredity, ontogeny, regeneration, consciousness and such-like have far outrun all scientific syntheses. But even in the inorganic realm, where (at least until lately) the classical mechanics held rigid sway, science has progressed only by adopting a deliberate, partial and one-sided survey. It may be good science, but it sometimes results in bad philosophy.

In connexion with recent research it will suffice to consider here very briefly the theories of molecular and atomic structure. Though the latter problem has attracted more attention, the former question (the structure of the molecule) is of equal philosophical importance. A good deal of unnecessary scepticism has been exhibited with reference to molecules. Most of the older Schoolmen seemed to hold that the substantial form of an inorganic body was co-extensive with any arbitrary piece. But the view has long since prevailed that the form is associated with a definite quantum, greater amounts being merely congeries of these substantial entities or molecules [1]. Indeed, the coarse-grainedness of matter is nowadays not a theory, but a fact, for science has made us acquainted with the complex micro-structure of apparently homogeneous bodies, such as wood and metals. Molecular motion, too, is now a familiar phenomenon in evaporation, in gaseous pressure, in diffusion which occurs even at the interface of two metals, in the Brownian movement (the agitation of microscopic grains in a liquid), which the Belgian Père Carbonelle, S.J., was the first to explain correctly. The brilliant researches of M. Perrin in this latter domain are an additional confirmation of the kinetic theory of gases. From this theory and analogous considerations it was estimated that about 250 million molecules placed in a row would stretch over an inch. Hence the individual molecule would seem to be for ever beyond our powers of perception. Within the last few years, however, it has been found possible to make the effects of an individual molecule directly

---

[1] For instance, St. Thomas : 'Tota forma substantialis ligni est in qualibet parte eius' (*In IV Sent.*, d. 10, q. 3, a. 3). 'In corpore naturali invenitur forma naturalis quae requirit determinatam quantitatem sicut et alia accidentia' (*In I Physic.*, l. 9).

appreciable [2]. Thus the problem of the existence or reality of molecules (the 'atoms' of the ancients) has now been finally relegated to the general epistemological question of reality.

Since the time of Dalton and Berzelius there is a special notation for molecules ; that of common salt, for instance, is denoted by NaCl ; *i.e.*, the juxtaposition of the two symbols for sodium and chlorine into which salt may be decomposed. This notation inevitably and deliberately suggests that a molecule of salt is merely the spatial juxtaposition of a sodium and a chlorine atom. This idea is further impressed by the constitutional formulæ introduced by Frankland and Kekulé (about 1852). The study of the carbon compounds led to the idea that the different atoms in the molecule were kept together, not by a mutual attraction of each by all the others, but by a linkage from atom to atom. Van't Hoff and Le Bel (1874) finally introduced the idea that the intra-molecular configuration of the atoms must be regarded as three-dimensional, and not merely in a plane ; the molecule of marsh-gas (CH_4), for instance, consists of a carbon atom at the centre of a regular tetrahedron at whose vertices are four hydrogen atoms.

These unanimous conclusions of chemists, reinforced by more recent discoveries to be mentioned presently, would seem to be the final *coup de grâce* to the Scholastic notions of substantial changes and forms ; for all chemical processes are thereby resolved into spatial regrouping of pre-existent entities. It is possible, indeed, to maintain that chemical formulæ have merely a kinetic reference ; *i.e.*, they indicate the past history and future behaviour of a substance without throwing any light on its static constitution. Thus the formula NaCl would simply mean that sodium and chloride can form salt and can again be recovered from it ; just as a sum of money can be deposited in a bank and again withdrawn from it, without necessarily implying the continual existence of the identical coins in the bank. Still, it is very difficult to escape the conclusion that the atoms do somehow exist in the molecule. How, for instance, can we explain the optical right- or left-handed deviation (of the plane of polarization of a transmitted light-ray) exerted by many substances, unless we assume a corresponding geometrical right- or left-handedness in the configuration of the molecule ? Furthermore, the recent experiments of Laue, W. L. Bragg and W. H. Bragg show that a crystal acts on X-rays as a solid diffraction-grating owing to the existence of sets of parallel planes of atoms in

---

[2] The effect of a single alpha particle (charged helium molecule projected with high velocity from a radioactive substance) has been made visible in three ways : (1) in Crookes' spinthariscope, by the bombardment of a zinc sulphide screen, the impact of each particle being indicated by a luminous splash ; (2) in an apparatus devised by Rutherford and Geiger in 1908, wherein the entrance of a single particle is indicated by the jerk of an electrometer ; (3) in C. T. R. Wilson's photographs of the path of a single particle, the flying particle ionising the gas-molecules in its path so that each becomes the centre of a visible globule of water.

the crystal. Hence it would appear that each component atom of a crystalline structure has a separate spatial existence.

On the other hand, this account fails utterly to explain the *real changes* which occur in chemical processes. It is in a sense true that sodium added to oxygen gives soda, or that water subtracted from alcohol leaves ether. But surely the addition precedes but does not constitute the chemical union ; the subtraction follows the chemical disruption. It would be quite ridiculous, for example, to tell us that common salt is a silvery metal plus a yellow poisonous gas, or that prussic acid is merely the sum of one atom each of carbon, hydrogen and nitrogen. Can any sane man believe that the difference in the properties of strychnine and theine is *explained* by the fact that they consist of the same elements only arranged in a different pattern ? The old objection of Aristotle is still pertinent [3] :

'When the components are divided into small particles (μικρά) and juxtaposed so intimately as to be sensibly indistinguishable, is there then composition at all or not ? . . . Since an aggregate (σύνθεσις) is not the same as a compound (μίξις), but different, clearly we cannot say that things are compounded when they remain unchanged in small particles. . . . Only relatively to the senses would things then be compounded ; the same thing would be a compound to a weak-sighted person but not so to a lynx-eyed man '.

Elsewhere he gives the essentials of his own solution, in terminology which can easily be applied to modern chemistry [4] :

'A compound which is existentially one, like a syllable and not like a heap, has Being as a whole. For a syllable is not merely its constituent letters (BA is not the same as B and A), neither is flesh simply fire and earth. After dissolution, in fact, the whole (syllable or flesh) no longer exists, but the constituents (letters or fire and earth) still exist. The syllable then is something ; not merely the letters, consonant plus vowel, but also *something more* (ἕτερόν τι). And flesh is not merely fire and earth or warm and cold ; it is something else besides. Now this something more cannot itself be a constituent element or composed of such elements. For if it were an element, the same difficulty would crop up. Flesh would then be composed of three (fire and earth and this other) instead of two ; and we should still have to search for the *something beyond*. . . . This is the substantial form (οὐσία) of each compound, its primary ground of being '.

Now this is precisely the argument of Scholastic Cosmology, the full admission of all chemical analyses and the assertion of *something else*. If it be true that the molecule is a spatial constellation of diverse atoms, we cannot indeed follow Aristotle and the Schoolmen

[3] *De gen. et corruptione*, i. 10, 327 *b*, 33 ff.
[4] *Metaphysica*, vii: 17, 1041 *b*, 11 ff.

in their contention that the inorganic compound is homogeneous (ὁμοιομερές). We must, in fact, treat the molecule as the Peripatetics treated the living body. ' A dead body ', says Aristotle [5], ' has exactly the same configuration as a living one ; but for all that it is not a man '. If, *per impossibile*, we could perceive a single water-molecule, it might perchance appear as two hydrogen atoms linked to one of oxygen ; but for all that the water-molecule is something more. It is *one* in a sense in which its spatial parts are not one, it has a unitary being analogous to that of a plant or animal [6]. A molecule may be conceived as a cluster of spatialized atoms, just as an organism is perceived to be a group of spatialized chemicals. In each case we have not only colligative or summational properties, but also indiscerptible specific qualities of the whole which cannot be distinctively predicated of or portioned out among the parts. We must, therefore, conceive (not imagine) a spatially complex and disparate aggregate as being, in some fundamental sense, one Being. This is the Scholastic theory ; it does not pretend ' to explain ' anything, it merely gives us a mental full-stop [7].

The preceding philosophical discussion of molecular complexity renders it unnecessary to apply similar considerations to the question of atomic structure. The relevant scientific facts and theories may therefore be briefly indicated. Hints of some underlying connexion between the different elements have long been recognized. For instance, the approaches of the atomic weights to whole numbers are too close and too frequent to be regarded as purely accidental. Mendeljew's famous periodic law (1869), permitting the elements to be grouped in families, showed clearly that the chemical elements are no random collection of disparate entities. But it is only within the past few years that we have obtained direct unequivocal evidence of something common to all the elementary atoms. Strange to say, this common constituent turns out to be the atom of electricity—the electron. Electrons, whose existence was suspected in electrolysis, were first discovered in a vacuum-tube (as cathode rays), but have since been found to be ubiquitous ; they are emitted, for instance, from hot bodies and from metals exposed to light. Auroras (northern lights) are probably due to electrons

---

[5] *De partibus animalium*, i. 1, 640 *a*, 35.
[6] Even the Schoolmen did not hold that the living body is a *continuum*. ' In animalibus quae movent seipsa est magis quaedam colligatio partium quam perfecta continuatio ' (St. Thomas, *In VIII Physic.*, l. 7).
[7] Père de Munnynck, O.P., appears to have been the first to realize that hylomorphism must be accommodated to modern atomic conceptions. He represents the molecule ' as a corporeal mass, whose quantity is essentially fixed, whose extension is determined, whose different parts are probably no more homogeneous among themselves than the arm and eye in the human body ' (*Compte rendu du congrès scientifique tenu à Fribourg*, 1897 : *Sciences philosophiques*, p. 450). M. Nys has also adopted the view that the molecule is heterogeneous, though probably not quite in the sense here outlined (*Cosmologie*, 1906, § 251 ; also *Revue néo-scolastique*, vol. 15, 1908).

ejected from the sun, and moving in spirals along the earth's magnetic lines. An electrically charged molecule or ion is one which has either lost or gained an electron ; an electric current is a stream of electrons.

After the finding of the X-rays (originating in a vacuum-tube where a swarm of moving electrons is suddenly stopped), the most sensational discovery is that of radioactivity. The rays which at the expenditure of electrical energy we can excite in a vacuum-tube are spontaneously emitted by the radio-elements. Radium, for instance, gives off three kinds of rays : (1) alpha rays, consisting of charged helium molecules (or atoms) moving with the enormous velocity of 12,000 miles a second ; (2) beta rays, which are electrons shot out with even greater speeds ; (3) gamma rays, which are probably X-rays caused by the starting of the beta-electrons. The special significance of radioactivity lies in the fact that it is the first recorded instance, not so much of the transmutation, as of the death and birth of elements. Apart from its unique features [8] the transformation of radium into helium and niton might be represented as a commonplace chemical equation ; and so might the subsequent exploits of niton and its congeners.

These and similar phenomena have led to the conclusion (1) that all atoms contain electrons, some of which may be lost without any alteration of chemical identity ; and (2) that, at least in the case of the radioactive elements, there is another set of electrons the loss of which changes them into different elements. More recent researches have justified this distinction between inner and outer electrons. The present view of the atom, which, of course, is vague and tentative, may be summarized as follows. Chiefly as a deduction from the scattering of high-speed particles in their transit through matter, Sir E. Rutherford has supposed that the atom possesses a concentrated positive nucleus wherein most of the mass resides. Furthermore, there is evidence that the nuclear charge changes by unity in passing from one element to the next ; so that if the elements are numbered in order of atomic weight, these ' atomic numbers ' will actually express the nuclear charge. Thus there is in the atom a quantity which is more fundamental and varies more regularly than the atomic weights. A similar simple relation has been found to connect some other properties of the elements ; for instance, the frequency of the characteristic X-rays of an element is proportional to the square of its atomic number. Hence there are atomic properties connected in a very simple manner

[8] Briefly, these are : (1) The change is absolutely independent of the physical and chemical environment ; (2) The associated energy is more than a million times greater than that accompanying any known chemical change ; (3) The rate of change follows the exponential law characteristic of monomolecular reactions ; (4) The spectrum of radium does not show that of helium.

with the nuclear charge, and presumably due to inner electrons [9]. There are other properties, such as gravitation and radioactivity, uninfluenced by chemical or physical agencies ; and these, too, must be mainly ascribed to the nucleus. But most of the ordinary physico-chemical properties of the elements change rhythmically with the atomic number or weight, *i.e.*, wax or wane periodically as we proceed along the list of elements ; and, moreover, they are not carried unchanged by the atom into its chemical compounds. These properties would seem, therefore, to be associated with the outer layer of electrons. If this conception of the atomic system be correct, it might be possible for elements with different atomic weights to be chemically identical ; and this is actually claimed to be true of some of the newly discovered elements.

The actual calculation of the distribution of the electrons in the atom is an extremely difficult problem : even when the conditions are artificially simplified its solution cannot be effected by the classical laws of dynamics. The real intra-atomic world would seem to be far more complicated than even our intricate model of a miniature solar system would lead us to suppose. Thus no theory of the atom has yet been devised to explain the series-laws of spectra. This complexity of the spectral lines is not the only clear indication of atomic complexity ; the very law of transformation of radioactive substances is a vivid proof. On the average a certain small proportion of the atoms—about one atom of radium in every ten thousand billion—break up every second. This rate is affected neither by external conditions nor by the past history of the atoms. Thus whatever be the age of a mass of radium, half of it will disappear in 2,000 years ; every atom which escapes destruction has an even chance of surviving for the next 2,000 years. We must conclude that the atom is itself a world subject to chance, *i.e.*, contains a vast number of irregularly variable factors, so that when a certain condition or coincidence chances to be realized in this infra-world a cataclysm occurs. The atom is the world writ small ; the universe is a large-scale atom.

A few final remarks may be made concerning the electron itself. Sir J. J. Thomson has shown that its mass is about 1/1800 of the mass of a hydrogen atom. As far back as 1881 he had pointed out that a moving electrified body possesses, in virtue of its charge, an additional mass ; just as a body moving through a liquid has an increased inertia. Moreover, this electrical mass increases with the velocity, as Kaufmann showed the mass of an electron to increase. Hence it has been concluded that the mass of an electron is entirely electromagnetic in origin [10]. The actual implications of

[9] The nucleus itself must consist of positively and negatively electrified bodies, for otherwise it is hard to see how a ready-made helium atom could be ejected from radium.

[10] In the sense that an electron would have no mass if it had no charge, *i.e.*, if it ceased to be an electron. It must be remembered that mass, as used in science, is merely a certain coefficient or number associated with a body.

this statement are very obscure. If the mass of ordinary matter is to be derived electromagnetically, it must be associated with positive electricity—of which little or nothing is as yet known. Moreover, there is a vicious circle in the current theory. The inertia of matter (perhaps the only kind we really know) is explained as due to the electromagnetic energy of moving electric charges ; and this, according to Maxwell's theory, is the kinetic energy of aether—which is therefore endowed with precisely that inertia which we started by repudiating.

To the philosopher the most important result of this analysis of molecule and atom is the fact of multiplicity and complexity. It has been shown above that the need for a real synthesis is only thereby increased. Once we realize the necessity of this synthetic factor and its perfect compatibility with a spatially heterogeneous complex—whether organism, molecule or atom—the actual details are of secondary philosophical importance. In the present state of science it is certainly advisable to keep an open mind concerning their validity and interpretations. The philosopher must be content to lag somewhat behind the man of science, for there are worse dangers than that of not being up-to-date.

The following expression of the views of Dr. Nys is taken from a recent letter addressed to Cardinal Mercier.

' As to the application of this scientific theory [of electrons] to cosmology, here in a few words is my opinion :

' (1) The electronic theory is a generally successful attempt at synthesis, but as yet it raises serious difficulties. Hence it is premature to wish to base upon it a cosmological conception of matter or to employ it as a conclusive argument against an adverse philosophical theory.

' (2) Anyway, this scientific synthesis can easily be reconciled with the Scholastic theory. In effect it results in a real and inevitable dualism, a plurality of primordial substances. Physicists admit, as primordial elements of the chemical atom, a positive nucleus and negative electrons, both linked to the central nucleus. Thus there are two constituents, two electrical elements described by the same name (electricity), but mutually irreducible. Now it is just as easy for a Thomist to conceive the formation of the world starting from a simple primitive dualism as to do so in terms of the eighty or a hundred simple bodies actually admitted by chemists.

' (3) Even if the two kinds of electricity were reduced to one, the diversity of the chemical species, in the Scholastic sense of the word, could still be maintained ; allotropy and polymerisation show us that the same matter, subjected to different influences, can be transformed into different species.

' (4) Finally, as is admitted by numerous writers, it is by no means established that the theory of electrons completely excludes the existence of extended matter in the ordinary meaning of the word '.

The following bibliography, which had no place in the Manual, may prove useful.

P. DUHEM, *Le mixte et la combinaison chimique*, 1902 ; *L'évolution de la mécanique*, 1905 ; *La théorie physique*, 1916[2].

W. WHETHAM, *Recent Development of Physical Science*, 1904.

SIR J. J. THOMSON. *Electricity and Matter*, 1904 ; *Corpuscular Theory of Matter*, 1907 ; *The Atomic Theory*, 1914.

SIR E. RUTHERFORD, *Radioactive Substances and their Radiations* 1913.

N. CAMPBELL, *Modern Electrical Theory*, 1913[2].

SIR O. LODGE, *Electrons*, 1906 ; *Modern Views on Matter*, 1907[2].

J. PERRIN, *Brownian Movement and Molecular Reality*, 1910 ; *Atoms*, 1916.

W. BRAGG, *X-Rays and Crystal Structure*, 1915.
  Les idées modernes sur la construction de la matière : Conférences faites en 1912, 1913.

The present writer has in preparation a work dealing with the relations of Scholastic Philosophy and Modern Science.